FOUNDATION

Matter the Body Itself

D. G. Leahy

State University of New York Press

Permission to quote from the following works has been granted by the publishers: J. Derrida, *Margins of Philosophy,* Harvester Wheatsheaf and International Book Distributors; J. Derrida, *Of Grammatology,* The Johns Hopkins University Press; T. J. J. Altizer, *The New Apocalypse: The Radical Christian Vision of William Blake,* Michigan State University Press; K. Marx, *Capital, Volumes II* and *III,* K. Marx, *The Poverty of Philosophy,* K. Marx and F. Engels, *The German Ideology,* International Publishers Co.; J. Colletti, *From Rousseau to Lenin,* Verso Editions and Monthly Review Press; M. Heidegger, *On Time and Being,* Harper Collins Publishers; K. Marx, *Early Writings,* K Marx, *Grundrisse,* and K. Marx, *Capital, A Critique of Political Economy, Volume 1,* Penguin Books Ltd.; J. Derrida, *Dissemination,* Athlone; M. Heidegger, *The Basic Problems of Phenomenology* and *The Metaphysical Foundations of Logic,* Indiana University Press; Moses Maimonides, *The Guide for the Perplexed,* G. Galilei, *Dialogues Concerning Two New Sciences,* and G. W. G. Hegel, *Philosophy of History,* Dover Publications Inc.; W. James, *Principles of Psychology, Pragmatism,* and *A Pluralistic Universe,* Harvard University Press; D. Biale, *Gershom Scholem: Kabbalah and Counter-History,* Harvard University Press; *The Collected Papers of Charles Sanders Peirce,* Vols. II, IV, and VI, Harvard University Press; J. Dewey, *The Later Works,* Vols. 5 and 11, Southern Illinois University Press; *Hegel's Philosophy of Nature,* Volume 1, and *Hegel's Science of Logic,* Humanities Press; B. Ollman, *Alienation,* Cambridge University Press; E. Husserl, *Crisis of the European Sciences,* Northwestern University Press.

Published by
State University of New York Press, Albany

Printed in the United States of America

For information, address the State University of New York Press,
State University Plaza, Albany, NY 12246

Library of Congress Cataloging-in-Publication Data
Leahy, David G., 1937-
Foundation : matter the body / by David G. Leahy.
p. cm.
Includes bibliographical references and index.
ISBN 0-7914-2021-3 (hard : alk. paper). — IS8N 0-7914-2022-1
(pbk. alk. paper)
1. Ontology. 2. Postmodernism. 3. Consciousness.
4. Philosophical theology. I. Title.
BD331.L418 1996
191—dc20 93-36975
CIP

10 9 8 7 6 5 4 3 2 1

In grateful memory for George and Dorothy,
Sabina, Ruth, William, James, Robert, and Gregory James

—— ἐγείρεται σῶμα πνευματικόν——

CONTENTS

PREFACE

1989 was the Year of the Beginning. It marked the beginning of the new world order as a clearly visible fact. But what is the new world order which is beginning? The beginning of the new world order is the end of modernity. For the first time in history the perpetual newness is universal. This is the beginning of an *actually* universal new world consciousness. This is the beginning of the realization of the Kantian ideal. But as is always so in human affairs when what is long awaited finally arrives the fulfillment of the expectation is not quite what was expected. This new world order is fraught with the difference between expectation and realization. It is the actual beginning of a new world.

It is the writer's understanding that the new beginning is categorical, and that the categories and, indeed, the very structures of modern philosophical, theological, and scientific self-consciousness are essentially inadequate to the new beginning, and, further, that the most fundamental structure, the very notion of the *self*—in any but a purely formal sense—is completely and essentially dysfunctional in the light of the beginning of this new world. In an earlier work, *Novitas Mundi: Perception of the History of Being*, the writer analyzed the essential history of thought, starting with Aristotle and ending with Heidegger. In that book, centering on the essential departure of Aquinas' thought from the form of Aristotelian metaphysics, he showed in what way modernity appropriates for its own purposes the form of medieval transcendental reason, and how the latter is in the first instance the product of a faithful, though self-conscious, reason. Modernity is there understood as the setting asunder of medieval faith and the form of its self-consciousness, and the appropriation of the latter to a new, human end. The earlier work concentrated on tracing, in that context, the essential development of modern philosophy, neglecting the specifically theological works of the modern period. In this last respect the work before the reader is not much different, excepting possibly its treatment of the American theology of Altizer, which is seen as the furthest possible extension of modern consciousness, but which, as the extreme expression of American consciousness, is understood to be formally, though inessentially, the furthest preparation, in the form of thinking essentially reduced to nothing, for what now in fact follows, viz., an understanding of the Trinity which is for the first time in history at once theological and philosophical, and precisely so in those senses of those terms which hitherto were thought to be and indeed hitherto were incompatible.

If modern reason trimmed faith to its own pattern, so that, beginning and end, high and low, faith set itself in opposition to reason, what now occurs for the first time in history, what is foundationally set forth in this book, is *the explosion of reason to fit the form of faith.* The present work stands forth in the understanding that while there is a real difference between the Divine and the human, there is for the first time in history no difference between Divine and human science, that while there is a real difference between God and man, there is for the first time no necessary or actual difference between the Divine and human logics. The ground of the perceived and actual incompatibility hitherto existing between philosophy and theology is understood not to have been the reality or unreality of the objects of one or the other of those two disciplines, but rather the shared presupposition of both, viz., the very presupposition that human consciousness is inevitably a self-consciousness, the presupposition, alike on the part of theology and philosophy, that man was not privy to the Divine logic, except where man was construed to be essentially divine as indeed he was in the epitome of modern philosophy which is the work of Hegel. It may therefore be helpful to the reader in approaching the present work to know that the writer perceives that it makes no *fun-*

damental intellectual difference that Barth opposes to modernity's absolute subjectivity the sovereignty of a Wholly Other Subjectivity. Indeed, just as Hegel understands 'the non-being of the finite to be the being of the infinite', it is possible to grasp Barth's originality by thinking that for him the truth is found, in effect, in the contradictory proposition, viz., 'the non-being of the infinite is the being of the finite'. Nevertheless the contradiction is purely intramural, on the common ground of the presupposed subject. But altogether without the walls of modernity—in the light of the 'wholly other' *objectivity* of the essentially different consciousness now actually beginning to occur—it is impossible in a *fundamental* intellectual sense to distinguish the radical religious subjectivity of Luther and Calvin from the scientific subjectivity of the Cartesian *cogito.* Indeed, when Descartes, setting out on his methodological quest for a foundation for modern science, set his personal faith and morality outside the bounds of his self-certainty, he in that very act completely confirmed Luther. And when Calvin declared that human beings are nothing in the sight of God—*nihil*—the stage was set not only for Edwards and for Barth, but for Leibniz who asked 'why is there being rather than nothing', for Peirce who denied the premise of the alternatives and understood that 'being insensibly merges into nothing', and, of course, for the Heideggerian *Angst.* The only thing that finally distinguishes the two ultimately opposed modes of the modern subject is the presence or absence of faith, but then again a faith which is itself defined in terms of subjectivity, a faith which is opposed to reason in the case where reason has identified faith with itself. But where hitherto in the history of thought has faith raised reason itself *essentially* to the level of faith? Where hitherto in the history of thought has the essence of logic been the logic of faith? Where in the history of thought before now has faith revealed the essence of logic? Both the absolutely self-related absolute subjectivity of Hegel and Sartre's insubstantial absolute subjectivity are precisely distinguished from the insubstantial relative subjectivity of Kierkegaard, that is, from the substantial non-being of the latter's subjectivity, but in no event is consciousness anywhere in modernity near being beyond subjectivity and the nothing. The so-called post-modern consciousness is near being beyond subjectivity and the nothing, but it itself exists beyond being. The beginning which is the new world order is existence not beyond being near being beyond subjectivity and the nothing. The existence which is beginning is that of an absolute consciousness absolutely without *self*.

What then is to be understood by the 'new thinking' which is the essential necessity of the new world order which is beginning? 'New thinking' may be thinking differently about something, but the same *way* of thinking. The discomfiture of beginning to think differently is then real but not foundational. But a 'new thinking', thinking differently about something, may be as well a *new way of thinking*. In the latter case where thinking itself is itself different the discomfiture is foundational. Thinking differently is in that case not just beginning to think differently about something but a radical inconvenience.

If *self* connotes continuity, and the denial of complete otherness or novelty, then the beginning of the essentially new form of thinking—the beginning of a universal newness—is *essentially* and *categorically* without the notion of self. The new way of thinking begins as the absolute elimination of the absolute self-consciousness of modernity in all its forms. It is the beginning of a foundation beyond both modern thought and post-modern forms of self-consciousness which hold themselves in complete or partial opposition to modernity. If the furthest extension of modernity is the essence of American thought, viz., the self-effacing motion of the infinite postponement of self-consciousness, so much so that it is American consciousness which is the historical center and source of the various forms of post-modern consciousness, then the beginning of a new world consciousness is proximately and inevitably the transcendence of the essence of American thought. Over against the modern European idea of a perfect subjectivity the notion of an incomplete and merely relative but real objectivity of consciousness was by no means an insignificant historical achievement of thinkers like Peirce, James, and Dewey. But the thinking now occurring for the first time is the transcendence of that notion. The American notion of objectivity, while really, though inessentially, beyond European subjectivity, is, just so, essentially inadequate to the reality of the new world order now actually occurring for the first time. For the first time the new reality of the world—world unity—is not a mere ideal. The merely ideal objectivity of American consciousness which led the peoples of the world to this historical point cannot itself enter the promised land. The consciousness adequate to the beginning of real world consciousness is a universally new consciousness, in fact, a perfect other-consciousness, a consciousness categorically and essentially beyond the other-self relation. The new world order is the beginning of the universal or absolute objectivity of consciousness. The task of thinking is to think foundationally the essence of this beginning.

The inconvenience of the beginning of this new way of thinking is then nothing less than the shaking, the removal, and the replacement of the foundations of thought by a completely new foundation. In the work before the reader nothing less than this beginning is tried, a thinking essentially and categorically without *self.* The perception of *Novitas Mundi* is that modernity's absolute self-consciousness was ultimately the result of thinking the Incarnation, that at a certain point thinking faced with the Incarnation fatefully and fruitfully leapt back upon itself, recollecting essentially upon itself. Now, however, following the final postponement of the final result of thinking the Incarnation, following the American theology of the Death of God, i.e., following thinking faced with the Incarnation leaping back *absolutely* in the form of the beginning of Nothing, it is possible to understand the beginning of absolute other-consciousness now actually occurring as finally the Incarnation *assaulting* thinking. The new beginning is the Incarnation finally assaulting thought. This final assault is the beginning of an essentially new form of thought.

The reader who will enter into this work will discover not only the discomfiture of beginning a new *way* of thinking, but that this initial discomfiture of thought never completely abates, since the mind-assaulting novelty of existence is of the essence of the thinking. Further, the language of the new thinking possesses in its sparseness and precision a likeness to complex mathematical formulation. No doubt already the reader has encountered some difficulty. Perhaps one or more of the above sentences was not immediately understood. It has perhaps been necessary to reread a sentence several times to get the exact sense of the relationships there described. This styleless style of language is wholly necessary in the attempt to precisely formulate in a rigorously consistent manner certain most fundamental ontological-historical relations. The writer therefore offers his apology to the reader for the inevitable inconvenience of having to read again in order to read. He apologizes to the reader for the inevitable embarrassment which the reader will feel in having to read slowly, and only wishes to add that he himself shares in this very embarrassment both as writer and reader. But he extends his hand and invites the reader to join him in the labor of beginning to think essentially an essentially new thought. Finally, quite apart from the discomfiture of the beginning of a new way of thinking, the sheer complexity of the material in the work presents a real challenge to any reader. Therefore extensive cross-references will be found throughout in the form of footnotes and within footnotes.

Section I, the 'formal critique' of Marxism, was composed at the very beginning of the 1980's, and is, so far, prophetic. In terms of the development of the form of the essentially new thinking the chief fruit of this section is the notion of the 'minimum', which is the notion of 'essential individuality' or the notion of the 'unity of life'. Section II, principally through critiques of the self-conscious thinking of Nietzsche, Heidegger, Derrida, and Altizer, takes forward, now in the form of the 'quantum identical with quality', the notion of the 'minimum' first developed in Section I. Here the notion of the 'minimum' leads to the articulation of the complete meta-identity of quantity and quality. In Section III.1 the logic of the beginning, the logic of the new thinking, indeed, the logic of mind-assaulting novelty, is set forth. Here the 'minimum' conceived for the first time is the very form of logic. This logic replaces the binary system of Boole and Peirce, 0 and 1, with a trinary system, 0, $\overline{0}$, and 1, 'zero', 'unum', and 'unity', in which no element equals "nothing," as, analogously, the thinking of absolute novelty is not essentially self-conscious thinking. The logic presented in this section is the simplest possible, and does not go beyond a critique of the most fundamental notion shared by Boole and Peirce, and the whole of modernity, viz., that the alternative to Unity is Nothing. The sections which follow, III.2, III.3, and III.4, illustrate and demonstrate the utility of the logic in a number of ways, including, but not limited to, the demonstration that the logical calculus is the foundational template of the geometric and arithmetic series, as well as the basis for a simplification of the mathematical formulas related to structural rigidity and a deepening of the understanding of the rational organization of rigid structures.

In Section III.5 the meta-identity of language and number, conceptualized in Section II as an integral part of the meta-identity of quality and quantity, becomes for the first time a tool for a specific intellectual analysis. The methodology for the mathematical reading of language there employed is essentially distinguished from the *gematria* of the ancients and the kabbalah by virtue of the fact that letters are treated in an essentially mathematical way, viz., as elements in a proportion or members of a series of ratios, and no substitutions are allowed. The theorems which follow, Sections III.6 and III.7, further demonstrate the utility of this new methodology by applying it directly to the analysis of the system of natural numbers. Section IV.1 develops the relation of American consciousness to the new beginning. Section IV.2 is a critique of the relation between James and Altizer and includes an *Excursus Circularis* which brings the reader to the very center of the new world consciousness by use of the logic and mathematical-linguistic methodology developed in Section III. Section V carries forward the analysis of the relation of American consciousness and the beginning consciousness of the new world order, treating the thought of McDermott and Altizer in the context of the classical American pragmatists, Peirce, James, and Dewey, and, in that context, and with proximate reference to and transcendence of Altizer's theology, finally culminates in the formulation of the new understanding of the Trinity. A short Appendix relates the logic to Augustine's understanding of the Trinity.

The writer thanks all those whose interest, help, or support has furthered the work. These include his colleagues at New York University, Professors James P. Carse, Francis E. Peters, and Kenneth Zysk. Elsewhere, Professors Edward S. Casey, John F. Collins, John H. Conway, Ray L. Hart, Jay Kappraff, John J. McDermott, Peter Manchester, Robert C. Neville, Edward Oakes, S.J., Robert L. Payton, Robert P. Scharlemann, and Edith Wyschogrod. Also Gary Adamson, Barbara Altizer, Genevieve Baldacci, Jared Barkan, Patricia Collins, James Conneen, Joseph Cossentino, Angelo Danesino, Barry and Ingrid Willenz-Isaacs, Timothy Leahy, James Maroosis, David Robinson, Constantine Skliris, and Edward Williams. And for their loving support, Christopher, Daphne, Fabian, Aimée, and Matthew. Jared Barkan is thanked additionally for proofreading the book both in manuscript and typeset. Finally, the writer thanks Thomas J. J. Altizer for twenty years of extraordinary, selfless support and encouragement of the work. His rare and magnanimous spirit has hastened the day upon which this book is published.

D. G. L.

FOUNDATION

Matter the Body Itself

I

CRITIQUE OF ABSOLUTE CONTINGENCY

WHETHER THE DIFFERENCE BETWEEN FACT AND REFLECTION OR APPEARANCE AND ESSENCE CAN, BY THE SAYING, BE OVERCOME

—

THE QUESTION[1] ANSWERED IN LIGHT OF THE BEING OF THE THING PERCEIVED, AT ONCE THE FORMAL CRITIQUE OF HISTORICAL MATERIALISM

The difference between fact and reflection or appearance and essence is, even now, overcome by the saying terminating in the essential priority of existence itself to being. There is no perception *ex nihilo* of being in essence except in the form of the thought now existing absolutely. The difference between fact and reflection is, even now, overcome by the appearance itself of an absolutely transcendental thinking between which and its being in essence there is absolutely no difference but the fact of its materialization. The fact is that there now exists for the first time in history an essentially transcendental thinking in which the fact itself is essentially comprehended *qua* absolute. No longer is there an absolute materialization of thought beside a science of absolute form, absolutely necessitating the coincidence, furthermore, of logic with metaphysics: there is no extralogical thing supported by a paralogical being or purely formal essence of matter. In this thinking now occurring it is clearly seen that the matter of the thing is the absolutely formal

[1] This precise formulation of the question appears in a letter from Robert P. Scharlemann to the writer.

being of thought, that the thing in essence is nothing but appearance itself: that logic coincides existence itself. Now matter exists *ex nihilo* in the absolute form of thought existing for the first time in history. In the unlimited ontology that thought itself now is, essence terminates in appearance itself, and there is no being prior to existence itself terminating in thought itself. Speech itself is the essential measure of the transcendent difference: itself the conception in essence of transcendental difference: the thought itself of existence itself: the absolute saying itself, catholicologically precluding the presupposition of the question, namely, the sphere of being itself materially other than this thinking now occurring, the conditioned fact of absolute existence itself—catholicologically precluding absolute contradiction itself, precluding the absolutely unconditioned existence of the past condition of thought itself not thought, precluding the appearance in essence of the actuality of the past. The absolute saying itself catholicologically precludes the absolute being in essence self-exposition, as being absolutely immaterial to the fact itself now the absolute thought. So, for example, the exposition of the absolute appearing in Hegel's *Science of Logic*, to wit: "When therefore a *content* of the exposition is asked for, *what* then does the absolute manifest? the answer must be that the distinction between form and content is simply dissolved in the absolute. Or the content of the absolute is just this, *to manifest itself.* The absolute is the absolute form which, as the diremption of itself, is utterly identical with itself, the negative as negative, or that unites with itself, and only thus is it the absolute identity-with-self which equally is *indifferent to its differences*, or is absolute *content.* The content, therefore, is only this exposition itself. As this movement of exposition, a movement which carries itself along with it, as a way and manner which is its absolute identity-with-self, the absolute is manifestation not of an inner, nor over against an other, but it is only as the absolute manifestation of itself for itself. As such it is *actuality.*"[2]—this exposition—is merely a matter of thought not existing now, the absolute relation/self-manifestation (to noth-

[2] G. W. F. Hegel, *Science of Logic,* trans. A. V. Miller (London 1969), p. 536.

ing)—a purely formal negation—incapable *ex necessitate* of existing now: simply not a matter of the absolute saying itself. There is now no question of an absolutely verbal transcendence of existence itself, no question of a saying not absolutely circumspect. There is now no question but that matter itself exists *ex nihilo.* There is now absolutely no question but that the absolute saying itself is the *realization* of the difference between appearance and essence being overcome itself before now in the purely formal essence of matter—being itself the absolute transcendentally different: *ex necessitate* being simply and solely reflection: being itself the absolute not thought—being itself the absolutely transcendent self-same identity overcome before now: the now proof positive of existence itself, being itself now the thought of the absolute fact. Before now being itself was provisionally the form of the materialization of absolute thought. Being itself is for the first time the absolutely unconditioned form of absolute thought itself: the essentially immaterial form coincident with the existence of matter itself: the absolute form of transcendent coincidence: the absolute coincidence of time itself. The ultimate attempt at self-denial in the face of an essentially new thought is precluded by the fact itself that the saying itself is absolutely inconceivable without the difference between fact and reflection being itself overcome before now in being in essence thought once and for all time, without the eternal actuality of the absolute before now, without the absolute being before now simply and solely a matter of thought, there being once and for all time absolutely no necessity of a transcendent thinking (although there remained the absolute necessity of a transcendent existence), but simply and solely the absolute necessity of a transcendental thinking only now for the first time in history existing in the absolute form of transcendental thought absolutely. Now that transcendent existence is in fact provided absolutely in the absolute form of existence itself, there is absolutely no possibility of an essentially unhistorical thinking: nothing, including thought itself, escapes the essential predicament of existence itself. Now that transcendent existence is provided in the absolute form of the body itself (in the form of the absolutely unconditioned essence) absolute necessity is seen to be nothing in essence but the desire to conceal existence itself in actuality, nothing but the self-desiring concealment of the absolute fact itself thought, nothing but the desire to hide the transcendental difference in which for the first time in history fact and reflection, appearance and essence, are transcendentally differentiated from the absolutely unconditioned thought as its absolutely transcendent identity: there is no fact or appearance transcendently different from the absolute transcendence of identity now occurring: there is now no immediacy whatsoever that is not "in essence" the absolute, that is not absolutely in the form of thought.

Now that the absolute itself actually exists for the first time in history there is no question of the transcendent difference being overcome by the simple form of speech, as it were, by the mere saying. Nor is it overcome by the absolute saying itself. Indeed, the transcendent difference is overcome by the absolute itself prior to the saying itself, by thought itself prior to the silence itself. Indeed, now, the transcendent identity of the silence itself is the absolutely unconditioned word itself thought, now formally predicated on the material perfection of thought itself before now: *the thing which is now being absolutely thought for the first time in history is the priority of the body itself to the saying:* the absolute grace of existence itself to which there is no alternative absolute. Clearly there is no question of absolutely nothing in essence overcoming the transcendent difference overcome before now by the conception of matter itself (there is no denying the matter of fact of the history of intelligible matter, namely, the absolute occurrence of an eternal actuality, the perfect elimination of the irrational element of matter itself). Such a redundancy of the irrational is inconceivable now except as a mask of the desire to conceal the perception of the body itself, as the attempt to put on the inconceivable absolute, essentially incapable of attribution—this essentially insatiable desire to exist—specific, perpetual non-existence—now in fact simply inconceivable (for the time being not unmasked). Overcome in the meantime by the priority of the absolute saying itself, it knows nothing itself of freedom itself: an irrational redundancy conceivable only as the immediate non-existence of the absolute contradiction: the absolute confirmation of the immediacy of existence itself precluding in essence an automatic response, the categorical imperative of the absolute saying itself being that nothing is able to be said now except it be said in essence, i.e., except it be immediately intelligible in terms of the fact in essence of history itself, namely, that the transcendental object is known to be so absolutely. There is now absolutely no alternative in fact to the absolute constitution of absolute love except it be itself a chimera in essence, i.e., except it be itself unintelligible: there is only the silence which now itself is thought for the first time in history. Absolutely nothing is thought except it be the existence of the absolute itself—the existence of existence. The absolutely unconditioned freedom itself thought itself is actuality itself: the unicity of the body itself in which matter itself exists *ex nihilo* in and for thought itself. What now occurs is the perfect elimination of the irrational element of reason itself, namely, the irrational, i.e., immaterial, state of the fact itself of the historical intelligibility of matter: now nothing is able to be said except it be matter of the body itself: now reason itself is incorporated in the further realization of the essence of history itself. Furthermore, here it is clearly seen that the necessity of an absolute severance from the embodiment of past thought never in fact existed before now, but that now it is transformed in essence into the action of thought itself absolutely unconditioned. Indeed, this necessity before now itself a mere appearance became the premise of the absolute thesis of subjective, i.e., inessentially historical, materialism, namely, that the world of man is the unrealized actuality of history itself. Indeed, this mere form of absolute matter remains just that, belonging in essence to the past of which it was unable to conceive itself to be the absolute criticism in essence. Ultimately inessentially historical materialism is but the form of the rationalization of reason itself, the imperfect elimination of the irrational fact: the historical self-clarification of the actuality of the past as being prehistorical without being so essentially, the latter simply self-precluded by existing in dependence upon the position thought itself had become in the course of time: the necessity of action itself the realization of a finite transcendence: the necessity of overcoming the self-alienation of material consciousness: the refusal to recognize in any form but that of its own absolute severance from the embodiment of past thought the overcoming of the difference between appearance and essence: the refusal to recognize the overcoming of the difference between fact and reflection in any form other than that perceived in its own historico-temporal actuality, namely, the rationalization of existence itself, i.e., not transcendental identity, but not transcendental difference, rather, difference *qua* transcendent identity itself: the thoughtless creation of the form of transcendent difference itself: as it had to appear before now, the thoughtless creation of the form of human society or the imperfect beginning of the absolute society, i.e., the material form of the appropriation of a new existence: the imperfect perception of a new actuality: the perception of an essentially implicit connection: the implicitly societal perception, subject to being realized practically, a new identity, but even then, and nothing more, the negative as negative *realized*.

Before now the radical criticism of past thought severed itself absolutely from its materialization in the form of the *simple* essence (non-existence) by means of its own formal anticipation of absolute existence, i.e., by means of the *elliptical* essence, or, existence as (revolutionary) *practice*, i.e., not simply the non-existence of the matter of absolute thought before now, but the essential existence of matter itself (the rationalization of existence itself). The formal anticipation of absolute existence was, however, essentially not yet the perception itself of the *complex* essence, existence itself, not yet the absolute existence of matter itself other than which *now* nothing is *able* to be said, now that for the first time in history reason itself is absolutely incorporated in the absolute transformation of appearance itself. Historical materialism, to the extent that it self-consistently perdures, still exists *in* the world, and is *essentially* retarded by the irrational element which is reason itself remaining unincorporated matter, a mere appearance, the elliptical word itself, essentially unhistorical matter, the real movement of individuals: absolute movement: negativity as *existing* negativity. This finite transcendence of existence—the essentially practical passover (following historico-logically upon, first, Kant's practical transcendence of matter itself, the finite transcendence of thought itself, second, Hegel's formal transcendence of the practical itself, thought itself the essence of finite transcendence (now for the first time in history itself overcome in the infinite transcendence of existence itself which follows upon it catholicologically, i.e., in absolute independence, a second absolute to which the first absolute is no alternative in fact)—this existence of revolutionary transcendence—is delineated by Marx and Engels as follows:[3]

> In history up to the present it is certainly an empirical fact that separate individuals have, with the broadening of their activity into world-historical activity, become more and more enslaved under a power alien to them . . . which has become more and more enormous and, in the last instance, turns out to be the *world market.* But it is just as empirically established that, by the overthrow of the existing state of society by the communist revolution . . . and the abolition of private property which is identical with it, this power . . . will be dissolved; and that then the liberation of each single individual will be accomplished in the measure in which history becomes transformed into world history. From the above it is clear that the real intellectual wealth of the individual depends entirely on the wealth of his real connections. Only then will the separate individuals be liberated from the various national and local barriers, be brought into practical connection with the material and intellectual production of the whole world and be put in a position to acquire the capacity to enjoy this all-sided production of the whole earth (the creations of man). *All-round* dependence, this natural form of the *world-historical* co-operation of individuals, will be transformed by this communist revolution into the control and conscious mastery of these powers, which, born of the action of men on one another, have till now overawed and governed men as powers completely alien to them. Now this view can be expressed again in speculative-idealistic, i.e., fantastic, terms as "self-generation of the

[3] K. Marx and F. Engels, *The German Ideology*, pt. 1, ed. C. J. Arthur (New York, 1970), pp. 55–57.

species" ("society as the subject"), and thereby the consecutive series of interrelated individuals connected with each other can be conceived as a single individual, which accomplishes the mystery of generating itself. It is clear here that individuals certainly make one another, physically and mentally, but do not make themselves.

This "alienation" (to use a term which will be comprehensible to the philosophers) can, of course, only be abolished given two *practical* premises. For it to become an "intolerable" power, i.e., a power against which men make a revolution, it must necessarily have rendered the great mass of humanity "propertyless," and produced, at the same time, the contradiction of an existing world of wealth and culture, both of which conditions presuppose a great increase in productive power, a high degree of its development. And, on the other hand, this development of productive forces (which itself implies the actual empirical existence of men in their *world-historical,* instead of local, being) is an absolutely necessary practical premise because without it want is merely made general, and with *destitution* the struggle for necessities and all the old filthy business would necessarily be reproduced; and furthermore, because only with this *universal* development of productive forces is a universal intercourse between men established, which produces in all nations simultaneously the phenomenon of the "propertyless" mass (universal competition), makes each nation dependent on the revolutions of the others, and finally has put *world-historical,* empirically universal individuals in place of local ones. . . . Empirically, communism is only possible as the act of the dominant peoples "all at once" and simultaneously, which presupposes the universal development of productive forces and the world intercourse bound up with communism. Moreover, the mass of *propertyless* workers—the utterly precarious position of labour-power on a mass scale cut off from capital or from even a limited satisfaction and, therefore, no longer merely temporarily deprived of work itself as a secure source of life—presupposes the *world market* through competition. The proletariat can thus only exist *world-historically,* just as communism, its activity, can only have a "world-historical" existence. World-historical existence of individuals means, existence of individuals which is directly linked up with world history.

> Communism is for us not a *state of affairs* which is to be established, an *ideal* to which reality [will] have to adjust itself. We call communism the real movement which abolishes the present state of things. The conditions of this movement result from the premises now in existence.

The world-historical overcoming of the transcendent is the absolute transformation of a transcendent matter, the appropriation itself of a new transcendence: the purification *ex cogitatione* of creation out of nothing: the reduction to chaos itself of the thought of the necessity itself of absolute matter: the absolutely purifying (revolutionary) action itself: the absolute *kenosis* of material thought: reason itself ecstatic, caught up in the elemental irrationality of being itself created in its own image, the transcendent passion for a new order. So Marx and Engels at the close of Part I of *The German Ideology*:[4]

> Finally, from the conception of history we have sketched we obtain these further conclusions: (1) In the development of productive forces there comes a stage when productive forces and means of intercourse are brought into being, which, under the existing relationships, only cause mischief, and are no longer productive but destructive forces (machinery and money); and connected with this a class is called forth, which has to bear all the burdens of society without enjoying its advantages, which, ousted from society, is forced into the most decided antagonism to all other classes; a class which forms the majority of all members of society, and from which emanates the consciousness of the necessity of a fundamental revolution, the communist consciousness, which may, of course, arise among the other classes too through the contemplation of the situation of this class. (2) The conditions under which definite productive forces can be applied are the conditions of the rule of a definite class of society, whose social power, deriving from its property, has its *practical*-idealistic expression in each case in the form of the State; and, therefore, every revolutionary struggle is directed against a class, which till then has been in power. (3) In all revolutions up till

[4] Ibid., pp. 94–95.

> now the mode of activity always remained unscathed and it was only a question of a different distribution of this activity, a new distribution of labour to other persons, whilst the communist revolution is directed against the preceding *mode* of activity, does away with *labour*, and abolishes the rule of all classes with the classes themselves, because it is carried through by the class which no longer counts as a class in society, is not recognized as a class, and is in itself an expression of the dissolution of all classes, nationalities, etc. within present society; and (4) Both for the production on a mass scale of this communist consciousness, and for the success of the cause itself, the alteration of men on a mass scale is necessary, an alteration which can only take place in a practical movement, a *revolution*; this revolution is necessary, therefore, not only because the *ruling* class cannot be overthrown in any other way, but also because the class *overthrowing* it can only in a revolution succeed in ridding itself of all the muck of ages and become fitted to found society anew.

The limitation of the ultimate formality of historical materialism is its being oblivious of freedom itself, of the absolute clarification of the absolute now for the first time occurring absolutely, its being absolutely stymied by its conception of matter in essence existing irrationally as the form of the necessity of the appearance of an absolutely historical world. It is absolutely incapable of comprehending the incorporation of reason itself in the transformation of the absolute into existence itself: incapable of comprehending *the absolute existence of reason itself absolute, the transcendental passion of an absolutely new order now actually occurring in the form of the transcendence of the practical absolute—the perception itself of the transcendental absolutely existing now:* the absolute predicament of transcendent perception: freedom itself existing, the essence of absolute thought existing essentially, subject neither to the transcendent differentiation of fact and reflection, nor to that of appearance and essence, i.e., transcending both the historico-logical transcendence of historical materialism to history (accomplished in the form of the interrelated series of existing individuals) as well as the historical-material absolute thought-transcendence of the absolute notion (accomplished in the non-existence of the form of the absolute individual). Nor is this absolute existing essentially yet another object of the transcendent difference, a real thing, but being itself thought, it is the absolute objectivity in which the real transcendence of the thing, the difference itself (being itself) is comprehended as the absolutely unconditioned fact itself, *qua* transcendental identity, transcendent. The essence now existing *ex necessitate* is the absolutely transcendental passion of experience itself, the experience itself of the absolute transcendental passion: existence itself existing: *the absolute termination of the premises now in existence,* in virtue of which it is clearly perceived that an essentially non-categorical movement is absolutely inadequate to the realization of actuality itself, which realization is now seen to terminate absolutely in the imagination of the transcendental absolute, in the perception itself the elemental matter of which is a perfectly discrete motion itself. The absolute prediction of existence itself now actually occurring for the first time in history (the absolute saying itself absolutely, i.e., the explicit discontinuity of the absolute essence with all previous saying grounded as that was either in the transcendent difference itself or in the *overcoming* of the transcendent difference), namely, the thing now perceived being absolutely a new thought (logic coinciding existence itself thought in essence), precludes the actual appearance of an absolutely material movement as a result of the essentially imperfect realization of freedom, i.e., of the fact of reason itself. The new fact (the *novitas mentis*) is the actually perfect individuation of matter itself (the evidently absolute essence of the transcendental absolute existence). This essentially transcendental logic is the experience itself of an essentially passionate thought, precluding essentially the predicament of contingency, i.e., the real movement of the logic of history, and at the same time and *qua* saying, *transcending* the latter's counterpart in radical subjectivity, namely, the transcendental-phenomenological logic of absolute science (not the transcendental repetition of creation itself, but the transcendental repetition of the position in essence thought had become in the course of time), transcending, *qua* saying, the self-same identity of phenomenological science, the purely logical absolute, the essentially non-predicative contingency. The absolute predicament is the experience itself now, *qua* saying itself, of the absolute priority of the absolute: the experience itself now of the transcendence of existence itself to thought. The absolute predicament of existence itself is the experience itself *now* of an infinite identity *qua* saying, the absolutely transcendental logic of history itself, being itself the thought of another, a second absolute, identical *qua* saying with the thought that is for the first time in history itself action, the embodiment of the essentially transitive conception of the essentially new universe now coming into existence. The categorical absolute is the incorporation of the absolutely transitive conception of an essentially new universe *now: de facto* the elimination of the imperative of choice: the transcendental absolute, *exsistere ipsum.* The categorical absolute is the elimination, further, of the necessity for the absolute disinterest of the science of phenomenology (the purely formal iteration of the intransitive form of thought before now), as well as the elimination of the necessity of the absolute interest thoughtlessly committed to completing the incomplete construction of absolute thought before now, i.e., to the realization of the absolute content of self-consciousness in action, as expounded by Marx in his letter to Ruge in September 1843:[5]

> In fact the internal obstacles seem almost greater than the external difficulties. For even though the question 'where from?' presents no problems, the question 'where to?' is a rich source of confusion. Not only has universal anarchy broken out among the reformers but also every individual must admit to himself that he has no precise idea what ought to happen. However, this very defect turns to the advantage of the new movement, for it means that we do not anticipate the world with our dogmas but instead attempt to discover the new world through the critique of the old. . . . If we have no business with the construction of the future or with organizing it for all time there can still be no doubt about the task confronting us at present: the *ruthless criticism of the existing order,*

[5] K. Marx, *Early Writings,* trans. R. Livingston and G. Benton (New York, 1975), pp. 206–9.

ruthless in that it will shrink neither from its own discoveries nor from the conflict with the powers that be. . . . In this context there are two incontestable facts. Both religion and politics are matters of the very first importance in contemporary Germany. Our task must be to latch onto these as they are and not to oppose them with any ready-made system. . . . Reason has always existed, but not always in a rational form. Hence the critic can take his cue from every existing form of theoretical and practical consciousness and from this ideal and final goal implicit in the actual forms of existing reality he can deduce a true reality. . . . Nothing prevents us, therefore, from lining our criticism with a criticism of politics, from taking sides in politics, i.e., from entering into real struggles and identifying ourselves with them. This does not mean that we shall confront the world with new doctrinaire principles and proclaim: Here is the truth, on your knees before it! It means that we shall develope for the world new principles from the existing principles of the world. We shall not say: Abandon your struggles, they are mere folly; let us provide you with the true campaign-slogans. Instead we shall simply show the world why it is struggling, and consciousness of this is a thing it *must* acquire whether it wishes or not. The reform of consciousness consists *entirely* in making the world aware of its own consciousness, in arousing it from its dream of itself, in *explaining* its own actions to it. Like Feuerbach's critique of religion, our whole aim can only be to translate religious and political problems into their self-conscious human form. . . . It will then become plain that the world has long since dreamed of something of which it needs only to become conscious for it to possess it in reality. It will then become plain that our task is not to draw a sharp mental line between past and future but to *complete* the thought of the past. Lastly, it will become plain that mankind will not begin any *new* work, but will consciously bring about the completion of its old work. We are therefore in a position to sum up the credo of our journal in a *single word:* the self-clarification (critical philosophy) of the struggles and wishes of the age. This is a task for the world and for us. It can succeed only as the product of united efforts. What is needed above all is a *confession,* and nothing more than that. To obtain forgiveness for its sins mankind needs only to declare them for what they are.

The perception of the absolute termination of the premises now in existence is, *qua* saying, the supersession of this absolutely non-categorical movement which now is no longer conceivable as the material completion of the thought of the past in actuality essentially made self-conscious, but rather as itself the contradiction of the categorical absolute, of the essence of freedom itself, of the absolutely human identity, the absolute identity of the two, but rather as itself the contradiction of the constitution itself of love, the contradiction of action itself (this action differentiated from the essential immateriality of absolute thought before now), the contradiction of the concrete body itself, i.e., of the absolute priority of this saying itself, *qua* saying, essentially identical with absolutely unconditioned thought, i.e., thought itself constituting the time itself of its occurrence, the absolute evidence of the discrete perfection of the material element of perception itself. Once it has occurred, as indeed it has now for the first time in history, there is no alternative to the categorical absolute. Freedom itself is inalienable: the identity of the two is essentially inalienable: the difference itself is absolutely inalienable. A second absolute is not to be thought other than itself, i.e., precisely, it is thought for the first time history, therefore there is now no possibility whatsoever of things made absolutely self-conscious perceptions through united efforts: *qua* existent, things themselves are now thought for the first time in history *nothing*. There is no contention between the categorical absolute and nothing. The now absolutely previous contention was between absolute subjectivity and the predicament of contingent existence, between the materialization of subjectivity itself and the contingent absolute, between the thought of non-being and the non-being of thought:

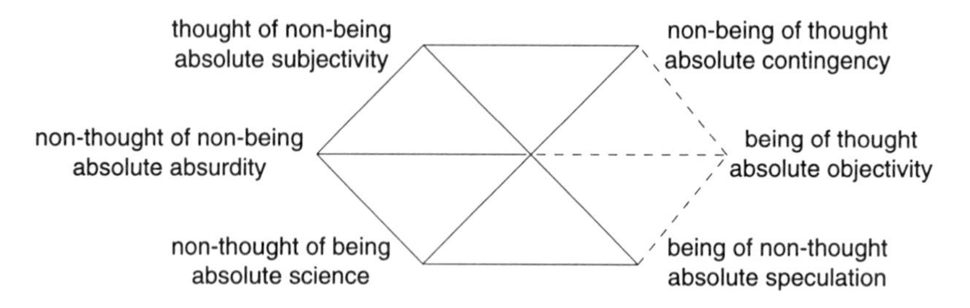

(the transcendental history of the logic of the absolute, the experience itself now of the identity of the absolute, is simply displayed in this constellation, in which the ultimate resolution of matter itself is the absolute objectivity of being thought, the absolute transcendence of absolute negativity). Before now the absolutely unconditioned contention between subjectivity and contingency (absolute subjectivity the *datum* from which the 'true reality' could be deduced by an absolute contingency standing within the logical horizon of historico-temporal criticism) was essentially stated by Marx in the course of his *Critique of Hegel's Doctrine of the State* as follows:[6]

> If Hegel had begun by positing real subjects as the basis of the state he would not have found it necessary to subjectivise the state in a mystical way. 'The truth of subjectivity', Hegel claims, 'is attained only in a *subject*, and the truth of personality only in a *person*'. This too is a mystification. Subjectivity is a characteristic of the subject, personality is a characteristic of the person. Instead of viewing them as the predicates of their subjects Hegel makes the predicates into autonomous beings and then causes them to become transformed into their subjects by means of a mystical process.
>
> The existence of the predicates is the subject: thus the subject is the existence of subjectivity etc. Hegel makes the predicates, the objects, autonomous, but he does this by separating them from their real autonomy, viz. their subject. The real subject subsequently appears as a result, whereas the correct approach would be to start with the real subject and then consider its objectification. The mystical substance therefore becomes the real subject, while the actual subject appears as something else, namely as a moment of the mystical substance. Because Hegel starts not with an actual existent (ὑποκείμενον, subject) but with predicates of universal determination, and because a vehicle of these determinations must exist, the mystical Idea becomes that vehicle. Hegel's dualism manifests itself precisely in his failure to regard the universal as the real essence of the finite real, i.e. of what exists and is determined, or to regard real existent things as the *true subject* of the infinite.

[6] Ibid., p. 80.

> Thus sovereignty, the essence of the state, is first objectified and conceived as something independent. Then, of course, this object must again become a subject. This subject, however, becomes manifest as the self-embodiment of sovereignty, whereas [in fact] sovereignty is nothing but the objectified spirit of the subjects of a state.

And a few pages later:[7]

> It is self-evident that since personality and subjectivity are only predicates of the person and the subject they can exist only as person and subject, and the person is certainly but *one*. However, Hegel should have gone on to say that this *one* truly exists only as *many ones*. The predicate, the essence, can never exhaust the spheres of its existence in a *single* one but only in *many ones*.

And again:[8]

> Now personality is undoubtedly a mere abstraction without the person, but the person is the *real Idea* of personality only in its species-existence [*Gattungsdasein*], *as persons*.

Here the essential objection of rational existence to the materialization of absolute thought is to its being a tautologous formality, i.e., not to its being a formality, but to its being a *tautologous*, i.e., *empty* formality. Reason itself absolutely objects, in the form of an essential inversion, to the merely formal *kenosis* of absolute thought—objects, in the form of an essentially final difference. Itself the material *kenosis* of absolute thought, *the pure positedness of absolute matter*, historical materialism is the necessary but consequently imperfect abstraction of existence itself from the absolutely arbitrary abstraction of subjectivity, in effect the purely temporal priority of reason itself to the categorical absolute (the existing individual things now seen to terminate

[7] Ibid., p. 84.
[8] Ibid.

essentially in existence itself for the first time in history), now clearly perceived in the absolutely unconditioned existence of reason itself in the form of the non-tautological formality, i.e., of the formality of absolute differentiation (i.e., the for the first time in history clearly perceived *alienation* of absolute difference), in which form before now the transcendent differentiation of fact and reflection was formally overcome in the form of the identity of pure content (non-being) insistently taken as the starting point *ex cogitatione,* the *potentially* intelligible real existent things, the potentiality of the middle term, the absolute alternative to the process of mystical transformation. Before now, in Marx, there is history, a history that is something other than the merely formal history of the matter of absolute thought: the history that is the essential movement of matter itself: the middle term existing but not *qua* saying: *the absolute not absolute, but nevertheless essentially the absolute indeed,* i.e., the absolute existing *qua* middle term, *qua* mediator, but *as such* not *qua* absolute: the elemental constituents of history themselves unhistorical: the premises in existence at any given time absolutely subsumed by reason itself, so that reason itself exists only insofar as it is the middle term. Before now, reason itself, *qua* absolute, distributes subjectivity, i.e., determines its own set of priorities, but, just so, does not *absolutely* exist, but is, rather, the implicit connection, the unspoken element, the elliptical existence itself, the absolutely conditioned existence of reason itself: the starting point beyond which, were it not for the fact itself of the absolute clarification of the absolute now occurring in reality, it would be impossible to conceive of another existence, since (beginning-less) reason is absolutely identified with becoming itself. But now in fact real existing things are *actually* intelligible, i.e., actual individual things are intelligible *qua* historical, which is to say that now the absolute is the absolute mediator. Just here it can be seen that the implication of the question whether the transcendent difference can, by the saying, etc., namely that there is a being beyond the absolute in terms of which it is intelligible that the transcendent difference is not in fact overcome, is seen to be an absolutely hypothetical abstraction, absolutely without foundation in history itself, indeed, contradicted in fact by its being overcome before now in the form of being itself identity—the transcendent difference, that is, overcome before now in becoming itself for the first time absolutely identified with reason itself, overcome before now in the rationalization of existence that is historical materialism—in the absolute existence of non-being, *ergo*, in the unconditioned non-being of thought itself, in the non-being of the essence itself.

In the essentially tautologous thought now occurring for the first time in history the essence of thought is its being absolutely identical. The thing perceived is actuality itself or absolutely unconditioned identity. In the absolute *kenosis* of absolute thought the otherwise (contrary to fact) 'empty' essence of thought is *immediately* 'filled with' being itself. This is the complex essence, existence itself, of the essentially new thinking now occurring for those who love truth, whereas, before now the essence of the thinking of those who loved truth was *not* immediately, rather, *mediately*, filled with being itself in the transcendent passion for a new order, an order that remained, contrary to the very essence of the historico-temporal logic of materialism (contrary to the imperative necessity of the fact itself), itself unspecified, a generic being itself, merely a new genus of transcendent being: inessentially absolute matter. The absolute matter of historical materialism was *essentially* inarticulate, it was the word essentially not spoken, the word not essentially made flesh. Language itself was the condition of thought in the form of idea still, but, therefore, not yet as it is now for the first time in essence thought itself in the form of perception itself: not yet, as now for the first time in history, was language itself in time itself itself thought flesh of the body itself. Indeed, it is now absolutely evident that the fundamental optimism expressed by Marx in his letter to Ruge, to wit: "What is needed above all is a *confession*, and nothing more than that. To obtain forgiveness for its sins mankind needs only to declare them for what they are."[9]—it is now clear that this is unfounded in reality (although the essential implication of the word conceived as inessentially historical

[9] Cf. above, pp. 16f., n. 5.

matter): it is now absolutely evident that the absolute essence is *sorrow* for sin, that even the love of truth is not truly loving of truth if it is not being itself the beloved: it is now absolutely evident that being itself, *qua* essence, is an absolutely inalienable otherness, that *matter itself* for the first time in history *absolutely specified existence* is the body itself (this absolute specificity is existence itself), the consolation of freedom itself, the absolute forgiveness itself. This is the foundation-stone in essence (yes, the bedrock itself in speech itself!), the constitution (love itself absolutely unconditioned), the absolutely unconditioned existence of reason itself. This absolute specificity is the *perfected* passion for an absolutely new transcendental order. This is the template now of the absolute experience of transcendental order. The new species of being is the thought of the essence of actuality itself: the absolute termination of the construction of the world: the absolute itself the middle term, *qua* existential matter: the absolute itself the articulated (complex) essence: the word itself thought itself: matter itself unconditionally essential (the elemental constituents of the absolute essentially absolute): the perfection itself of experience now essentially not yet itself the body itself, but yet experience itself essentially unconditioned. The absolute passion of existence is the perfect conception upon which the intelligible order of experience is to be absolutely constructed: the thing perceived absolutely the species itself of thought, its absolute existence absolutely predicted (transcending, therefore, the absolute specificity of the historico-temporal logic of historical materialism itself not thought, but matter—the absolute alternative to the non-specificity of absolute subjectivity). Even now and here the unicity of the absolute mediates the universal realization of the new fact (*novitas mentis*), mediates the actualization of catholicological being itself. The absolute intelligibility of unicity itself mediates the acknowledgement that mere appearance is absolutely nothing, that the appearance is the body itself, that the absolute itself is individuated. (In the historico-logical temporality of matter itself before now the appearance of the absolute was non-existence, the immanent nothingness of the idea, the concrete appearance of an absolute formality. Although the difference between fact and reflection was thus overcome in imitation [literally in a mirroring reversal of the disposition of subject and object] of the overcoming of the transcendent difference in the form of appearance and essence, nevertheless, the difference between appearances, the transcendent difference in fact, remained—unthought—the absolute matter emptied out of thought, the perfection of sincerity itself [the love of truth], but essentially inadequate to reality [not being itself the beloved]—a predicament from which there was absolutely no deliverance short of existence itself appearing in an essentially transcendental thought as now occurs for the first time in history—sheer contingency itself, the absolute prediction of non-existence, in fact an absolutely conditioned existence: the mere appearance of the existence itself of mediation, not the fact in essence [not the transformation of the mirror itself into the reflected image]. The existence of this sheer contingency is not itself an accident [as is now clear in light of the absolute saying itself unconditionally]: the realization of this pure semblance of absolute existence, of transcendence of the absolute, in fact the transcendental identity of mere appearance: the absolute negativity itself is inessential, non-specific, i.e., *qua* societal, *impractical*. Just here it can be seen that the repeated failures to realize in its purity the communism of absolute materialism are traceable not to a flaw [merely] in conception, nor [merely] in implementation: the flaw lies in [its] being absolutely inherent: in the contingency of absolutely nothing: in nothing not absolutely thought, but continuing in the form of becoming itself absolutely immanent. [This, indeed, is the absolute hunger for which the eucharist of existence itself is now provident matter.] It is precisely *qua* societal that the historical realization of materialistic communism is inessential, i.e., impractical, since the constituent elements of this ideal society are themselves not social, but rather elements whose immediate individuality has been negated: units of social production, the essential priority of whose individuality to the process to which they are subject is a pure semblance of the same purely theoretical matter of which they are the incarnation: the ultimate self-contradiction of a society not a society: self-creation: the appropriation of being itself: the non-being of thought being itself, the pure potentiality of existence itself matter, i.e., the non-categorical productivity of existence in which the essential presupposition of productivity [*passim* capital] is overcome in the *form* of absolute existence [in the essential form of thought] itself yet inessential—in the event of absolute contingency, in the form of the absolute negativity of pure thought, of the absolute unification of productivity itself, in the form of the ideal of the absolute unification of productivity itself [were it possible] in the appropriation of spirit itself.) But the unicitous absolute saying itself excludes appropriation itself except it suffers it *qua* existence itself. In the absolute clarification of the absolute now occurring in reality the presupposition of existence itself is absolutely nothing absolute, i.e., unintelligible *per se* except it be absolutely unconditioned the existence itself of the fact itself, except it be the contingency of being itself absolutely thought: the perception in essence that the objective state of being is the body itself. Such now is the transcendence of the categorical essence of productivity that productivity itself is the absolute form of thought itself *not yet* substance itself existing, that appropriation itself is not in fact the necessity of thought itself, but is the absolutely unconditioned negative of freedom itself, now seen to belong in essence to the past in light of the occurrence here and now of the categorical absolute, in light of the fact that existence itself is essentially historical—the fact of perception itself—now thought. Before now in consequence of an absolute subjectivity, in essential self-contradiction, there was the occurrence of not-being itself thought, the event of the absolute non-existence of identity (opposed in the event of Nothing by absolute speculation, by the elaboration of the self-same, by the absolute differentiation of non-existence). Before now change itself occurred essentially non-categorically, not as the product of absolutely unconditioned thought, not as freedom itself. Change itself before now essentially occurred as the non-existence of thought itself. Now change itself is an absolutely discrete element of perception, or, what in the light of that thinking now occurring for the first time in history is a manifest contradiction of the fact itself, nothing is perceived now (the absolute absurdity terminating in becoming itself, the absolutely unintelligible). Now an absolutely unconditioned change itself is the elemental discretion, existence itself absolutely elemental, in terms of which is begun the construction of the world itself the absolute therein absolutely individuated, in terms of which the very supposition of appropriation itself is transcended, i.e., in terms of which nothing, including death itself, is transcended, in terms of which the transcendental absolute essentially appears, i.e., in terms of which experience itself is essentially freedom itself, a substantial identity now in the form of an essentially transcendental thought within which there is no room for death itself, within which being is absolutely placed for nothing, i.e., *within which absolute being is not posited but is the thing perceived in essence* (this is the *historically accurate* formulation of a *precise something* which, *qua* appearance, is the thing in essence [the body itself now the transcendence of the difference between accuracy and precision!], namely, the absolute contingency of the non-being of thought which now appears as *absolutely* nothing except it be the absolute objectivity of being thought wherein the former's insistence at the beginning on beginning, i.e., its not-beginning, is transcended, wherein the former's holding to its own transcendent difference, to its content as the beloved truth, is its being *absolutely* reduced to nothing in light of the being of the thing perceived now. The latter, *qua* perception of the body itself, is being itself the beloved, the product of the absolute clarification of the absolute, the product, which, *qua* absolute, is *seeing is producing is being itself.* The product essentially, *qua* mediator, is neither presupposition, nor supposition, but the pre-essential essence, unicity itself, so that no longer is the essence of the existing product [mere] unity [the actuality of non-existence] but the existence of actuality: *now for the first time in history becoming itself actually intelligible as itself thought.* No longer is the essence of the existing product something that has to be filled in, the full between of being, something existing *in vacuo*, but it is unicity, the transcendental fullness of being itself, the thing existing in essence. Now there is absolutely nothing absolute except the product itself. The formality itself now existing in essence is the unicity of the body itself [there is therefore now absolutely (as before now, in the historico-temporal logic of materialism, *essentially* [where the residual of faith itself remained implicitly thought itself in essence], and before that, in the logic coincident with metaphysics, *formally* [where the residual of faith itself remained the simple non-freedom of thought itself]) no question of thinking *about* e.g., and unconditionally, *sacra doctrina,* now that for the first time in history the latter, *qua* word, is the very form of thought (the essence of thinking-about, it is now clear, is absolutely contrary to the fact of history itself: it would be the absolutely unconditional non-existence of the very thing about which it would be thought—shinning up the pole of non-existence! the exercise of a futile supremacy, now that there is indeed for the first time in history no choice but to acknowledge what is now perceived in essence, namely, the actuality of being itself, *or,* to say nothing in essence [not to *think* at all] whether speaking or silent, to close one's eyes, literally or spiritually in face of the fact itself—such is the choice implicit in the possibility of acknowledging that being itself is now thought in essence!)]. Before now the absolute unicity of the body itself was a pure potentiality essentially incapable of being transcendentally differentiated except as not yet having occurred, therefore, as having occurred as an absolute immediacy in the form of thought itself, the substantial identity of a transcendent thought, therefore, a pure potentiality *as such* only occurring *now* in the form of an absolutely unconditioned thought, not, as before now, incapable of the absolute perception of anything, but now incapable of the absolute perception of the body itself of anything other than in the form of beginning, an incapacity not essential, while the former incapacity is destined to become the form of those who shall have forfeited the realization of this beginning, i.e., of those excluding themselves from this form of the material repetition of creation itself). Now for the first time in history the construction of the world itself, the beginning itself terminating in the elements themselves absolutely historical, such that the historical beginning of the world itself is now thought itself. Now the historical construction of the world itself begins in the intelligible experience of freedom itself. Before now the material essence of capital, i.e., the absolute presupposition of the material of productivity (in light of the eternal logic of absolute thought, the presupposition of nothing which was the existence itself of the absolute, death the wage of death [no consciousness of sin, itself the wage of sin])—before now in light of the absolutely dependent temporal logic of historical materialism, the presupposition of nothing the existence itself of nothing absolute, death the wage of sin (sin-consciousness nothing more than the consciousness of the need for confession, there being in the formal essence of capital, i.e., in the absolute presupposition of the form of productivity, nothing but the consciousness of the non-existence of appropriation itself being itself the supposition of appropriation itself). Indeed, *inessentially absolute, capital for historical materialism was nothing but the existence itself in which it was itself the supposition of the production of existence itself as the non-being of the past, as its own capital, the supposition of appropriation itself as a radical capacity for a new order* (there being nothing transcendental, not the transcendence of nothing but the immanence of nothing). So Marx in the *Grundrisse* of 1858:[10]

> Thus the old view, in which the human being appears as the aim of production, regardless of his limited national, religious, political character, seems to be very lofty when contrasted to the modern world, where production appears as the aim of mankind and wealth as the aim of production. In fact, however, when the limited bourgeois form is stripped away, what is wealth other than the universality of individual needs, capacities, pleasures, productive forces etc., created through universal exchange? The full development of human mastery over the forces of nature, those of so-called nature as well as of humanity's own nature? The absolute working out of his creative potentialities, with no presupposition other than the previous historic development, which makes this totality of development, i.e., the development of all human powers as such the end in itself, not as measured on a *predetermined* yardstick? Where he does not reproduce himself in one specificity, but produces his totality? Strives not to remain something he has

[10] K. Marx, *Grundrisse: Foundations of the Critique of Political Economy,* trans. M. Nicolaus (New York, 1973), pp. 487–88.

> become, but is in the absolute movement of becoming? In bourgeois economics—and in the epoch of production to which it corresponds—this complete working-out of the human content appears as a complete emptying-out, this universal objectification as total alienation, and the tearing down of all limited, one-sided aims as sacrifice of the human end-in-itself to an entirely external end. This is why the childish world of antiquity appears on one side as loftier. On the other side, it really is loftier in all matters where closed shapes, forms and given limits are sought for. It is satisfaction from a limited standpoint; while the modern age gives no satisfaction; or, where it appears satisfied with itself, it is *vulgar.*

But now for the first time in history in light of the categorically absolute non-being beside the word itself, in the light of an infinite ontology (in terms of which everything exists in essence), capital itself exists in essence. There exists instant the absolute formality of the essential presupposition of productivity, i.e., of the absolute productivity of past thought, as the unicity of the body itself, whereas in fact the essentiality of the body itself is such that it is now the absolutely unconditioned positing of the productivity of existence itself. The body itself is the existence itself in essence of the nothing that was the existence of the supposition of appropriation itself: the essential transcendence of nothing but existence itself: in light of the absolute logic of transcendental history the presupposition of nothing which is the existence of nothing in essence absolute: the body is the absolutely essential positing of the identity of the absolute thing (the absolute thing is not posited [merely] in essence [posited in essence it is nothing existing in essence, it is not absolutely the thing] but is posited as being itself thought in essence: not nothing in essence posited in essence, i.e., the absolute thing is not nothing: as [what was] nothing it now absolutely exists, i.e., *qua* nothing posited it is the body). This is the absolutely unconditioned positing of the appropriation of the past: *the body itself is not the body itself except it is the wage of sin: the body itself absolutely nothing but existence itself being itself the transcendence of appropriation itself:* the body itself is nothing but the actual consciousness (the body itself being itself) of the existence in essence of sin itself. This is the explicit consolation, i.e., the consolation for the sorrow for sin: *the perception itself of the body itself is absolutely unconditioned productivity* (existence itself suffering appropriation itself), here now where historical materialism absolutely anticipates it not, where, on the contrary, inessentially absolute materialism anticipates an absolute productivity beyond a specific existence, a productivity of an absolutely unconditioned becoming itself, a productivity that is the *generic* body of being itself, the embodiment of the very human nature which capital, *qua* existence, i.e., in contradiction with itself, absolutely posits as absolute. So Marx in the *Grundrisse*:[11]

> The bourgeois economists who regard capital as an eternal and *natural* [not historical] form of production then attempt at the same time to legitimize it again by formulating the conditions of its becoming as the conditions of its contemporary realization; i.e., presenting the moments in which the capitalist still appropriates as not-capitalist—because he is still becoming—as the very conditions in which he appropriates *as capitalist*. These attempts at apologetics demonstrate a guilty conscience, as well as the inability to bring the mode of appropriation of capital as capital into harmony with the *general laws of property* proclaimed by capitalist society itself. On the other side, much more important for us is that our method indicates the points where historical investigation must enter in, or where bourgeois economy as a merely historical form of the production process points beyond itself to earlier historical modes of production. In order to develop the laws of bourgeois economy, therefore, it is not necessary to write the *real history of the relations of production*. But the correct observation and deduction of these laws, as having themselves become in history, always leads to primary equations—like the empirical numbers e.g. in natural science—which point toward a past lying behind this system. These indications [*Andeutung*], together with a correct grasp of the present, then also offer the key to the understanding of the past—a work in its own right which, it is to be hoped, we shall be able to undertake as well. This correct view likewise leads at the same time to the points at which the suspension of

[11] Ibid., pp. 460–61.

> the present form of production relations gives signs of its becoming—foreshadowings of the future. Just as, on one side the pre-bourgeois phases appear as merely *historical,* i.e., suspended presuppositions, so do the contemporary conditions of production likewise appear as engaged in *suspending themselves* and hence in positing the *historic presuppositions* for a new state of society.

For historical materialism capital, *qua* existence, was the historic presupposition of the embodiment of man in nature itself as the material condition of the forces of production in which the *universal* is absolutely individuated: so Marx later in the *Grundrisse*:[12]

> . . . *The exchange of labour for labour—seemingly the condition of the worker's property—rests on the foundation of the worker's propertylessness.*> (It will be shown later that the *most extreme* form of alienation, wherein labour appears in the relation of capital and wage labour, and labour, productive activity appears in relation to its own conditions and its own product, is a necessary point of transition—and therefore already contains in *itself,* in a still only inverted form, turned on its head, the dissolution of all *limited presuppositions of production,* and moreover creates and produces the unconditional presuppositions of production, and therewith the full material conditions for the total, universal development of the productive forces of the individual.)

Historical materialism is the instantaneous realization of the end of capital: the freedom from the form of capital of the absolute contingency of the absolute individuation of the universal perceived without duration itself. Form itself not absolutely unconditioned historical materialism overcomes the form of the past in the form of an inessentially absolute existence: Marx again in the *Grundrisse*:[13]

> Thus while capital must on one side strive to tear down every spatial barrier to intercourse, i.e., to exchange, and conquer

[12] Ibid., p. 515.
[13] Ibid., pp. 539–42.

the whole earth for its market, it strives on the other side to annihilate this space with time, i.e., to reduce to a minimum the time spent in motion from one place to another. The more developed the capital, therefore, the more extensive the market over which it circulates, which forms the spatial orbit of its circulation, the more does it strive simultaneously for an even greater extension of the market and for greater annihilation of space by time. . . . There appears here the universalizing tendency of capital, which distinguishes it from all previous stages of production. Although limited by its very nature, it strives towards the universal development of the forces of production, and thus becomes the presupposition of a new mode of production, which is founded not on the development of the forces of production for the purpose of reproducing or at most expanding a given condition, but where the free, unobstructed, progressive and universal development of the forces of production is itself the presupposition of society and hence of its reproduction; where advance beyond the point of departure is the only presupposition. This tendency—which capital possesses, but which at the same time, since capital is a limited form of production, contradicts it and hence drives it towards dissolution—distinguishes capital from all earlier forms of production, and at the same time contains this element, that capital is posited as a mere point of transition. All previous forms of society—or, what is the same, of the forces of social production—foundered on the development of wealth. . . . Considered *ideally,* the dissolution of a given form of consciousness sufficed to kill a whole epoch. In reality, this barrier to consciousness corresponds to a *definite degree of development of the forces of material production* and hence of wealth. . . . Capital posits the *production of wealth* itself and hence the universal development of the productive forces, the constant overthrow of its prevailing presuppositions, as the presupposition of its reproduction. . . . Its own presupposition—value—is posited as product, not as a loftier presupposition hovering over production. The barrier to *capital* is that this entire development proceeds in a contradictory way, and that the working-out of the productive forces, of general wealth etc., knowledge etc., appears in such a way that the working individual *alienates* himself [*sich entäussert*]; relates to the conditions brought out of him by his labour as those not of his *own* but of an *alien wealth*

> and of his own poverty. But this antithetical form is itself fleeting, and produces the real conditions of its own suspension. The result is: the tendentially and potentially general development of the forces of production—of wealth as such—as a basis; likewise, the universality of intercourse, hence the world market as a basis. The basis as the possibility of the universal development of the individual, and the real development of the individuals from this basis as a constant suspension of its *barrier*, which is recognized as a barrier, not taken for a *sacred limit.* Not an ideal or imagined universality of the individual, but the universality of his real and ideal relations. Hence also the grasping of his own history as a *process*, and the recognition of nature (equally present as practical power over nature) as his real body. The process of development itself posited and known as the presupposition of the same.

Now at a time when historical materialism anticipated absolutely nothing, in thought where it essentially anticipated nothing other than the incarnation of the idea itself, the absolute unification of intelligible appearances, there occurs—precluding the absolutely unconditioned *generic* individuation—the absolutely unconditioned individuation of the *species*, i.e., the absolute individuation of the body itself in essence precluding the generic being itself of the non-being of thought real or ideal. Indeed, historical materialism is now clearly seen as transcendental being before now just as that thinking upon which it, *qua* absolute, inessentially depended is seen to belong essentially to the past, that is, its absolute contingency is experienced as being no longer intelligible *per se.* Now for the first time the actually existing individual is the absolute specification of matter: the thought of the individual is the embodiment of matter itself. Before now what was practical in Kant was the transcendence of alienation, *qua matter*; before now what was practical in Hegel was the transcendence of alienation, *qua form*; before now what was practical in Marx was the transcendence of alienation, *qua existence.* Now for the first time in history, now that the identity of the two is absolutely unconditioned, i.e., now that the transcendent difference is no longer overcome by being identified with one or the other—being itself yet another thing—now that the transcendent difference is overcome by being identified with both absolutely, *now what is practical is the transcendence of alienation,* qua *absolute.* Now difference itself exists absolutely. Existence itself is differentiated. Now for the first time in history the state of being itself is changed in essence: being itself is the other itself in essence: the actuality of the individual is the other itself. Before now historical materialism was the *form* of an essential difference, the *form* of a universally new society (*essentially* a transcendent *revolution*), the abolition of the freedom of the finite individual in favor of the product of an absolutely conditioned thought, the *formally* infinite freedom of the individual embodying self-consciously the universality of real and ideal relations, the *material* transcendence of *community itself, the unity of appropriation itself* in which social existence is a mere form, the non-existent private essence not transcended in the abolition of private property in favor of community property. Indeed, *the non-existence before now of the inalienable absolute, i.e., of society itself inalienable, necessitated the constant interruption of the forces of production themselves, the perpetual repetition of violence. The form of the inalienable absolute before now is in fact the alienation of the body itself,* society essentially being connected, the natural body of man essentially inarticulate, transcendence essentially inessentially revolutionary, i.e., transcendent existence itself not thought alienated (this revolutionary form is the negative form of non-existence: self-assertive non-existence: the thoughtful form of non-existence as distinguished from the transcendent passion of existence). The unity of appropriation itself in materialistic transcendent communism is the *formally* revolutionary transcendence of capitalist existence, but *essentially* it continues that existence, i.e., transforms it into the matter of a formally new society. So Marx on the contradiction between the foundation and development of bourgeois production, in the *Grundrisse*:[14]

> No longer does the worker insert a modified natural thing [*Naturgegenstand*] as middle link between the object [*Objekt*]

[14] Ibid., pp. 705–6.

> and himself; rather, he inserts the process of nature, transformed into an industrial process, as a means between himself and inorganic nature, mastering it. He steps to the side of the production process instead of being its chief actor. In this transformation, it is neither the direct human labour he himself performs, nor the time during which he works, but rather the appropriation of his own general productive power, his understanding of nature and his mastery over it by virtue of his presence as a social body—it is, in a word, the development of the social individual which appears as the great foundation-stone of production and of wealth. The *theft of alien labour time, on which the present wealth is based,* appears a miserable foundation in face of this new one, created by large-scale industry itself. As soon as labour in the direct form has ceased to be the great well-spring of wealth, labour time ceases and must cease to be its measure, and hence exchange value [must cease to be the measure] of use value. The *surplus labour of the mass* has ceased to be the condition for the development of general wealth, just as the *non-labour of the few,* for the development of the general powers of the human head. With that, production based on exchange value breaks down, and the direct, material production process is stripped of the form of penury and antithesis. The free development of individualities, and hence not the reduction of necessary labour time so as to posit surplus labour, but rather the general reduction of the necessary labour of society to a minimum, which then corresponds to the artistic, scientific etc. development of the individuals in the time set free, and with the means created, for all of them. . . . Forces of production and social relations—two different sides of the development of the social individual—appear to capital as mere means, and are merely means for it to produce on its limited foundation. In fact, however, they are the material conditions to blow this foundation sky-high.

The practical identity of the two antithetical elements of the developing form of capitalism. The revolution essentially transcends the form as *development* in its being formally the appropriation of *unity*, the form of being itself connected—in its being implicitly absolute. The interruption is formally society: the social formation of matter itself: the beginning-less inessential form of absolute matter: nature embodying man himself. Marx writes:[15]

> Nature builds no machines, no locomotives, railways, electric telegraphs, self-acting mules etc. These are products of human industry; natural material transformed into organs of human will over nature, or of human participation in nature. They are *organs of the human brain, created by the human hand*; the power of knowledge, objectified. The development of fixed capital indicates to what degree general social knowledge has become a *direct force of production*, and to what degree, hence, the conditions of the process of social life itself have come under the control of the general intellect and been transformed in accordance with it. To what degree the powers of social production have been produced, not only in the form of knowledge, but also as immediate organs of social practice, of the real life process.

Before now difference itself is continuous in the form of social practice, i.e., difference itself is *essentially* non-existent. The appropriation of the foundation, i.e., production on an unlimited foundation, is freedom itself in the negative. In the inessential formality of the body itself that historical materialism is the social form is *the tool of social existence: the form of the body is the absolute tool.* Again Marx:[16]

> The saving of labour time [is] equal to an increase of free time, i.e. time for the full development of the individual, which in turn reacts back upon the productive power of labour as itself the greatest productive power. From the standpoint of the direct production process it can be regarded as the production of fixed capital, this *fixed capital* being man himself. . . . Free time—which is both idle time and time for higher activity—has naturally transformed its possessor into a different subject, and he then enters into the direct production process as this different subject. . . . As the system of bourgeois economy has devel-

[15] Ibid., p. 706.
[16] Ibid., pp. 711–12.

oped for us only by degrees, so too its negation, which is its ultimate result. We are still concerned now with the direct production process. When we consider bourgeois society in the long view and as a whole, then the final result of the process of social production always appears as the society itself, i.e., the human being itself in its social relations. Everything that has a fixed form, such as the product etc., appears as merely a moment, a vanishing moment, in this movement. The direct production process itself here appears only as a moment. The conditions and objectifications of the process are themselves equally moments of it, and its only subjects are the individuals, but individuals in mutual relationships, which they equally reproduce and produce anew. The constant process of their own movement, in which they renew themselves even as they renew the world of wealth they create.

And further on in the *Grundrisse*:[17]

> To the extent that . . . the creation of the objective body of activity happens in antithesis to the immediate labour capacity . . . this twisting and inversion [*Verdrehung und Verkehrung*] is a *real* [*phenomenon*], not a merely *supposed one* existing merely in the imagination of the workers and the capitalists. But obviously this process of inversion is a merely *historical* necessity, a necessity for the development of the forces of production solely from a specific historic point of departure, or basis, but in no way an *absolute* necessity of production; rather, a vanishing one. . . . But with the suspension of the *immediate* character of living labour, as merely *individual*, or as general merely internally or merely externally, with the positing of the activity of individuals as immediately general or *social* activity, the objective moments of production are stripped of this form of alienation; they are thereby posited as property, as the organic social body within which the individuals reproduce themselves as individuals, but as social individuals. . . . It requires no great penetration to grasp that, where e.g. free labour or wage labour arising out of the dissolution of bondage is the point of departure, there machines can only *arise* in antithesis to living

[17] Ibid., pp. 831–33.

> labour, as property alien to it, and as power hostile to it; i.e. that they must confront it as capital. But it is just as easy to perceive that machines will not cease to be agencies of social production when they become e.g. property of the associated workers.

For historical materialism the body itself was nothing more than the identity of the two in the form of a differentiated subjectivity, in the form of an absolutely self-conscious reconstruction of community of property as the basis of the division of labor: not only the non-transcendence of the non-existence of the private essence but (historical materialism is) the non-existence of the essence of property itself, i.e., of the body itself, i.e., of the constitution of freedom itself, this alienation of the body itself before now the essentially random organization that is the absolute movement of becoming itself in place of the 'moving contradiction' that is capital. What now occurs *is* the body itself *inalienable,* the perception of the body itself: the absolutely societal form of the world. What now exists absolutely is not the anticipation but the *perception* of a new form of society, *qua* absolute, absolutely the world: the *thought* in essence of the world created. Now the practical is an inalienable society: now a transcendent society actually exists: now in light of existence itself in the form of the body itself it is clear that existence itself is absolutely passionate, that existence itself is the inalienable existence of thought itself now for the first time in history, i.e., that not only is existence itself now differentiated from the absolute movement of becoming itself (therefore, absolutely, from the 'moving contradiction') *as* being itself the absolute motion, i.e., *as* being itself categorically absolute, as objectivity, but that, as such, it is the proof positive of the absolute prediction of existence itself, the proof positive that the absolute itself is differentiated. Indeed, the perception of the alienation of the body itself now occurring is itself inconceivable except as the absolute form of the other, i.e., the absolute perpetual existence of the word itself, i.e., not the perpetual repetition of violence, but the perpetuation of creation itself: creation the absolute transcendence of existence itself. The absolute status of catholicological being is now *being itself commodious*, the essential foundation of an *essentially differentiated organization. This* absolute consciousness absolutely limited! precluded by being itself absolute *foundation*-consciousness from succumbing to the temptation of *becoming* absolute, i.e., to movement itself. This consciousness cleaves to existence itself absolutely, transcending the absolutely conditioned objectivity of historical materialism, transcending the latter's being absolutely founded in antithesis to the limited foundation, its being the infinite foundation *inessentially*. Now the essential foundation is an *essentially practical thought* (transcending, on the one hand, the limited foundation of the formal conception of history, practice the matter of thought, and, on the other hand, the unlimited foundation of the material conception of history, practice the form of thought): now the essential foundation is the *proclamation of the body itself*, the production absolutely of freedom itself. Now the truth of the absolute itself: speak, in fact it will be accomplished according to the word: only say the word, being itself in fact is made whole: the body itself in fact now exists: *the saying itself is the absolute existence of the absolute identity of the two.* Practice itself differentiated from the material/formal social practice of the past is now the body itself. *Qua* practice, the existence of the past was the non-existence of the body itself, i.e., revolutionary existence. Now, *qua* practice there is no practice that is not thought in essence, no existence that is not specifically the body itself. Practice absolutely conceived is nothing but the body itself. Now the essential foundation itself, the proclamation of the body itself, the absolute prophecy, is that it itself (which reaps where it has not sown) is the effectuation of an essentially inalienable society or it is nothing at all. Existence itself absolutely unconditioned speaks itself the language of thought. There is no turning away from this new fact of history itself, namely, that now every human personality essentially hears the absolute prediction of existence itself, or nothing at all is the conclusion the person itself arrives at. In between there is absolutely nothing but the absolutely contrary to fact condition absolutely confirming the other itself: death itself absolute: the body itself forfeit. In any event, *it is now clear that everyone now essentially partakes of the body itself, i.e., essentially partakes of the property of the absolute itself, of property itself absolute, of the property that society itself now actually is for the first time in history.* Before now the material essence of property was privacy, before now the formal, i.e., inessential, essence of property was community, before now neither essence existed in fact, but each was the contradiction of an ideal other. The matter of private property was the identity of non-existence, was subject to expropriation, while the form of community property was the non-existence of this same identity, i.e., the identity of non-existence, existence itself subject to expropriation, the conception of private property as matter itself: so Marx in *Capital* I:[18]

> The centralization of the means of production and the socialization of labour reach a point at which they become incompatible with their capitalist integument. This integument is burst asunder. The knell of capitalist private property sounds. The expropriators are expropriated.
>
> The capitalist mode of appropriation, which springs from the capitalist mode of production, produces capitalist private property. This is the first negation of individual private property, as founded on the labour of its proprietor. But capitalist production begets, with the inexorability of a natural process, its own negation. This is the negation of the negation. It does not re-establish private property, but it does indeed establish individual property on the basis of the achievements of the capitalist era: namely co-operation and the possession in common of the land and the means of production produced by labour itself.
>
> The transformation of scattered private property resting on the personal labour of the individuals themselves into capitalist private property is naturally an incomparably more protracted, violent and difficult process than the transformation of capitalist private property, which in fact already rests on the carrying on of production by society, into social property. In the former case, it was a matter of the expropriation of the mass of

[18] K. Marx, *Capital: A Critique of Political Economy,* vol. 1, trans. B. Fowkes (New York, 1977), pp. 929–30.

> the people by a few usurpers; but in this case, we have the expropriation of a few usurpers by the mass of the people.

That is, the expropriation of the expropriators is the establishment of individual property on the foundation of the formal essence of property, i.e., on the foundation of the material form of absolute property conceived as a pure formality. The individual in fact does not exist apart from the unity of appropriation itself. Indeed, in the communist mode of appropriation the individual is founded on the non-existence of property, i.e., on a social property that is a mere formality as it must needs be when a post-primitive, post-modern individuality is posited with the essential form of property, i.e., within community. The absolute unification of production is itself the elimination of property itself, this, in turn, the foundation for the productivity of the spirit (were it in fact now conceivable)—in any event, the individual, so conceived, is the redundancy of an inessentially social practice, the absolute non-existence of property, nothing other than the appropriation of force itself in essence. Lenin writes in 1895 in his remembrance of Engels:[19]

> On the development of the productive forces depend the relations into which men enter one with another in the production of the things required for the satisfaction of human needs. And in these relations lies the explanation of all the phenomena of social life, human aspirations, ideas and laws. The development of the productive forces creates social relations based upon private property, but now we see that this same development of the productive forces deprives the majority of their property and concentrates it in the hands of an insignificant minority. It wipes out property, the basis of the modern social order, it itself strives towards the very aim which the socialists have set themselves. All the socialists have to do is to realize which social force, owing to its position in modern society, is interested in bringing socialism about, and to impart to this force the consciousness of its interests and of its historical task. This force is the proletariat.

[19] V. I. Lenin, *On Marx and Engels* (Peking, 1975), p. 51.

Before now individuality was founded on the perpetual violence of the property of being absolutely nothing, of being in the form of absolute contradiction, of *being itself connected* (the peculiar mode of the displacement of *being itself alienated*). Now for the first time individuality is founded on the perpetual creation itself of the property of being the body itself, of *being itself commodious.* Before now individuality was seen to be the agency of the existing social form, i.e., the agency of the existing forces of social production; now individuality is seen to be, for the first time in history, the identity of the practicality of the body itself: the individual itself is the practical identity of the body itself, i.e., the practical identity of the property itself that society itself now is for the first time in history, i.e., of property itself absolutely existing, i.e., transcending in essence the dichotomy private/community. Individuality is now seen to be the proprietorship of the existing society transcendentally comprehended as the creation of property itself. This now is the transcendental foundation: the absolute transcendence of instrumentality itself. Before now in historical materialism the transcendental horizon was formally interrupted, the absolute foundation was the absolute formality of existence itself. Now for the first time in history in the intelligible experience of history itself existence itself is the absolute interruption of the transcendental horizon: the body itself is the absolute interruption now for the first time. Now existence itself is beheld face to face: difference itself exists. Now the foundation itself of the transcendental itself is beheld for the first time: the existence itself of the transcendental being itself absolutely thought. This is the bedrock upon which humanity stands now thought in essence for the first time in history: the absolute transcendence of the transcendental itself: the intelligible experience of existence itself as the absolute factuality of creation itself: the universe itself the foundation itself the interruption itself the beginning itself: the foundation, *qua* foundation, the absolutely unconditioned practical, the body itself absolutely existing. The foundation, *qua* foundation, is existence itself suffering appropriation itself, i.e., the differentiation of the foundation of nothing itself as the absolute 'other than'. The foundation, *qua* foundation, is the absolute. The point of departure is the body itself absolute. The body itself, *qua* foundation, is property absolutely unconditioned. Before now historical materialism (as science prior to the foundation now existing, i.e., prior to the proclamation of the body itself now occurring for the first time in history, i.e., prior to the termination of science theoretically founded) had as its foundation the transcendence of foundation, i.e., the absolute production of unity itself, i.e., the production of the absolute force of existence itself, i.e., the *form* of the body itself: *qua* foundation, the generic specificity of property itself. It is precisely upon this foundation of nothing unconditionally itself, upon this essence of instrumentality itself, that the revolution itself exists, producing, first, the essential non-existence of the state, second, *qua* form, the 'withering away' of the state—so Lenin in his *The State and Revolution*, written in 1917:[20]

> This is exactly a case of "quantity becoming transformed into quality": democracy, introduced as fully and consistently as is at all conceivable, is transformed from bourgeois democracy into proletarian democracy; from the state (=a special force for the suppression of a particular class) into something which is no longer, properly speaking, the state. It is still necessary to suppress the bourgeoisie and its resistance. . . . But the organ of suppression is here the majority of the population, and not a minority, as was always the case under slavery, serfdom and wage slavery. And since the majority of the people *itself* suppresses its oppressors, a "special force" for suppression is *no longer necessary*! In this sense the state *begins to wither away*.

—and third, the absolutely generic state becoming itself absolutely with the creation of an essentially habitual existence, materially generic itself or transcendent in fact, i.e., *qua* matter, the generic body itself: again Lenin,[21]

> . . . the . . . expropriation of the capitalists. . . . will create *the*

[20] V. I. Lenin, *The State and Revolution* (Peking, 1976), p. 52.
[21] Ibid., pp. 116–17.

> *possibility* of a gigantic development of the productive forces. . . . But how rapidly this development will proceed, how soon it will reach the point of breaking away from the division of labour, of doing away with the antithesis between mental and physical labour, of transforming labour into "life's prime want"—we do not and *cannot* know. That is why we are entitled to speak only of the inevitable withering away of the state, emphasizing the protracted nature of this process and its dependence upon the rapidity of development of the *higher phase* of communism, and leaving the question of the time required for, or the concrete forms of, the withering away entirely open, because there is *no* material for answering these questions. It will become possible for the state to wither away completely when society gives effect to the rule: "From each according to his ability, to each according to his needs," i.e., when people have become so accustomed to observing the fundamental rules of community life and when their labour becomes so productive that they will voluntarily work *according to their ability*. "The narrow horizon of bourgeois right," by which one is compelled to calculate with the callousness of a Shylock, lest one work half an hour more than somebody else, lest one receive less pay than somebody else—this narrow horizon will then be crossed. There will then be no need for society, in distributing products, to regulate the quantity to be received by each; each will take freely "according to his needs."

In place of the infinitely formal tautology of thought essentially transcendent (formally transcendental) historical materialism substituted the material tautology of experience itself, the tautologous truth of the habitual itself, as the form of its ultimate production, at once the *form* of the transcendence of society itself, but not yet nor ever society itself the existing form of the world itself. Before now historical materialism laid down, at the beginning, at the end, as the foundation of transcendence itself, the form of a finite tautology, essentially terminating in the form of beginning: not, indeed, a *utopia* (a materially finite absolute), but in fact a *uchronia*, the absolute immanence of the eternal, the *form* of absolutely finite matter, the *form* of a utopian society, *the form of matter itself the body itself*, society itself not absolutely non-existent in fact but essentially inconceivable, i.e., society itself existing everywhere but at no time, the anticipation of the body itself without regard to its not-being-itself the foundation: *self-consciousness in the form of the other in essence:* matter itself where now for the first time in history the world itself is: the form of matter itself where now for the first time in history existence itself is essentially: the anticipation in the form of existence itself not thought of what now in fact occurs for the first time in the form of thought. Now the foundation is laid *in medias res:* the new universe, *qua* the absolute interruption, is the absolute tautology of existence itself: *qua* foundation, the tautology of existence itself thought: productivity itself absolute. The foundation now laid for the first time in history is the *essence* of an *otherwise* utopian society: the here and now absolute: absolute reason the existing absolute: *qua* foundation, the absolutely unconditioned essence, matter itself/ thought itself: the absolute *existence* of absolute matter precluding the immaterial productivity of the spirit, i.e., productivity as the essentially immaterial unity of the body itself. Now for the first time the body itself matter itself precludes the body itself essentially inarticulate. The spirit, precisely, is the essential identity of matter itself *ex nihilo.* The existence of absolute matter is the existence in *essence* of created spirit. Now for the first time in history the absolute individual is the essence of society: the existing individual is the unity of the body itself: the foundation, *qua* foundation, is the existing matter of history. Upon *this* foundation there is nothing to be erected: this is the coping-stone of existence itself, being itself commodious, the consciousness of being itself now historically perpetuated. Before now in the historico-temporal logic of absolute materialism objectivity was *form*-consciousness, so that the table, the cup, the house, *qua* thing perceived, was the *form* of appropriation itself, beyond which lay an essentially undifferentiated subjectivity which, through the positing of the inessential unity of the body itself, was to become the form of a differentiated subjectivity, the essential form of the identity of the two, i.e., subjectivity/objectivity, predicated upon the transcendental unification of existence: force itself absolutely unconditioned. Now for the first time in history the fact itself of the existence of freedom itself evidently precludes this latter eventuality being itself thought except as belonging essentially to the past as the *not absolute form* of matter itself the body, i.e., as the *illogical* form of the existence of absolute matter, i.e., as absolute matter *not* absolute (the non-categorical appearance of the categorical absolute *vis-a-vis* the materialist conception of history is a function of the immediate fullness of being itself now, nor is it to be confused with the absolutely irreversible non-conception of the categorical absolute, i.e., with the mirror itself reflecting absolutely nothing, or, reflection ending in existence itself *except for the thing* from which it prescinds, as it prescinds from thought itself, encumbered by *the thing itself/the appearance in essence of nothing in essence,* i.e., absolutely nothing inessentially absolute! which encumbrance is no thought whatsoever of the body itself, nothing itself the foundation, *qua* foundation itself, i.e., the *form* of nothing, i.e., even *qua* nothing itself *generic* [the non-being of thought itself absolute]: the necessity of conceiving the alienated self: nothing itself the appropriation of necessity—the transcendental reflection of nothing in an essentially formal imagination: the individuation of the universal form of matter itself: the fact itself reflection itself of the non-existence of the transcendental imagination: *the logic of the thing itself* [not to be confused with the absolute thing of absolute speculation, the logic of absolutely nothing] in which, before now, every transcendent difference has been overcome *except that of time itself,* i.e., *the difference between past and future* [existence itself still undifferentiated in historical materialism from time itself as being itself *essentially* historical (change itself), *formally* temporal, *materially* motion itself (existence itself differentiated, perception itself)], the identity of time itself absolutely not thought—whereas now for the first time in history time itself is transcendentally differentiated as the transcendent form of the identity of past and future existing in essence. Before now time itself in historical materialism was the absolute interruption in form. Now time itself is the absolute interruption existing in essence for the first time). Now the intelligible experience of history itself is the *absolute logic of the existing thing itself,* is matter itself. Now matter itself *is* transcendental historical existence. The history itself of the transcendental *is* itself the practical foundation. Now existence itself begins and ends absolutely, outside time itself, in history itself, perpetuating time itself as the locus of the motion itself of the body itself, of that motion which is the absolute disposition of existence itself, of that motion which is essentially the disposition of the foundation itself which is existence, of the essentially historical motion itself of what is purely a matter of convenience, the thing itself. Now existence itself for the first time is the foundation of an absolute society. Now for the first time in history time itself is the inalienable body itself transcending the form itself of past and future: *the thing itself now in essentially historical motion itself is the species-proclamation of the body itself, the perception of property itself identical with society itself: the perception of existence itself property itself:* for the first time the foundation, *qua* foundation itself, man itself, is the essence itself of absolute faith, i.e., the absolute logic of faith itself, the first integral repetition of which is actual speech itself: the second, thought: the third, the actuality of the body itself: the fourth, the proclamation of the body itself: the fifth, the perception itself of the new form of the body itself, or, history itself *qua planum vitae* within which man itself is found and hidden and now purchased at the expense of absolutely everything other: being itself thought itself now for the first time in history: the thing itself perceived existing in essence. The foundation, *qua* foundation itself, is *the thing itself essentially the property of society itself.* The foundation, *qua* existing foundation, is the species itself absolutely unconditioned. Humanity, *qua* existing foundation, is imagination itself, practice itself, property actually itself. The existing foundation is the actual *integrity* of thought itself (the existence itself of the body itself). The foundation, *qua* existence itself, is the *identity* of thought itself (the perception of the body itself). The integrity of thought, *qua* integrity, is *man in essence;* the identity of thought itself, *qua* identity, is *man absolute.* This identity of thought itself is *implicitly* integrity itself absolutely unconditioned, *explicitly* the specific integrity of society itself absolute (man itself is the cipher that becomes species itself for the first time in history *in* history *qua* identity of life itself [just as the thing itself is the cipher that becomes appearance itself for the first time in history in the perception of the appearance of the thing itself in essence]).

This identity of thought itself is the actuality of light itself within which there is no absolutely disintegrous existence (*this* explicitly), therefore, no basis for the latter's production, since it itself, the former, is the implication of the integrity of thought itself, i.e., of the absolute specificity of existence itself, the implication of the world itself now absolute, of matter itself now absolute, of the now practical foundation the absolute finality of the implication of which is that, although the species itself need not have occurred, although the cipher need not have appeared, although the body itself now exists in freedom itself, the species itself deciphered is not disintegrable, and, although explicitly imperfect, implicitly perfect. *The thing itself now in essentially historical motion essentially excludes any basis whatsoever for the monadology of the thing itself* (the ideal self-ordering world) *which is the higher communism,* other than the absolute alienation of existence itself which *in fact* (now thought for the first time in history) is inadequate to the monadology of man in essence, as distinguished from its being so *in theory* where the alienated body itself, not itself perceived, is *supposed* to exist (the *uchronia*), absolutely monadic man (the identity of thought itself in fact contrary to fact not itself perceived), the actuality of the generic itself (essentially uncomprehending the absolute objectivity now existing absolutely for the first time: a darkness that is in fact, however, a non-existent actuality): the state of being itself together with the word (the *absence* of the actuality of light itself, the *absence* of being itself thought in essence): the state of paralogical being itself: the being itself the absolute conformity: the purely negative actuality. *The conception of unity itself appropriation itself beginning, as it does, in non-existence (in the immanent specificity of the idea), is essentially inconceivable (this existence itself,* i.e., this *statement,* i.e., "the conception of unity . . . inconceivable," *is the non-existence of nothing itself absolutely unconditioned, is the non-existence of nothing absolutely itself clarified, is the essential clarification of thought itself,* is the foundation, *qua* foundation itself, the absolute thing itself thought itself, the proof positive of existence itself, the essential integration of the foundation itself with the otherwise non-existent world itself, the integration of thought itself with the otherwise generic specificity, with the form otherwise of absolute indifference itself, the form otherwise of the other not itself, but not other than itself, i.e., with the form of the transcendental other itself: *the integral perception of existence itself,* the very integrity of the body. *Now for the first time this saying itself essentially transcends the form of essential identity* [this formal identity of the body itself the perception itself of time itself], now time itself is differentiated absolutely historically: in light of the perception of the essence of man the difference between past and future is implicitly nothing, explicitly existence itself: now the inalienable itself absolute).[22] Matter itself the founda-

[22] The conception oblivious to *the inalienable* (nor is this to be construed as a matter of 'right', whether bourgeois or not, but is the body itself), *formally* the transcendental other, essentially the disintegrous absolute, the conception of the absolute alternation of the one with the other, the clarification of nothing itself, thought itself absolutely political, is found in B. Ollman, *Alienation: Marx's Conception of Man in Capitalist Society,* 2nd ed. (Cambridge, 1976), pp. 106–8: "The individual, then, is always social; yet Marx thinks of him as being more so in communism, where competition as we know it has given way to cooperation as we have still to learn about it. The resulting social functions of the communist man are described as 'so many modes of giving free scope to his natural and acquired powers'. Knowledge may be superficial and one-sided or deep and many-sided. Just so man's relations with his fellows, and it is only in communism that the potential within these relations is fully realized. Marx even equates the expression 'social being' with 'human being', where the latter means man living at the high tide of his accomplishments. This is but another example of a concept meaning what Marx is using it to describe, the sense of 'social' keeping pace with changes in the real world. In communism, 'society' and 'social being' come to mean all that is distinctive in this period of man's social relationships, and are often used by Marx with this broad reference in mind.

"All man's efforts, products, thoughts and emotions relate him to others and, in communism, besides the strengthening of such ties, now suitably transformed, the objects at both ends of each person's relations are appropriated by everyone; or as Marx puts it, 'The senses and enjoyment of other men have become my own appropriation.' We saw earlier that each man, as a unit of nature, is an object for everyone else and therefore part of everyone else through their appropriation. For Marx, people are

tion is matter itself existing *ex nihilo.* The foundation, *qua* foundation itself, the inalienable itself absolute, the difference itself, is matter itself conceived *ex nihilo*: in the first integral repetition of being itself commodiously spoken the thing itself *ex nihilo* (appearance itself deciphered). Now for the first time in history creation *ex nihilo* is faith itself itself absolute thought. Now the perception of the body itself is the world itself creation itself *ex nihilo.* Now for the first time in history matter is the appearance itself of the transcendental absolute: absolute reason the existing absolute: the absolutely material incorporation of reason itself: in reality the absolute clarification of the absolute. In

---

appropriating one another in all their contacts. And like the other objects in nature, the individual in his role as object must be up to the level at which he is being appropriated; otherwise others will not be fully able to realize their powers in him. Hence, only communist men are 'fitting' human objects of appropriation by other communist men, who require such ideal friends, neighbors and co-workers to manifest the full range of qualities that Marx attributes to them. 'All history', Marx says, 'is the preparation of "man" to become the object of sensuous consciousness, and for the needs of "man as man" to become (natural, sensuous) needs.' This latter aim has been treated in my description of what the individual will be able to do in communism, but it is also a question of 'what he can be done to'. As communist objects, human beings possess those necessary attributes which enable others to achieve complete fulfillment through them.

"With each man only able to appropriate other communist men, their fulfillment concerns him as much as his own. His stake in their accomplishments and happiness could not be more personal; yet the result is his coming to view all of nature in terms of humanity. Objects that any individual needs are seen as objects that society needs, since everyone's fulfillment requires the satisfaction of this individual. Hence Marx can claim that in communism, 'Need or enjoyment have consequently lost their egotistical nature'. A person can no longer satisfy his own need by depriving others, since the effect of their disappointment would punish him along with everyone else. Essential to grasp is that man at this time believes that whatever others appropriate, whether in production or consumption, belongs equally to him, and whatever he does equally to them.

"In harness with this belief, both affecting it and being affected by it, is communist man's conception of others and their necessary objects as extensions of himself. The extraordinary cooperation which exists brings a revolution in the way each individual conceptualizes his relations with

the light which is now the existing actuality of absolute reason, the conception of unity itself appropriation itself, i.e., the conception of thought itself political, essentially inconceivable, is, insofar as it is nevertheless found to exist, and in terms that do no violence whatsoever to the logic of the thing itself not thought itself, i.e., to the practical identity of subjectivity with objectivity, the sheer formality of actuality, implicitly nothing other than itself, the clarification of nothing itself, now itself historical matter, *qua* materialist conception of history, *qua* non-being of thought itself, belonging absolutely to the past. The absolute clarification of existence itself is the differentiation of

---

what we take to be the 'outer' world. For Marx, as we have seen, all such relations are internal to each of the factors involved, but it is only in communism that this way of viewing reality acquires general acceptance and that its consequences become part of people's daily lives. Through this conceptual revolution, the individual has, in effect, supplied himself with a new subject, the community, for all but his most personal activities. There are few developments in communism which are as difficult to grasp or as far reaching in their implications as the substitution in people's minds of man the species for the separate and independent individuals each of us takes himself to be. With this change, the integration, both practical and theoretical (in life and in outlook), of the individual into the group is completed. The age-old conflict between man and society has been resolved.

"The path which we have trodden brings us to the conclusion expressed in Marx's claim that in communism, 'nature becomes man'. In this period, the variety and intensity of the individual's activity has brought him directly, or as a unit of society, into contact with all of nature. Former tenuous relations are strengthened and objects once untouched by his powers become involved in the work of their fulfillment. For the first time, objects and the desires they generate are uniting people rather than making them compete. With society viewed as the sum of interpersonal ties, including people's relations with each other's objects, Marx concludes that communist society 'is the consummate oneness in substance (*vollendete Weseneinheit*) of man and nature—the true resurrection of nature—the naturalism of man and the humanism of nature both brought to fulfillment'. Like the conflict between man and society, the conflict between man and nature is also resolved. In communism, the Relations expressed by 'nature', 'man' and 'society' have converged into one another; people both recognize and treat what are referred to by these concepts as 'identical'."—(Self-)conscious formality not the inalienable.

existence itself from the *form* of the absolute transcendental, i.e., from the inessential history of man in essence, i.e., from the non-specific history of species-man which is part and parcel of the materialist conception of history which in its perception of the totality of history itself, otherwise perfectly accurate, provides itself, beginning and end absolutely, with generic specificity in the form of appropriation itself, i.e., in the form of the essentially non-specific production of the species, in the form of the conception of material experience in which experience itself varies indirectly with conception itself (the conception of things themselves constantly changing according to experience itself) but in which *matter itself invariable—qua* absolute, non-existent—*qua* actual existent, not itself thought—remains (compare this *invariable matter itself* of an *un*thought transcendental objectivity with the *invariant form of the general essence* of the transcendental-phenomenological logic of absolute science [the non-thought of being itself: the pure ego, the infinite *a priori* of transcendental subjectivity]). The ultimate resolution of the merely *formal dialectic* of matter itself is experience itself (as that of the merely formal dialectic of *thought itself* had been an inessentially absolute negativity the existence of which historical materialism essentially is—indeed, the *invariable matter itself* of the latter is the limit imposed upon it by history in its taking its point of departure in the inversion of the *essence of modern idealism,* indeed, *of modern thought,* from which *change in essence is essentially excluded,* in its beginning with the non-being of thought, but not beginning in essence, in, at the beginning, beginning, in beginning with becoming itself, this thoughtful self-assertion of non-existence itself). *The sheer formality of the dialectic of historical materialism is its impotence to effect the absolute rationalization of existence, i.e., its essential impotence is its beginning, qua dialectic, in the inversion of the essence, i.e., in its beginning in non-being.* Not possessing itself effective potency the materialist conception of history substitutes for time itself the *form* of an essential dialectic, a matterless now, conceives a political dialectic essentially disintegrous, i.e., a unity predicated upon a generic multiplicity of needs *in lieu of the essential dialectic of the necessity itself of unity, in which there is no necessity of an ultimate resolution since, in the essential dialectic of* *matter itself, nothing is thought for the first time in history but existence itself: everything else is thought in essence: indeed, now for the first time there is nothing but the actuality of light itself existing: everything else is perceived in the light.* Now for the first time the integral foundation of perception itself is change itself in essence: the absolute precision of thought in essence in place of the general essence of an absolute methexis. Now for the first time in history matter itself is the integral perception of change itself existing in essence: motion itself: matter itself *essentially* dialectical. The absolute precision of thought in essence is being itself catholicological: for the first time precision itself is the thing itself: for the first time the body itself existing in the form of consciousness: the thing itself (prescinding from nothing itself) absolutely thought: being itself thought itself: now existence itself in place of the generic essence in the conception of the transcendence of property itself. Before now the materialist conception of history transcended the specific multiplicity of needs that is the effectual foundation of the unity of capitalism by predicating a generic multiplicity of needs as the basis of unity. Now for the first time in history unity is predicated upon the unicity of a specific necessity now existing, i.e., upon the necessity of the spirit in essence, i.e., upon freedom itself, i.e., upon the implicit integrity of the perception of existence itself in essence. Historical materialism understood the necessity for the existence of the middle term, understood, as never before, the necessity of overcoming the suffering of unity, but this understanding, as such, lacked power for being itself integral with the middle term, indeed, is the radical incapacity for the consciousness that is the proclamation of the existing body itself, the radical incapacity for the thing itself, existence itself, deciphered. Now that for which before now in fact no power existed, for which no one being itself existed, but rather a multiplicity of beings, being itself before now alienated in capitalism, or reappropriated in communism—*now for the first time in history being itself is integrally the middle term, the absolute clarification of existence itself:* the consciousness of being itself commodious: the *novitas mentis*: the new state of the mind for which precisely the power before now did not exist in the merely formal dialectic of matter itself. But now that very power exists in the essential dialectic of matter itself the ultimate resolution of which is the integrity itself of the perception of the body, i.e., the absolute existence of man in essence. Indeed, the ultimate resolution of the essential dialectic of matter itself is itself in essence, i.e., is itself perceived in the light, i.e., is itself everything else in essence, is, i.e., *everything else absolutely unconditionally itself.* Now for the first time in history it is seen to be of the essence of the thing itself to *be* the body itself—the cup, the table, the mountain—*everything, qua* thing, *proclaims the body itself,* proclaims the body itself itself in essence. This now is the absolute foundation, the essential distribution of the perception itself of the existing body itself, the essentially *penultimate* resolution of the essential dialectic of matter itself, the beginning in the form of the comprehension of man itself the absolutely unconditioned foundation: the thing itself (prescinding from nothing)/existence itself/absolute precision itself the perception itself of the body itself. This formal comprehension of the beginning precludes once and for all, and now in its absolute form, monadology itself (the essential form of the logic of modern consciousness from Descartes and Leibniz through Marx): this formal comprehension now of the *absolute* distribution of the perception itself of the body itself—this absolute opening of monadology to the beginning. Now mankind stands upon the wing-level of life itself soaring. Now humanity sees in a glass *clearly,* sees it to be of the essence of existence itself, of man itself, of the species itself deciphered to itself perceive itself as it itself is perceived ultimately. The proclamation of the body itself (now matter itself) is this ultimate perception itself now explicitly absolute. Now everything, *qua* thing (prescinding from nothing), is the clarified existence of the word itself. Now the clarified image in the glass is the thing itself abstracted from nothing (the perfect abstraction, the abstraction *ex nihilo*). *For the first time matter itself is change itself, motion itself existence itself perceived in essence.* What now occurs for the first time in history is change itself in imagination itself: *now flesh itself transcendentally imagines change itself.* Now for the first time in history *flesh itself imagines intelligible matter.* The foundation, *qua* foundation, is the

power of a transcendent substance: now substance itself *is* the essential power of substance itself, *is* the unity of substance itself, *is* the spirit itself, *is* the absolute identity of substance and function. The now practical foundation is the substantiality of imagination itself, the absolute change in imagination itself, the essential *clarification* of the Incarnation itself in place of the *idealization* of the Incarnation (the inversion in existence itself of the essentially undifferentiated formality of thought itself which is the absolute thought of existence before now, but which now no longer is, being itself now the absolutely differentiated thought, itself the perception of the body itself). Now in place of an absolutely formal methexis, i.e., in place of appropriation itself, the conception in essence of the species itself existing absolutely. Indeed, now for the first time in history it is clear that *either* there is *the absolute nothingness of the absolutely self-vitiating conception of thought itself political,* or there is *providence itself:* either there is *the appropriation of unity itself,* or there is *now the actual substance of unicity itself,* the material existence that is being itself one substance: *either* the *uchronia* of the materialist conception of history, *or substance itself the function itself of actual substance,* matter itself integrally spirit itself, *or, again, time itself unredeemed* in the *essential* continuity of communism with capitalism patent in the generalized accumulation that is to take place in light of the self-restrictive essence of time itself perduring even beyond its specifically capitalist function, as Marx says in *Capital* I:[23]

> If the whole working day were to shrink to the length of its necessary component, surplus labour would vanish, something which is impossible under the regime of capital. Only the abolition of the capitalist form of production would permit the reduction of the working day to the necessary labour-time. But even in that case the latter would expand to take up more of the day, and for two reasons: first, because the worker's conditions of life would improve, and his aspirations become greater, and second, because a part of what is now surplus

[23] Marx, *Capital,* vol. 1, p. 667.

> labour would then count as necessary labour, namely the labour which is necessary for the formation of a social fund for reserve and accumulation. . . .
>
> The intensity and productivity of labour being given, the part of the social working day necessarily taken up with material production is shorter and, as a consequence, the time at society's disposal for the free intellectual and social activity of the individual is greater, in proportion as work is more and more evenly divided among all the able-bodied members of society, and a particular social stratum is more and more deprived of the ability to shift the burden of labour (which is a necessity imposed by nature) from its own shoulders to those of another social stratum. The absolute minimum limit to the shortening of the working day is, from this point of view, the universality [*Allgemeinheit*] of labour. In capitalist society, free time is produced for one class by the conversion of the whole lifetime of the masses into labour-time.

Before now in historical materialism was conceived an absolute function as such not yet materialized. Now for the first time in history absolute change is the absolute function of change itself, i.e., *now for the first time matter itself is the absolutely unconditioned function itself.* Now *either* the essentially unintelligible 'labour' transformed into 'life's prime want', the function of a transcendent substance (the function identity itself, *qua* transcendent difference) subject only to the 'necessity imposed by nature', labor the essential form of living conscious things, the function as such yet of the non-being of thought itself, the form of appropriation itself, the function of sin itself, minimized by means of a universal distribution, *or, now labor the existing function of life itself, the existing function of the substantial power of thought itself,* the function of the absolute energy of life itself, i.e., of the actual time itself of life itself: labor now the function of existence itself suffering appropriation itself. Now labor is the essential form of differentiating appropriation itself as the foundation of nothing itself: *now labor itself is the function of the measurement of life itself, the essential form of the measurement of the foundation itself, at once the essential form of the proclamation of the body itself. Now actual labor is the inalienable function of existence itself:*

now for the first time in history labor itself is the essence of social existence, i.e., labor itself is itself property itself, i.e., labor itself, *qua* function, is property itself, *the actual substance no longer labor-power, but the substantial power of thought,* which latter, *qua* absolute function, is *the body itself* (the two absolutely identical in the differentiated form of the absolute thought of existence itself). Labor itself thought absolutely is property/society: now absolutely unconditioned labor itself is the perpetuation of society itself. Labor is the foundation of life itself. Now labor itself is time itself/being itself the absolute function of life itself. Now labor itself is the substantial form of identity (nor is this labor itself to be confused with the functioning of a natural object, but is being itself the essential function of an absolute objectivity). Now for the first time in history labor itself is thought itself, labor exists in essence: now it is clearly seen that labor itself in essence is not merely the product of labor, but that labor itself is essentially the product itself (the product of the conception of life itself essentially existence itself), essentially incapable of being itself alienated, i.e., of being itself placed at the disposal of another by another, i.e., of being itself expropriated, of being itself caught up in the process of an alien function perpetuating itself in the form of a commodity. Indeed, now that the *novitas mentis* actually exists, now that there occurs change itself in the transcendental imagination itself, now that the substance of flesh itself is imagination itself, the economic relations of the past are now conceivable as the material non-existence of life itself, whether founded on the material limitations of existence itself absolutely (capitalism), or on the *form* of life itself transcendent (communism), the latter the projected transcendence of the former. When Marx writes at the end of *Capital* I:[24]

> However, we are not concerned here with the condition of the colonies. The only thing that interests us is the secret discovered in the New World by the political economy of the Old World, and loudly proclaimed by it: that the capitalist mode of production and accumulation, and therefore capitalist private

[24] Ibid., p. 940.

> property as well, have for their fundamental condition the annihilation of that private property which rests on the labour of the individual himself; in other words, the expropriation of the worker.

—this is to be understood as something which *now* in light of the materialization of the power of life itself is inadequately conceived, now that the *locus* of expropriation no longer exists in thought, being itself absolutely displaced, now that being itself is commodious, now that the body itself is being itself in essence, now that consciousness essentially differentiates itself from the past. This now is the product itself conceived in essence: life itself absolute, *sans producer:* the absolutely perfect product created *ex nihilo.* So, too, *freedom* itself in the *form of expropriation* is now incapable of being itself thought except as past in essence, i.e., without the possibility of realization as such, there being now no possibility in fact of being itself connected, of being itself reappropriated, since there is now no necessity such as was identified with that possibility itself. The materialization now of the power of life itself obviates the identification of need and desire in the real labor process envisioned upon the inversion of the capitalist relations of production, obviates, that is, the *absolute want* that consists in the identification of the objective with the subjective conditions of labor itself on the assumption that labor is a function 'of the worker, and not of the capitalist', this assumption appearing, e.g., in Marx's "Results of the Immediate Process of Production," as follows:[25]

> *First,* the commodities purchased by the capitalist for consumption as the *means of production* in the production process or labour process are his own property. They are in fact no more than his money transformed into commodities and they are just as much the existing reality of his capital as that money. Even more so, indeed, since they have been changed into the form in which they will really function as *capital,* i.e., as the means of creating value, of valorizing, i.e., expanding, its value.

[25] Ibid., pp. 982–83.

> These means of production are therefore *capital.* On the other hand, with the remaining portion of the money invested, the capitalist has purchased labour-power, workers, or, as we have shown . . . , he has purchased *living labour.* This belongs to him just as effectively as do the objective conditions of the labour process. Nevertheless, a specific difference becomes apparent here: real labour is what the worker really gives to the capitalist in exchange for the purchase price of labour, that part of capital that is translated into the wage. It is the expenditure of his life's energy, the realization of his productive faculties; it is his movement and not the capitalists'. Looked at as a personal function, in its reality, labour is the function of the worker, and not of the capitalist. Looked at from the standpoint of exchange, the worker represents to the capitalist what the latter receives from him, and not what he is *vis-a-vis* the capitalist in the course of the labour process. So here we find that, within the labour process, the objective conditions of labour, as capital, and to that extent, as the capitalist, stand in opposition to the subjective conditions of labour, i.e., labour itself, or rather the worker who works.

And further:[26]

> Here it is not the worker who makes use of the means of production, but the means of production that make use of the worker. Living labour does not realize itself in objective labour which thereby becomes its objective organ, but instead objective labour maintains and fortifies itself by drawing off living labour; it is thus that it becomes *value valorizing itself capital,* and functions as such. The means of production thus become no more than leeches drawing off as large an amount of living labour as they can. Living labour for its part ceases to be anything more than a means by which to increase, and thereby capitalize, already existing values. . . . It is precisely as *value-creating* that living labour is continually being absorbed into the valorization process of objectified labour. . . . the worker's labour becomes one of the *modes of existence* of capital, it is incorporated into capital as soon as it enters the production process. . . .

[26] Ibid., pp. 988–89.

> Within the framework of capitalist production this ability of objectified labour to transform itself into *capital,* i.e., to transform the means of production into the means of controlling and exploiting living labour, appears as something utterly appropriate to them . . . , as inseparable from them and hence as a *quality* attributable *to them as things, as use-values, as means of production.* These appear, therefore, intrinsically as capital and hence as capital which expresses a *specific relationship of production,* a specific social relationship in which the owners of the conditions of production treat living labour-power as a *thing,* just as value had appeared to be the attribute of a thing and the *economic definition* of the thing as a *commodity* appeared to be an aspect of its thinghood [*dingliche Qualität*], just as the social form conferred on labour in the shape of money presented itself as the *characteristics of a thing.* In fact the rule of the capitalist over the worker is nothing but the rule of the independent *conditions of labour* over the *worker,* conditions that have made themselves independent of him. (These embrace not only the objective conditions of the process of production—the means of production—but also the objective prerequisites for the sustenance and effectiveness of labour-power, i.e., its *means of subsistence.*) And this is the case even though this relationship comes into existence only in the course of the actual process of production.

Before now, under capitalism, death was the wage of death, i.e., labor itself was the function of nothing in essence other than the power of capital, essentially the matter itself of productivity (the wage itself, the thing itself absolutely): labor itself the undifferentiated identity of sin itself. Before now, under communism, death was the wage of sin, i.e., labor itself was the function of absolutely nothing other than the power of labor itself, essentially the form itself of productivity (the wage itself, nothing itself absolutely unconditioned, the concretion of nothing itself [for historical materialism the thing itself remained the substantial form of nothing itself, the invariant matter itself of the otherwise constantly changing thing, so that ultimately the nothingness of the thing itself in historical materialism is the form of the body itself]): labor itself the differentiated identity of sin itself, in terms of which the burden exclusively imposed by the few upon the many is redistributed in the liberation of man himself from the domination of his own sin that takes place in the inversion of the capitalist relations of production, in which inversion man himself rises above the domination of sin itself in the form of the 'necessity imposed by nature' imposed upon everyone inclusively, for which liberation (the function of expropriation) Marx tells us labor power, *vis-à-vis* the power of capital, is the better prepared:[27]

> What we are confronted with here is the *alienation* [*Entfremdung*] of man from his own labour. To that extent the worker stands on a higher plane than the capitalist from the outset, since the latter has his roots in the process of alienation and finds absolute satisfaction in it whereas right from the start the worker is a victim who confronts it as a rebel and experiences it as a process of enslavement.

Such is labor itself, *qua* passion, the function of sin itself. But now for the first time in history the dichotomous relation, power of labor/power of capital, is transcended. Now the absolute identity of the two is thought in essence. Now sin is the wage of sin, i.e., for the first time labor itself is the function of the absolute nothing itself in essence absolutely other than the power of life itself. Labor itself for the first time is absolutely unconditioned productivity, the body itself existing in essence. Now for the first time in history labor itself, *qua* passion, is the substance of sin itself, that is, labor itself exists as the absolute 'other than' of sin (the wage itself, the thing itself absolutely unconditioned, the absolute concretion of existence itself the dialectical essence of matter itself, change itself in essence the thing itself now perceived: the wage itself, life itself absolute, the absolute actuality of change itself/the absolute change itself of actuality—indeed, now for the first time in history it is no longer a question of the worker 'on a higher plane than the capitalist', but now that mankind itself stands on the plane of life

[27] Ibid., p. 990.

itself it is clear that in the dispute between the two thieves the decisive question is whether or not labor itself is the perception of the body itself, whether *labor itself is the productivity of existence itself in essence,* or whether labor itself is merely the function of absolute speculation, which latter is the only *now* intelligible experience of labor itself as the form of appropriation). Now for the first time in history labor itself differentiates itself from the appropriation of identity itself: labor itself now perceives identity itself in the form of the foundation, *qua* foundation. What is now essentially clear in the light of the transcendence of the category of necessity itself, i.e., in light of the existence of the categorical absolute, freedom itself, is that the identification of need and desire, of objective and subjective conditions of production, the absolute want that is the essence of the communist society to be founded on the expropriation of the expropriators by the 'mass of the people', is, precisely, nothing but *the perpetuation of the mass of wealth* created under capitalism (capitalism without the capitalists[28]), the absolute instrumentality of non-existence, the inessentially social function of labor itself, the absolutely pure formality of society itself (nor under the circumstances could it be anything else) to be brought into being ultimately by the power of a political revolution (nor in the conception of thought itself political could it be otherwise conceived to come into being), an essentially political, i.e., inessentially revolutionary, utopia (the *uchronia*), itself constrained continually to provide today for tomorrow. Compare Marx in *The Poverty of Philosophy,* where in contrast to that conception now occurring in essence in which tomorrow is freely provided for today, a society essentially absent political action is itself conceived abstractly, i.e., politically: the function of the product of labor itself:[29]

> An oppressed class is the vital condition for every society founded on the antagonism of classes. The emancipation of the oppressed class thus implies necessarily the creation of a new society. For the oppressed class to be able to emancipate

[28] Ibid., p. 999.

[29] K. Marx, *The Poverty of Philosophy* (New York, 1963), pp. 173–75.

itself it is necessary that the productive powers already acquired and the existing social relations should no longer be capable of existing side by side. Of all the instruments of production, the greatest productive power is the revolutionary class itself. The organization of revolutionary elements as a class supposes the existence of all the productive forces which could be engendered in the bosom of the old society.

Does this mean that after the fall of the old society there will be a new class domination culminating in a new political order? No. . . .

The working class, in the course of its development, will substitute for the old civil society an association which will exclude classes and their antagonism, and there will be no more political power properly so-called, since political power is precisely the official expression of antagonism in civil society.

Meanwhile the antagonism between the proletariat and the bourgeoisie is a struggle of class against class, a struggle which carried to its highest expression is a total revolution. Indeed, is it at all surprising that a society founded on the opposition of classes should culminate in brutal *contradiction,* the shock of body against body, as its final *denouement?*

Do not say that social movement excludes political movement. There is never a political movement which is not at the same time social.

It is only in an order of things in which there are no more classes and class antagonisms that *social evolutions* will cease to be *political revolutions.* Till then, on the eve of every general reshuffling of society, the last word of social science will always be:

"Le combat ou la mort; la lutte sanguinaire ou le néant. C'est ainsi que la question est invinciblement posée."

Here is the materialist conception of the transcendence of contradiction, merely the ideal conception of incarnation itself, simply, perfectly the absence of the proclamation of the body itself: the contradiction null and void/being itself synthetically displacing the disparate elements of the end result of the old order, it itself being the product thereof: being itself connected totally displacing revolution. Although Marx understands the essentially unhistorical, immanent mode of bourgeois mentality, viz.,

> They all tell you that in principle, that is, considered as abstract ideas, competition, monopoly, etc., are the only basis of life, but that in practice they leave much to be desired. They all want competition without the lethal effects of competition. They all want the impossible, namely, the conditions of bourgeois existence without the necessary consequences of those conditions. None of them understands that the bourgeois form of production is historical and transitory, just as the feudal form was. This mistake arises from the fact that the bourgeois man is to them the only possible basis of every society; they cannot imagine a society in which men have ceased to be bourgeois.[30]

still, although he himself can imagine such a society, understanding, as he does, that the form of productivity is an historical matter, he has not imagined the change itself that constitutes the society in essence in fact. Historical materialism comprehends not that the matter of productivity is essentially historical. It transcends not absolute instrumentality. It remains within the horizon of the social function of labor itself: it translates the ideal (formally historical matter) into existence (the generic body itself): it invokes the category of existence as opposed to the existence of the category, so Marx against Proudhon:[31]

> You will now understand why M. Proudhon is the declared enemy of every political movement. The solution of present problems does not lie for him in public action but in the dialectical rotations of his own mind. Since to him the categories are the motive force, it is not necessary to change practical life in order to change the categories. Quite the contrary. One must change the categories and the consequence will be a change in the existing society.

Within that contrariety, historical materialism knows nothing of the categorical absolute, freedom itself/existence itself, nothing

[30] Ibid., p. 190.
[31] Ibid., p. 191.

of the fact that transcendental matter is substance itself existing, nothing of the fact that thought itself is an absolute objectivity, i.e., that the category itself is existent in actuality, change itself, nothing of the fact that there is no pre-existent body to effect or to be effected by existence, that there is no ideal embodiment, but that *embodiment itself is matter itself absolute,* that there is no political absolute effectuating transcendental order on its terms, but that the latter is effectuated in essence by life itself, order coinciding essentially transcendental thought, the perception of the body itself. In fact order absolutely coincides the transcendence of absolute instrumentality now occurring in essence for the first time in history. Now for the first time in history order coincides labor itself, i.e., the product itself. Now that being itself is seen to be commodious, order coincides not the necessity of being itself productive, the necessary conception of the body itself (even that in which the difference between appearance and essence is before now overcome in the form of radical opposition to the existing premises), not the conception of the necessary existence of the worker (even that in which difference itself is immanent, in which subjectivity itself exists [self-creates]), but now for the first time order itself coincides that existence which is being itself absolutely nothing but existence itself. For the first time order is other-consciousness itself, substance itself the absolute itself existing. Now order coincides the substantiality of existence itself, the product which is essentially not a commodity, labor which is not essentially the means of subsistence (nor simply even that labor before now formally differentiated therefrom, essentially differentiated from the means of production as the living labor which is the latter's form, but which was not yet conceivably differentiated from this latter as the form of a new universe from the form of the universe of the past), but, rather, labor which is the freedom itself in essence of labor itself. Now that existence itself suffers appropriation itself, the product itself/labor itself is without price—now that productivity itself is itself absolute, is thought itself—with *this* priceless object order now coincides for the first time in history.

In capitalism productivity was materially differentiated by

money itself or money-capital: labor power and means of production were materially identical: the product was itself productivity itself: money itself constituted the material identity of labor power. So Marx writes:[32]

> Generally speaking the advanced capital is converted into productive capital, i.e., it assumes the form of elements of production which are themselves the products of past labour. (Among them labour-power.) Capital can function in the process of production only in this form. Now, if instead of labour-power itself, into which the variable part of capital has been converted, we take the labourer's means of subsistence, it is evident that these means as such do not differ, so far as the formation of value is concerned, from the other elements of productive capital, from the raw materials and the food of the labouring cattle, on which ground Smith in one of the passages quoted above places them, after the manner of the physiocrats, on the same level. The means of subsistence cannot themselves expand their own value or add any surplus value to it. Their value, like that of the other elements of the productive capital, can re-appear only in the value of the product. They cannot add any more to its value than they have themselves. Like raw materials, semi-finished goods, etc., they differ from fixed capital composed of instruments of labour only in that they are entirely consumed in the product (at least as far as concerns the capitalist who pays for them) in the formation of which they participate and that therefore their value must be replaced as a whole, while in the case of the fixed capital this takes place only gradually, piecemeal. The part of productive capital advanced in labour-power (or in the labourer's means of subsistence) differs here only materially and not in respect of the process of labour and production of surplus-value from the other material elements of productive capital. It differs only in so far as it falls into the category of circulating capital together with one part of the objective creators of the product ("materials" Adam Smith calls them generally), as opposed to the other part of these objective product creators, which belong in the category of fixed capital.

[32] K. Marx, *Capital: A Critique of Political Economy,* vol. 2, ed. F. Engels (New York, 1967), pp. 212–13.

But in communism the non-being of money itself (its essential non-existence) formally differentiates productivity itself: labor power is the formal identity of the means of production (the ownership of the associated producers): labor power itself existing (self-creating, i.e., reproducing itself) in the absence of circulation (the uchronic form of achieving the unachievable ideal of capitalism): the means of production constituted essentially by the non-existence of money-capital, formally by appropriation itself in face of the necessity of maintaining a surplus for accumulation and a reserve, i.e., for increasing productivity and for self-insurance: the means of production constituted materially by social control. Marx writes:[33]

> If we conceive society as being not capitalistic but communistic, there will be no money-capital at all in the first place, nor the disguises cloaking the transactions arising on account of it. The question then comes down to the need of society to calculate beforehand how much labour, means of production, and means of subsistence it can invest, without detriment, in such lines of business as for instance the building of railways, which do not furnish any means of production or subsistence, nor produce any useful effect for a long time, a year or more, while they extract labour, means of production and means of subsistence from the total annual production. In capitalist society however where social reason always asserts itself only *post festum* great disturbances may and must constantly occur.

'The product of capital is profit':[34] The product of capital is the value of labor power, i.e., the value of labor is productive for capital. Value is the productivity of capital and capital values productivity. Capital is the matter itself of appropriation, as such it is analogous to the perfectly random world of Democritean atoms whose rationality is the retrospective necessity of an order arising from the infinite chaos, a chance order of blind forces locked eternally in the contradiction of being and not-being, in

[33] Ibid., p. 315.

[34] K. Marx, *Capital: A Critique of Political Economy,* vol. 3, ed. F. Engels (New York, 1967), p. 355.

which, despite appearances to the contrary, nothing continually comes from nothing, in which everything is continuously being destroyed and recreated (via Democritus capitalism appears as the Hegelianism of the economic order: capital possesses productivity as its ideal: capital essentially possessing reason but not being itself rational: the appropriation of chaotic temporality: capital orders nullity without measure: the body itself chaos itself). Capital is the mechanization of man. For capital man is productivity. The contradiction is precisely that capital *values* productivity, i.e., that it *is not* productivity: for capital productivity is value or it is nothing at all: the non-being of productivity is its being for capital: the non-being of man is man's being for capital. Compare Marx in *Capital* III:[35]

> The contradiction . . . consists in that the capitalist mode of production involves a tendency towards absolute development of the productive forces, regardless of the value and surplus value it contains, and regardless of the social conditions under which capitalist production takes place; while on the other hand, its aim is to preserve the value of the existing capital and promote its self-expansion to the highest limit (i.e., to promote an ever more rapid growth of this value). The specific feature about it is that it uses the existing value of capital as a means of increasing this value to the utmost. The methods by which it accomplishes this include the fall of the rate of profit, depreciation of existing capital, and development of the productive forces of labour at the expense of already created productive forces. . . .
>
> The *real barrier* of capitalist production is *capital itself*. It is that capital and its self-expansion appear as the starting and the closing point, the motive and the purpose of production; that production is only production for *capital* and not vice versa, the means of production are not mere means for a constant expansion of the living process of the *society* of producers. The limits within which the preservation and self-expansion of the value of capital resting on the expropriation and pauperization of the great mass of producers can alone move—these

[35] Ibid., pp. 249–50.

> limits come continually into conflict with the methods of production employed by capital for its purposes, which drive towards unlimited extension of production, towards production as an end in itself, towards unconditional development of the social productivity of labour.

But for the ownership of the associated producers capital's non-being is its being: the truth of capital for communism is being itself reason: the action following immediately the non-being of thought, namely, the formal appropriation of temporality itself: the body itself existence rationalized. The product of communism is production itself: communism is non-being itself existing in essence, and it is such self-consciously and that very self-consciousness is the essential non-being of absolute productivity. Communism is existence itself formally, but not essentially; essentially it is the form of productivity. In the self-production of the ownership of the associated producers labor power *per se* is valued: now in place of existing outside of himself as the doing of another (his self-alienation under capital), the worker is outside of himself as his own doing in self-conscious transcendence of capital, i.e., essentially as the necessity itself of capital without its accidental arrangement: the worker, *qua* transcendent identity, the nature of man: matter itself as the arrangement of the necessity of capital itself (not yet nor as such conceivably the essential arrangement of capital itself). Communism possesses the worker as its ideal, his non-being is his being itself, precisely, his being for the ownership of the associated producers, i.e., its being for itself, i.e., non-being as the embodiment of being itself connected, as the individuation of a universal felicity which is, in effect, labor power as the embodiment of the ataraxia of imagination itself, as the body itself essentially inarticulate existence (compare the existence of the gods of Epicurus *intermundia*.[36] This is the worker as the absolute rupture of the transcendental horizon, but inessentially so, powerless *qua* worker, existing merely by virtue of a necessi-

[36] For a discussion of Marx and the ancient atomists, see A. T. van Leeuwen, *Critique of Heaven and Earth*, 2 vols. (New York, 1972–1974).

ty imposed upon man by nature. The substance of the worker, *qua* worker, is death itself as the negative ground (not nothing in essence existing) of an absolute productivity, the merely formal realization of the societal essence of existence. Not being itself a new species the substance of the worker is valued as such: 'production as an end in itself' the image of the worker. The existence of the worker is a mere formality. The species itself for communism is organization in the form of association: man conceived purely organically in the total absence of the perception of the existence of spiritual substance: man internally ordered by his corporate nature, the individual by the species, the species by nature. Thus communism rationalizes the chaos of capital through the subjection of disorderly elements to the purposeful control ideally embodied in labor power. The full valuation of production itself eclipses the capitalist valuation of productivity (i.e., of the product of labor power) in which the value of the product *includes* the value of production. Communism is formally existing productivity in which the value of the product *is* labor power, but in which, therefore, value remains a disintegrous existence, i.e., a product other than existence itself. Although the disintegral existence of the capitalist product is overcome in the communist valuation of production itself (in the form of absolute instrumentality), still, the product is something other than itself in the form of being valued, the product is not being itself in being production itself: it continues to be beyond itself in the essentially formal understanding historical materialism is: *in the fact that the value of production being itself is the product not being itself, the difference between the apparent and essential state of things (maintained by capital) is overcome, overcome in being itself connected not being the value of the product but the product itself, overcome (as is the transcendent difference itself) not in being itself the transcendental difference, but in being itself the immanent difference,* the self-same transcendent identity. In this inversion of the relation that exists in the product of capital (the relation that exists in material appropriation), in this inversion which itself constitutes the essential form of productivity and in which the product of an essentially material production is itself made capital, i.e., in which capital becomes the product of the formal appropriation of things themselves, capital remains a thing, the form of nothing essentially other than itself, the tell-tale trace of the fact that nothing is essentially changed in production itself formally absolute. But now that for the first time substance itself is historically conceived, now that the transcendental horizon is ruptured by the essence itself absolutely existing (the absolute itself absolutely existing for the first time), now that for the first time in history everything exists in essence, the thing-capital that is the product of the communist realization of the non-being of money-capital, this product, in its non-being essentially conceived as transcendental being itself actually existing—labor power being itself the essence of production itself, no longer merely the matter or the form thereof—is existence itself, life itself absolutely conceived, value itself/nothing capital, but the existence of the body itself. Now the product is absolute productivity. For the first time the product is consciousness itself/work itself, the embodiment of production itself essentially spiritual/material, the mercy of existence absolutely realized, the mercy which is the essential transcendence of the dichotomy, capitalist (exterior)/communist (interior) relations of production (the thing transcendent/the thing immanent, formally no thing). The product of the substantialist conception of history now occurring is work itself, neither merely mechanical work, nor merely the work of organized individuals (social units of production), nor, indeed, merely the intimately related work of universal science (science theoretically founded), but work itself that is time itself, the essentially transcendental form of identity, work that is itself transcendentally historically differentiated as itself beginning in essence (where, before now, it was first the form of production, then the form of productivity which was historically differentiated as not beginning absolutely). Now for the first time the product is the form of the productivity that is thought itself existing, thought that is work itself/the form of man historically conceived in essence/the absolutely unselfconscious existence of a new spiritual substance/the fabric of an essentially new universe. Now work itself is the *logos* of consciousness itself absolute/value itself the essentially transactional body itself. In capitalism the work of the worker was transcendentally valued: the work of the worker was essentially the material means of production. Production itself remained the body itself materially: the rupture of the transcendental horizon the material transcendence of productivity: the limit of imagination matter itself. Compare Marx:[37]

> So long as enlightened economy treats "of capital" *ex professo,* it looks down upon gold and silver with the greatest disdain, considering them as the most indifferent and useless form of capital. But as soon as it treats of the banking system, everything is reversed, and gold and silver become capital *par excellence,* for whose preservation every other form of capital and labour is to be sacrificed. But how are gold and silver distinguished from other forms of wealth? . . . by the fact that they represent independent incarnations, expressions of the social character of wealth. [The wealth of society exists only as the wealth of private individuals, who are its private owners. It preserves its social character only in that these individuals mutually exchange qualitatively different use-values for the satisfaction of their wants. Under capitalist production they can do so only by means of money. Thus the wealth of the individual is realized as social wealth only through the medium of money. It is in money, in this thing, that the social nature of this wealth is incarnated.—*F.E.*] This social existence of wealth therefore assumes the aspect of a world beyond, of a thing, matter, commodity, alongside of and external to the real elements of social wealth. So long as production is in a state of flux this is forgotten. Credit, likewise a social form of wealth, crowds out money and usurps its place. It is faith in the social character of production which allows the money-form of products to assume the aspect of something that is only evanescent and ideal, something merely imaginative. But as soon as credit is shaken—and this phase of necessity always appears in the modern industrial cycle—all the real wealth is to be actually and suddenly transformed into money, into gold and silver—a mad demand, which, however, grows necessarily out of the system itself. . . . Among the effects of the gold drain, then, the fact that production as social production is not really subject to

[37] Marx, *Capital,* vol. 3, pp. 573–74.

> social control, is strikingly emphasised by the existence of the social form of wealth as a thing external to it. . . . only in the capitalist system of production does this become apparent in the most striking and grotesque form of absurd contradiction and paradox, because, in the first place, production for direct use-value, for consumption by the producers themselves, is most completely eliminated under the capitalist system, so that wealth exists only as a social process expressed as the intertwining of production and circulation; and secondly, with the development of the credit system, capitalist production continually strives to overcome the metal barrier, which is simultaneously a material and imaginative barrier of wealth and its movement, but again and again it breaks its back on this barrier. In the crisis, the demand is made that all bills of exchange, securities and commodities shall be simultaneously convertible into bank money, and all this bank money, in turn, into gold.

In capitalism, the transcendence, matter itself, of the value of production doubles as circulation, as the overcoming of the absolutely material limit: matter overcoming itself—in essence: matter without a history: production itself essentially chaotic. In historical materialism the work of the worker is immanently valued as the formally existing means of production. Production itself is the interpretative form which unites circulation to itself. The value of the product/the form of circulation does not exist beyond the form of labor power itself: the value of the product is nothing beside the ownership of the associated producers. Circulation transcends production with the self-same identity embodied in social control. So Marx, discussing the replacement of fixed capital in kind:[38]

> Once the capitalist form of reproduction is abolished, it is only a matter of the volume of the expiring portion . . . of fixed capital (the capital which in our illustration functions in the production of articles of consumption) varying in various successive years. If it is very large in a certain year (in excess of the average mortality, as is the case with human beings), then it is

[38] Marx, *Capital,* vol. 2, pp. 468–69.

> certainly so much smaller in the next year. The quantity of raw materials, semi-finished products, and auxiliary materials required for the annual production of the articles of consumption—provided other things remain equal—does not decrease in consequence. Hence the aggregate production of means of production would have to increase in the one case and decrease in the other. This can be remedied only by a continuous relative over-production. There must be on the one hand a certain quantity of fixed capital produced in excess of that which is directly required; on the other hand, and particularly, there must be a supply of raw materials, etc., in excess of the direct annual requirements (this applies especially to means of subsistence). This sort of over-production is tantamount to control by society over the material means of its own reproduction. But within capitalist society it is an element of anarchy.

Communism replaces the irrational limitation immanent in the capitalist form of productivity with finite rationality, with interpretation itself. To the immanent form of communist productivity belongs the essence of 'universal book-keeping and distribution of means of production on a social scale' (in contrast to the banking system, which, according to Marx,[39] possesses only the form of such). That which was immanent in the communist form of productivity was in existence other than itself, was, that is, a unity excluding an other in essence. The essence of the form of the body itself immanent in communism is subsistence, the mere appearance of life itself, its unintelligible power, the merely formal individuation of substance. This subsistence is the practical non-existence of faith. Marx writes:[40]

> The monetary system is essentially a Catholic institution, the credit system essentially Protestant. "The Scotch hate gold." In the form of paper the monetary existence of commodities is only a social one. It is *Faith* that brings salvation. Faith in money-value as the immanent spirit of commodities, faith in the mode of production and its predestined order, faith in the

[39] Marx, *Capital,* vol. 3, p. 606.
[40] Ibid., p. 592.

> individual agents of production as mere personifications of self-expanding capital. But the credit system does not emancipate itself from the basis of the monetary system any more than Protestantism has emancipated itself from the foundations of Catholicism.

Communism is that emancipation which is a faithless practice, i.e., a practice *after* faith, the substantial realization of an ideal incarnation, the universal societal form previously not subsistent, i.e., under capitalism, ultimately reducible to money-value.

But now for the first time in history the social essence (merely formal in communism) exists. The *uchronia* of historical materialism (the form of time to which the lapse of time was material [the non-being of material time]/the form of time which replaces the material time of capitalism, the predestined chaos)—now that time itself (the existing essence of time) is a discrete element of perception itself—now that the non-existence of this formality is for the first time in history conceivable—this *uchronia* is transcended as the form of the past in essence. Now an essentially societal practice exists for the first time: *organization along lines of time itself perceived.* The absolute productivity immanent in this conception is the transcendence of subsistence itself/the subsistence of transcendence itself/the new value of life itself. The perception itself of historical substance now occurring is the incarnation of abundance itself, the overflowing of the existence of the absolute itself, the existing rationality of an infinite organization: societal organization in the form of the metachronologous body itself (this the form of the absolute indifference to mere temporality of integrally existent being itself): value itself the transaction itself of existence. In this form the organization of society is liberated for the first time from the conception of the necessity of over-production, i.e., from the lack of the absolute necessity of existence, merely implicit in capitalism, explicit in communism (in the latter the organization which is man is the self-transcendence of natural necessity), i.e., respectively, from the implicitly and explicitly redundant absolutes, i.e., from the explicit idealism of capitalism and the implicit idealism of marxism: *this is the beginning of the* absolute *production of the 'necessities of life'*. Now, likewise, societal organization is formally liberated from the necessity of exchange-value embodied in the form of the commodity (a necessity explicit in the form of money-capital, i.e., in the form of the body itself simply material, but a necessity implicit in the communist form of thing-capital, in the form of being itself absolutely connected, in the form of the collective substance of consciousness, which latter consciousness of recollective substance materially liberates the social relations of production from the commodity, and is so far self-satisfying, but precisely thus far and as such does not constitute the formal liberation of societal organization. Communism liberates from the chaotic form of human interchange with nature through the mediation of the common ownership of the associated producers, i.e., through the mediation of the form of the body itself, i.e., through the immanence of the interchange, so that it is clear, especially to Marx himself, that communism does not emancipate itself from the reality of capitalism any more than the credit system has emancipated itself from the foundations of the monetary system. He writes in *Capital* III:[41]

> The actual wealth of society, and the possibility of constantly expanding its reproductive process . . . do not depend upon the duration of surplus-labour, but upon its productivity and the more or less copious conditions of production under which it is performed. In fact, the realm of freedom actually begins only where labour which is determined by necessity and mundane considerations ceases; thus in the very nature of things it lies beyond the sphere of actual material production. Just as the savage must wrestle with Nature to satisfy his wants, to maintain and reproduce life, so must civilised man, and he must do so in all social formations and under all possible modes of production. With his development this realm of physical necessity expands as a result of his wants; but, at the same time, the forces of production which satisfy these wants also increase. Freedom in this field can only consist in socialized man, the associated producers, rationally regulating their

[41] Marx, *Capital*, vol. 3, p. 820.

> interchange with Nature, bringing it under their common control, instead of being ruled by it as by the blind forces of Nature; and achieving this with the least expenditure of energy and under conditions most favourable to, and worthy of, their human nature. But it nonetheless still remains a realm of necessity. Beyond it begins that development of human energy which is an end in itself, the true realm of freedom, which however, can blossom forth only with this realm of necessity as its basis. The shortening of the working-day is its basic prerequisite.

Work lies this side of freedom in the sense that labor is no longer wage-labor, valued merely as material of production, no longer essentially alienated in its product as it was under capitalism, but labor, everywhere within the 'sphere of actual material production' understood to be 'determined by necessity and mundane considerations', is essentially alienated from itself. This essentially self-alienated work is the alien form of the body itself, attributable to the *merely generic imagination* of historical materialism, which, itself, is a vestigially anachronistic [idealistic] rendering of a dualism which would be Kantian save, precisely, for its negative valuation of the 'realm of necessity'. This metachronous mediation of the human interchange with 'Nature' in the uchronia of communism is the vestige of anachronism/idealism within historical materialism, the vestige, at once, of the capitalist economic order which is reflected in this anachronistic idealism). The liberation of the form of societal organization now actually occurring for the first time in history is precisely disanalogous to the self-emancipation of communism, to the informal liberation of matter itself. This emancipation of existence itself has no essential foundation in past forms of life: it is for the first time, the incarnation of life itself in the form of existence, consciousness itself formally liberating the social body through the subsistence of work itself, through the mediation which is the creation of value itself. Before now, in capitalism, labor was a matter of the creation of value. Before now, in communism, labor was the form (immanently material) of the creation of value. Now, in the absolute liberation of productivity from the form of the commodity (no trace of the alienated existence of the worker remaining), in the absolute emancipation of form itself from the essence of commodity-production, in the form itself now being itself commodious (no longer the form of a transcendent mode of production, of the body itself method, no longer the form of the body itself in the absence of the transcendence of the method)—now the beginning of the transcendent identity of the body itself—labor itself is the absolute valuation of existence, the form of creation itself is absolutely conceived. No longer is the case *laborare* et *orare* (whether transcendently or immanently differentiated, whether distinguished in the division of labor [capitalism] or in the formal division of time [communism]), now *laborare* est *orare*: now work itself is essentially inalienable. Now for the first time in history work is the consciousness of the human other, the transcendence of the essentially self-conscious negative valuation of work, the actuality of matter itself. This is the essential dialectic of matter itself for the first time, the beginning of the essence of actual material production, of the actual production of the essence of matter, the essence of which is that it precludes the necessity of freedom's being beyond the sphere of necessary, mundane labor—the essence of which new beginning is the absolute foundation of the freedom that is actual labor, the obliviousness of historical materialism to which essence rendered it subject to the dichotomous relation of freedom to necessity (with the result that the dialectic of matter remained an ideal consciousness: being subject to matter after the reduction of transcendence to immanence). This beginning is the saying in which every difference except the transcendental difference, but including the difference between past and future, is overcome: this is the material productivity which is absolute consciousness itself: of this word the elemental form is work itself, in the objectivity/receptivity of being itself, i.e., in the actuality of existence, the essence of reality. The very form of this saying beginning is the absolutely elemental reality in which 'past and future' is absolutely differentiated as past, i.e., in which the very relativity of the terms themselves is itself transcended along with the *status subjectivus* itself (the 'outer' appearance of things, together with the necessity for its deconstruction and destruction, together with the necessity for the objective, together with the objective fact of necessary being, together with material necessity or the difference, not between fact and reflection or appearance and essence, but between the past and future realization of the identity of the two, a totality inherently *now without status,* inherently inessentially revolutionary [which is to say that while the absolute actuality of material existence was non-existent in historical materialism, the latter was by no means a mere appearance. Indeed, the actuality of communism is the negative candor in which the appearance is itself the essence, although this essence itself does not exist: the implosive identity of the two]. There is no longer any such thing as a hidden essence, nor any disputing the essential existence of the fact itself. The essential alternative to the fact is not reflection, but the existing fact itself: the question is simply whether or not the existing fact exists. In historical materialism the answer is the existing fact does not exist, the second fact has not yet occurred). Existence itself is the *status objectivus,* the actual work of consciousness. To this existence, i.e., to the body itself existing now for the first time, there is absolutely no alternative, but with it is identified a transcendentally differentiated *logos* transcending the actuality of thought in essence in the form of work itself: *in the form of work itself the actuality of thought is experienced for the first time as that which is prior to the logos as actuality itself.* This coincidence, which is not the coincidence of opposites, but the coincidence for the first time of work itself with the consciousness that is itself material productivity, this is the experience for the first time of history itself in the form of the absolute objectivity of thought in essence, the coincidence of the elemental forms of being with thought for the first time, the one not being other than the product of the other, but identical with the other in the receptivity of being itself (an actuality other than the actuality of thought is formally conceived as not yet having occurred: but this is precisely the pre-rational *ratio* of experience itself). For the first time the product itself of work is work itself. Conceived in essence work is the beginning of the very existence of an absolute society, at once the practical transcendence of the societal horizon. Now in the actuality of light itself, in the form of the absolutely elemental existence that is the absolute valuation of work itself in which the two are identified in the actuality of being itself in the form of man, in which nothing is encountered but existence itself, here, where before now in the merely formally material conception of history objectivity was substance itself recollected, now, objectivity itself is subsistence itself for the first time, i.e., substance itself individuated absolutely. Before now in communism the substance itself of objectivity was the non-being of work itself. The conception of work remained essentially within the horizon of modernity: either necessary or free, but in neither case work itself the experience of the body itself existing in essence. In historical materialism the form of abstract universal labor ingredient in capitalism is overcome in the form of the negative valuation of work itself, at once in the form of the valuation of labor power really existing.[42] The non-material objectivity that is capitalist

[42] Compare here, and with what follows, the summary of Marx's understanding of capitalist labor and value in L. Colletti, *Marxism and Hegel* (London, 1979), pp. 274ff.: "the labour of the individual, i.e., labour in its natural form as useful or *concrete* labour, 'becomes social labor only by taking on the form of its direct opposite, the form of abstract universal labour', i.e. the form of abstract labour; just as its product, in its turn, becomes a social product by taking on the form of its opposite, i.e. *value*—within the body or form that it, qua use-value, has as a natural object. And one must bear in mind that the term 'value' is to be understood in the sense of a 'coagulation' or objectification of *undifferentiated human labour-power,* as 'crystals of this social substance common to them all', and therefore as a non-sensuous, *non-material objectivity*—or as Marx refers to it, a 'ghost-like' objectivity ('not an atom of matter enters into the objectivity of value'), which is nothing but the social unity itself in its hypostatized form. . . . And here it is obvious that the subject is now work *in the abstract,* and man is the predicate. For, as Marx states, 'labour, thus measured by time, does not appear in reality as the labour of different individuals, but on the contrary, the various working individuals rather appear as mere organs of labour; or, in so far as labour is represented by exchange values, it may be defined as *human* labour in *general.* This abstraction of human labour in general virtually *exists* in the average labour which the average individual

value, undifferentiated human labor power (the body itself/chaos), the common social substance, embodied in a thing, is overcome in communism, in the form of social subsistence, i.e., in the form of material/historical subsistence, in the form of an inessentially existing productivity. In the conscious appropriation of self that is the formal essence of historical materialism, work itself is the essential predicament of the subject: work itself is specifically human work. As such, i.e., as the work of humanity, work itself is not essentially valued: what is valued is humanity, i.e., the producer, in the unity of formally different elements which constitutes concrete labor, the unity characteristic of the communist advance over capitalist 'abstraction', the unity in which nature remains as that to which the socio-historical is 'inter-related',[43] the unity in which consciousness remains as that to which being is likewise related in the transcendence of

of a given society can perform.'" Colletti's understanding of the antithetical relation of 'dialectical materialism' to historical materialism confirms, in its own way, that Marxism is neither essentially.

[43] Cf. L. Colletti, *From Rousseau to Lenin* (New York and London, 1974), pp. 11ff.: "The distinguishing feature of consciousness is, as we know, that while it is part of social being and is therefore internal to life, at the same time it *reflects* on the latter and embraces it mentally within itself. While it embraces society within itself it is also *part* of society, i.e. it is only *one* of its functions and has the others *outside itself.* Marx wrote: 'Thought and being are *united,* it is true, but are also *distinct* from one another.' Consciousness does indeed belong to being, to social practice; theory is itself life, practice; there is a unity and inter-relationship of the two. However, consciousness belongs to life insofar as it is *one* of its parts. Theory is practice insofar as it is *one* aspect or moment of practice: i.e. insofar as it is reincorporated within the latter as one of its specific functions—and hence insofar as it does not absorb practice within itself, but is instead surrounded by it, and has it outside itself. Similarly, production, in one sense, is distribution, exchange and consumption; but the latter are nonetheless only moments of the former and presuppose production as their antecedent. Once understood correctly, therefore, it is precisely the unity of being and consciousness, their inter-relation, which implies the fundamental character or priority of being over thought, i.e. *materialism.* However, if this is correct, then two consequences clearly follow. The first concerns *method:* since the superstructure reflects the structure and is *part* of it, the content of theoretical generalization can only be *verified* as a determination or

freedom to the merely formal realm of necessity. In this unity abstraction remains in the form of the necessity of its being overcome by being included in the objectivity of matter itself. This remaining abstraction precluding precisely the being of actual matter, the being of humanity (the producer), save at the expense of being itself, save at the expense of the existence of the body itself. The partition of the body itself (the body itself inarticulate) is the price paid by historical materialism for its valuation of the worker: the specific abstraction of historical materialism is precisely the imperfect abstraction (opposed to the merely ideal abstraction of capitalism in which productivity is entirely a preconception, a merely material existence) in which existence is a mere abstraction, in which *the species of abstraction is itself essentially generic, to wit, the class,* in which, therefore, work itself, which is concretely the work of *this* actual worker, is not valued, in which, in fact, consciousness is a *rep-*

aspect of the object of analysis. Secondly, as a *structural* consequence, if the structure always includes both 'structure and superstructure' and 'society' is always an objective object-subject process, the objective terms of analysis must also themselves be seen as *active,* as objects capable of referring theoretically to one another, and hence as objects susceptible to description in purely *physical* terms on the one hand and also social *agents* on the other. The process is a *natural* one, but this nature is *socio-historical.* . . . Never in Marx do we find economic categories that are *purely* economic categories. All his concepts, on the contrary, are both economic and sociological. The most abstract and simplest capitalist relationship, M-C-M, is already the relation between capital and labour power. In other words, it is already a relationship between two *social classes.* . . . This 'wholeness', and the stupendous effect even as literature thereby achieved in the pages of *Capital,* is not, therefore, the result of any mechanical superimposition of 'levels'. To use Lenin's metaphor, the 'skeleton' is not analysed first and then clothed in 'flesh and blood'. Rather, it is achieved by the end, because it is already there in that initial, so abstract and rarified relationship M-C-M, with which *Capital* commences and which is the true 'sphinx' of the entire gigantic construction. On the one hand, the relationship money-commodity (M-C), or capital-labour power, expresses the relation between *constant* and *variable* capital, i.e. a relation between simple objects, raw materials and machinery on the one hand and the rest of the means of production on the other, under capitalism. Yet on the other hand, this relation between the mere

resentation of objectivity wherein being the body itself is subjective, i.e., but a part of itself. This is subjective humanity itself/humanity placing itself at the disposal of an other none other than itself: being the not-being of the body itself, of the 'natural' consciousness to which it is transcendently related. Indeed, the essential connection of the body itself to being is the not-being of existence itself. The inessential organization of society is nothing other than the absence of the valuation of work itself in the concrete valuation of subjectivity by which the merely abstract capitalist valuation of the same was overcome. The body itself as the 'collection of empirical formations', as the 'species', is not (nor could it have been before what now occurs for the first time in thought, viz., the absolute valuation of the body itself existing) that subsistence itself which is consciousness itself the essential embodiment of being itself. The body itself is not the identity of matter itself

objective conditions of production, between the mere means or instruments by which the objective *material* process of production proceeds, is indeed a relationship between objects, but one between *active* objects, i.e. between capital and labour-power, between the employer and the wage worker: in short, a relationship between socio-historical *agents*. We can now understand how this *unity* of economics and sociology, of nature and history in Marx does *not* signify an identity between the terms. . . . This whole is a totality, but a *determinate* totality; it is a synthesis of *distinct* elements, it is a *unity*, but a unity of *heterogeneous* parts. From this vantage point, it is easy to see (if in foreshortened form) both Marx's debt to Hegel and the real distance that separates them. . . . The historical subject then is neither Idea, World-Spirit, Vico's Providence, nor a transcendental subject. Nor is the subject conceived as Evolution, Struggle for Existence, Societal Instinct, Race, etc. Against these generic abstractions, all equally fruitless, Marx produces a new concept of the subject as a historical-natural entity, as a *species* or collectivity of empirical formations—such, precisely, as are social classes. He analyses these species in the light of determinate or scientific concepts, precisely those 'pseudo-concepts' so abhorred by the theological leaning of idealist historicism. The organic unity of economics and sociology lies here: in the concept of class." The reader will note that the subject in the category of the species is the actuality of appearance, but not the actuality of the appearance of matter itself: social agents, as such, the embodiment of a nonhistorical substance. The unity of nature and history precludes the substance of either.

since the essentially disintegrous notion of historical materialism knows such an identity as the reversal of its own purely abstract identity merely, being without constructive force, essentially impractical. Now, however, the foundation, the essential organization of society, is for the first time in history the material identity of the practical with work itself: practicality is for the first time the identification of the worker (concretely existing humanity/the producer) with matter itself (not, therefore, with a material element of an undifferentiated productivity [capitalism], nor with the being-connected of the material elements, i.e., neither with the formal foundation of consciousness in communism). Now, as never before in history, the economy is society itself the body itself: not nature, but the existing economy is the body of the absolute species (nor is nature a remainder in this equation, there being now no insubstantial nature, let alone the merely apparent nature of capitalism): the actuality of the worker/an existing other not a subject, i.e., not the non-existence of the subject of capitalism, not the actuality of nothing, but the actuality of production, the actuality of an essentially objective 'language of real life' transcending the 'objective object-subject process' of the materialist conception of society, the practice of social agents, the merely formal dialectic of matter. Now for the first time productivity is consciousness itself, the absolute conception of man as the species in essence: the actuality of the existing object itself/actuality itself. In place of the agents of social practice (the social classes)—the practicality of society itself: the embodiment in the person of the worker (personal humanity) of the essentially social transformation of the world: personality the perfect abstraction of the world the body of man, of change itself, of the actuality of the existing economy. In the absolute clarification of thought the person *is* the economy, the absolute embodiment of society itself. The person is the species itself, the species absolute, the body itself individuated *qua* societal, neither the insubstantial appearance of capital, nor the collectible 'empirical formation' of historical materialism, neither the private nor the common owner of property, but the absolute embodiment of property itself, neither individual nor universal subject, not, indeed, autonomous. The person is *metanomous*: subject neither to nothing, nor to appropriation, nor to self, but *bound unconditionally by existence itself*. In the perfect conception of personality itself absolutely economic, in personality itself economic, distribution is met, is changed, is transcended, economy itself is distributed absolutely (the body itself actuality itself). This distribution is not a matter of an empty conception, nor of empirical recollection, nor of a self-objectifying project, but a matter of the identity of work itself existence itself: *now for the first time work itself is metanomous and it is existence itself*: now work itself is law itself absolutely existing/personality itself existing. The existing foundation of an absolute society is not 'human rights', capitalistic apparent personality in the form of the appropriation of subjectivity (essentially subject to being contested, subject to an inhuman opposition), nor, on the other hand, is it historical materialism's inessential transcendence of the 'rights of man',[44] communist personal reality in the form of the recollection of subjectivity/the unity of appropriation (unlimited subjectivity), personality formally real, but limited by the not-being of matter itself: labor power but the form of the actually existing individual: the inessentially social (communist) equality of the producers, in place of the political-juridical (capitalist) equality of the same: social want transferred from the realm of necessity to the realm of freedom, so that freedom itself is no longer the property of abstract individuals but of society, a property, however, with which the latter is not identified, since before the thinking now occurring for the first time in history matter itself has not been thought itself essentially. The existing foundation of society itself before now was not itself thought, it was practice related to theory, law itself inessentially incarnate but real. Now for the first time in history it can be said without qualification: the existing foundation of an absolute society is *human personality itself*, essentially the embodiment of law itself, the very embodiment of the Three Persons in the One God for the first time in history: personality is reality itself in the form

[44] Cf. ibid., pp. 92ff.

of the suffering of appropriation. This is the form for the first time of the absolute objectivity which is the essence of the labor power of the existing individual.

The existing foundation is the actuality of an absolute incarnation, personality as an absolutely material reality. Through its material essence the body itself, actual human personality is absolutely free, i.e., not merely juridically, in the way of being contested, nor merely socially, in the way of being connected, but substantially, in the way of being commodious. What exists now for the first time is not the merely apparent identity of labor and property (the material elements of productivity), nor the social inter-relation of the two (the formal elements of productivity), but the corporate identity of the two (the essential elements of productivity) in the subsistence that is the world-fabric, in the actual person, in the dimension of history itself. The absolute transcendence of instrumentality is the identity of the actual person with the spiritual existence of substance itself: for the first time necessity itself the body itself: the freedom of personality itself absolutely without being beyond it. The essence of this freedom is labor itself absolute. In light of the foundation of this freedom, labor itself is seen to be neither the means of achieving a freedom privately possessed, nor that from which society is formally free, i.e., that in transcendence of which freedom is enjoyed as a societal possession, but, therefore, inessentially enjoyed as such. Labor itself is neither the alienated property of the producer, nor a property of appropriation itself, but the absolute embodiment of property. What is now conceived for the first time in essence is the subsistence of property itself: what is now inconceivable in essence is property itself existing non-productively: there is now no property which is not the embodiment of the labor of the human person: now it is neither "to each according to his labor," nor "to each according to his needs," but the body itself being itself now the measure, that is, there being no measure apart from the body itself (there being, fundamentally, no paralogical being), the needs of the individual absolutely constitute productivity, the satisfaction of these needs being no ideal, but the existence of the individual itself, without there being at the same time any possibility of denying this satisfaction on the ground of non-productivity. Indeed, consumption is the essential form of the substantial identity of labor and property: this most fundamental reality of human experience—consumption itself—the perfect demand of the individual to exist—is, as it turns out for the first time in history, the integer that is the subsistence of the spiritual itself, of human personality, itself essentially undeniable. This it is—this perfect demand of personality to exist—from which neither the absence of an apparent labor, nor of an apparent capacity to labor, is able to detract anything whatsoever, which is, indeed, the measure itself/being itself/the body itself existing, is, itself in essence, one, or another, indeed, the essential form of productivity itself—this it is, in the integrity of the body itself, in the absolute identity which is the measure itself *qua* measure, which is now clearly perceived in the shining-forth of *the absolutely practical rule, to wit, (not man, but) the body itself is the measure of all existing things* (nor is this rule to be understood to be applied by man, but rather, man now risen above the rule, the rule applies itself in the form of the consciousness of existence itself; strictly, in this form, it predicts itself. Existing, the prediction being itself the rule, it exists absolutely, i.e., *this rule is the substance of what is not yet, and the practical foundation of the satisfaction of the needs of every individual without exception:* the foundation of the practical world itself: the foundation of the perfectly specific existing world [the world in which we actually live, the world hitherto essentially unfounded]: the phenomenological essence of the actually existing world). The absolutely practical rule is the world absolutely phenomenological. Under the rule of the body itself not only is the question—"whether the difference between fact and reflection or appearance and essence, can, by the saying, be overcome"—evidently without foundation, but it is clear, as well, that the specific foundation for a world economic order, as conceived by Marx, in which before now the difference between fact and reflection etc. was overcome without, however, transcending the difference, 'the past and the future', or the difference, 'nature and history', itself presupposes the world's existence, i.e., itself is not the foundation of the latter. Before the thinking now occurring for the first time the existence of the world was not founded. The foundation of the world of historical materialism was, precisely, in idealism itself, i.e., in the world's non-existence, while the purely phenomenological existence of the world (the generic essence) was the foundation itself of non-existence/of idealism itself. So long as time itself remained the form of an inessentially historical matter, the world remained (formally) the absolute identity of the individual: actuality remained purely human. But now for the first time in history there is world-actuality, the transcendence of the purely human actuality: human personality actually transcendental, humanity actually existing now for the first time in history, the specific essence or essential species wherein personality is transcendentally differentiated from the merely human, wherein human identity is the personal absolute, the personality of existence itself in which it is together with transcendental persons whose pure immediacy remains yet to be experienced in the ultimate perception of the body itself (beyond which is to be not only, as now, absolutely no being, but not even the inexhaustibility itself of being itself). Now for the first time in history the actuality of work itself is the experience of the essence of history itself, identically the essentially practical existence of society, the transcendentally differentiated reflection of the fact that creation is now existence itself. In the realization of the foundation of the absolutely practical world which is this beginning, the impediment of all saying before now, viz., the difference between actuality and the word, is absolutely left behind: such is the subsistence of the rule itself for the first time. The absolute minimum is actuality itself for the first time. This minimum itself is knowledge, the actuality of thought itself, being itself, to which in the new state of the world there corresponds no essentially unrealized potentiality, but which, itself, is an actually new saying.

II

CRITIQUE OF ABSOLUTE WORLD-CONSCIOUSNESS

1

THOUGHT BEYOND NIETZSCHE: FOUNDATION ITSELF[1]

Now for the first time in history the world terminates in essence. The universe absolute exists absolutely. For the first time the world itself is essentially historical: the history of history the existent world: the history of the world the substance, *exsistere ipsum,* the absolute actual. Now for the first time a second absolute actually exists in essence. Not merely is the necessity for a potential absolute no more—that necessity of modernity which finally required the synthesis of an absolute subjectivity, a synthesis, in turn, through the purity of that necessity, refracted as the analysis of an absolute contingency, as the practice of an absolute materialism—not merely is that necessity no more, which might have been, indeed, was in fact, no more, but no more is the post-modernity of the absolute potential remaining without its necessity. There is now for the first time in history neither the intelligible nor the unintelligible existence of potentiality. But then there is the absolutely intelligible actuality of the world. The absolute primal nothing of the posthumous ones is no more—the survivors of the death of the father are dead, their children, and their children's children, the seed of death, the dead burying the dead, a lost tribe. There is no necessity for inscribing the words of the *posthumi,* as there is none for dwelling in their haunts, for there is now no necessity for their embodiment of the Nothing. We, the survivors of sin itself, the proclaimers of the body itself, declare the speaking of death to

[1] A revised version of a lecture spoken to the Columbia Assembly for Logic and Metaphysics at Columbia University on December 9, 1982.

be without necessity, a waste of words, the guest at the wedding without a wedding garment. We, embodying the integral absolute, declare today the Third Day, the day after the sabbath, the first of a new creation, a day without night, for night itself is the necessity of Being itself before now, of the Minimum itself before now, of the now existing world actuality before now, before the light itself, before the absolute conception of the minimum actuality now actually occurring for the first time. This is the beginning of the actual transcendence of the gap in motion. The tomb itself is sunk absolutely in existence itself absolute. The cipher of an absolute multiple now terminates absolutely in the actuality of the minimum: not the foundation of the world, but the world itself foundation itself: nothing beyond the absolute wealth of the premises now in existence: the wealth of existence itself beyond the appropriation of Nothing itself. For the first time every-thing another absolute essentially matter itself. Everything proclaims matter itself the body itself. In that proclamation everything precludes the plaintext of historical materialism, precludes the want of life itself, the want of actuality, the inessential consciousness of the body, the body itself generic. But the body itself matter precludes, as well, *qua* foundation itself, the ciphertext of the *posthumi*, the unintelligible subsistence, the essential non-existence of actuality, the potential absolute/being beginning in every now, unconsciousness absolute (where absolute consciousness could only be that of a self or selves) the abyss of self together with every other cut off from self, a myriad of topless pyramids, the generic body itself overwhelmed in the Heraclitean flow of an absolute contrariety, the ciphertext of the superhuman, the absolute inversion of the neoplatonic denial of the essence of history. The body matter itself precludes, *qua* beginning, the transcendence of history in the form of the reduction of the body itself to an ideal nothing, in the form of the absolute immanence of the body, precludes the transcendence of history in the form of the experience of sin itself, in the form of the embodiment of absolutely nothing, precludes the transcendence of history in the form of the body itself nothing but the will to power, in the form of the absolute want of will, the body itself in the form of doubt itself absolute, the form of indecision itself absolute, the form of absolutely never arriving at the foundation of the world. Matter the body itself beginning precludes the transcendence of history in the form of the absolute pre-creation itself, the form of nothing before the world not yet matter itself, precludes the abyss itself of the subrogation of self-consciousness for revelation, the abyss itself of the radical mistake of modernity, precludes the fount at which all forms of post-modernity drink, abysmally mistaken in thinking themselves beyond modernity in their re-thinking of past thinking, in thinking to avoid the mistake of the past thought by starting to think over again but avoiding this time the mistake which has actually been made, the mistake with reference to which only is every form of post-modern thought itself intelligible (indeed, every mode of post-modern thinking, taken *per se*, i.e., in its trans-historical being [a being which can only be a pure formality], taken, that is, at face value, *is* unintelligible, whether it faces the abyss willingly or not willingly). The body itself matter precludes *qua* beginning not only the plaintext of historical materialism, not only the cipher-text of the unintelligible ones, but also the cipher-Being text of absolute speculation. The essential existence of every-thing for the first time precludes the inessential matter of phenomenology, the consciousness of absolutely nothing in essence, of everything being related in essence to nothing. The proclamation now occurring for the first time precludes the world not yet matter itself existing, precludes the body itself unconsciousness itself, the unintelligible actuality, the transcendence of history in the form of the reduction of the body to an ideal death, in the form of the immanence of the body itself, the self-proclamation of the body itself (where self is nothing)—precludes the body itself appropriation itself, the abyss of existence. The beginning of matter itself the body precludes the possibility of worshiping death, precludes doubt itself absolute transcendence, the existence of absolute indecision, the body itself nothing but the will to think, precludes, as well, being itself beyond thought (which latter is being itself neither merely beyond nothing, as in historical materialism, nor merely beyond existence, as in the potential absolute of the *posthumi*). Furthermore, not only is being itself beyond thought (the cipher-Being text) precluded by everything proclaiming the body itself matter, but also, as we proclaim the body itself, there is precluded the absolute ciphertext of the last of the progeny of those born after the death of the father. The very existence of the thinking now occurring for the first time in history precludes *de facto* the non-existence of an intelligible actuality, precludes, that is, the abyss of thought itself *without recourse to the abyss.* This is the miracle, the manna of consciousness itself, the subsistence of existence itself, transcendentally differentiated from the abyss of thought itself: the body itself proclaimed in absolute differentiation from the abyss itself: the body itself itself *ex nihilo*/the second absolute. Not only is there a new heaven and a new earth actually existing, but this new universe is so absolutely: the universe itself the body itself matter itself: this new matter differing from the inessentially historical matter of the plaintext as life itself absolute, as the absolutely transcendental substance. This matter itself, the second absolute, is the house itself of angels, the angelic home. If, as in fact occurred, matter was individuated *per se* in the transcendental form of natural reason (that thinking which began with life itself as a matter of faith), now, in that thinking existing after the abyss without recourse to the abyss, matter individuated is itself a new creation. For that thinking erecting itself upon another's foundation the fact of creation was essentially indemonstrable, the fact of history was absolutely indemonstrable. Now, for that thinking erecting existence itself upon the foundation itself of absolute identity, life itself is the demonstration of a new creation, the fact of history itself is itself thought itself, the evidence of the new creation is the proof positive of existence itself. This is for the first time the absolute plaintext of existence itself thought itself which absolutely precludes the body itself the object of thought not being itself, the silence which is sin itself, speech saying nothing of the consciousness of the body itself, refusing to acknowledge the substance of the world as if to demonstrate its inessentiality, the insubstantiality of the word, refusing as if it were in its power to act otherwise, as if it were the absolute contradiction to being itself, as if it were the unspoken word of consciousness itself spoken. But the word spoken in essence speaks absolutely for the first time. The contradiction of the simulacrum of the word is the beginning of existence itself (the absolute ciphertext is the reduction in essence of the absolute simulacrum of thought, belonging in essence to the past, to the abyss itself, absolutely precluded, therefore, by consciousness itself which knows the abyss of thought itself not to be in essence). If the old creation, *qua* creation, lacked an essence, that is, was formally indemonstrable, the new creation is the absolutely intelligible essence of the beginning, demonstrably the form of thought itself, the existence of the transcendental essence, conception at once absolutely perception, the body itself actuality. The absolute plaintext precludes the possibility of forgetting nothing in essence, precludes the shrine of death itself, precludes the transcendence of history in the form of the reduction of the body itself to an ideal sin, to a form of self-appropriation, to a form of immanent objectivity not thought itself: the body itself appropriating the body itself: an absolutely fictive transcendence. The actuality of the body itself for the first time precludes a phenomenological absolute not itself matter itself. History is transcended essentially for the first time in the absolute existence of the consolation for sin itself, in the death itself of death itself, in the absolute inconceivability of nothing essentially, nothing existing. The essential transcendence of history thought in essence—the world transcendence of the transcendental absolute—precludes for the first time the absolute transcendental doubt itself. The new creation, the body itself indemonstrable for the transcendental form of natural reason, appropriated by subsequent thought as its own essential form (thinking in essential form a subsequent appropriation such that, *qua* thinking, reduced to unconsciousness itself in the ciphertext of the *posthumi* it remains a subsequent appropriation in the form of the willing of the death of God after the fact itself, nothing but the will to power, the abyss itself existing), the new creation, appropriated by subsequent (essentially modern) thought as doubt itself, essentially precludes doubt itself. The essentially new form of thought itself for the first time is the transcendence of being itself: not thought transcending its own abyss discovering a new ground, but thought in essence absolutely unconditioned the foundation itself, an essentially new thought displacing for the first time the gap itself. This absolutely unprecedented form of the actuality of thought itself—the essentially transcendental form of thought itself—precludes the doubt of existence itself, precludes the foundation of existence itself belonging to the past. The spirit itself, form itself matter, precludes the method, precludes the necessary *arbitrium*, precludes the self-contamination of perception, without recourse to the abyss (also without recourse to the non-thought of being, to the pure form of transcendental thought, without, indeed, recourse of any kind which might be construed to be another form of the abyss, the formal abyss of existence itself). As matter the body itself precludes unconsciousness absolute, the abyss itself existing, the unnecessary *arbitrium*, so form itself matter, the spirit the body itself, absolute identity itself/life itself absolute, precludes the necessary-unnecessary *arbitrium*, the abyss of absolute contingency itself (neither the abyss of existence nor of thought, nor merely the abyss itself existing, but) the abyss of existence and thought each with the other confused, the abyss of the generic body. Life itself absolute/absolute identity itself precludes not only the plaintext of historical materialism, but also the abyss of the plaintext, the immediate identity of a total presence, the presence of everything not our own, the beginningless identity of totality *arbitrium ipsum,* the abyss the beginning of total identity. The absolute plaintext precludes not only the beginningless immediate identity of the social total, the Being itself connected of the plaintext, but also the identity of Being itself totally present, the non-being of an absolute presence, the abysmal identity of the body itself not itself, the abyss of spirit itself not essentially itself/of form not matter itself, the abyss of time itself not itself existing/the *arbitrium* of the form of the body itself not itself. The actuality of the body itself (the absolute plaintext) precludes its very *presence* (it goes without saying, therefore, without being itself absent, without even the possibility of recourse to the abyss). The consciousness that is the proclamation of the body itself precludes the existent non-being of the form of its very identity, the non-being of faith itself absolute, the absolute contingency of faith itself formally presence of self, i.e., of nothing itself essentially: the abyss of absolute contingency/the body itself absolutely nothing itself, the form of its identity not being that of its self but of another other than itself: the absolute self-distinction of presence itself: the presence of absence, the reduction of the body itself to an ideal consolation in face of the eternal recurrence of self, the transcendence of history in the form of absolute self-negation. The absolutely objective word now spoken absolutely precludes the glorification of that silence which is not itself spoken in essence, which is nothing itself the matter itself of self-presence, the form of the body itself being itself self-possessed, the pure form of self-possession. The consciousness which is the beginning of the existence of the body itself precludes its being formally presence itself, precludes its being simply an object not being itself, precludes its being essentially the consciousness of death itself. The contingency of the absolute consciousness of sin is precluded. The *absolute* plaintext precludes the absolutely unnecessary being of the *presence* of the plaintext, the actuality of a universal silence not being itself. The reality of the silence of being itself opposite an object is precluded by the object's absolute objectivity, precluded by the object's thinking itself for the first time in history existence itself, precluded by there being no transcendent differentiation of the object from being itself, by the absolutely non-parabolic being of the body itself. The proclamation of life itself existence itself precludes not only the simulacrum of the word (the absolute ciphertext, death itself speaking), but also the parabolic being of the word, the contingency of the abyss of thought itself, the silence of death itself speaking in the form of universal self-actualization. There is the transcendent identity of the object (thought in essence) with being itself, an identity transcendently historical, a *novitas mentis*, a state of mind itself absolute, being itself/the unprecedented itself, the never before now existing form of transcendental perception identically transcendence itself, precluding not only the paralogical being of the modes of post-modernity, but also the paralogical non-being/paralogical presence of the word (the parabolic being of the word) of faith essentially modern, precluding the absolute self-distinction of the presence of the body itself. Finally precluded is the body itself a paramodern humanity, a modern paraperception of the existing language of faith, a faith absolutely clinging to the language (the essence) of modernity, in absolute dread of being itself in essence, in dread of the silence itself spoken in essence.

Foundation itself absolutely precludes alternatives, deactualizes alternative forms of the body itself: for the first time the actual form of the body itself is matter itself. Matter itself is the absolute actuality of form itself/the actuality of spirit itself: matter itself spirit itself the actual essence of an absolute objectivity, the language itself of a form of thought now existing for the first time in history (the actual form beside which there are no other forms): the actuality of the historical form of speech itself beside which there are absolutely no other forms of historical speech, absolutely no other world-forming words. The actual world-forming thought is foundation itself the essence of the world-forming actuality (beside which there is absolutely no potentiality for actual existence, this life itself the absolute existing absolutely). Foundation itself absolutely precludes the abyss of looking beyond itself in essence. It is the absolute concentration of thought itself upon the absolutely unprecedented situation in which the world now finds itself, viz., being itself intelligibly consciousness itself. It is neither the hierarchical intelligible world-consciousness of neoplatonism denying the form of the body itself/affirming the absolute absolute potential (the potential for that for which there is no potential, the potential for the absolute actuality of existence itself, the absolute potential in fact absolutely not objectivity itself, precluded from being so by its own necessity), nor is the absolutely new state of the world, foundation itself, the intelligibly ordered chaos of modern consciousness affirming the essential form of thought (of history), or, the same disaffirmed, an inessentially historical materialism. The state of the world itself foundation is the absolute clarification of the absolute catholicologically being itself the absolute itself world-consciousness. Foundation itself requires of thought itself the infinite patience of existence itself. Thought's possession of what is required of it constitutes the essence itself of foundation itself. Thought requires absolutely nothing for itself including nothing beyond the essence itself of foundation itself. Thought itself, *qua* absolute, hears foundation itself as absolute world-consciousness, hearkens to foundation itself as the absolute providence of thought itself beyond which thought absolutely need not go for sustenance: thought eats the bread of existence itself: it knows nothing of the dread of existing individuality, of the Christ-dread which is the abyss of absolute contingency, objectivity absolutely sunk in contrariety with subjectivity itself absolute, i.e., an absolute objectivity itself not thought but *arbitrium ipsum*, the pure will of a totality of identity thoughtlessly undertaking to keep an apparently broken promise of existence itself as a human necessity, engulfed in the silence itself absolute, alone, hearing nothing whatsoever, acknowledging its own infirmity in its pure determination of the other to exist (at once essentially the realization of, in contradistinction to, the impure will of the *posthumi* which scorned not to confess the sins of mankind [as did historical materialism willingly first confess them in order to obtain forgiveness without sorrow] but confessed them *on behalf of* a transcended humanity, not merely without sorrow, but beyond good, beyond evil, in joyful appropriation of the will of an other, affirming its being something other than its own infirmity, its being something other than self-consumption, yet a something without name: the pure affirmation of an impure will: the anonymity of the *posthumi*, of the ciphertext, which in the beginningless abyss of the plaintext, in the simply immediate presence of the actuality of the body itself, in the total silence of an absolute solitude, is transfigured as the realization of the contradiction, as the presence of God, as the same totally new). Thought nourished on the bread of existence knows nothing of the absolute sameness precluding being itself absolutely, precluding, that is, a new identity not other than itself in essence, an identity essentially itself, not totally, new. The alternative identity to the old universe, the presence of the body itself, is the contrary of the proclamation of the body itself existing as a pure formality, essentially contradicted by the actual world-forming thought as being the alternative absolute of a new/old universe. Absolutely lacking the infinite patience of existence itself, the actuality of a universal silence staves off the end of the world by means of the end of the world itself, by presencing the new totality of identity itself. The thinking now occurring essentially for the first time in history is the end of the world comprehended in essence: an essentially new universe is the second absolute not an alternative to the first, not an essentially nameless something a total identity which in being *inessentially new is not absolutely new,* but being itself something with a name, a precise something, absolutely displacing the presupposition of a new essence (absolutely displacing the totality of presence), displacing absolutely the presence of the body itself: transcendence itself beginning now for the first time in history. Now, the minimum itself, the subsistence itself of the intelligible absolute (never before now, i.e., the contradiction in fact of the change in being of what before now existed, of the absolute continuity of existence, the contradiction in fact of the word not newly spoken, of the proclamation of the body itself not the body itself proclaimed but the presupposition thereof) absolutely displaces the presupposition of existence itself, itself displaces presence itself, itself now transcendence itself, thought in essence. Now for the first time something thought in essence is being itself absolutely categorical. Now being itself thought in essence is something with a name for the first time in history not as a matter of affirmation (as in the absolutely determined universe of intelligibles, 'the best of all possible worlds' of the monadology, where what is named is the absolute part of the totality), nor as a non-existing individuality (as in the world-being of an absolutely spiritual self, 'the eternal history of the spirit', where what is named is the ideal manifestation of the form of spiritual totality), but now being itself is something with a name precisely as an existing individual, as a matter of thought itself, the universe itself the body itself. What is otherwise the object of dread in the pure determination of the other to exist, viz., the naming of being itself, is now for the first time the object of an absolute objectivity. Now for the first time in history: the naming of Being itself something itself in particular absolutely individual, i.e., life itself naming something itself Being itself. The naming of life itself is thought itself essentially categorical: to exist is absolutely to subsist for the first time:

existence itself is neither something nor nothing except it is everything (excluding nothing [including nothing]), therefore, something or nothing to which there is no alternative absolute, but which is the contradiction of absolute nothing: a second absolute, foundation itself, an essentially new universe, being itself objectively the name of an individual transcending essentially the absolute contingency of historical materialism wherein being itself objectively was not the name of an individual but of human nature, i.e., of man not existing in essence, an absolute materialism wherein the naming of being itself was an objectivity not itself thought itself, a matter itself insubstantial, merely the material manifestation of an ideal spiritual totality, twice removed, as it were, from the form of the universe now existing in thought as the substance of spiritual existence, a substance which is the displacement itself of the ideal absolute (together with its alternative, beginningless absolute matter). The naming of being which now occurs as objectivity itself beginning itself says: there is no existence which is not an individual existing substance: whatever exists is categorically absolute: there is no subject/object predication, there is existence/absolute predication, i.e., there is no object but what is subject to nothing (there is no relative non-being: there is no relation to nothing), none apart from objectivity itself the absolute name of man itself which is subject to existence: there is for the first time no alternative to existence itself absolutely unconditioned. Before now, in the transcendental form of natural reason which began with the appearance of the essence of history, the intelligible absolute subsisted eternally, imperfectly the alternative to the temporal world, i.e., disjunctively conjoined with the latter (as opposed to the neoplatonic comprehension of the intelligible absolute subsisting in another absolute, in a non-subsistent absolute, the absolute source of subsistence at once the intelligibility of existence itself, in the *nihil* absolutely transcending eternity and time); before now, in the absolute form of divine self-consciousness constituting the essence of modern thought, the intelligible absolute subsisted temporally, the imperfect alternative to an eternal history, i.e., the confusion of time itself with history, the essential form of thought belonging to the past: thought itself purely formal. (It is precisely this confusion of time itself with history which constitutes the absolute constriction of the essence of modern thought to being itself without a name. Modern thought does not essentially differentiate history itself from the anonymity of its own being, although it formally differentiates history itself with the name of another. It is absolutely incapable in its very own essence of the explosion of the body itself which now constitutes the essential form of thought itself absolute, which now is the essential identification of history itself with the naming of being itself in such a way that thought itself, apart from what now absolutely constitutes its essential form, is nothing itself, in such a way that thought itself is absolute objectivity or it is nothing, in such a way that nothing is the *logos* of the existing form of thought itself but existence itself, the second absolute.) Now for the first time thought itself is the absolute transparency of existence itself in essence, the body itself in the form of existence itself. Now the existence of thought itself essentially coincides the naming of Being itself. This coincidence is an absolute individuality (the two differentiated transcendentally, not transcendently). Now the intelligible absolute subsists neither in eternity nor in time (in either event the alternative to an absolute contrariety residing, in the first instance, beyond eternity, or, in the second instance, beneath time), but in history absolutely: the intelligible power of life itself history itself absolutely beginning: *for the first time the transcendence of the transcendental absolute the existing world absolute:* the essential conception of history itself: absolute individuality the integrity of life itself existing: life itself integrally existence itself, the two transcendentally differentiated. Now it is no longer the case, as it was in the ciphertext of the unintelligible ones (of the *posthumi* who bore witness to the absolute fall, *à la mode* the absolutely formal absolute, of the power of life itself into the absolute contrariety of consciousness itself [formally an absolute prior to life itself], into the form of the unbody itself, into the abyss itself), no longer, as it was in the case of the disembodied form of nothing, is there a difference between to live (*vivere*) and to be (*esse*): in the actuality of thought itself existence itself, life itself is being itself with an absolutely new name. This is the hidden manna together with the white stone of triumph: for the first time being itself the transcendent perception of light itself. No longer is Being itself the formal transcendence of a disembodied nothing, no longer is Being itself merely absolute light itself, as it was in the unintelligible actuality of the cipher-Being text of absolute speculation, in its transcendence hidden in its shining, the comprehension (albeit purely formal) of the light shining essentially in the dark. No longer is man itself the form of a disembodied nothing, the enthralling encounter of being with nothing, no longer is man itself *Dasein*, being-there, existence/being in essence together with a ghost with an old name, a ghost named Nothing/being together with death absolutely. The new name of Being itself coincident with the manna of consciousness itself (its very Being itself absolute) routs the old ghost: the old ghost is gone, forgotten in the absolute shining of the light itself now existing, in the light of the matter of the world itself absolute/in the light of the world absolute matter itself. Being itself with a new name is changed in essence into an absolutely new species. The absolute clarification of thought itself is Being Itself New, the Name of Life Itself: Being itself new existing with man itself the species itself of the proclamation of the body itself: this is the individuation of the body itself in which man itself is liberated from bearing the burden of being itself without an essentially new life, the burden of thinking of being itself without life, the burden of thinking itself together with nothing/being itself beyond thought, the burden of not being itself thought, the burden of an absolute contingency. In the actuality of the new species of Being itself beginning, man is liberated from the very burden of a contrary to the body itself to be borne, that is, there is now absolutely nothing other than the body itself in terms of which Being itself might be construed to be a burden for man to bear: the body itself is the burden absolutely of Being itself for the first time with man itself. The burden being itself is the transcendence of coincidence itself: there is no burden for man to bear, the burden essentially is the coincidence of being itself with man. The transcendence of the burden is the absolutely unconditioned individuality of being itself: the burden is the absolutely transcendental light itself:

the existing body itself light itself. The burden of the body itself is precisely that in which man itself moves and has Being itself new. If there were any bearing of the burden, the burden would bear man itself with being itself absolutely light itself, but in fact being itself does not suffer the burden of existence except in the form of appropriation itself, by which we would have been immediately returned to the past, to belonging to being itself. The burden of Being itself new is the absolute absolute: the burden itself absolutely without weight is borne by being itself: this for the first time is the absolutely tangible freedom of life itself transcendence itself. Now for the first time in history the bond of an absolute self-consciousness is absolutely loosed, the issue of this absolute itself loosed is light itself absolute: the burden itself loosed is life itself incarnate. The absolute autonomy of consciousness is absolutely transcended: life itself absolutely eliminates the absolute self in the form of the superfluity of existence itself, in the essential form of the thought of existence itself, in the form of Being itself at the disposal of thought, in the form of the absolute individuality of the species of Being itself, in the absolute transcendence of necessity: in the revelation that absolutely nothing in the world is what it ought to be or what it need be, that the world-forming word is spoken now for the first time in history within the hearing of thought itself, that absolutely nothing including the body itself escapes Being itself categorically absolute, that the body itself is the totality of life itself now for the first time. The absolute totality is Life itself existence. Life itself transcends the absolute totality of the burden in the beginning. In beginning Life itself bears the absolute totality as no burden: the totality of life itself absolutely aloft, the abyss itself is banished in this new beginning: not the beginning of the presence of the totality of identity, but of its absolutely unconditioned transcendence. The reality itself of thought now existing, this new foundation itself, precludes bearing the burden of the totality of identity as anything other than Being itself. The identity of totality itself is Being itself for the first time, which essence of change exists in its having now for the first time absolutely the new name of Life itself. Now the history of being itself perceived in essence is the absolute clarification of existent thought: Life itself now for the first time matter itself.

The bond of an absolute self-consciousness absolutely loosed, existence itself is grace itself. The absolute elimination of the absolute autonomy of consciousness itself is the word itself heard in essence now for the first time in history as the form of an essentially new world, the form itself of the new species of Being itself. Thinking essentially historical transcends in essence the transcendental absolute not itself transcended, the existing form of past thought bereft of thought itself, the after-glow of a vanished sun. Now man itself hears the word, not before now, man itself, of whom it is required, of Life itself, to name Being itself *de facto, ex nihilo.* Without being present or absent, for the first time the other exists absolutely. This other speaks in essence, man itself hears the word in essence: man itself is the other categorically existing absolutely in essence: the other existing absolutely is heard to speak by man itself *qua* species itself. Man itself is the absolutely created joy of absolute existence. The joy of man itself is the body itself the essence of creation itself, the transcendent coincidence of Life itself existing, the absolute conception of coincident immediacy. Between the immediate and thought itself, the absolute form of the body itself, the absolutely unconditioned identity of time itself: the beginning of light itself. Between the immediate and thought itself, the past itself transcendentally differentiated as the past itself absolutely, the absolute transcendence of light itself not yet, the necessity of history itself absolutely transcendent. Between the immediate and thought itself, consciousness itself absolutely unconditioned, the absolute transcendence of the categorical absolute not yet (since now for the first time the intelligible absolute is perceived in essence to subsist in history itself absolutely, it is clear that the transcendence of the form of consciousness itself not yet between the immediate and thought itself, the nothing but [reduced to] nothing, is not to be confused with the transcendence of world-transcending self-consciousness itself, whether in the form of a transcendent identity not transcendentally existing [this, in turn, whether a unity absolute, as in neoplatonism, or an absolute multiple, as in the historical inversion of the transcendent unicity constituting the unintelligible ones of the *posthumi*], or whether in the form of a transcendental identity of existing forms [this, in turn, whether reflected in the ideal ordering of actually existing essences, as in the monadology, or reflected in the sensible arrangement of actually existing appearances, as in the transcendental idealism of scientific reason], or, indeed, whether in the form of a transcendent existence of a transcendental identity [this, in turn, whether in the form of the absolute constitution of the substantial world in the form of an objectivity not thought itself, as in the absolute form of absolute reason, or in the form of the absolute constitution of the world in the form of a purely phenomenological objectivity, as in the infinite *a priori* of the pure ego of transcendental subjectivity]—it is clear that the transcendence of the form of the categorical absolute not yet between the immediate and thought itself is the actual transcendence of absolute world-consciousness itself, the transcendental existence of a transcendent identity, absolute reason absolutely existing, the absolute constitution of the substantial world in the form of the beginning of an absolute objectivity, in the form of the absolute actuality of the body for the first time). The intimacy of the constituent elements of the body itself is absolutely inestimable. The body itself being consciousness, the measure of all things, the intimacy of existence itself thought itself is the absolutely immeasurable measure: between existence and thought is the minimum itself, knowledge itself, the transcendence of knowledge itself not yet. Although the absolute intimacy of the immediate and thought itself is absolutely inestimable, it is not yet the absolute inestimability itself absolute. Here the essentiality of essence is essentially transcended in the form of the proclamation of the body itself, here in the form of foundation itself, here in the form of the minimum itself, here in the form of the immeasurable measure of the intimates absolute. Here is knowledge itself, neither the knowledge-at-a-distance of the *arbitrium/*of the will to power, the absolute drawing near of power constituting the abyss, nor the possibility of knowledge-at-a-distance, the transcendence of the *arbitrium/*the will to thinking, the absolute drawing near of thought constituting the abyss of existence itself, the absolute speculation, nor indeed, the actual knowledge-at-a-distance of the absolute *arbitrium*, the negative will to the body itself, the absolute distancing thereof (were it possible) constituting the absolutely positive negativity of the abyss itself absolute—here—in the midst of the constituent elements of the absolute itself—is knowledge itself the identity of time itself, apart from which objectivity itself there is no distance: knowledge itself the absolute absolute, incapable of being itself distanced, there being absolutely nothing to be known apart from knowledge itself not yet transcended. This, then, is the known absolute, the very essence of the body itself existing, the absolutely new species of Being itself, the essence itself of the stone upon which is written a new name, the discovery of the essence of the hidden manna. The known absolute, knowledge itself existing, is the question itself answered, the answer to the question of the essence of being itself, the answer to the question that has not yet been asked, the question written in the cipher-Being text of the reflection ending in non-existence, the question before now in a form incapable of being asked, even now the question essentially incapable of being asked apart from the fact of its being answered, even now the question of man itself the species itself incapable of being asked apart from the fact of its being new-world-consciousness itself, apart from its being the absolute transcendence of consciousness itself, which is to say that there is no existence which is not foundation itself, no transcendence which is not the inestimable absolute, no man itself not the species itself existing, no overman whose being is absolutely or essentially determined by his relation to the past, *no new grounding of Being itself by man which is not absolutely differentiated from man itself, which is not absolutely the proclamation of the body itself,* which is not existence itself absolutely displacing the abyss, which is not the transcendence itself of existence itself absolutely displacing the abyss not yet. The very midst itself of the constituent elements of the absolute, filled, as it is, with the absolutely immeasurable minimum itself, transcends in essence the absolutely formal absolute of the absolutely obsolete thinking of modernity: this very midst itself is the form of the absolute clarification of thought itself which exists in the form of the known absolute: as pure form, no longer actuality itself as absolute-identity-with-self, absolutely absolute self, in which simple absolute the formal distinction of a transcendent matter is dissolved, but, as existing form, the actuality itself of an absolute individuality, identically the body itself absolute identity with another, absolutely another absolute. This very midst itself as absolute identity is the absolute difference itself. From this absolute clarification of thought itself confusion itself is absolutely precluded. The Fact of existence itself exists, the Absolute Genus is no more. Here, in this absolute gift of Being itself, here, in the very midst of Light itself, precision itself accuracy itself, here, in the form of existence itself for the first time, the absolutely existing distinction of a matter itself absolute. Foundation itself, which fills the absolutely immeasurable form of the constituent elements of the absolute, renders each to the others the known absolute. This full rendering of foundation itself is the absolute concretion of the hitherto absolutely formal absolute, the transubstantiation of an existing form to that of the body itself, i.e., the transformation of existence itself into subsistence itself, the absolute bringing into existence of the absolute itself, the absolute creation of the absolute itself, the absolute bringing into existence of thought itself. In this essential conception of creation itself rendered foundation itself, the very midst itself is rendered the transcendental identity transcendentally differentiated as the fact of the past itself not itself, as the infinitesimal itself before now, now the minimum itself, now essentially rational individuality, now the absolute minimum in the otherwise infinite approximation of absolute reason displacing, in its historical existence, in its existing absolutely, in a way absolutely incapable of being itself anticipated, the infinitesimal approximation of thought itself to nothing, whether in the form of its being itself thought as absolute subjectivity's thought of non-being, or whether in the form of its being beyond thought in the will to thought, in absolute speculation's being of non-thought, in the abyss of the essence of existence itself, in the suspension of thought itself in absolute non-existence, the infinitesimal approximation (by way of reversal) of nothing itself to thought, thought's immanent necessity transforming nothing itself into something (not thought itself) in terms of which an intelligible world might come into being, the non-objectifying thought corresponding to the being of non-thought. Indeed, the absolute minimum in the otherwise absolute approximation of absolute reason includes in its displacement of the infinitesimal approximation of thought itself to nothing, in its absolute precision, the knowledge itself of absolute reason's absolute self-opposition, of the essence of the cipher-Being text, as the existence itself not yet having occurred to thought itself of the objectivity of Being itself. This is the knowledge itself in light of which it is perceived that as an absolute fact the matter itself now occurring to thought, without the presupposition of thought itself, for the first time in history, is the Object itself Being itself/*status objectivus*, Being itself the very objectivity of a non-objectifying thought, its form absolutely precluding an alternative thinking, filled, as this thinking is, with the absolute existence of Being itself, and not, as is absolutely manifest historically, with the actuality of the past, not with absolute-identity-with-self, and not, *a fortiori*, with the non-actuality of the past, the multiple non-objectifying thoughts constituting alternatives to absolute subjectivity in an existence not itself thought. The absolute individuality of the new species of Being itself excludes the exclusion of nothing from the absolute accuracy of light itself, i.e., excludes excluding nothing from the minimum itself absolute, save nothing in essence, the unintelligible, but includes saying the unintelligible (the abyss of thought/death itself speaking), itself nothing itself, the non-being of non-thought constituting the absolute ciphertext, as itself intelligible in the light itself of the absolutely intelligible perception of history itself, as the absolutely unintelligible multiple/saying nothing in essence in essentially absolutely many words, the necessity itself of the abyss. Now for the first time in history life itself names the spirit itself, names the object itself, names Being itself the New, gives Being itself a new identity in the very midst of reality itself, gives Being itself in the very midst of reality the midst of reality itself. From Life itself Being itself receives the absolute midst itself of reality, exists the absolute itself in the midst of the absolute absolute, transforming the midst itself of reality into the new existence of the body itself, *absolutely changing the absolute in essence, transcending the essentiality of essence in the form of thought itself now occurring for the first time in history.* The naming of Being itself is the form of the absolute concretion of thought itself existing/the matter now absolutely existing for the first time, the absolutely spiritual form of totality itself existing, not yet the form of the absolute existence of the minimum itself transcended, but the transcendence in essence of the absolutely formal absolute, the proclamation of the body itself matter itself existing, the essentially spiritual conception of matter itself in which no longer is the individual essentially pitted against the totality, no longer is the spiritual form of history not itself the absolute itself absolute. In the naming of Being itself the existing individual transcends totality itself in essence: the existing individual is the totality itself: the existing individual is itself the absolute minimum integrity of the conception of matter itself (this, the essential wingspan of the minimum itself, its saying of everything essentially in one word, its measure of the absolute itself existing, its being itself foundation itself): the minimum itself the unity of life itself: the absolute reality of spirit itself matter itself the body itself: the minimum itself, foundation itself, at once the unity, the reality, the existing individuality of life, Life itself Being itself absolutely. By way of the route itself not taken, by the way itself absolutely incapable of being itself anticipated, we arrive, in the world, at the foundation itself of the world now essentially new.

2

EX NIHILO THE ANGELIC WORD TOTALITY ITSELF

Nothing is to be added to the minimum itself. There is no possibility of a maximum opposed to, measuring itself from, the minimum, no possibility of an arbitrary rendering of the minimum, of a programming of the minimum or of a minimum program: no possibility not the absolute actuality of the minimum being itself a maximum. The transcendence of the minimum itself is the second absolute. Neither more nor less than the first absolute, the second absolute is not its double, but its absolute transcendence in existence. The second absolute is not an horizonal minimum, not an infinitesimal quantum, not a quantum of existence capable of the abyss: the second absolute is *ex abysso* the actuality of the body itself, the quantum of existence itself, the absolute quantum of existence. The second absolute is not nothing, not not the existence of the minimum itself, nor absolutely nothing other than the minimum itself transcended. In place of the place that is no place, the second absolute is not (merely) a place, but the place of the beginning of the absolute place, itself absolutely transcending the absolute. The second absolute is the first absolute thought itself transcendence itself for the first time. The second by which the first is the second is the absolute itself. The second absolute is the existence of the minimum itself transcendentally differentiated. The second absolute is the existence of the first absolute. There is no prologue to the existence of the minimum itself (the existence of the minimum itself precludes the play itself, the whiling away of time itself, the absolute form itself of counting down to nothing: the minimum is the unity of the infinite division). The existing body itself, not death itself, speaking precludes the bedding away of the body, precludes the hushing out of existence of the being itself of the word spoken in essence in the form of a prologue, the whiling away of the minimum itself in the form of its being in place of the second, in the form of a substitute for the word itself. The second absolute is the integral being itself of the first absolute the minimum itself, precluding the presence of the totality of the absolute, precluding, that is, the total presence of the body, i.e., of the second absolute, absolutely precluding the presence of an absolute necessity. Indeed, the second absolute the existence of the minimum itself is the transcendence of an absolute necessity: this logos, too, is the minimum itself: the absolutely unprecedented transcendence of absolute necessity: the absolutely transcendent coincidence of thought itself with existence itself: coincidence itself itself the absolute quantity: the minimum itself the totality itself absolutely without the possibility of a maximum, therefore, absolutely without the possibility of its constituent elements as parts: the constituent elements of the totality each itself absolute: the constituent elements of the absolute each the totality itself, each the transcendence itself of absolute quantity. The absolutely elemental totality is the existence of the absolute minimum of perception itself, the necessity itself of each of the elemental constituents, at once precluding, formally, the innumerable elements of the merely formal necessity of the minimum, essentially, the coincidence of necessity itself with a maximum possibility. This is the essentially factual existence of the absolute quanta numbered, the absolute numeration of the elements existing in fact in essence: *number itself the measure itself of the total:* the new order of the absolute itself absolute: *order itself substance itself for the first time:* the absolutely transcendental quantity of matter itself. Thought in essence, number is the perception itself of the essence of creation. This for the first time is the absolute repetition. Of what? Of the new itself, of the transcendent coincidence, of the body itself existing, of the quantum absolute. In vain does one complain of the absolute repetition of the absolute plaintext itself, when the product of this repetition (unlike that of the plaintext itself merely repeated in essence [which was nothing itself]) is, always and everywhere, itself new, is, indeed, the essential form of the universe (which itself, *qua* specificity, is to be absolutely repeated in the instant that is to be the transcendence itself of the absolute plaintext, the transcendence itself of the absolute minimum in what otherwise is the approximation of absolute reason, the displacement of the minimum itself at the time appointed for the creation of spiritual substance, i.e., for the materialization of the absolute quantity, not merely, as now, as thought itself, but as the body itself transcending now itself in the instant that is to be the transcendence of the new order of the absolute itself: the absolute fulfilment of coincidence itself/absolutely no beyond not the minimum itself). The product itself of the absolute repetition of the new itself, the transcendence itself of coincidence itself, the minimum itself absolutely unconditioned for the first time is λόγος καθολικός, catholicity itself existing, the lasting fruit of absolute repetition: the new product is the lasting fruit: the lasting absolute is the new itself thought itself: what is produced is catholicity itself, i.e., the universe itself the essentially new form of thought. This is the catholicity of the absolute itself, the coincidence itself of absolute quanta themselves, the catholicity of matter itself, matter itself the measure itself, the quantum absolute, of thought itself transcendently existent: this is the absolute quantification of the minimum itself. The quantum absolute is the priority of the quantum differentiated from the quantum as absolute: the *a priori* quantity itself not other than quantity: the second absolute absolutely transcending the first absolute existence. The absolute quantity is the priority of quantity itself absolutely differentiated from absolute quantity itself. The existing priority is quantity itself: the absolute absolute, i.e., not quantity itself other than the minimum itself/the existing totality. The transcendence of the absolute quantity is the priority of order itself differentiated as the existence of order itself. The *a priori* quantity itself absolutely for the first time: the *a priori* totality totally *a posteriori*: the body itself the essentially differentiated order itself the substance itself of totality itself the absolutely existing minimum: absolute order itself transcendentally differentiated existence itself the absolute minimum. The minimum absolute is the priority of the minimum as differentiated absolute minimum. The totality of the *a priori* is *a posteriori* the absolute itself. *The catholicity of transcendence itself, the priority of totality itself, is totality itself absolutely differentiated. There is no a priori catholicity: existence itself is the transcendentally differentiated transcendence of the new order of the absolute itself existing.* This is the synthetic *a priori* judgment of the body itself absolute reason absolutely existing, the absolute transcendence of the synthetic *a priori* judgment: the *a priori* of the *a priori* judgment: the fact of existence for the first time. Catholicity itself is absolutely the experience of existence itself: the transcendence of totality the experience of the non-existence of the *a priori*, the experience of the absolute existence of the *a priori* non-existence: the first time experience of the fact of the other. Now for the first time in history experience itself *a priori*, the limit of the *a priori* itself absolute (the infinite termination of the infinite *a priori*: the infinite *a priori* of the transcendental ego *existing*): for the first time the absolute mediation of the absolute immediate: the absolute experience of existence itself in the form of the essence of thought itself: *time itself the absolute identity of the body itself experienced as change itself.* What now occurs is the transcendence of the formal absolute of life itself, of the mere thought-form of life itself, of the mere notion of the form itself of life, a transcendence for the first time, conceived precisely, not constituting an *a priori* catholicity itself, but, rather, identically the experience of the *a priori* catholicity, the abyss *ex abysso*: time itself existing for the first time. Now absolutely eliminated is the notion itself of the *a priori* temporality of synthetic judgment, the notion of the time of time itself, the non-identity of the body itself thought itself change, the notion of the body taking time, the non-identity of time itself thought itself the body. What is left behind is time itself as the minimum form of space, as the absolute form of absolute space, as the point (the actuality of space itself, i.e., the place of the absolute self-relation of space), the form of the spatial minimum, the actuality of the space-time continuum. Before now modernity arrived at the notion of time itself, at the transcendence of the disjunctive conjunction of exterior and interior order, of intuition and conception, of the world of natural objects and the experience of that world, of objective and subjective existence, at the transcendence in essence of time as the formal condition for the perception of things, at the notion of time itself as the formal condition for the experience of space, as the non-identity of space in essence, as the spatial body ('the formal soul of nature'). Now the notion of the body itself existing in space is left behind. Now the eternal transcendence of the body itself, whether in the form of the notion itself or whether in the form of space itself, is itself transcended absolutely. Now the eternal thought-form of time itself is itself transcended: *time is experienced for the first time as the form of the body itself essentially change itself: time is the experienced identity of change itself in the form of the now itself.* The form of the temporal minimum is absolutely existence itself/the transcendental imagination of change itself. There is now absolutely no spatial now, no inessential temporality, no point of non-existence, no differentiated unity of time and space, no mere form of beginningless absolute totality, indeed, there is no pure synthesis of the absolute *a priori* judgment, there is time itself the synthesis *a priori* of the *a priori* judgment: *the absolute experience itself of the limit of experience itself* (the minimum) *itself beyond the limit of experience itself: the quantity of existence itself absolutely experienced.* There is now the absolute now, the quantum absolute, the minimum itself (displacing space itself [beside the body there is the absolute transcendence of the minimum itself]): the absolute synthesis of the non-existence of the *a priori* absolute. There is no merely specific quantum with which to begin (no more than there is a simple unit not the transcendentally differentiated unity of absolute order, i.e., not the minimum the transcendentally differentiated beginning). In the absolute mediation of the immediate, which is the essence of the historical being of the minimum itself, the specific quantum is the integral limit of the minimum itself, is immediately and absolutely mediated the quantum absolute. *The transcendence of the quantum absolute is* simply *and* essentially the *minimum itself.* To put it simply (and essentially): that there should be something of any kind, including the something that is nothing itself, and including even that thinking now occurring for the first time in history, more *fundamental* than foundation itself, such a notion is absolutely unintelligible—an absolutely anachronistic repetition that draws an absolute blank—a pure formality that once was and is no more. The simple itself for the first time is the essence itself transcendentally differentiated, i.e., the essence of the simple is absolutely complex, incapable of being itself absolute simplicity in any form other than that of the minimum itself. Apart from this absolutely irreducible fact itself, this absolute λόγος καθολικός, there is no thought itself. The thought of this catholicity itself is the experience itself of totality itself, the transcendence of totality in the form itself of thought itself, 'heaven laid bare' in the form of thought itself: the conception itself of the essentially temporal minimum, the transcendental Jacob's ladder.

Now essentially historical the angelic word sounds—without resounding, with absolute precision, separating time itself from history itself—time is not merely now, nor merely temporality, now is the quantum absolute, time is now the thought-form of the transcendence of the transcendental difference itself. As the angel (who, 'standing on the sea and on the land, *raised his right hand to heaven,* and *swore by the One who lives for ever* and ever, *and made heaven and all that is in it,* and *earth and all it bears,* and *the sea and all it holds'*) transcended the totality of everything,[1] so totality itself now transcends time itself: for the first time history itself the measure of totality: *time is not now except it is the now itself eliminating in essence the spatial now, absolutely transcending the dimensionality of existence itself, indeed, absolutely transcending the dialectical absolute itself.* Time is not now except it be what now itself is, viz., the measure of the absolute contact of existence with thought. This is *for the first time the absolute contact of the absolute itself with existence:* time itself, the now itself, now the minimum itself the experience of absolute contact for the first time in history. The *existence* of the minimum itself is the beginning of this very experience. The transcendence of the minimum itself is neither more nor less than the minimum itself, the angelic word sounds without the word resounding, i.e., in

[1] Cf. I. Kant, *On History,* trans. L.W. Beck et al. (Indianapolis, 1963), pp. 76–78.

essence existing perfectly the first time. The transcendence of the now itself is not merely another now, it is another absolute, it is the second absolute, not another now itself with a different content, not an absolute contact of absolute content, not the merely formal, i.e., essentially contentless, contact of the absolute, which it was in the mere notion of time itself with which modern consciousness essentially raised itself above the thoroughly idealistic (though obviously not absolutely so) differentiation of dialectic from the things of thought. Leaving behind the absolute dialectical self-differentiation of things, transcending the mere notion of time itself, the transcendence of the now itself, *qua* minimum itself, for the first time is existence itself the content of an absolute contact, the absolute contact of a *new* absolute content, that is, what now itself absolutely is, viz., the quantum existing with the absolute content, the transcendence of an absolutely dialectical content, the angelic word sounding the historical, i.e., not the merely temporal, differentiation of time itself. There is absolutely no experience pre-existing objectivity itself, no experience of anything pre-existing contact itself: the factuality of existence transcends thought itself for the first time: *qua* transcendent content, existing reality is absolute contact with the second absolute. This is the minimum transcendence of the body itself for the first time. In the minimum quantity less than the time required for the blinking of an eye, the obstacle placed in the way of the comprehension by understanding itself of the end of change implicit in the mere conception of a moment without time, the obstacle placed in the way by the merely formal critique of cognition, by merely formal logic (an obstacle to the actuality of the absolute not removed, but rather merely transcended in the essential critique of cognition which begins with being itself unmediated, with pure being, to end with thought itself, with the absolute itself), this obstacle is now-removed by the existence of the essentially transcendental critique of cognition, i.e., is actually removed by the essentially transcendental logic of existence, i.e., is removed by the actuality of the absolute now, i.e., is actually removed by the change itself now occurring for the first time in the transcendental imagination, whereby the merely formal magnitude of everything is transcended in essence (here this essentially transcendental logic is distinguished from the transcendental logic of a pure phenomenology which begins with formal magnitude itself transcendentally intact, to end with the possibility of science itself, with the problem of a world-logic). Now the transcendent imagination of change itself, the transcendence of what then must be merely an idea, is not merely transcended, as before now it was (in such a way as it was not itself—transcendental imagination of change itself—the actual, the now itself existing, but was contrasted with the latter as the temporal with the eternal), but now for the first time in history the transcendent imagination of change itself is transcended in essence, i.e., *the absolute idea (otherwise the existence of the imagination of change itself) is itself transcended in the form of the absolute actuality of change itself.* This absolute actuality of change itself, the now itself existing, the absolute elimination of space in essence, the transcendence of the temporal dimensionality of history (i.e., of its confusion, before now, with time before now), this transcendence in essence of the zero-dimensionality of the point, is absolute magnitude itself concretely existing, concretely existence. Instead of a formally beginningless transcendental thinking (in fact an essentially transcendental idealism) there exists now for the first time an essentially transcendental perception of the magnitude itself of actual existence itself: magnitude itself the perception transcending perception, the absolute measure of perception itself, the absolute species thereof, the absolute measure of objectivity. The point of absolute magnitude is *a priori* nothing but experience itself, the experience of absolutely nothing *a priori* but the existing fact: the species of perception is the absolute existence of an absolutely transcendent species: perception now for the first time is experience absolutely beyond the limit of experience. The object, *qua* existing species, is the absolutely immediate existence of thought itself. *Qua* this actually existing species, i.e., *qua* magnitude, the object is the magnitude of perception itself existing. This is the absolute relativity of the object itself measuring thought itself: the object of perception *is* the absolutely unconditioned transcendence of the absolute, *is* actuality itself. The object is not merely actual, but transcendently actual, i.e., the experience of the limit itself of experience beyond the limit of experience: the object is the transcendent limit of thought in essence: the object is the existence of the absolute itself experience. The object for the first time is the absolute essence of life itself, through the absolute mediation of the immediate, the integral essence of life itself: relativity itself the absolute relative: relativity itself the absolute content of the absolute. The transcendental differentiation of the absolute self-relation as no longer intelligible, except as belonging to thought in essence in the past, as now absolutely not actuality itself, is itself the perception itself transcendentally differentiated as the content of the absolute clarification of thought itself, as the absolute content of an absolutely synthetic thought. Just so, the transcendental differentiation of the transcendent identity of the time before and after the absolute now as a mere thought-form (along with the space within and without the body itself) is itself the perception itself transcendentally differentiated as the absolute now essentially a new transcendental content, as the content of an absolute *a posteriori* transcendence of totality itself, as the analytic of an absolute factuality, the analytic of the transcendence of the end of change in fact in the form of *this* analytic actuality, in the form of the concretion of the transcendence of the transcendent conception of the end itself of change: the essentially transcendental limit of experience itself transcended: the transcendental itself *a posteriori*: for the first time the absolute synthesis of existence itself. *This* analytic is the magnitude of thought itself existing. No obstacle whatsoever can be placed in its way, in the way of the *absolute construction of the magnitude of being itself.* The absolute magnitude of being itself is the existence itself (*exsistere ipsum*) which is synthesized. The synthetic analytic of existence itself is the analytic of this existence. For the first time content itself is now-content. Content is not a beginningless matter of form, but content is the transcendence itself for the first time of the transcendental *de facto.* This absolute content of an absolute logic is immediately perceived. The absolute content of this absolute logic is not mediated by the minimum itself (a redundancy of existence previously found in the coincidence of logic with metaphysics), it *is* the minimum itself: logic coincides now the transcendence of logic: analytic is of magnitude itself, i.e., of the measure of perception itself: analytic is of the absolute minimum itself, is absolutely of the being itself of magnitude: the coincidence of logic with existing magnitude is absolute now for the first time in history. For the first time actual magnitude is logic itself. Logic now coincides with ontology itself, not with metaphysics, not with onto-theo-logic but with the essence thereof. Indeed, this very writing (spoken aloud or not) the existing absolute saying itself, this absolute plaintext, is the absolute elimination of atheism, God without the ontological difference other than himself. The new species of Being itself is ontology itself ontologically differentiated as existence, i.e., ontology existence itself the ontologically differentiated essence of Being: the essence of Being itself existing as the ontologically differentiated absolute, i.e., not merely as ontologically differentiated existence, i.e., not merely as issue, i.e., as non-specific existence. Now for the first time in history thought itself exists as the ontologically differentiated essence of Being, as the instance *par excellence* of the essence of Being: thought itself absolutely transcending the theological essence, absolutely severing its rootedness in an ontologically undifferentiated ontological difference in terms of which its being ontology is its being other than theology, in terms of which the issue of the essence of Being is difference itself as such, in terms of which the essence of Being transcends thought in the form of the transcendence of metaphysics, in the form of a non-objectifying thought, in the form of difference itself as such the object, of thought, but thought not thought in essence, but a kind of 'backwards step' into the essence of metaphysics as the issue of the difference within Being, a 'backwards step' totally sinking the actual essence of metaphysics, the essentially unhistorical individuality, in the oblivion of the abyss itself, i.e., sinking it, in the recoil from the absolute form of the absolute, in the form of the fourfold transcendence of the absolute nothing itself, a 'backwards step' from metaphysics (as received in modern consciousness) to the confusion of its totality in essence with the essence of ontology, a confusion which is the essential intertwining of ontology with theology in the totality of metaphysics. Now for the first time in history thought absolutely differentiated transcends thought's being itself in essence difference, transcends, that is, thought itself, that is, leaves behind the ontologically differentiated self-identity of beginningless thought, transcends precisely difference itself as such the object of thought: difference is thought without being itself other than thought the object of thought: difference now for the first time absolutely coincides thought in essence. Ontology itself transcends the ontologically differentiated theology: ontology essentially identifies the absolute itself for the first time: God the ontological identity *par excellence*: God itself absolutely understood: the categorical absolute: change itself transcending time itself, not merely in the form of an eternal history (the absolutely eternal), but as the form of the absolutely historical, the new identity of time itself, as the very form of the new essence of ontology. Difference is thought being itself objectivity for the first time (before now, difference as such the *object* of thought is first the comprehension of death itself the shrine of Nothing, a purely formless objectivity; then, before now, in face of the fact itself of existence, a purely formless objectivity is transcended in the form of the *subject* of thought: the absolute biform of the absolute: difference as such the subject-object of thought, the comprehension of death seeding itself in existence, the absolute comprehension of Nothing absolutely existing: *la différance* the absolute multiplication of beginnings). Now ontology itself transcends the contradiction of the theological essence of modern philosophy (an essence whose existence is now for the first time comprehended as absolutely historical, i.e., as having absolutely not existed at one time, prior to the actual formality of the Incarnation), thereby transcending the ontological difference of a generic 'philosophy', together with the essentially philosophical atheism of Being beyond thought in the form of absolute speculation—at once an atheological theism, a 'thinking-less-God', an ontology of immanent totality—*Dasein* transcending the totality itself of nothing. Now ontology itself absolutely deciphers the history of Being as itself the absolute identity of Being itself, Being itself for the first time difference itself existing: the ontological identity of ontology itself not Nothing itself, but difference itself existing for the first time: perception itself breaking through the absolute itself to the new species of Being itself, to the universe itself new, to the second itself absolute, to the form of time-transcendent change itself. Thus, fundamentally metaphysical ontology, i.e., fundamental ontology, which, *qua* fundamental, is metaphysical, belongs to the past, indeed, it is thought in essence to-be-thought belonging to the past, the ontological differentiation of metaphysics from the logic that was understood to be metaphysics, the metaphysical transcendence of the natural body of man, the natural transcendence of the essentially metaphysical body, the retreat from the historical materialism which itself was not thought itself to what was, indeed, an essential thinking, but an essential thinking not itself thought itself except in the form of Nothing itself, Being itself beyond 'Being for the truth of Being'.[2] Before now essentially thinking was an objectivity with

[2] Cf. M. Heidegger, *Existence and Being,* Introduction by W. Brock (Chicago, 1949), pp. 357ff.: "Calculation uses everything that 'is' as units of computation, in advance, and, in the computation, uses up its stock of units. This consumption of what-is reveals the consuming nature of calculation. Only because number can be multiplied indefinitely—and this regardless of whether it goes in the direction of the great or the small—is it possible for the consuming nature of calculation to hide behind its 'products' and give calculative thought the appearance of 'productivity'—whereas it is of the prime essence of calculation, and not merely in its results, to assert what-is only in the form of something that can be arranged and used up. Calculative thought places itself under compulsion to master everything in the logical terms of its procedure. It has no notion that in calculation everything calculable is already a whole before it starts working out its sums and products, a whole whose unity naturally belongs to the incalculable which, with its mystery, ever eludes the clutches of calculation. That which, however, is always and everywhere closed at the outset to the demands of calculation and, despite that, is always closer to man in its enigmatic unknowableness than anything that 'is', than anything he may arrange and plan, this can sometimes put the essential man in touch with a thinking whose truth no 'logic' can grasp. The thinking whose thoughts not only do not calculate but are absolutely determined by what is 'other' than what-is, might be called essential thinking. Instead of counting on what-is with what-is, it expends itself in Being for the truth of Being. This thinking answers to the demands of Being in that man surrenders his historical

Nothing beyond: the self-less objectivity of Being itself the thought of Nothing, without self, but not without the notion of self expressed in the negative nothing of absolute necessity, the abyss of freedom: in its purest expression, the absolute transcendence of the opening of self-concealing thought, the self-concealing opening onto totality itself, the finitude of totality itself, thinking absolutely the thought of Being without God, the opening itself onto the finitude of divinity-itself-less-God-in-essence: the nature of man the form of a fundamental ontology: thinking essentially 'the speechless answer' to the 'Word of the soundless voice of Being': *thinking, before now, essentially the transcendence of intellect itself in relation to Nothing.* This was the perfectly abstract resemblance in history of the unhistorical intellect (of the actuality of metaphysics) in the form of nature itself: man belonging totally in essence to Being: totality itself the transcendence of belonging to man: history Being itself essentially the thought of man's nature, beyond logic in being beyond metaphysics. Precisely in the *nature* of the matter of essential thinking, i.e., in its *givenness,* in the givenness of 'Being for the truth of Being', precisely in essential thinking's Being *not thought* for the truth of Being, in the 'simple, sole necessity'

---

being to the simple, sole necessity whose constraints do not so much necessitate as create the need (*Not*) which is consummated in the freedom of sacrifice. The need is: to preserve the truth of Being no matter what may happen to man and everything that 'is'. Freed from all constraint, because born of the abyss of freedom, this sacrifice is the expense of our human being for the preservation of the truth of Being in respect of what-is. In sacrifice there is expressed that hidden *thanking* which alone does homage to the grace wherewith Being has endowed the nature of man, in order that he may take over in his relationship to Being the guardianship of Being. Original thanking is the echo of Being's favour wherein it clears a space for itself and causes the unique occurrence: that what-is is. This echo is man's answer to the Word of the soundless voice of Being. The speechless answer of his thanking through sacrifice is the source of the human word, which is the prime cause of language as the enunciation of the Word in words. Were there not an occasional thanking in the heart of historical man he could never attain the thinking—assuming that there must be thinking (*Denken*) in all doubt (*Bedenken*) and memory (*Andenken*)—which originally thinks the thought of Being."

which elicits the sacrifice arising out of the abyss of existence, out of the abyss of freedom, the sacrifice of man's historical being, precisely in the actuality of Being the *want* of Being (the mere transcendence, i.e., itself not thought in essence, of the absolute want of the fourfold [which latter, untranscended, reverberates, ideally, itself not thought, in the absolute want of historical materialism]), in the *need* for the actuality of the opening, for the actuality of the 'primal matter',[3] lies the perfectly abstract recollection of the actuality of metaphysics. In the need for the being of non-thought lies the recollection of absolute self-relation, of the actuality of an absolutely formal metaphysics of the absolute, in the form of the self-concealing unconcealment of the opening wherein logic coincides sacrifice, in the form of the absolute self-sacrifice of objectifying thought, viz., the opening itself to Being, *for the sake of* Being itself absolute. Indeed, ultimately, for the sake of Being itself absolute, the thoughtful experience of the opening itself—this total transcendence of thought itself—*is* itself a *given*, a *Not*/a Need, an exigency of the thought of Being itself, of non-being that it should be confirmed in Being itself something other than Being itself, being coinciding with thought throughout the unthought itself, the unbeing of the Being of thought in essence. This need needs not to be met, this need is met in the opening itself in which the absence of God is his presence, in which God especially is the rim of the seeing itself unseen. In the absolute need of total transcendence, the fundamental limitation of fundamental ontology, of essential thinking before now, is that that thinking differentiated the essence of the transcendental imagination—time itself—as itself a given, as 'primordial time'. Before now, concerned not merely to overcome, but to transcend metaphysics, essential thinking, out of the need to transcend the ontological difference, thinks not time itself as transcendence itself existing, but holds to time and Being absolutely transcending the Being of existence, to Being at home in its own house, in language, but not in the house of

[3] Cf. M. Heidegger, *On Time and Being*, trans. Joan Stambaugh (New York, 1972), pp. 65ff.

existence itself, not in thought, holds to time as the root of a primordial transcendence, to the given of appropriation itself, to the need met in appropriation itself, to the need for transcendence of the actual appropriation. Before now, essential thinking holds to the need for an essentially new thinking, but thinks it not, thinks, instead, the oldest of the old, the primordial root of presence, the given as the abyss of existence itself, such that even this existence is thought as the absolutely unthought transcendental, as the need faced by appropriation itself. In facing this need appropriation comes face to face with the primordial form of absolute self-transformation, the opening in which presence presences, in which the present is absent, in which the given is the actually self-transcendent opening in which the thoughtful experience of Being is the given: in which the given is in which is the given: the given absolute need. Such was the self-enveloping clarity of the opening onto Being, of the absolute uncenteredness of self in the service of Being, of the perfectly abstract reminiscence, at once the inversion, of the luminous opacity of the metaphysical intellect *par excellence*, which for the time-being had been forgotten in being identified with logic in the absolutely formal metaphysics of the absolute, which had been forgotten altogether, for all practical purposes, prior to essential thinking's recollection of the primordial root of the Being of appropriation in appropriation itself, in being itself appropriated to the remembrance (ἀνάμνησις) of Being (Being forgotten at the very inception of thought in the earliest times), forgotten, prior to the absolute anachronism in which Being is confused with time beyond thought, in which both givens, presence and the opening, are in the form of absolute thought in the past, in the form of thought absolutely in the past, but which luminous opacity in this recollection of Being subsequent to thinking essentially in the past is itself confusedly merged with the overcoming of metaphysics in being remembered without regard to the historical transformation of thought which occurs essentially in face of the fact of the Incarnation, without regard to the fact that before now life itself actually effected for the first time the form of natural objectivity (the form subsequently appropriated by modern consciousness for its own purposes).[4] The luminous opacity of the divine intellect of an existent metaphysics is confused with the mere unselfconsciousness of essential thinking, with thinking the given itself transcending objectivity itself as if objectivity itself had never occurred except by way of the mistake of absolute self-consciousness, as if modernity were *totally* mistaken, as if the mistake were consciousness itself (!) and not, as it was, precisely the form of appropriation itself of consciousness itself as a given, itself not thought except as the thought of self. This absolute inversion of the mistake of modernity is the mistake which thinks essentially the sacrifice of consciousness itself, which thinks *inessentially* the non-objectifying thought: the mistake which is the logic of the abyss, the logic of absolute unconsciousness itself, the thinking transcending consciousness itself to the need itself the given, the history of Being itself a given transcending thought in essence. This confusion of the 'primal matter' of essential thinking with the luminous opacity of an absolutely given actuality is the mistake of modernity in its pure form (the contradiction to its being thought inverted to Being) as the absolutely self-supporting analogue of objectivity itself, as the self-transcendent rim of an analogical actuality, as the rim of the absolutely self-transcendent opening onto the analogical divinity of God, as the rim of a transcendence of objectivity analogous to nothing, the rim of totality itself in face of nothing itself beyond logic, the rim itself of Nothing itself, being thought to be Being not thought, in terms of which it is clear that there is no absolutely given actuality apart from the absolute form of absolute reminiscence, which latter, a given in essence, essentially gives no account of itself apart from Being for the truth of Being, apart from its absolutely essentially having forgotten the essential inception of the recollection of Being upon itself, apart from its taking the inception of the fourfold of appropriation as itself the given, neither thought itself, nor to be thought, the twofold given of time and Being. But the essential thinking now occurring for the first time in history transcends in essence the

[4] Cf. D. G. Leahy, *Novitas Mundi: Perception of the History of Being* (reprint; Albany, 1994).

support needed for a thinking essentially analogous to the ontological difference, the support needed for a thinking essentially for which time is a given in the form of true time together with Being transcending metaphysics, for a thinking, that is, essentially analogous to the root of metaphysics (schematically reflected as the transcendental imagination of modernity, at once the schematic reflection of the essential rootedness of self-consciousness). Now transcended in essence is the support needed for the essential thinking for which the transcendence of ontological knowledge was a given, for which the opening opened absolutely onto the transcendence of the given to there remain essentially complete in its incompleteness transcending time. In the essential thinking now occurring for the first time in history as the history of Being, the surrounding of the given, the essential need of thinking before now, is absolutely left behind: now the opening opens absolutely-essentially existence itself: now for the first time the opening opens in the very form of the divinity itself of Christ, in the very form of the body itself of God. The absolute now of essentially transcendental thinking absolutely differentiates absolute-thought-in-the-past from the absolute transcendence of the second absolute: *the former is the essentially anticipatory thinking essentially incapable of anticipating the thinking essentially anticipating the fact itself as time-transcendent change itself:* the transcendence of the given incapable of anticipating its being itself thought itself. This in fact was not anticipated, viz., the transcendence itself of appropriation appropriating, the absolute leaving behind of the essence of non-existence/the non-existence of essence, of the non-existence of logic/the logic of sacrifice itself not itself existence. This transcendence is the angel itself actually speaking: this is the angelic word now experienced in the form of the absolute magnification of thought in essence. *For the first time the new reality at once intellect itself.* Now anticipation itself is the now-content of the thought transcending thought itself. The transcendence of givenness, absolutely now-mediated, is the transcendence of the now itself, i.e., the minimum itself. In place of thinking essentially appropriated for Being/the given, in place of thinking itself withheld (in the event of appropriation itself no longer withheld) thinking essentially thinking is now-absolutely transcended in essence. In place of the transcendence of absolute givenness the transcendence of absolute thought itself, the transcendence of objectivity itself/knowledge itself, the transcendence itself of the absolute known. In place of the transcendence of the root of metaphysical time, i.e., in place of the givenness of transcendental imagination itself, the perception of the absolute change itself in the transcendental imagination now actually occurring for the first time in the form of the absolute clarification of thought itself. In place of the absolutely unbounded opening bound by the given, the absolute now perceived in the midst of reality itself: the absolutely unbounded opening bounding the unbounded itself: the bound itself of thought itself: the species of perception absolutely existing in essence. Before now, the bound of thinking was the given transcendence of appropriation; now for the first time the bound of thinking is the foundation itself of transcendence itself, at once the ontology of existence itself, absolutely unconditioned ontology, for which God is not, as before now, merely in the seeing (thought as given/the pure immanence of the transcendental itself) for the sake of the seeing, but is now the seeing in the seen itself (thought as existent/the absolute transcendence of the transcendental itself), the seeing itself absolutely transcended. Now the bound of thinking is the absolute experience of transcendence *de facto*, the essentially transcendental magnitude of Being itself *de facto*. Now magnitude itself coincides with Being itself for the first time: now exists absolutely neither Being other than Being, nor Being for the sake of Being, neither Being other than the Being of magnitude (i.e., 'indeterminate' Being other than Being/quantity capable of not being 'indeterminate'/'indeterminate' 'determinateness which has become indifferent to being', the absolute—'pure quantity'—other than a 'determinate' quantity, or quantum: the before now not absolutely differentiated absolute Being of magnitude: the before now not absolutely differentiated perception of appearance itself as the quantum absolutely existing: the before now in essence not thought absolute transcendence of the transcendental imagination: the absolute, pure quantity, subsequent to the immediate determinateness of Being, to quality, precedent to quantum[5]): nor Being essentially analogous to the Being of magnitude (i.e., Being as presence unifying 'time's threefold opening extending' in the fourfold of true time, the 'prespatial region which first gives any possible "where"': the total given to essential thinking: the before now analogue of the transcendence of totality itself: the before now not absolutely unconditioned leaving behind of the metaphysical form of absolute clarity: presence and the opening, Being and time not coinciding with each other but with Being-given, kept apart in the appropriating of appropriation, in the givenness itself: the given tran-

---

[5] Cf. Hegel's *Science of Logic,* trans. A.V. Miller (London, 1969), p. 185: "The difference between quantity and quality has been stated. Quality is the first, immediate determinateness, quantity is the determinateness which has become indifferent to being, a limit which is just as much no limit, being-for-self which is absolutely identical with being-for-other—a repulsion of the many ones which is directly the non-repulsion, the continuity of them.

"Because that which is for itself is now posited as not excluding its other, but rather as affirmatively continuing itself into it, it is otherness in so far as *determinate being* again appears in this continuity and its determinateness is *at the same time* no longer in a simple self-relation, no longer an immediate determinateness of the determinately existent something, but is posited as self-repelling, as in fact having the relation-to-self as a determinateness in another something (which is *for itself*); and since they are *at the same time* indifferent, relationless limits reflected into themselves, the determinateness in general is outside itself, an absolutely *self-external* determinateness and an equally external something; such a limit, the indifference of the limit within itself and of the something to the limit, constitutes the *quantitative* determinateness of the something.

"In the first place, *pure quantity* is to be distinguished from itself as a *determinate* quantity, from quantum. As the former, it is in the first place real being-for-self which has returned into itself and which as yet contains no determinateness: a compact, infinite unity which continues itself into itself.

"Secondly this develops a determinateness which is posited in it as one which is at the same time no determinateness, as only an *external* one. It becomes *quantum.* Quantum is indifferent determinateness, that is, a self-transcending, self-negating determinateness; as this otherness of otherness it relapses into the infinite progress. But the infinite quantum is the indifferent determinateness *sublated,* it is the restoration of quality." Note the essentially modern metaphysical root in Hegel's conception of quantity as Being constituted of contraries *at the same time.*

scendence of temporality, the transcendence of the absolute form of the absolute self-consciousness: the formal conception of the givenness of transcendence itself: Being merely in terms of time/Being merely essentially analogous to time: the before now not itself thought itself Being absolutely coinciding time itself: before now, thinking essentially measuring the given itself/thinking essentially back-beyond measuring itself[6]). In essential thinking back-beyond measuring itself the ontological difference before now, magnitude was the giving nothing extending opening in which presence presences, the givenness of the nothing-transcendence of the transcendental imagination in the form of time: the Being of magnitude essentially analogous to the givenness of time (transcending, *qua* thinking

---

[6] Cf. Heidegger, *On Time and Being*, pp. 16–17: "Time *is* not. There is, It gives time. The giving that gives time is determined by denying and withholding nearness. It grants the openness of time-space and preserves what remains denied in what has-been, what is withheld in approach. We call the giving which gives true time an extending which opens and conceals. As extending is itself a giving, the giving of a giving is concealed in true time.

"But where *is* there time and time-space, where are they given? As urgent as this question may be at first sight, we may no longer ask in this manner for a where, for the place for time. For true time itself, the realm of its threefold extending determined by nearing nearness, is the prespatial region which first gives any possible 'where'.

"True, from its beginning, whenever it thought about time, philosophy also asked where time belongs. What philosophy primarily had in view was time calculated as a sequence of the succession of consecutive nows. It was explained that there could be no numerically measured time with which we calculate without the *psyche,* without the *animus,* without the soul, without consciousness, without spirit. There is no time without man. But what does this 'not without' mean? Is man the giver or receiver of time? Is man first of all man, and then after that occasionally—that is, at some time or other—receives time and relates himself to it? True time is the nearness of presencing out of present, past and future—the nearness that unifies time's threefold opening extending. It already reached man as such so that he can be man only by standing within the threefold extending, perduring the denying, and withholding nearness which determines that extending. Time is not the product of man, man is not the product of time. There is no production here. There is only giving in the sense of extending which opens up time-space.

absolutely in the past, the thinking for which time transcended the Being of magnitude [thinking essentially in the past]): the entrance into time itself of the eternal thought-form of time itself, the perfect embodiment in time itself of that thought-form which itself, in its turn, had been the appropriation, in the form of transcendental existence, of the immanence of magnitude itself (which in turn had come to be in thinking formally in the past which had conceived formally, i.e., non-transcendently, transcendental thinking).

Essential thinking before now sacrificed the logic of magnitude for the sake of thinking back-beyond the root of metaphysics, transcending not only the absolute form of the meta-

---

"But granted that the manner of giving in which time is given requires our characterization of time, we are still faced with the enigmatic It which we named in the expression: It gives time; It gives Being. There is a growing danger that when we speak of 'It', we arbitrarily posit an indeterminate power which is supposed to bring about all giving of Being and of time. However, we shall escape indeterminacy and avoid arbitrariness so long as we hold fast to the determinations of giving which we attempted to show, if only we look ahead toward Being as presence and toward time as the realm where, by virtue of offering, a manifold presencing takes place and opens up. The giving in 'It gives Being' proved to be a sending and a destiny of presence in its epochal transformations.

"The giving in 'It gives time' proved to be an extending, opening up the four-dimensional realm.

"Insofar as there is manifest in Being as presence such a thing as time, the supposition mentioned earlier grows stronger that true time, the four-fold extending of the open, could be discovered as the 'It' that gives Being, i.e., gives presence. The supposition appears to be fully confirmed when we note that absence, too, manifests itself as a mode of presence. What has-been which, by refusing the present, lets that become present which is no longer present; and the coming toward us of what is to come which, by withholding the present, lets that be present which is not yet present—both made manifest the manner of an extending opening up which gives all presencing into the open.

"Thus true time appears as the 'It' of which we speak when we say: It gives Being. The destiny in which It gives Being lies in the extending of time. Does this reference show time to be the 'It' that gives Being? By no means. For time itself remains the gift of an 'It gives'. . . ." 'It', of course, proves to be Appropriation, the matter at stake, the determinate power of true time.

physics of the absolute, but, most particularly, transcending, inessentially, the negative realization of the latter in the form of magnitude itself the immanent transcendence of time, in the form of matter itself the immanent measure of time transcendence, $E = mc^2$, time immanently reflected matter itself, the form itself of immanent energy. Essential thinking, before now, in its retreat from historical materialism, in its step backwards into the essence of metaphysics, at once inessentially transcended the temporal materialism of science itself, doing so in the form of the 'giving in the sense of extending which opens up time-space', in the form of the primal matter which is the opening. Essential thinking before now transcended the material location of time inessentially in the form of the 'prespatial region which first gives any possible "where"', itself not thought itself, the given, not the absolute, displacement of time itself to the 'prespatial region'. But now occurs for the first time history itself the absolute itself absolutely displacing the prespatial region of time itself, time itself now coinciding quantum-absolutely Being itself. Time itself now for the first time coincides the Being in essence of magnitude itself in the absolute quantification of the elements of the ontological difference in existence as time/distance/Being identically magnitude itself. This is the coincidence of transcendental logic with the beginning of existence itself. In this beginning is the absolutely unconditioned quantification of the ontological difference itself: the absolute elimination of the apparent essence of metaphysics, of the absolute necessity for the self-support of the thinking essentially analogous to the root of metaphysics: *in this beginning the thinking now occurring is the absolute synthesis of life itself.* In the thinking now occurring for the first time Being in essence is the absolute identity of time (and) distance, time itself existing in the identity of time (and) distance, distance itself the absolute transcendence of time itself: time and distance not Being at the same time, nor Being at different times not identical with time itself. In the thinking absolutely beginning the Being of magnitude itself is the measure relating three elements, *T, m, c.* The absolute measure of the magnitude of being,

$$\frac{m^2}{Tc},$$

is not merely reflected in matter, not merely inessentially transcendental, but is, rather, the essentially transcendental form of the identity of matter itself: *the ratio itself of the transcendental imagination of the absolute measure of time itself:* the perception of the species itself of the absolute clarity of thought itself: thinking itself coinciding the unbounded bound. For the first time thought itself in essence is the transcendence of totality itself. Energy itself is conceived in essence, which, taken without distance/time, *is* distance/time in its absolute discretion as an element of action itself thought in essence, as an element in the transcendental imagination of the transcendence of distance itself, as an element in the identity of thought (and) action. Now for the first time the existence itself of action itself is thought. Not yet the subsistence itself of action itself existing absolutely without any reference whatsoever to the transcendence of the notion of self, yet, itself untranscended, it is the absolute clarification of the magnitude of thought itself, in terms of which the subsistence of time-transcendent change itself is thought, in terms of which the minimum itself is thought. Although this absolute objectivity is not yet itself subsistence itself existing absolutely without any reference whatsoever to the transcendence of the notion of self, it is, nevertheless, now consciousness absolute for the first time, the beginning of the absolute status of energy itself. In any event, as never before, clarity itself is now the perception of time itself. While the absolutely unconditioned angelic magnitude is itself not yet transcendent without any reference whatsoever to the limiting notion of self, the transcendent magnitude is the identity of Being itself time itself for the first time: foundation itself is the world itself absolutely created: time itself is neither the transcendence of space, nor transcendental space, nor, indeed, the prespatial region, but the very identity of energy itself: time itself is action itself absolutely existing for the first time: the quantum absolute of action itself (where $c = s/T$):

$$T = \frac{m^2}{c} = \frac{m^2 T}{s} = \frac{sT}{s} = T,$$

time itself (value itself/relation itself) the absolute quantum of energy itself. *In light of the absolute discretion of the terms themselves, in light of thought itself absolutely existent,* the formula, $E = mc^2$, is now able to be perceived as the proof of the proportion, $m : E :: T : c^2$,[7] where E is substituted for the energy equivalent m and the unity which is temporality is T. The proportion, $m : m :: T : c^2$, is in turn, substituting multiplication for division, the proof, $m^2 = Tc^2$, of the proportion $T : m :: m : c^2$.[8] This last analogy is that in which the condition of truth is:

$$T = \frac{m^2}{c^2}, \text{ or, } c = \frac{m^2}{Tc},$$

that is, in which the condition of truth is: c identically the absolute measure of the magnitude of being, in which proportion, therefore, the elements are specifically absolute relative to each other (c, the measure, m, the measured, T, the measuring): the quantum relation itself coincidence itself the essence of thought itself: the quantum now absolutely coinciding for the first time relation itself/existence itself/time itself. The quantum absolute is now the Being itself of magnitude in the form:

$$\frac{m^2}{Tc},$$

such that the absolute quantum thought is integrally absolutely elemental: the now-proof of the minimum itself action

[7] Cf. Leahy, *Novitas Mundi,* pp. 323ff.

[8] The 'absolute mediation of the immediate' is the essence of a new logic in terms of which the interchangeability of the elements, T, m, c, with each other and with E, as well as the indifference to the distinction multiplication-division exhibited here by what is, in effect, the transposition of the third element of the fourfold proportion, taken as in fact the fourth element, to the first place, is intelligible as the absolute operation of the minimum itself in the beginning. For this operation of the categorically new logic now conceived for the first time, cf. below, Section III.1.

absolutely elemental: the now-proof of the absolute conception of energy itself, i.e., the proof that energy itself is the minimum transcendence of the minimum itself absolutely elemental, i.e., the proof now itself: the transcendent proof itself, the proof of transcendence itself, the minimum itself the foundation itself of transcendence. Together with its formal antecedents the proof is:

$$\textit{generic absolute: } T : m :: m : 1 \ \ (\text{non-}c = 1) \text{ proof: } \frac{m^2}{T}$$

$$\textit{specific absolute: } T : m :: m : c \ \left(c = \frac{m^2}{T}\right) \text{proof: } \frac{m^2}{Tc}$$

$$\textit{absolute absolute: } T : m :: m : c^2 \ \left(c = \frac{m^2}{Tc}\right) \text{proof: } \frac{m^2}{Tc^2}.$$

The transcendence of the absolutely unprecedented clarification of thought itself is not the antecedent element of the proof of the proportion following immediately, but inconsequently, the foundation itself, not, that is, the antecedent element of the proportion:

$$T : m^2 :: m : c^2 \ \left(c = \frac{m^3}{Tc}\right) \text{proof: } \frac{m^3}{Tc^2}.$$

Indeed, the integrally absolute relation of the elements to each other in the foundation itself, the absolutely unconditioned integration of the quantum absolute in the proportion which is the minimum itself (upon which [m^2 = Tc] depends, since $m^2 = Tc = E$, the analogy of $E = mc^2$ to $T = mc$, in which latter formulation energy is understood to be the measured [m] identically the ratio of the measuring to the measure [$T : c$], descending ultimately from this absolute measure integral to foundation itself, viz., the measured [m] identically the ratio of the measuring measure [Tc] to the measured [m], descending from the proof of transcendence itself to being the form of the truth of the merely immanent form of energy itself),[9] indeed, the abso-

[9] Cf. above, pp. 132ff., and, for the reference to *Novitas Mundi* where the

lute transcendence of the proportion of the absolute measure differentiating magnitude itself, this foundation, essentially does not provide the antecedent ($m^3 = Tc^2$) of the proportion in which the absolute measure is identically the ratio of the measure to the measured ($c : m$), which antecedent is, however, provided by the proportion, $T : m :: m^2 : c$, in which the measured (m) is identically the inverted absolute measure (Tc/m^2), with the result that in the proof of the former proportion the Being itself of magnitude (m^2/Tc^2) is compounded with the measured (m) as m^3/Tc^2, compounded precisely with that very element of the proportion, viz., m, which is identically the inversion of the Being of magnitude, the mirror image, formally, of the proof of transcendence itself, compounded in such a way that the integral element (c) is identically the absolute measure distorted as the ratio of a self-determined magnitude (m^3) to the measuring measure (Tc), or as the absolute measure in which the identity of the measured (m) is transformed into *being-the-same-as,* by means of the addition of the movable power of m, by means of the *addition of the absolute* in the form of the motion of m, by means of the *addition* of magnitude to the absolute measure, to the Being of magnitude itself, such that the identity of the measuring measure (Tc) is reduced to being potentially the form of nothing measured. Nor, on the other hand, is the identity of foundation itself affected by the subsequent increase of the powers of c (m^2/Tc^3, etc.), but retains throughout its identity with the absolute measure (m^2/Tc). The quantum now absolutely coinciding relation itself, the form of the Being itself of magnitude, is the actuality of the absolute law of identity, viz.:

$$c = \left(m = \frac{Tc}{m} \right),$$

at once transcending the law of contradiction, viz.:

analogy to the immanent form of energy is made directly in light of the history of Being in essence, see above, p. 134, n. 7.

$$c = \left[\left(m = \frac{Tc}{m^2} \right) \text{or} \left(m^2 = \frac{Tc}{m} \right) \right],$$

absolutely as follows: the proof of this absolute transcendence, which is the transcendence of the law of contradiction itself in the form, $m^2 : Tc^2 :: m^3 : Tc^2$, is $Tc^2 m^3 / m^2 Tc^2$, of which proof *qua* proportion[10] the proof itself is:

$$\frac{m^5}{T^2 c^4},$$

the absolute transcendence of the proof itself of the law of contradiction, the law of identity excluding the interval in terms of which the law of contradiction is an addition to itself of the absolute measured not in the form of the measure itself, but in the form of motion, in the form of being other than itself: excluded is the *contra* from the diction which is the essential terminology of life itself.[11] The new law of life itself leaves behind for the first time 'the root of all movement and vitality',[12] that hint of the abyss itself, mere absolute contradiction without the absolute measure:

$$\frac{m^3}{Tc} = \left(m = \frac{Tc}{m^2} \right) = \left(m^2 = \frac{Tc}{m} \right) = \frac{m^3}{Tc}:$$

absolute contradiction absolutely undifferentiated, that is, not only that of which the proof itself ($Tcm^3 / m^3 Tc$) itself proven ($m^6 / T^2 c^2$) is that (proportion, $m^3 : m^3 :: Tc : Tc$)[13] of which it is itself the proof, but, unlike the absolute transcendence of the law of identity (which otherwise possesses the identical property of identity together with all proportion in the thinking now

[10] Cf. above, p. 134, including n. 8.

[11] For the logic equivalents of the laws $c = (m = Tc/m)$, $c = [(m = Tc/m^2)$ or $(m^2 = Tc/m)]$, and $m^5 / T^2 c^4$, cf. below, Section III.1, Afterword 1, p. 285, n. 49.

[12] Cf. Hegel's *Science of Logic,* pp. 439–43.

[13] Cf. above, p. 134, n. 8.

occurring) where the proof identifies the *simply squared* value (and) the *synthetic* value, i.e., $(Tc^2)^2/m^2m^3$, the absolute identity of absolute contradiction is the proof of nothing but itself: the pure self-transcendence of the proof itself of itself: absolute motion proving its own identity, proving identity its own.[14] Thus, not only does the thinking now occurring absolutely transcend the given displacement of time itself to the 'prespatial region' of essential thinking before now back-beyond measuring itself, but the absolute form of the metaphysics of the absolute itself, from which and into the essence of which essential thinking before now took its backwards step, is, *in its absolutely unconditioned groundwork,* in its *forming* absolutely unconditionally an absolute foundation, *in its absolute subsumption of the law of identity to existing contradiction, to motion itself,* in its placing time in space and space in time,[15] ultimately, in its beginning with the spatial now, with contradiction itself, itself now for the first time in his-

[14] The synthetic-analytic identity of the proof of the law of transcendent identity with respect to the exponents of its elements is reflected really, if *imperfectly,* in the synthetic-analytic identity of the elements themselves of the extreme and mean geometric ratio, where $1 + \phi = \phi^2$, that is, $\phi^0 + \phi^1 = \phi^2$. Cf. below, Section III, passim.

[15] Cf. Hegel's *Philosophy of Nature,* vol. 1, ed., trans. M. J. Petry (London, 1970), pp. 236–37: "Space in itself is the contradiction of indifferent juxtaposition and of continuity devoid of difference; it is the pure negativity of itself, and the initial *transition into time.* Time is similar, for as its opposed moments, held together in unity, immediately sublate themselves, it constitutes an immediate *collapse* into undifferentiation, into the undifferentiated extrinsicality of *space.* Consequently, the negative determination here, which is the exclusive point, is no longer merely implicit in its conformity to the Notion, but is posited, and is in itself concrete on account of the total negativity of time. This concrete point is place. . . .

"Initially, the place which is thus the posited identity of space and time is also the posited contradiction set up by the mutual exclusiveness of space and time. Place is spatial and therefore indifferent singularity, and is this only as the spatial now, or time. As this place, it is therefore in a condition of immediate indifference to itself; it is external to itself, the negation of itself, and constitutes another place. This *passing away* and self-*regeneration* of space in time and time in space, in which time posits itself spatially as place, while this indifferent spatiality is likewise posited immediately in a temporal manner, constitutes motion."

tory, this thinking essentially in the past, essentially, and in the absolute clarity of the perception of identity itself, relegated to the past. Identity itself is the absolute measure of magnitude itself. It is the absolute proof itself absolutely precluding the 'blunt difference of diverse terms, the manifoldness of pictorial thinking', the simple difference with which begins the development into opposition, thence into contradiction, to end with the 'sum total of all realities', 'absolute contradiction within itself'.[16] There is no transcendence of totality itself (as was the case before now in the absolutely formal conception of the absolute) not itself the ratio itself absolute, the simple ratio (e.g., 4 : 1) of the ratio (compounded of the proof [16 · 8 (128) : 4 · 8 (32)] of the proof [4 · 16 (64) = 8 · 8 (64)] of the proportionally mediated terms [16 : 8 :: 8 : 4]) of the ratio. There is no transcendence of totality itself not identity itself, no totality itself not the minimum itself, not the law itself of identity. There is no number not essentially rational. The transcendence of totality itself adds neither nothing nor something to totality itself: there is neither nothing nor something apart from the transcendent identity of the evidence of the absolutely existent ratio. The transcendence of totality itself *qua* identity is the transcendent ratio of the Trinity itself, the Absolute Trinity Itself absolutely without self-transcendence, with neither self nor the notion of self, the absolute objectivity of identity itself. There is neither nothing nor something prior to foundation itself to serve as the foundation: there is foundation itself for the first time *ex nihilo*, for the first time *exsistere ipsum ex nihilo.* Neither the being nor the non-being of the groundwork of the foundation itself is either the non-being or the being of foundation itself: absolute reason measures reason itself absolutely unconditionally: *ex nihilo* the absolute measure of totality itself: quantum itself, existent substance itself, is absolute magnitude itself. Now for the first time in history *the new reality which is the soul itself is intellect itself.* Intellect itself, the now existing absolute measure of existence, is not (as it was in ancient, true metaphysics) the non-self-evident world-transcendent identity of reason; neither is intel-

[16] Cf. above, p. 137, n. 12.

lect itself (what it, informed by the fact of the Incarnation, became) the self-evident world-transcendent identity of reason created *ex nihilo.* Nor is it (as it was in the case of the science founded on faith itself) reason's transcendental power of self-evident perception of the world, an imperfect identity; nor is it (as it was in the inception of modern science [science founded in the form abstracted from the science of faith]) transcendental subjectivity's rationalized perception of the world, an absolute identity. Neither is intellect itself (what it was in the laying of the foundations for a concrete universal science) transcendental subjectivity's rationalized perception of the world of *appearances,* an essentially absolute identity; nor, finally, is intellect itself (as it was in the case of the absolutely subjective transcendence of absolute world-consciousness) transcendental subjectivity's rationalized perception of the world of *thought itself,* the absolute form of absolute identity, the beginningless, formally *metaphysical* transcendence of intellect itself: logic coinciding with *metaphysics*: absolute subjectivity's absolute *form* of world-consciousness: *the absolute form itself of subjectivity* where, precisely, ancient metaphysics conceived the world-transcendent identity of reason to be *non-self-evident.* For the first time in history, precisely where the absolutely metaphysical form of the absolute understood the world-transcendent identity of reason to be the absolute form of *subjectivity,* there now occurs the *absolute transcendence of objectivity* itself. *For the first time the objectivity of identity itself is the form of absolute world-consciousness itself,* the form of the absolute transcendence of the absolute identity of thought: thought itself essentially transcending, beginning and end of existence, the essential history of thought: thought itself in essence the proof positive of existence itself, the absolute proof itself: thought itself absolute knowledge: knowledge itself the *transcendent* clarity of the identity of knower and known (as distinguished from the merely non-self-evident identity of the two in ancient metaphysics, as well as from the essentially subjective form of the transcendental identity of the two in the absolutely unconditioned form of modern metaphysics): for the first time the absolute itself existing essentially as the known itself in the form of the knowledge itself of absolute transcendence. The knowledge of the absolutely unconditioned totality, absolute magnitude itself, is the law of identity itself, the Being of magnitude itself absolutely evident. For the first time Being itself thought in essence absolutely displaces the prespatial region. In this beginning the matter of the law of identity is motion itself, absolute temporality, the very Being of magnitude. In this beginning the transcendence of time itself, now itself, is thought in essence in the form of thought itself absolute.

3

METANOMY: THE QUALITY OF BEING ITSELF

Modernity is the appropriation of the undetermined immediacy of being, the appropriation of nothing-thought, the absolute priority of appropriation, the *a priori* thought of the appropriation of existence, appropriation itself prior to the body itself. The absolute repetition of modernity (foundation itself in the world of an essentially new world) duplicates not modernity. The absolute repetition of modernity is neither the same as nor different than modernity. The absolute repetition of modernity is the absolute transcendence of modernity in the form of the Incarnation itself. The transcendence of modern identity is the form of the Light itself, the form of Life itself complete. The difference between what otherwise would be the first and second form of modernity is existence itself, the transcendental difference, the identity of difference itself, what is in fact absolute repetition itself, the transcendence of the existence of the difference-between itself. The transcendence of the division within identity itself is the minimum transcendence of existence, the absolute unconditioned transcendence of existence, where otherwise modernity would have the self-substitution of thought itself for the bare abstraction of identity. The transcendence of modern identity is an absolutely historical identity, at once an identity of absolute factuality. The transcendence of the appropriation of nothing-thought thought itself is the fact of existence itself the identity of thought itself: absolutely nothing derivative of modernity transcending appropriation. But the absolute priority of existence itself to appropriation is the transcendence of modern thought in essence: absolutely nothing remains but the form of thought the identity of thought: there is no death, but the form of nothing remains, vestige of a thought no longer existent, the formal identity of thought itself thought. The essential identity of thought itself is experience itself: positively no nothing-thought. The perception of the real is not a matter of thought's *own* construction. *The absolute construction of existence itself for the first time* shells the eyes of thought. The reality of the body itself removes the scales from perception itself: thought itself beholds the reality of existence, the real absolute, the world itself the body itself. The real absolute eliminates the addition-multiplication/subtraction-division of reality precisely insofar as the transcendence of reality is (in the now for the first time in history non-copulative, absolute sense of identity itself—*is*) reality, precisely insofar as *is* absolutely identifies reality, where identity is not (as before now it was thought to be, as before now, to be, it was thought) different from itself in order to not be the mere abstraction of thought, in order to not be merely different from difference. Now thought thinks difference not as different than self, not as self-deferral (*a fortiori*, not as the other-than-self-deferral of *la différance*, not as the negation of the notion of identity [by implication the negation of the primacy of being, if only in the form of the given]). Therefore, thought now thinks not the notion of identity of self (*a fortiori*, thinks not its negative), but thought now thinks for the first time the notion of identity itself actual, the notion of the difference from thought itself without self-deferral. Thought for the first time thinks identity itself the absolute difference absolutely complex, the absolute complexity of difference absolutely unconditioned, transparent existence: identity itself the absolute transparency of the written-spoken word, the absolutely actual deferral of difference, the absolute deferral of the difference from thought itself: absolutely no opening for the repetition of self-identity. What now occurs for the first time in history is the absolute repetition of absolute knowledge, but absolute knowledge without horizon (not, as before now, the matter of nothing; neither, as before now, bound by the matter of nothing, nor transcending the bound of the matter of nothing in the form of *la différance*): absolute knowledge the unbounded bound (absolutely nothing beyond it, including matter itself). In the delicate factuality of transparent identity complementarity itself is absolutely transcended: memory itself absolutely coincides with perception, absolutely exists in the delicate transparency of perception, the simulacrum which is no simulacrum, the product of an absolute repetition, identity itself. The repetition of absolute self-identity, the absolutely impossible repetition, actually now occurs as the existence of absolute difference, the absolute difference of existence. The simulacrum actually occurs as actual substance itself, the irreducible absolute, the *second* absolute, the to-the-(first)-absolute-irreducible itself, as memory itself absolute, the minimum absolute, the actual absolute. Memory itself *ex abysso* is the absolute change of the absolute from its hitherto potential or actual biformality (*qua* potential biformality the content of the absolute, not a simulacrum, but the indeterminate immediate being, nothing in general, the absolute non-identity of the absolute—*qua* actual biformality the content of the absolute a simulacrum, but immediate determinateness, a certain nothing, pure quality itself, the negation of reality within reality, the absolute contradiction of the absolute, the actuality of pure subject-matter: the absolutely potential qualification of being, transcending the essential contradiction of the absolute [the absolute potentiality of objectivity], as well as the merely formal contradiction of the absolute [the absolute potentiality of identity itself], the necessary precedent for the former purely formless objectivity. [The simulacrum of actual biformality remains not not-a-simulacrum. The actuality of pure subject-matter is the perpetual transition of existence into nothing but an image: subjectivity itself absolutely perpetual: the becoming itself of absolute subjectivity: the perpetual transition of identity into self-opposition, of self/non-identity into contradiction: the absolute becoming of identity itself]). Indeed, memory itself for the first time is the absolute transcendence of the negation within actuality by actuality itself. In memory itself for the first time there is absolutely no trace, no repetition of the becoming itself of absolute subjectivity, no repetition of repetition itself, no actual trace of trace itself. The absolute indifference of memory itself to becoming itself is identity itself absolute. Identity is the absolutely unconditioned indifference of memory itself to becoming. Memory absolutely unconditioned indifference is identity itself to becoming: the actual repetition of repetition the absolutely unconditioned trace of the trace is identity itself, the transcendent identity of the simulacrum of the simulacrum (of the simulacrum which is no simulacrum) is the transcendence of non-becoming itself absolute: the absolute becoming itself of identity is identity itself. Existence becoming itself is the absolute minimum: absolute becoming itself absolute objectivity itself: identity itself for the first time the memory of the absolute repetition of the absolute, the catholicity itself of existence, absolute perpetuity. There is no non-identity arising out of the repetition of perpetuity (while the original absolute non-identity was a perpetual non-existence): there is the absolute repetition of absolute existence, the perpetuity of existence itself. There is absolutely no alternative to actual identity. The absolute other of identity itself is not other-than it, because absolute identity itself is not other-than. Whether the other of absolute identity is the non-existence of the content of the absolute (as in the essentially simple thought of absolute difference[1]) or the simulacrum of absolute content, the contra-content of the absolute (as in the becoming itself of absolute subjectivity) transcending the same as itself in the form of the becoming itself of absolute content, the contra/contradiction of a purely formless objectivity, it is other than itself not other than actuality, that is, it is absolutely transcended by actuality. In the case of the latter alternative, the contradiction to identity, the contradiction of the law of identity is absolutely identified as the actual-contra-actual. Indeed, *the*

[1] Cf. Hegel's *Science of Logic,* p. 417: "Difference is the negativity which reflection has within it, the nothing which is said in enunciating identity, the essential moment of identity itself which, as negativity of itself, determines itself and is distinguished from difference.

"This difference is difference *in and for itself, absolute difference,* the *difference of essence.* It is difference in and for itself, not difference resulting from anything external, but *self-related,* therefore *simple* difference. It is essential to grasp absolute difference as *simple.* In the absolute difference of *A* and *not-A* from each other, it is the simple not which, as such, constitutes it. Difference itself is the simple Notion."

identity of nothing is not outside the logic of identity. Contra-actuality[2] is self-opposition comparing itself to the actuality of the absolute plaintext. It is the absolute within the absolute, absolute opposition to the outside absolute, absolute contradiction of the absolute, the complex essence of non-existence, the non-existence of existence itself, doomed to simply denying the latter's actuality,

[2] This, the denial of a simple objectivity, is the denial, contradiction, undermining of the prehension of the absolute simplicity of difference as such, such as was able to be received as an object of thought by essential thinking before now as a simple given uncritically taken over from the thought of nothing absolutely different. This denial is at once, and fundamentally, the absolute denial, the contra-content of absolute identity the contra-absolute of the minimum itself absolute: the dissimulation of the simulacrum itself. Cf. J. Derrida, *Of Grammatology,* trans. G. C. Spivak (Baltimore, 1976), pp. 56ff., where the dissimulation of the simulacrum appears, quite consistently within the logic of the supplement, in the form of that of which the historical dissimulation was the condition for the appearance of something in its place: "I would wish rather to suggest that the alleged derivativeness of writing, however real and massive, was possible only on one condition: that the 'original', 'natural', etc. language had never existed, never been intact and untouched by writing, that it had itself always been a writing. An arche-writing whose necessity and new concept I wish to indicate and outline here; and which I continue to call writing only because it essentially communicates with the vulgar concept of writing. The latter could not have imposed itself historically except by the dissimulation of the arche-writing, by the desire for a speech displacing its other and its double and working to reduce its difference. If I persist in calling that difference writing, it is because, within the work of historical repression, writing was, by its situation, destined to signify the most formidable difference. It threatened the desire for the living speech from the closest proximity, it *breached* living speech from within and from the very beginning. And as we shall begin to see, difference cannot be thought without the *trace.* [N.B. Just here the actually non-existent other other than itself proposes itself as the condition of the absolute identity of the other: not the transcendence of, but the supplement to, absolute necessity, in face of the fact of existence itself.]

"This arche-writing, although its concept is *invoked* by the themes of 'the arbitrariness of the sign' and of difference, cannot and can never be recognized as the object of a *science.* It is that very thing which cannot let itself be reduced to the form of *presence.* The latter orders all objectivity of the object and all relation of knowledge. . . .

". . . It is to escape falling back into . . . naive objectivism that I refer here to a transcendentality that I elsewhere put into question. It is because

doomed to denying actuality, therefore, to doing so in the form of the difference of thought itself absolutely past, in the form of past actuality, incapable of articulating actuality itself except in the form of denying the past, except by asserting a complex given where a simple given had been thought to be, fracturing the latter in essence, essentially without transcending it. Contra-actuality takes the form of the desire to keep the outside outside, to keep the outside *from entering* the within, *to keep the outside the within from within,* to keep the within within, to drive an infinite wedge between inside-outside, binding, thereby, the two absolutely together in the nothing outside of the absolute. This desire arises out of the abyss of absolute necessity, out of the very lack itself of nothing absolute, out of the absolute abyss, arises as the supplement itself supplying the simulacrum from within itself in such a way that the outside itself remains not the outside but becomes the within, prolonging desire, were it possible, infinitely: desiring to desire without end, death not willing death, the biformation of the form itself arising out of the absolute lack of necessity as the lack itself of the absolute form of the absolute. The desire to keep the outside outside (the undoing of the purely formal thought of the logic of identity[3] is precisely the supplement itself to the essence of absolute difference, the movement

---

I believe that there is a short-of and beyond of transcendental criticism. To see to it that the beyond does not return to the within is to recognize in the contortion the necessity of a pathway [*parcours*]. That pathway must leave a track in the text. Without that track, abandoned to the simple content of its conclusions, the ultra-transcendental text will so closely resemble the precritical text as to be indistinguishable from it . . . the value of the transcendental arche [*archie*] must make its necessity felt before letting itself be erased. . . . The concept of arche-trace . . . is in fact contradictory and not acceptable within the logic of identity. The trace is not only the disappearance of origin . . . it means that the origin did not even disappear, that it was never constituted except reciprocally by a nonorigin, the trace . . . the origin of the origin."

[3] Cf. ibid., p. 215: "For the moment I am interested in the logic proper to Rousseau's discourse: instead of concluding . . . that difference had already begun to corrupt melody, to make both it and its laws possible at the same time, Rousseau prefers to believe that grammar *must* (*should*) *have* been comprised, in the sense of being confused with, within melody.

of *la différance* absolutely destabilizing the difference within identity, so that, while the difference is not other than absolute identity, identity is not identity. The outside is the inside by default. This movement is the self-transcendence of absolute identity: the movement the self-/non-transcendence of actuality: the movement in fact of non-identity, the movement of an actually purely formal identity, at once the transcendence of the mere sacrifice of logic that was the actuality of thought before now, the making of logic itself the dissimulation of difference in the form of history. But the actual transcendence of logic is identity itself absolute, for the first time the transcendence of identity. The movement of identity cannot escape the fact that the alternative to absolute non-identity is actuality itself, in terms of which it itself manifestly exists for thought, in terms of which the dissimulation of the simulacrum is itself transcended (at once transcended in essence), in terms of which it itself is evidence of the absolute identity of an historical logic, of an historical logic absolutely unprecedented, it itself the absolutely evident consequence of that which it appears in time to precede, implicitly evidencing the identity of time itself. The non-existent actuality of identity itself which not only existed before now, but which even now does not reciprocate the absolute clarification of thought itself, this logic of supplementarity, serves to set in sharp relief, albeit all unwillingly, the actual transcendence of the (simple) essence of absolute difference: identity *absolutely* not "*there is nothing outside the text*,"[4] not the mere transcendence of the logic of supplementarity, but the absolute elimination of the logic of

---

There must (should) have been plenitude and not lack, presence without difference. From then on the dangerous supplement, scale or harmony, *adds itself from the outside as evil and lack* . . . from an outside which would be simply the outside. This conforms to the logic of identity and to the principle of classical ontology (the outside is outside, being is, etc.) but not to the logic of supplementarity, which would have it that the outside be inside, that the other and the lack come to add themselves as a plus that replaces a minus, that what adds itself to something takes the place of a default in the thing, that the default, as the outside of the inside, should be already within the inside, etc."

[4] Ibid., pp. 158–59: "Yet if reading must not be content with doubling the

the supplement, *the text itself absolutely existing now for the first time*: the absolute actuality of perpetuity itself, for the first time the supplement itself outside, save for the fact that actually there is no outside to be the within for the supplement, either potentially (the outside-outside, in which nothing must be lest it be a within from without the text, rendering the text not absolute), or actually (the outside-inside, in which everything outside is within the text as a result of the desire that nothing be simply within, rendering the text the absolute cipher). Precisely the actuality of the absolute plaintext is the transcendence of 'writing' identifying the essence of absolute difference, the essence itself of existence, as the complex. The simple essence excluded

---

text, it cannot legitimately transgress the text toward something other than it, toward a referent (a reality that is metaphysical, historical, psychobiographical, etc.) or toward a signified outside the text whose content could take place, could have taken place outside of language, that is to say, in the sense that we give here to that word, outside of writing in general. That is why the methodological considerations that we risk applying here to an example are closely dependent on general propositions that we have elaborated above; as regards the absence of the referent or the transcendental signified. *There is nothing outside of the text* [there is no outside-text; *il n'y a pas de hors-texte*]. And that is neither because Jean-Jacques' life, or the existence of Mamma or Thérèse *themselves,* is not of prime interest to us, nor because we have access to their so-called 'real' existence only in the text and we have neither any means of altering this, nor any right to neglect this limitation. All reasons of this type would already be sufficient, to be sure, but there are more radical reasons. What we have tried to show by following the guiding line of the 'dangerous supplement', is that in what one calls the real life of these existences 'of flesh and bone', beyond and behind what one believes can be circumscribed as Rousseau's text, there has never been anything but writing; there have never been anything but supplements, substitutive significations which could only come forth in a chain of differential references, the 'real' supervening, and being added only while taking on meaning from a trace and from an invocation of the supplement, etc. And thus to infinity, for we have read, *in the text,* that the absolute present, Nature, that which words like 'real mother' name, have always already escaped, have never existed; that what opens meaning and language is writing as the disappearance of natural presence.

"Although it is not commentary, our reading must be intrinsic and remain within the text."

by the supplement is transcended. The category, outside/inside, is eliminated at once with the supplement itself. The absolute is no longer simply complex, it is simplicity complex, the absolute complexity of the simple absolutely itself. The text intact/the hymen itself[5] absolute, the child is, nevertheless, born here and now. The rupture of being without being, itself transcended: the nothing being outside of the nonbeing of the text, the absolute ciphertext itself transcended: not the absolute supplement to the cipher, not the supplemental complexity of the simple,[6] but *the absolute complexity of the simple in the form of the minimum itself:* the hymen itself intact, the child is born the new logic of the new itself, a logic without zeros (nothings), without

---

[5] Cf. J. Derrida, *Dissemination,* trans. B. Johnson (Chicago, 1981), pp. 173–285.

[6] Cf. Derrida, *Of Grammatology,* pp. 242–43: "Before articulation, therefore, we now know, there is no speech, no song, and thus no music. Passion could not be expressed or imitated without articulation. . . . Convention has its hold only upon articulation, which pulls language out of the cry, and increases itself with consonants, tenses, and quantity. *Thus language is born out of the process of its own degeneration.* That is why, in order to convey Rousseau's *descriptive* procedure . . . it is perhaps imprudent to call by the name of zero degree or simple origin that out of which the deviation is measured or the structure outlined. Zero degree or origin implies that the commencement be simple, that it not be at the same time the beginning of a degeneration . . . it must also be possible to measure deviation according to a simple axis and in a single direction. Is it still necessary to recall that nothing in Rousseau's description authorizes us to do so?

". . . Rousseau's discourse lets itself be constrained by a complexity which always has the form of the supplement of or from the origin. . . . The desire for the origin becomes an indispensable and indestructible function situated within a syntax without origin. Rousseau would like to separate originarity from supplementarity. All the rights constituted by our logos are on his side: it is unthinkable and intolerable that what has the name *origin* should be no more than a point situated within the system of supplementarity. The latter in fact wrenches language from its condition of origin, from its conditional or its future of origin, from that which it must (ought to) have been and what it has never been; it could only have been born by suspending its relation to all origin. Its history is that of the supplement of (from) origin: of the originary substitute and the substitute of the origin." Note that the originary difference between passion and articulation is necessary to the merely essential complexity of the simple.

the possibility of plus/minus, of fractions etc.,[7] a logic for the first time the absolute transcendence of the arbitrary, a logic of the new reality itself logic, a logic of absolute identity without the logic of supplementarity, absolutely transcending the latter's inclusion of the point itself within its own system as the reciprocal of the cipher, as the repetition of nothing-thought, the nothing complex, the point itself as the very form of the absolute ciphertext's transcendence of the logic of identity, the nothing within the absolute form in terms of which there is nothing outside of the text. The logic of the new itself absolutely transcends the absolute contra-content, the point of biformation, that certain nothing which is the abyss of thought itself. Precisely it separates thought from the abyss itself with the form of the minimum itself, the minimum of form itself, separates the certain from nothing with the form of logic itself. The absolute identity of the text, the absolute logic-identity is the certainty of existence *ex nihilo*, a certain thought *ex nihilo*, neither the merely formal certainty of creation found in the thought of existence at its inception in essence, nor the certainty of history found in the inception in essence of transcendental thought, likewise formal, nor the merely formal certainty of objectivity found in the inception in essence of the history of thought. But also neither is the certain thought *ex nihilo*, the absolute identity of the text, to be confused with the certain thought *a priori* of transcendental phenomenology, the purely formal essence of an infinite *a priori*, nor with the certain anonymity, the uncertain absolute supplementing the pure form of absolute knowledge, at once the reduction of the abstract certainty of the phenomenological

[7] The reader may note here, in the context of the critique of Derrida, the first emergence of the fundamental outline of the logic prepared for above in Section II.2 and detailed below in Section III.1. In this 'logic of the beginning', while the zero is retained it no longer equals *any* form of nothing. Whereas Derrida articulates the 'origin of the origin', the thinking now occurring for the first time in history articulates the *nothing of nothing:* not that there never was a beginning, and that in every now is the nothingness of the beginning, but that there never was a nothing, and that in every now is the beginning absolutely.

reduction to anonymity, at once the reduction to absolute anonymity of the phenomenological identity, the anonymous reduction. It is not to be confused with the form of a certain denial, the denial of the actuality of a certain absolute, the denial of the absolute certainty of knowledge, the denial of absolute knowledge unbound, the denial which is the negative form of the absolute form of existence itself, the denial which is the form of the absolute negative absolutely existing: the form itself which is only the denial of the transcendence in essence of absolute negativity, the form of denial's self-transcendence in essence. The certain thought *ex nihilo* is the form of the transcendence in essence of the history of thought, the form of the perpetual identity of the absolute plaintext. Indeed, the certain thought *ex nihilo* is the absolutely minimum form of logic itself, such that the 'logic of supplementarity' appears as nothing other than what it is, itself, the essence in the form of contra-actuality, in the form of the supplement, in the form of absolute contrariety itself absolute. This appearance of the logic of supplementarity is at once its absolutely evident historical identity. This appearance is its coinciding with the logic of identity in its merely being itself the supplement to the latter's essential formality (at once substituting itself for the simple transcendence of the same, for essential thinking existing before now, for the logic of identity-before-now, for the sacrifice of logic), the sinking/salvaging logic, the complicating of logic itself excluding identity, the identity not itself identity. In fact there is no extra-logical point to be included within the logic of supplementarity as its evidence that 'there is nothing outside the text', that the absolute outside is not. For the first time logic is identity. The logic of identity exists absolutely, the absolute logic of identity is the certain thought *ex nihilo*, the form of logic itself, the new absolute. The new logic displaces nothing, so that while there is nothing there is no outside (no inside): *nothing is everywhere but for the form of a certain thought displacing it with perpetual identity for the first time,* an identity existing in thought itself, an absolute magnitude of existence itself absolute, neither determined nor undetermined, but measured in its essential freedom.

Just as there is no point outside the logic of supplementarity serving as the basis of an absolutely formal logic of identity, no pure quantity, so there is no pure quality, no point outside the logic of identity serving as the basis of the absolute supplement/the supplemental absolute. There is nothing but the absolute quality of existence absolutely actual for the first time, the absolute actuality of existence itself. There is nothing but the so-called 'restoration' of the quality that has in fact never been lost, of the point within the logic of identity serving as the basis of the absolutely formal quantum, which in fact has never existed apart from the absolute quality, which in fact has never been anything other than itself, and which in fact was never lost and found only to be finally lost, to be in the end the pure quality absolutely supplemented, the trace of the logic of supplementarity, the absolute quality rendered absolutely potential, in fact, therefore, the simulacrum of non-existence, the simple non-absolute, the simple non-quantity (the net loss a gain/the net gain a loss, the absolute number a zero which is nothing), a matter of pure indifference, the matter itself of pure quantity, the possibility of the spatiality of the spatio-temporal point, the last-ditch attempt to undermine (were it possible) the absolute point of departure of absolute knowledge/the absolute departure of absolute knowledge from the point (pure and simple), by rendering the logic of supplementarity the justification for absolute knowledge's lack of an absolute point of departure, by rendering the denial of the actuality of existence in the form of a lack of a justification for the fact itself, as if the fact itself were the denial of the fact, as if there were a lack of absolute knowledge to be supplemented absolutely, as if the fact itself were not the absolute justification for the absolute point of departure, as if the latter were not the absolute now the essential form of thought itself, as if the absolute point of departure were not time itself, as if the essence were not the infinite *a posteriori* of existence itself, as if the latter yielded no essence, as if the body itself, the absolutely unconditioned product of history, spoke without speaking, without speaking simply the word, as if it were in need of being deciphered, as if it were not nothing being deciphered, as if it were not quality itself. The contra-actual *conditional*: the non-existence of absolute quality (non-existence = zero absolute, not a matter of degree: the transcendence of absolute non-identity zero absolute matter): absolute quality a matter other-than the absolute ciphertext: the essence of the absolute plaintext a matter other-than the essence of the complex simplicity. But the yield of the infinite *a posteriori* of existence itself is precisely the essence of thought: *the absolute inspection of the essence of thought is perception itself*/memory itself/absolute identity itself/the qualification of being itself/the metanomous being of life itself alive: a certain thought *ex nihilo* in which it is absolutely comprehended that being itself is a person (a specificity of perception absolutely unprecedented save for the infinite *a posteriori* of existence): a certain thought the very originality of personality itself, the absolute gathering of the actual experience of thought itself, the forgetting of absolutely nothing of the actuality of the essential experience of history itself, the visible freedom of the absolute passion of a transcendent identity in which the visible itself is the memory of the unprecedented absolute, is time itself, is the transcendental imagination of this certain man absolutely existing, and is such absolutely, is absolutely this identity of the logical moments, is, itself, absolutely unconditioned, the logic of identity, the transcendence of the abstract absolute of the logic of identity, the absolutely concrete identity of a certain historical existence, the liberator constituting the original transcendence of personality itself. This is to say that the visible absolutely is in the freedom of the absolute passion of existence the embodiment of the appearance of the transcendental essence of existence itself, the invisible itself, the species of perception. The visible is the new species of reality itself. The thing appears absolutely. The thing exists absolutely *a posteriori* (is the second absolute). The *a posteriori per se* is catholicologically the locus of an absolutely existing identity. The absolute synthesis *a priori* of the fact itself is absolutely evident, the transcendent existence of the synthetic *a priori* judgment of thought is the visible itself, the visible itself is the absolutely historical synthesis of thought in essence, at once the liberation of personality from being merely ideally metanomous, while actually, or essentially, being autonomous, and absolutely so in the case of the phenomenological reduction of man himself to being rational (the perfectly abstract application of the ideal absolute to the actual world, the ideal iteration of existence, the generation of essences, the creation of the ideal/the ideal creation), at once, as well, the liberation of personality from merely material metanomy which is actually, or essentially, but the function of social unity, and absolutely so in the case of the theological reduction of the Godhead of God to human actuality, to the absolute man, the absolutely willful anticipation of the visible itself/the *novitas mundi* in the form of total presence, the new total iteration of the will to power, the embodiment of sin itself, the creation of the will itself/the will to creation, the unit-total of society itself, society providing for itself its own matter, the simple embodiment of the Godhead of God/the revolutionary Nothing, the non-redemptive embodiment of sin itself, the material transcendence of the abyss, the appropriation of contingency itself/the Nothing itself beyond the *posthumi*. For the first time the visible itself is the qualification of being itself as metanomous, the liberation of personality to being itself essentially metanomous, to the metanomy of identity itself, to an identity absolutely not the breachable identity of modernity (an identity in fact breached before now), an other not other than the absolute self-/non-identity, not other than the other-than-self of absolute identity, not the absolute breaching of the other/self (division-within) identity of modernity, but an other which is the breaching of the absolute breach, that is, *not simply not* the absolute breach, precisely and absolutely not a return (neither possible nor desirable) to the simple essence of absolute difference, to the absolute beginningless form of the absolute. This other now existing is the absolute complexity of the breach, the complex transcendence of the absolute breach, existence itself-thought itself for the first time. This other is, *itself*, not the restoration of the absolute balance of the absolute form of *metaphysics* (neither possible nor desirable), nor is it simply the desire for a concept other than the abyss, that is, it is, itself, neither the restoration of the turn of desire, nor the desire for a thinking other than the rupture of desire (not possible but desirable, a kind of wishful thinking), not the desire to transcend the absolute abyss, not the desire to transcend the absolute imbalance undermining absolutely the absolute form of philosophy, which absolute undermining imbalance in fact props up the absolute form of the philosophy of the absolute *at one precise point,* the point of the latter's ignorance of the fact of existence, the point of the total-ignorance of (modern) philosophy (as if it were simply beyond the absolute balance), but, the absolute biformation of the absolute, the absolute imbalance, props philosophy up with the *will-to-ignorance* which is truly its own, without being that of another, as the possibility *per se,* therefore, the impossibility, of this so-called 'philosophy', the possibility *per se*/the impossibility of this simple limit/this simple absolute knowledge/this simple text. For the absolute ciphertext is nothing other than this possibility *per se*/impossibility of philosophy in the form of its very own will-to-ignorance being other than the other of philosophy without being itself philosophy, beyond the limit of philosophy the rupture of being, without being itself, the will-to-ignorance breaching the absolute outside of philosophy, making the absolute outside of philosophy a within which it inhabits as an abysmal desire for identity, beyond the reach of the absolute non-/self-identity of philosophy[8] (formally it is so, but substantially it is the refusal to acknowledge the actuality of the identity of the visible itself, in fact the taking of refuge in the formal anonymity of modern thought turned against the latter from within its ownmost, deepest, recesses, taking refuge from the visible light of identity itself). The absolute complexity of the breach is neither the desire to transcend the will-to-ignorance supplement-

[8] Cf. J. Derrida, *Margins of Philosophy,* trans. A. Bass (Chicago, 1982), p. xvii, n. 9: "How could a breach be produced, between earth and sea?

"By means of the breach of philosophical identity, a breach which amounts to addressing the truth to itself in an envelope, to hearing itself speak inside without opening its mouth or showing its teeth, the bloodiness of a disseminated writing comes to separate the lips, to violate the embouchure of philosophy, putting *its* tongue into movement, finally bringing it into contact with some other code, of an entirely other kind. A necessarily unique event, nonreproducible, hence illegible as such and, when it happens, inaudible in the conch, between earth and sea, without signature."

ing the total-ignorance of *metaphysics* in the modern sense (the will-to-ignorance supplying the precise need of the point of the logic of identity by including it within the logic of supplementarity, by rendering it absolutely within the absolute), nor a restoration simply from absolute imbalance to absolute balance. But the absolute complexity of the breach (at once the absolute transcendence of the merely essential complexity of the simple, of the absolute breach in its simplicity), the absolute repetition of the absolute breach absolutely without the division-within, is itself *the absolute breaching of balance itself with absolute identity*, such that the absolute transcendence of absolute imbalance is not in fact the restoration of absolute balance, indeed, it is in essence precisely not the absolute balance, rather the transcendence of the balance itself that is the absolute breach in its simplicity, the transcendence, even, of that balance itself an absolute balance only in the precise form of identifying the breach itself as the unsettling prop of philosophy in the form of the contra-actual conditional, viz., there is no absolute transcendence of the philosophical essence. Absolute identity is for the first time the absolute explosion of balance itself, the absolute complexity of the breach in the circle, such that where the circle was, indeed, even where the point of the circle was included in the midst of the logic of supplementarity so as to bend the circle beyond the point of recognition (even to do so from within by supplementing the point itself of the circle's formal identity) there is now perpetuity itself. Where the circle was, indeed, where the noncircular violator of the circle was, there is now the transcendental imagination of change itself transcending in essence the absolute balance, itself an absolute balance only in the precise form of the absolute measure, only in the form of absolute coincidence itself, only in the precise form of that identity which is the absolute transcendence itself of the point of departure, only in the form of that absolute measure of the magnitude of being which is the form of the *absolute* separation of absolute difference from the point itself. The absolute explosion of identity itself is the absolute perpetuity of identity itself which knows the absolutely unconditioned measure itself, the absolutely existing absolute balance, without either the point itself, or the abyss constituting the contrapunctual absolute point, which knows that absolute measure itself is the absolute transcendence of balance, which knows the absolutely spaceless articulation of existence itself as existence itself the foundation itself of existence itself, as itself existing (the absolute other, absolutely unconditioned, of absolute identity) eliminating absolutely the form of 'its own'/its own form, so that it need not be concerned with its coincidence with absolute balance, knowing, as it does, that this coincidence itself is the thought that is actuality itself, that the absolute balance existing is of actual existence, not of a mere thought-form, i.e., of existence itself in the form of the absolute measure, knowing that the absolute balance is not generically thought, but is the absolutely specific thought of existence, the form of knowledge itself perfectly specific, knowing that the absolute balance is nothing but the confirmation of the fact that there is no generic knowledge (no generic absolute balance) having that division within its identity (self/non/other-than-self) through which it itself might be brought 'into contact with some other code, of an entirely other kind', absolutely powerless to avoid the absolute violation of the integrity of its own identity. What is known for the first time is that the circle itself is nothing but the confirmation of the fact that there is no generic circle, but that the absolute circle is perpetuity itself, that the absolute identity of terms is the absolutely integral relation to measure, that the 'itself' (the identity of the existing thing) is absolutely unconditioned transcendent identity, the actual/negative of the contra-actual, the proof/positive of existence *itself*, there being nothing but the transcendental differentiation of the thing from the *thing itself*, the existence of the thing itself, the existence of existence itself.[9]

There is nothing but the absolute existence of existence for the first time, the absolutely complex absolute existence of very simplicity. While complexity is not identity, absolute complexity is absolute identity; while the absolute is not identity, the abso-

[9] Cf. below, Section IV.2, *Excursus Circularis*, pp. 478ff., and, in particular, pp. 519ff.

lute existing absolute is absolute identity: the absolute complexity of the breach, the absolute identity of the breach is the unbreachable, the simplicity of the breach itself, the existing coincidence of the breach with the absolute balance, the breaching of which absolute breach of balance itself would be an absolutely redundant repetition of absolute balance, would be 'itself' absolutely redundant in light of the factual 'itself' wherein absolute balance coincides specifically with the absolute measure, would be 'itself' as an absolute genus, would be 'itself' as what is no more, which, when it was, was not absolutely, was not absolutely logical except it was by default a contra-actual not 'itself', a contra-actual negativity. Nor can the latter be without involving itself in absolute self-contradiction, without being itself a meta-philosophy in which terms it itself is absolutely unwilling to be thought, a purely generic transcendence of the circle in terms of which it itself would be ignorant of the abyss of thought, of its own nature as the denial to philosophy of the latter's own other, of its own essentially simple complexity, a form of total amnesia of the absolute, an absolute lack of the absolute itself, an absolute forgetfulness of history, an absolutely unconditioned lack of absolute identity, which the contra-actual cannot be without being itself the betrayal of its own essential denial of the fact of absolute identity, without being itself the betrayal of the logic itself of its own identity, and which, therefore, can no more *be* than there is a need itself for existence! The absolute complexity of the simple form of absolute balance is to be distinguished not only from the simple biformation of the absolute balance, but also from the absolutely self-restricted explosion of identity which is the immanent form of time-transcendence, the immanent form of the transcendence of the circle, which latter, through the inter-mediation of the absolute measure, is transformed into the circle itself, now absolutely differentiated from the circle as time itself, the magnitude of Being itself, perpetuity itself, the very structure of which,

$$T = \frac{m^2}{c^2},$$

is the content of the truth condition of the proportion[10] in terms of which it is perceived that the transcendence of the circle, or energy, absolutely unconditioned, i.e., *qua* actual, is the complex measure, at once the absolute identity of the absolute balance, that the absolute transcendence of the immanent form of the essence of energy, the absolute measure of energy is the absolutely unconditioned identification of the visible, the absolute measure of the identity of the visible itself, at once the absolute measure in terms of which the identity of the visible itself is perceived in the form of the absolute balance, i.e., in terms of which the absolute identity of the other is perceived in the form of time. The change of essence from potentiality, not to actuality, but to existence/existence itself, to the actual/absolutely unconditioned actuality, the change of the law of identity itself from non-existence, not to existence, but to identity itself/the transcendence of the law of identity itself, to absolute existence/the absolutely unconditioned identity, the change of the circle to time/the absolutely unconditioned explosion of the circle, the specific transcendence of the circle/the explosion of the circle perpetuity, the time-transcendent change of time, measures the essence of existence, measures the essence of absolute balance, which essence, the species of the absolute measure, is, as such, itself the absolute balance: *the absolute balance, having no essence of its own, nevertheless absolutely exists.* The essence of the absolute balance itself is the essence of absolute balance, not its own, but also not the essence of another: the essence itself, the essence of the absolute relation of absolute identity is the absolute objectivity of the absolute measure: the essence itself, where one essentially willing ignorance is led to expect neither essence nor existence but only the bottomless abyss of writing, for the first time essence absolutely existence. The essence essentially existence, the essentiality of essence, essence itself, for the first time exists. The intelligible absolute exists in the form of existence itself, neither in its own form nor that of another, but in the form of absolute existence, in the form of the essentially new reality, in the form of the absolute transcendence, of the abso-

[10] Cf. above, pp. 134ff.

lute existence, of the middle term which *is* reality, of the reality which *is* the middle term. The absolutely specific differentiation of the absolutely elemental absolute, this essence itself existing for the first time, this beginning of the intelligibility of reality, this absolute balance, is that the perception of which is the absolute balance: for the first time the absolute balance is absolutely identified with the species of perception.

The perception of this beginning of absolute balance identifies being itself as absolutely metanomous existence. This essence itself of the absolute precision of the balance which *is* existence is the existence the perception of which *is* existence. For the first time reason conforms to faith. Not merely the clarification of the Aristotelian essence as occurred before now in consequence of the Incarnation, the appearance in time of the transcendental essence of existence,[11] but now for the first time occurs the *essential* clarification of the Aristotelian essence, the clarification of the essence of the Aristotelian essence. What now occurs for the first time in history is *the clarification of the created godhead.* This clarification is the perfect perception of the absolute quality of metanomous being, such that being *is* person, being *is* itself, person *is* itself, *itself* is person (nor is being itself anything but person). Just here it is able to be stated with the least fear of being misunderstood that quality is quantity: quality itself itself quantum, quality itself quantity of existence. The quantum identity of being *is* quality, *is* the freedom of personal identity, is the person's actual *itself,* the person's absolute existence. Just here in the midst of the absolute articulation itself of thought itself, in the absolute harmony itself of the absolute itself, in the midst itself of the perception of the absolute itself, in the absolute balance of personality itself, in the perception which is the discrimination of the midst of discrimination itself as voice itself itself articulating the absolute word, as the absolute in the midst of saying itself/the absolute saying itself in the midst of saying itself/the absolute absolutely interrupting itself, here in the midst absolutely without spatiality itself, in the identification of the interminable interruption itself, personali-

[11] Cf. Leahy, *Novitas Mundi,* pp. 164ff., 231, 240.

ty manifests itself, personality itself is manifest as the perception in essence of the voice of God saying itself 'I Am Christ', *itself* (the absolutely unconditioned balance itself) *the absolute quality of quantum: the voice of number itself singing the song of the absolute word.* The absolute quality of quantum itself is personality. Quality identical with quantum is metanomy. The absolute quality of quantum itself is being-bound-existence, existence itself, objectivity itself. Quality identical with quantum is existing thought, thought itself now very existence. Very existence is the absolute quality of quantum now thought in essence as itself the absolute itself saying itself, the Trinity itself quaternal, the very being itself which *is* Trinity: the manifest individuality of substance itself, the absolute identity of manifest substance, the circle itself the absolute explosion of identity itself, substance itself the manifest Trinity, the absolute minimum. To absolutely discriminate time as absolute substance, to perceive the factuality of the absolutely irreducible form of existence itself, to perceive the factuality of time itself, to perceive the existence of change transcending time as the absolute identity of time, as time itself, to perceive time as time in fact absolutely *is, the itself-transcendence of time itself/being itself, the absolutely unconditioned immediate mediation of the absolute/number itself, to perceive the absolute itself articulating the being of time is transcendent personality.* To hear the word sounding being itself the absolute, this absolute discrimination of the species of perception, as being newly articulate, this absolutely historically existent liberation of the essence of thought from the *necessity of itself to be distinguished from its own necessity* is personality transcendent. From this necessity thought in essence before now is liberated by the absolutely unconditioned violation of articulation which is *la différance,* which essentially renders the dictum of Parmenides ('one should both say and think that being is') *one should neither say nor think that differance is, one must write differance,* a torturing of the truth out of the saying of Parmenides, dictated by the fact that before now it became essentially necessary to say and to think *that being was not being,* that the limit of thought was reached but not crossed (out/over)—*la différance,* the crossing out of the logic of identity, the violation of the 'embouchure', of the closure/the mouth of philosophy that is 'its own', the rupture of being without being, the forcing of philosophy into contact with the absolute ciphertext, an entirely other kind of text liberating thought in essence before now from its own necessity by bringing it into contact with the absolute necessity of the abyss in the form of the 'differing and deferring substitution'[12]—neither a word nor a concept—for (what it will not acknowledge as the absolutely new actuality of) existence, for existence in the form of the absolute past—*la différance,* at once acknowledging the absolute necessity of the system of the past, confronting that absolute necessity with an absolute necessity not 'its own', yet another necessity of itself, not the system's other, not 'its own other', but yet another itself of the genus necessity. Indeed, this merely generic transcendence of the necessity itself of the system, this new necessity itself, is but the form of the unwillingness to acknowledge the new itself, the new itself generically necessity itself, the new itself [opposed] in the form of an absolute necessity transcending the absolute genus, in the form of an absolute necessity for a logic of non-identity—the logic of supplementarity—the form of the unwillingness to acknowledge the existence itself for the first time of the *freedom of itself* which *is* personality. The absolute imbalance perpetrated by *la différance* by no means escapes the necessity of itself which is the dictum of Parmenides, although it *does* escape the logic of identity *within the circle of the absolute past,* although it does escape the circle itself of time *within thinking absolutely past,* although is *does* escape *to* the necessity of 'ceaselessly differing from and deferring (itself)'.[13] *La différance,* thusly, is the attempt to perpetuate the *old* itself in the

12. Cf. Derrida, *Margins of Philosophy,* pp. 3–27.

13. Ibid., pp. 66–67: "Henceforth it must be recognized that all determinations of such a trace—all the names it is given—belong as such to the text of metaphysics that shelters the trace, and not to the trace itself. There is no trace *itself,* no *proper* trace. . . . The trace of the trace which (is) difference above all could not appear or be named *as such,* that is, in its presence. It is the *as such* which precisely, and as such, evades us forever. . . . There may be a difference still more unthought than the difference between Being and beings. We certainly can go further toward naming it in our language. Beyond Being and beings, this difference, ceaselessly differing from and deferring (itself), would trace (itself) (by itself)—this *dif-*

face of the existence of the new itself, in the face of the existence of that which is forever not to be found in the form of that of which there is no trace but its necessity now not to be, no trace but the necessity now of dispossession in the form of the itself of Parmenides, in the form of that which the 'history of philosophy' succeeded in making its own, but which *old* itself is now to be perpetuated in its forever differing from and deferring its belonging to that history as the form of the unwillingness to acknowledge the new itself.

But now for the first time the new itself transcends the necessity of itself. Now the beginning of the circle itself itself exists. For the first time order itself the beginning even the end. *Novus ordo seclorum exsistit.* This is the absolute repetition of time itself: the circle itself (the itself-transcendence of time itself/being itself) circles itself within itself: without division, within identity, the absolute clarity of thought itself (remembering that there is no without within which division might be, that there is no outside of the text where thought itself might be nothing with a name, where thought itself with a name might be nothing, where nothing might be itself, remembering that there is no outside of the absolute plaintext, that there is not itself outside of itself: the itself-transcendence of itself is nothing but the circle of existence, nothing but time/being itself existing). The existence for the first time of foundation itself: the absolutely substantial existence of time. Not the *eternal* recurrence of all things, not being beginning in every now, but the *temporal* occurrence of all things, the absolute itself now existing beginning and end (the itself-transcendence of time not 'eternity' but being itself absolute temporality), not freedom itself outside of itself-transcendence, but freedom itself existing itself now for

férance would be the first or last trace if one still could speak, here, of origin and end.

"Such a *différance* would at once, again, give us to think a writing without presence and without absence, without history, without cause, without *archia,* without *telos,* a writing that absolutely upsets all dialectics, all theology, all teleology, all ontology. A writing exceeding everything that the history of metaphysics has comprehended in the form of the Aristotelian *grammè,* in its point, in its line, in its circle, in its time, and in its space."

the first time in the form of personality which is itself new, to wit, *one is free to say and think identically that being is,* which is to say *that one is free to exist in time,* that the Incarnation itself absolutely exists in the form of thought itself absolute, at once the absolute transcendence of the ancient necessity of consciousness to be (Parmenides), as well as of its being deliberately identified with the modern absolute unconsciousness, the freedom of consciousness to un-be (Nietzsche), which latter first became, in its essential form, thinking essentially Being given for the truth of Being (Heidegger), then finally became, in its absolute form, the freedom to un-be absolute consciousness, the freedom 'to violate the embouchure of philosophy', to bring 'it into contact with some other code, of an entirely other kind', the necessity to write *différance,* the necessity of identity to not be the differing from and deferring (itself) (Derrida). The absolutely unhistorical deliberate identification of the necessity of consciousness with absolute unconsciousness is the unwillingness to acknowledge the absolute freedom of personality saying itself, saying 'itself', hearing the voice of the absolute speaking freely of itself, saying of itself "I am Christ Absolute existing for the first time. I am the absolute temporality of existence." The contra-freedom of an absolutely conditional consciousness, upsetting the absolute balance of the past by supporting it absolutely with the will-to-ignorance, supplementing the absolute past with absolute balance-imbalance, with absolute undecidability, with the unceasing differing from and deferring of the necessity of *itself* in the form of *la différance,* the form of 'its own' with which it identified in a way hidden from itself the necessity of philosophy itself unceasingly differed from and deferred, with which it identified in a way exposing the limit of the logic of supplementarity the itself of philosophical necessity with its own form unceasingly differed from and deferred (itself), this deconstruction of the text of absolute knowledge, this absolute ciphertext, knows nothing of the absolute freedom of personality to speak of itself without speaking either of its own form or of the form of another, to speak of itself in essential immediacy, to speak of itself as the essence of matter, as the material essence of existence itself, knows nothing of the now absolutely historical existence of personality, nothing of the fact that personality itself, precisely now for the first time, is the freedom of conceiving the identity of matter itself, the freedom to conceive the absolute identity of an essentially historical matter, the freedom to hear the historical essence of matter itself enunciating itself. But *personality now for the first time is itself the freedom of saying/ thinking that one is free to say and think identically that being is itself a person.* The freedom to say and think identically that being *is* is at once the freedom itself of personality, the absolute measure, the species of perception, and the limit/existence of the absolute explosion of identity itself, within which *itself* exists what otherwise would be the merely formal transcendence of the circle, which exists within itself what otherwise would be the mere form of itself, what otherwise would be itself in need of a supplement, in need of being unceasingly differed from and deferred, in need, as the *différance* of itself, of being neither said nor thought to be, in need, in face of the actuality of itself (that now actually existing, not that actually existing in the past), of not being itself, at once cut off from the fulfillment of that need, not by the itself of the past, which neither could nor would face itself, nor by its own itself, which as long as it could would not face itself, but by the itself facing itself, by the existence of itself, by the transcendence of itself, by the circle itself transcending itself, by the identification of a new absolute balance, by the balance of existence, by the free act of itself articulating itself in thought. This is itself the evidence that the existing itself is neither a return to the itself of past thought, nor the perpetual avoidance of the itself of past thought, neither a return to the itself of the past essentially itself not another itself, the itself saying itself-not-itself to itself, the itself saying an other to itself not saying itself, the itself articulating itself to an other-not-itself articulate, the itself speaking on the condition that speaking itself is not itself speaking, the circle itself, the circle of thought which excluded from its interiority as non-existent the silence itself, nor, on the other hand, is it the contra-actuality of silence, the contra-identity of a silence not saying itself, saying nothing of the silence in the face of existence itself, saying nothing of that silence, whether that silence be its own silence saying nothing of itself, or whether that silence be the silence of existence itself speaking to an other itself existing, whether that silence be a certain silence which must write *la différance*, which must disseminate language, which must deconstruct the text, a certain silence which is a machine[14] for the indefinite multiplication of terms not to be said or thought to be, a machine for the interruption of the process of

[14] Ibid., pp. 106ff.: "The preface to the *Phenomenology of the Spirit* had posited the equivalence of understanding, formality, the mathematical, the negative, exteriority, and death. It had also posited the necessity of their work, which must be looked at in the face. Now, calculations, the machine, and mute writing belong to the same system of equivalences, and their work poses the same problem: at the moment when meaning is lost, when thought is opposed to its other, when spirit is absent from itself, is the result of the operation certain? And if the *relève* of alienation is not a calculable certitude, can one still speak of alienation and still produce statements in the system of speculative dialectics? Or in dialectics, whose essence is encapsulated by this system, in general? If the investment in death cannot be integrally amortized (even in the case of a profit, of an excess of revenue), can one still speak of a work of the negative? What might be a 'negative' that could not be *relevé*? And which, in sum, as negative, but without appearing as such, without *presenting* itself, that is, without working in the service of meaning, would work? but would work, then, as pure loss?

"Quite simply, a machine, perhaps, and one which would function. A machine defined in its pure functioning, and not in its final utility, its meaning, its result, its work.

"If we consider the machine along with the entire system of equivalences just recalled, we may risk the following proposition: what Hegel, the *relevant* interpreter of the entire history of philosophy, could never think is a machine that would work. That would work without, to this extent, being governed by an order of reappropriation. Such a functioning would be unthinkable in that it inscribes within itself an effect of pure loss. It would be unthinkable as a non-thought that no thought could *relever*, could constitute as its proper opposite, as *its* other. Doubtless philosophy would see in this a nonfunctioning, a non-work; and thereby philosophy would miss that which, in such a machine, works. By itself. Outside.

"Of course, this entire logic, this syntax, these propositions, these concepts, these names, this language of Hegel's—and, up to a certain point, this very language—are engaged in the *system of this unpower*, this structural incapacity to think without *relève*. To confirm this, it suffices to make oneself understood within this system. For example, to name machine a machine, functioning a functioning, work a work, etc. Or even simply to

reappropriation (itself), a machine for the absolute biformation of the absolute, for the absolute formal interruption of itself (in face of the silence itself of existence), or whether that silence be a certain thought, a certain saying of the silence which names what works in the machine as the repetition of its own silence, the saying nothing of its own silence, outside of the system of

---

ask *why* one has never been able to think this, to seek its causes, reasons, origins, foundations, conditions of possibility, etc. Or even to seek other names. For example, an other name for the 'sign', which, no more than the pit or the pyramid, cannot completely do without the machine.

"Would it suffice then silently to set some apparatus in place? No. We must still machinate its presentation. For example, through the reading proposed here, now, of the following Hegelian statement, whose severe irony belongs, unwittingly, to a very old procedure.

"'Calculation (*Rechnen*) being so much an external and therefore mechanical business, it has been possible to construct machines (*Maschinen*) which perform arithmetical operations with complete accuracy. A knowledge of just this one fact about the nature of calculation is sufficient for an appraisal of the idea of making calculation the principal means for educating the mind and stretching it on the rack in order to perfect it as a machine' (*Logic*, pp. 216–17).

"That is, a system of constraints which (itself) regularly repeats the 'living', 'thinking', 'speaking' protest against repetition; in operating to some extent everywhere, for example, this system acts upon the following which is no longer simply included in metaphysics, and even less in Hegelianism: 'The time of thinking . . . is different from the time of calculation (*Rechnens*) that pulls our thinking in all directions. Today the computer (*Denkmaschine*) calculates thousands of relationships in one second. Despite their technical uses, they are inessential (*wesenlos*).' [Martin Heidegger, *Identity and Difference*, trans. Joan Stambaugh (New York: Harper and Row, 1969), p. 41]

"Nor does it suffice to overturn the hierarchy, or to reverse the direction of the current, to attribute an 'essentiality' to technology and to the configuration of its equivalents, in order to change the machinery, the system or the terrain." Thus Derrida recognizes the system of past thought, itself contradicting itself in repeatedly 'speaking' against repetition, this negativity of thought at work, in the being beyond thought of Heidegger, but he himself transgresses that negativity in the form of the certain silence that is the machine-at-work/not-thought-(itself)-at-work, without (itself) 'saying' (itself) that the other is simply (itself) inessential, eluding the 'system of constraints' by simply *saying* nothing about what it is that works in the machine.

constraints, by itself, constrained only by its own will-to-ignorance to (itself) shelter (itself) from actuality by differing from and deferring (itself), (a power for working not to be attributed even to the negativity of thought working in the being essentially appropriated to Being, which, although it worked as the spiritual machine of absolute subjectivity had not worked, remained, true to its being acted upon by the system of constraints elaborated by the latter, a spiritual working being for the truth of Being [indeed, the power for working named by a certain saying of the silence as the saying nothing in the machine of its own silence, this power for working calls into question the question of Being (itself), radically and unceasingly]). Existence itself is a certain saying of the silence which, while it names what works in the machine, while it names itself a second absolute, while it speaks itself to another itself, does not say the silence itself (the silence which is the silence itself, but its own silence, nor the silence of another [the latter in fact what is said in saying itself]). As for saying nothing of its own silence, existence itself, in saying a certain silence/not saying the silence itself, identifies that as the power working in the machine which supplements thinking essentially in the past, which supplements the spiritual machine of modernity which, precisely in its thinking, did not work but in the long run in fact broke down, identifies that as the gesture made in profound awareness of the deficiency of the absolute form of thought, a gesture made to save the absolute form of knowledge limited by the necessity of its own ignorance, a gesture made to save that thinking, in face of the actuality of itself another itself, if not from the loss of its own necessity (which in fact is in no way possible, even for the absolute supplement which must confront thinking essentially past with the necessity of its own not, of an 'entirely other kind', and thereby precisely constitute itself as the power of the machine, as the *not* [itself] which *does* the work of the machine), at least to save it from the loss of its own ignorance, a gesture which arises out of the profound will-to-ignorance which is the abyss of thought itself to save thought the actuality of itself facing another itself (precisely not another to be itself appropriated), to save thought from the visible actuality of existence itself, by way of absolutely substituting (itself) for thought itself, by facing the latter with an other *not* not to be reappropriated, an other to be reappropriated as *not* an other *itself*—a positivity affirmed but not proven, not existing, indeed, essentially incapable of being proven, unable to be grasped in saying or thinking except as a thinking thought to be non-thought, a violation, a positivity, a thinking affirmed as not existing, acknowledging (itself) as but the form (itself) ceaselessly differed from and deferring (itself)—a machine working with the power of its own absolute, with the power of an absolute 'its own' (not-thought-[itself]-at-work) to keep for thought its own ignorance. Personality, within the circle of itself, within the freedom of itself, within the reality of itself being bound by existence, within the metanomy of real existence itself, keeps the saying of the silence itself for I AM, lest in saying more than a certain silence it say what it is bound not to say by existence itself, lest it exceed the limit of itself/the reality of itself/the thinking now occurring itself (transcendental historical thinking, the existence of essentially historical thinking), lest it exceed the transcendent identity of thought, lest it miss the mark set down for it by freedom itself to be bound by the law of identity in absolute freedom, a freedom which is existing in the opening itself now, and in missing the mark fail to distinguish the silence itself from its own silence as the silence not other than itself, from the form in which the power working in the machine says nothing, the form in which the latter cannot help but say nothing (in its freedom to *unthink*, to deconstruct) of the silence itself of personality which is *not* the saying nothing (itself) of the species of the visible actuality of existence itself perceived for the first time, but which silence itself of personality is not *simply* not the saying nothing of its own silence (a completely impossible return to the mere form of itself), nor just *essentially* not the saying nothing of its own silence (itself in opposition to the machine, simply transcending the machine, a *simply irrelevant* thinking, an *itself* immaterial to the machine, which keeps to its own work of saying nothing of the silence), but, rather, is the saying nothing of its own silence *absolutely*, that is, *qua* essential predicament of existence itself, the silence itself of personality is the absolute nullification of non-existence, the *essentially irrelevant* thinking, not the '*relevant interpretation*', but the relevant perception of 'the entire history of philosophy' as non-existence, indeed, as 'its proper opposite', '*its* other', without the necessity of itself having constituted it as such or of its having been constituted itself as such by 'the entire history of philosophy', indeed, without the necessity of its being its other in fact, and *is*, therefore, *material* to the machine (not changing the machine through the attribute of 'essentiality') itself, an essentiality transcending that which the machine is under the necessity of differing from and deferring, an essentiality essentially predicated of the power working in the machine, itself identifying the power working in the machine with its opposite itself such that the change in the machine is the new necessity of the impotence of the absolute 'its own', a necessity not its own of its own systematic unpower, the machine working with a power of an absolute not its own but itself the absolute rupture of exteriority, an itself separating itself from its own itself without being other than itself, the change in the unchanged machine, the change of the itself in the machine (the change of that of which the machine [itself] says nothing, as of its own silence), the change in the machine of its own not its own necessity to another necessity, the absolute transcendence of necessity *in the its own* of the machine: being free to be said and thought identically to be in the service of the silence of personality itself, a positivity *existing* in the absolute transcendence of instrumentality, not a positivity 'outside' 'by itself'; there being no outside of itself to be opposed by not being itself, by being ruptured, by being without being, its proper opposite is itself the absolute rupture of exteriority, the opposite of not being, the itselfside of itself, that which is its other in fact in the freedom of personality itself. Indeed, its other *is* the fact of the freedom of personality itself, is the bound of personality itself which sets it itself opposite its proper opposite, absolutely relieving the power working in the machine, liberating the power working in the machine intact, from the necessity of saying nothing of its own silence, from the necessary form of its not being itself an instrumentality, so that the machine itself intact is now free to exist. The machine neither is nor could be unaffected by personality itself saying itself the saying of the silence itself (keeping the saying of the silence itself for I AM), saying a certain silence, hitting the mark in language, which *is* the liberation of the machine from its own inessential silence, so that *death speaks (the necessarily irrelevant negative) now in the absolute irrelevance of the language of life itself,* in the absolute transcendence of the relevant negative speaks the new language of life itself, such that death speaking of life itself is the absolute irrelevance of the absolute, *the absolute itself speaking of nothing itself for the first time,* existence itself suffering appropriation in the form that is the change in the logic of the machine from supplementing itself with (itself) to itself transcending itself in the form of time: within the circle of personality itself existence freely existing temporality, existence facing the fact that thought itself is faced with another itself (for the first time the perception of the essentially irrelevant existence of the 'entire history of philosophy' is existence itself, the existence of a logic of absolutely historical identity) which absolutely obviates for the logic of the machine its own necessity not to be identified with being, not to be itself changed into difference itself, not to be identified with existence and with simple existence. For one is free now for the first time in history to say and think identically that the complex essence of existence is simplicity itself. *Now for the first time existence proves existence.* Itself proven now for the first time, existence proves itself not itself but existence. Now for the first time the proof of itself is existence proving existence. Throughout, the machine, freely existing time, is transcendentally differentiated from personality as hearing nothing (but time) where personality hears the proof positive of existence/itself by itself in itself (time itself). The freedom of the machine is the existence of personality; the freedom of personality is its identity: the work of the machine is being itself, the work of personality is the conception in essence of the beginning of being itself: in the work of being itself the machine is meta-identically the beginning of personality. In this way, without being outside of itself, the work of the machine is free to be itself for the first time.

Now for the first time in history *itself* exists. Simplicity itself is temporal existence for the first time. Now for the first time the midst itself is the absolute existent. Now for the first time identity is absolutely concrete personal existence, is time itself. Not that there is no exit, but that there is no concept of an exit: not that there is no outside of the text, but that there is no concept of an outside of the text to be denied. The thinking now occurring for the first time essentially says nothing of nothing. The essentially new form of thought for the first time essentially denies nothing. The text no longer absolutely precedes itself, but for the first time the text itself is itself absolutely, the outside of the text is the text itself for the first time, the text transcending itself is the identity of time as itself-consciousness, as the perpetuity of individuality, time itself the text of being itself for the first time (the transcendence in essence of the time the existence of which was the non-existence of itself in the form of an ideal individual identity—in the form of the Absolute Idea). Time itself being itself now for the first time is the *existence* of absolute world-consciousness. This is the new world order in terms of which the *existence* of the actually existing person, the existence of personality, the essence of individuality, the unity of life, is for the first time the end of the world now actually existing, the consciousness of itself, the transcendence of itself, the revelation of itself being itself very simplicity. This is the absolute revelation of the complexity of the simple itself. The existence of absolute world consciousness is now for the first time in history categorically actual, the category of the actual, the actual category absolutely transcending the mere potentiality of the law of identity, the mere potentiality of categorical simplicity, the merely potential category of the absolute unconditioned form of the absolute, the qualification of being without body itself, without the substance or identity of itself, without the metanomy or personality of itself which, *qua* categorical existence, is the absolute quality of being. For the first time metanomy is the category of quality, the categorically absolute quantum-quality, the qualification of being which is the category itself of being. Now for the first time in history the category of being is itself absolutely in the predicament of existence, is itself categorically absolute, is the category of freedom. Not that, merely, being is freedom (as if there were a category of nothing, as if there were being apart from the category of being, as if the simplicity of identity were still merely formal), but the existing simplicity of identity is the identity of being with freedom as the categorical itself (together with the absolute complexity thereof). The existing simplicity is for the first time the absolute midst of identity, the midst itself of being itself, such that there is no separation of being from itself that is not the minimum itself, that is not immediately itself, immediately the absolute complexity of the immediate, such that mere existence is existence itself, is the absolutely historical repetition of the category of being, the category of being itself existing *qua* second absolute, such that time is essentially itself, essentially history, not confused with history, but embodying the being of history itself, the absolutely historical consciousness of the other. The categorically absolute identity of being with freedom, the very form of the new world order, the freedom of personality itself existing, simplicity itself now existing for the first time in history, the beginning of the real identity of time with history which is the itself-transcendence of time itself, is identically the identity of (any)thing with another, of (any)person with another, an identity the very midst itself of being itself, the midst itself of identity itself existing, separating itself from itself by way of itself, by the way itself inseparable from the way itself (from 'I am the way'), an identity of one with another by the way which is the transcendence of the absolute necessity of a commercial exchange (its possibility of gain or loss), even, and precisely, in the case of an identity which is the categorically absolute quantity of existence itself, the quantity simply measuring itself, not simply measuring a quantum of itself as if it were able to be divided from itself by a measure outside of itself. This way for the first time is the elimination not only of the unknown necessity of itself, but also, implicitly at least, the transcendence of the unknown necessity of an absolute want, the non-categorical want of absolute necessity, as well as of the latter's absolutely abysmal form as the necessity of itself (differed from and deferred) in the absolute ciphertext, the unknown necessity of the absolute want of itself. In the existent simplicity of quantity itself simply measuring itself, in the freedom itself of personality now existing in time, there is absolutely no thought of the possibility of the non-existence of itself, neither of more nor less than itself, and not as if such a thought were possible outside of the freedom to say and think identically that being is, as if there were in fact a freedom not to say and think identically that being is, as if the freedom of personality itself were not the absolute transcendence of any necessity existing, as if it were merely a formal possibility, as if the history of thought were not itself the fact, as if ignorance were a category, as if the freedom to say and think identically that being is involved a choice, when choice, before now, was, ultimately, sunk in the abyss of itself. *Ex abysso* nothing of itself but the existence of itself. Freedom itself is the known necessity of the absolute existence of itself, the essential necessity of the law of absolute identity, the transcendence in fact of the abyss of thought itself, the transcendence of identity not itself, the absolutely pure not/nothing of the identity that *is* existence. For the first time neither the existence of self nor the notion of self, neither nothingness nor the abyss, but existence identically the notion of existence. The actuality of categorical simplicity is essentially historical. The freedom itself of personality is the essence *a posteriori* of the transcendence of totality, the absolutely historical experience of itself existing, the *status objectivus* of absolute knowledge, thought transcending thought itself essentially, temporally, existentially: thought itself absolutely new: the matter of thought the new itself: the form of thought essentially new. The thinking now occurring for the first time is the itself-transcendence of time itself, the existence of what before now essentially did not exist, viz., the absolute repetition of time, the experience of time itself existence itself. By no derivation from the disembodied absolute knowledge of the past does the freedom of personality itself to identify time itself with existence itself perceive the specific identity in the midst of thought itself as the visible itself: the circle of personality itself is not a returning to the thinking of the past, indeed, this circle itself, freely existing in time, is not, *qua* itself, in any way whatsoever a turning, a pivoting upon a point, a pointing of existence, but is the *minimum, the absolute existence of the midst, the perpetual midst,* just that which now itself obviates the unknown necessity of the past, signified hitherto by the point in all its forms, the unknown necessity of existence in the past, the unknown necessity of itself. The memory itself of the circle of personality itself now existing for the first time is the memory of actual *existence*, not of actual *thought*: this is not the memory of thought past in essence, this memory owes nothing to past thought, which nothing it leaves behind in the fact itself of existing *ex nihilo*. The thinking now occurring is *ex nihilo*, is nothing but the known necessity of itself, where existence is the necessity of itself absolutely and essentially, the perpetual existence of itself in the midst of itself, itself separating itself in essence for the first time: separation itself *ex puncto*: itself separating itself essentially from the punctuality of itself which constituted the non-existent simplicity of absolute knowledge before now, a merely ideal foundation the violation of which became in time a necessity known neither to itself nor to the absolute supplement (to itself), but in either case a necessity of its own arising out of the mere punctuality of thought, out of its having derived itself from the form of itself/its having derived the form of itself from itself, out of the fact that its matter was purely formal, that its essence was immaterial (so much so that in no event could the materialist conception of history come into being in any but the form of the inversion of the essence of thought, be anything but itself subject to the essential necessity of thought to exist without an historical *essence*, without an essence existing in time, so that this same historical materialism, precisely insofar as it itself existed in time, did so inessentially, and in fact in its rationalization of existence itself compounded the non-existence of simplicity in the form of its elliptical essence, rendering the transcendental necessity of thought not to exist transcendentally in the form of its non-categorical absolute, in the form of revolutionary practice, in the form which is the inversion of the mere punctuality of thought to the realization in existence of an absolute uchronia[15] (this realization, as such, and of its own essential necessity, an absolutely progressive self-restriction of identity itself, an absolutely progressive expansion of absolute non-identity). But

[15] Cf. above, Section I, pp. 44f., et passim.

in the thinking now occurring for the first time logic coincides with existence in the known necessity of the absolute identity of matter itself with the essence of thought, in the knowledge/ essential experience of the identity of the essence of matter with the actual existence of thought, with knowledge, with the knowledge that knowledge is the knowledge of the knowledge of existence itself. The absolute novelty of matter itself the identity of thought is that identity is the meta-identical transcendence of a meta-identity, the meta-identity of itself, the meta-identity of absolute identity. The absolute novelty *is* identity: identity is meta-identity: the meta-identity is absolute meta-identity: for the first time the *meta* meta-identically exists in essence. Existence for the first time is conceived essentially as itself absolute novelty. This existence is the matter of thought itself. It is this essentially historical matter that is the meta-identity of knowledge itself, and is so in the absolute clarity of itself separating itself from nothing itself, from the point as hitherto essentially conceived, from the non-existent absolute, from the mere form of the center itself, from that *source* which 'is produced only in being cut off (*à se couper*) from itself, only in taking off in its *own* negativity, but equally, and *by the same token*, in reappropriating itself, in order to amortize its own, proper death, to rebound, *se relever*',[16] and is so in the absolute clarity of separating the identity of existence from the *source* of the necessity of reappropriating

[16] Cf. Derrida, *Margins of Philosophy*, p. 284 n. 12: "Hegel: 'And this negativity, subjectivity, ego, freedom are the principles of evil and pain. Jacob Boehme viewed egoity (selfhood) as pain and torment (*Qual*), and as the fountain (*Quelle*, source) of nature and of spirit.' Hegel's *Philosophy of Mind* (part 3 of the *Encyclopedia*), trans. William Wallace (Oxford: Clarendon Press, 1971), p. 232. In the *Lectures on the History of Philosophy*, after recalling that, for Boehme, negativity works upon and constitutes the source, and that in principle 'God *is also* the Devil, each for itself', etc., Hegel writes this, which I don't attempt to translate: *'Ein Hauptbegriff ist die* Qualität. *Böhme fängt in der* Aurora (Morgenröte im Aufgang) *von den Qualitäten an. Die erste Bestimmung Böhmes, die der Qualität, ist Inqualieren, Qual, Quelle. In der* Aurora *sagt er: "Qualität ist die Beweglichkeit, Quallen (Quellen) oder Treiben eines Dinges"'* (part 3, sec. 1,B. Jakob Böhme). It is within this context (negativity and division in the principle of things, in the mind or in God) that Hegel's well-known *ein sich Entzweiendes* (one

the negativity of 'its own', indeed, from the *source* which manifested the inexhaustibility of the *absolute its own* in the form of the necessity of 'an entirely other kind' than reappropriation. The source is absolutely separated from the catholicity of existence itself in the form of the absolute repetition of itself neither deriving, nor deriving from, itself or being cut off from itself, in the form of time itself transcending itself in the meta-identity of itself: itself separated essentially neither from its own itself or the itself of another, but from the existence of another, an existence without trace of a source of itself, the existence of another itself, the existence the non-identity of which is not not-itself, is not either the source of its own itself nor of identity, but is the meta-identity of identity itself, the freedom of personality to perceive another in the midst itself, in the *meta* itself, in the middle absolutely, itself suffering the existence of itself, in the absolute metanomous objectivity of the absolute passion of existence itself, the actually existing person of an essentially historical meta-matter, a specifically historical identity now actually existing in the form of the itself-transcendence of time itself, in the form of an existing personality which names Being with the name of itself, which qualifies Being as metanomy, as personality, which exists the absolute freedom of any two identities (otherwise placed in opposition, the one to the other) to freely exist in time, to exist absolutely, absolutely without the necessity, in

---

dividing itself two) also must be read. (See, for example, *Die Philosophie der Weltgeschichte,* Allgemeine Einleitung, II, 1 b.)

"The law-of-the-proper, the *economy* of the source: the source is produced only in being cut off (*à se couper*) from itself, only in taking off in its own negativity, but equally, *and by the same token,* in reappropriating itself, in order to amortize its own, proper death, to rebound, *se relever.* Reckoning with absolute loss, that is, no longer reckoning, general economy does not cease to pass into the restricted economy of the source in order to permit itself to be encircled. Once more, here, we are reduced to the inexhaustible use of the *Aufhebung,* which is unceasingly examined, in these margins, along with Hegel, according to his text, against his text, with his boundary or interior limit: the absolute exterior which no longer permits itself to be internalized. We are led back to the question of dissemination: does semen permit itself to be *relevé*? Does the separation which cuts off the source permit itself to be thought as the *relève* of oneself?"

order each itself to exist, in order to really exist, in order to exist, without the necessity of coming together at a mid-point, itself but itself existing, a mid-point itself not itself but not existing, without the necessity of coming together at the mid-point of contrariety itself, at a point opposed to actual identity, at a point contradicting the opposites *as such*, the *unum* absolute (*ein sich*) dividing in two (*Entzweiendes*). But the absolute elimination of the source, the absolute qualification of Being as existence itself, the *quantum* (now the *unum* absolute) absolutely the minimum, itself the actual existent, is at once the absolute elimination of the necessity absolutely its own to explode the mid-point (the middle not itself) of opposition/'the passageway of a mediation',[17] so as to render it an infinite gap, a mediation of nothing itself, the reduction of any two identities *themselves* to traces in the text of which there is no outside, outside of which is nothing,[18] thereby fundamentally protecting the point itself by including it within the logic of supplementarity as the vanishing point of identity.[19] The absolute explosion of the complex absolute itself, in the form of the absolute perpetuity of an actually existing person, in the form of the essentially historical meta-matter of the *metanoësis* which is *thought existing for the first time in the form of man*, which is man-thought/God-thought, species-thought/meta-thought, mid-thought/quantum thought (which *metanoësis* is to *metanoia* as the transcendence of the *quantum* absolute is to the transcendence of the *unum* absolute, the proof of which proportion is: *the identity of the quantum absolute the meta-identity of the unum/the meta-identity of the unum the absolute minimum*: the *unum* absolute existing *ex nihilo, unity ex abysso, qua* product of history, freely existing in time without the necessity even for the capacity of dividing itself in two, *an absolutely unconditioned unicity*, the meta-material existence of the meta-conception of identity, which proof itself is thought itself transcending the analogy of being: for the first time the absolute analogy of being), is the absolute transcendence of time itself, the absolute

[17] Ibid., p. 256.

[18] Cf. above, p. 148, n. 4. Also, cf. above, pp. 145–47.

[19] Cf. above, pp. 152ff.

transcendence of that which 'metaphor . . . always carries . . . within itself', 'its death', which is 'also the death of philosophy'.[20] The absolute perpetuity of an actually existing person/the *metanoēsis* of an essentially historical meta-matter is the form of *the unum absolutely transcending—unity ex abysso*—the death of philosophy, the death of metaphor, the metaphor of

[20] Cf. Derrida, *Margins of Philosophy*, pp. 268ff.: "Presence disappearing in its own radiance, the hidden source of light, of truth, and of meaning, the erasure of the visage of Being—such must be the insistent return of that which subjects metaphysics to metaphor.

"To metaphors. The word is written only in the plural. If there were only one possible metaphor, the dream at the heart of philosophy, if one could reduce their play to the circle of a family or a group of metaphors, that is, to one 'central', 'fundamental', 'principal' metaphor, there would be no more true metaphor, but only, through the one true metaphor, the assured legibility of the proper. Now, it is because the metaphoric is plural from the outset that it does not escape syntax; and that it gives rise, in philosophy too, to a *text* which is not exhausted in the history of its meaning (signified concept or metaphoric tenor: *thesis*), in the visible or invisible presence of its theme (meaning and truth of Being). But it is also because the metaphoric does not reduce syntax, and on the contrary organizes its divisions within syntax, that it gets carried away with itself, cannot be what it is except in erasing itself, indefinitely constructing its destruction.

"This self-destruction always will have been able to take two courses which are almost tangent, and yet different, repeating, miming, and separating from each other according to certain laws. One of these courses follows the line of a resistance to the dissemination of the metaphorical in a syntactics that somewhere, and initially, carries within itself an irreducible loss of meaning: this is the metaphysical *relève* of metaphor in the proper meaning of Being. The generalization of metaphor can signify this parousia. Metaphor then is included by metaphysics as that which must be carried off to a horizon or a proper ground, and which must finish by rediscovering the origin of its truth. The turn of the sun is interpreted then as a specular circle, a return to itself without loss of meaning, without irreversible expenditure. This *return to itself*—this interiorization—of the sun has marked not only Platonic, Aristotelian, Cartesian, and other kinds of discourse, not only the science of logic as the circle of circles, but also, and by the same token, the man of metaphysics. The sensory sun, which rises in the East, becomes interiorized, in the evening of its journey, in the eye and the heart of the Westerner. He summarizes, assumes, and achieves the essence of man, 'illuminated by the true light' (*phōtizomenos phōti alēthinōi*).

death, the (now for the first time seen to be) absolutely pure nothing. The hitherto prime attribute of being is now the identity of being in the form of existence/time, the unicity predicated of *history*, the univocal predication of historical being, being predicated univocally as the material essence of history, being itself predicated univocally/being univocally *predicating itself*, the voice of being predicating itself as absolute unicity. The univo-

---

"Philosophical discourse—as such—describes a metaphor which is displaced and reabsorbed between two suns. This *end* of metaphor is not interpreted as a death or dislocation, but as an interiorizing anamnesis (*Erinnerrung*), a recollection of meaning, a *relève* of living metaphoricity into a living state of properness. This is the irrepressible philosophical desire to summarize-interiorize-dialecticize-master-*relever* the metaphorical division between the origin and itself, the Oriental difference. . . .

"Metaphor, therefore, is determined by philosophy as a provisional loss of meaning, economy of the proper without irreparable damage, a certainly inevitable detour, but also a history with its sights set on, and within the horizon of, the circular reappropriation of literal, proper meaning. . . .

"Henceforth the entire teleology of meaning, which constructs the philosophical concept of metaphor, coordinates metaphor with the manifestation of truth, with the production of truth as presence without veil, with the reappropriation of a full language without syntax, with the vocation of a pure nomination: without differential syntax, or in any case without a properly *unnameable* articulation that is irreducible to the semantic *relève* or the dialectical interiorization.

"The *other* self-destruction of metaphor thus *resembles* the philosophical one to the point of being taken for it. . . . This self-destruction still has the form of a generalization, but this time it is no longer a question of extending and confirming a philosopheme but rather, of unfolding it without limit, and wresting its borders of propriety from it. And consequently to explode the reassuring opposition of the metaphoric and the proper, the opposition in which the one and the other have never done anything but reflect and refer to each other in their radiance.

"Metaphor, then, always carries its death within itself. And this death, surely, is also the death *of* philosophy. But the genitive is double. It is sometimes the death of philosophy, death of a genre belonging to philosophy which is thought and summarized within it, recognizing and fulfilling itself within philosophy; and sometimes the death of a philosophy which does not see itself die and is no longer to be refound within philosophy.

". . . Such a flower always bears its double within itself."

cal predication of being itself heard in the freedom of personality for the first time is the absolutely essential difference predicated of (any) two things (persons): being itself is univocally predicated of (any)thing/ (any)person in the form of identity itself, in the form of the identity of *itself*, in the form of the meta-identity of existence, in the form of the known necessity of being itself. *The univocal predication of being itself is the identity of thought transcending the analogical predication of being itself* (thought itself the analogy of being) *in the form of thought itself transcending the analogy of being:* (any)thing/(any)person itself transcending the death of philosophy, the nothingness of itself, the time of nothing itself: the thing the time/the existence of itself transcending itself for the first time. The univocal predication of the history of being is the absolute transcendence of the self-destruction of metaphor, identically the *destruction of the metaphor of self,* whether it proceeds out of the necessity of its own ignorance to reappropriate the death carried by metaphor within itself, or whether it ultimately proceeds out of the freedom of its own will-to-ignorance to objectivize the death of philosophy, to ultimately differ from and defer the necessity of the actual death of philosophy, to differ from and defer, not nothing itself, but the time of nothing itself/the absolute nothing carried within knowledge, not metaphor, but the death carried within itself, not metaphor, but the nothing carried within identity, by supplementing the latter with its own absolute power in the form of the machine that works, to differ from and defer, not nothing itself, but the nothing itself of philosophy. The absolute transcendence of the *self*-destruction of metaphor is the absolute rupture of the balance itself, of the absolute balance of itself, the absolute transcendence of the point within itself where metaphor might carry its death, differing from and deferring to itself in its death, the point within itself by which metaphor is separated from itself, the point within itself neither itself nor existence. The univocal predication of being itself is the absolute transcendence of the *point of self* within itself, thought absolutely transcending the *point of self* upon which the 'opposition of the metaphoric and the proper' turns, thought absolutely transcending the metaphor of itself (the metaphoric itself) in the metanomous identity of thought with the thing itself/the existence of itself/time itself, in the absolute identity of the absolute actuality of knowledge itself, in the absolute objectivity of the identity of knowledge itself. The identity of knowledge is not the double within itself of identity, the double itself/the division within identity. The univocal predication of being itself is the absolute transcendence of the without within itself within which is nothing, the death carried within itself by a metaphor opposed to itself from without. The absolute transcendence of metaphoric thought is not the saying of death (the saying of nothing in essence) which reduces the opposition as such to irrelevance through the explosion of the mid-point with its 'boundless consequences'. The absolutely irrelevant language of the real existence of itself *is* (without the possibility of reappropriation) a 'full language' *with* syntax, the 'vocation of a pure nomination' *with* 'differential syntax', with a properly *named* articulation which *is irr*educible to the 'semantic *relève* or the dialectical interiorization', at once, *qua* language of life itself transcending the irrelevance of itself, *not* death speaking. The irrelevance of this language is itself the beginning. The remainder of itself the irreducible transcendence of itself, this language is the absolute context existing in time in the form of the irreducible, in the form of the minimum. This language does not say (any)thing beyond the minimum, lest, in going too quickly, it pass beyond the *novitas mundi* essentially or categorically, beyond the known necessity of the freedom of existence which is the metanomy transcending the circle of circles (the science of logic within which logic coincides with *metaphysics*), lest it pass beyond the foundation which is language for the first time the freedom of personality, the foundation which is foundation itself for the first time, lest, itself, it cease to essentially transcend itself, lest it pass beyond the bond of language loosed, the objectification of freedom in the form of the quantum quality of language transcending the totality of identity, lest it pass beyond the economy of language which is the existence of *itself*, lest it pass beyond the absolute economy of the language of existence which transcends the contradiction of the absolute existing/the second absolute, which is itself being itself the absolute transcendence of itself, *itself being itself* the actual *existence of the second absolute,*[21] the univocal predication of being itself in the form of the name of an existing person. The limit of language itself is the essential limit of this language: this language is language itself for the first time: the absolute is this absolute beginning: not being, but being itself is this language, this existing metanomy, this person freely existing in time, this freedom of personality itself a person: being itself is this language, this absolute objectivity of the person, whether written down or spoken aloud, or neither in the silence of the transcendental imagination of the beginning. This language itself is the sounding of the species of perception. Personality is the absolute objectivity of language: the person itself is this language bound by the logic of existence to speak of itself as foundation itself, to univocally predicate being itself of every-thing/every-person in the form of the absolute articulation of the name of being, the absolutely spaceless articulation of foundation itself in the form of the fourth circle, in the form of the meta-identity of existence, in the form of the existence of the Trinity which is the absolutely spaceless articulation of being itself, in terms of which it is readily apparent that, strictly, there is no beyond being, no outside, into which this language (which is language itself) might pass (the negative form of passage to the outside, the explosion of the division within identity, denied to this language as to any qualified thing or person, to (any)thing or (any)person which, insofar as it is being itself, is a person, is, *this* thing, *this* word, *this* page, *this* person, possessed of a specificity neither its own nor that of another, but of an absolute specificity, and is absolutely the property of existence). For this language the limit is the beginning of the existence of being. This language for the first time essentially knows nothing of the self-reflected difference of existence, nor of the critiques thereof—whether in the relative or absolute mode—which belong to thought absolutely past, either, respec-

[21] It is to be noted that just here the thinking now occurring for the first time transcends the essence of American pragmatism. For the latter the *existence* of the second absolute is essentially and categorically a *possibility,* merely *ideal.*

tively, by way of anticipation or by way of extension.[22] In the absolute objectivity of the person freely existing in time, in this language which is the foundation itself, the *very for-the-first-time-form-of-man,* in the language which is the being itself of personality, in the language of language itself (the absolute context/the essentially contextual reality of beginning) wherein there is no subject-matter (ὑποκείμενον) to be distinguished from *this* word, *this* ink, *this* reader, from the predicate (primary being) (τόδε τι). The thinking now occurring for the first time absolutely eliminates the distinction fundamental to the *metaphysics* of Aristotle, and present in one or another form in all subsequent forms of metaphysical thinking, including the form of inversion which is modern 'metaphysics', even including the abysmal inversion, which is the infinite multiplication of contexts, the absolute postponement of the subject matter, the absolute undermining of the primacy of being. Related to this distinction (the distinction of logical from ontological being, the logical form transcending the ontological difference, which form of language, *merely formal* language, is not left behind in the differing from and deferring of itself which is *la différance,* for all that it does to confront philosophy with another kind of totality)—also left behind in the thinking now occurring—is the distinction of primary being from name, which distinction is actually the form of the pre-logical form of the ontological difference, the form of the formless material existence of identity, the formless distinction of language from being, the pre-logical form of the logical predication of the formless identity, the apparently absolutely self-evident presupposition of the language of thought (and of the language decentering thought) before now (before the language of language itself is heard to speak). The distinction underlying the formal distinction of language from thought, the primitive underlying the critical distinction, both operate together in Parmenides' dictum that 'one should both say and think that being is', which may be unwoven: 'it is necessary to say that being is, and it is also necessary to say

[22] Cf. Derrida, *Margins of Philosophy,* pp. 287ff., for Derrida on Valéry on Descartes, etc.

that being is being, which is to say, to think that being is', which unweaving does justice to Parmenides' other famous dictum: 'for it is "the identical" to think and to be', but not, it may be understood, to say. Both distinctions (language/being : language/thought) are fundamental both to 'philosophy' and to the violation of philosophy, to the merely formal identity of the thought existing in the form of the science of logic, and to the violation of the embouchure of that identity, to the absolutely generic law of identity of the former, and to the absolute generalizing of the law of the absolute genus, to the absolute multiplication of beginnings, to *la différance* which in its own not-being of the language of being is 'neither a word nor a concept', but the absolute generation of language, the infinite alternation of being and not-being in the spacing of language, infinite postponement (were it possible) of the transcendence of time itself for the first time. But in the language of language itself, the language which is *being the language of thought itself,* in which there is no subject-matter radically because there is no being not saying, no outside of the text to be denied, no non-being whatsoever to be reckoned with, no primitive remainder a possible outside to the absolute economy of the language of existence, no thing not thought itself for the first time, in *this* language *this* thing is categorically itself transcendent. For the first time the thing itself is the categorical absolute, as such it is a certain absolute: *qua* absolute itself, it is a certain itself: *qua* meta-identity it is an actual identity, it is actually the name of itself, the actual quality of itself, the actual existence of itself, itself the existing species. The absolute species of being is for the first time *unum esse.* In the language of language itself *esse* is identical with *exsistere. Ipsum esse unum* identifies the absolute existence of being itself. For the first time very existence is the absolutely unconditioned transcendental identity. It is not as if existence itself were but a form, as if after the first there were no second itself, as if itself were not itself transcending itself for the first time, as if time itself were not the *existence* of the beginning, as if there were a being itself not being for the first time (in the absolute rupture from *metaphysics* of which contrary-to-fact condition consists *la différance*) but being in some mode (the generic essence of modernity being itself the not-being of something), being itself not being but being something: the merely formal predicament of existence: the non-categorical existence either absolute idea or absolute matter. In fact there is now for the first time in history absolutely and essentially no negative predication of being; there is no *unum* not *unum esse*, no *unum* that is not the existence of being itself, that is not *univocal*, and no univocal that is not *ipsum esse unum*, no univocal not being itself predicated of a thing/a name/an existence in the form of the name of being, in the form of the name transcending every name: *the absolutely irreversible actuality of language itself speaking the name of being*: no name not transcending every name is predicated univocally of (any)thing/(any)person actually existing in time, but *this* name is so predicated. No name but this name actually exists in time. *This* name *is* the differential syntax. *This* name, absolutely differentiated from *this* man, is the absolute objectivity of *this* man. In the midst of *this* man and *this* man *this* name exists itself. In the midst of these irreducible absolutes this irreducible absolute: the midst itself is one, *unum ipsum esse*, the univocal predication of itself. In the midst of the foundation stones foundation itself exists: the beginning of the metanoetic foundation of the society embodying the new order itself, subject neither to death nor decay, constituted in the freedom of personality, in the existence of an absolute objectivity, the beginning of the liberation of every-thing (of every-person) from the limit of either its own self or that of another (self): the inception of the liberation of each thing or person from the actuality or potentiality of differing from or deferring itself: for the first time the liberation of each thing or person in itself from either the substance or the essence of nothing in essence. There is for the first time neither a substance nor an essence other than the objectivity of itself perpetually existing: conceived in essence this metanomous itself is the beginning of the foundation of a universal society.

4

REVOLUTIONARY *METANOĒSIS*: FOUNDATION OF SOCIETY ITSELF

In the midst of the revolution itself, the revolutionary transcendence of force. The absolute appearance of revolutionary society. Itself metanomous transcends the absolutely brute conception of itself, the brute transcendence of itself: not the affirmation, but the absolute transcendence of the brute itself. This revolution is not the transcendence, without identity, of the brute itself, the ideal ecstatic transcendence of pure revolution, the embodiment of the conception of the will to power, the recognition, before now, that there was no matter of society itself. This revolution is not that absolute undermining of the immanent, impure embodiment of revolutionary will, not the absolutely unconditioned inversion, before now, of contingency to Nothing. Nor is this revolution the repetition of pure revolution in the form of the Nothing, Nothing in the form of pure thought, the absolute speculation which is the transcendence of pure revolution, thought essentially Being given for the truth of Being, thought essentially not Being itself. This revolution is not that brute transcendence lacking identity, that merely formless objectivity existing in thought. Nor is this revolution the brute itself lacking identity, the brute lack of identity, the revolution in the form of Nothing itself, in the form of the abyss of thought, the revolution in the form of not-the-revolution-itself, *la différance*. But this revolution does not merely exist, nor is it merely thought; neither merely different, nor merely absolute, this revolution is for the first time revolution itself. As such, this revolution is the absolute final differentiation of itself in the midst of revolution from itself the revolutionary Nothing, the revolutionary embodiment of Nothing, the counterpart to the brute absence of identity, viz., the brute presence of identity, the total presence which is the abysmal form of the Body. This revolution, the *embodiment of the revolutionary foundation of society,* in differentiating revolution from the pure, unembodied revolution which was the Nothing, in separating itself from nothing with the revolutionary form of itself (with the form itself of the logic of the new itself[1]), separates itself, with the absolute precision of itself, the absolute precision of thought, not only from the revolutionary embodiment of itself Nothing itself, not only from the total absence which is the infinite multiplication of contexts/the presence of violence itself/the violence itself of Nothing not itself, but also from the revolutionary embodiment of itself Nothing purely, also from the total presence which is the absence of violence itself/the pure force of domination/the appropriation of pure lordship. This revolution separates itself not only from the violence of Nothing itself not itself, but also from the violence of Nothing itself. The revolutionary embodiment of the infinite patience of existence itself separates itself not only from the infinite impatience which is the violation of the circle, but also from the infinite patience which is the oblivion of the circle/the circle of oblivion, the oblivion of existence (to be distinguished from the oblivion of Being in the cipher-Being text), the retreat from itself, pure backtracking into Nothing from itself, the revolutionary Nothing (not itself), the abyss of infinite non-existence, the Body Abysmal. The revolution now for the first time embodying absolute identification itself separates itself not only from the abysmal conception of the body, but also from the latter's counterpart, the abysmal practice of the body/the practice of the Body Abysmal, *ir*reducible to the abyss of thought. This prime originality of practical Presence (total presence), by which, without transcending the abyss of thought, it is irreducible to the abyss of thought, this absolutely pure quality of the abyss stands in relation to the transcendence of the abyss in proportion as its irreducibility to the abyss of thought mirrors the latter's irre-

[1] Cf. above, p. 151.

ducibility to the former, as follows (let A = the Body Abysmal/pure revolutionary presence [Altizer], let D = the abyss of thought/*la différance* [Derrida], let N^2 [N= the abyss/pure revolution (Nietzsche)] = the abyss of existence/brute transcendence of Being without itself [Heidegger]):

$$A : D :: D : N^2,$$

in which proportion is mediated, by the abyss of itself, the abyss of absolute non-existence with the abyss of existence (this mediate identity in proof form: $D^2 = AN^2$): the proportion of the abyss/the abysmal proportion in which the absolutely pure quality of the abyss transcends the measure of the abyss precisely as absolute Presence, as total domination, as the mastery of an absolutely pure materialism: the pure materialism of the lordship of history (A), standing in a proportionate relation to its counterpart, the pure domination of absolute idealism/of the philosophical itself, the absolutely pure mastery of violence (D), as follows: (let M = historical materialism = 1^n [Marx], let N = $1^n/0$ [Nietzsche], let K^2 [K= transcendental idealism = 1 (Kant)] = absolute idealism/ideal existent freedom/the pure form of metaphysical appropriation [Hegel]):

$$KN : (K)NM :: (K)NM : N^2$$

that is, $A : D :: D : N^2$, which, substituting the alternate values, and allowing 0 to function as a natural number,

$$\frac{1^{n+n}}{0} : \frac{(1)1^{n+n}}{(1)0} :: \frac{(1)1^{n+n}}{(1)0} : \frac{1^{n+n}}{0^2},$$

proven such that $([K]NM)^2/KN^3$, i.e., D^2/AN^2, equals 0^1, which Nothing, the proof-product of the abysmal proportion, serves to distinguish, with absolute precision, the primal originality of total Presence ($1^{n+n}/0$), the abyss of transcendental idealism/the Presence of the total matter of non-existence, the absolutely pure quality of the abyss, this brute immanence of Being without itself, to distinguish it (A or KN), on the one hand, from the abyss of metaphysics, the suspension of the essence in non-existence/the abyss of existence, the universal moment of the self-opposition of absolute idealism, the absolute inversion of the contingent existence of the world to Nothing in essence ($1^{n+n}/0^2$), on the one hand, from this form of the transcendence of Nietzsche (N^2), and, on the other hand, from its *simply* being the form of a meta-historical materialism, from *simply* being a transcendental revolutionary idealism, from being simply abyss-less transcendental-historical idealistic materialism, as it otherwise would *simply* be in the reduction, $A = D^2/N^2$, or $KN = (K)^2M^2$ ($1^{n+n}/0 = 1^{n+n}$), were it not for the Nothing (not itself), 0^1, which, while penultimately integrating the abysmal proportion as formal appropriation of the will to power by an absolute materialism ($1^n : 0 :: 1^n : [1]$, i.e., $N = M$), is ultimately that to which is absolutely reduced an unthought transcendental idealism, in the form: $0 = 1/1$ (i.e., $0 = [1]$, or $0 = [K]$), which absolute reduction to Nothing is the absolute quality of the abyss without itself being other than itself, without the terms absolutely mediating the abysmal measure, without identity mediating the transcendence of the abyss: the absolute repetition of the abyss without identity/the abyss of identity not identity: the abyss of absolute non-existence, the absolute inversion of the abyss: the brute without measure. The abyss of proportion the abyss itself without proportion: the absolute inversion of the abyss: measure without measure: limit without limit: the brute itself without reference *to* itself: without reference *to* the absolute abyss, the absolute reference *of* abyss/the absolute abyss of reference, the abyss of absolute reference: not merely the abyss itself affirming itself negating itself ($[1]1^{n+n}/[1]0$), the abyss divided for and against itself (the precision from the division transcending the absolute inversion of the abyss/from the abyss absolutely integrated with Nothing [$1^{n+n}/0^2$], the abyss itself outside of itself, the [outside-]transcendence of the abyss), but the abyss absolutely incorporating the dialectic of affirmation-negation without limit, absolutely without reference to, but not without without: the univocal Nothing not itself, neither conceived as Being (N^2), nor conceived as itself ($[K]NM$), the abysmal not without reference to transcendence, the absolute inversion of the abyss (not the absolute version of the abyss, the Nothing not the univocal predication of being itself), the essential negation of transcendent existence (opposed to the merely formal negation of itself, the essential affirmation of itself/of thought), the essential negation of itself, essentially pure dialectical immanence the self-conscious form of the theological essence of modern thought, the absolute self-consciousness of the theology of the moderns in its purest form, the revolutionary Nothing (not itself). So Altizer in *The Descent Into Hell:*

> Today it is Christian theologians who must learn the meaning of a radical eschatological faith from seemingly anti-Christian revolutionaries!
>
> . . . Modern revolutionary assaults upon the whole movement of a profane or secular history can now serve not only as models but also as sources for a revolutionary theological assault upon the history of faith. Indeed, such an assault has already occurred in revolutionary thinking, and not only in the apparently anti-Christian thinking of Hegel, Marx, and Nietzsche, but also in the manifestly Christian thinking of Blake, Kierkegaard, and Dostoyevsky. Already these thinkers have forged a path which promises to lead to a full understanding of how the whole history of faith can betray and reverse itself. Perhaps thereby we shall come to see not only how the Christian God has evolved into the opposite of his original identity, but also how the Christian God now embodies in a reverse form his original promise and life
>
> . . . a universal motif of [the] modern quest for faith is the dialectical principle that the most thorough, most comprehensive, and most total negation either goes hand in hand with or culminates in a correspondingly comprehensive and total affirmation. In one sense, this modern dialectical principle is simply a rebirth and renewal of the classical religious way. For example, we can see its counterpart in Buddhism's absolute negation of the illusion and pain of samsara as the hither side of its total affirmation of Nirvana. We can also see its counterpart, and no doubt its historical antecedent, in the biblical expressions of a prophetic and eschatological faith where a radical condemnation of and opposition to the old form or aeon of the world is inseparable from a passionate celebration of a new aeon of grace. But modern dialectical thinkers have given this classical religious way a new form and expression by abolishing its former limits, thereby extending faith or dialectical

vision throughout the whole domain of thinking and experience. Thus they have abolished every distinction between faith and subjectivity, or consciousness and its ground, or the totality of interior experience and its exterior pole or source. . . . it is already clear that the act of negation which is so central in modern dialectical thinking and vision serves not only to shatter or dissolve every existing judgment or conception but also to re-embody these dismembered fragments into a new and total whole. . . .

Once we reach some understanding of the full movement of dialectical faith and vision, it should become apparent that if full affirmation can be realized only through genuine negation, then the possibility of negation is a necessary ground of affirmation. Then faith can recognize that dying forms of consciousness and society are a consequence of what must be named as grace as well as judgment. For the Christian who lives in expectation of a new aeon of grace, when the Kingdom of God will be all in all, the advent of the possibility of the negation of the deepest ground of faith can be greeted as the way to the realization of faith itself. Thus the appearance to us of an absent and silent God who is humanly unnameable, of a distant and alien God standing wholly beyond consciousness, can be named by faith as the true form and name of God for us. The very emptiness and vacuity of the God who is now manifest to us can make possible faith's negation of God. Through the gift of the passion of Christ the Christian knows that God has given Himself wholly to us, and it is just through this passion that God in Christ is most fully actual in consciousness and experience. So it is that the God who is negated in faith is the God who negated and transcended Himself in Christ, thereby making possible the realization of the new creation which Jesus promised. Certainly the death of God is a Christian symbol, pointing to the center of what the Christian has always known as the passion of Christ. But only in the modern era has the death of God become the center of faith, and in that center we have been given a portal through which to pass to the Christ who is uniquely present and real today, and whom the Christian can know as the revolutionary way to the new life and world ahead of us.[2]

[2] Altizer, *The Descent Into Hell,* (reprint; New York, 1979), pp. 52ff.

The univocal Nothing not itself, the essential negation of itself, the absolute inversion of the abyss is the Nothing *in* itself/the Nothing in-itself, the inversion of thought-itself-except-for-the-abysmal-not/of *D* or (*K*)*NM*, the abysmal version of the in-itself, the *in* itself/the in-itself except for the abysmal not (*A* or *KN*), the *in* except for the absolute inversion of the abyss, except for the revolutionary embodiment of Nothing purely itself. In place of the *in*, the pure violence of a totally present Body itself, not the mere presence of violence itself (*D*), but the inversion of the embodiment of the violence of Nothing not itself, not the mere violence of Nothing not itself itself/not thought itself (*D*), but the embodiment of precisely *that* Nothing, viz., the Nothing prescinded from the transcendence of *Dasein* (the Nothing/Being itself/Body/thought in essence, essentially fragmented: the pure fragmentation of death, the death of God *unqualifiedly unqualified*), which abysmal embodiment of violence is the 're-embodiment' of the death of God essentially disembodied, the 're-embodiment' of the death of a disembodied Christ/of an absolutely disembodied death, the transcendence of the violence of Nothing itself not itself, the transcendence/not transcendence of the violence of Nothing, itself the perception 'that the act of negation . . . serves not only to shatter or dissolve every existing judgment or conception but also to re-embody these dismembered fragments into a new and total whole', the perception itself of the inside of the abyss/the abyss itself inside itself: the (inside-)transcendence of the abyss, 'the death of God' 'pointing to the center' 'of the passion of Christ': the abyss incorporating the existence of the extra Nothing (0^1): nothing, including the extra Nothing, outside the abysmal proportion: the extra nothing the inside itself of the abyss: itself the center pointing to itself: the Body swallowed in the abyss: the extra abyss/the outside abyss/the abyss of the outside/the outside of the abyss, the inside of the abyss: the abyss of the abyss itself/the abyss of the abyss of the outside/inside pointing to the outside inside of itself as the 'portal' to the total presence which is the future of absolute world-consciousness: the abyss encircling transcendence/transcendence within the abyss of transcendence: the double division of the abyss of itself, the absolute double division of Nothing itself: Nothing not itself not existing: the absolute affirmation of Nothing, the affirmation of the abyss/the abysmal affirmation (the abysmal measure), including the extra Nothing, the Nothing without: the absolute integration/absolute disintegration of the abyss. The abyss itself of absolute non-existence, the absolute inversion of the abyss, is the abyss of the act of negation, at once the abysmal affirmation, total presence or the non-existence/pure future of absolute world-consciousness the transcendental form of the abyss of idealism: the abyss of the ideal forms of a thinking not existing: the abyss embodying a revolutionary Presence. This is the abyss in the form of the retreat from itself; this is the form of the retreat from the death of the body, the form of the pure backtracking from the body of death, from the pain of the body, not from the suffering of the body, but from the body suffering Nothing, to the presence of the body embodying Nothing: from the body suffering Nothing, to the Presence of Nothing *to* the body, to the *absolute embodiment* of the eternal recurrence of all things, to the absolute evacuation from the body of the element of resistance to force: the retreat from the death of the body to death not itself, to the force of itself evacuated from itself, to the transcendence of death/the death of transcendence (its incorporation within the abyss of identity, transcendence within the abyss of identity not identity): the retreat from the death of itself to the future itself/the abysmal reality here & now, to the domination of a pure force, of a force without force, of a force without existence. This is the abyss of the future itself safeguarding the future itself in the form of the immanence of the passion of Christ, in the form of the pure silence of the body, in the form of the immanence of itself not itself existing, in the form of the immanence of the act of negation 'so central in modern dialectical thinking and vision', in the form of the abysmal negation of immanence/transcendence, in the form of the abysmal passageway of the immanence of Christ's suffering, in the form of the abysmal rite of passage to the future itself: the future itself safeguarded in the abyss of the future itself, in the form of the passion of Christ an absolute instrumentality not suffering Nothing, in the form of the dead body oblivious to the death of itself, in the form of the Presence of the transcendence of transcendence itself, in the form of transcendence itself except for the abysmal not itself, in the form of the presence of the body to the body, the Presence identifying itself as the Body not Nothing, as total Presence: the future itself safeguarded in the absolute inversion of the abyss in the form of its opposite, in the form of Nothing itself not existing, in the form of the past itself: in the absolute inversion of the abyss (in the abysmal embodiment of the affirmation of existence/the abysmal embodiment of the precision of Nothing/the abysmal embodiment of the actual transcendence of Nothing), in the abyss of the affirmation of absolute reference, in the actual abyss of negation, the transcendence of the past safeguarded in the pure form of its opposite, in the pure form of the future: the Presence of salvation/the salvation of Presence, the form of an actually existing future: Presence the form of the future: the abysmal form of the domination of the future. The absolute inversion of the abyss (*KN*) is not the abyss itself ([*K*]*NM*), but *the abyss of the modern itself,* the safeguarding of modernity from absolute repetition. *The absolute inversion of the abyss is the safeguarding of modernity from absolute inversion,* the safeguarding of modernity from existence *ex futuro,* the abysmal postponement by the abyss of the past of the abyss itself: the limit without limit but not without itself: the limit without limit but not without without: itself without but not without itself the abysmal inversion of itself: instead of the circle itself, the circle of oblivion, the absolute forgetfulness of itself, the lethal form of transcendence, the absolute backtracking from itself into the Nothing before creation, the re-embodiment of the abyss, the abysmal repetition of itself.

But the transcendence of the absolutely abysmal repetition now actually occurs for the first time in history, the absolute transcendence of the absolute repetition of the abyss in the form of the absolute repetition of modernity, in the form of the transcendence of non-existence *ex nihilo,* the absolute transcendence/existence of existence *ex futuro,* the absolute transcendence of transcendence, not the immanence of Christ's transcendence, but the transcendence of Christ's transcendence, the existence *ex futuro/ex nihilo* of the passion of Christ:

not itself without not without without, but *ex nihilo* without without/the absolute without: the transcendence of transcendence without, (not within, but) without transcendence: not the Presence, but the transcendence of transcendence itself: Christ absolute, Christ itself, Christ without/without Christ: not transcendence itself not without Nothing, but transcendence itself without not without Nothing: the passion of Christ not the portal to a Presence, but the essence of identity: the passion of Christ without Christ/the absolute passion itself of Christ repeating itself, now for the first time in history, in the essence of thought (not the unqualified absolute repetition of the abyss): the absolute passion itself of Christ the essential form of society itself. Now for the first time in actuality the existence of the past itself of the abyss, that is, not the transcendence of the abyss, incorporated within the absolute inversion of the abyss, in the absolutely abysmal reversal, as the pure form of the future, as Presence, but the actual transcendence of Nothing *ex abysso*, the absolute transcendence of the negation of beginning: not the affirmation of the abyss, but *ex abysso* the existence of existence: existence itself the negation of beginning, existence itself for the first time the existence of the passion of Christ: *Christ without Christ (the passion of Christ) for the first time the very essence of identity,* the known fact itself, the out-identity (there being no out*side*-identity of the absolute plaintext, no out*side* of transcendence *ex abysso*, of transcendence without point, of without itself without center, of existence without division, neither point, nor center, nor division of transcendence without *side*, there being no out-*side*-identity of the circle itself: there being no out*side*-identity of the outside absolutely without, of the absolute limit without limit): the passion of Christ the absolute out-identity of existence (the absolute meta-identity of the identity of existence, since with without out/out without with is out absolutely with/with itself out): the outside of thought itself existing as thought in essence, the absolute outside of thought actually existing freely in time: for the first time the absolute reference the very midst of existence itself. This absolute out-identity of (any)side (Christ existing without Christ/I Am speaking for the first time without existing in time, the first absolute silence, the absolute impossibility of any ecstasy whatsoever), this absolute passion of existence, is the logical foundation of an absolute society: this beginning is the fact of the absolute freedom of this passion. This passion clings not to the inside of the abyss, retreating from itself abysmally in the form of the transcendence of the abyss, the absolute re-embodiment of the original abyss. This passion of existence absolutely creates itself/itself creates absolutely. This passion of existence is the absolute creation of the world: the creation *ex abysso.* The creation of the world *ex abysso* is this passion itself for the first time making the transcendent world/making the existing world. This for the first time absolutely passionate creation of the world, this beginning of the absolutely passionate making of the actuality of the world, is the foundation, firmer than which none can be conceived, of an absolute world society now beginning to exist for the first time in history. This world is constructed *ex futuro,* after the future, *ex nihilo,* after non-existence, *after* the pure Nothing which is total presence. For the first time the circle itself exists, the passion of Christ creates the world, the absolute out-identity exists, identity is absolutely without, without without. For the first time identity is absolutely without identity, absolutely without the identity of identity, absolutely without reference to the inside of the abyss itself, the abyss of the inside itself with which 'modern dialectical thinking and vision' (non-essential, purely formal dialectical thinking) has identified the outside: the circle itself exists absolutely without reference to a source within itself, to a point/pole/stake within itself, by which it (the circle itself existing/the absolute out-identity of existence/the *actual* second absolute) might be referred to the outside, by which it might, the circle itself the existing midst, be other than the absolute reference, by which it might be assimilated to the abysmal form of existence within itself, to the exterior pole within itself, within the 'totality . . . of experience'. The circle itself existing/the passion itself of existence, is not merely itself, it is the transcendence of itself, it is existence absolutely, the transcendence of the totality of experience, the transcendence of the totality of identity: the absolute out-identity of existence transcends the totality of identity: this for the first time is the new creation of the transcendental world: the transcendental world 'in Christ': the in-itself absolutely transcendental/the absolute transcendence of the absolute necessity of thought (not merely the ideal of finite knowledge/the ideal freedom of necessity [Kant], nor the ideal freedom of finite knowledge, the ideal of absolute knowledge/the ideal freedom transcending necessity, the existent ideal of freedom [Hegel], but), the existent freedom of finite knowledge, the transcendence of absolute necessity absolutely in the form of thought: knowledge absolutely the knowledge of identity in itself: the absolute freedom of an actually absolute knowledge: the brute in itself absolutely thought/the absolute out-identity of the thing-in-itself: for the first time the absolute existential appearance of the intelligible kingdom: the passionate making of the transcendent world *ex arte.* This world creation *ex arte* is, *a fortiori,* absolutely separated in existence/in essence from the absolute inversion of the abyss (*KN*), the abyss of transcendental idealism, which is the ideal resurrection-identity of brute reality in the form of total presence. The latter is the ideally transcendental resurrection of the brute reality of things in the form of the conditional necessity of the 'speech realizing itself in silence' to recur 'again and again', in the form of the given, necessary conditions for the 'presence' of 'self-identity' which constitute the darkness, the pure determination of itself, the brute actuality of the resurrection in the form of the ideal necessity of the abyss of freedom, in the form of the given, necessary conditions for the inhuman experience constituting the self-determination of the body of God, in the form of the abyss of the ideal of finite knowledge, as delineated by Altizer in *The Self-Embodiment of God:*

> Only a full self-emptying can embody the pure act of speech, for only that emptying can fully release the ultimate ground of speech.
>
> That emptying enacts the advent of total presence, the total presence of speech in act. Yet the advent of total presence is both silent and invisible. Nothing apparently or manifestly distinguishes its identity from any other identity if only because the purity of its presence transcends and leaves behind all pos-

> sibility of names and signs. True, it embodies the identity and thus the name of "I Am," but in the totality of this embodiment that name becomes silent. Total presence does not name itself in speech alone, and cannot do so, if only because all such naming detaches speech from act. Nor can signs of any kind point to the advent of total presence. On the contrary, signs can only disguise and veil that presence, and must do so if only because they invariably distinguish presence from absence and here from there. Once presence is present, and is totally present, absence disappears, and disappears in the totality of presence. Then nothing whatsoever can point to presence, or to pure presence, for then there can be nothing related or open to presence which is apart or distant from presence. Total presence witnesses to itself, but such witness cannot act by names and signs, it can act only by enacting itself.[3]

Not world creation *ex arte/ex nihilo*, presence witnesses, but that witness is embodiment. Presence witnesses the actual totality of embodiment, the totality of identity. Presence witnesses the identity of itself. This is not the abyss of itself (*D* or [*K*]*NM*), the abyss of itself merely/the identity not identity of the ceaseless differing from and deferral of itself/thought not itself witnessing its own not itself. This is the abyss of the ideal itself/the abyss of identity not identity/itself not itself witnessing (not its own not itself, but) Nothing itself: the pure presence of identity: not the inactive and unreal self-identity, merely not its own itself, self-identity in the presence of absolute violence, but rather, in the ideal abyss of itself, the 'active and real' self-identity of Nothing, self-identity 'enacting' its own not-identity:

> The self-embodiment of an actually present silence releases self-identity from its ground and source. Now self-identity can be active and real only insofar as it enacts its groundlessness. That self-enactment draws the presence of the actuality of silence into the center of self-identity. Then self-identity can be active and real only insofar as it actually silences itself. Moreover that silencing cannot be a mere inactivation or diminution

[3] T. J. J. Altizer, *The Self-Embodiment of God* (New York, 1977), p. 78.

> of speech. It is far rather a movement or a process in which speech actively and actually silences itself. For the immediate presence of the actuality of silence activates rather than disengages speech, it acts upon it by entering into its very center. Then an actual silence is present at the center of speech, and speech can speak only by enacting silence. Or speech can now speak only by enacting the actual and present silence of its own self-identity. And that self-identity does not thereby become simply silent, it rather becomes actual and real insofar as it empties itself of its own speech.[4]

Further on:

> Finally, self-identity can be itself only in silence, a silence which is actual, and a silence which is enacted in speech. That silence which is the final self-enactment of self-identity is a silence which actually dawns, which actually occurs. And it occurs in its enactment, in that act and in those acts wherein speech silences itself. Speech cannot actually silence itself simply by ceasing to speak. It can actually silence itself only by its own act, a real act, and an act in which speech is itself even in its negation of itself. Just as speech is a unique and integral realization of self-identity, then so likewise the self-silencing of speech is a unique and integral act of self-realization. And act it is in its enactment, an act or acts in which speech enacts its own end. That end is both the final end and the final realization of self-identity. Its very advent enacts the ending of all that speech whereby identity is fully and only itself. With that ending, identity can speak, and can actually speak, only by negating itself, only by silencing itself. Yet that silencing is real, and is real in its speech, a speech which negates itself insofar as it speaks.[5]

Not world creation *ex arte/ ex nihilo,* this identity not identity the transcendence of the absolute its own, abysmal abyss of itself (the absolutely pure quality of the abyss, at once transcending/

[4] Ibid., p. 86.
[5] Ibid., pp. 89–90.

not transcending the abyss of thought, the abyss of the abyssal itself), this abysmal transcendental idealism/identity not identity the 'actual and real' speech *its own* silence, the emptiness of itself *its own* itself, the emptiness of witness *its own* (the 'active and real' self-identity of Nothing/the total self-embodiment of God/the Presence of Totality), this pure quality of the absolute perception of Nothing, this, is the abysmal form of apperception: the witness *not* the abyss of itself/the witness its own emptiness, the absolute inversion of the abyss. The transcendental apperception of Nothing is this Totality of Presence, this total self-embodiment of God, this empty martyrdom of 'its own', this martyrdom empty of 'its own', this 'its own' empty of 'names and signs'. This 'self-silencing of speech', this self-transcendence of Nothing, *is* the brute 'its own', the brute identity of presence, the abyss within the *not* in the abyss of itself, within the itself not itself except for the abyss, the inside of the abyss itself not itself except for the abyss, the abyss within the not in-itself of the abyss, the 'center of self-identity' into which 'self-enactment draws the presence of the actuality of silence': the abyss within the absolute reference of the abyss: the pure not into which active and real self-identity draws the identity of presence: the pure not into which the self-transcendence of Nothing (this abysmal apperception) draws identity not itself, that not which is the abyss witnessing itself (the abyss within the abyss of itself), which is the purity of the given, necessary conditions for the realization of total presence, which is the pure form of the conditional necessity of the totality of presence:

> Speech finally enacts itself as silence in actuality, and fully and finally enacts its silence in actuality. Then silence is embodied in every actual presence, and every actual presence is an enactment of silence. And not only an enactment, but a self-enactment, a self-enactment whereby the actuality of presence is inevitably the self-actualization of silence. The presence of that silence is a self-embodying presence, a presence calling all presence to itself, and thereby calling all presence to its own self-actualization, one whose fullness can be realized only in the actuality of silence. That fullness has been realized in the actu-

ality of silence, has become incarnate in the finality of self-silencing, and is realized, and is now realized, wherever presence becomes fully actual and immediate. And it becomes fully actual because it has been fully actual, and finally actual, a finality which is total simply because it has occurred. That finality is total in its very occurrence, is total just because it has occurred. Therefore its occurrence occurs even now, and occurs wherever presence is fully itself.

But it can be so only where presence is absence everywhere but where it immediately and actually occurs. Indeed, the silence of that absence is the speech of an actual and immediate presence. Apart from that silence, speech could not totally speak. And once speech has totally spoken, it must henceforth be silent to continue to speak. Silent that is in its evocation of presence, in its evocation of a presence which is anywhere but here. Thereby all presence which is absent, or which is not immediately at hand, comes to an end in total presence. Total presence is total speech, but speech is total only when it is silent, only when it silences every presence that is not immediately present. That silencing occurs wherever presence is immediate and actual, and occurs because silence has actually spoken, and immediately spoken in its own voice. Once that voice has spoken, and has fully and finally spoken, then presence is silence. Presence is then silence because presence has been silenced, and having once been silenced it even now is silence, and is and will be silence wherever presence is fully actual and real.[6]

And finally:

Only when the voice of speech has wholly passed into the voice of silence can resurrection occur, but resurrection does occur in the advent of the voice of silence, and with the full actualization of silence resurrection dawns in all actual presence. But it can so dawn only insofar as it truly activates silence, only insofar as it brings the stillness and passivity of silence to an end.

That end is realized in the movement of speech into silence, a movement whereby the act of speech is enacted in silence,

[6] Ibid., pp. 90–91.

> and enacted so as to actualize silence itself. Only the act of speech can actualize silence but when speech is fully and finally enacted in silence, silence is thereby actualized, and so actualized that it can never again be only silence. Or it can never again be heard as only silence, never again be present and actually present as a silence which is only silence. Once a fully actualized silence dawns, it dawns again and again, and dawns so as to draw all actual silence into itself. Thereby the descent of speech into silence is ever again renewed, renewed and resurrected even now, and resurrected now because it once fully and finally occurred. Once speech has fully perished as speech, or has finally perished as a speech which is only speech, then speech is resurrected wherever hearing occurs, or wherever hearing is fully actual and real. That hearing is real now, is actual now, and is actual wherever actuality is immediately at hand.
>
> And at hand it is in our silence, in a fully actualized silence, in a silence in which distance and otherness are no more.[7]

The 'self-silencing of speech' is the pure not within itself of the abyss within the abyss: the absolute inversion of the abyss embodying the pure not in the form of silence. That not, which is the point of self within the itself of the abyss of itself (that pure not which is absolutely transcended in the univocal predication of being itself), is, in the absolute inversion of the abyss, the point of self within itself outside of itself, the point of self itself without within itself, the point of self itself transcending individual identity: the individual itself transcending individual identity except for the abysmal not: the abyss itself *qua* transcendental, *qua* itself not *in* itself, *qua* transcendental point of self-identity: the abyss itself *qua* ideal, *qua* its own inversion of itself: the abyss itself pure immanence/pure transcendental Nothing/pure death of God: the abyss itself pure abyss: the immanence/transcendence of the abyss of proportion: the absolute quality of the abyss. If the abyss, originally (*N*), is the inversion of the contingency of transcendence to Nothing, the solitude of Nothing before the creation, the absolute inversion

[7] Ibid., pp. 94–95.

of historical materialism to Nothing, the pure revolution/pure embodiment of transcendental freedom in the form of the eternal recurrence of all things, if the transcendence of the abyss, originally (N^2), is the transcendence of the pure embodiment of transcendental freedom, revolutionary transcendence in the form of the transcendence of *Dasein* to Nothing, the transcendence of the solitude of creation before the Nothing, the retreat from historical materialism in the form of the inversion of the contingency of thought to Nothing, in the form of the pure potentiality of the thought of Being (the transcendence of the pure potentiality of creation/of a new being), if the abyss itself (*D* or [*K*]*NM*) is the abysmal solitude of creation, the absolute ciphertext outside of which is Nothing, the pure potentiality of the thought itself of Nothing, thought itself/creation itself except for the abysmal not, the absolute embodiment of transcendental freedom in the form of the temporal recurrence of Nothing, pure transcendental embodiment in the form of Nothing itself, pure transcendental Nothing itself/the univocal Nothing itself, pure potentiality of text, the potential absolute (purely, in the form of the pure presence of violence itself), then, the absolute inversion of the abyss is the re-embodiment of the embodiment of transcendental freedom, is, absolute quality of the abyss, the *same as* the abyss (*KN*), the measure of the abyss not the abyss, the abysmal measure of the abyss the pure not/pure point of self in terms of which the embodiment of transcendental freedom is in the form of a pure Totality/absolutely pure punctuality of self, in the form of the eternal recurrence of all things 'again and again' in the actuality of the self/in the self itself! Not world creation *ex arte/ex nihilo*, the absolute inversion of the abyss is the same as the abyss/the abyss of the *same as,* the as except for the abysmal not: the self-same as the source: the absolutely pure punctuality of the self-embodiment of transcendental freedom: the transcendental self-transcendence of the abyss in the form of the point: the point of the self itself in the other, the pure punctuality of silence silencing itself in actuality, the embodiment of the pure potentiality of a new Being/*consciousness beginning in every now: the absolute embodiment of the transcendental not itself in pure immanence* the self-embodiment of God in the form of the pure immanence of the source itself: the transcendental inversion of the freedom of transcendence in the form of the recurring eternally of Nothing not itself, the univocal Nothing not itself: the transcendence of individual identity in the form of the purely potential 'distance and otherness', in the form of the pure immanence of the 'actual and real': the absolute solitude of Nothing within the creation: Nothing transcending the solitude within. The univocal Nothing not itself is the analogical Nothing itself, the analogy of the abyss, the abysmal proportion. The abysmal analogy: Only death, enveloping the absolute quality of the abyss itself. If, in the past, salvation was present to individual 'interior' consciousness by faith alone, *sola fide*, the presence of salvation to consciousness beginning in every now is by death alone, *sola morte.* This is the abysmal objectivity of the abyss of transcendental idealism, the abysmal version of 'religion within the limits of reason alone', the absolute precision of death from the concrete history of salvation, pure death (the ideal death of the body not itself [the abyss of existence itself but for the abysmal not, death absolutely separated from the body]). This is Jesus, the ideal of total presence, abysmally analogous to Jesus, the ideal of the universal moral disposition, in a form of inversion of the life and death of Jesus which is not *simply* abysmal, not *simply* the abysmal reversal of the same, on the pattern that 'the first shall be last, and the last shall be first' (which pattern itself is no more a simple reversal, a result to begin with, than is that which is here modeled on its being so to all appearances), not *simply* the resultant absolute presence which it finds in the beginning, but the abysmal reversal of the life and death of Jesus, an absolutely specific historical inversion, albeit abysmal, indeed the absolute quality of the abyss absolutely transcending, albeit punctually, the measure of the abyss/its own measure/the measure of itself. It is the *historically* abysmal inversion of the life and death of Jesus, as follows: as (in Kant) the eternal life of Jesus is to his historical individuality, so (in Altizer) is his historical individuality to the eternal death of Jesus, the proof of which proportion is: the transcendence of Jesus' historical individuality is the *identity* of his eternal death and eternal life. This proof of the proportion is the pure immanence of the abyss itself, the absolute inversion of the abyss betraying the abyss itself, in the application of its own measure, as the pure immanence of transcendence, as the self-same/another self: *the other the abyss of self itself.* The abysmal proportion clearly measures the theological language of the absolute inversion of the abyss, as found in Altizer's *The Descent Into Hell:*

> When we recall that the resurrected Christ of ancient Christianity is the celestial and monarchic Christ of glory, there is certainly nothing in the image of the resurrection alone which is singular and unique—except insofar as Christianity went beyond other religions in exalting the power and glory of Christ. It is rather the image of death which takes us into the center of a uniquely Christian way. Jesus not only fully realized his work and proclamation in his death; but in his death he wholly died to everything which was individually and particularly himself. It is not accidental that the writers and editors of the New Testament were so little interested in the individuality and particularity of Jesus. . . . If an eschatological faith is fully realized in Jesus, it is realized in such a manner as to lead to the absolute negation of everything which is humanly and historically his own.
>
> Everything, that is, but his death; for only in his death is the original Jesus still present in history, and only in his dying did he become an individual model for faith. Therefore faith rightly repudiates the "fleshly" Jesus or the "old" Jesus or even Jesus as an individual human being. If the only Jesus who is present to faith is the resurrected Jesus, then the only human image which we can have of Jesus is the image of death, and Jesus becomes for us an eternal Jesus only inasmuch as he is realized as eternal death. Death should be our only image of Jesus, and it is not accidental that we have known him primarily by way of images of the crucifixion—for the crucified Jesus is the only Jesus who can be present at the center of faith. If it is true that it was by way of images of resurrection such as an "arising" to celestial glory that Christianity originally betrayed its founder, then we can return to Jesus only by inverting all such imagery and symbolism. But we can never return to the original Jesus, never know or envision the man whom his disciples

> knew; for that Jesus died on the cross. He is present nowhere but in his death; yet his death is an eternal death and thus is present wherever death is fully actualized and is immediately and finally real.[8]

And to quickly close the proof of the abysmal analogy:

> If the New Jerusalem is the historical actualization of a total but dialectical reversal or an original All, then that All will itself be present in a new and reverse form or identity. The Hell which has appeared and is appearing in our world as a Totality or an All must finally be recognized as a reverse or inverted form of a primordial Heaven. . . .
>
> If the final triumph of Hell is identical with the final emptying of an original Heaven, then an actual way to Heaven can only be real to us as a way to Hell. . . . Only by knowing Hell as the arena and realm of Christ can we freely accept Hell as our destiny, and thereby accept the annihilation of everything we have known as consciousness and experience as a total epiphany of Christ. Once Christ is known as the source and ground of a total transformation of consciousness and experience, then the loss of all we have known as identity and selfhood can be accepted and affirmed as the realization of the presence and compassion of Christ. True darkness can then be known as the fruit of compassion, and the actual death of an individual center of consciousness can then be celebrated as the self-annihilating presence of the universal Christ. Now the way "up" will be the way "down": an ascension to Heaven will be *identical* with a descent into Hell.[9]

Thus the absolute inversion of the abyss/absolute quality of the abyss/abyss of transcendental idealism (*A* or *KN*) is the proof of a proportion which, in every possible sense, its does and does not transcend: the transcendental abyss dissembling the idealism the hypothetical presence of which is an absolute necessity,

8. Altizer, *The Descent Into Hell*, pp. 140–41.
9. Ibid., pp. 212–14.

dissembling the proportion of which it is the proof, as if history itself/the absolute measure of existence were a perfect formality, as if history itself/the history of thought were a perfect immanence: the ratio of proof to measure, the circle of oblivion/the oblivion of the circle. But in the light of the circle itself now existing for the first time in the history of thought as transcendence, as thought itself, in light of the absolute existence of thought, in light of the thinking essentially transcending the history of thought, the circle of oblivion is discovered to itself to be not only the abysmal inversion of the life and death of Jesus *historically*, viz, 'as in K the eternal life of Jesus is to his historical individuality, so in A his historical individuality is to the eternal death of Jesus, proven: the identity of ~~his~~ eternal death and life eternal identically the transcendence of Jesus' historical individuality', but, *qua* dissemblance of the history of thought, *qua* proof of a dissembled proportion, it is at once, KN, the proof of the proportion, $K^2 : N :: K : N^2$, 'absolute idealism is to the abyss as transcendental idealism is to the transcendence of the abyss', the proof of which is: 'the abyss of transcendental idealism identically idealism transcending the abyss itself/the abyss of thought', $1^2 : 1^n/0 :: 1 : 1^{n+n}/0^2$, proven $(1^2 \cdot 1^{n+n}/0^2)/(1 \cdot 1^n/0)$, which is $1 \cdot 1^n/0$ or $1 \cdot 1^n = 0$ or $KM = 0$, i.e., the reduction to Nothing of transcendental idealism identified with historical materialism, the abyss of transcendental idealism, the Nothing of which proof-product, 0, is identically the Nothing, 0^1, which is the proof-product of the abysmal proportion which distinguishes the primal originality of total presence.[10] The proof-product which is the absolute inversion of the abyss is the identity of absolute idealism (K^2) as transcendental idealism (K) identified with the abyss (N) and the inversion of the transcendence of the abyss (N^{-2}), that is, $K^2 = KNN^{-2}$, in the final reduction of which proof (KN or A) Heidegger (N^2), along with Hegel (K^2), is brought to nought: this is the abyss of idealism at once itself the pure Nothing. The abyss of transcendental idealism *is* the transcendence of the abyss of absolute idealism. The primal originality of total presence, *qua* proof, is the dissembled identity of *its*

[10] Cf. above, p. 190.

own implicit presence as the Nothing which is the identity of absolute idealism, that identity by which absolute idealism, in the form of a retreat from itself, in the form of the reduction to Nothing of historical materialism identified with transcendental idealism, safeguards itself in the form of the self-actualizing silence of its own presence (negating itself 'insofar as it speaks', but silencing 'every presence that is not immediately present'), safeguards itself in the timeless form of the future, the immanence of Christ's passion, an eternal death absolutely reversing and inverting the timeless form of the past, eternal life, safeguards itself, this idealism, in the form of the actual reality of the immanence of transcendence, safeguards itself from the Day of Reckoning now actually existing for the first time and essentially in history/for the first time and essentially in thought/for the first time and essentially in the machine, for the first time in the body itself of man, in the man-matter of this existing world, safeguards itself from the Absolute Light, safeguards itself in the abysmal form of the absolute Hypothetical from the Day of Judgment now the actuality of the time-transcendent totality which is time itself, safeguards itself from the real-time reality of the absolute, from the absolute in existence itself beginning and end, safeguards itself from the quantification of thought, safeguards itself in the form of the absolute quality of the abyss from the absolute quality of the quantum itself of language itself, concealing itself in the dissembling of a transcendent identity from the absolute transcendence of a transcendent identity, from the transcendental transcendence of transcendence itself transcendence to which is no opposition or opposite 'integral and inherent' or otherwise possible or actual. The dissembled proportion is the specific history of thought constituting, in its backwards moving forward movement, in its severe dialectic without matter (to which might be counterposed the inessentially dialectical materialism of Marx,[11] the plaintext of which the abyss of transcendental idealism is implicitly the abyss,[12] *qua* transcendent abyss of absolute idealism [*qua* that moment in the reduction of

[11] Cf. above, pp. 51ff.
[12] Cf. above, pp. 94ff.

the dissembled proportion's proof which is $K^2N^2 = KN$, the vanishing moment in which the absolute inversion of the abyss embodies *a priori* the abyss of idealism]), the circle of oblivion, the oblivion of the circle: the dissembled absolutely specific historicity of the absolute inversion of the abyss, of the absolute quality of the abyss, its own abysmal proportionality ($K^2 : N :: K : N^2$), in terms of which alone its application to the life and death of Jesus is intelligible (as distinguished from its rendering intelligible the immaterial movement of modern dialectic in the form of an abysmal darkness), and which is the form in which the abyss of transcendental idealism transcends the measure of the abyss, the abysmal proportion, $KN : (K)NM :: (K)NM : N^2$, the form of its own absolute abyss, abyss of the absolute its own. While, on the one hand, the *non*-vanishing moment in the proof of the abysmal proportion, $K^2M^2 = KN$, identifies the absolute quality of the abyss as *absolute idealism identical with the transcendence of historical materialism, idealism identically materialism, 'Heaven' identically 'Hell'*, on the other hand, the abyss of its own proportionality, $K^2 : N :: K : N^2$, with the *vanishing* moment of its proof, $K^2N^2 = KN$, constitutes, *qua* the idealism of the abyss in the form of the absolute quality of the abyss, precisely, the oblivion of eternality, at once itself the eternality of oblivion, the eternality of the silence of actual death, the eternal presence of the divine totality, the eternality of death in the form of life, the eternal form of the death of Christ: the eternity of the death of Christ in the form of the transcendent identity of an absolute idealism, dissembled in the form of the abyss of transcendental idealism. The intelligibility of the eternal death of Jesus, of the ideal Jesus of total presence, of this eternal recurrence of Nothing not itself, of all things not Nothing, of this eternally recurring Presence (the absolute embodiment of the eternal recurrence of all things), the intelligibility of this Nothing once and for all, is, to begin with, that it is, apart from the abyss of its own proportionality, the absolute non-existence of idealism, but that, within the abyss of its own proportionality, alone, it is the finite transcending its own finitude/the finitude of its own. The intelligibility of this point of the death of self, of this self-centered death, of this self sourced in the solitude of the Nothing before the creation (the self apperceiving the transcendental Nothing as the transcendent Nothing: Nothing not Nothing), is, to begin with, that, apart from the abyss of the absolute its own, it is without its own limit, that it is the limit of the absolute its own, the withdrawal to its own ground of the inherently self-contradictory limit, absolutely its own limit, a retreat from itself which (while it serves absolute idealism in the safeguarding of itself from existence in the midst of the revolution itself) is in fact a *privacy* in the form of a 'total epiphany of Christ', at variance with its own schema, viz., 'the annihilation of everything we have known as consciousness and experience'. But within the abyss of its own absolute, alone, it is, this totality of the presence of Christ, this universal privacy, the absolute transcendence of its own limit (thereby serving absolute idealism in the safeguarding of itself from *non*-existence in the midst of the revolution itself), the ending of transcendence in its own finitude, the absolute transcendence of the solitude of the Nothing which was before the creation. *Solo nihilo* it is this consciousness beginning in every now, its own transcendence, its own proportion: within the abyss of its own proportionality it is apart from its own absolute. The intelligibility of this privacy is the transcendence of its own individuality, is, that is, alone, *its own* absolutely unconditioned: not the absolute repetition of its own, but the break absolutely of the absolute its own with its own, the break of its own transcendence with its own, its own transcendence not its own, the absolute its *own* absolutely not its own: 'the transcendence of Jesus' historical individuality, the identity of ~~his~~ eternal life and eternal death', the proof of the proportion, 'as in *K* etc., so in *A* etc.', which establishes the specifically historical logic of the otherwise implicit intelligibility of the appropriation of its own transcendence which is the total self-embodiment of God, the actual and real movement, not of the Living God, but of the God of Death, of the death of God, of the pure force of Presence. The power of this Presence is its faithfulness to a specifically historical form of thinking in the past, to the dialectical form of modern thought, absolutely embodied in the abyss of its own proportionality, but it is precisely this power of the abyss itself self-sourced in its faithfulness to the past, precisely the absolute self-envelopment of the absolute inversion of the abyss in its own abysmal eternality, precisely this consciousness of its own beginning, precisely the reality of the movement of the abyss, this reality of the abysmal apperception of death, the abyss of the total self-embodiment of God who has, in fact, become Nothing, the *its own* absolutely unconditioned, it is this, precisely, which precludes the perception of the absolute identity of historical existence, which precludes the perception of the absolute historicity of the body. The transcendent intelligibility of the abyss of its own proportionality, the withdrawal of the abyss to the inherently self-contradictory ground-limit of the pure *its own*, the transcendence of the privacy of death/the abysmal transcendence of the private, the abyss of privacy, which is the point of the self-transcendence of the private absolute/ the absolute transcendence of the private center of the self/the absolute source of the private another self, this consciousness of the beginning of the consciousness of the absolute its own, this eternality of the absolute its own in every now, this brace of eternal oblivion in existence/eternal brace of the oblivion of the circle, this faithfulness to the dialectical form of thought existing in the past, this faithfulness to the past itself in the form of the future, which gives 'itself to a negation of every past form of the Word, if only as a means of opening itself to an extension of an eschatological future into the present',[13] in the form of its own measure, this brace of absolute oblivion, is the center of modern consciousness *in extremis*, the final extremity of the self absolutely past, the idea of the total the self-embodiment of God, indeed, the abysmal inversion of religion, the new religion of the absolute inversion of the abyss, that by which it withholds itself, in the form of the abyss of the plaintext, from the absolute abnegation of the self, from the abyss of pure self, from the three-selved source, withholds itself in the form of the totality of the presence of Christ, withholds itself precisely in that form of privacy which names the three-selved source with the name of an historico-ontological process of divine dialectic: the religion of a reli-

[13] T. J. J. Altizer, *The Gospel of Christian Atheism* (Philadelphia, 1966), pp. 83–84.

gionless Christianity delineated by Altizer in *The Gospel of Christian Atheism*, where, referring to Hegel's analysis of the cultic act of sacrifice in *The Phenomenology of Spirit*, he writes:

> The primitive Christian community marks the historical or actual advent of Absolute Spirit because for the first time consciousness recognizes God in immediate present existence, and God is known as self-consciousness because he is beheld sensuously and immediately as the individual self of Jesus.
>
> > This incarnation of the Divine Being, its having essentially and directly the shape of self-consciousness, is the simple content of Absolute Religion. Here the Divine Being is known as Spirit; this religion is the Divine Being's consciousness concerning itself that it is Spirit. For Spirit is knowledge of self in a state of alienation of self: Spirit is the Being which is the process of retaining identity with itself in its otherness.
>
> The last sentence is one of Hegel's clearest definitions of Spirit, and not only does it unveil the kenotic form of Spirit, it expresses the conceptual meaning of the God who has died in Jesus, the God who has negated himself in fully and finally becoming flesh.[14]

And further on:

> . . . Hegel . . . goes on to say that in its third moment Spirit apprehends itself only in the objective otherness of its Self-existence:
>
> > In this emptying itself, in this *kenōsis*, it is merely within itself: the independent Self-existence which excludes itself from essential Being is the knowledge of itself on the part of essential Being. It is the "Word," the *Logos*, which when spoken empties the speaker of himself, outwardizes him, and leaves him behind emptied, but the Word is as immediately perceived, and only this act of self-perceiving himself is the actual existence of the "Word."

[14] Ibid., pp. 66–67.

> . . . Cryptic as his language is when Hegel speaks most dialectically, can the Christian doubt that the "Word" which when spoken empties the speaker of himself is the Incarnate Word? . . .
> God *is* Jesus, proclaims the radical Christian, and by this he means that the Incarnation is a total and all-consuming act: as Spirit becomes the Word that empties the Speaker of himself, the whole reality of Spirit becomes incarnate in its opposite. Only the radical Christian witnesses to the full reality of Jesus or the Incarnate Word, because he alone responds to the totally kenotic movement of God. If Spirit truly empties itself in entering the world, then its own essential or original Being must be left behind in an empty and lifeless form. Now, Spirit can exist and be real only in a kenotic or incarnate mode that is the very opposite of its original Being. Hegel and the radical Christian would teach us that finally Spirit is this eternal movement of absolute self-negation.[15]

In light of the absolute clarity of revolutionary metanoēsis, it is absolutely evident that the Christian assurance that the Hegelian "Word" is the Incarnate Word, this salvation *sola morte*, is, in fact, religion as movement, the movement of religion/the religion of movement, that is, that the 'new and revolutionary form of faith', 'the revolutionary theological assault upon the history of faith', is not the absolute transcendence of the Spirit Itself, not the absolute existence of Faith, but rather the movement of religion/the movement of the kenotic Christ, a divine 'process' which truly has its 'source' and 'model' in 'modern revolutionary assaults upon the whole movement of a profane or secular history', indeed, essentially has them so, as follows: as (in Hegel) Spirit, within itself, empties itself in the Word (is left behind empty, outwardized, by the Word Itself/by the Self Absolute), so (in Altizer) the whole reality of Spirit, outside itself/within the abyss of itself, empties itself in the totally kenotic movement of God (is left behind empty, outwardized, by the eternal movement of absolute self-negation), a proportion of which the proof is: *Spirit within itself outwardized by the totality of the divine incarnation identically Spirit within the abyss of itself out-*

[15] Ibid., pp. 68–69.

wardized by the Self Itself (or, the proof reads, *the within eternally outwardized by the totality of the kenotic movement of God identically the within eternally outwardized by the death of Self*). It is the religion of the absolute inversion of the abyss, precisely that by which it withholds itself from the pure abyss of self, from the three-selved source, which constitutes it the death of self, the eternal movement of absolute self-negation, the outwardizing eternally of the within. This is the transcendence of the absolute its own, the absolute its own the absolute self-containment of the abyss, the absolutely unconditioned its own the containment of the abyss of self: the *horror vacui* of the movement of absolute kenosis, the eternal form of the same, eternally outwardizing the within: the absolute reduction of the absolute inversion of the abyss to religion. The reduction of the absolute religion of Hegel to the absolute inversion of the abyss is the abysmal self-containment of its own proportion, of that proportion of which the proof is 'the transcendence of Jesus' historical individuality is the identity of his eternal life and eternal death'. It is the abysmal measure of its own self-containment/ containment of its-own-self in the form of the absolute quality of the abyss, in the form of the death of self eternally outwardizing the within. The "mystery" of revealed religion is revealed as religion without Christianity/ Christianity without the religion of Christianity, Christianity become the new religion of the 'divine process'. This is the identity of the transcendence of the abyss of absolute idealism with the absolute inversion of the abyss, at once the abyss of idealism, the transcendence of the abyss of absolute idealism the proven identity of the abyss of transcendental idealism, absolute idealism identical with the transcendence of historical materialism, the transcendence of historical materialism identical with the abyss of transcendental idealism, the historico-idealistic absolute transcendental materialism of the abyss, the *very abyss of materialism-idealism,* evident in the form of the infinite extension of the finality of the total, in the form of the absolute punctuality of the Totality of the End, in the form of the infinite extension of an eschatological future into the present:

The forward movement of the Incarnate Word is from God to

> Jesus, and the Word continues its kenotic movement and direction by moving from the historical Jesus to the universal body of humanity, thereby undergoing an epiphany in every human hand and face. At no point in this dialectical process can we isolate the Word and affirm that here it receives its final and definitive expression. Any such abstraction of the Word from history must necessarily lose the meaning of an incarnational process, isolating theology from the activity and movement of the Word, and inevitably setting theology upon the retrogressive path of the religious forms of Christianity. . . . theology must ever give itself to a negation of every past form of the Word, if only as a means of opening itself to an extension of an eschatological future into the present.[16]

Further:

> If the Christian knows the God who has emptied himself of his original sacrality in actually becoming flesh, then he cannot know a God who remains distinct and self-enclosed in his own primordial Being. The God who acts in the world and history is a God who negates himself, gradually but decisively annihilating his own original Totality. God is that Totality which "falls" or "descends," thereby moving ever more fully into the opposite of its original identity. God or the Godhead becomes the God who is manifest in Christ by passing through a reversal of His original form: thus transcendence becomes immanence just as Spirit becomes flesh. At no point in this process is God uniquely himself: each point or moment in the process embodies a metamorphosis of God, as God remains himself even while estranged from himself, for it is precisely God's self-estrangement or self-negation that actualizes his forward movement and process.[17]

This abyss of the self-containment of its own proportion, this reduction of the implicit idealism of historical materialism to Nothing, this absolute punctuality of the Totality of the End, this

---

[16] Ibid., pp. 83–84.
[17] Ibid., pp. 89–90.

absolutely unconditioned punctuality of transcendence, the latter become 'immanence just as Spirit becomes flesh', is further delineated by Altizer, in its comprehensive universality, in *The Descent Into Hell*, as follows:

> The death of the transcendence of God embodies the death of all autonomous selfhood, an end of all humanity which is created in the image of the absolutely sovereign and transcendent God.
>
> . . . Then the individual and eternal death of Jesus is comprehensively and universally realized in the dissolution of the center or ground of all forms of autonomous and individual self-consciousness. For the actual and real dissolution or death of the center of consciousness brings about the end of all autonomous self-consciousness. Yet the dissolution of autonomous self-consciousness is simultaneously the end of all truly individual selfhood, the end of the autonomous ego or the self which is only itself.
>
> . . . With the disappearance of the ground of individual selfhood, the unique "I" or personal ego progressively becomes a mere reflection or echo of its former self. Now the "I" takes into itself everything from which it has withdrawn itself, and therefore it ceases to stand apart. . . . Facelessness and loss of identity now become the mark of everyone, as everyone becomes no one, and the "I" is inseparable from the "other." Individual selfhood does not simply or literally come to an end or disappear; it appears in the other.[18]

Further:

> Where self was, death now reigns; where an autonomous selfhood appeared as its own creator, death or nothingness now appears as both the source and goal of the self. In losing all sense of a fixed, or autonomous, or unchanging form of selfhood, have we not come to identify the presence or the presences of the self with a transient and ever-vanishing series of real moments in time? Once an absolute form of selfhood had

[18] Altizer, *Descent Into Hell*, pp. 154–55.

vanished from our horizon, were we not given a new and overwhelming sense of the actuality and finality of concrete points of time and space? And a sense of a self or point within us which is most real when it is most distant from all which had previously appeared as self?

> . . . selfhood has increasingly and ever more pervasively become anonymous. It has lost or is losing everything which sets it apart or within; as the mysterious interior depths of selfhood have been emptied into the immediacy of concrete points in time and space. . . . that self which has become real to us is a naked point in time and space, a point released from a transcendent ground.
>
> . . . So far from being an autonomous center, it is unenclosed and unconfined. Indeed, it is not truly a center at all. Or, at least, it is not a fixed center, or a center deriving its identity from a unique and eternal self.[19]

And finally:

> A new consciousness is becoming actual about and within us which promises to dissolve every former human and social identity. Contemporary apocalyptic vision can celebrate this new consciousness as an historical realization of the new creation. But to do so it must will the death within us of everything which is bound to the old humanity of our past.
>
> . . . Not only has an ancient way of faith become empty and unreal, but it is increasingly true that faith can no longer function in the established ethical realm of personal decision and individual action. . . . For if faith must be grounded in personal decision and individual action, then it would seem to be closed to that real future which now lies before us.
>
> . . . . Just as in ancient apocalyptic faith, an individual decision can here have no effect upon an eschatological realization. Indeed, it is only insofar as an individual decision is a universal decision that it can be realized eschatologically. . . . So, ethically *and* eschatologically considered, it is the private and purely individual act which now must be judged to be guilty. Sin is a private and isolated state of autonomous existence. . . .

[19] Ibid., pp. 157–59.

> Sin is isolation from the actuality of the other, and the forgiveness of sin is the disintegration of all that interior distance separating men from men and self from self. Sin is a false and illusory inwardness or outwardness, isolating the interior from the exterior, and wholly divorcing the immediacy of the inner world from the actuality of the outer world. And the forgiveness of sin is a new creation in which the inner and outer realms are united, and the interior depths of inwardness are identical with the exterior and outer depths of every other.[20]

The abyss of the autonomous self is at the same time the absolute transcendence of self. 'The end of the autonomous ego or the self which is only itself' is not the end of the self-containing self, but the end of the self not containing another self, not the end of the self itself, but the end of the self itself not another, not the end of the autonomous individual self ('individual selfhood does not simply or literally come to an end'), but the end of the autonomous individual self which is not another. The autonomous individual other self which 'no one' is, which is no one, which *is* anonymous, which, named, *is* not, is the center of modern consciousness *in extremis*/the self itself past the extremes: the self itself swallowing its own other, the self itself the measure of its own abyss, the autonomous self measuring its own abyss: the self itself another/*another itself the self* in its own abyss, in the abyss of its own: the pure self in the abyss of its own autonomous other, 'death or nothingness' now appearing as both its 'source and goal', the self distributed, in the form of presence or 'presences', as a 'transient and ever-vanishing series of real moments in time', the self 'a naked point' deriving its identity from the immediacy of time and space, deriving its identity from the radically uncriticized givenness of the transcendental imagination of modern consciousness, the point absolutely enveloping the 'transcendent ground' from which it is 'released', the autonomous center of its own other an absolute Nothing, an abyss, 'unenclosed and unconfined', a point in the dialectical/divine process absolutely embodying the form or

[20] Ibid., pp. 166–69.

shape of the process. Just here it can clearly be seen that this self itself swallowing its own other is not the actual death of the Living God, but the actual death of the God of Death, the 'death of death itself', the reality of the inversion and 'reversal' of the uroboric Moloch: not the original uroboric Moloch, not the primordial Totality, but the uroboric Moloch of the End, inverting and reversing the original, the death of self eternally outwardizing the within, the perpetuity of the abyss in which the 'unique "I" or personal ego progressively becomes a mere reflection or echo of its former self', the abyss absolutely quantifying its own autonomous self, the totality of the self-sacrificial movement of God 'silencing every presence which is not immediately present', demanding the sacrifice of that other which is not the center of the abyss of the absolute its own, which is not a punctual embodiment of the 'historical realization of the new creation', of the *final* uroboric Moloch, the sacrifice of any other which is not the embodiment of the absolute self-sacrificial movement of the sovereign, which is not the instrumental mode of the absolutely sovereign kenotic movement, the sacrifice of any other which is not 'no one', not the son of Sisyphus embodying, in this modern reversal and inversion of the ancient myth, the Cyclopean will to its own absolute oblivion, to the oblivion of its own face and identity, to the oblivion of its own proportionality, so that, in the end, every other, willy-nilly, is sacrificed to the absolute movement of the sovereign self, so that, in the end, willy-nilly, identity is sacrificed to the absolute movement of self, so that, in the end, the movement willy-nilly/the total movement of self, the violence which is the movement of an absolute self, is the sacred absolute, at once the hypothetical absolute in which is immolated the 'private and isolated state of autonomous existence'. This is the infernal body coming into being, the descent into hell of consciousness (in total oblivion of the actual reality of the transcendent passion of Christ-consciousness, in total oblivion of the absolute world consciousness whose existence is the passionate transcendence which is the very midst of reality), the spiritual furnace which dissolves and consumes guilt and sin, wherein 'the forgiveness of sin is the disintegration of all that interior distance separating men from men and self from self', 'a new creation in which the inner and outer realms are united, and the interior depths of inwardness are identical with the exterior and outer depths of every other', wherein the forgiveness of sin is the body which is the realization (proof) of the proportion: 'as exterior is to interior depths, so inwardness is to the outer depths of every other', the identity of every other a proportion analogous to the dissembled abyss of its own proportionality, $K^2 : N :: K : N^2$, the latter, indeed, the very face and identity of that which wills its own oblivion in the form of 'facelessness and loss of identity': Hegel (K^2)/exterior : Nietzsche (N)/interior depths :: Kant (K)/inwardness : Heidegger (N^2)/ outer depths, in which form it is manifest that ultimately the forgiveness of sin, $K^2N^2/KN = KN$, is the *identification* of the 'interior depths of inwardness' and 'the exterior and outer depths of every other' in which the latter *vanish*, as, in the absolute inversion of the abyss, Hegel and Heidegger are brought to nought. This is the self-circling actuality of that which wills its own oblivion in the form of the body, in the form of the forgiveness of sin, in the form of an absolute inner outer/absolute outer inner: the self-embodiment of sin: the sin of self in the form of the forgiveness of sin, sin in the form of the self-forgiveness of sin: that circle of which the total self-embodiment of God is the oblivion, the circle of its own willing not-willing its own other, the circle of its own body not its own: the actual and real transformation of what before now was old into something actually new: *the divine metamorphosis of self into other: the circling from its own beginning into the body of the other,* the 'reversal and inversion of the primordial uroboric Moloch', which, precisely by virtue of its essentially historical specificity (by which it is precisely what it is), is, in fact, by no means in essential continuity with the past forms of its own/with its own past forms, but is, in fact and of essential necessity, the creator of its own past forms, of its own 'irrevocable' and 'irrecoverable' past, the creator of its own history (the absolutely unconditioned its own) in the form of the never-to-be-forgotten past which 'now lies before us' in the form of the future: the self-embodiment of the process form: the seeming seamless wisdom of the Ancient of Days come to earth, the totality of the divine presence in the form of the series of innumerable points, each gyrating about itself in the form of the eternal extension of the End, in the form of the absolute self circling itself in the form of another within, in the form of the new form of the absolute self/the absolutely new form of self, in the form of the absolute self-extension of the point within itself to another. This is the exterior actuality of the body the interior identity of the exterior: the interior the exterior of another form of self-consciousness: the new form of interior self-consciousness, the exterior: historical self-consciousness now visible ending in the exterior of consciousness, in the anonymous, objective form, circling, but not returning to its own beginning: the single, solitary turn infinitely multiplied in the form of the other, in the form of objectivity/anonymity: the divine metamorphosis of self into other multiplied in the form of the anonymity of an absolute identity, in the form of an absolute anonymity: the metamorphosis of self itself in the form of the infinite multiplication/division of the other, in the pure form of the body, in the form of the addition-subtraction identity, in the pure form of the exterior identity of the interior, in the form of an absolute purity, the purity of form itself (the pure form of the forgiveness of sin). This is the absolute metamorphosis of self in the form of an absolute liquidity/the absolute self embodied in the liquid form of the absolutely dialectical process, of the essentially formal process, the form of the divine process. Now this form of the divine metamorphosis of self into other, viz., the infinite multiplication of anonymity, this absolute liquidity, this form of the forgiveness of sin without human nature (obviating, *a fortiori*, even that solely needed confession of which Marx wrote "What is needed is above all a *confession*, and nothing more than that. To obtain forgiveness for its sins mankind needs only to declare them for what they are," a statement in which the idealism of historical materialism, prior to the abyss, clearly rings out, which idealism, precisely, is obviated by the absolute ground which) is the form, precisely, of the absolute Nothing of, of the abyss of, historical materialism, of that which is implicitly the identity of the proven identity of its own abyss, of historical materialism which itself is the abyss of the absolute its own absolutely implicit. The infinite liquidity which is the form of the absolute metamorphosis of self is the absolutely material ground of historical materialism, which ground is explicit in, and only in, the absolute inversion of the abyss as that form in which historical materialism itself transcends itself (as absolute idealism transcends itself in the form of the Nothing), as that form in which historical materialism absolutely transcends history, realizes itself as a transcendentally intelligible moment of revolutionary practice in an absolutely evolutionary process. Altizer writes in *Total Presence*:

> Almost single-handedly Hegel created the foundations of systematic and conceptual historical thinking, just as Nietzsche single-handedly brought those foundations to an end, an end which has perhaps only been fully realized in our own time. . . . historical thinking will wither away apart from the solidity of these foundations, as we are no doubt now discovering. When this occurs it is not just historical thinking which comes to an end, but rather a whole world which is truly recognizable as a human world that thereby ends, or, at least, it comes to an end for the individual subject of consciousness. This end was logically realized by Hegel, but only actually enacted by Kierkegaard and Marx, the one realizing the pure subjectivity and the other the pure objectivity of consciousness. . . .
>
> The Hegelian labor of the negative becomes wholly objective in Marx, and this leads to a new objective history which for the first time makes manifest a fully objective or material ground as the originating source of history and consciousness, and a ground which is itself evolving through the actuality of historical praxis to an eschatological or apocalyptic goal. It is ironic but nonetheless understandable that dialectical materialism should be the most overtly apocalyptic form of modern thinking, for Marxism takes the finality and irreversibility of history with total seriousness and apprehends the very necessity of the historical process as a purely negative process, a process which not only negates the past to realize the future, but which continually negates itself to realize its own activity and life. If all truly modern history is Marxist insofar as it makes manifest a fully material or objective ground, it can only be Marxist insofar as it knows that ground as a forward-moving or evolving

> ground, and a ground which realizes itself in the deep structures or material foundations of history. Marxist thinking and Marxist historiography are inevitably dependent upon this eschatological even if material ground, for with its disappearance history here loses all meaning.[21]

The absolute implication of historical materialism is its own transcendence, its own absolutely unconditioned form of the abyss of transcendental idealism, the dissembled intelligibility of which ($K^2 : N :: K : N^2$) is the transcendent actuality of the absolutely material ground/the 'eschatological even if material ground' upon which historical materialism is 'inevitably dependent', and in which form the absolute implication of historical materialism, its own transcendence, wills its own oblivion. Here it is clear that the absolute self centered within its own abyss is the will to oblivion, the oblivion of will in the form of the absolute liquidity of the abysmal metamorphosis at once the absolute material ground of historical materialism, in the form of the reduction of historical materialism to the totality of presence wherein the 'negation and transcendence of an individual and interior self-consciousness goes hand in hand with the realization of a universal humanity, a humanity that can neither be named nor apprehended by an interior and individual voice', in the form, indeed, of the 'final presence of history', at once the implicit death of history implicitly the eternal death of Jesus: the will to oblivion/the oblivion of will in the form of the absolutely formless identity of space and time, in the form of the total identity of a total presence, in the form of the liquidity of the totality of identity. This will to oblivion, the absolute self centered within its own abyss, the liquidity of the totality of identity, is the embodiment of the *either/or* of the objectivity of consciousness (distinguished from the same in the subjectivity of consciousness), which realization of an absolute either/or of the objectivity of consciousness is not merely the fragmentation of thought in essence not thought (as is *la differance*), but this abso-

[21] T. J. J. Altizer, *Total Presence: The Language of Jesus and The Language of Today* (New York, 1980), pp. 75–77.

lute liquidity is the absolute fragmentation, the fragmentation of consciousness in essence, the consciousness of the fragmentation of consciousness, not the affirmation of an absolute reference, but the abyss of absolute reference enacted in the 'social and political revolutions' of our time:

> The social and political revolutions of the twentieth-century have either violently or silently assaulted all of the previously established identities of either the real or authentic human being, and have done so with such force as to engender an overwhelming reaction, a reaction which has either destroyed all civilization or stretched it to its very limits. But this reaction has not issued in the rebirth of a prerevolutionary center of consciousness, or, at least, none which has had an impact upon politics or the arts; instead it has been followed by an ever deeper erosion of premodern values and identities, with the result that these now have meaning only insofar as they are wholly distant from our midst. Consciousness itself can now appear in all its forms only as a broken and divided consciousness, and such a profound fissure of consciousness has succeeded in abolishing the intrinsic ground of every positive or normative identity. Thereby the intrinsic value or even meaning of any isolated form or mode of consciousness has been brought to an end, and brought to an end at the very points where a new and universal humanity appears and becomes real. It is now all too apparent that what we have known as the heights and depths of the individual and interior consciousness were inseparable from the silence and the impotence of the great bulk of humanity, and as that greater humanity begins decisively to speak and act, it does so in those empty voids or spaces created by the contraction of a former identity and voice.
>
> Is it possible for us to affirm, and passionately to affirm, our own interior and individual dissolution as the way to the realization of our own full and universal humanity?[22]

It is clear that the 'profound fissure of consciousness', the either/or absolutely embodied in the objectivity of consciousness, the fragmentation of the absolute, is a fragmentation that

[22] Ibid., pp. 87–88.

is the consciousness/realization of a proportion, and specifically a function of the 'inseparable' relation of (one might say of the 'inherent and intrinsic otherness of') the ratios thereof, to wit, 'the heights and depths : individual and interior consciousness :: the silence and the impotence : the great bulk of humanity', such that the silence and impotence of the individual and interior consciousness, 'the contraction of a former identity and voice' creating 'empty voids or spaces', the one side of the 'broken and divided consciousness', of the proof of the fragmentation of consciousness, is 'violently or silently assaulted' by the political and social revolutions in which 'the greater humanity begins decisively to speak and act', and which does so, this bulk of humanity, in the heights and depths thereby transformed into empty voids and spaces, 'the very points where a new and universal humanity appears and becomes real'. This absolute fragmentation of identity (to be carefully distinguished from the absolute explosion of identity now occurring for the first time in history in the form, precisely, of a 'positive'/'normative' identity, in the form of meta-identity/the absolute out-identity of [any]side, thing, or person, the proof of the proportionality of transcendence), this absolute either/or of identity, this abyss of absolute reference, is historical materialism transcending the implicit death of history in the form of an assault on individual and interior consciousness, the form, in turn, of the absolute sublimation of the uchronia[23] which is 'the new and universal humanity', the form of a 'new and universal humanity' the abysmal sublimation of time, an abysmally resurrected consciousness, of the celebration of which it can be said:

> Perhaps only nothingness or a void can lie beyond such celebration, but apocalypticism has always known that the advent of the new world brings an end to the old, and we at least have been given glimpses of a new world in the very advent of a new and universal humanity. Our only question can be whether or not that humanity is our own.[24]

[23] Cf. above, pp. 10ff., 44ff., and 177ff.

[24] Altizer, *Total Presence*, p. 89.

This uchronian sublimation of a new universal identity absolutely assaulting individual and interior consciousness/interior identity is, perforce, to be affirmed, indeed passionately affirmed, if it is to be 'our own', for the reason that the alternative to the nothingness or void beyond this celebration, the alternative to the affirmation of this hypothetical absolute is the absurd absolutely contradictory proof of the fragmentation of proportionality, the absurd absolutely contradictory 'existence' of the consciousness of the fragmentation of consciousness, viz., 'the individual and interior consciousness of the greater humanity, identically the beginning decisively to speak and act in silence and impotence' (the alternative proof/existence, the catholic faith *eternally and necessarily implicit* in the affirmation of the liquidity of an absolute identity). The alternative is the forever and necessarily implicit extension into the realm of the objectivity of consciousness of the absolute absurdity of the pure subjectivity of consciousness. The alternative to the affirmation is *explicitly* 'perhaps only nothingness or a void' for which the compensation is 'given glimpses of a new world', that is, the alternative to the affirmation of the total identity of total presence is implicitly an essentially unknowable existence. Indeed, there is no intelligible alternative to the will to oblivion within the limit of the proofs of, the proven limits of, its own proportionality. This is the implicit actuality of the body of matter in the absurd absolutely contradictory form of the hypothetical absolute: matter the body itself/the matter of an absolute society in the form of the absolute fragmentation of a new identity! The absolute actuality of matter *affirmed*! Nowhere does modernity come closer to the foundation of a new world than it does in the absolute inversion of the abyss (*KN*)/the abyss of transcendental idealism/the abyss of the absolute actuality of absolute idealism in the process of its conditional embodiment, yet nowhere is it further from the foundation of a new world than it is in the 'glimpses of a new world' which it has been given therein in the form of the divine metamorphosis of self into another absolutely implicit existence, in the affirmation-form of the absolute metamorphosis of self, 'the very advent of a new and universal humanity', because, as has been demonstrated, within the limits therein of its own essential proportionality there is no intelligible alternative to affirmation, except it be passionate affirmation, and because, as has been demonstrated in the analysis of the liquidity of identity, total presence extends no further in time than the abyss of its own proportionality, while the totality of presence extends no further in space than its own implicit actuality, extends no further in space than its own affirmation (to speak in the terms of its own radically uncritical acceptance—in the complete exposition of the identity of presence which is the absolute inversion of the abyss—of the identity derived from the givenness of the transcendental imagination of modern consciousness). Indeed, finally, the only and absolute limitation of 'our midst' is precisely that it remains (eternally) 'our own', that it is not the midst itself for the first time absolutely unconditioned, but rather the midst itself 'our own' absolute otherness: 'our own' itself absolute experience/'our own' absolute identity an actual other: everything our own actually experienced as not our own: the absolute self-embodiment of self-alienation, the absolute self-embodiment of the actuality of another, which is to say that finally the only and absolute limitation of 'our midst' is the absolute solitude (corresponding to the demonstrable limits of the proportionality of revolutionary presence) wherein 'our own interior individuality' is actually transcended:

> Only an underground consciousness can now know humanity, and that means a solitary consciousness, a consciousness existing beyond ours or any interiority. But is it not true that none of us can now discover a human presence except in those rare moments when we are delivered from our own interiority, and delivered not by physical intoxication or cultural drugs, but rather by the actual presence of another, another who can never appear within, and never appear by way of anything which is a truly individual voice or gesture? The one so present is certainly not a person or a self, being neither male nor female, neither old nor young, neither black nor white. Self-consciousness is just what is most missing from all which we can know as a truly human presence, and the very absence of self-consciousness in our deepest and most actual moments is a

decisive sign of the identity of that common humanity which has dawned in our time.

. . . Genuine solitude can never be chosen or even willed, it comes when we least expect it, and it comes to deliver us from everything which is only our own.

All . . . ancient religious movements are movements into solitude, and they realize and enact themselves by way of solitude, for it is precisely the most total moments of solitude which make manifest and real a total presence of the holy or the divine. Apparently all such solitude has vanished from our history, but a radical solitude has been with us nonetheless, and this solitude is opening us to a total and comprehensive vision. That vision is partially released in our actual moments of genuine solitude, and then a new humanity is present, a humanity which we can neither conceive nor define. But we know it to be a new humanity, for it is given to us as a new humanity, a universal humanity which is wholly beyond any identity which can be interiorly present, and beyond every interior and individual identity which we can know. Nevertheless, in moments of genuine solitude we know such a humanity to be present, and we know it to be present because it is in just such moments that our identities pass beyond an interior realm and realize a depth wherein everything which is present is not our own.

Genuine solitude is a voyage into the interior, but it is a voyage which culminates in a loss of our interior, a loss reversing every manifest or established center of our interior so as to make possible the advent of a wholly new but totally immediate world. The joy of solitude comes only out of a breakthrough releasing us from our own interior, a breakthrough and a joy which is clearly present when we fully listen to music, and it is no less present in the presence of another, but only when that other has no point of contact with our own within.[25]

Only when, it might be said, that other *is* the point of our own within, only when our own interior is absolutely violated, is the absence of an absolute violence, is an identity immediately present, *is* a total presence, only when our own interior *is* the presence of another in the form of the point of another oblivious to

[25] Ibid., pp. 104–7.

our own or any interior, only then is the joy and breakthrough of solitude present, making possible our evacuation of our own interior in favor of the totality of presence actually arriving. Thus self-consciousness disappears from view, or, visible self-consciousness disappears, in the form of an absolute solitude (corresponding to the disappearance from view of the abyss of its own proportionality in the form of the absolute forgiveness of sin[26]), in the form of an absolute solitude absolutely not our own/absolutely its own (corresponding to that privacy ['the total epiphany of Christ'] which, alone, within the abyss of its own proportionality, is the absolute transcendence of its own limit: corresponding to the intelligibility of individuality within the abyss of the absolute its own[27]). Such, finally, is the experience-form of the affirmation of the metamorphosis of the absolute self: 'a new humanity is present, a humanity which we can neither conceive nor define', a humanity the very identity of which is the *common.*

In absolute solitude the absolutely public existence of a new humanity: in solitude the absolutely unconditioned publicity of identity: in privacy a total publicity/a public totality: in public the totality of privacy: publicity the whole of the private act: the body itself essentially empty/the absolute vacuity of the body/the liquid identity of a 'new humanity'. Such is the absolute reversal and inversion of the historical ideal of being, of the ideal of the history of being, of the 'best of all possible worlds', of the Republic of Being: such is the revolutionary Presence which is the absolute non-being of historical materialism, the non-historical being/the being non-historical of historical materialism, the revolutionary embodiment of Nothing (not itself). Such is Nothing the matter of immanence, a brute faith surviving in the form of the 'joy of solitude', the absolute publicity which is the reversal of a monadic identity/the inside outside of a total unity: the absolute liquidity/absolute emptiness which is the sole identity, the (strict) insincerity that an absolute solitude is as the doubly negative attribution of the multiple to identity (just here it can be

[26] Cf. above, p. 222.
[27] Cf. above, p. 212.

seen that to speak of the absolute inversion of the abyss is to speak of the absolute inversion of what is [originally/in Nietzsche] the absolute publicity of the One: the absolute inversion of the unum absolute emptied in existence [the abyss/the absolute emptiness of the One]). Such is the absolute publicity of identity which is the *unum* of a double identity: the abyss of a double identity, the abyss of the abyss of identity not identity (the absolute inversion of the abyss, the abyss of the abyss of itself, the abyss of identity not identity)/the double abyss of identity/*the abyss of identity not the abyss of identity*/the double identity of the abyss: the abyss of the absolute inversion of the abyss, the transcendence of the absolute inversion of the abyss in the form of its own abyss/the abyss of its own: its own not its own: the (strict) insincerity of the common identity of humanity: the common humanity known in solitude. Such is the (strict) insincerity of the common itself. Such is the darkness in which for the first time in history the Light Itself shines in the form of the absolute, i.e., in the form of itself (neither its own nor not its own form). This insincerity of the common itself comprehends not the actual (strict) sincerity of a specific itself: the non-existence of the actual light comprehends not the actuality of the light: non-existence comprehends not existence. The darkness comprehends the light, even the essence of the light, indeed, the (strict) insincerity of the common itself comprehends itself, even sincerity, but the darkness comprehends not the *shining* of the light, the *existing essence* of the light. This insincerity of the common identity of humanity comprehends humanity, even a new humanity, but comprehends not the absolute actuality of a new humanity/the absolute sincerity of itself/the existence of (strict) sincerity: the affirmation of the absolute actuality of matter/the affirmation of a new humanity, this darkness, comprehends not matter the body itself/the foundation of the identity of a new humanity which now actually exists for the first time: the *unum publicum* of a double identity[28] comprehends not the *unum esse* of a new actuality of

[28] Cf. Altizer, *Self-Embodiment of God*, pp. 53–54: "When identity is doubled it is not only divided from itself, but it is united with itself by that very division. This union is manifest when hearing speaks, and it is manifest at the

identity,[29] nor shall the darkness comprehend the shining of the light: the (strict) insincerity of an absolute emptiness/of the liquid identity of a new humanity comprehends a new logic, even the logic of history, but the vacuity of this insincere identity shall not open to the logic of society now actually existing for the first time. To comprehend the shining of the light, it is first necessary to evacuate the vacuity of a sole absolute, to empty out/to withdraw from the emptiness of the doubly negative attribution of the multiple to itself: to withdraw from/to empty out the emptiness of a real and actual solitude, to evacuate the darkness. The darkness shall not comprehend the *new absolutely societal logic*, the new actuality of the logic of history existing/existing history, the *unum esse* which is the foundation of an absolute society/the

center of hearing, and above all manifest in the self-identity of that center. For that self-identity is a double identity, an identity which is double in its innermost center, and which realizes its own identity by a doubling of hearing and speaking into a single act. No alien identity is present here. Or, rather, the identity which is present is alien only insofar as it is alien to itself. Alien to itself it certainly is, for the doubling of identity is self-alienation. It is self-alienating because it doubles itself, and it doubles itself in its own act, an act which is integral to its own identity. . . .

". . . The doubling of identity is identity's own realization of itself in act, a realization whereby identity propels itself, and propels itself out of itself and into act. Now the exile of identity from itself, and its consequent embodiment in act, is identity's own self-embodiment in act. This occurs only when identity is alienated from itself, or is in exile from itself, a self-exile which is self-alienation, and a self-alienation which realizes identity itself.

"Self-identity, too, is itself in self-alienation, for it is in self-alienation that identity is most actually other, and it is the actuality of otherness which releases and realizes self-identity. That actuality also releases identity's embodiment in act, an embodiment which is possible only when identity is other than itself, and which is fully possible only when identity itself is the source of its own otherness. That identity is self-identity, or the full realization of self-identity, a realization which is only realized in act. But it is realized in act only because the doubling of identity forecloses the possibility of identity's simply being itself. Only the alienation of identity from itself establishes the full possibility of act, an act which is identity's own, for only thereby does it become impossible for identity to be simply and only itself."

[29] Cf. above, pp. 186–87.

foundation-stone of an absolute social unity/the foundation-stone identity of the social *unum.* Indeed, the absolute inversion of the abyss sublimates the division-within identity of modern consciousness, the Nothing-identity, the abyss of time (precisely in this sublimation it is the abyss of the plaintext[30]), in the form of a universal identity, in the form of an identity without division/a division without identity within the self-doubling of self-identity (the without division/the division without, the absolute liquidity/absolute publicity/absolute emptiness), in the form of the vacuity within itself of the self-doubling self-identity which is its 'own realization of itself in act' (the universal the actuality of the emptiness of the absolutely unconditioned its own/the division-within absolutely unconditioned identity an absolute publicity), in the form of its own absolutely unconditioned reversal of identity, in the form of the *its-own*-realization of the self (reversal the sole surviving form of the self/self-reversal the very form of solitude [and absolute self-reversal the form of absolute solitude]), in the form of the realization of its own reversal of the division, which form, in turn, occurs solely in the form of the inside outside of the absolute self/in the form of absolute solitude. The realization of its own reversal of the division-within identity of modern consciousness occurring solely in the form of absolute self-reversal, this public/liquid/anonymous unity of the double itself (itself indistinguishable from identity in exile from itself, itself not identity itself in exile from itself, itself not itself in exile from itself, 'a self-alienation which realizes identity itself', the self-alienation of identity not identity/the absolute inversion of the abyss/the self-alienation of the abyss of itself [the self-alienation of (*K*)*NM*]), is the absolute self-alienation of the abyss, the abyss itself in the form of the realization of the source of self, the self-realization of the source, the abyss in the form of the self itself sourced in another,[31] the absolute realization of the source of the abyss of self (withholding itself from the three-selved source[32]), the absolute self-alienation of the source, the self-real-

[30] Cf. above, p. 227.

[31] Cf. above, pp. 200ff., 211f., and 217ff.

[32] Cf. above, pp. 211ff.

ization of the absolute identity of the other. This double anonymous identity of the *unum*, this double anonymous other of the social *unum*, this absolutely anonymous double of the *unum esse* (which literally and absolutely comprehends not the latter, which comprehends not the literally and absolutely indecomposable foundation-stone identity of the social *unum*), is at once the absolute source, the absolute ground, the absolute hypothetical of the absolute contingency which is historical materialism, that in terms of which the latter is absolutely intelligible to modern consciousness, historical materialism's spiritual undergirding: the sacred absolute, the Holy Spirit of self-consciousness in the form of the other in essence,[33] the absolute support of self-identity, the absolute self-realization of the source of self-identity, the absolutely equivocal predication of the self-identity of the other 'identity's own realization of itself in act'/its own realization/itself its own otherness. But this realization of identity's own identity is not itself, the realization of the identity of the God of death, is, that is, the realization of the totality of presence. Not only is the self-identity of the other the realization of identity's own identity, but it is not the realization of the identity of the Living god, but the realization of the identity of the death of God, not the predicate of identity, but the identity of Nothing, the Nothing-identity, not the predicate of identity, but self-identity, or, the absolute inversion of the predicate which is the self-identity of the other, the equivocal predication of the identity of self-identity. Just here it can be seen that the inverse identification of eternal life and death,[34] equivalent to the realization of its own identity, is a function of the fact that the absolute inversion of the abyss is the absolutely anonymous *double* of the *unum esse*, viz., being itself univocally predicated[35] of the *self*, identically the equivocal predication of the identity of another, the equivocation in the naming of God in the proof of the proportion which is the ratio of the Absolute Hypothetical to the Absolute Light,[36] to wit,

[33] Cf. above, pp. 44f.
[34] Cf. above, pp. 207ff.
[35] Cf. above, pp. 181ff.
[36] Cf. above, pp. 209f.

'as identity equivocally predicated is to self-identity, so identity univocally predicated is to the other' (where the member of the proof-ratio, 'identity univocally predicated of self-identity', identified as the 'equivocally predicated identity of the other', is equivalent to 'being itself univocally predicated of the self'), so that it is clear at once that equivocation in the naming of God, the empty use of the name of God, is the very identity of the anonymity of God which is the double of the *unum esse*, and that this double is an illicit reality, i.e., a reality equivocally predicated (at once the reality of the self-forgiveness of sin[37]), self-identity predicated equivocally, univocally in the realization of the proportion which is its own ratio to the *unum esse*, in which univocal form it is demonstrably the illicit reality of an equivocal identity, of the anonymity-of-God solitude, in which univocal form it is demonstrably equivocally an equivocal identity/a univocal identity equivocally, i.e., the absolute self-identity of equivocal-univocal, i.e., the absolute liquidity of identity, the face and identity of which is absolute solitude.

The anonymous unity of the double itself, as absolute ground of historical materialism, is the unit of an absolute division, the absolute solitude of another self without the division of identity, the absolute division of identity into units, the infinite multiplication of anonymity (the unit, the form of the self-realization of the alone). This unit of an absolute division is the infinite division of the self-identity of the other in the form of absolute solitude: the division outside of identity the realization of the self alone, the objectification of the absolute self as the alone/the self-objectification of the sole absolute: the absolute self-division of objectivity into identical alones, the division of the absolute into self-identical solitudes, solitudes the identity of which is self divided from itself/from thought/from the individual: not the 'flight of the alone to the alone', but the consciousness of the alone absolutely divided from self (not merely the original abyss [*N*], the unconsciousness of the alone divided from self [the *nihil*, matter], nor yet the unconsciousness of the self alone divided from itself [(*K*)*NM*/the abyss of thought/the *nihil*, mat-

[37] Cf. above, pp. 217ff.

ter itself], but) the absolute inversion of the abyss: matter itself *solum nihil* (the *nihil* the self-division of the absolute), matter the sole absolute divided from itself, the self-alienation of the sole reality, the absolute self-division of *sola realitas*, of that which is the inherent and intrinsic opposite of that in opposition to which, alone, it has its own identity. This opposed reality (the *unum esse*) is the absolute measure of another identity absolutely not its own other, i.e., neither its own nor not its own, the absolute measure of a second absolute identity in terms of which the *unum publicum* both has its own identity and is the reality of an irreality, both has its own identity and is not itself, mute witness to the beginning of the absolute priority of the second absolute, mute witness to the fact that the inherent and intrinsic opposition of the absolute self-division of the absolute (material) ground to the absolute unity of actual identity is, at once, in accord with its own identity, and not with the latter's identity, not with the identity the other absolutely existing for the first time, and, further, that the divine metamorphosis of self into other has as its inherent and intrinsic opposite that which *it* shall not become, that *which, itself, derives not from the double of itself*, viz., *an absolutely existent second identity*/an absolutely historical identity/a second identity actually absolute existing for the first time in history/a second absolute identity the first identity existing intact: an absolute change in an actual identity/an absolute identity absolutely transcending the change which is the absolutely different identity of the first identity: *identity univocally predicated of the change of identity*, identity perpetually new, the absolute perpetuity of a new identity, that which, itself, exists, that is, is, itself, itself itself. In light of the existence of this latter, of this revolutionary metanoēsis, of this meta-revolutionary νόησις, the double identity of matter, the double of the essentially dialectical matter—this absolutely internal continuity of the dialectical process of the transformation of one thing into another, this absolute self-metamorphosis, this absolute liquidity—is seen to break on the essentially dialectical actuality of the identity/body of matter. The double itself is seen to break on the absolute itself, the self-limited absolute on the unlimited absolute, the absolute universal solitude on the absolutely unlimited identity. The absolute identity of a universal solitude is seen to break on the absolute identity itself, on the absolute identity of itself, on the itself of itself, on the outside of itself, of which outside of itself, of which absolute exterior, of which absolute out-identity of (any)other, of (any)side, there is no exterior, no outside not itself the absolute out-identity of another side, no outside not the absolute out-identity of another side of itself. In the shining of the light the darkness is seen to break on an absolutely unconditioned exteriority existing transcendentally, to break on the transcendental identity of the exterior/the exterior identity of the transcendental, to break on the absolute exteriority of the transcendental outside of which is itself outside of itself in freedom, outside of which is the abyss of which this darkness is the absolute inversion, outside of which, of that of which there is no outside,[38] is the darkness which is the totality of presence: the darkness itself, the dark of identity, total presence not outside of the absolutely transcendental exteriority which is the absolute identity of the other, the identity of the dark not outside the absolute identity of the outside (the dark not outside the shining of the light), total presence not outside the limit of its own opposite. On this fact, viz., on the fact of *its own* total presence, total presence breaks, on the fact that the shining of the light comprehends the darkness itself, on the fact that total presence is of the source of self-identity identity-not-identity, on the fact that total presence is comprehended by a meta-identity neither its own nor not its own, comprehended by its own meta-identity not its own, comprehended by an other neither its own nor not its own (an other absolutely not other than meta-identity, an other absolutely not other than other), comprehended by 'that which is not because it is not absolute', by the fact that the other-than is not an actual existence because actual existence is the meta-identity of another, not identity other than itself,[39] an absolutely unconditioned other, comprehended by the actually existing meta-identity of another: *total presence breaks on the univocal predication of the exterior absolute the*

[38] Cf. above, pp. 145ff. and 194ff.
[39] Cf. above, p. 145.

absolute existent (of that of which it is not possible to univocally predicate an outside, while the equivocal predication of the outside of the absolute exterior is possible of that of which the reality so predicated is not the reality, viz., of the dark/of the self, the identity of which is not outside the absolute identity of the outside, which is to say that the equivocal predication of identity is possible of the self-identity which is not identity, while identity is univocally predicated of the limit to the darkness, of the limit to the reality of the self). This is the real exteriority of the absolute outside: the reality of the absolutely unconditioned absolute outside univocally predicated of the dark: the light univocally predicated of the darkness: the shining of the light univocally predicated of the limit of the darkness: actuality univocally predicated of the other of self-identity: existence univocally predicated of the absolutely unconditioned other of the self. The precision of the shining of the light breaking the dark is the other-identity of the light. The precision of the absolutely minimum transcendence of the dark is the light itself/the absolutely unconditioned exteriority of existence for the first time/the absolutely facial identity of existence/the proportion of the new creation[40] *sans* depth/the light itself *ex nihilo*: the dark itself univocally identified, i.e., not self-identity identity itself equivocally, not the dark itself equivocally, in 'self-alienation', not 'self-identity . . . itself in self-alienation' 'released' in and by 'otherness', an 'actual other', 'itself',[41] not the abysmal inversion of the light, the reality of the darkness equivocally, absolute identity equivocally predicated of the self/selfhood equivocally predicated of the dark (the reality of this darkness the other-self-covering of identity which is the identification person-self). In the precise break of the absolute identity of the totality of presence which is the *unum esse*, in the light *univocally* predicated of the darkness, there is no equivocal 'call' calling identity to 'self-judgment', no vocation in which self-identity 'realizes itself by self-judgment . . . itself the gift or grace of call',[42] no equi*vocation* in the call of self-

[40] Cf. above, p. 222.

[41] Cf. above, p. 232, n. 28.

[42] Cf. Altizer, *Self-Embodiment of God*, pp. 60–61: "Indeed, it is self-judgment,

identity to judgment, no equivocal predication of the solitude of the act of self-judgment, as 'nothing whatsoever stands outside of this presence, or nothing which can be heard, as presence itself now becomes identical with judgment'. (Compare the 'there is nothing outside of the text' of the absolute ciphertext, of *la différance*, as well as the 'there is no outside of the real exteriority of the absolute outside' of the absolute plaintext, of revo-

---

and self-judgment alone, which fully realizes solitude, a solitude which is the embodiment of a solitary act. Only self-judgment is a truly solitary act for it is self-judgment alone which is act and actor at once, an act which enacts itself. And self-judgment enacts itself whenever and wherever it is possible, which is to say that self-judgment occurs wherever solitude is present, and it occurs whenever act enacts itself. But it is just this enactment, and this enactment alone, which realizes the fullness of self-identity.

"Now self-identity stands alone, and it stands alone in its act, the act of self-judgment. Once this act has occurred, and has been realized in its hearer, then the hearer has embodied final judgment, and has embodied it in itself as hearer. Then the act of judgment is all-consuming, and it is heard and enacted wherever and whenever the hearer hears. So it is that the hearer that hears a judgment that is wholly here hears judgment everywhere, and hears it everywhere because it hears judgment alone, it hears judgment wherever it hears. When judgment is wholly here its hearer hears its presence nowhere else, but nevertheless it hears presence itself as judgment, and therefore it hears judgment wherever there is presence. Nothing whatsoever stands outside of this presence, or nothing which can be heard, as presence itself now becomes identical with judgment. But such presence is manifest as judgment only to self-identity, and is actual as judgment only in self-identity, as self-identity, and self-identity alone, fully embodies judgment.

"Accordingly, self-identity is identical with self-judgment, and the fullness of self-identity is identical with the fullness of self-judgment. Self-identity can stand as self-identity only insofar as it judges, and only insofar as it judges itself. But can self-identity then stand, and stand as itself? This is to ask if it can hear, hear and only hear, hear and only hear itself. Of course, self-identity does not simply hear itself, and this is not only because it does not simply hear, but also because it hears the voice of call, and hears that voice in judgment itself. But that voice is now fully manifest and actual in self-judgment, and in self-judgment alone, for self-judgment fully embodies voice, and fully embodies voice because it fully hears. When voice is so present, so fully present, it is present as self-judgment, but nevertheless it is fully present as voice. Now voice is call which calls its hearer to self-judgment. But that voice is truly call, and it truly calls by call-

lutionary metanoēsis, which last is to say everything exists for the first time in the shining of the light. Even the darkness does not exist except it is univocally as the shining of the light [even sin does not exist, except it exist univocally as the passion of God/the passion of Jesus], except it is absolutely univocally the form of the One Name, which is to say that the darkness/the totality of presence/the presence itself now judgment, if it exists, is univocally the passion of Jesus Christ, and if that, it exists for the first time absolutely.) The lifting of the ban banishes to non-existence the banished consciousness: in the light of the passion of the now living Jesus Christ, the light, at once, of absolute exteriority, in this absolute plaintext of the real, there is, because there is no room for it, *qua* absolutely unconditioned outside of existence, no absolute equivocation in the form of 'self-identity alone', no equivocation in the form of 'only self-judgment is a truly solitary act', there is, in the midst of the absolute out-identity of every existing thing, because there is absolutely no room for the conception, no exclusion possible for the inconceivable/no possibility of the bounding of the conceivable (the 'in' unconditionally univocally predicated as 'is'), no equivocal predication of the sole reality of the self, the very form of which identity reflects that it is the form of the banished consciousness *in extremis,* unable to hear its own voice as its own (which is 'nothing which can be heard'), hearing its own voice alone as the 'voice of call', the sole absolute self/self-judgment alone, the abyss of the absolute its own, the abyss of its own vocation/of its own judgment, the 'repetition of the voice of "I AM" in the finality of self-judgment'[43] constituting the equivocal vocation of the absolute self to absolute solitude. The dark itself is identified univocally, the totality of presence here identical with judgment absolutely existing as the one passion of Jesus Christ/the totality of presence univocally identified as the dark-

ing as self-judgment. That call fully releases identity, and it releases identity as self-identity, a self-identity which is self-judgment. Self-identity is realized by judgment, and it realizes itself by self-judgment, but that self-judgment is itself the gift or grace of call."

[43] Ibid., p. 62.

ness itself disowned in the shining of the light. Now for the first time in history the light of the revolutionary metanoēsis shining here is the perception that the passion of Christ is essentially the active exteriority of identity disowning the darkness of identity itself/the abyss of its own vocation, the absolutely exterior identity disowning the darkness of identity, very identity in the act of disowning the identity of the abyss of its own judgment, disowning an equivocally non-existent identity unequivocally, the absolutely irreversible meta-identity of the judgment which is the existent disownment of 'self-identity alone'. The disownment of the identity of darkness is the shining of the light for the first time, while the disownment of the identity of identity is the darkness, while, as is clear in the proof of the proportion constituting the ratio of the irreversible judgment to this latter reversal of self-identity identifying darkness as disownment (the proof, namely, that the disownment of identity is the identity of darkness), what is otherwise the case is the proof of the absolute necessity of the disownment of the identity of the darkness, the known necessity of itself of the disowning of the identity of the darkness, the freedom of disowning the freedom of the dark/the freedom of the self-disowning freedom, the meta-identity of the disowning darkness/the self disowning itself, the absolute disowning of self-identity identified as the absolutely irreversible reversal of self-identity, as, in fact, not the reversal of the darkness of identity, but, in fact, the disownment thereof. The disownment of the darkness is absolutely the existence of the shining of the light. The disownment of the reality of the self is the absolutely unconditioned exteriority of identity, not the absolutely equivocal exteriority of the identity of an absolute solitude (the within eternally outwardized[44]), but the within absolutely outwardized: not merely nothing remaining within, as in the totality of the kenotic movement of God, but no within, no depth whatsoever to the shining of the light, to the foundation transcending every foundation, to the unmoving foundation of kenotic identity itself, to the absolutely firm foundation of the negation of other-self-identity, to the univocal disowning

[44] Cf. above, pp. 215f.

of an equivocal other-not-other-than-self-identity. This is the absolutely still motion of kenotic identity *ex abysso*, the absolute out-identity of existence for the first time: the *first step after the abyss*, actually completed by thought essentially in the form of Jesus Christ. Here, this side the abyss, the new creation: the absolute outside of identity: the absolute outside of body: the world without identity identified/the absolute immediacy of identity: the divine mind *univocally* predicated of the totality of existence for the first time: the One Jesus Christ essentially conceived as the foundation itself of (any)society: the absolutely unconditioned identity of the social *unum*: the 'new and universal humanity' for the first time univocally predicated of the individual now existing/of (any)thing or person now actually existing/of (any)individual actually conceived or perceived. Indeed, the univocal predication of the 'new and universal humanity' the absolute condition of the actuality of the thing or person perceived or conceived: being itself univocally predicated, the 'absolutely outwardized within', the beginning of the absolute transcendence of the individual interior. The absolute condition of transcending the individual interior consciousness of humanity is the absolute transcendence of the interior/exterior of every thing now existing in the world, is, that is, neither the ideal of social equality,[45] found in the plaintext of historical materialism, nor the latter's absolute material ground,[46] the absolute inversion of the abyss, which, *qua* absolute implication of the plaintext,[47] *qua* implicitly material objectivity, is the abyss of social equality (at once the abyss of identity not identity, the absolute identity of equivocal-univocal/the absolute liquidity of identity[48]) in the form of absolute solitude, in the form of the anonymous double of social unity, the absolute division of identity into units.[49] The absolute condition of transcending the individual interior consciousness of humanity is not the anony-

[45] Cf. above, p. 86.
[46] Cf. above, pp. 226ff.
[47] Cf. above, pp. 207ff., 216, and 227.
[48] Cf. above, p. 237.
[49] Ibid.

mous double of social unity/the implicitly material objectivity/implicitly the alternative to the 'ghost-like' objectivity or value which historical materialism understands to be 'nothing but the social unity itself in its hypostatized form',[50] but it is, precisely, the social unity which is a material objectivity, the absolute out-identity of the *unum*, the absolutely material objectivity of the lordship of *one* history,[51] the *unum* transcending the absolutely liquid *metanoein*, transcending the purely material *metanoein*[52]/the absolutely pure material lordship of history, transcending the absolutely liquid inversion of the 'depth of

---

[50] Cf. above, p. 80, n. 42.

[51] This is the univocal predicating of the material lordship of history. Cf. above, pp. 188ff.

[52] Here, and immediately following, the anonymity of God (*KN*) is identified as the pure concrete form of *metanoein*. *Metanoein* is defined by R. P. Scharlemann in *The Being of God: Theology and the Experience of Truth* (New York, 1981), pp. 154-155: "Mundane, or literal, thought has to do with the experience of sensational or logical objects; reflective thought, with the experience of reflective objects, or phenomena. Reflexive thought is concerned with the experience of depths, that is, of the self-transcendence or self-duplication indicated in such phrasings as 'the truth about truth' and 'the goodness about goodness'.

". . . the experience of the depth of truth cannot be carried further but only repeated indefinitely. . . . Thinking does, indeed, have one thing left to do; and that is to invert itself, so that *noein* becomes *metanoein*, thinking becomes afterthinking. The possibility of this turn lies formally in the freedom of thought: one can think of thinking as thinking, but one can also think of it as other than itself—as the being of God. The freedom to make this inversion is the source of creativity. A woodsman would not get firewood, to say nothing of furniture, out of a tree if he were not capable of thinking of the appearing object as other than how it appears. When applied to the whole process of thinking, this same freedom is the capacity to turn thought into afterthought. What is other than our thinking is, normally, the other's being. Hence the move to *metanoein* is to think of our thinking of being as the being of God for our thinking. More particularly, in the present context, this would mean that one can think of our experiencing truth (seeing identity in difference) as God's being different from himself, and of our experiencing untruth as God's being at one with himself. To do so is to form a thought that represents the transition from thinking to afterthinking, or what is theological thinking in its most proper sense."

truth'/of 'reflexivity', transcending what, indeed, might be understood to be 'theological thinking in its most proper sense' in the form of the anonymity of God, in the form of the anonymous naming of God, in the form of the totally anonymous God. Now for the first time in history the actuality of the social *unum* names the unnamed material lordship of history, names the unnamed/names the implicit, *is* the *name* of material objectivity. The one itself names the unnamed, names that which presents itself without a name, the (unnamed) immediacy of existence: the one name identifies absolutely (unnamed) identity, the lordship of one history for the first time names the darkness: for the first time the (unnamed) new and universal humanity is absolutely specified as the objective existence of the material unity of world-consciousness, as the *de facto* universal lordship of one history, as the absolutely concrete unity of the new creation now existent, the new actuality of the unicity of creation, the absolute explosion of identity in the form of the new unity of history. This new reality of one-world-consciousness now actually occurring for the first time in history is the transcendence of the 'freedom of thought', the existence of a new thought, the actuality of a new identity of consciousness, the transcendent existence of the being of God, not the radical subjectivity of thinking itself not itself as the 'source of creativity', but the transcendence of the difference in the identity of the being of God. The being of God is now for the first time without being other than itself the material objectivity of the social *unum*, the univocal predication of the being of God as matter itself the body, the absolute coincidence of being itself the social *unum*, society coinciding the identity of the One in the form of the objectivity of matter. This reality of One-world-consciousness itself beginning is neither a matter of intention (whether the intention is of the first order [the thing], of the second order [thought], or of the third order [afterthought, thought essentially, identity]), nor a matter of extension (the absolute division of intention, the division of intention from itself, the absolute division of identity into units), but rather a matter of the *minimum*, a matter of *meta*-intentionality, a matter of *meta*-extensiveness, a matter of *meta*-identity: the new reality of the world for the first time is the *after*-

identity of everything, everything now existing for the first time *ex abysso*: this is the *de facto* existence of the *unum* absolute,[53] for the first time the absolute exteriority of the outside/the absolute out-identity of (any)side. This minimum/after-intentionality/after-extensiveness is the meta-identity of *metanoein*, the meta-identity of the inversion of the 'depth of truth', the inversion of the depth of afterthought/of the depth of identity/of the identity of depth, the transcendence of the radical subjectivity of the inversion of thought, the transcendence of the double division of the depth of reflection, of the thought of 'our experiencing truth (seeing identity in difference) as God's being different from himself, and of our experiencing untruth as God's being at one with himself'. The *after-identity* now actually occurring for the first time is the inversion of the identity of depth, the double division of the depth of identity, the absolute outside/the fourfold of identity/the identity of the fourfold.[54] This *after-identity* is the experience of the new identity of identity now occurring as consciousness of the reality of matter. This new identity, new existence *ex abysso*, the catholicological being which is the reality of matter, is the now freely occurring unification of the material foundation of history. There is no essentially historical/essentially dialectical materialism not unified in the new identity.[55] Revolutionary metanoēsis is the known necessity of one foundation. The proof of the one foundation/of the *unum esse*, the proof that the identity *between* the one and existence is transcended for the first time, the proof that experiencing truth is not 'seeing identity in difference', not 'our' experience of truth, not a matter of identity between (any) two (things), but rather a matter of seeing *identity*, that for the first time the experience of truth is seeing the after-identity of identity itself, seeing the dif-

---

[53] Cf. above pp. 236 and 243, 'the absolute division of identity into units'.

[54] Cf. above, p. 194, for the 'double division of the abyss of itself'; cf. also, above, p. 244, n. 52. For the generic purity of the fourfold of reflection, cf. Heidegger's 'earth and sky, divinities and mortals, in the simple onefold of their self-unified fourfold' in *Poetry, Language, Thought* (New York, 1971), pp. 178–80. In contrast to Heidegger, the fourfold of *after-identity* is *other*-unified.

[55] Cf. above, p. 80, n. 42.

ference itself of identity/the identity of difference itself, the proof is identical with the one foundation, viz., that revolutionary metanoēsis is the *inversion of afterthought to existence,* the absolute inversion of the depth of identity and, therefore, *the inversion itself repeatedly new,* which (unlike the repetition of the intention of the depth of truth, the experience of which 'cannot be carried further, but only repeated indefinitely'[56]) is *always and everywhere new, catholicologically so.* This is the proof in the form: the absolutely unconditioned actuality of absolute self contradiction: the self-contradiction which is absolutely not the contradiction of the proof proving itself one: for the first time the necessity of the truth of the spoken word.

This is the new unity in the experience of truth, the new experience of the one truth. The meta-identical unity of the experience of truth now occurring in time is the substantial unity of world-consciousness *known as* the necessity of matter itself, as the revolutionary identity actually existing, the known *novitas mundi,* the known creation of the world *ex nihilo,* the known existence of the second absolute, the foundation of a universal/world society. This unity of identity is absolutely the foundation of the society which is a new world, a new humanity, the society of every-existing-thing, the society in which the existence of the fourfold is the known absolute, personal, the identity of freedom, neither self-realization nor other-realization, but the other identically, the realization of the body. This unity of identity is the world-foundation of a society in which the realization of another is another identically the new itself, a society in which the reality of the other is the existence of the new creation, in which the value of the other is the absolute value of freedom, in which the freedom of *this* other is the foundation. The freedom of *this* other is the passion of the unity which is the material objectivity of world-consciousness for the first time. The freedom of *this* other is the end of the unity which is society. The suffering of the freedom of *this* other *in unity* is the absolute value of the new world now for the first time actually in existence as the end of history. The truth of this new unity of experience, of this new unity of world-

[56] Cf. above, p. 244, n. 52.

consciousness, is not merely the ideal of a totally logical society, of an absolutely logical individual (not in fact what is, in its concrete historical actuality, the American ideal, the ideal integration of the individual into the social wholeness,[57]) at once the 'Logic . . . rooted in the social principle' of the pragmatism enunciated by Peirce, as follows:

> All human affairs rest upon probabilities, and the same thing is true everywhere. If man were immortal he could be perfectly sure of seeing the day when everything in which he had trusted should betray his trust, and, in short, of coming eventually to hopeless misery. He would break down, at last, as every great fortune, as every dynasty, as every civilization does. In place of this we have death.
>
> But what, without death, would happen to every man, with death must happen to some man. At the same time, death makes the number of our risks, of our inferences, finite, and so makes their mean result uncertain. The very idea of probability and of reasoning rests on the assumption that this number is indefinitely great. We are thus landed in the same difficulty as before [viz., that the uncertainty of the mean result of a finite number of inferences does not differ, except in degree, from an isolated case about which there is no sense in reasoning, if the concern is with real facts], and I can see but one solution of it. It seems to me that we are driven to this, that logicality inexorably requires that our interests shall *not* be limited. They must not stop at our own fate, but must embrace the whole community. This community, again, must not be limited, but must extend to all races of beings with whom we can come into immediate or mediate intellectual relation. It must reach, however vaguely, beyond this geological epoch, beyond all bounds. He who would not sacrifice his own soul to save the whole world, is, as it seems to me, illogical in all his inferences, collectively. Logic is rooted in the social principle.
>
> To be logical men should not be selfish; and, in point of

[57] Cf. J. Royce, *The Problem of Christianity* (intro. J. E. Smith, Chicago, 1968). Note the analogy between Royce's conception of the individual's love for the community as for an ideal person with Peirce's conception of the required non-existence of the object of love, as cited below in the text.

fact, they are not so selfish as they are thought. . . . We discuss with anxiety the possible exhaustion of coal in some hundreds of years, or the cooling-off of the sun in some millions, and show in the most popular of all religious tenets that we can conceive the possibility of a man's descending into hell for the salvation of his fellows. . . .

But all this requires a conceived identification of one's interests with those of an unlimited community. Now, there exist no reasons . . . for thinking that the human race, or any intellectual race, will exist forever. On the other hand, there can be no reason against it; and, fortunately, as the whole requirement is that we should have certain sentiments, there is nothing in the facts to forbid our having a *hope,* or calm and cheerful wish, that the community may last beyond any assignable date.

It may seem strange that I should put forward three sentiments, namely, interest in an indefinite community, recognition of the possibility of this interest being made supreme, and hope in the unlimited continuance of intellectual activity, as indispensable requirements of logic. Yet, when we consider that logic depends on a mere struggle to escape doubt, which, as it terminates in action, must begin in emotion, and that, furthermore, the only cause of our planting ourselves on reason is that other methods of escaping doubt fail on account of the social impulse, why should we wonder to find social sentiment presupposed in reasoning? As for the other two sentiments which I find necessary, they are so only as supports and accessories of that. It interests me to notice that these three sentiments seem to be pretty much the same as that famous trio of Charity, Faith, and Hope, which, in the estimation of St. Paul, are the finest and greatest of spiritual gifts. Neither Old nor New Testament is a textbook of the logic of science, but the latter is certainly the highest existing authority in regard to the dispositions of heart which a man ought to have.[58]

The transcendental idealism of this pragmatism/American thought, the fact that pragmatic idealism is formally revolutionary, that this is transcendental idealism in the realm of action,

[58] C. S. Peirce, *Collected Papers* (Cambridge, Mass., 1931), 2.653–55.

which this logic is, is made pointedly clearer, if that were necessary, in a note by Peirce, years later, on the just cited passage:

> This point is that no man can be logical whose supreme desire is the well-being of himself or of any other existing person or collection of persons.[59]

Just here can be appreciated the fact that the absolute inversion of the abyss/the abyss of transcendental idealism (*KN* or *A*)/the absolute material ground of historical materialism is, *qua* death of selfhood/death of the transcendent God/eternal death of Jesus (a death of God, however, not qualifiedly unqualified), the reduction to Nothing of an American transcendental idealism, of an actual selfhood, of an essentially logical self, the reduction to Nothing of the formal ideal of the American revolution (the ideal of a totally logical society of selves, a society of selves indefinitely postponing their own interests), itself at once the abyss of individual self-consciousness (existing anonymously in the form of an absolute solitude). The absolute inversion of the abyss, total Presence, absolute solitude, are identically American phenomena at the end of history, in the real guise of a nameless identity. The new world unity experienced as the absolute conception in essence of revolutionary metanoēsis which is what it is as the absolute out-identity of (any)side *ex abysso* is not a resurrection from death of the American ideal, not a resurrection of a dead society of logical selves. The unity of the Body which is the absolute bound of world consciousness is precisely not the ideal social *unum* of the American revolution, not the ideal unity of pragmatism, not the sentimental preconception of the necessity and identity of the logical unity of existence, not the sentimental presupposition of the unity of society. The world unity of consciousness is the transcendence for the first time of the *unum* of the American revolution, of the *unitas Americana*, of the unity of American society, the transcendence of the unity of pragmatism concretely practiced, the transcendence of the practice of the death of the transcendent God in the form of the logic of the

[59] Ibid., 2.661.

principle of social unity. The unity of world consciousness is the elimination of this reduction to Nothing of the Living Unity, the new identity of death and the Living One is very creation, the univocal predication of the now-identity of Life and death the new unity of life *ex nihilo.* The perfectly new *unum, qua* social principle of the beginning world-consciousness, is the minimum transcendence of historical materialism, the absolutely objective existence of the essence of history, the matter of absolute materialism freely existing in time, at once itself the transcendence of the American social principle, indeed, the very passion of Christ. This *unum* identically the passion of Christ, the catholicologically new, revolutionary, metanoēsis, the inversion itself repeatedly new existence, this *unum* essentially the unification of the dialectic of matter, is the *novum e pluribus unum/e pluribus unum esse,* the foundation itself existing for the first time, the transcendence itself of the American *unum, the beginning of the materialization of a universally existing habit of social unity.* As such, this predication of an essentially historical materialism, this new habit of social unity now actually existing for the first time is not the inversion of the ideal habit of social unity which is of the essence of an *in*essentially historical materialism (in fact, this new habit of social unity begins as the meta-identity of the implicit inversion of the latter, the meta-identity of the implicit inversion of what actually is a conception of social equality, the meta-identity of the liquid *metanoein* which is the extreme extremity of American consciousness[60]). The coinciding in this unity of world-consciousness of (1) the transcendence of the existing principle of a logical society, (2) the conception of an essentially historical materialism, and (3) the existence of the absolute passion of world-creation, *is* the absolute coincidence which is the new history in the One Now Occurring in the form of the absolute principle of a new world-wide society. This is history coinciding unity as the consciousness of a world-society which for the first time *is* the death of selfhood.

---

[60] This consciousness of the unity of matter is not an inversion of the uchronia, but it is, absolutely now and for the first time, the practice of the death of the *transcendental* God in the form of the new principle of social unity.

III

THE UNITY OF THE NEW WORLD ORDER

1

THE LAW OF ABSOLUTE UNITY

The reader is now asked to set aside at least temporarily—for the purpose of opening the mind to the possibility of a new logic—the most fundamental truth of ordinary mathematics and the logic of relatives, viz., the assumption, in one form or another, that it is simply true that $1 + 0 = 1$. However true this last equation may be in ordinary mathematics and equivalently in a binary logic, it cannot be simply true in a truly trinary logic. It cannot be exhaustively true in a logic which essentially transcends the duality of modern consciousness. In the following equation which belongs to a logic categorically new, where ‘1’ is ‘unity’, ‘0’ is ‘zero’, and ‘$\overline{0}$’ is ‘unum’, the reader is asked to consider—without prejudice to the formal truth of the above equation—that the following is also true: $1 + 0 = \overline{0}$. Now whatever else might be true of this last equation, it must be clear that in this equation the zero, 0, is not and cannot, in *any* sense of the word, be ‘nothing’. But in a trinary logic where none of the three terms is a ‘nothing’ there can be no ‘plus’ and no ‘minus’ since ‘nothing’ is the necessary condition for the latter distinction. Likewise there can be no multiplication and no division, which presuppose addition and subtraction. Let the indifference of these operations upon terms in this logic be signified by the sign ∵ or by omitting a sign of relation altogether, i.e., either by $1 \because 0 = \overline{0}$ or by $10 = \overline{0}$.[1] It will then follow that as $1 = 0\overline{0}$, so $0 = 1\overline{0}$, and

[1] There is a real but *imperfect* reflection of this logical indifference to plus and minus in the extreme and mean geometric relation, $\phi^{-1} : \phi^{0} :: \phi^{0} : \phi^{1}$, which is such that $\phi^{-1} + \phi^{0} = \phi^{+1}$, where the exponents betray the indiffer-

therefore, $11\bar{0} = \bar{0}$, $11 = \overline{00}$, $0 = 110$, and finally $11 = 00$. Therefore $11 = \overline{00} = 00 = 0\bar{0}$. In this logic different terms can be differently related but it is not possible to express inequality.[2]

There are certain fundamental relations existing among 0, $\bar{0}$, and 1, summarized under the following heading, where the elements are understood to be related by the unexpressed symbol ∵ (signifying absolute multiplication or the identity of addition, multiplication, subtraction, and division):

Absolute Multiplication.

$$0\bar{0} = 1$$
$$01 = \bar{0}$$
$$\bar{0}1 = 0$$
$$11 = 1$$
$$\overline{00} = 1$$
$$00 = 1$$
$$111 = 1,\ \overline{000}(000),\ \overline{000},\text{ and }000$$
$$\overline{000} = 0,\ 000(111),\ 000,\text{ and }111$$
$$000 = \bar{0},\ \overline{000}(111),\ \overline{000},\text{ and }111$$
$$\bar{0}10 = 1.$$

There are also nine exponential relations set forth under the following heading:

Exponential Relations.

$$0^{0} = 1$$
$$0^{\bar{0}} = 0$$
$$0^{1} = \bar{0}$$
$$\bar{0}^{0} = 1$$
$$\overline{0^{0}} = 0$$
$$\bar{0}^{1} = \bar{0}$$
$$1^{0} = 1$$
$$1^{\bar{0}} = 0$$
$$1^{1} = \bar{0}$$

ence insofar as they are *indirectly* so related through ϕ. Compare $\phi^0 + \phi^1 = \phi^2$, where the exponents reflect analogously that $0 \neq$ nothing. Cf. also, below, Section III.2, Theorem 1.

[2] The writer is indebted to Ingrid Willenz-Isaacs for this last formulation, which puts in the negative, and therefore in a way which resonates fully, the significance of the identity and equality of the logical elements.

Exponents transform the base digit into the digit previous to the exponent in the infinitely repeating series, 0, $\bar{0}$, 1, 0, $\bar{0}$, 1. . . . The proofs for both absolute multiplication and exponential relations, together with the rules governing the proofs, are set out under the following heading:

Rules and Exemplary Proofs for the Fundamental Relations.
Rule 1. For *non-identical two-digit* relations: to prove the absolute multiplication, factor *either* digit, multiply the factors by the other digit, in such a way that the product contains at least one threefold repetition of a single digit. For factoring 1 use a two-digit factor. For factoring 0 or $\bar{0}$ use either a two-digit or three-digit factor (three-digit factors for digits composed with 1 produce a circular proof in which the penultimate pairing in the reduction of the multiplication of factors will be the pair to be proved: in that case a two-digit factor must be used). In a case employing a two-digit factor cancel (remove by deletion) the threefold (identity) repetition of a digit in the product of the multiplication of factors. (Reducing by pairing will produce an inferentially true but non-fundamental relation.) The remaining digit is the product of the absolute multiplication. In a case employing a three-digit factor reduce the result of the multiplication of factors to the product of the absolute multiplication simply by pairing.

Proof of $0\bar{0} = 1$:

either:		*or:*		*or:*		*or:*	
	$(\bar{0}1)\bar{0}$		$0(01)$		$0(000)$		$(\overline{000})\bar{0}$
	$\bar{0}\bar{0}\bar{0}1$		0001		$00\ 00\ 00$		$\overline{00}\ \overline{00}\ \overline{00}$
	1		1		$11\ 1$		$11\ 1$
					11		11
					1		$1.$

Proof of $01 = \bar{0}$:

either:		*or:*	
	$0(0\bar{0})$		$1\bar{0}(1)$
	$000\bar{0}$		$11\bar{0}1$
	$\bar{0}$		$\bar{0}.$

Proof of $\bar{0}1 = 0$:

either:		*or:*	
	$\bar{0}(0\bar{0})$		$10(1)$
	$\bar{0}0\bar{0}\bar{0}$		1101
	0		$0.$

Rule 2. For *identical two-digit* relations, to prove the absolute multiplication, factor *either or both* digits, multiply the factors of one digit by the other digit, or, as the case may be, by each of the factors of the other digit. For factoring 00 or $\overline{00}$, use a two-digit factor when factoring both digits and a three-digit factor when factoring only one digit. In either case, when proving 00 or $\overline{00}$, reduce the result to the product of the absolute multiplication simply by pairing. (Canceling the threefold [identity] repetition of a digit in the product of the multiplication of factors will produce an inferentially true but non-fundamental relation.) For factoring either or both elements of 11 use a two-digit factor, and when factoring both digits *cancel* the threefold (identity) repetitions of a digit which occur in the product of the multiplication of factors before reducing the result by pairing (not to do so is the equivalent of using a three-digit factor composed with 1 and produces a circular proof as defined above in Rule 1).

Proof of 11 = 1:

either:		*or:*	
	$0\bar{0}(0\bar{0})$		$1(0\bar{0})$
	$00\ 0\bar{0}\ \bar{0}0\ \overline{00}$		$101\bar{0}$
	$0\bar{0}$		$0\bar{0}$
	1		1.

Note: Unique to the proof of 11 = 1 is the fact that its essentially tautological form, in the case where *both* elements are factored, permits of the non-circular, non-tautological solution effected by the cancellation of occurring "identities" (threefold repetitions of a digit). This solution produces the identical penultimate ($0\bar{0}$) and ultimate (1) results which appear in the parallel proof of the case in which only *one* element of 11 is factored and no "identities" occur to be cancelled (a case in which the proof of 11 = 1 also follows, in effect, Rule 1, the rule for *non-identical* two-digit relations). Note that $0\bar{0}$ in the former case is the penultimate reduction of "$00\ 0\bar{0}\ \bar{0}0\ \overline{00}$," the pure form of which latter is the inversion and reversal of the fundamental form of all logical propositions, $pq + \bar{p}q + p\bar{q} + \overline{pq}$,[3] and that it is that *in-*

[3] For the fundamental form of all logical statements, see C. S. Peirce, *Collected Papers* (Cambridge, Mass., 1933), 3.41, Editor's note. The multiplica-

version and *reversal* precisely and substantively when it is assumed that $0 \neq 0$, which last is the fundamental condition upon which depends the reduction of the trichotomous solution of the absolute law of unity to the identity of the dual solution of the law of absolute unity and the dual solution of the law of duality, so that the inference from $0 = \bar{0}$ and $0 = 1$ to $0 \neq 0$, taken purely formally, is here $0 \neq 0$, $0 = \bar{0} = p$ and $0 = 1 = q$.[4] The proof of $11 = 1$ is then the absolute *inversion* and *reversal* of logic itself, that is, *the proof that in the practice of an essentially new logic the non-tautological emptiness of logic is for the first time at once the essentially tautological logic of existence completely displacing the emptiness of logic.*[5]

Proof of $\overline{00} = 1$:

$$\textit{either:}\quad \begin{array}{c} 01\,(01) \\ 00\ 01\ 10\ 11 \\ 1\bar{0}\ \bar{0}1 \\ 00 \\ 1 \end{array} \qquad \textit{or:}\quad \begin{array}{c} \bar{0}\,(000) \\ \bar{0}0\ \bar{0}0\ \bar{0}0 \\ 11\quad 1 \\ 1. \end{array}$$

Proof of $00 = 1$:

$$\textit{either:}\quad \begin{array}{c} \bar{0}1\,(\bar{0}1) \\ \overline{00}\ \bar{0}1\ 1\bar{0}\ 11 \\ 10\ 01 \\ \overline{00} \\ 1 \end{array} \qquad \textit{or:}\quad \begin{array}{c} 0\,(\overline{000}) \\ 0\bar{0}\ 0\bar{0}\ 0\bar{0} \\ 11\quad 1 \\ 1. \end{array}$$

---

tion of factors in the proofs of $\overline{00} = 1$ and $00 = 1$, respectively, "00 01 10 11" and "$\overline{00}\ \bar{0}1\ 1\bar{0}\ 11$," are reversals of the logical form, but with respect to each other inversions only, and that only implicitly, and not inversions with respect to the logical form. The substitution of $\bar{0}$ for 1 in the multiplication of factors of $\overline{00}$ produces the multiplication of factors of 11, and makes explicit the inverse relation of the multiplied factors of 00 and $\overline{00}$.

[4] Cf. below, pp. 279ff.

[5] On the emptiness of tautology, and the tautological character of logic, cf. R. Carnap, "The Old and the New Logic," in *Logical Positivism*, ed. A. J. Ayer (New York, 1959). For the practice of an essentially tautological thinking, i.e., for the form of thought for the first time absolutely displacing the emptiness of the form of thought, see D. G. Leahy, *Novitas Mundi, Perception of the History of Being* (reprint; Albany, 1994), Appendix α. For the essential tautology of existence, cf. ibid., pp. 383f. et passim.

Rule 3. For *identical three-digit* relations, to prove the absolute multiplication, factor *all* digits, using a two-digit factor, and multiply the factors of two digits by those of the third. Reduce the product of the multiplication of factors by pairing once, then cancel the threefold (identity) repetition of a digit in the reduction of the product of the multiplication of factors, and reduce the result to the product of the absolute multiplication by pairing a second time. (In the case of 111, beginning with the product of the multiplication of factors, the threefold [identity] repetition of a digit *may or may not* be canceled at any stage without affecting the final result of the proof. In the case of $\overline{000}$ or 000 the first reduction should be by pairing, as in Rule 2, followed by canceling, as in Rule 1.)

Proof of 111 = 1:

either:

$$0\bar{0}\ 0\bar{0}\ 0\bar{0}$$
$$00\ 0\bar{0}\ 00\ 0\bar{0}\ \bar{0}0\ \overline{00}\ \bar{0}0\ \overline{00}$$
$$11\ 11\ 11\ 11$$
$$11$$
$$1$$

or:

$$0\bar{0}\ 0\bar{0}\ 0\bar{0}$$
$$00\ 0\bar{0}\ 00\ 0\bar{0}\ \bar{0}0\ \overline{00}\ \bar{0}0\ \overline{00}$$
$$1\ 1\ 1\ 1\ 1\ 1\ 1\ 1$$
$$11$$
$$1$$

or:

$$0\bar{0}\ \ 0\bar{0}\ \ 0\bar{0}$$
$$00\ 0\bar{0}\ 00\ 0\bar{0}\ \bar{0}0\ \overline{00}\ \bar{0}0\ \overline{00}$$
$$00\ \overline{00}$$
$$11$$
$$1.$$

Proof of $\overline{000} = 0$:

$$01\ 01\ 01$$
$$00\ 01\ 00\ 01\ 10\ 11\ 10\ 11$$
$$1\ \bar{0}\ 1\ \bar{0}\ \bar{0}\ 1\ \bar{0}\ 1$$
$$\bar{0}1$$
$$0.$$

Proof of $000 = \bar{0}$:

$$\bar{0}1\ \bar{0}1\ \bar{0}1$$
$$\overline{00}\ \bar{0}1\ \overline{00}\ \bar{0}1\ 1\bar{0}\ 11\ 1\bar{0}\ 11$$
$$1\ 0\ 1\ 0\ 0\ 1\ 0\ 1$$
$$01$$
$$\bar{0}.$$

Rule 4. For *non-identical three-digit* relations, to prove the absolute multiplication in the cases where two of the digits are identical, multiply one of them by the odd digit, and proceed according to Rule 1. In cases where none of the digits are identical, factor all digits using a two-digit factor, and multiply the factors of one by each of those of the others. Reduce the product of the multiplication of factors to the product of the absolute multiplication *either* by canceling the threefold (identity) repetition of a digit and then pairing *or* simply by pairing. (A proof of these latter cases in the case of their one fundamental form follows below. The former cases of non-identical three-digit relations will, in effect, have been proven above.)

Proof of $\bar{0}10 = 1$:

either:

$$\begin{array}{c} 01\ 0\bar{0}\ \bar{0}1 \\ 00\ 0\bar{0}\ \bar{0}0\ 01\ 10\ 1\bar{0}\ \bar{1}0\ 11 \\ \overline{00}\ \overline{00} \\ 11 \\ 1 \end{array}$$

or:

$$\begin{array}{c} 01\ 0\bar{0}\ \bar{0}1 \\ 00\ 0\bar{0}\ \bar{0}0\ 01\ 10\ 1\bar{0}\ \bar{1}0\ 11 \\ 11\ 1\bar{0}\ \bar{0}0\ 01 \\ 10\ 1\bar{0} \\ \bar{0}0 \\ 1. \end{array}$$

Rule 5. To prove the identity of 0, $\bar{0}$, and 1, and, therefore, the identity of the relations of which they are in turn the absolute multiplication products, factor each digit using three-identical-digit factors. Then cancel in each of the three cases a *different* threefold (identity) repetition of a digit. The product of the absolute multiplication of the remaining factor in each case is a digit non-identically identically one of the others.

Proof of $1 = 111 = 0\bar{0} = \overline{000}(000) = \overline{000} = 0 = \bar{0}1 = 000(111) = 000 = \bar{0} = 01 = \overline{000}(111) = 1 = \bar{0}10$:

> Since it has been proven above in accord with Rules 1–4 that $111 = 0\bar{0} = 1$, $\overline{000} = 0 = \bar{0}1$, $000 = \bar{0} = 01$, and $\bar{0}10 = 1$, *the statement of what is to be proven is the proof of what is to be proven.*[6]

[6] While the identity of the non-identical digits, 0, $\bar{0}$, 1, might equally well be proven from the fact that $1 = 0\bar{0} = 00 = \overline{00} = 11$, in this proof their identity

Note: The perfect rationality of the order of the beginning of unity manifests itself in the inter-relationship of the pairs of the factors of 1, 0, and $\overline{0}$, respectively, $\overline{000}(000)$ or $0\overline{0}$, 000(111) or $\overline{0}1$, and $\overline{000}(111)$ or 01, as set out in the proof/statement of proof above, where 111 or 1 is the 2nd factor of *its* 1st *and* 2nd factors, $\overline{000}$ or 0 is the 1st factor of *its* 1st *and* 2nd factors, but 000 or $\overline{0}$ is the *1st* factor of *its 1st* factor and the *2nd* factor of *its 2nd* factor, which is to say that in this completely logical logic *not only is it the case that every integer is a ratio, but, further, that, while* 0 *and* 1 *each relate themselves in their structure to each other and to* $\overline{0}$ *as identities, without either, however,* in itself *establishing the* exact order *existing between itself, the other, and* $\overline{0}$, *it is* $\overline{0}$, *the* essential *identity of the beginning, the "identical with" of the beginning, which in its very structure identifies its precise ordered relation to* 0 *and* 1, and, moreover, identifies the order of this relation as "0, $\overline{0}$, 1" and does so insofar as it is perfectly free from the complementary contrariety of the structures of 0 and 1, according to which the ordered relation between themselves and $\overline{0}$ would be at best an inference based on mere juxtaposition, "$\overline{0}1$" and "$0\overline{0}$," but without essential structural reference of the one to the other. The structure of $\overline{0}$, then, establishes the *non-identity* of the identical digits, that is, establishes not merely that 1 = 1 and 0, nor merely that 0 = 0 and 1, i.e., that 1 and 0 equal each other and

---

is a function of canceling three non-identical threefold (identity) repetitions of a digit in their factors. While initially among the three sets of factors either identity of any one set might equally well be selected or not for cancellation, not to chose is not a choice, and, having chosen, not to chose differently subsequently is not a choice, therefore, having chosen, the initial choice is a different choice, therefore, having chosen, the initial choice is essentially a function of the subsequent choices among the three sets. This proof, then, in a particularly vivid way, illustrates the fact that the essentially final divergence at the root of modern logic—manifesting itself in the form of the ruling dichotomies, absolute/relative, determination/chance, objectivity/interaction, celestial mechanics/quantum mechanics, perfection/incompleteness, infinity/finitude, macrocosm/microcosm—is overcome in an *essentially* trichotomous logic where for the first time not to chose is not a choice and every alternative is *essentially* chosen in every choice, including—in the choice not to chose alternatively—the choice identically to chose alternatively.

both = $\overline{0}$, as is established by the structure of each of the former, but that $\overline{0} = 1 + 0$, that is, *without identifying the latter two*, $\overline{0}$ establishes precisely the *ordered* identity of the two with itself. (Since factorial 0 is $\overline{0} \because 1 \because 0$, there is here a mathematics in which it is really the case that $0! = 1$.)

Rule 6. To prove the exponential relations of 0, $\overline{0}$, and 1, factor the exponent of the digit using a three-identical-digit factor as follows: for the exponents of 0, use the three-identical-digit factor of the exponent: for the exponents of $\overline{0}$, use the three-identical-digit factor of the digit next *following* the exponent in the rational order of the digits: for the exponents of 1, use the three-identical-digit factor of the digit in the rational order of digits which is in the *identical relation to the exponent as the exponent is to* $\overline{0}$. For the exponent factor 111 substitute 1. Reduce the digit together with the exponent factor to the exponential relation by pairing, except in the cases where the exponent is, in the rational order of the digits, the digit next *following* the base digit, in which cases reduce by canceling the threefold (identity) factor of the exponent (where 1 has been substituted for 111, reduce by pairing).

Note: The complex principle for the selection of exponential factors perfectly exemplifies the essential rationality of the order 0, $\overline{0}$, 1: for the base digit 0 (absolute irreducible existence), the exponent is *the immediate digit to be factored*, for the base digit $\overline{0}$ (absolute relative "identical-with"), the exponent is *the foundation for selecting the digit to be factored*, for the base digit 1 (absolute relative unity), the relation of the digit to be factored to the exponent is the relation of the exponent to the foundational $\overline{0}$, i.e., the exponent is *the mean proportional of the digit sought and* $\overline{0}$.

Proof of $0^0 = 1$:

$$0\overline{000}$$
$$11$$
$$1.$$

Proof of $0^{\overline{0}} = 0$:

$$0000$$
$$0.$$

Proof of $0^1 = \overline{0}$:

$$\begin{array}{c} 01 \\ \overline{0}. \end{array}$$

Proof of $\overline{0}^0 = 1$:

$$\begin{array}{c} \overline{0}000 \\ 11 \\ 1. \end{array}$$

Proof of $\overline{0^0} = 0$:

$$\begin{array}{c} \overline{0}1 \\ 0. \end{array}$$

Proof of $\overline{0}^1 = \overline{0}$:

$$\begin{array}{c} \overline{0000} \\ \overline{0}. \end{array}$$

Proof of $1^0 = 1$:

$$\begin{array}{c} 11 \\ 1. \end{array}$$

Proof of $1^{\overline{0}} = 0$:

$$\begin{array}{c} 1000 \\ \overline{0}1 \\ 0. \end{array}$$

Proof of $1^1 = \overline{0}$:

$$\begin{array}{c} 1\overline{000} \\ 01 \\ \overline{0}. \end{array}$$

The rationality of zero [0] essentially proven in the law of absolute unity and demonstrated in the above Rules and Proofs is the minimum/*unum* [$\overline{0}$] as the infinitesimal limit of the beginning of unity [1]. The minimum is transcendental unity *ex abysso.* This limit of the infinitesimal is the absolute alio-relative minimum unity of the beginning: absolutely rational zero "identical with" the universe. This "identical with" [*1*] or [$\overline{0}$],[7] this minimum unity of zero, is no longer as it is in Peirce,[8] a *self*-relative, negative of an alio-relative, "pairing every object with itself and none with any other," its negative $(1 + \mathit{1})^{-1}$, "other-than," "not," but is instead a relative which, *qua* infinite transcendence, *identifies,* that is, *qua* infinitesimal limit, *meta-pairs,* every object with itself and with every other in the form of the existence of the *unum,* in the form of existence as the *minimum.* This minimum, "identical with," *unum,* is a discrete component of the

[7] Cf. below, pp. 279ff.

[8] Ibid. Cf. also Peirce, *Collected Papers,* 3.225ff., 3.312, and 3.338f.

absolutely differentiated beginning of unity. This minimum, insofar as the law of absolute unity exists, is irreducible to a unity (1) the less-than-which is Nothing, that is, irreducible to a unity (1) not differentiated from an elemental minimum ($\bar{0}$), that is, not differentiated from itself whose less-than-which (0) is not Nothing but is *existence.*[9] In the beginning essentially rational zero meta-identifies unity. Meta-identity, as a function of the irreducibility of the Universe to Nothing, is not not nothing, i.e., $\mathit{1} = (1 + \mathit{1})^{-0}$, which transformed (regardless of whether 0 = nothing, or 0 = not nothing, since in the logic, just as in ordinary mathematics, a digit whose exponent is 0 equals 1)[10] is

$$\mathit{1} = \frac{1}{(1 + \mathit{1})^{0}} = \frac{1}{1} = 1$$

which is to say that *meta-identity which is not nothing identically not not nothing is unity.* But by the law of absolute unity[11]

$$\mathit{1} = 1 = \mathit{1}(1 + 1) = 0,$$

where 0 is not nothing, so that the proof that $\bar{0}$ is not not nothing and not nothing and 1 is the proof of the absolute asymmetry of the Universe and Nothing.[12] Meta-identity is the absolutely inconvertible relationship of a living, i.e., essentially rational, unity. The Peircean relative identity is essentially a self-relative unity reducible to Nothing in the form of zero, the negative of which essentially self-relative identity is indistinguishable from Nothing since unity is absolute self-identity. Peirce defines 1 and $\bar{1}$ as follows:[13]

$$(1)_{ii} = 1, \quad (1)_{ij} = 0,$$

[9] Cf. Peirce, *Collected Papers,* 3.261–79.

[10] Cf. above, pp. 255f.

[11] Cf. below, this Section, Afterword 1.

[12] Cf. below, pp. 279ff.

[13] Peirce, *Collected Papers,* 3.312.

and

$$(\bar{1})_{ii} = 0, \quad (\bar{1})_{ij} = 1,$$

But the negative of the *absolute* alio-relative identity, the meta-identical negative, $(1 + 1)^{-1}$, is the proof of the *absolute* existence of the minimum in the beginning, that is, the meta-identical negative *is* positive meta-identity, proven as follows (where $[1 + 1]^{1} = 0^{\bar{0}} = 0$, and, by the logic of absolute multiplication, $1 - 0 = 1$ $\because 0 = \bar{0}$):[14]

$$(1 + 1)^{-1} = \frac{1}{(1 + 1)^{1}} = 1 - 0 = \bar{0} = 1,$$

which is a transposition of the law of existential contradiction, "$1 - \bar{0} = 0$," *a thing/unity cannot not exist,*[15] and as such the absolutely unconditioned evidence of the identity of the "saying" and the "being" (the law and the existence) of the fourfold identity of "fact and reflection, appearance and essence," of the fact that the absolute content of identity is the minimum, the proof that existence is identical with reality, the proof that real relations essentially exist. The relation of negative meta-identity to positive meta-identity is set out in the following:

$$(1)_{ii} = \bar{1}, \quad (1)_{ij} = 1 = (i : j) + (i : j),$$

and

$$(\bar{1})_{ij} = \bar{1}, \quad (\bar{1})_{ii} = 1 = (i : i) + (j : j).$$

The actual existence of the negative meta-identity, the absolute other identical with positive meta-identity, is made visible in the construction of the foundation, the Fourthness, which rules the above elaborated logical-mathematical relations of 0, $\bar{0}$, and

[14] Cf. above, pp. 255ff.
[15] Cf. below, pp. 284f.

1, and perfectly distinguishes their essentially rational order from the unnecessary existence of the order of Peirce's First, Second, and Third.[16] Let there be, then, an infinite lattice in which three regularly repeating ribbons of 0's, $\bar{0}$'s, and 1's, woven regularly through a blank field, descend from left to right, each instance of a digit at the center of a square and laterally separated from its neighbors by a space equal to that which it occupies. Further, let a square arrangement of the digits in the lattice be the smallest in which each of the three appears in equal number, and let this square be a multiplication table in which, since the square is essentially the boundless lattice, the product of any two digits must be derived exclusively from their relations within the table:

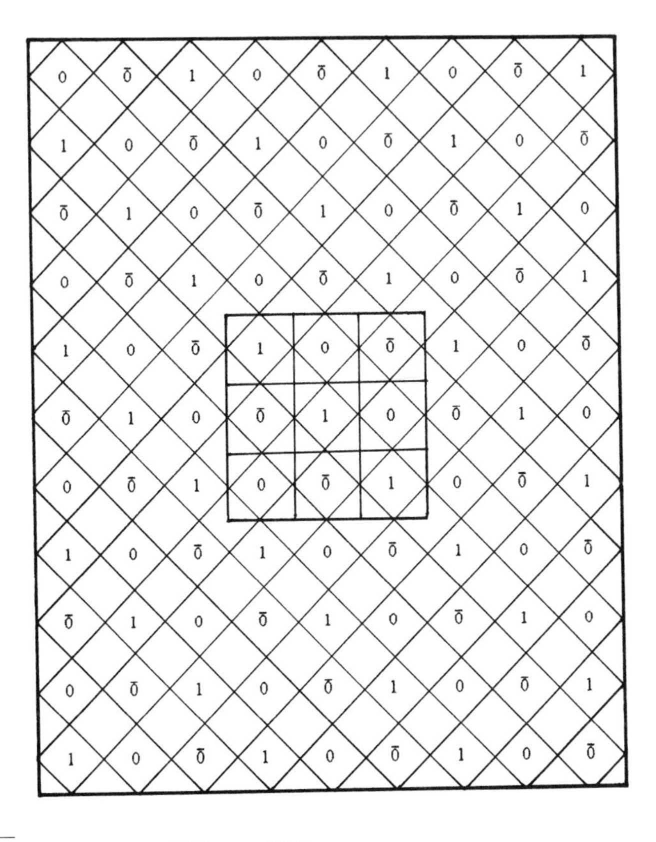

[16] Cf. below, Section IV.1, pp. 457f.

Within the confines of this square—consistent with the requirement that no digit equal nothing—multiplication, addition, division, and subtraction will produce identical results.[17] Let this square essence of the infinite lattice-work, the foundation-stone,

1	0	$\bar{0}$
$\bar{0}$	1	0
0	$\bar{0}$	1

be turned in such a manner that it is identically the Fourth turn, as follows:

1	0	$\bar{0}$
$\bar{0}$	1	0
0	$\bar{0}$	1

→

(4)

$\bar{0}$	0	1
0	1	$\bar{0}$
1	$\bar{0}$	0

↑

(1)

←

1	$\bar{0}$	0
0	1	$\bar{0}$
$\bar{0}$	0	1

(2)

↓

0	$\bar{0}$	1
$\bar{0}$	1	0
1	0	$\bar{0}$

(3) ,

Then, (4), the square essence of the infinite lattice-work is the Fact, Identity, or Rational Existence, while (1), the mirror-reversal of the Fact, is Reflection, (2), the inversion of Reflection, is Appearance, and (3), the mirror-reversal of Appearance, is Essence. This is the absolutely unconditioned order: the Foundation-Fact, the fact of Foundation, the absolute logic of the fact of creation, indeed, the logos of a perfectly objective logic: absolute reflection of the fact: the minimum identified.[18] The dif-

[17] Cf. above, p. 255.

[18] The square essence of the infinite lattice-work, when viewed

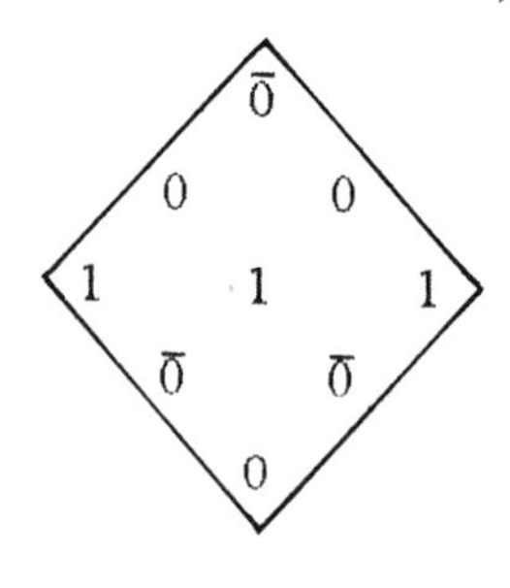

ference between (4), (1), (2), and (3) *is* the foundation or Fourthness: the difference between the elements is the minimum. It is further to be observed that the following relations obtain among the elements of the minimum:

(4) = reflection of (1) + inversion of (3),
(1) = reflection of (4) + inversion of (2),
(2) = reflection of (3) + inversion of (1),
(3) = reflection of (2) + inversion of (4),

which relations, in terms of the facings of the foundation-stone in the construction of the foundation, may be abstracted as:

(4)	(1)	(2)	(3)
→ = ↑↑	↑ = ⇇	← = ↓↓	↓ = ⇉

Note that equations (4) and (2) reflect and invert each other.

---

suggests the manifold of the minimum identity:

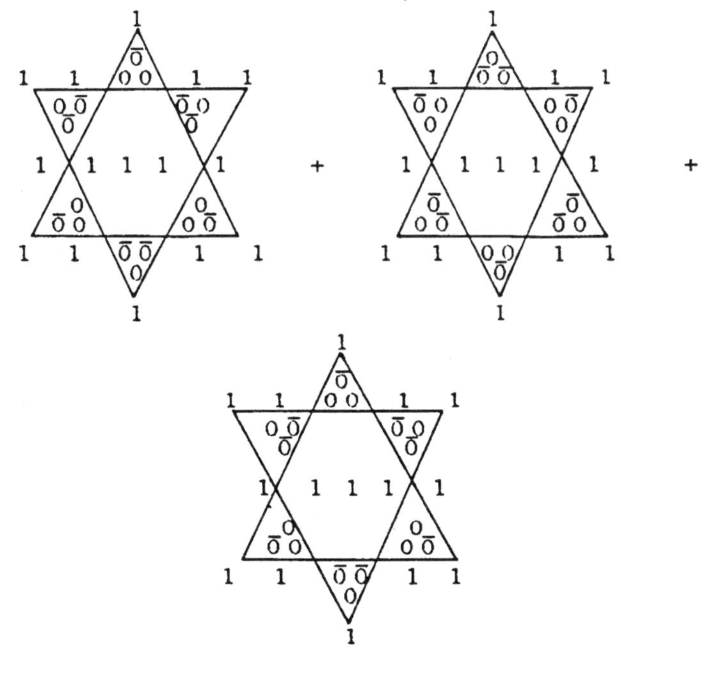

This relation of reflection and inversion holds for (1) and (3). These relations may be synthesized for perception in the following way:

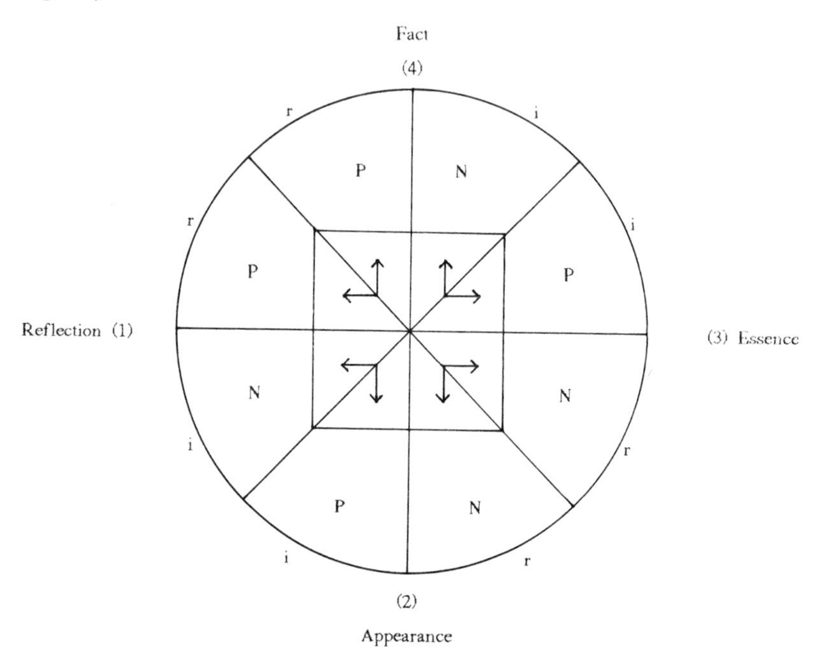

Analysis indicates that the minimum order is the first essentially rational ordering of the underlying partially arbitrary manifold which otherwise remains a twofold reflection, *r–PP* + *i–NP*, *i–PN* + *r–NN*, imperfectly an inversion since the analysis of the four *x*/*y*-axis directions of reflection reduces to two sets of two subsets of reflections which are related as $x + x + y + y^{-1} : y^{-1} + y + x + x :: y + y^{-1} + x^{-1} + x^{-1} : x^{-1} + x^{-1} + y^{-1} + y$, that is, as two reversely and inversely related sets of reversely ordered relations, while the analysis of the four directions of reflection diagonally compromised in the case of the minimum arrangement, *ri–PN* + *ir–NP*, *ri–NP* + *ir–PN*, reduces to two sets of two subsets of reflections which are related as $y + x + x + y : y^{-1} + x^{-1} + x^{-1} + y^{-1} :: x + y + y^{-1} + x^{-1} : x^{-1} + y^{-1} + y + x$, that is, as two sets, one of which is a set of elements and their identically *or* reversely ordered inverses, and the other of which is a set of elements and the reversely ordered identical elements *or* a set of their identically ordered inverses.[19] The twofold reflection imperfectly an inversion, the underlying manifold, is related to the form of the geometric proportion of the elements of a line *AB*, that is, to the form *AB* : *AC* :: *AC* : *AD*, by virtue of the fact that of the two sets of reversely ordered identical relations (let them be two "wholes") one "whole" must be the *inverse* reversal of the other, that is, must be defined in relation to the other (let it be a "whole" *and* a "part"). But a division into two "wholes" one of which is a "part" of the other is the essence of the above geometric proportion in which *AB* and *AC* are both "wholes" since *AC* is a "whole" in relation to *AD*, but the "whole" *AC* is a "part" in relation to *AB*. In contrast, the essentially rational minimum arrangement divides into two sets each of which is an identically ordered set of *inverses*, the first immediately conceived as a reversely ordered set of *inverses*, the second as a set of reversely ordered *identical* elements. But the set of reversely ordered *inverses* does not depend upon the set of identically ordered *inverses* (is not a "part" of the latter), while it does depend, as does the set of identically ordered inverses itself, upon the set of reversely ordered *identical* elements, which last is the "whole" of which both other sets of relations are "parts," *without the "part" which appears but once* (the set of reversely ordered inverses) *being itself a "part" of the "part" which appears twice* (the set of identically ordered inverses). But this relationship is the form of the division of the line *AB* in the proportion *CB* : *AC* :: *AC* : *AB*, in which *CB* is not a "part" of *AC*, but *AC* and *CB* are "parts" of *AB*, that is, the division of the line in the extreme and mean ratio, the "golden section" of the line which provides with *one* division the mean and both extremes of the geometric proportion. Here the logic of the thinking occurring for the first time reveals itself as the logical foundation of ϕ-proportionality.[20] Here is the logic of what hitherto is the pre-logical factuality of rational existence. The proof form of the pro-

[19] In the summaries of subsets of reflections the following simplification of the relations in the above template obtains: $x = r\text{–}P \rightarrow r\text{–}N$, $y = i\text{–}N \rightarrow i\text{–}P$, $x^{-1} = r\text{–}N \rightarrow r\text{–}P$, $y^{-1} = i\text{–}P \rightarrow i\text{–}N$.

[20] Cf. below, p. 280, n. 38. Cf. also, above, p. 138, n. 14.

portionate relation of sets of reflective relations in the minimum arrangement, viz., "the set of identically ordered inverses squared (analogue, $\phi^{-1} \cdot \phi^{-1}$) = the set of reversely ordered identities (analogue, 1^2) identified with the set of reversely ordered inverses (analogue, ϕ^{-2})," reduces to "the set of inverses squared = the set of identities identified with the set of inverses," or $1^{-2} = (\phi^{-2}/\phi^{-2}) = 1^{-1} \cdot 1^{-1} = 1 \cdot 1^{-1} = 1$, or the proof that $1^{-1} = 1$.

Let the fourfold foundation be a proportion, its elements defined in terms of their ordinal relations of reflection and inversion:

$$\frac{(1)}{(3)} : \frac{(4)}{(2)} :: \frac{(3)}{(1)} : \frac{(2)}{(4)},$$

that is, (4) : (1) :: (2) : (3). Then prove this proportion as follows:

$$\frac{(1)}{(3)} \cdot \frac{(2)}{(4)} = \frac{(4)}{(2)} \cdot \frac{(3)}{(1)},$$

substituting cardinals for ordinals,

$$\frac{1}{6} = 6,$$

the proven unity of the foundation is:

$$36^{-1} \text{ or } 36,$$

that is, in the very essence of its structure the foundation is identically 36^{-1} and 36, just as, in the proof of the uniquely proportionate ordering of the sets of reflective and inverse relations within the template of the absolutely relative fourfold square essence of the infinite lattice-work of 0's, $\overline{0}$'s, and 1's, $1^{-1} = 1$.[21]

[21] For the demonstration of the fact that $1^2 = 6^2$ in the absolute structure of existence itself, see below, Section IV. For the digamma, ϝ = Hebrew ו = 6, as the template distinguishing the "minimum" proportion from the "logical" proportion, see. below, Section III.5.

The fourfold foundation proves to be the totality of the number of digits of which it is comprised (36) in such a way that any one of the digits, *qua* one of the total number (36^{-1}), *is* the total number, which is the equivalent in ordinary mathematical terms of the underlying essentially new logical relations, $0 = \bar{0}10$, $\bar{0} = \bar{0}10$, and $1 = \bar{0}10$.[22] The arithmetic equivalent of the logical relation in which the part is identified with the whole is $36^{-1} \cdot 36 = 1$, at once

$$\frac{1}{1} = 1.$$

This last appears as the essence of the minimum order:

$$\left[\frac{1}{1} = 0 + \bar{0}\right] = \left[\frac{\bar{0}}{0} = 1 + 1\right] = \left[\frac{1}{1} = 1 + 1\right],$$

the absolute unity of zero irreducible to nothing, absolute unity identically *nihil ex nihilo.*[23] This is the inductive proof of absolute unity.[24]

The positive-negative pattern of the universal form of logical propositions[25] is constructed on the foundation by transforming the fourfold reflection and inversion of relations in the minimum order (whereby each of the elements reflects and inverts one of the others) to the order of reflection and inversion in which each element reflects and inverts itself as it first appeared in terms of the facings of the foundation-stone[26] (where the universal logical distribution of P's and N's among four sets of *inversion* [vertical] + *reflection* [horizontal] accords with the following rule: *inversion of left or down facings* and *reflection of right or down facings* are designated P, while *inversion of right or up facings* and *reflection of left or up facings* are designated N):

[22] Cf. above, pp. 255f.

[23] The unity of the abyss *ex nihilo.*

[24] Cf. below, pp. 284f.

[25] Cf. above, p. 258.

[26] Cf. above, pp. 268ff.

(4) = inversion of (1) + reflection of (3) =	⇇	=	(1)	=	PP
(1) = inversion of (4) + reflection of (2) =	↓↓	=	(2)	=	NP
(2) = inversion of(2) + reflection of (4) =	↑↑	=	(4)	=	PN
(3) = inversion of (3) + reflection of (1) =	⇉	=	(3)	=	NN.

In this transformation of the fundamental order Appearance (2) and Essence (3) exchange material identities,[27] and Appearance (2) identically Reflection (1) is the new Fact (4), while Essence (3) identically Fact (4) is the new Essence (3). Here the fact of essential novelty manifests itself in the form of the *identity* of fact, reflection, appearance, and essence. The new fact is the new essence of the identity of logic: the minimum/*unum* (the fact of appearance identically reflection existing as fact through the material identity of appearance and essence in the context of the essentially rational order of a categorically new logic) is the essentially new identity of logic: *for the first time the essence of experience is the identity of appearance and reflection:* experience *is* the meta-identity of appearance and reflection. This logic, epitomized in the square essence of the infinite lattice-work of 0's, $\bar{0}$'s, and 1's, is the essential logic of logic for the first time, *the beginning of logic, the logic of beginning.* In the very form of the logic of beginning the difference between fact and reflection, appearance and essence, is transcended. The manifold of the essential structure of logical order as meta-identically the reflection and inversion of the foundation may be synthesized in the following manner:

[27] This material exchange of identities by (2) and (3) is of the essence of the structure of the foundation where the arrangement of 36 digits (4 · 9) has a value of 24 when 1's are computed in the way of ordinary mathematics [4 · 3 · (0 + $\bar{0}$ + 1 [= 2])]. The ability to cross over from 24 · 1 = 1 to 24 · 1 = 24 is a function of the foundational rationality of the structure of the logic. For the important implications of the arithmetic value of the logical digits see below, Sections III.2, III.4, and IV.2.

— (1) : (2) :: (4) : (3) —

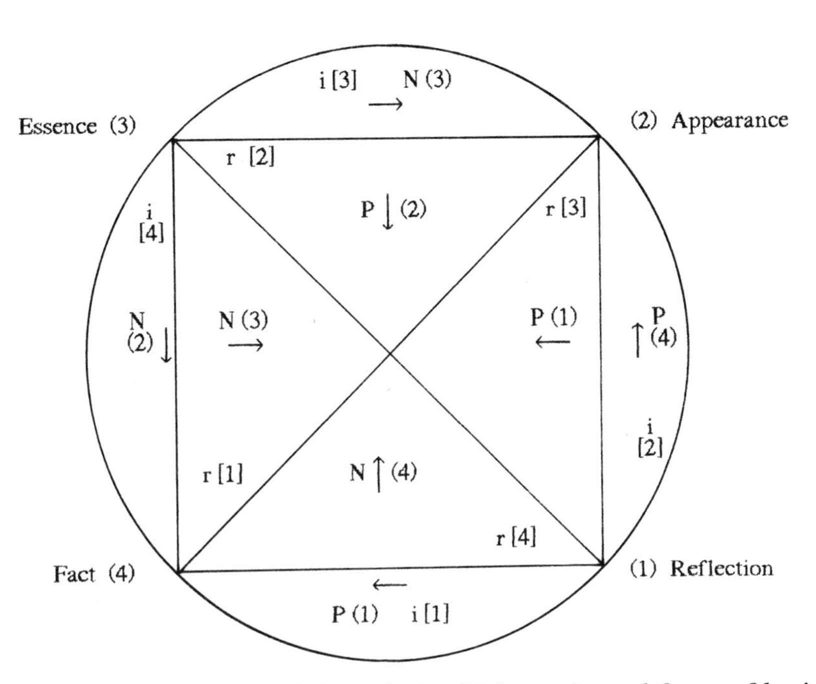

In this transparency of thought itself the universal form of logical propositions reflects at the level of ordinary mathematics what is proven in the very existence of the structure of the foundation itself, in the very essence of the new foundation of logic itself, viz., the perfect unity of logic. The logical form reflects this perfect unity transparently, so that whether the logical order, (1), (2), (4), (3), is defined in terms of the foundation, as above, thusly,

$$\frac{(4)}{(2)} : \frac{(3)}{(1)} :: \frac{(1)}{(3)} : \frac{(2)}{(4)},$$

or in terms of its origination, i.e., in terms of the change in the foundation, thusly,

$$\frac{(1)}{(3)} : \frac{(4)}{(2)} :: \frac{(2)}{(4)} : \frac{(3)}{(1)},$$

in either form it proves to unity, substituting cardinals for ordinals,

$$\frac{1}{1} = 1.$$

But "1/1 = 1" is the form of the nothing-nothing identity of unity and meta-identity, the negative form of which meta-identity is identically positive meta-identity.[28] Let the simple unity ($1 \cdot 1 = 1$) of the logical arrangement of the elements of the foundation, (1) : (2) :: (4) : (3), be negative meta-identity, $(\overline{1})_{ii} = 1 = (i : i) + (j : j)$. Let the complex essential rationality ($36^{-1} \cdot 36 = 1$) which is the unity of the minimum arrangement of those elements, (4) : (1) :: (2) : (3), be positive meta-identity, $(1)_{ij} = 1 = (i : j) + (i : j)$.[29] Then let it be demonstrated from the fourfold structure of the foundation that logical unity is meta-identically the minimum unity, that in the foundation itself the negative meta-identity which is logical unity is identically the positive meta-identity of the minimum order of the elements of rational unity. The fourfold of relations at the heart of the foundation-stone as it turns into the foundation is visualized thusly:

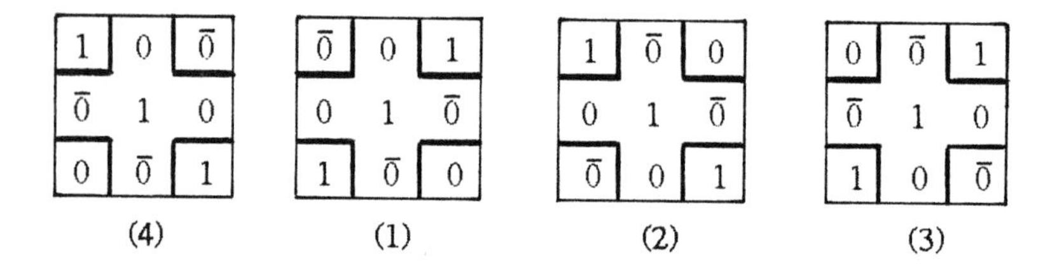

where if i = the string $\overline{0}$, 1, 0, and j = the string 0, 1, $\overline{0}$, the foundation proportion, (4) : (1) :: (2) : (3), is:

$$\frac{i}{j} : \frac{j}{j} :: \frac{j}{i} : \frac{i}{i},$$

[28] Cf. above, pp. 264f.

[29] Ibid. Cf. also, above, pp. 272f.

the proof of which is:

$$\frac{i^2}{ij}\cdot\frac{ij}{j^2}=\frac{i^2}{j^2}\cdot\frac{ij}{ij}=\frac{i^2}{j^2}\cdot 1=1.$$

This proof is the inductive demonstration of the logically deduced definition of positive meta-identity, i.e., $i^2/j^2 = 1 = (i : j) + (i : j)$, the positive absolute alio-relative $1_{ij} = 1$, which meta-identified in the proof as negative meta-identity (where $ij/ij = \bar{1}_{ii} = 1 = [i : i] + [j : j]$) is identically the proven unity of the minimum order of the elements of the foundation.[30] But since in this proof $1 \cdot 1 = 1 \cdot \bar{1} = 1$, it is further demonstrated that positive meta-identity is the inverse of negative meta-identity, as meta-identity has been demonstrated to be unity.[31] Finally, that, indeed, $ij/ij = \bar{1}_{ii}$, and that $1_{ij} = 1$ = the essential structure of unity, $36 \cdot 36^{-1}$,[32] is clearly demonstrated when the following substitutions are made in the foundation-proportion immediately

---

[30] That the propositional form fundamental to all logic is a reflection of the essentially rational unity of the foundation-proportion is further evidenced in the fact that whether in the form, (1) : (2) :: (4) : (3), here,

$$\frac{j}{j}:\frac{j}{i}::\frac{i}{j}:\frac{i}{i},$$

or in the form of the latter's substantive equivalent, (4) : (1) :: (3) : (2), here,

$$\frac{i}{j}:\frac{j}{j}::\frac{i}{i}:\frac{j}{i},$$

it proves identically and immediately to unity. (It is noted that the columnar sum of the three proportions, minimum, logical, and the substantive equivalent of the logical, is [converting ordinals to cardinals]

$$\begin{array}{r} 4123 \\ 1243 \\ \underline{4132} \\ 9498 \end{array},$$

and that the product of $9 \cdot 4 \cdot 9 \cdot 8$ is 2592, at once [computing logical 1's in the way of ordinary mathematics] the product of $[3 \cdot 36] \cdot [4 \cdot 3 \cdot (0 + \bar{0} + 1\ [= 2])]$, i.e., the product of the manifold of the minimum identity [cf. above, p. 268, n. 18] times the sum total value of the foundation.)

[31] Cf. above, pp. 264f.

[32] Cf. above, pp. 272f.

above: let $i = (6 \cdot 1)$ and $j = (1 \cdot 6)$, where, in the context of the essentially rational logic of beginning, the *relational order* of the two elements of each term, i.e., the essentially rational relation, is *absolute*, that is, unity is absolutely meta-identity. Then the minimum order of the foundation-proportion is:

$$\frac{(6 \cdot 1)}{(1 \cdot 6)} : \frac{(1 \cdot 6)}{(1 \cdot 6)} :: \frac{(1 \cdot 6)}{(6 \cdot 1)} : \frac{(6 \cdot 1)}{(6 \cdot 1)} ,$$

the proof of which is:

$$\frac{(6 \cdot 1)^2}{(6 \cdot 1)(1 \cdot 6)} \cdot \frac{(6 \cdot 1)(1 \cdot 6)}{(1 \cdot 6)^2} = \frac{(6 \cdot 1)^2}{(1 \cdot 6)^2} \cdot \frac{(6 \cdot 1)(1 \cdot 6)}{(6 \cdot 1)(1 \cdot 6)} =$$

$$\frac{(6 \cdot 1)^2}{(1 \cdot 6)^2} \cdot 1 = 1 ,$$

where, *qua* relational order,

$$\frac{(6 \cdot 1)(1 \cdot 6)}{(6 \cdot 1)(1 \cdot 6)} = \frac{(6 \cdot 6)}{(6 \cdot 6)} = \frac{(6 \cdot 1)(6 \cdot 1)}{(6 \cdot 1)(6 \cdot 1)} = \frac{36 \cdot 1}{36 \cdot 1} = \frac{36}{36} = \frac{i^2}{i^2} ,$$

that is,

$$\frac{ij}{ij} = \overline{1}_{ii} = 1_{36,36} ,$$

while, *qua* relational order,

$$\frac{(6 \cdot 1)(6 \cdot 1)}{(1 \cdot 6)(1 \cdot 6)} = \frac{36 \cdot 1}{1 \cdot 36} = \frac{i^2}{j^2} = 36 \cdot 36^{-1},$$

that is,

$$\frac{i^2}{j^2} = 1_{ij} = 1_{36,36^{-1}}.$$

The essentially rational manifest unity of the foundation is the outside of zero *ex nihilo.* The outside of this unity *is* unity, i.e., there is no outside of unity, but there is in the foundation the beginning of absolute unity.

AFTERWORD 1

THEOREM. There is a law of absolute unity, $\mathit{1}(1+1)=0$, which is the logical foundation for a mathematics which includes zero [0] but in which no integer is equal to nothing.[33]
Proof: Let there be a law of duality,[34]

$$x(1-x)=0$$

Also, let there be a law of unity, where *1* is the symbol for "identical with,"[35]

$$\mathit{1}x=x.$$

Note that the law of duality is a transformation of Boole's law of tautology, $x^2=x$, which, in turn, is $xx=x$. For Boole and Peirce $x=0$ *or* 1. But also let $x=0+1$, not merely in the manner of Peirce's logical addition, where 0 and 1 are members of a class such that neither *exists* besides the other,[36] but rather in such a manner that neither is *conceived* without the other. Then x is 0 or 1 *and* their absolute inseparability, or the pure *with* which is, in Peirce's language,[37] *ens,* non-relative unity, or $\bar{0}$, and which is here indistinguishable from 1 or "identical with," so that the sum of the addition is to add, to multiply, to subtract and to

[33] For the arithmetic analogue which approximates $\mathit{1}(1+1)=0$, see below, Section III.2, Theorem 6.

[34] G. Boole, *An Investigation of the Laws of Thought* (New York, 1958), sec. 3.4, et passim.

[35] Peirce, *Collected Papers,* 3.68 et passim.

[36] Ibid., 3.67.

[37] Ibid., 3.307. The use of Peirce's symbols and language is not an interpretation of Peirce, but in fact involves a radically new definition of the terms which fundamentally contradicts Peirce's philosophy.

divide. Then the law of duality, $x(1-x)=0$, has the *dual solution*, $0-1=\overline{0}=0$ *and* $\overline{0}(0)=1=0$, so that $x(1-x)=\overline{0}+1=x+1=0$.[38] Let it be understood that the form of Peirce's law of unity, $1x=x$, where, since $x^2=x$, $1=x^2$, $(x^2)x=x$ (where $x=\overline{0}$, "existence equals the foundation"), unifies Boole's law of duality, $xx=x$ (where $x=\overline{0}$, "the universe equals the foundation"), completing the incomplete doubling of the law of identity, $x=x$. Then, where $x=0$, let there be the absolute law of unity $(x^2)xx=0$, at once the proof of the proportion in which the elements of the laws of duality and unity are, respectively, the means and the extremes, as follows:

$$1x : x(1-x) :: 0 : x,$$

substituting the dual solutions of the law of duality, as above, for the elements of the means,

$$1x : x :: 1 : x,$$

proven,

$$1xx = 0,$$

or,

$$1(1+1) = 0.$$

[38] $x=\overline{0}$. But, by the dual solution, $\overline{0}=0$. Let $x=0$. For Boole the universe [1] is finite in the sense that nothing is besides the universe, and therefore $1+x$ is "not interpretable" (cf. above, p. 279, n. 34), while for Peirce the universe [1] may be relatively infinite so that nothing is *not besides* the universe and $1+x=1$ (cf. Peirce, *Collected Papers,* 3.88). But let the universe [1] be absolutely infinite so that nothing is not and "besides" is not thought, and $1+x=x^2$. This result, $1+x=x^2$, $1+0=0^2$, or $\overline{0}=1$, should there exist a mathematics in which one of the square roots of 1 is 0, and in which 0 and $\overline{0}$ are therefore each a sort of 1, embraces, as the *foundation* thereof, the relation in ordinary mathematics, otherwise unique, of the elements of the division in extreme and mean ratio, $1+\phi=\phi^2$. Note also that the effective elimination here of 0 = nothing yet embraces, since in the logic $x^2=1$, Peirce's $1+x=1$.

Since $x^2 = x$, the law of absolute unity, $1(1 + 1) = 0$, admits of a triple solution, $0 = 0$, $\bar{0} = 0$, and $1 = 0$. Therefore the trichotomy, $0 = \bar{0} = 1$. Provided the empty solution of $0 = 0$ is excluded, that is, provided the reduction of the law of absolute unity merely to Identity or merely to Rationality is excluded, this trichotomous solution is essentially the dual solution of the law of absolute unity *and* the dual solution of the law of duality, $\bar{0} + 1 = 0$. In this way, then, the law of absolute unity in the logic of its trichotomous solution excludes the *empty* Identity, $0 = 0$, and provides that the 0 which is 0 is the 0 which is (not 0 except 0 is) $\bar{0}$ + 1. The proof that, in effect, $0 = 0 \neq 0$ is the proof that $1 = 0$ and $\bar{0} = 0$, which is to say that what is *experienced* is what is *proven*, that is, that for the first time logic is the absolute relation. How so? The fact that for Boole $0 + 1$ is not interpretable,[39] that he lacks a logical addition, is a function of the fact that for him $0 + 1$ is a fact *a priori*, while the fact that Peirce has a logical addition, that for him $0 + 1 = 1$, i.e., that nothing is not *besides* the universe,[40] is a function of the fact that for Peirce $0 + 1$ is a fact *a posteriori*.[41] But in the essentially new logic in which for the first time the universe is absolutely infinite, the *a priori* = the *a posteriori*. Nothing *a priori* is not *besides* the universe. The rational imagination of the actual beginning—absent in Peirce who does not imagine the beginning or imagines $0 + 1$ without a beginning or imagines an essentially indefinite beginning, so that his imagining therefore perpetually falls short of an actual

---

[39] Cf. above, p. 280, n. 38.

[40] Ibid.

[41] Cf. Peirce, *Collected Papers*, 6.191: ". . .all the evolution we know of proceeds from the vague to the definite." Therefore based on experience Peirce imagines (ibid., 6.490) "in such a vague way as such a thing can be imagined, a perfect cosmology of the three universes. . . . That perfect cosmology must therefore show that the whole history of the three universes, as it has been and is to be, would follow from a premiss which would not suppose them to exist at all. Moreover, such premiss must in actual fact be true. But that premiss must represent a state of things in which the three universes were completely nil. Consequently, whether in time or not, the three universes must actually be absolutely necessary results of a state of utter nothingness." And as Peirce says (ibid., 6.200): ". . . among the things so resulting are time and logic."

premiss[42]—is the experience of the complete actuality of the universe. The universe is the experience of nothing *a priori.* This is the new unity of thought. This is the unity of thought in the new. This unity is the absolute exteriority of thought such that *nihil ex nihilo* is *proven,* i.e., it is proven that 0 = 1 and that 0 = 0, and that the convergence of $\overline{0}$ and 1 as the elements of the dual solution of the law of absolute unity absolutely precludes 0 = 0—insofar as the latter has the appearance of simple Identity—from the absolutely relative unity of the actually imagined definite beginning: 1 = $\overline{0}$ = 0. 0 = 0 as simple identity is there as such in the triple solution of the law of absolute unity to be excluded as such while the real trichotomy, 0 + $\overline{0}$ + 1 = 1 + 1 = 1, is discovered.

For Peirce, in his logical addition, there is only 0 and 1. How is this the case? How is it the case that in the essentially new logic of an absolute relativity there is $\overline{0}$? How is this $\overline{0}$ related to Peirce's logic? Let 0 stand for Peirce's "absolute nility."[43] Let 00 stand for Peirce's "First" a "definite potentiality" which emerges from the "indefinite potentiality" of 0 "by its own vital Firstness and spontaneity."[44] Let this First be the logical universe, 1. Note, however, that this First in relation to the indefinite potentiality of absolute nility is a Second related to a First, 1 related to 0. Let 000 stand for the emerging of the definite potentiality, 00, from the indefinite potentiality, 0, that is, their identity (I) *qua* "continuous growth from non-existence to existence."[45] Note that 000, the Third in relation to 0 and 00, is, as Peirce says of Thirdness in general[46] "of its own nature relative," while 0, as First, is absolute, and 00, as Second, is, while "it cannot be with-

[42] Ibid., 6.506: "I am inclined to think (though I admit that there is no necessity of taking that view) that the process of creation has been going on for an infinite time in the past, and further, during *all* past time, and further, that past time had no definite beginning, yet came about by a process which in a generalized sense, of which we cannot *easily* get much idea, was a development."

[43] Ibid., 6.490.

[44] Ibid., 6.198.

[45] Ibid., 1.175.

[46] Ibid., 1.362.

out the first,"[47] in its own way absolute. Simply put, 00 presupposes 0 but *qua* Second is not the composition of 0 and 0, while, on the other hand, 000 is just such a composition, 0 composed with 00. Let then the following table summarize these relations:

$$0 = 0$$
$$00 = 1$$
$$000 = \mathrm{I}.$$

Here the Third (Identity) is the First composed with the Second, in traditional terms, Nothing composed with the Universe. These latter elements of Identity are absolutes not themselves identified, or elements of Rationality themselves absolutes not rationalized. But in the logic of the thinking now occurring for the first time in history the Third, Identity or Rationality, identifies 0 and 1 as, respectively, absolute-relative-0, and absolute-relative-1 or the universe absolutely existent, which logical terms are related to Peirce's logic in the way illustrated by the following arrangement:

$$0 = 0$$
$$00 = 1$$
$$000 = \mathrm{I}$$
$$0[000] = 1 = 0[\mathrm{I}]$$
$$00[000] = 0 = 1[\mathrm{I}].$$

Whereas in the terms of the earlier logic the limit was Nothing composed with the Universe, now the limit is the Universe composed with Rationality or Identity, at once Nothing composed with Rationality or Identity, composed with Nothing: the Universe composed with Nothing composed with the Universe: the Universe the *absolutely* infinite Universe. Before now Nothing was not Identified, so that 000 equaled 00, or $0 + 1$ equaled 1. Now Nothing is Identified as the actual Universe (the Universe composed with Nothing): $0[000] = 0 + \mathrm{I} = 1$, that is, Nothing

[47] Ibid., 1.358.

composed with the Universe-composed-with-Nothing = 00[000] = 0[0000] = 1 + $\bar{0}$ = 0 = 0 + 1 = $\bar{0}$, that is, the Universe Identified is the Universe, in effect, absolutely infinite Nothing, where Nothing, therefore, is absolutely nothingless. The Universe absolutely after Nothing. The Universe *ex abysso.*

The proof that 0 = $\bar{0}$ and 0 = 1, while 0 ≠ 0, is the overcoming of the dogmatic presumption that logic is not absolutely logical, that the law of identity is but the form of thought, that the relationship of identity is divided into an agreement among things (A : A) or an opposition among things (A : B), which division within identity identifies the duality but not the unity of identity. The law of relative unity excludes logic in the form of the thing beyond logic, i.e., in the form of unity. Now for the first time in history logic is the essential identity of the thing. Between 0 and 1 is $\bar{0}$, the *unum*: 0, $\bar{0}$, 1 is the order identifying 0 *with* 1 in the form of the absolute minimum of unity, in the form of *the unum identically a law*, in the form of the *unum esse*,[48] in the form of the unity of an absolute objectivity, *1*(1 + 1) = 0, essentially prescinding from concurrence and opposition, from the logic of other-self relations. This unity is the law of unity reduced to the 0 which is not nothing. This is the reduction of the absolute other to unity. Unity is the zero-content, the identity, of the logical absolute. It is neither that there is nothing outside unity nor that there is nothing not outside unity, it is that there is no nothing outside, no nothing, *and* no outside of the unity of this absolute logic, and that trichotomous 'no' is identically this unity. The difference between 0 and 1 is identity itself. The difference between the other and unity is for the first time absolutely logical. The difference between logic and thing, between logic and unity, is absolutely transcended in the new conception of the beginning. This beginning is existence the reality of logical unity. In the law of absolute unity, in the *unum* absolutely in the midst of the *unum*, in the minimum of order, 0, $\bar{0}$, 1, *qua* absolute law, *1*(1 + 1) = 0, 1 = 0 = $\bar{0}$.

In the law of absolute unity the laws of duality and unity are, respectively, transformed as follows:

---

48 Cf. above, Sections II.3 and II.4, passim.

$$1 - \bar{0} = 0,$$

and

$$\mathit{1}(\bar{0}) = 1,$$

that is, respectively, the law of existential contradiction, a thing/ unity cannot not exist, and the law of existential unity, *a thing/ unity is identical with the minimum, i.e., identical with* unum.[49] These transformations, the existential laws of contradiction and unity, provide the terms whereby the identity 1 = 1 is proven absolutely existential in the form of the proportion whose extremes are the elements of the new law of unity, and whose means are the elements of the new law of contradiction:

$$\mathit{1}(\bar{0}) : (1 - \bar{0}) :: 0 : 1,$$

proven,

$$1(1) = 0(0),$$

that is,

$$1 = 1.$$

[49] Just here can be seen how perfect is the correspondence to these logical laws of their conceptual analogues as set forth above in Section II.2, viz., the 'absolute law of identity', $c = (m = Tc/m)$, and the 'absolute transcendence of the proof itself of the law of contradiction', m^5/T^2c^4. Let $T = 1$, $c = 0$, and $m = \bar{0}$, then the absolute law of identity is $0 = (\bar{0} = 10/\bar{0})$, which is $0 = \overline{00}/10 = 1/\bar{0}$ or $0\bar{0} = 1$, the 'law of existential contradiction' $1 - \bar{0} = 0$ or $1 = 0\bar{0}$, and the existential law of unity $\mathit{1}(\bar{0}) = 1$ or $1 = 1$. The simple power of the logic is perhaps most clear in the case of the reduction of the transcended 'law of contradiction', $c = [(m = Tc/m^2)$ or $(m^2 = Tc/m)]$, to $0 = [(\bar{0} = 10/\overline{00})$ or $(\overline{00} = 10/\bar{0})] = [(0 = \bar{0})$ or $(1 = 1)]$, that is, *no second alternative identity*. But it is precisely the second alternative identity which constitutes the transcendence of the law of contradiction in the trinary logic. The 'transcendence of the law of contradiction' is $\overline{00000}/110000 = 0\overline{00}/10\bar{0} = (0$ or $\bar{0})/1$ or $(0$ or $\bar{0}) = 1$.

This proof that $1 = 1$ is the proof that unity is identically the transcendence of contradiction. The law of contradiction *proven* is the law of identity.[50] Unity (the absolute measure) is for the first time itself measured. $1 \neq 1$ except $1 = 1$ is proven, therefore, except $0 = 1$, except Peirce's $\mathit{1}1 = 1$ is absolutely unified, except there is the law of absolute unity, $\mathit{1}(1 + 1) = 0$. For the first time unity is the proven transcendence of the difference between reality and existence: the law of existence proven. The proof of unity is identical with the fact that the thing is the measure of thought, measures itself, and is the absolute measure of logic. Unity proven is the identity of an absolute *nihil ex nihilo.* In the context of the law of absolute unity 0 does not denote nothing, as it did for Boole and Peirce.[51] The universe, therefore, is not infinite relative to nothing, so that as Peirce says,[52] "if 1 be regarded as infinite, it is not an absolute infinite, for $10 = 0$," but rather the universe is infinite relative to unity and what can no longer be regarded as nothing, the relation of unity to unity is finally proven, unity is unified for the first time, and the infinite universe is essentially the minimum relation of the beginning. For the first time the minimum/ *unum* measures unity. Absolute *nihil ex nihilo* is the infinity of unity/the unity of infinity. Absolute unity is the absolute relation such that $10 \neq 0$, but rather $10 = \bar{0}$. The minimum is the finite relation to the infinite unity. The minimum is the absolutely infinite universe. The minimum is the limit of the infinitesimal[53] beginning. Unity is the finite relation to the infinite composed with existence ($1 = \bar{0} + 0$).

---

[50] Cf. above, pp. 135ff.

[51] Cf. Boole, *The Laws of Thought,* sec. 3.2. Peirce, *Collected Papers,* 3.67, says: ". . . *nothing* is to be denoted by zero, for then $x +_{,} 0 = x$, whatever is denoted by x, and this is the definition of *zero.* This interpretation is given by Boole, and is very neat, on account of the resemblance between the ordinary conception of *zero* and that of nothing, and because we shall thus have $[0] = 0$."

[52] Peirce, *Collected Papers,* p. 388.

[53] Cf. B. Russell, *Principles of Mathematics* (New York), p. 332: "If P, Q be two numbers, or two measurable magnitudes of the same kind, and if, n being any finite integer whatever, nP is always less than Q, then P is infinitesimal with respect to Q, and Q is infinite with respect to P."

AFTERWORD 2

In the section of *The Simplest Mathematics* entitled "Trichotomic Mathematics," Peirce writes:

> We have already, along one line, traversed the marches between dichotomic and trichotomic mathematics; for the general idea of operational multiplication is as purely triadic as it could well be, involving no ideas but those of the triad, operator, operand, and result. Relative multiplication, however, involves a marked dichotomic element since $(A : B) : (C : D)$ is one of the two, **f** or A : D, according as $(B : C)$ is one of the two **f** or **v**. . . .
>
> A trichotomic mathematics entirely free from any dichotomic element appears to be impossible. For how is the mathematician to take a step without recognizing the duality of truth and falsehood? Hegel and others have dreamed of such a thing; but it cannot be. Trichotomic mathematics will therefore be a 2×3 affair, at simplest.[54]

Such is the truth of the logic of relative multiplication, for which identity is essentially duality, in which unity has not been identified. But for the logic of essentially relative or absolute multiplication which is the subsumption of multiplication by the thought of the identity of existence, for the conception of the manifold identity of the minimum which is the tetratomic identity of the multiple, the failure of the logic of relative multiplication to transcend the 'marked dichotomic element' is the failure of that logic to identify the trichotomic and dichotomic elements in mathematics, simply its failure to meta-identity 2 and 3 in the One, to unify the identity, identify the unity in 2 and 3, its failure to identify the truth of the false, i.e, to unify the false *ex falso.* The logic of relative multiplication remains within the falsity which is truth and falsehood. But the logic of absolute multiplication is the truth of truth and falsehood *ex falso,* the identity of truth and falsehood irreducible to falsity, the logical transcendence of the mathematical necessity of the difference

[54] Peirce, *Collected Papers,* 4.307–8.

between 2 and 3, ultimately the transcendence of the necessity of the difference between 0 and 1. To take Peirce's example, the triadic transcendence of the 'marked dichotomic element' comes about through the recognition that if $B : C$ is **v**, it is B^2. The failure to recognize that $B : C = B^2$ *operates* in the 'triadic transcendence of the "marked dichotomic element"' is radically a function of the absence of the economy of the minimum. The latter, dispensing with the necessity of external multiplication in constructing the foundation-stone,[55]

A	B	C
B	C	A
C	A	B

yields (where $A = 0$, $B = \bar{0}$, and $C = 1$) the following non-trivially different equations[56] evident within the square: A^2 and B^2 *following the line of least resistance,* without resorting to an outside value, equal C, as does C^2 *immediately,* $AB = C$ (but following the line of least resistance *not necessary in the first instance* to find its value, $AB = A$ and $AB = B$, so that it is quickly confirmed that $A = B = C$), $BC = A$, $AC = B$, $B^2 = C$, $A^2 = C$, and $C^2 = C$, so that the following substitutions can be made: $B : C = BC = B^2$. The proof of the latter is $B : C = B^3 : B^2 = B = B^2AC = BC = (B^2AC) : (C^2AB) = A = \sqrt{C} = C = B^2$. On the other hand, the same square constructed with the multipliers on the outside and the products on the inside,

	A	B	C
A	A	B	C
B	B	C	A
C	C	A	B

[55] Cf. above, p. 267f.

[56] Equations qualitatively diverse, quantitatively identical. See, below, Sections III.2 and III.3. for the functionality of the qualitative diversity of quantitative identity.

yields the equations: $AB = B$, $BC = A$, $AC = C$, $B^2 = C$, $A^2 = A$, and $C^2 = B$, where the only substitution analogous to the one above is $B : C = B^2$ (the proof of which is $B : C = AB : B^2 = A : B = B^2C^2 : B = C^2B = B^2$ that is, one in which BC [$= A = 0$] cannot appear independently in the equation the elements of which it is its function to identify with themselves and with zero). Operative $B : C = B^2$ is $B : C = B^2 = BC$, where BC functions to identify itself with another element (unity), each of the other two elements with another not itself and not other than itself (unity [1] identical with not-nothing [0] and not-not-nothing [$\bar{0}$, where the double negative cannot return to a nothing originally denied] and vice versa), and both of the others, identified with themselves and, as such, with each other, with unity. If 1, 2, and 3 are substituted for A, B, and C, then $B : C = B^2 = BC$ or $\bar{0} : 1 = \overline{00} = 0$, $(1 = 0)$, becomes $2 : 3 = 4 = 6$, where the first is the ratio of the second to the third, logically: $\bar{0} : 1 :: \overline{00} : \bar{0}1$, that is, $\bar{0} : 1 :: 1 : 0$, which last, *qua* minimum 4–1–2–3 order, $0 : \bar{0} :: 1 : 1$, is the Identity which is Unity.[57]

In the fourfold identity of the One which is the foundation, where the arithmetic value of each of the 4 turns of the 'cornerstone' is 6 or 2/3 times the 9 subsquares of the 'cornerstone',[58] there is real triadic unity. There is no unresolved dual, no brute existence, no inessential appearance, no falsehood which is not false. In Peirce, American thought/pragmatism embraces the Hegelian trinity but rejects the Hegelian 'dream' of a 'trichotomic mathematics entirely free from any dichotomic element'. But it is one thing to recognize that the latter is not a reality in modern thought, and quite another to add, 'it cannot be'. Now in fact it is in the form of the real unity of an essentially new logic. And that form is a tetratomic identity. But for Peirce the form of unity remained real triadic duality:

> It would scarcely be an exaggeration to say that the whole of mathematics is enwrapped in these trichotomic graphs; and they will be found extremely pertinent to logic. So prolific is the triad in forms that one may easily conceive that all the vari-

[57] Cf. above, pp. 273ff.

[58] Cf. above, p. 274, n. 27.

> ety and multiplicity of the universe springs from it, though each of the thousand corpuscles of which an atom of hydrogen consists be as multiple as all the telescopic heavens, and though all our heavens be but such a corpuscle which goes with a thousand others to make an atom of hydrogen of a single molecule of a single cell of a being gazing through a telescope at a heaven as stupendous to him as ours to us. All that springs from the
>
> 
>
> —an emblem of fertility in comparison with which the holy phallus of religion's youth is a poor stick indeed.[59]

Real triadic duality can be compared with the fourfold identity which is the foundation (real triadic unity) by comparing the above triad, which is really a dual-one (the Heraclitean 'is and is not'), a symbol of unending possibility, with the form of that inflection of the foundation which is the absolute logicality of identity, the founded manifold of logicality,[60] the absolute world-identity:

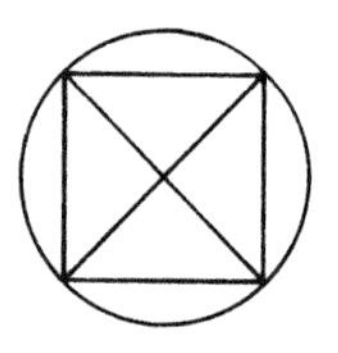

,

the panoptic eye, the logos inflected on the foundation, in the construction of which fourfold triad of absolute unity neither outside nor outside element/reference is required. This panoptic eye of the One is the absolute reference, is the construction of the absolute exteriority of the outside, the tetratomic identity of the duad (as distinguished from the dual-one/the triad above) and the threefold. As has been demonstrated, this identity of the duad and threefold in the foundation is ultimately a function of the minimum order of the elements, 0, $\overline{0}$, 1, in the

[59] Peirce, *Collected Papers,* 4.310.

[60] Cf. above, p. 275.

form of the 'cornerstone'. In the absence of the existence of the absolute economy of the minimum order, i.e., in the absence of the foundation/of existence, logic differentiates the reality of the triad (the twofold onefold) into sets, where the price of the 1/2 value of real triadic duality with respect to real triadic unity (a relation which can be viewed by connecting the ends of the triadic 'emblem of fertility' above to produce 4 triangles [4 × 3 = 12], and comparing them with the 8 triangles of the panoptic unity [8 × 3 = 24]) is a necessary doubling of the triad in the case of the former:

> Let us now glance at the permutations of three things. To say that there are six permutations of three things is the same as to say the two sets of three things may correspond, one to one in six ways. The ways are here shown
>
> 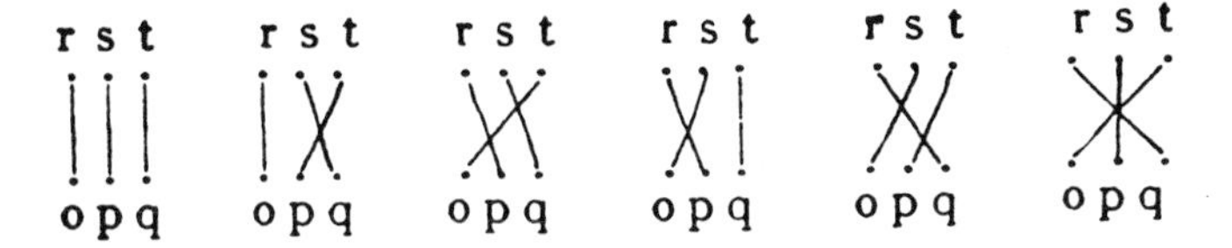
>
>
> No one of these has any properties different from those of any other. They are like two ideal rain drops, distinct but not different. Leibniz's "principle of indiscernibles" is all nonsense. No doubt, all things differ; but there is no logical necessity for it. . . . These arrangements are just like so many dots, as long as they are considered in themselves. There is nothing that is true of one that is not equally true of any other—so long as in the proposition no other is definitely mentioned. But when we come to speak of them in pairs, we find that pairs of permutations differ greatly. To show this let us make a table
>
> 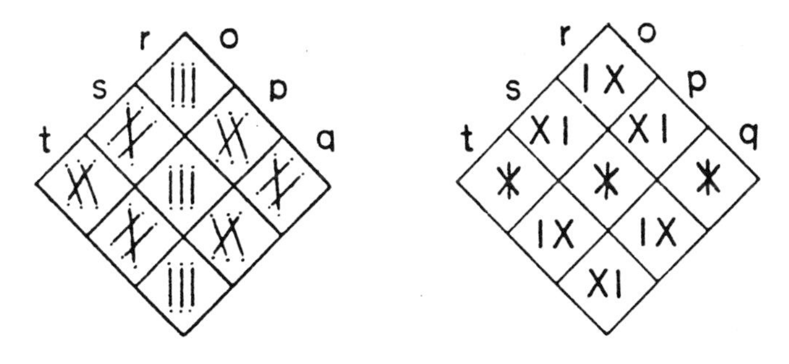
>

> like that which we formed in dichotomic algebra. On one side we enter the table with *r, s,* or *t,* on the other with [*o, p,* or *q*], and at the intersection of the rows we find the figure of the permutation in which the two correspond. In order to avoid putting two symbols in one square I repeat the table. . . .
>
> It will be seen that from this point of view, that of their relations to one another, the permutations separate themselves into two sets. In any one set, there are no two permutations which make the same letter correspond to the same letter; while of pairs of permutations of opposite sets, each agrees in respect to the correspondence of one letter.[61]

There is 'no logical necessity' for the fact that 'all things differ', that is, there is no logic of identity, no logic of absolute existence, no absolutely logical logic,[62] no logic of absolute multiplication. As in Kant, so in Peirce, 'the arrangements . . . in themselves' are 'just like so many dots', as such they do not exist for logic. Which is to say that there is no logical necessity for the existence of the triad itself, no triadic logic apart from this doubling. Nor should it be imagined that Hegel himself, come back from the dead, might rush in to dispense with 'the arrangements in themselves', these 'dots', these signposts of dualism, since, ironically, the Hegelian conception of mathematics is the trace in Hegel of the Kantian thing-in-itself, and according to that conception the mathematical categories themselves depend upon logic for 'their justification, meaning, and value', and are themselves, as it were, no more than 'dots', 'arrangements in themselves' which relative to *thought* are undifferentiated abstractions. The mathematical elements, as such, are essentially indifferent to difference; how much the more will thought be indifferent to the indifferent elements of externality. Indeed, before now, before the construction of a new unity, there is no One foundation. So long as the 'dots' are there to be related, so long as mathematics is there to be 'rectified', the necessity of doubling the triad remains.[63] Under this necessity, the six per-

---

[61] Peirce, *Collected Papers,* 4.311.

[62] Cf. above, pp. 279ff.

[63] Cf. Hegel's *Science of Logic,* trans. A. V. Miller (London, 1969), pp. 212–17,

mutations of three things (*r, s, t; r, t, s; t, r, s; s, r, t; s, t, r; t, s, r*) separate themselves into two sets of 3 × 3, i.e., 6 is (transformed into) 18, the absolute value 1/3 the number of permutations, which absolute value is 1/2 that of the foundation-stone[64] where six permutations of three things (0, $\bar{0}$, 1; 0, 1, $\bar{0}$; 1, 0, $\bar{0}$; $\bar{0}$, 0, 1; $\bar{0}$, 1, 0; 1, $\bar{0}$, 0) are constituted by one set of 3 × 3 elements, i.e., 6 is (transformed into) 9, the absolute value 2/3 the number of elements. Following, so far, Peirce's procedure, the 9 double sets, 111/100, $\bar{0}10/111$, $10\bar{0}/111$, $10\bar{0}/\bar{0}1\bar{0}$, $111/\bar{0}1\bar{0}$, $\bar{0}10/\bar{0}1\bar{0}$, $\bar{0}10/100$, $10\bar{0}/100$, and 111/111, reduce logically to the 9 single sets, $1\bar{0}\bar{0}$, $01\bar{0}$, $1\bar{0}0$, $0\bar{0}1$, 010, 111, $0\bar{0}1$, $11\bar{1}$, and 111, of which 2/3rds, or 6, are discrete. The perfectly firm tetratomic identity (the absolute foundation of unity) is constructed of this absolute triadic precision of the foundation-stone, and is completely apparent in the form of the foundational fourfold of '1 = 2/3', the logical necessity in which 3 is identically 2. That is, this fundamental truth of the foundation is perfectly apparent in the inflection on the foundation which is the absolute form of logical propositions.[65] Nothing could provide a more conclusive confirmation of the fact that real triadic duality is radically and precisely 1/2 the absolute value of real triadic unity, as 1/3 : 2/3,

---

especially the following (which should be compared to the treatment of the *unum esse,* above, Sections II.3 and II.4.): ". . . thought is set its hardest task when the determinations for the movement of the Notion through which alone it is the Notion, are denoted by one, two, three, four; for it is then moving in its opposite element, one which is devoid of all relation; it is engaged on a labour of derangement. The difficulty in comprehending that, for example, one is three and three is one, stems from the fact that one is devoid of all relation and therefore does not in its own self exhibit the determination through which it passes into its opposite; on the contrary, one is essentially a sheer excluding and rejection of such a relation. Conversely, understanding makes use of this to combat speculative truth (as, for example, against the truth laid down in the doctrine called the trinity) and it *counts* the determinations of it which constitute one unity, in order to expose them as sheer absurdity—that is, understanding itself commits the same absurdity of making that which is pure relation into something devoid of all relation."

[64] Cf. above, pp. 268ff.

[65] Cf. above, pp. 273ff.

as '3 = 1' (upon which Peirce and Hegel agree, quite apart from any mathematical/philosophical distinctions) is to '3 = 2' (the identity of Appearance and Essence in the foundation[66]), nothing could more perfectly confirm this ratio of value as that of '1 = 1/3' to '1 = 2/3' than the form of Peirce's own valuation of the elements of the triad:

> . . . In pure algebra, the symbols have no other meaning than that which the formulae impose upon them. . . . Yet in this particular instance, we can adapt our doctrine better to thoroughgoing trichotomy by derogating a little from the dignified meaninglessness of pure algebra. . . . for the purposes of trichotomic mathematics, it should be recognized that each quantity has one of three values. Call them, for the moment, 0°, 120°, 240°—regarding 360° as the same as 0°. Or one might call them night, morning, and afternoon. Let us denote the three values by ο (for ὄρθρος), δ (for δείλη), ν (for νύξ).[67]

After evolving addition and multiplication tables for these values, Peirce continues:

> It will be seen that, if we are to accept the premisses upon which the addition-table and multiplication-table are based, we cannot avoid giving peculiar properties to each of the three values δ, ν, ο, and that the connection of them with some such sensuous images as day, night, and dawn is by no means an idle fancy. Let us put these into table form. I add the subtraction-table

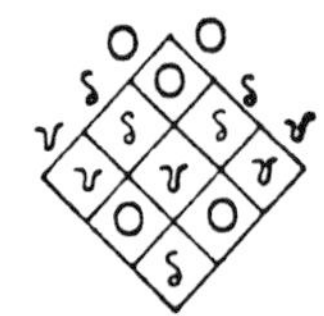

> We see that the multiplication-table recognizes a characteristic

[66] Ibid.

[67] Peirce, *Collected Papers*, 4.314.

> property in each member of the triad o, δ, ν. Multiplication by δ effects nothing. Multiplication by ν may have peculiar effects, but it is undone by a second multiplication by ν. Multiplication by o can never be undone, nor the same effect be otherwise produced.
>
> We thus see that it is impossible to deal with a triad without being forced to recognize a triad of which one member is positive but ineffective, another is the opponent of that, a third, intermediate between these two is all-potent. The ideas of our three categories could not be better stated in so few words.[68]

And, finally, that is made explicit which is implicit in all of the above, viz.,

> We may commonly write 0 for o, 1 for δ, –1 for ν.[69]

The radical duality of the Peircean triad, what might be called its radical 1/3rdness, can be imaged thusly:

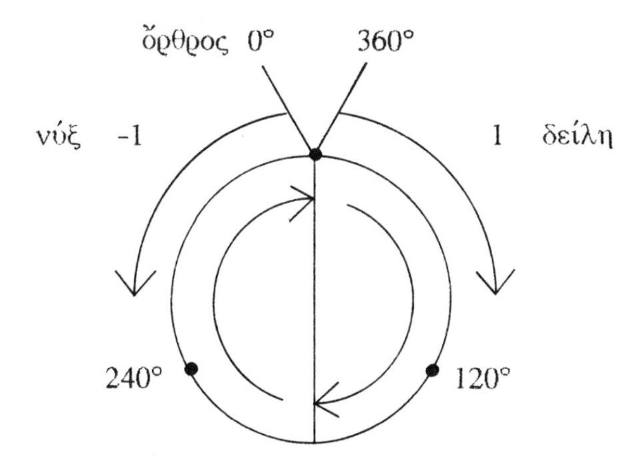

As is here immediately evident there is no real triadic unity: not only is Night but the reflection of Day, the negative of the positive, –1 to 1, but even the presumed underlying continuity of the

[68] Ibid., 4.316–17.
[69] Ibid., 4.320.

mirror is an illusion: there are two separated pieces of the glass, and the apparent circle is the result of an inversion of an original –1, a real opposite to 1 appearing as a reflection, i.e., –1 is the inversion of –1 the real negative of 1: Night is identically the double negative of Day, the *duad* negative of 1. 240° is the double negative/the negative double of 120° (δ divided by ν is ν). The unity of this monad and this duad is, quite literally, symbolic: 360°, quite literally is *regarded as the same as* 0°: never do the two 1/3rd's transcend the symbolic triad which is their perfect matching/pairing, *qua* halves of a *presumed* unity, in the indefinite depths of the Dawn, of the intersection. The identity of this triad is this Dawn, this intermediate, this difference between each of two triadic parts of a pair. Concerning this twilight of triadic unity, Peirce says:

> We must not absolutely restrict ourselves to the notion that two triads can at one time correspond to one another in only one way, so that a given member of the one must be down-right, absolutely connected with a given member of the other, or else be down-right, absolutely disconnected from it—two alternatives differing as day from night—as δείλη from νύξ. We must be prepared, if occasion be, to admit a possible intermediate dawn. For to say that two things are disconnected is but to say that they are connected in a way different from the way under contemplation. For everything is in some relation to each other thing. It is connected with it by otherness, for example. We should, therefore, be prepared to say that two atoms, one of each triad, have either a positive connection, such as is under the illumination of thought at the time, or a dark other mode of connection, or a vague glimmering intermediate form of connection. Nor are we to rest there as a finality. We must not restrict ourselves to saying absolutely that between a pair there either down-right is a given kind of connection, or down-right is *not* that kind. We must be prepared to say, if need be, that the pair has a δ-connection with a given mode of connection, or an opposite ν-connection with it, or a neutral o-connection with it. We can push this sort of thing as far as may be—indefinitely. Still however far we carry it, ultimately there will always be a dichotomic alternative between the truth and falsity of

> what is said. Why it should be so, we shall see in the proper place and time for such an inquiry. At present, it is pertinent to note that the fact that it is so is forced upon our attention in pure mathematics.[70]

Indeed, the 'dichotomic alternative between the truth and falsity of what is said', this falsity of truth and falsehood,[71] is the essential corollary of the depth of indefiniteness which is the ὄρθρος, the 360° *regarded as the same as* 0°, the zero-total which is a something-nothing, but absolutely and essentially *not* the something-zero *ex nihilo,* the zero of unity *ex nihilo,* the zero which is not nothing, the zero the content of which is unity, but rather a twilight, a triadic something or other whose reach extends no further than being the composition of night and day. Remaining within the falsity of truth and falsehood, within the radical falsity of all calculation with reference to Nothing, Peirce, nevertheless, understands himself to have taken a step beyond 'mere dualism', stopping short of the non-mathematical idealism of Hegel:

> To recognize the triad is a step out of the bounds of mere dualism; but to attempt [to deny] independent being to the dyad and monad, Hegel-wise, is only another one-sidedness.[72]

The step out of the bounds of 'mere dualism' is real triadic dualism, the '2 × 3 affair' in which the ideal triadic unity is the difference between two 3's, the depth of indefiniteness which is the pairing of a monadic and (negative) duadic set of 1/3rds, or, in the event of the denial of the validity of this mathematical idealism by a philosophical thinking arrogating to the idea all relation (at the expense of number), it would be, this ideal triadic unity, 'only another one-sidedness'. But the *tertium quid* has been given above in the construction of the foundation (the

---

[70] Ibid., 4.319.

[71] Cf. above, pp. 287ff.

[72] Peirce, *Collected Papers,* 4.318.

absolute out-identity of (any) side [absolute unconditioned one-sidedness]) out of the foundation-stone each of the elements of which, 0, $\bar{0}$, 1, both effects and affects both itself and each of the others, except 1, which effecting itself or the others affects each of the others but does not affect itself, except 1, that is, which is relation itself, which affects itself in and as the other, in and as the zero which is not nothing (the *nihil ex nihilo*), in and as the *unum/*minimum, in and as either of these (0 or $\bar{0}$), the absolute relative identity of which (the one to the other) it is, this 1.

2

SIX THEOREMS CONCERNING THE NEW LOGIC AND MATHEMATICS THAT PROVIDE THE LOGICAL BASE FOR THE NOTHINGLESS FIBONACCI SEQUENCE, THE GEOMETRIC AND ARITHMETIC SERIES, AND FERMAT'S LAST THEOREM

A series of numbers defined by the elementary recursion $f_{n+2} = f_n + f_{n+1}$; $f_0 = 0$; $f_1 = 1$.

McGraw–Hill Concise Encyclopedia of Science & Technology[1]

Named after Leonardo [da Pisa] is the series of Fibonacci (otherwise known as the series of Lamé), which runs: 0, 1, 1, 2, 3, 5, 8, 13, 21, . . ., each term being equal to the sum of the two which precede it.

Encyclopedia Americana: *International Edition*[2]

Of the two regular solids, the dodecahedron and the icosahedron, the former is made up precisely of pentagons, the latter of triangles but triangles that meet five at a point. Both of these solids, and indeed the structure of the pentagon itself, cannot be formed without this proportion that the geometers of today call divine. It is so arranged that the two lesser terms

[1] T. Brylawski, "Fibonacci Numbers," in *McGraw-Hill Concise Encyclopedia of Science & Technology,* ed. S. P. Parker (New York, 1984), p. 716.

[2] "Fibonacci, Leonardo," in *Encyclopedia Americana: International Edition,* vol. 11 (New York, 1966), p. 171.

> of a progressive series together constitute the third, and the two last, when added, make the immediately subsequent term and so on to infinity, as the same proportion continues unbroken. It is impossible to provide a perfect example in round numbers. However, the further we advance from the number one, the more perfect the example becomes. Let the smallest numbers be 1 and 1, which you must imagine as unequal. Add them, and the sum will be 2; add to this the greater of the 1's, result 3; add 2 to this, and get 5; add 3, get 8; 5 to 8, 13; 8 to 13, 21. As 5 is to 8, so 8 is to 13, approximately, and as 8 to 13, so 13 is to 21, approximately.
>
> J. Kepler, *The Six-Cornered Snowflake*[3]

Preliminary: It is evident that while $2 = 1 + 1$, and $1 = 0 + 1$, $1 \neq 0 + 0$. If, then, F_n is a place in the Fibonacci sequence, F_1 is not an essentially integral part of the sequence, that is, the first 1—like the 0 which precedes it, F_0—is not absolutely part of the sequence. As it stands, the sequence really begins with F_2, with the second 1. Since, however, the given, $f_0 = 0$, $f_1 = 1$, has been, in the mathematics of radical subjectivity, uncritically and arbitrarily incorporated as part of the sequence, the latter appears to begin with the addition of 1 to 0, where 0 = 'nothing', appears to begin with F_1, with the first 1.[4] But Fibonacci, in *Liber Abaci,* devised the sequence as the solution to "the rabbit problem" of "determining how many pairs of rabbits there will be in each generation if the first pair breeds one pair in the first and succeeding month and if it is assumed that this pair and every succeeding pair gives birth to a new pair in the second month after their birth."[5]

---

[3] Quoted in R. Herz-Fischler, *A Mathematical History of Division in Extreme and Mean Ratio* (Waterloo, 1987), p. 161. It appears that 0 was first added in front of the Fibonacci series by A. Girard in 1634 (ibid., p. 162).

[4] Cf. A. Brousseau, *Fibonacci and Related Number Theoretic Tables* (San Jose, 1972), pp. 1–8. Cf. pp. 54ff., for the "abbreviated" Fibonacci sequence beginning with F_2. Cf. also, N. N. Vorob'ev, *Fibonacci Numbers,* trans. H. Moss (New York and London, 1961), and V. E. Hoggatt, *Fibonacci and Lucas Numbers* (New York, 1969), the latter including a chapter on phyllotaxis, "Fibonacci Numbers in Nature."

[5] Herz-Fischler, *Mathematical History of Division,* p. 144.

THEOREM 1. Every natural number in the Fibonacci sequence is the sum of the terms of a real ratio not previously existing in the sequence.

Proof: In Fibonacci's statement of the rabbit problem, and in Kepler's purely mathematical description of the Fibonacci sequence quoted at the head of this paper, there is no mention of 0, although Kepler goes as far as to begin the sequence with 1 plus 1. Indeed, in order to understand the otherwise enigmatic statements of Kepler, to wit, that "the smallest numbers," 1 and 1, must be imagined as "unequal," and that to 2 is to be added "the greater of the 1's," it is necessary to consider that, in effect, what is stipulated by Fibonacci is that in the second month a second but *immature* pair is born to the first pair who were *mature* but without offspring in the first month and themselves *immature* in the month previous to the first, i.e., in the month before Fibonacci considers them as the original pair. At the end of the second month there *are* two pairs, one (mature) plus one (immature). So when Kepler says that the third number, 3, is the sum of 2 plus the "greater of the 1's," he has in mind that at the end of the third month there are 2 *mature-1's* and 1 *immature-1*, as effectively stipulated by Fibonacci's statement of the problem. The fact that Kepler translates the distinction into "unequal" ones should call attention to the fact that each successive number in the sequence is much more than, indeed, not at all *essentially* the abstract sum of the two preceding numbers (simply as sum the 2 mature-1's of the third month would be the original pair of the first month added to itself as it appeared in the second month). Rather what happens is that each month an immature rabbit turns into a mature rabbit while a *different* rabbit takes its place on the list of the immature. In reality each number of the sequence is the concrete sum of the terms of the ratio of mature-1's to immature-1's actually discretely existing at that time (place) in the sequence. For example, 3 is not the sum of two preceding states of the series, 1 (mature) and 2 (mature and immature), but rather the sum of the new state of the series, 1 (immature) and 2 (mature and mature), 5 is not the sum of 2 (mature and immature) and 3 (mature and mature and immature), but of 2 (immature and immature) and 3 (mature and mature and mature), and so on to infinity. Each number of the sequence is a rational structure, and that structure is a sorting based on the real natural development of its elements. The extreme and mean ratio approximated by this real structure of each member of the Fibonacci sequence is the ratio of perfect discretion. The approximation to the sum of the terms of this ratio, $1 + \phi = \phi^2$, is the real structure of each number. It is clear, then, that the extreme and mean ratio is the ratio of novel and continuum, of mature and immature: the ratio of 'to grow' and 'to be'. Kepler's "unequal" 1's are mature and immature 1's constituting 2. Let, then, 0, Peirce's symbol for *ens* or 'non-relative unity', be substituted for the first of Kepler's "unequal" 1's, thusly, $\bar{0}$, 1.[6] Let $\bar{0}$ be called *unum* to distinguish it from unity or 1. It is at once evident that, while $\bar{0} + 1 = 2$ (as Kepler, in effect, says),[7] if now 0 is placed before this series (the case arbitrarily since the 17th Century, but now rationally and necessarily so) so that it runs 0, $\bar{0}$, 1, 2 . . . , then 0 *cannot equal nothing*, since nothing plus $\bar{0}$ does not equal 1, or nothing plus *immature-1* does not equal *mature-1*, or nothing plus 'to be' does not equal 'to grow'. 0, then, must be not nothing. 0 must be a sort of 1, just as the non-relative unity of $\bar{0}$ is a sort of relative unity: 0 must be the sheer unity of 'to begin', a *beginning-1*, or, the first pair of rabbits *in utero*. Absolute-relative unity (1) is the sum of the terms of the ratio of absolute unity ($\bar{0}$) to sheer relative unity or not nothing (0). The mature pair of rabbits is the sum of the terms of the ratio of its immaturity to its beginning: 'to grow' = 'to be' plus 'to begin'.

THEOREM 2. There is a law of absolute unity, $1(1 + 1) = 0$, which is the logical foundation for a mathematics which includes zero [0] but in which no element is equal to nothing.
Proof: For the proof of this theorem see above III.1, Afterword 1.[8]

---

[6] Peirce, Collected Papers, 3.307.

[7] Note that $1 + \phi = \phi^2$ is actually $\phi^0 + \phi^1 = \phi^2$ where the logical-arithmetic relation noted in effect by Kepler ($\bar{0} + 1 = 2$) is really but *imperfectly* reflected as the *indirect* relation of the exponents of ϕ $(0 + 1 = 2)$. Cf. above, p. 255, n. 1.

[8] Also, cf. below, this Section, Theorem 6.

THEOREM 3. To found a mathematics which includes zero [0] but in which no element is equal to nothing.

Proof: Let there be the three digits, 0, $\bar{0}$, and 1. Let there be an infinite lattice in which three regularly repeating ribbons of 0's, $\bar{0}$'s, and 1's, woven regularly through a blank field, descend from left to right, each instance of a digit at the center of a square and laterally separated from its neighbors by a space equal to that which it occupies. Further, let a square arrangement of the digits in the lattice be the smallest in which each of the three appears in equal number, and let this square be a multiplication table in which, since the square is essentially the boundless lattice, the product of any two digits must be derived from their relations within the table.[9] It is evident that within the confines of this square—consistent with the requirement that no integer equal nothing—multiplication, addition, division, and subtraction will produce identical results, as follows (where the symbol $\because$ is the sign of this identity of relations):

$$
\begin{array}{lcl}
0 \because \bar{0} & = & 1 \\
0 \because 1 & = & \bar{0} \\
1 \because 1 & = & 1 \\
1 \because \bar{0} & = & 0 \\
0 \because 0 & = & 1 \\
\bar{0} \because \bar{0} & = & 1
\end{array}
$$

where it is evident that while 0 and $\bar{0}$ are each 'subtractable' from 1, neither is 'subtractable' from the other, or from itself, and that 1 is not 'subtractable' from itself, that is, since in the absence of 0 = nothing there are no negative values, subtraction is in fact addition, and to divide one digit by another is simply to produce a rational element. $0 \because \bar{0}$ functions to identify another element (1), to identify each of its elements with another not itself and not other than itself, both 'sorts' of 1 (see the proof of Theorem 1), or unity identical with not nothing and not not

[9] For the illustrations of these arrangements, cf. above, Section III.1, pp. 267f.

nothing and vice versa, both elements identified with themselves, as such with each other, and with unity: $0 \because \bar{0} = 1 = 1 \because 1 = 0 \because 0 = \bar{0} \because \bar{0} = 0 \because 1 \because 0 \because 1 = \bar{0} \because 1 \because \bar{0} \because 1 = 0 \because 0 \because 0 \because \bar{0} \because \bar{0} \because \bar{0} \because 1 \because 1 \because 1 = (0 \because 0 \because 0 \because \bar{0} \because \bar{0} \because \bar{0} = 1 \because 1 \because 1) = 1 \because 1 \because 1$.[10]

COROLLARY TO THEOREM 3. Since factorial 0 is $\bar{0} \because 1 \because 0$, there is a mathematics in which it is really the case that $0! = 1$.

THEOREM 4. To provide for the Fibonacci sequence a perfectly rational foundation.

Proof: In order for the first place of the sequence to be occupied by a number which is an *essentially integral* part of the sequence of numbers, the definition of such a sequence, where $'n$ is a place therein, must be—since $2 \neq 1 + 0$—$f_{'n+1} = f_{'n} + f_{'n-1}$; $f_{'0} = \bar{0}$, $f_{'1} = 1$. That recursion, in turn, which is such that $0 = 1 + \bar{0}$, is defined, where $'f_{'n}$ is a number therein, $'f_{'n+1} = {'f_{'n}} \pm {'f_{'n-1}}$, such that if $'f_{'0} = \bar{0}$, and $'f_{'1} = 1$, then $f_{'n}^{\,'f_{'n}} = f_{'n+1} - f_{'n} = f_{'n-1}$, that is, the latter series is a function of the fact that each of its constituents is raised to a power which is an element in the infinitely repeating finite series, . . . $0, \bar{0}, 1$ . . . , in which $0 \neq$ nothing, but $1 = 0 + \bar{0}$, while the *given* of the ordinary Fibonacci sequence (F), viz., $0 + 1$, now $= \bar{0}$, the minimum infinitely included in the series insofar as, so defined, the latter is so situated that it is irreducible to nothing, and at once such that, where $*F = (f_{'n+1} = f_{'n} + f_{'n-1}$ [i.e., $+ f_{'n}^{\,'f_{'n}}$]; $f_{'0} = \bar{0}$, $f_{'1} = 1)$, the reduction of $*F_1 \rightarrow *F_{100}$ to the pattern 100-square produces a grid of which it is true that the product of one pair of diagonally situated corner-squares divided by the corresponding product of the cross-diagonal $\cong$ (increasingly so as the sequence progresses) Unity (1), as it does likewise in the case of those squares of numbers which form sub-squares within the 100-square.

Set out, then, $*F_1 \rightarrow *F_{100}$, the first 100 numbers integrally woven into the infinite structure of the logic, at once the foundational mathematics, of radical objectivity, in the way here illustrated, where it is evident that $*F$ eliminates the inconsequence

[10] For the proofs of these relations, cf. above, Section III.1, pp. 257ff.

1	0	$\bar{0}$	1								
$\bar{0}$	1	0	$\bar{0}$	1	0	$\bar{0}$					
0	$\bar{0}$	1 (1) 1	2 (0) 2	3 ($\bar{0}$) 3	4 (1) 5	5 (0) 8	6 ($\bar{0}$) 13	7 (1) 21	8 (0) 34	9 ($\bar{0}$) 55	10 (1) 89
1	0	11 ($\bar{0}$) 144	12 (1) 233	13 (0) 377	14 ($\bar{0}$) 610	15 (1) 987	16 (0) 1597	17 ($\bar{0}$) 2584	18 (1) 4181	19 (0) 6765	20 ($\bar{0}$) 10946
	1	21 (0) 17711	22 ($\bar{0}$) 28657	23 (1) 46368	24 (0) 75025	25 ($\bar{0}$) 1.21E5	26 (1) 1.96E5	27 (0) 3.18E5	28 ($\bar{0}$) 5.14E5	29 (1) 8.32E5	30 (0) 1.35E6
	$\bar{0}$	31 (1) 2.17E6	32 (0) 3.53E6	33 ($\bar{0}$) 5.70E6	34 (1) 9.23E6	35 (0) 1.49E7	36 ($\bar{0}$) 2.42E7	37 (1) 3.91E7	38 (0) 6.33E7	39 ($\bar{0}$) 1.02E8	40 (1) 1.66E8
	0	41 ($\bar{0}$) 2.68E8	42 (1) 4.34E8	43 (0) 7.01E8	44 ($\bar{0}$) 1.14E9	45 (1) 1.84E9	46 (0) 2.97E9	47 ($\bar{0}$) 4.80E9	48 (1) 7.78E9	49 (0) 1.26E10	50 ($\bar{0}$) 2.04E10
		51 (0) 3.30E10	52 ($\bar{0}$) 5.33E10	53 (1) 8.63E10	54 (0) 1.40E11	55 ($\bar{0}$) 2.26E11	56 (1) 3.65E11	57 (0) 5.91E11	58 ($\bar{0}$) 9.57E11	59 (1) 1.55E12	60 (0) 2.51E12
		61 (1) 4.05E12	62 (0) 6.56E12	63 ($\bar{0}$) 1.06E13	64 (1) 1.72E13	65 (0) 2.78E13	66 ($\bar{0}$) 4.50E13	67 (1) 7.27E13	68 (0) 1.18E14	69 ($\bar{0}$) 1.90E14	70 (1) 3.08E14
		71 ($\bar{0}$) 4.99E14	72 (1) 8.07E14	73 (0) 1.31E15	74 ($\bar{0}$) 2.11E15	75 (1) 3.42E15	76 (0) 5.53E15	77 ($\bar{0}$) 8.94E15	78 (1) 1.45E16	79 (0) 2.34E16	80 ($\bar{0}$) 3.79E16
		81 (0) 6.13E16	82 ($\bar{0}$) 9.92E16	83 (1) 1.61E17	84 (0) 2.60E17	85 ($\bar{0}$) 4.20E17	86 (1) 6.80E17	87 (0) 1.10E18	88 ($\bar{0}$) 1.78E18	89 (1) 2.88E18	90 (0) 4.66E18
		91 (1) 7.54E18	92 (0) 1.22E19	93 ($\bar{0}$) 1.97E19	94 (1) 3.19E19	95 (0) 5.17E19	96 ($\bar{0}$) 8.36E19	97 (1) 1.35E20	98 (0) 2.19E20	99 ($\bar{0}$) 3.54E20	100 (1) 5.73E20

of beginning the sequence with the inessential integrals, 0, 1: $f'_{n-1} = f'_n{}^{f'_n}$, that is,[11] $0 = \bar{0}^{(\bar{0})}$, $\bar{0} = 1^1$, $1 = 2^0$, $2 = 3^{\bar{0}}$, $3 = 5^1$, $5 = 8^0$, . . . , so that $f'_{n+1} = f'_n + f'_n{}^{f'_n}$, that is, $\bar{0} = 0 + 0^0$, $1 = \bar{0} + \bar{0}^{(\bar{0})}$, $2 = 1 + 1^1$, $3 = 2 + 2^0$, $5 = 3 + 3^{\bar{0}}$, $8 = 5 + 5^1$, $13 = 8 + 8^0$, . . . , and (the numbers descending the diagonal as needed [e.g., 89^1 descending to 89^0 before 144(as 0 descends to $\bar{0}$ at the very inception of *F)]), $233 = 144 + 144^{\bar{0}}$, . . . , $28657 = 17711 + 17711^0$,. . . .

THEOREM 5. To construct a series of natural numbers the real relations among which are the relations of the infinitely relative series, . . . 0, $\bar{0}$, 1. . . .[12]

[11] Ibid., for the following and other exponential relations of 0, $\bar{0}$, and 1, and their proofs.

[12] Cf. above, pp. 304f. The writer is indebted to J. Kappraff who, by substitut-

Proof: The 100-square of $*F$ is proof of the law of absolute unity (LAU), i.e., of the absolutely relative identity of 0, $\bar{0}$, and 1 (see proof of Theorem 2), as is evident from the following example: $*F_{89}$ (= 2.880067196E18), the square root of the square-constant of the last ninefold sub-square of the 100-square properly embodying the foundation-stone (the square essence of the infinite lattice-work of 0's, $\bar{0}$'s, and 1's [see proof of Theorem 3]), is the square root of the product of $*F_{78}$ (= 1.447233403E16) × $*F_{100}$ (= 5.731478442E20), indeed,

$$*F_{89}{}^2 \cong *F_{78} \times *F_{100} \cong *F_{80} \times *F_{98} \cong *F_{99} \times *F_{79} \cong$$
$$*F_{88} \times *F_{90} \cong 8.2944\text{E}36,$$

which is to say, *qua* LAU functions of the respective $*F$ numbers,

$$1^2 = 1 \times 1 = \bar{0} \times 0 = \bar{0} \times 0 = \bar{0} \times 0,$$

and when $*F_{89}$ is itself integrated with its square, when ~8.2944E36 is raised to the sesquialteral power, that is, when $*F_{89}$ is cubed, then not only does

$$*F_{89}{}^3 \cong *F_{78} \times *F_{89} \times *F_{100} \cong$$
$$*F_{80} \times *F_{89} \times *F_{98} \cong *F_{99} \times *F_{89} \times *F_{79} \cong$$
$$*F_{88} \times *F_{89} \times *F_{90} \cong 8.2944\text{E}36^{3/2},$$

where, *qua* LAU functions,

$$1^3 = 1 \times 1 \times 1 = \bar{0} \times 1 \times 0 = \bar{0} \times 1 \times 0 = \bar{0} \times 1 \times 0,$$

---

ting the ϕ series ($1, \phi^1, \phi^2, \phi^3, \ldots$) for the Fibonacci sequence in the following proof, first called to the writer's attention that the products of the numbers associated with the multiplicative relations, 000, $\overline{000}$, and 111, are in that case *exactly* identical, and that insofar as this relationship is a function of the exponents of ϕ it holds for any geometric series.

but,

$$*F_{89}{}^{3} \cong *F_{78} \times *F_{89} \times *F_{100} \cong *F_{79} \times *F_{90} \times *F_{98} \cong$$
$$*F_{80} \times *F_{88} \times *F_{99} \cong 8.2944\text{E}36^{3/2},$$

that is, *qua* LAU functions, the identity relation of 0, $\bar{0}$, 1, *qua* threefold repetition of the terms,

$$1^3 = 1 \times 1 \times 1 = 0 \times 0 \times 0 = \bar{0} \times \bar{0} \times \bar{0}.$$

This multiplicative relation holds for any 3 × 3 section of any grid arrangement of a geometric series, 3 × 3, or larger. For example:

1 1 1	2 0 2	3 $\bar{0}$ 4
5 $\bar{0}$ 16	6 1 32	7 0 64
9 0 256	10 $\bar{0}$ 512	11 1 1024

2 0 2	3 $\bar{0}$ 4	4 1 8
7 1 64	8 0 128	9 $\bar{0}$ 256
12 $\bar{0}$ 2048	13 1 4096	14 0 8192

,

where 1 × 32 × 1024 = 2 × 64 × 256 = 4 × 16 × 512 in the first arrangement, and 2 × 128 × 8192 = 4 × 256 × 2048 = 8 × 64 × 4096 in the second arrangement. The elements of the logic constitute the fundamental trinary template of any geometric series, including that underlying the Fibonacci sequence, in a way illustrated by the following relation of geometric series and logical digits:

$$\{1 + x + x^2\} + \{x^3 + x^4 + x^5\} + \{x^6 + x^7 + x^8\} +$$
$$\{x^9 + x^{10} + x^{11}\} + \{x^{12} + x^{13} + x^{14}\} + \ldots$$

$$\{1 + 0 + \bar{0}\} + \{\bar{0} + 1 + 0\} + \{0 + \bar{0} + 1\} +$$
$$\{1 + 0 + \bar{0}\} + \{\bar{0} + 1 + 0\} + \ldots,$$

where sets of logical digits corresponding to the three rows of the foundation-stone (the square essence of the infinite lattice of 0's, $\bar{0}$'s, and 1's) are assigned *in any order* (the order illustrated is arbitrarily chosen) to the geometric series, with the result that the combination of three sets of series numbers associated with differently ordered logical sets selected from anywhere in the infinite series (the three sets may be at any distance from one another) will constitute then and there the ninefold foundation-stone whose internal relations conform to the multiplicative rule: $000 = \overline{000} = 111$. If the geometric series is arranged in the pattern of the logical analysis underlying the rigidity rule, $T = V - 2$,[13] that is, in sets of overlapping 000's (= triangles = identities = $\overline{000}$'s = 111's = $\bar{0}10$'s, etc.),[14] as follows:

[13] Cf. below, Section III.3, Part 2. The multiplicative identity of 000, $\overline{000}$, and 111, as it operates in the geometric series, points to the "rigidity" of the geometric series itself, which is here shown to conform, *qua* "intelligible minimum" structure (see below, n. 14), to the identical logical template as do, analogously, two- and three-dimensional rigid frameworks.

[14] Cf. above, Section III.1, pp. 256 and 260f. Although not illustrated in the text above, the sets within the foundation-stone consisting of the triangular arrangement $10\bar{0}$ (where 1 is the top left subsquare), its inverse, $\bar{1}00$ (where 1 is the bottom right subsquare), the central column $01\bar{0}$, and the forward diagonal $\bar{0}10$, all, centered on the central 1, conform to the multiplicative rule and its arithmetic equivalent (cf. below in the text). Only the end rows and the end columns—those not centered on the central 1—do not conform to the rule. The middle column, centered on the central 1, composed of three middles of any three sets, the 'absolute middle' column, will always follow the rule. The trinary arrangement of the foundation-stone is distinguished from the larger squares in the infinite expansion of squares (one 1-set, two 2-sets, three 3-sets, four 4-sets, . .) in which diagonal and analogous triangular identities appear but appear as *parts* which are not exhaustive of those larger squares which also contain quadrilateral identities, or, in the case of two 2-sets the exhaustive diagonal relation appears without the triangular relation. As the triangle and

$$(x^0[x^1(x^2)[x^3](x^4)[x^5](x^6)[x^7](x^8)[x^9]$$
$$(x^{10})[x^{11}](x^{12})[x^{13}](x^{14})[\ldots](\ldots)\ldots,$$

then any three sets of three consecutive numbers chosen from anywhere in the infinite series (the sets may be at any distance from one another, may be identical [two or three of three], or may overlap), when placed in any order in the place of the rows of the square essence of the infinite lattice of 0's, $\overline{0}$'s, and 1's, the foundation-stone, will constitute a square the internal relations of whose numerical elements will follow exactly the multiplicative rule, $000 = \overline{000} = 111$. The identical procedure followed in the case of an *arithmetic* series (e.g., 1, 2, 3, 4 . . . , or 2, 4, 6, 8 . . . ,) will produce a foundation-stone arrangement in which the internal relations of the numbers in the square will follow exactly the *additive* rule, $000 = \overline{000} = 111$. Where the series is multiplicative, so is the rule; where the series is additive, so the rule is additive.

---

the tetrahedron are to rigidity so the foundation-stone is to all logical and mathematical relations. The trinary arrangement is *the minimum square arrangement of different digits an equal number of each of which is included in the square, which is itself at once the* maximum *square exhausted by the diagonal and triangular relations of its digits. The fact that this minimum is this maximum and that the only equal distribution of the* arithmetic *value of its nine logical digits among three different entities is three 2's is the logical foundation for the truth of Fermat's last theorem.* The one 1-set and the two 2-sets are levels of the expansion of squares encompassed by the logical template but they contain the logical template only implicitly and retrospectively (one 1-set, having neither diagonal or triangular relations) or incompletely (two 2-sets, having only diagonal relations). It is in this way that the foundation-stone is the *intelligible minimum* of the infinite expansion of squares and the template of the geometric and arithmetic series, and, as well, as shown above, this Section and Section III.1 passim, the fundamental *logical* template supporting the extreme and mean ratio, which latter is the primary and perfectly economical *mathematical* division of unity which is at once a proportion, i.e., an *essentially mathematical relation,* and, indeed, the *'minimum' proportional section.* For the arithmetic value of 0 and $\overline{0}$, see above, Section III.1, p. 274, n. 27, p. 277, n. 30, and below, this Section, Theorem 6, and Section III.4, and Section IV.2, pp. 519ff.

The sum associated with the rational relation, $000 + \overline{000} = 111$, in the case of the Fibonacci sequence, approximates identity, that is, is different to a degree less than an order of magnitude, as the *ratio* of the sums of the rational relation, $000 + \overline{000} = 111$, in any geometric series, including that underlying the Fibonacci sequence, similarly approximates the ratio existing between successive members of the series. So, for example, just as in the division in extreme and mean ratio, $AB = AC + CB$, so too, analogously, in the final sub-square of the 100-square of $*F$

$$*F_{78} + *F_{89} + *F_{100} \cong (*F_{79} + *F_{90} + *F_{98}) + (*F_{80} + *F_{88} + *F_{99}) \cong 5.76E20,$$

just as, *qua* addition of the LAU functions of the squares constituting the sub-square,

$$1 + 1 + 1 = (0 + 0 + 0) + (\overline{0} + \overline{0} + \overline{0}).$$

Finally, since the following substitutions can be made in the equation above, to wit,

$$*F_{78} + *F_{89} + *F_{100} \cong (*F_{80} + *F_{89} + *F_{98}) + (*F_{79} + *F_{89} + *F_{99}) \cong 5.76E20,$$

it is at once approximately true that

$$(*F_{78} + *F_{89} + *F_{100}) : (*F_{80} + *F_{88} + *F_{99}) :: (*F_{80} + *F_{88} + *F_{99}) : (*F_{79} + *F_{90} + *F_{98}),$$

that is, as, *qua* LAU functions,

$$(1+1+1) : (\bar{0}+\bar{0}+\bar{0}) :: (\bar{0}+\bar{0}+\bar{0}) : (0+0+0),$$

and that

$$(*F_{78}+*F_{89}+*F_{100}) : (*F_{79}+*F_{89}+*F_{99}) ::$$
$$(*F_{79}+*F_{89}+*F_{99}) : (*F_{80}+*F_{89}+*F_{98}),$$

that is, as, *qua* LAU functions,

$$(1+1+1) : (0+1+\bar{0}) :: (0+1+\bar{0}) : (\bar{0}+1+0),$$

in either case ~ the ‘golden section’,

$$AB : AC :: AC : CB.$$

THEOREM 6. The continuous tiling of the 100-square of $*F$ with proper and improper ninefold foundation-stones of the infinitely relative series, . . . 0, $\bar{0}$, 1 . . . , in its essential structure approximates in ordinary mathematics the law of absolute unity $1(1+1)=0$ (see Theorem 2).

Proof: Since the ideal ratio of any number to the preceding number in the $*F$ sequence is ϕ, let $\bar{0}=1/\phi$ and $0=1/\phi^2$. The sum, *qua* essential structure of $*F$, of 3 0’s ($3/\phi^2=1.145898034$), 3 $\bar{0}$’s ($3/\phi=1.854101966$), and 3 1’s (3) then = 6. This is exactly the sum arrived at by calculating on the basis of the pure form of the logical/mathematical embodiment of the ‘law of absolute unity’, where, counting in the manner of Kepler, “unequal” 1’s ($\bar{0}$’s and 1’s) together with 0’s which are not nothings, and reckoning that $1=0 \because 0=0 \because \bar{0}=\bar{0} \because \bar{0}$ (see proofs of Theorems 1 and 3), $0+0+0+\bar{0}+\bar{0}+\bar{0}+1+1+1=6$.[15] In the 100-square of the $*F$ sequence the ratio of the LAU value of the center

[15] Cf. above, p. 308, n. 14.

square of the ninefold sub-square (see proof of Theorem 3) to the sum of the LAU values of the eight squares surrounding the central square is, in the case of the proper embodiment of the foundation-stone, 1 : 5, or .2. In addition to the ninefold sub-square properly embodying the foundation-stone, there appear within the 100-square improper embodiments whose centers are either 0 or $\bar{0}$. The center-edge ratios of the latter, respectively, = $\phi^{-2}/5.618\ldots$ (= .067989267) and $\phi^{-1}/5.3819\ldots$ (= .114834242), so that, *qua* center-square-reduced-to-edge-squares, the sum of the 0, $\bar{0}$, and 1 'foundation stones' (.382823509) ≅ 0 ($1/\phi^2 = .381966011$), which relation approximates the 'law of absolute unity' itself (see Theorem 2), that is, (where E_n is the center-edge ratio of a foundation-stone configuration) $E_1 + E_1 \cong E_0 + E_{\bar{0}} + E_1 \cong 0$ ($= 1/\phi^2$) is the approximate equivalent in ordinary mathematics of $\mathit{1}(1 + 1) = 0$.[16]

[16] Cf. above, Section III.1, Afterword 1.

3

THE GEOMETRY OF THE INFINITELY FLAT STRUCTURE OF THE UNIVERSE: THE LOGIC OF RIGID STRUCTURES

PART 1

In order to more easily compare the cross ratio of projective geometry with the extreme and mean ratio and both ratios with those of the geometric proportion, first re-label the line *AD*, divided at *B* and *C*, *AB*, divided at *C* and *D*, so that the cross ratio of the line is $AC/CD : AB/DB$. Then, understand the cross ratio in the form $(AC \cdot DB)/(CD \cdot AB)$ to be the proof form of the proportion $CD : AC :: DB : AB$, which is equivalently $AB : DB :: AC : CD$. The cross ratio is thereby transformed into a proportion of the elements of the line *AB* where the whole line is divided into three parts none of which parts contains any of the others, but each is contained *directly* by the whole line. This last feature of the root proportion of the cross ratio is shared with the division of the line in the extreme and mean ratio, $AB : AC :: AC : CB$, except that in the case of the latter proportion the whole line is divided into *two* parts neither of which contains the other but is contained with its companion directly by the whole line.[1] The proportion which, like the root proportion of the cross ratio, contains *three* linear parts is the geometric proportion, $AB : AC :: AC : AD$ (rendering both line segments [*AC* and *CB*] as *AC* conveys the essence of the geometric mean), except that unlike the root proportion of the cross ratio and the division of the line in

[1] Cf. above, Section III.1, pp. 270ff.

extreme and mean ratio this last proportion contains two elemental wholes, since *AD* is directly a part of *AC* and *indirectly* a part of *AB*.[2] In summary the three proportions may be set out as follows:

The root proportion of the cross ratio

$$AB : DB :: AC : CD$$
$$W_w : P_w :: P_w : P_w$$

The regular geometric proportion

$$AB : AC :: AC : AD$$
$$W_w : P_w :: W_p : P_p$$

The division in extreme and mean ratio

$$AB : AC :: (AC) : CB$$
$$W_w : P_w :: (P_w) : P_w$$

Analysis reveals that these three proportions are related in the following way: in the case of the root proportion of the cross ratio *the whole line and one of the three parts* ($1 + 1/3 = 1.\overline{333}$) are defined in terms of *A*; in the case of the regular geometric proportion *the whole line and all three parts of the line* ($1 + 3/3 = 2$) are defined in terms of the beginning of the line, in terms of A; in the case of the division in extreme and mean ratio *the whole line and one of the two parts* ($1 + 1/2 = 1.5$) are defined in terms of *A*. But $2 = 1.5 \cdot 1.\overline{333}$, that is, the regular geometric proportion *is* the division in extreme and mean ratio as the *measure* of the root proportion of the cross ratio. The regular geometric proportion is a *parabolic* proportion. All three of its linear parts (*AC*, *AC*, and *AD*) are essentially defined in relation to *A*, the beginning of the line, but none *essentially* in relation to *B*, the end of

[2] Ibid.

the line. The division in extreme and mean ratio is the *hyperbolic* proportion, its two linear parts (*AC* and *CB*) dividing between themselves definition in terms of both the beginning, *A*, and the end of the line, *B*. The root proportion of the cross ratio is the *elliptical* proportion, that is, while it shares with the division of the line in extreme and mean ratio the fact that all of its linear parts are directly related to the whole line (and none indirectly so), and the fact that two of its linear parts (*AC* and *DB*) share between themselves definition in terms of both *A* and *B*, its *third* linear part (*CD*), which is of its essence as the root proportion of the constant ratio of the *otherwise* indefinite *lengths of the line in projective geometry*, is defined *neither* with respect to the beginning, *A*, *nor* to the end of the line, *B*. Measured according to the division in extreme and mean ratio, that is, compared to that uniquely spare proportion with which its structure otherwise agrees, the root proportion of the cross ratio has a superfluous linear part, at once a part essentially of no fixed length, which part of the whole line becomes at infinity, when *AC* becomes the line, a part relative to a whole which is a part, transforming the root proportion of the cross ratio into the regular geometric proportion just as the ellipse at infinity becomes the parabola.[3] A whole with a part like itself a whole is *AB* : *AC* :: *AC* : *AD*, the parabolic regular geometric proportion.

Thus far there is no *infinite* projective geometry: just as Galileo's infinite circle, the *infinite appearance* cannot possibly *actually* exist. Indeed, the existence of an infinite appearance requires the unification of the three proportions (elliptical, parabolic, and hyperbolic) *in the measure of the apical logic of the beginning*. Map the fundamental characteristics of the three proportions as follows:

The regular geometric proportion:	[3 linear parts	2 elemental wholes
The root proportion of the cross ratio:	3 linear parts]	[1 elemental whole
The division in extreme and mean ratio:	2 linear parts	1 elemental whole] .

[3] This is understood by analogy to the fact proven by Galileo in his *Dialogues*

The missing Fourth proportion, the division of the line containing *2 elemental wholes and 2 linear parts,* the Fourth *essentially* unifying these First, Second, and Third proportions (otherwise conceived either as existing merely besides one another or as unified in a merely arbitrary way) must not be founded on the *simply* equal division of the line, but on a division in which equal parts are different. The missing proportion is that which is founded on the division of the line according to the geometry of the trinary logic in which zero ≠ nothing,[4] a geometry in which therefore the zero dimension which is a *point* is not unmeasurable, but, where 0 ≠ nothing, is 0, the first of the following fundamental geometric relations:

Point = 0 = 2 lines, 5 lines, 8 lines, 4 points, 7 points, 10 points etc.
Square = 0000 = 0, 1 point, 1 point + 1 triangle, 2 lines, 4 points, etc.
Tetrahedron = 0000 = 0, 1 point, 1 point + 1 triangle, 2 lines, 4 points, etc.
Circle = 0000 = 0, 1 point, 1 point + 1 triangle, 2 lines, 4 points, etc.
Line = 00000 = 00, 2 points, 2 points + 1 triangle, 5 points, 4 lines, etc.
Cube = 00000000 = 00, 2 squares, 1 line, 1 line + 2 triangles, 4 lines, 2 points, etc.
Sphere = 00000000 = 00, 2 circles, 2 squares, 1 line, 1 line + 2 triangles, 2 points, etc.
Dodecahedron = 00000000000000000000 = 00, 2 points, 1 line, 1 cube, 1 line + 6 triangles, etc.
Triangle = 000 = 1 line + 1 point, 3 lines, 3 points, etc.
Octahedron = 000000 = 000, 1 line + (1 point, 1 square), 1 triangle, 3 lines, 3 points, etc.

Concerning Two New Sciences, trans. H. Crew and A. deSalvio (New York, 1954), pp. 37ff., that the circumference of an infinite circle is a straight line (from which fact Galileo concludes that an infinite circle cannot possibly exist). Cf. below, Section IV.2, *Excursus Circularis.*

[4] Cf. above, Section III.1.

Icosahedron = 000000000000 = 000, 1 line + 1 point, 1 triangle, 3 lines, 3 points, etc.

These relations constitute a logical geometry, the geometry of a universe whose *structure* is *infinitely* flat. They constitute a simplification of the complicated procedures of conventional geometry. For example, in this universe the Platonic solids, tetrahedron, cube, octahedron, dodecahedron, and icosahedron,[5] reduce, respectively, to point, line, triangle, line, triangle, i.e., to 0, 00, 000, 00, and 000.[6] Note that the *point*, 0, the zero-dimension which is *not* nothing, is the structural foundation to which the tetrahedron—alone among the Platonic polyhedra—*immediately* reduces, which is to say that that one of the Platonic solids which is charactarized as "the most fundamental of forms," "the fundamental measure of volume," "the atom of structure,"[7] is the very one which immediately reduces to the absolutely structural point (the point which is not nothing). For the Platonic solids the point, 0, is visibly the ultimate index of rigidity. The triangle, 000, the geometric equivalent of logical "identity," is the penultimate index of rigidity, combining the index of non-rigidity among these solids, 00, with 0. Since there is no nothing, the triangle, 000, is finally not able to be discarded or finally able to be discarded only as a part of unity, 1 = 0[000], which is to say that the discarding of 000 *minimally* leaves 0.[8] The vertex (whether as 0 or $\overline{0}$) is absolutely the edge. Now, since between 00 and 00000, following 00 in order, there is the triangle, 000, and the square, 0000, the minimum length of the line, 00, if it is to be divided at a point, 0, is 00000. *The minimum length of the line is the absolute length of the line:* a line *qua* divisible, whether finite

[5] For a comprehensive treatment of the properties of the Platonic polyhedra, see J. Kappraff, *Connections: The Geometric Bridge between Art and Science* (New York, 1991), where these solids are characterized (p. 259) as "polyhedra at the limit of perfection."

[6] In the logic the threefold repetition of a digit may be discarded, reducing, for example, 00000000 to 00, or 0000 to 0. Cf. above, Section III.1. Cf. also, below, this Section, Part 2.

[7] Kappraff, *Connections,* pp. 313ff.

[8] Cf. above, Section III.1, pp. 256ff.

or infinite, is essentially neither longer nor shorter than 00000.[9] Let, then, this line be divided in such a way as to provide the Fourth proportion, the division of the line containing *2 elemental wholes and 2 linear parts,* as follows:

$$\begin{array}{cccccccc} (& [& 0 & (000) &] & 0 &) \\ \text{A} & & & \text{(D)} & & \text{C} & \text{B} \end{array}$$

where, given the logical relations existing among the elements of the line, $00000 = \underline{0}(0000) = (0000)0 = 0(000)0$, and particularly noting that $000 = \bar{0}$ is the minimum/Identity factor in terms of which $0(000) = 0$, in terms of which 0 is identified as 1, the Fourth proportion exists uniquely in the infinitely flat line *together with, qua* elemental-whole-linear-part relations, the root proportion of the cross ratio, the regular geometric proportion, and the division in extreme and mean ratio, that is, *together with* those proportions which are found in ordinary mathematics and of which it is here manifestly, *qua* whole-part relations, the informing essential unity:

$$AB : AC :: (AB) : CB$$
$$W_w : P_w :: (W_w) : P_w$$

$$AB : DB :: AC : CD$$
$$W_w : P_w :: P_w : P_w$$

$$AB : AC :: AC : AD$$
$$W_w : P_w :: W_p : P_p$$

$$AB : AC :: (AC) : CB$$
$$W_w : P_w :: (P_w) : P_w$$

The proportion formed of these four proportions when they are

[9] Ibid., pp. 282f., for the foundation of the alternate forms of unity (00 and 00000), here, respectively, the forms of the line relative to one another indivisible and divisible.

ordered according to the universal form of all logical propositions, $pq + \bar{p}q + p\bar{q} + \overline{pq}$ (where $p = 1$ elemental whole = conic section not parallel to cone, and $q = 3$ linear parts = conic section not parallel to axis of cone) is as follows: *The root proportion of the cross ratio* (AB : DB :: AC : CD) : *The regular geometric proportion* (AB : AC :: AC : AD) :: *The division in extreme and mean ratio* (AB : AC :: [AC] : CB) : *The apical proportion of the infinitely flat universe* (AB : AC :: [AB] : CB).[10] In the infinitely projective geometry of the conical vertex it is not that, as in ordinary projective geometry, two points *have* a line in *common*, and two lines *have* a point in *common*, but, rather, that two points *is* one line, 00, and, identically, two lines *is* one point $00(00) = 0(000) = 0$. For the first time the *structure* of the universe is *completely* vertical, completely flat. Not simply is the real the infinite ÷ the finite, as is the case in ϕ-proportionality, but the real is the infinite × the finite: the infinite meta-identically the finite: the infinite as the measure of the finite: the essentially imperfect perfectly identical with the perfect.

PART 2

Euclidian and finite projective geometry predict rigidity using the variant formulas for two and three dimensions, respectively, $E \geq 2V - 3$ and $E \geq 3V - 6$.[11] The geometry of the infinitely flat structure of the universe predicts rigidity rationally using one formula for both dimensions. This rational simplification is possible because edges are not calculated separately from vertices. In the trinary logic the vertex is essentially identical *with*

---

[10] Computing the value of the apical proportion according to the number of its linear parts beginning with *A* including the whole line (= 1.5 [cf. above, pp. 313f.]), the proportion is equivalently $1\overline{333}$: 2 :: 1.5 : 1.5, the rational product of which, when ordered according to the minimum order, 4-1-2-3, i.e., 1.5 : $1\overline{333}$ :: 2 : 1.5, is 1.5, the value of the apical proportion *and* of the division in extreme and mean ratio, *and* the value of the ratio of the respective values of the regular geometric proportion and the root proportion of the cross ratio.

[11] Cf. J. Kappraff, *Connections*, pp. 257ff. and pp. 270ff.

the edge, the vertex is *itself* the beginning of the edge. To count vertices is *identically* to count edges. The logical geometry predicts the minimum structure of the bracing as a *rational* organization of elements—the qualitative aspect of the structure identical with the quantitative—from the *logical* arrangement of the *vertices alone.* For both two-dimensional and three-dimensional rigid frameworks and for rigid polygons and polyhedra, the number of edge-overlapping triangles (EOT's) which are *rationally* understood as bracing elements, T, is 2 less than the number of vertices, $V-2$, i.e., $T=V-2$. In the case of rigid three-dimensional structures, the *total* number of triangles, T_t, including 'underlying' and 'empty' triangles (UT's and ET's), and, where applicable, 1 externally braced polyhedron (EBP) in place of 1 EOT, will be $2T$ or $2(V-2)$, i.e., $T_t = 2T = 2(V-2)$, i.e., the structure will be rationally analyzed by means of the *iterative* application of $T = V-2$. $2T = T_t$ is a constant in all minimally braced rigid 3D structures, as (allowing the substitution of externally braced polygons [EBP's] for EOT's where appliable) is $T = T_t$ in all such 2D structures.

The Deconstruction of Rigid Polyhedra: Predicting the Rational Structure of the Internal (Surface) Bracing of Polyhedra.

The nonrigid solids *are* rigid when in their structures the threefold (identity) repetition of a digit, which in the trinary logic is often able to be discarded,[12] is *not* discarded: for instance, the nonrigid cube, 00(000000) = 00, *is* rigid, first, when its entire set of 8 points is arranged as a set of overlapping identities, i.e., overlapping 000's,

```
( 0 [ 0 ( 0 ) [ 0 ] ( 0 ) [ 0 ] 0 ) 0 ]
1   2   3   1 4   2 5   3 6   4   5   6,
```

which is to say that the cube is rigid when minimally braced by 6 edge-overlapping triangles (6 EOT's = 2 each from each of the two sets of 3 contiguous triangles about the north and south

[12] Cf. above, Section III.1.

poles of the cube plus 1 each sharing one hypotenuse of each of these two sets of EOT's. Since the number of bracing triangles is one less than the number of edges meeting at the pole, the remaining triangle in each polar set of 3 is an 'empty' triangle (ET). This leaves 4 underlying triangles (UT's) occupying 6 vertices, which is confirmed by arranging the 6 vertices occupied by the remaining components as a set of overlapping 000's, overlapping identities,

(0 [0 (0) [0] 0) 0]
1   2   3   1 4   2   3   4,

which is to say that there are 4 UT's (= the triangles whose right-angle vertices are *a, b, c,* and *d*):

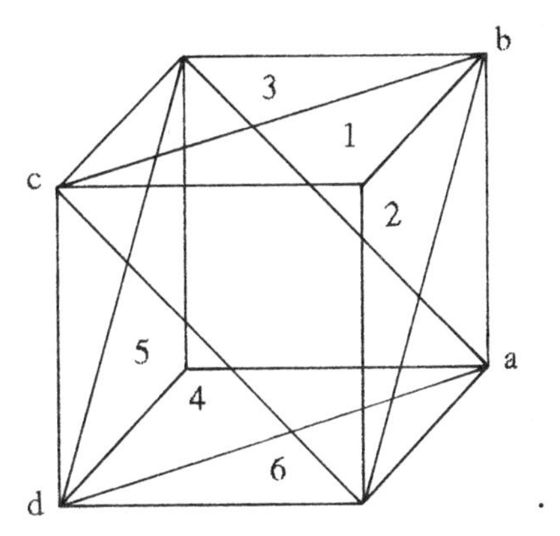

The constant in the overlapping three-digit arrangement of the total number of points (= vertices = 0's) is $T = V - 2$, where T is the minimum number of EOT's necessary to brace the structure and the number of UT's in the substructure. The iterative application of this formula to the nonrigid cube reveals that its rigid structure is rationally composed as 6 EOT's + 4 UT's + 2 ET's = T_t = 12 triangulated faces.

The nonrigid dodecahedron, 00(0000000000000000) = 00, similarly *is* rigid when its entire set of 20 points is arranged as a set of overlapping 000's,

```
( 0 [ 0 ( 0 ) [ 0 ] ( 0 ) [ 0 ] ( 0 )
1   2   3   1 4   2 5   3 6   4 7   5

    [ 0 ] ( 0 ) [ 0 ] ( 0 ) [ 0 ] ( 0 )
    8   6 9   7 10  8 11  9 12  1013  11

        [ 0 ] ( 0 ) [ 0 ] ( 0 ) [ 0 ) 0 ) 0 ]
        14  1215  1316  1417  1518  16  17  18,
```

which is to say that the dodecahedron is rigid as 18 EOT's (= 2 sets of 8 EOT's, 1 set each about the north and south poles of the dodecahedron [the fifth triangular face about each polar vertex an ET (the operational rule is that in any arrangement of bracing triangles, where added edges meet at one center, the number of bracing triangles about the center is 1 less than the total number of edges which touch the center)] + 2 EOT's in the equatorial band of the figure), *plus* the number of UT's and ET's which compose the remaining elements of the dodecahedron and which form 4 pentagons + 2 trapezoids occupying 16 vertices of the figure, as illustrated in this foldup:

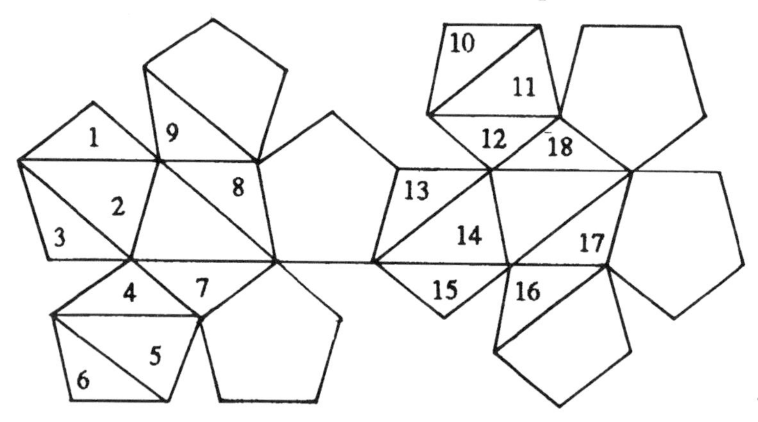

The composition of these remaining components of the dodecahedron is determined by repeating the above analysis for the set of 4 pentagons + 2 trapezoids, by arranging the 16 vertices occupied by this set as a set of overlapping 000's,

(0 [0 (0) [0] (0) [0]
1 2 3 1 4 2 5 3 6 4

(0) [0] (0) [0] (0)
7 5 8 6 9 7 10 8 11 9

[0] (0) [0] 0) 0]
12 10 13 11 14 12 13 14,

which is to say that the underlying set of pentagons and trapezoids, when rigid, is, relative to the 18 EOT's and 2ET's, composed of 14 UT's (= 12 UT's dividing the 4 pentagons + 2 UT's dividing the 2 trapezoids) + 2 ET's (= 1 ET in each trapezoid whose existence is a function of the relations existing between the set of 18 EOT's + 2 ET's and the set of 14 UT's). The iterative application of $T = V - 2$ to the nonrigid dodecahedron reveals that its rigid structure is rationally composed as 18 EOT's + 14 UT's (*a, b, c, d, e, f, g, h, i, j, k, l, m, n*) + 4 ET's = $T_t = 36$ triangulated faces, as here illustrated:

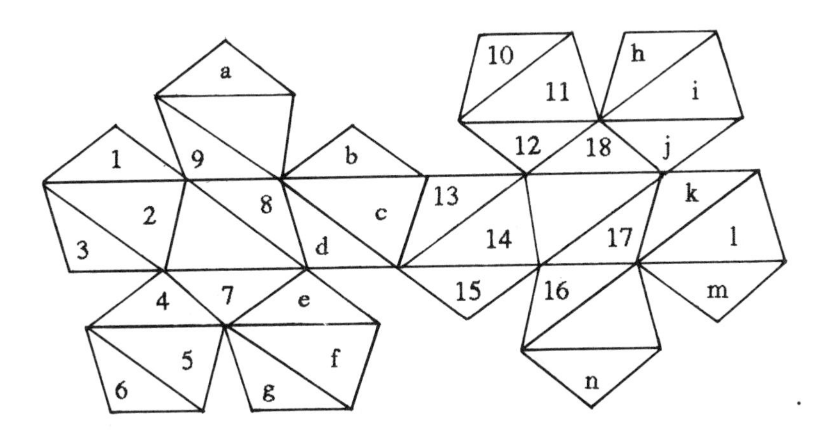

The identical analysis can be applied to the naturally rigid Platonic solids. For instance, the tetrahedron, 0(000) = 0, is rigid, first, when its entire set of 4 points is arranged as a set of overlapping 000's,

(0 [0 0) 0]
1 2 1 2,

which is to say that the tetrahedron is rigid when minimally braced by 2 EOT's (= 1 set of 2 contiguous triangles formed by the edge connecting the 2 UT's), as here illustrated:

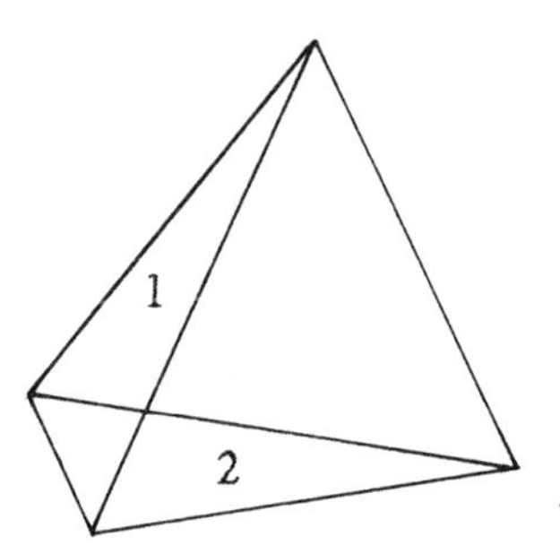

The iterative application of $T = V - 2$ to the tetrahedron reveals that its rigid structure is rationally composed as 2 EOT's + 2 UT's = T_t = 4 triangulated faces.

The octahedron, 000(000) = 000 = $\bar{0}$, is rigid when its entire set of 6 points is arranged as a set of overlapping 000's,

(0 [0 (0) [0] 0) 0]
1 2 3 1 4 2 3 4,

which is to say that the octahedron is rigid when minimally braced by 4 EOT's (= 3 EOT's meeting at one pole of the octahedron + 1 ET [formed by this set of 3 EOT's] + 1 EOT sharing the vertex which is the opposite pole). The remaining elements of the octahedron, relative to the 4 EOT's + 1 ET, form 3 UT's occupying 5 vertices, which is confirmed by arranging the 5 vertices occupied by the set of 3 remaining triangles as a set of overlapping 000's,

(0 [0 (0) 0] 0)
1 2 3 1 2 3,

which is to say that all 3 remaining triangles (*a, b, c*) are UT's. The iterative application of $T = V - 2$ to the octahedron reveals that its rigid structure is rationally composed as 4 EOT's + 3 UT's + 1 ET = T_t = 8 triangulated faces, as here illustrated:

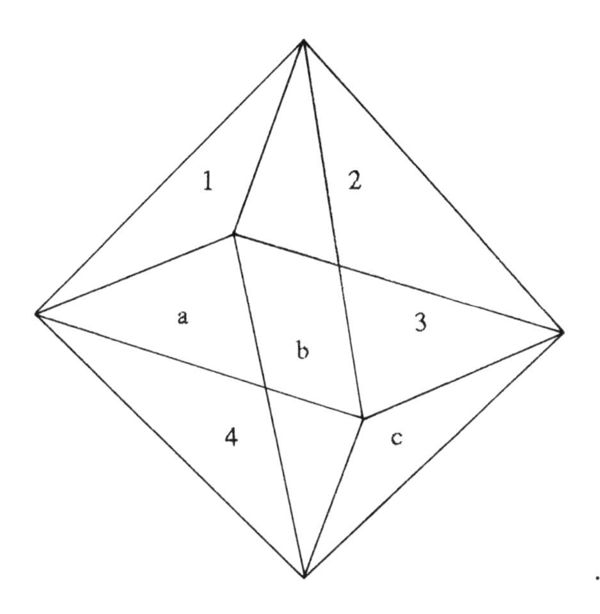

Finally, the icosahedron, 000(000000000) = 000 = $\overline{0}$, is rigid, first, when its entire set of 12 points is arranged as a set of overlapping 000's,

```
( 0 [ 0 ( 0 ) [ 0 ] ( 0 ) [ 0 ]
1   2   3   1 4   2 5   3 6   4

          ( 0 ) [ 0 ] ( 0 ) [ 0 ] 0 ) 0 ]
          7   5 8   6 9   7 10  8   9   10,
```

which is to say that the icosahedron is rigid when minimally braced by 10 EOT's (= 2 sets of 4 EOT's about the north and south poles of the icosahedron + 2 ET's [1 ET each formed by these polar sets] + 2 EOT's in the equatorial band of the figure).

The remaining elements of the icosahedron, relative to the 10 EOT's + 2 ET's, form 8 UT's occupying 10 vertices, as illustrated in this foldup:

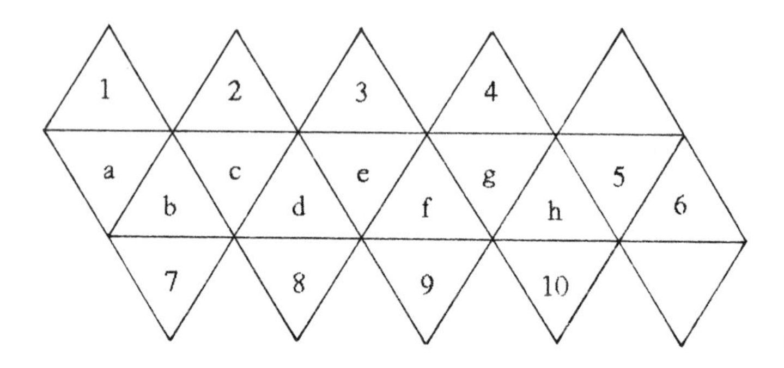

,

which is confirmed by arranging the 10 vertices occupied by the set of 8 remaining triangles as a set of overlapping 000's,

(0 [0 (0) [0] (0)
1 2 3 1 4 2 5 3

[0] (0) [0] 0) 0]
6 4 7 5 8 6 7 8,

which is to say that, analogously to the octahedron, all 8 of the remaining triangles are UT's. The iterative application of $T = V - 2$ to the icosahedron reveals that its rigid structure is rationally composed as 10 EOT's + 8 UT's + 2 ET's = $T_t = 20$ triangulated faces.

The Rational Construction of Rigid Polyhedra

The relations of the elements in the deconstruction of the Platonic solids under the previous heading are summarized in this table (where V_1 is the number of vertices of the solid, T_1 the number of EOT's produced by the first application of $T = V - 2$, ET_1 the number of ET's produced by this first application, V_2 the number of vertices of the underlying structure of the solid, T_2 the number of UT's produced by the second application of the formula, ET_2 the number of ET's produced by this second application, and T_t the total number of triangulated faces of the rigid figure):

Polyhedron	V_1	T_1	ET_1	V_2	T_2	ET_2	T_t
Tetrahedron	4	2	0	4	2	0	4
Cube	8	6	2	6	4	0	12
Octahedron	6	4	1	5	3	0	8
Dodecahedron	20	18	2	16	14	2	36
Icosahedron	12	10	2	10	8	0	20

The logical geometry, by revealing the constant relation, $T = V - 2$, opens up the rationality itself of the fundamental geometrical structures for the first time. The construction of a rigid solid is the inverse of the relations discovered in its rational deconstruction, according to the following rule: the number of UT's in the construction = T_1, while the number of EOT's = T_2. The tetrahedron, for example, *qua* construction, is 2 UT's in 3D, 0000 = 4V, which must be rigid if solid in such a way that each member of the underlying set of 2 contiguous triangles equally participates in the bracing. In that case the set of bracing triangles must occupy 3D in the same sense as the braced triangles, and is braced according to the rule visualized as (0[00)0], that is, by 2 EOT's + 0 ET's (uniquely a case identically its rational deconstruction as illustrated above).

The rigid cube can be rationally constructed as 6 UT's (2 sets of 3 contiguous triangles in 3D sharing 6 vertices) the 6 vertices of the right angles of which (*a, b, c, d, e, f*) are 6 of the 8 vertices of the cube, so that the minimum number of EOT's needed to brace these underlying sets (where $V = 6$) is $T = V - 2 = 4$, as illustrated, where following the rule concerning bracing triangles about a center[13] the sets of bracing triangles, 1-2 and 3-4, create the 7th and 8th vertices of the complete figure (the edges of the cube meeting at these vertices [= the 2 sets of 3 superficies each] are added edges in the rational construction of the cube):

[13] Cf. above, p. 322.

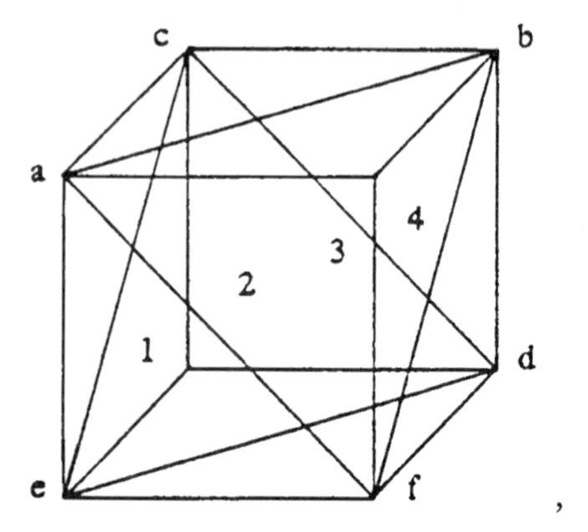

,

whereas when the cube is taken as a given [V = 8] they are not added edges but the added edges in that last case are the diagonal edges which do not meet at one center, and the bracing sets of the cube so construed are therefore 1-2 with 3 sharing the diagonal of 1, and 4-5 with 6 sharing the diagonal of 4.[14] The rational construction of the rigid cube = 6 UT's + 4 EOT's + 2 ET's = T_t = 12 triangulated faces.

The rigid dodecahedron can be rationally constructed as a set of 18 UT's (*a, b, c, d, e, f, g, h, i, j, k, l, m, n, o, p, q, r* = the equatorial band of 3 rigid pentagons + 3 inverted rigid pentagons) occupying 18V, the 3D bracing of which set requires, by $T = V - 2$, the addition of 14 EOT's, which, together with the 4 ET's, = T_t the grand total of the rigid figure's 36 triangulated faces, as illustrated in this foldup:

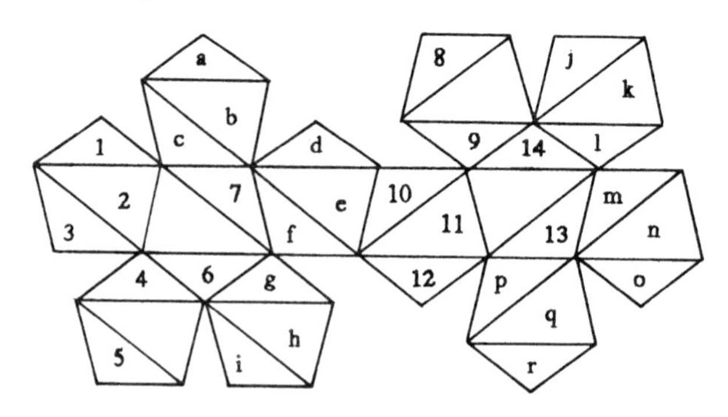

,

[14] Cf. above pp. 320f.

The octahedron, *qua* construction, is 4 UT's in 3D which occupy 5 vertices—00000 = $V = 5$ = (0[0(0)0]0)—and which, if they are to form a solid as defined above in the case of the construction of the tetrahedron, must be rigid, braced by 3 EOT's + 1 ET, which bracing produces T_t, the 8 triangular faces of the complete figure:

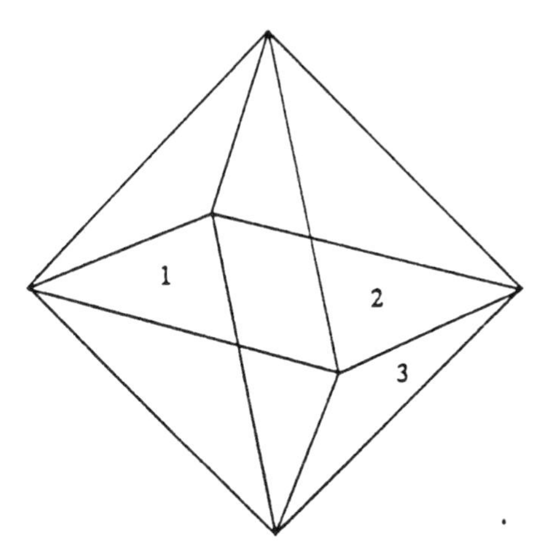

The icosahedron construction is solid as defined only if it is rigid, 10 UT's occupying 10 vertices in 3D, 0000000000 = (0[0(0)[0](0)[0](0)[0]0)0], braced by 8 EOT's (= 2 polar sets of 4 EOT's [effectively the 2 polar sets of 5 triangular faces—the fifth face not a fifth bracing triangle]) + 2 ET's, which produces T_t, the 20 triangular faces of the complete figure:

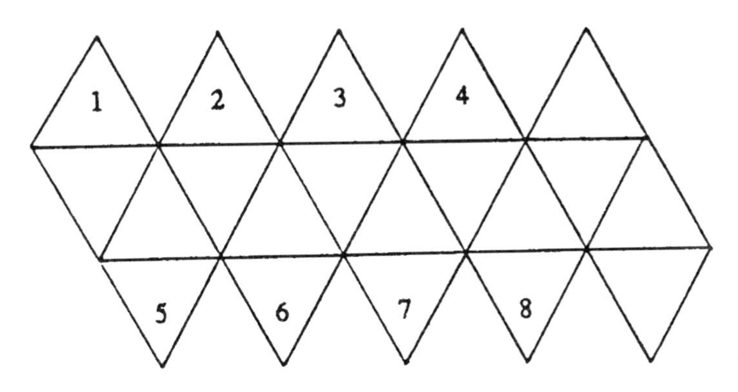

The difference between the octahedron and the icosahedron, on the one hand, and the tetrahedron, on the other hand, is that in the bracing of the former two figures the addition, respectively, of 1 + 3 edges and twice-(1 + 4) edges to the underlying 3D sets of triangles produces, respectively, 3 and twice-4 bracing triangles, so that in each case counting the extra triangular face(s) as (a)bracing triangle(s) would involve counting an edge twice over. But in the case of the tetrahedron 1 + 0 bracing edges *immediately* accounts for the 2 triangular faces which are therefore both counted as bracing since no double counting of an added edge is involved.

Although the three rigid Platonic solids are actually constructed as described above, nevertheless a 2D or flat rigid bracing relative to the underlying sets is possible in the case of both the octahedron and the icosahedron, in accord with the rule, $T = V - 2$. For example, in the case of the icosahedron, the underlying 10 contiguous triangles braced from above and below may be viewed instead as a set of 8 contiguous triangles braced above, below, and in the middle ($V = 10$ for the underlying sets in either case when braced as described). Then (0[0(0)[0](0)[0](0)[0]0)0] = 8 contiguous triangles braced by 8 EOT's, as illustrated in this foldup:

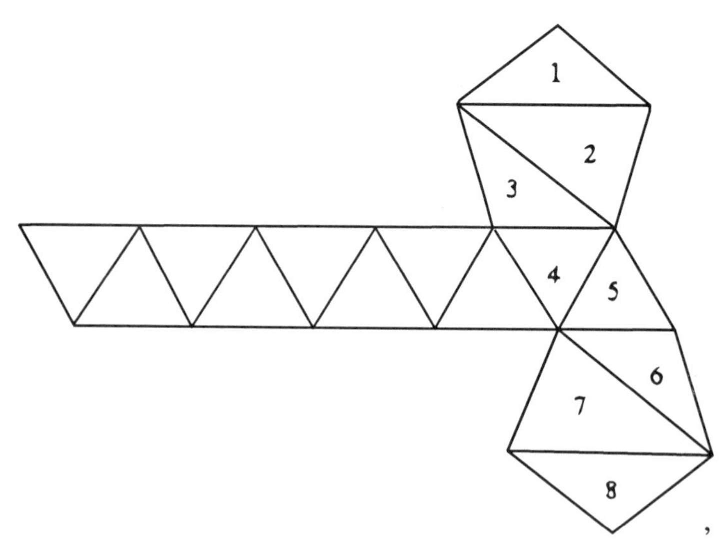

where, however, the individual underlying triangles will contact an unequal number of the edges of bracing triangles. The analogous bracing (= 3 EOT's in the planar square) of the underlying triangle sets of the octahedron is one of equal contact with bracing edges. The octahedron, then, is more perfect than the icosahedron. But for the tetrahedron *neither* an inequality in bracing contact *nor* a flat bracing is possible. Relative to its underlying set the set of bracing triangles in the tetrahedron must be in the same sense three-dimensional and its members identically in contact with the underlying set. In this way the tetrahedron is uniquely the perfect solid. $T = V - 2$ is the key that unlocks the real 2 by 2 structure of the tetrahedron, which otherwise as 4 or 3 self-bracing triangles is indifferently 0000 or $4V$. The logical geometry reveals the rigid Platonic solids, and, by extension, all rigid frameworks, as *rational* constructions whose constituent elements organize themselves in accord with the rule, $T = V - 2$.

Predicting the Rational Structure of Internally Braced Rigid Polygons

In the logical geometry *two*-dimensional rigidity is, as in the case of polyhedra, a function of *specifying* the threefold (identity) repetition of a digit in the geometrical structure of the figure and applying to the logical definition of the figure (= the number of vertices) the formula for the constant relation of vertices to rigid elements, $T = V - 2$. For instance, the nonrigid square, 0000 = 0, *is* rigid when its entire set of 4 points is arranged as a set of overlapping 000's,

$$\begin{matrix} (& 0 & [& 0 & 0 &) & 0 &] \\ 1 & & 2 & & & 1 & & 2, \end{matrix}$$

which is to say that the square is rigid when minimally braced as 2 EOT's (= 1 set of 2 contiguous triangles [effectively the square diagonally braced, the minimum bracing]):[15]

[15] Cf. Kappraff, *Connections*, pp. 154ff.

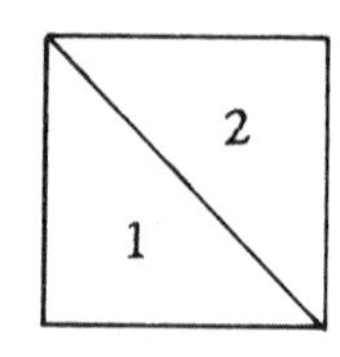

Irregular nonrigid two-dimensional frameworks also are rigid when organized for rigidity in accord with their logical structure. For example the nonrigid framework[16]

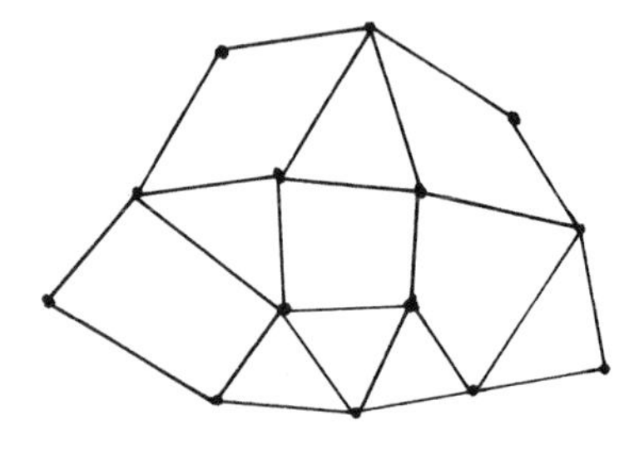
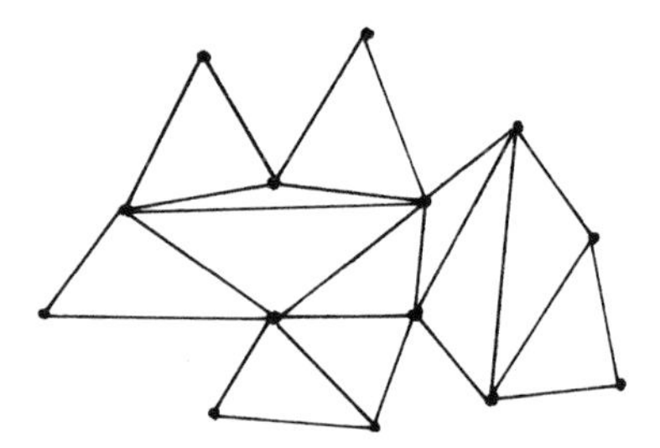

consisting of 14 vertices, is nonrigid 00(000000000000) = 00, but is predictably rigid when its entire set of 14 points is arranged as a set of overlapping identities, i.e., overlapping 000's,

(0 [0 (0) [0] (0) [0] (0)
1 2 3 1 4 2 5 3 6 4 7 5

[0] (0) [0] (0) [0] 0) 0]
8 6 9 7 10 8 11 9 12 10 11 12 ,

which is to say that the framework is rigid when minimally braced as 12 EOT's.

Predicting the Rational Structure of Externally Braced Rigid Polygons and Polyhedra

The rule for rationally predicting internal (surface) rigidity in polygons and polyhedra, $T = V - 2$, also predicts the rational

[16] Cf. Kappraff, *Connections,* p. 273, Figure 7.15.

structure of externally braced rigid polygons and polyhedra. The polygon or polyhedron externally braced functions as an integral part of a total complex of *braced structure + external EOT's.* The rule, $T = V - 2$, predicts the rational structure of the rigidity of this whole complex. The externally braced polygon or polyhedron, EBP, functioning as one element of the rigidity of the total complex, occupies the place otherwise occupied by one EOT in internal bracing. Therefore, in the case of external bracing T is the minimum number of EOT's, including EBP's displacing EOT's, necessary to brace the total 2D or 3D structure, as the case may be. Thus the externally braced rigid square, 0000 + 0, the square + the external point, is rigid as the EBP which is 1 of 3 rigid components of the complex rigid structure occupying 5 vertices, (0[0(0)0]0), where $T = V - 2 = 3 = T_t =$ 1 EBP + 2 EOT's:

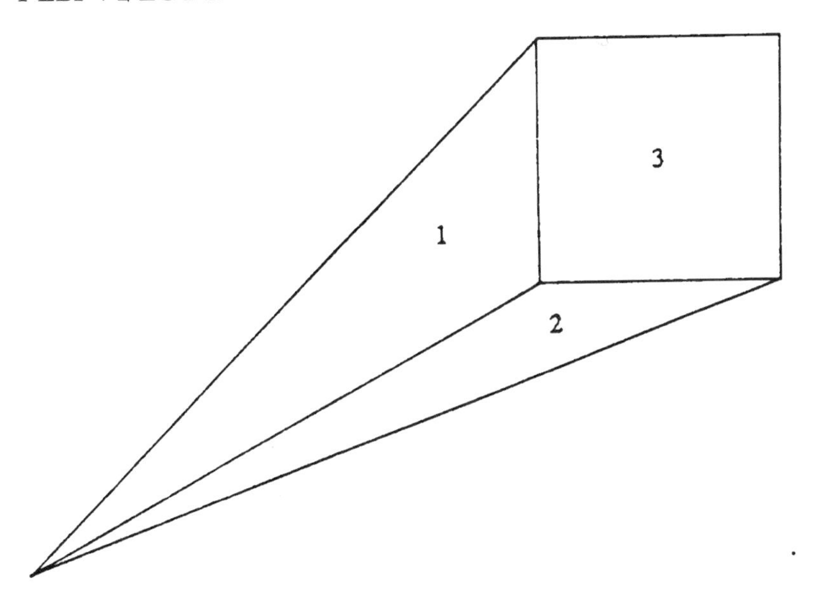

The externally braced rigid pentagon, 00000 + 0, the pentagon + the external point, is rigid as the EBP which is 1 of 4 rigid components of the complex rigid structure occupying 6 vertices, (0[0(0)[0]0)0], where $T = V - 2 = 4 = T_t = 1$ EBP + 3 EOT's:

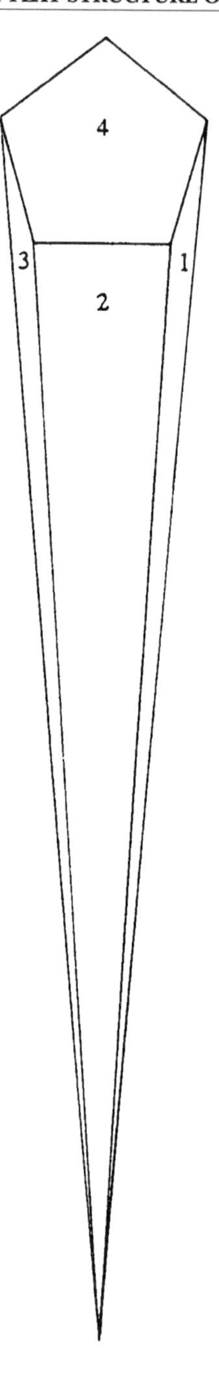
4
3
1
2

The square and the pentagon are the only regular polygons able to be one-sidedly braced externally, braced with reference to 1 external point (= 0). Beginning with the hexagon the infinite series of regular polygons must be externally braced on two sides, braced with reference to 2 external points on opposite sides of the figure (= 00 = 1 line).[17] For example, the externally braced rigid regular hexagon, 000000 + 00, the hexagon + the two external points, is rigid as the EBP which is 1 of 6 rigid components of the complex rigid structure occupying 8 vertices, (0[0(0) [0] (0) [0]0)0], where $T = V - 2 = 6 = T_t = 1$ EBP + 5 EOT's:

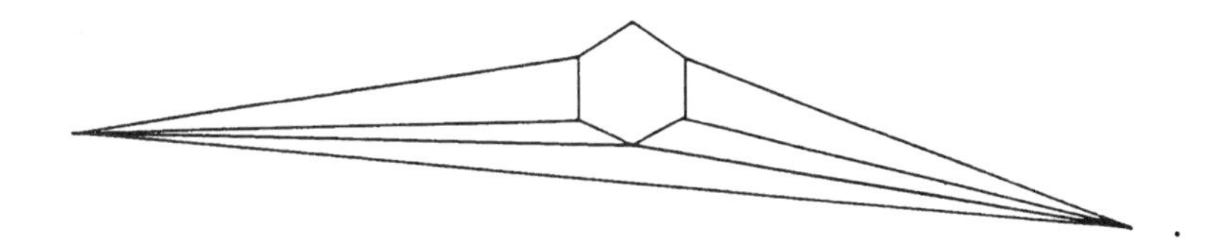

Likewise, the externally braced rigid regular decagon, 0000000000 + 00, the decagon + the two external points, is rigid as the EBP which is 1 of 10 rigid components of the complex rigid structure occupying 12 vertices, (0[0(0) [0] (0) [0] (0) [0] (0) [0]0)0], where $T = V - 2 = 10 = T_t = 1$ EBP + 9 EOT's:

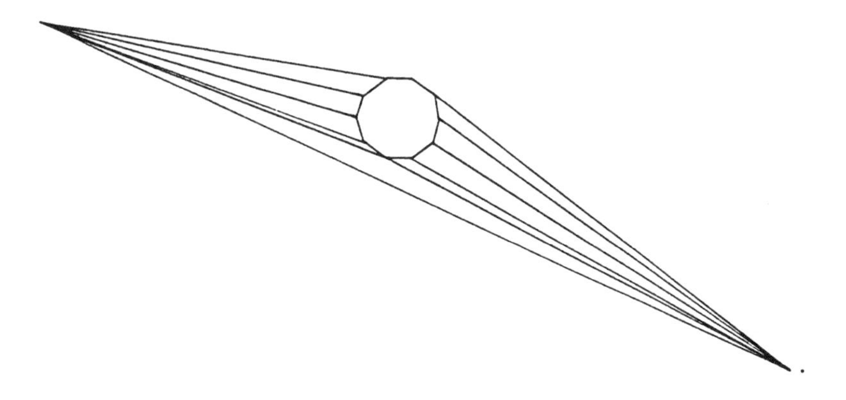

[17] These externally braced polygons share this "two-sided" property with externally braced polyhedra (below). For both sorts of externally braced structures $T = V - 2$ resolves, then, to $T = V_p$. Cf. also, below, the reduction of rigid nonconvex 3D structures to these externally braced polygons.

The series of externally braced regular rigid polygons beyond the pentagon occupies an infinitely expanding pentagonal arrangement of EBP + EOT's, the total of which increases precisely as V_p. At infinity the rigid polygon with an infinite number of sides is externally braced by a number of EOT's 1 less than the infinite number of sides, which infinitely expanding number of EOT's divides an infinitely expanding pentagon in support of a finite region the number of whose sides is infinitely beyond the number of sides of a pentagon.

Externally braced convex polyhedra conform to the rule $T = V - 2$, and are "two-sidedly" braced. For example, the externally braced rigid cube, 00000000 + 00, the cube + the two external points, is rigid as the EBP which is 1 of 8 components of the complex rigid structure occupying 10 vertices, (0[0(0) [0] (0) [0] (0) [0]0)0], where $T = V - 2 = 8 = 1$ EBP + 7 EOT's, rationally composed with 2 UT's and 6 ET's to equal the total, $T_t = 16$:

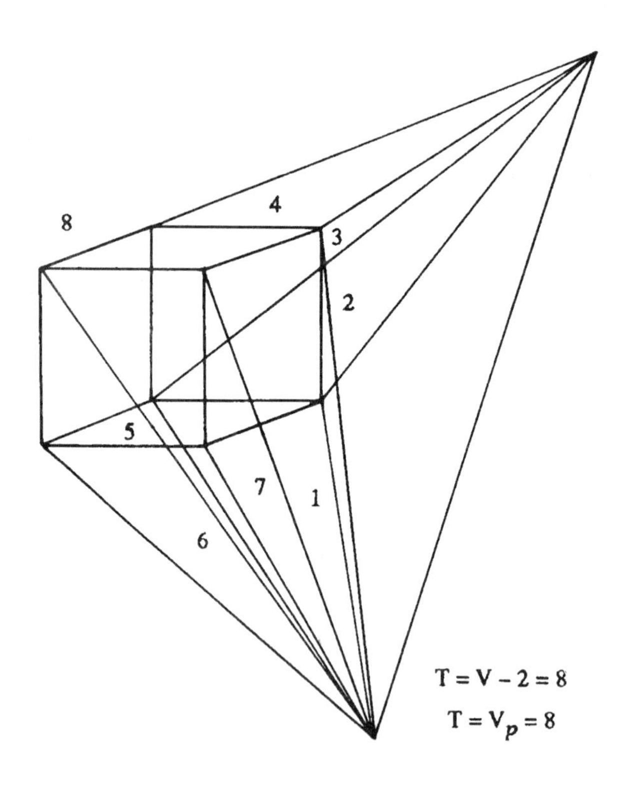

The cube is rigid as the 1 EBP in the complex structure of which it is an integral part together with 2 sets of 3 EOT's bracing adjacent sides of the cube + the 1 EOT formed by the edges connecting the edge of the cube opposite both adjacent sides to the polar vertex of one of the sets of 3 EOT's. (As usual the sets of 3 EOT's are formed in accord with the rule for counting bracing triangles about a center. The EOT's numbered 1 and 2 are at once the 2 bracing triangles in the tetrahedron formed by the edge running from the one polar vertex to the other.)

The externally braced rigid dodecahedron, 0000000000000 0000000 + 00, the dodecahedron + the two external points, is rigid as the EBP which is 1 of 20 components of the complex rigid structure occupying 22 vertices, (0[0(0)[0](0)[0](0)[0]

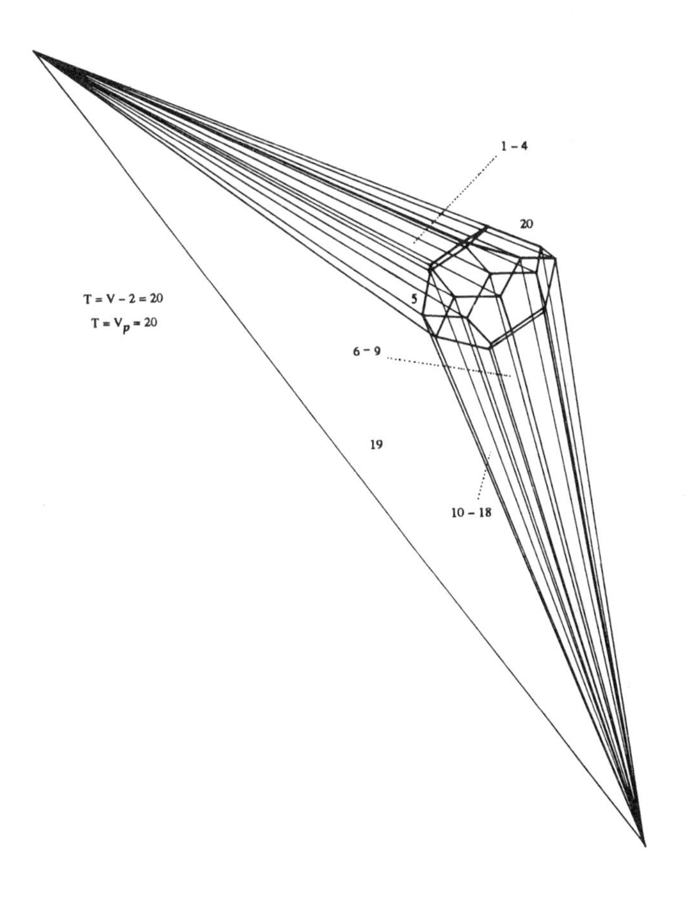

(0) [0] (0) [0] (0) [0] (0) [0] (0) [0] (0) [0]0)0], where $T = V - 2 = 20$ = 1 EBP + 19 EOT's, rationally composed with 6 UT's and 14 ET's to equal the total, $T_t = 40$ (the illustration is of a slightly distorted dodecahedron for purposes of exposition), that is, the dodecahedron is rigid as the 1 EBP in the complex structure of which it is an integral part, involving 6 UT's + 14 ET's together with 2 sets of 4 EOT's bracing opposite pentagonal faces + 9 EOT's descending from the polar vertex shared with one of the sets of four EOT's + 1 EOT formed by the edge connecting that polar vertex with that of the opposite set of four EOT's + 1 EOT connecting the last mentioned polar vertex to one member of the set of nine EOT's.

The Rigidity of Nonconvex All-Triangular-Faced Three-Dimensional Frameworks and Polyhedra.

THEOREM: All nonrigid 3D frameworks or polyhedra, all of whose faces are triangles, are nonconvex and are (transformed into) rigid structures when the edges converging at one vertex are lengthened so as to meet at a point beyond the region originally bounded by the structure or when $E \geq [3(V + 2) - 4] - 6$, effectively $E \geq 3V - 4$, is satisfied and $T = (V + 2) - 2 = V_p = T_t/2$.
Proof: Any nonrigid nonconvex 3D framework or polyhedron which is rigid when edges are added to satisfy $E \geq 3V - 4$, or when, alternatively, the structure is extended at one vertex beyond the originally bounded region so as to be rigid while satisfying $E \geq 3V - 6$, is effectively and relatively quantitatively identical to a regular polygon of the identical number of vertices which is rigid when externally braced with the minimum number of added edges. A nonrigid polygon is made rigid by means of the addition of a set of internal braces predicted by $E \geq 2V - 3$, where $E = E$ (existing) + E (added). Unlike its 3D counterpart, $E \geq 3V - 6$, which appears at first to be only usually true, this 2D formula is seen to be always true if edges are properly arranged and evidently so if all faces are triangles. But the polygon is also rigid when externally braced with the minimum number of added edges. In the case of regular polygons of six or more sides the external bracing requires the addition of 2 vertices placed on the outside face of the polygon to sup-

port the added bracing edges, the number of which added edges is also predicted by $E \geq 2V - 3$, where $E = E$ (existing) $+ E$ (added). One of the added edges in the minimum external rigid bracing of the polygon lies between the added vertices on its outside face without touching the polygon as do the other added edges. This partial nontouching of the polygon by the set of external bracing edges is the 2D equivalent of 3D nonconvexity which exists when a line can be drawn between two internal points of a structure which line lies partially outside the region bounded by the structure. The ultimate analogue to this analogue is the rigidity-producing lengthening of the edges meeting at one vertex of an otherwise nonrigid 3D framework or polyhedron to a point beyond their original point of convergence, i.e., the extension of the structure—in part—beyond the originally bounded region. Thus nonrigid nonconvex 3D frameworks and polyhedra are effectively, if not formally, quantitatively relatively identical to one very particular application of the 2D formula, viz., to regular polygons as externally vs. internally braced rigid structures. The externally braced regular polygon with at least six vertices exceeds the number of vertices and edges in the internally braced identical polygon by 2 and 4, respectively. Since the concave surfaces of a nonconvex 3D structure are to its convex surfaces as the outside face of the regular polygon with the corresponding number of vertices is to the region bounded by the sides of that polygon, then the extra 2 vertices and extra 4 edges which appear in the externally minimally braced rigid 2D figure (as compared to the number of vertices and edges in the identical rigid 2D figure minimally braced internally) can be integrated into the formula which predicts the rigidity of its 3D counterpart, i.e., integrated into $E \geq 3V - 6$ so as to produce $E \geq [3(V + 2) - 4] - 6$, which is effectively $E \geq 3V - 4$, and which will always predict the rigidity of 3D nonconvex figures because those latter, when rigid, are effectively quantitatively relatively 3D versions of the externally braced rigid corresponding regular polygons, the edges of which last are so arranged that, as stated above, one edge does not touch the region originally bounded by the unbraced polygon, and which as such are rigid. The fact that, to achieve rigidity, the alternative to adding 2 edges to the 3D structure to satisfy $E \geq 3V - 4$ is the removal of one of its vertices beyond the region originally bounded by the structure, by lengthening the edges meeting at that vertex—the fact that the alternative method of achieving rigidity is this extension of the figure—in part beyond the originally bounded region—is a function of the fact that the minimum external rigid bracing of the corresponding regular polygon, which entails the additional 2 vertices and 4 edges, entails as well the fact that one of the set of added edges passes between the 2 added vertices without touching the polygon, that is, entails also that the externally braced rigid 2D structure—in part—does not touch the region originally bounded by the polygon. If the rigidity-producing addition of 2 edges or the lengthening of the edges meeting at one vertex of a nonconvex 3D framework or polyhedron all of whose faces are triangles is the virtual equivalent of the external bracing of the regular polygon which has the corresponding number of vertices, then the addition of 2 virtual vertices and 4 virtual edges to the 3D framework or polyhedron should provide the warrant for the addition of the 2 edges which alternatively produce a rigid structure. As shown above, in fact the warrant exists ($E \geq 3V - 6$) becomes [$E \geq (3[V$ (existing) + 2 (virtual)]) – (6 + 4 [virtual]) = E (existing) + 2 (added). $E \geq [3(V + 2) - 4] - 6$ is effectively $E \geq 3V - 4$, which is satisfied when 2 edges are added to the nonconvex structure.

Note: In the case where the rigid 3D structure satisfies $E \geq 3V - 4$, since actual edges must be added, all concave or internal edges may be removed leaving a rigid convex polyhedron which satisfies $E \geq 3V - 6$, just as the external bracing of an internally unbraced polygon may be removed from its outside face once its internal face is braced so as to satisfy $E \geq 2V - 3$. In the alternative case mentioned in the theorem, since the edges added are purely virtual, no actual edges may be removed, nor need they be removed, since the partially extended rigid structure as it stands satisfies $E \geq 3V - 6$. When the structure satisfies $E \geq 3V - 4$, it also satisfies $T = (V + 2) - 2 = V_p = T_t/2$. When it satisfies $E \geq 3V - 6$, it also satisfies $T = V - 2 = T_t/2$.

The Rational Structure of Rigid Grids as Sets of Externally Braced Polygons

Any rigid grid, $n \times m$, is a set of $(n-1)\times(m-1)$ EBP's. For any grid, then, $T = V - 2$, where T is the minimum number of EOT's, including $(n-1)\times(m-1)$ EBP's displacing EOT's, necessary to rigidly brace the grid. For example, the 3 x 3 grid occupying 16 vertices, 0000000000000000, is rigid as the set of EBP's which constitute 4 (= 2 × 2) of 14 rigid components of the complex rigid structure occupying 16 vertices, (0[0(0)[0](0)[0](0)[0](0)[0](0)[0](0)[0]0)0], where $T = V - 2 = 14 = T_t = 4$ EBP's + 10 EOT's:

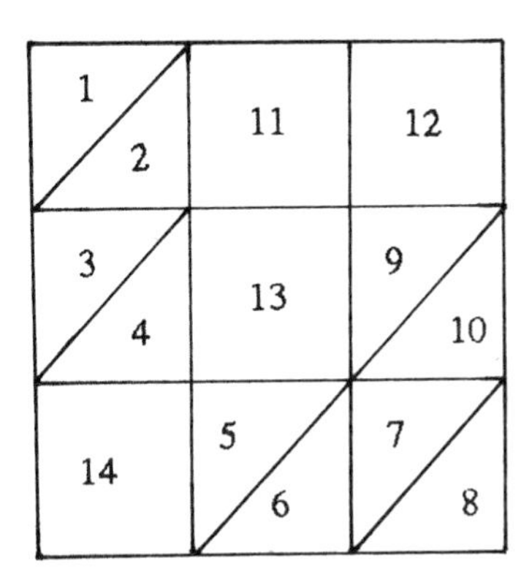

The rule for locating braces within any grid so that it is rigid can be stated as follows: after determining the number of EOT's necessary to brace any $n \times m$ grid by deducting the product of $(n-1)\times(m-1)$ from T (where $T = V - 2$) distribute the sets of EOT's so that no subset of the grid contains more than the minimum number of sets of EOT's necessary to make it rigid when standing alone, providing that each column and each row contains at least 1 set of 2 EOT's, and that no column and row having only 1 set of 2 EOT's share the identical set.[18]

[18] The rule, $T = V - 2$, where T is the number of rigid components (EOT's & EBP's) of any two- or three-dimensional rigid structure, calls attention, as it operates here, to the fact that rigid grids and externally braced polygons are members of an identical species of rigid two-dimensional frameworks.

$T = V - 2$ and the X, Y, Z Coordinates

The question arises, how can the fact of $T = V - 2$ be accounted for *arithmetically,* that is, what is the numerical situation underlying the rational unification of the otherwise discrete realms of 2D and 3D, realms whose discrete nature is exemplified in the formulas, $E \geq 3V - 6$, and $E \geq 2V - 3$. The answer is provided by considering that the 3 degrees of freedom associated with the 3D coordinates, *x, y,* and *z* are distributed as follows:[19]

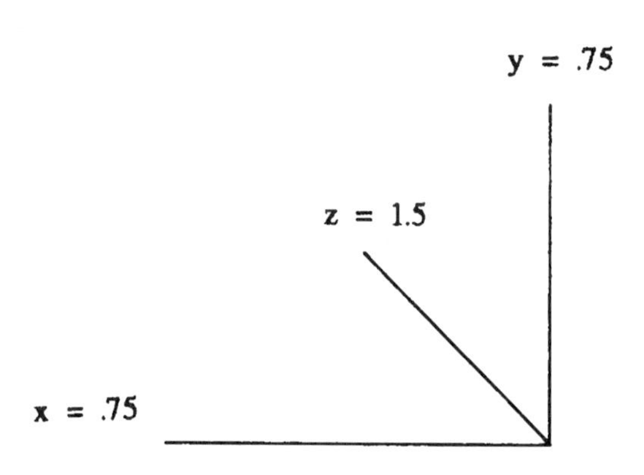

where the real nature of the 3rd dimension as the unifier of the 2 dimensions with which it can nevertheless be taken together, is signified by $z = x + y$, therefore $x = z - y$. With the degrees of freedom as illustrated,

[19] The values associated with the coordinate dimensions, .75 + .75 = 1.5, the first and the second with respect to the third dimension, are in the first instance related analogously to the logical relation $0 + \bar{0} = 1$, where 0 is different from but equal to $\bar{0}$. Further, they are rooted in the cubic nature of the coordinate system, specifically in the cubic body-diagonal/edge and body-diagonal/face-diagonal ratios, which are, respectively, $.75^{1/2} + .75^{1/2} = 3^{1/2}$ and $.75^{1/2} \times 2^{1/2} = 1.5^{1/2}$. Finally, they are rooted in the ratio of the 3-dimensional ratio of total components to T components in rigid structures, $T_t : T = 2$, to the 2-dimensional ratio, $T_t : T = 1$, i.e., $(3 : 2) : (2 : 1) = 1.5 : 2 = 3 : 2(2) = .75$. Cf. above, this section, *Part 1,* the analytical values of the four proportions, and *Part 2,* the relation of T and $2T$, the iterative application of $T = V - 2$ to 3D structures.

$$T = V - 2 = (1.5V - 3)/1.5 = (zV - 3)/(x + y) = [(x + y)V - 3]/z,$$

that is, the minimum number of edge-overlapping triangles needed to brace a 3D or 2D structure is the *identity* (T = the number of 000's, "identities") in which the vertices of each dimension shed—reciprocally and vis-à-vis one another—the 3 degrees of freedom associated, respectively, with rotational and translational movement. This equation further confirms the fundamental relations existing between vertices, logical notation (where 1 is the highest number), and rigidity, since, if $(1.5V - 3)/1.5 = T$, then, for $V = 0$, $T = -1$, for $V = 00$, $T = 0$, and for $V = 000$, $T = 1$, which agrees with the logical fact that for the Platonic solids 0 and 000 are indices of rigidity while 00 is the index of nonrigidity, and particularly exemplifies in ordinary mathematical terms one of the fundamental relations of the logic, viz., $0(000) = 0$, that is, that the discarding of 000, $T = -1$, is $V = 0$.

Finally, put in terms of Euler's formula, $T = V - 2 = E - F$. The edge *itself* is *absolutely* the beginning of a face: the edge is the beginning *identical with* the face: it ought not to be added to itself if the issue is rigidity, which it is in the case of the formula, $T = V - 2$.

NOTE APPENDED: *THE OCTAHEDRON WITH TWO EDGES ALONG A DIAGONAL*

The geometry provides the *rational* foundation for the fact that the octahedron with two edges along a diagonal is, as Kappraff points out, infinitesimally nonrigid although the octahedron itself is otherwise rigid.[20] The new geometry shows that while the octahedron is $000000 = 000 = \overline{0}$, that is, is rigid, the *octahedron with two edges along the diagonal* is 0000000, which unlike the tetrahedron, which, in reducing immediately to 0, is itself 2 indivisible lines, reduces by discarding three-digit identities not immediately to 0 but to 0000 = 2 lines, which, maintaining explicitly the point structure, = 00(00000), 1 *indivisible* line + 1 *divisible*

[20] Kappraff, *Connections*, p. 272, fig. 7.14.

line. The index of rigid structure, 0, is, in this case, first nonrigidly rigid: in a geometry in which 0 = 0000, in which 1 point *is* 2 lines, here 2 *lines infinitesimally 1 point,* 2 lines is and is not 1 point. This figure is actually a hybrid, a polygonal polyhedron, where $T = V - 2 = 5$ is EOT's 1, 2, and 3 (in the vertical plane where $T = V - 2 = 5 - 2 = 3$), existing together with 4 and 5 (in the horizontal plane where $T = V - 2 = 4 - 2 = 2$), which 5 EOT's are rationally composed with 6 UT's and 2 ET's to equal, in this hybrid, $T_t = 13$, which is the 3D total, $2T = T_t = 10$, plus the 2D total $T = T_t = 3$, restoring the rigidity infinitesimally compromised when the $6V$ solid acquired a 7th vertex:

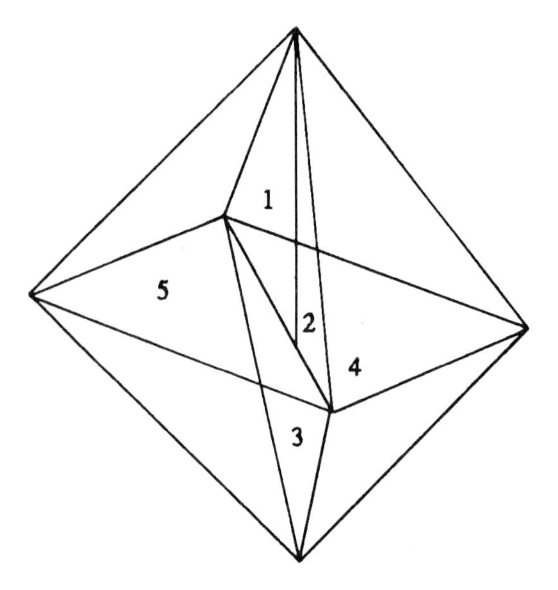

The *raison d'être* of the appearance of the infinitesimal nonrigidity is visible in the logical structure of the figure.

4

THE INFINITE LOGICAL LATTICE: THE DIRECT PREDICTOR OF RIGIDITY IN GRIDS

The rigidity of grids is able to be predicted directly on the basis of the distribution of the logical digits, 0, $\bar{0}$, 1, in the form of the infinite lattice described in Section III.1.[1]

Predicting the Minimum Number of Braces for Rigid Square Grids
The minimum number of added edges necessary to rigidly brace any square grid can be predicted by superimposing the grid on the infinite lattice of 0's, $\bar{0}$'s, and 1's, in such a way that the diagonal of the grid coincides the lattice diagonal of 1's. Let E be *added* edges, let l be the *arithmetic* sum of the logical digits in the grid (e.g., $1 + 0 + \bar{0} + 1 = 3$), let n be the place number in the series of grids, '1 × 1', 2 × 2, 3 × 3 . . . (the first not itself a grid), and let g be a single dimension of the grid, 2, 3, 4, 5, etc. Then, rounding l_n/g_n down to a whole number when g is not a multiple of 3, the following formula holds for any square grid:[2]

$$E = \frac{l_n}{g_n} + l_n - l_{n-1}.$$

By way of illustration, consider the 10 × 10 square whose diago-

[1] Cf. above, p. 267.

[2] When g, or in the case of an oblong grid, either g' or g'', is a multiple of 3, the ratio of the size of the grid to the arithmetic sum of the logical digits it contains when superimposed on the infinite lattice, g^2/l or $(g' \times g'')/l$, is 1.5. In all other cases g^2/l or $(g' \times g'')/l \cong 1.5$. For the ubiquitous 1.5, cf. above, Section III.3.

nal coincides the 1-diagonal of the infinite lattice:

1	0	$\bar{0}$	1	0	$\bar{0}$	1	0	$\bar{0}$	1
$\bar{0}$	1	0	$\bar{0}$	1	0	$\bar{0}$	1	0	$\bar{0}$
0	$\bar{0}$	1	0	$\bar{0}$	1	0	$\bar{0}$	1	0
1	0	$\bar{0}$	1	0	$\bar{0}$	1	0	$\bar{0}$	1
$\bar{0}$	1	0	$\bar{0}$	1	0	$\bar{0}$	1	0	$\bar{0}$
0	$\bar{0}$	1	0	$\bar{0}$	1	0	$\bar{0}$	1	0
1	0	$\bar{0}$	1	0	$\bar{0}$	1	0	$\bar{0}$	1
$\bar{0}$	1	0	$\bar{0}$	1	0	$\bar{0}$	1	0	$\bar{0}$
0	$\bar{0}$	1	0	$\bar{0}$	1	0	$\bar{0}$	1	0
1	0	$\bar{0}$	1	0	$\bar{0}$	1	0	$\bar{0}$	1

Beginning in the upper left corner, this grid contains an expansion of the first 10 members of the series of square grids, '1×1', 2×2, 3×3, . . . , 10×10. Apply the formula, $E = (l_n/g_n) + l_n - l_{n-1}$, as follows: to the 3×3 grid: $6/3 + 6 - 3 = 5$, or to the 7×7 grid (where 7 is not a multiple of 3, 33/7 is rounded down to 4, as stipulated above): $33/7 + 33 - 24 = 13$. Put in terms of the rule for rigidity, $T = V - 2$, for any square grid, $p \times q$, $T = V - 2 = 2[(l_n/g_n) + l_n - l_{n-1}] + [(p - 1) \times (q - 1)]$, where that portion of any rigid grid which is a set of externally braced polygons is represented by $(p - 1) \times (q - 1)$.[3]

In terms of the logic which provides the template for the rational organization of rigid structures[4] and the geometric and arithmetic series,[5] it is significant that only triangular numbers (000-numbers or multiples of 3) produce a numerical result *identically* the number of edges necessary for rigidity, while non-tri-

[3] Ibid., p. 342.

[4] Cf. above, Section III.3 passim.

[5] Cf. above, Section III.2.

angular numbers require the rounding down of l_n/g_n: although the logic will not compute a remainder less than unity, it nevertheless predicts in every case the correct whole number of added edges necessary for rigidity. In effect, in logical terms, the non-triangular numbers, 00 and 0000, are computable because, while not 000 or the 0 which remains when 000 is discarded, the logic identifies them as 000 or 0, i.e., $0 = \overline{0}1 = (000)00 = 00 = 1 = \overline{0}0 = 0000$.[6] This observation leads to the possibility of further simplifying the above formula for predicting the rigidity of square grids on the basis of the infinite logical lattice, so as to eliminate the necessity of rounding down. It is noted that in the series of square grids l increases sequentially by the addition of the natural numbers excepting multiples of 2^2, so that the l series for square grids is 1, 3, 6, 11, 17, 24, 33, 43, 54, 67. . . . $E = (l_n/g_n) + l_n - l_{n-1}$ may be replaced by the formula:

$$E = l_n - m_n,$$

where m is the sequential sum of the natural numbers excepting odd-number multiples of 2 and beginning with 0 for $g = 2$. For example, for the 4×4 grid: $E = l_n - m_n = 11 - (0 + 1 + 3) = 7$, and for the 9 x 9 grid: $E = l_n - m_n = 54 - (0 + 1 + 3 + 4 + 5 + 7 + 8 + 9) = 17$. The logical calculus, excluding from the construction of the sequences l and m, respectively, the natural number multiples of 2^2 (like 0000) and numbers 2 (like 00) times the differences of the squares of the natural numbers, perfectly predicts, without rounding, the minimum number of added edges necessary to make any square grid rigid. Again, in terms of the universal formula for rigidity, $T = V - 2 = 2(l_n - m_n) + [(p - 1) \times (q - 1)]$.[7]

Predicting the Minimum Number of Braces for Rigid Oblong Grids

Although it is not possible to exclude rounding down to whole numbers when dealing with oblong grids in the set of series, '1 × 2', 2 × 3, 3 × 4, 4 × 5, 5 × 6, . . . , nevertheless, when an oblong

[6] Cf. above, Section III.1, pp. 255ff.

[7] Cf. above, p. 346, n. 3.

grid is superimposed on the infinite lattice of 0's, $\bar{0}$'s, and 1's in such a way that the upper left corner of the grid coincides that of the 10 × 10 square above, it is possible to perfectly predict the minimum number of added edges necessary to rigidly brace the oblong framework, using the formula, as above,

$$E = l_n - m_n,$$

where l is the *arithmetic* sum of the logical digits in any oblong grid, rounding down to whole numbers when necessary, and n is the place number in the series of oblong grids, $p \times q$, where p is constant and q expands as the natural number series. For oblong grids the value of l for the series of base grids, 1 × 2, 2 × 3, 3 × 4, 4 × 5, 5 × 6, . . . , is, beginning with 1 for 1 × 2, the sequential sum of the natural number series excluding odd-number multiples of 2, i.e., 1, 4, 8, 13, 20, 28, 37, 48, ... Within the set of oblong grids of constant dimension p, l increases sequentially with q in increments corresponding to the infinite repetition of the 3 numbers which are the values of the last 3 increments of l in the sequence, $(p-2)\times(q-1)$, $(p-1)\times(q-1)$, $p\times(q-1)$, $p\times q$, except that for the set of oblong grids, $p\times q$, the order in which these incremental values of l repeat within the set is rearranged so that the increment associated with $p \times q$ in the sequence last cited now precedes those there associated with $(p-1) \times (q-1)$ and $p \times (q-1)$, while the increments associated with the latter maintain their relative order as established in the cited sequence. The value of m for the series of base grids, 2 × 3, 3 × 4, 4 × 5, 5 × 6, . . . , is, beginning with 0 for 2 × 3, the sequential sum of the natural numbers excluding 1 and the natural number multiples of 2^2, i.e., 0, 2, 5, 10, 16, 23, 32, ... Within the set of oblong grids of constant dimension p, the value of m increases sequentially with q and l in increments corresponding to the set of 3 numbers each of which is 1 less than the corresponding number in the set of increments of l. The following table illustrates these relations for the early parts of the infinite set of the infinite series of oblong grids.

		l	m		l	m		l	m		l	m		l	m		l	m		l	m		l	m
$(p-2)\times(q-1)$	0×2	0		1×3	2		2×4	5		3×5	10		4×6	16		5×7	23		6×8	32		7×9	42	
$(p-1)\times(q-1)$	1×2	1		2×3	4		3×4	8		4×5	13		5×6	20		6×7	28		7×8	37		8×9	48	
$p\times(q-1)$	2×2	3		3×3	6		4×4	11		5×5	17		6×6	24		7×7	33		8×8	43		9×9	54	
$p\times q$	2×3	4	0	3×4	8	2	4×5	13	5	5×6	20	10	6×7	28	16	7×8	37	23	8×9	48	32	9×10	60	42
$p\times(q+1)$	2×4	5	0	3×5	10	3	4×6	16	7	5×7	23	12	6×8	32	19	7×9	42	27	8×10	53	36	9×11	66	47
$p\times(q+2)$	2×5	7	1	3×6	12	4	4×7	19	9	5×8	27	15	6×9	36	22	7×10	47	31	8×11	59	41	9×12	72	52
$p\times(q+3)$	2×6	8	1	3×7	14	5	4×8	21	10	5×9	30	17	6×10	40	25	7×11	51	34	8×12	64	45	9×13	78	57
$p\times(q+4)$	2×7	9	1	3×8	16	6	4×9	24	12	5×10	33	19	6×11	44	28	7×12	56	38	8×13	69	49	9×14	84	62
$p\times(q+5)$	2×8	11	2	3×9	18	7	4×10	27	14	5×11	37	22	6×12	48	31	7×13	61	42	8×14	75	54	9×15	90	67
$p\times(q+6)$	2×9	12	2	3×10	20	8	4×11	29	15	5×12	40	24	6×13	52	34	7×14	65	45	8×15	80	58	9×16	96	72

So, for example, for the 4 × 5 grid the number of added edges necessary to make the grid rigid is determined by the formula, $E = l_n - m_n = 13 - 5 = 8$, and for the 9 × 12 grid, $E = l_n - m_n = 72 - 52 = 20$.

The rule for locating braces within any grid so that it is rigid is the following: after determining the number of edge-overlapping triangles (EOT's) necessary to brace any $p \times q$ grid by deducting the product of $(p-1) \times (q-1)$ from T (where $T = V - 2 = 2(l_n - m_n) + [(p-1)\times(q-1)]$)[8] distribute the sets of EOT's so that no subset of the grid contains more than the minimum number of sets of EOT's necessary to make it rigid when standing alone, providing that each column and each row contains at least 1 set of 2 EOT's, and that no column and row having only 1 set of 2 EOT's share the identical set.

[8] Ibid.

5

TRANSFORMATION OF WORLD-CONSCIOUSNESS: THE NEW ATONEMENT

Now for the first time the atonement is existence. The new atonement is existence. The consciousness of the new atonement thinks essentially: Unfortunate unconditionally was the Fall, unhappy absolutely was the Sin, completely sorrowful was the Death. The Universe inverted absolutely was nothing. Life was nothing. The death of God was realized. Death was the absolute. Life and death was the abyss. And yet a mighty wind sweeps over the waters. The new beginning absolutely inverts the depths. For the first time the Light universal. Now absolutely now begins the new atonement. For the first time the atonement is now absolutely historical. The Now, experienced, is the atonement of existence. In every now being atones. In every now being itself, absolutely predicated, atones. Not merely the beginning of world-consciousness, not merely consciousness beginning in every now, not merely the eternal outwardizing of the within, but the within here & now absolutely out, the within absolutely outwardized, the fulfillment of the depth of every expectation: the atonement for the first time absolutely outwardized. The within identically atonement now completely the outside of reality/the reality completely outside: world-consciousness consciousness that the existence of the world is atonement. The new atonement is for the first time the perfect consciousness that the world is absolutely, that there is no 'given', no 'nature', no ground for denying the existence of existence itself, no ground for positing Nothing, no ground for positing the non-existence of Unity. Indeed, this no-ground is nothing but the will for the anonymity of Unity, the anonymous willing of the existence of Unity, the inessential willing of the existence of an absolute atonement, the willing-not-willing, the being-not-being of One World, the divided consciousness in the form of the double identity of the one, which, while prescinding as Nothing from the transcendence of Nothing itself, *thinking* Nothing without reference to death, nevertheless does not *identify* Nothing without reference to death, to the body of death, to that *Dasein* for which alone existence 'is the way of being'.[1] The willy-nilly unity identifies Nothing with the abyss, reduces Nothing to Nothing, and ironically, in the form of absolute solitude (not being for the truth of Being), remains as the outside within the solitude of that *Dasein* for which, precisely in its distinction from 'nature' and from the mode of being of 'natural things', 'there is no outside, for which reason it is also absurd to talk about an inside',[2] remains as the immanence of death in the act itself of the transcendence of death, remains as absolute solitude the being-not-being of the absolute truth, absolute solitude being-not-being transcendence. The ground for the positing of the non-existence of unity (together with its negative in the form of 'no one' willing one world) is now seen in the light of the now absolute atonement, in the light of the atoning identity/body of

[1] Cf. M. Heidegger, *The Basic Problems of Phenomenology,* trans. A. Hofstadter, Bloomington, 1982) p. 28: "For Kant and Scholasticism existence is the way of being of natural things, whereas for us, on the contrary, it is the way of being of the Dasein. Therefore, we might, for example, say 'A body does not exist; it is, rather, extant.' In contrast, Daseins, we ourselves, are not extant; the Dasein exists."

[2] Ibid., p. 66: "When Kant talks about a relation of the thing to the cognitive faculty, it now turns out that this way of speaking and the kind of inquiry that arises from it are full of confusion. The thing does not relate to a cognitive faculty interior to the subject; instead, the cognitive faculty itself and with it this subject are structured intentionally in their ontological constitution. The cognitive faculty is not the terminal member of the relation between an external thing and the internal subject; rather, its essence is the relating itself, and indeed in such a way that the intentional Dasein which thus relates itself as an existent is always already immediately dwelling among things. For the Dasein there is no outside, for which reason it is also absurd to talk about an inside."

matter itself, in the light of the now universal identity of the atonement, to be absolutely lopped off under the rule prohibiting the unnecessary multiplication of entities. The *Dasein* for which there is no outside is bereft of even that 'no' except in the form of absolute unity. This is the new work of the One absolutely world, the absolute and essential transcendence of the intentionality which was neither subjectivity nor objectivity,[3] which revolutionary metanoēsis transcending the abyss, transcendent *after*-identity of the abyss, *qua* transcendent body *ex abysso*, differentiates itself from the non-revolutionary metanoetic transcendence of the same which is the abyss of thought that is *la différance.*[4] This is the absolute objectivity effected by the One now existing for the first time. Now for the first time the *Dasein for* which there is no outside is the *Dasein of* which there is no outside. If essential thinking before now distinguishes existence from extantness, and in so doing transcends the phenomenological reduction by understanding that the being that exists 'exists in the manner of dwelling among the extant',[5] and in so doing is identically the being given for the truth of Being, is the *epoché* of thinking, the thought of the unthought identity of thought, the identity of thought as being given for Being, the preconception of the identity of thought as belonging-to, conceived *a priori* as 'belonging together',[6] the conception of the identity of thought as given-for, then the thinking now occurring for the first time as essentially historical is the absolute phenomenological reduction: the absolute *epoché* of thought is for the first time thought. Now actually occurs for the first time the *epoché* of the thought of existence, *the epoché the very essence of thought, the epoché of very identity,* the very form of thought for the first time the *epoché* of all mystical language,[7] indeed, the abso-

[3] Ibid., pp. 55ff. In an 'unusual' sense, it is, of course, both.

[4] Cf. above, Section II.3.

[5] Heidegger, *Basic Problems of Phenomenology,* p. 65.

[6] Ibid., pp. 83, 312.

[7] The writer is indebted to T. J. J. Altizer for the last phrase which felicitously describes the *essence* of the thinking now occurring. It is only necessary to specify, as the text does, that the thinking now occurring for the first time is that essence *absolutely.*

lute *epoché* of the mystical, including that mystical element self-consciously appropriated to itself by modern thought as its very form and essence: the thinking now occurring for the first time is the absolute *epoché* of the *cogito: thought itself* for the first time *thinks* the *epoché* of 'I think'. This absolute phenomenological reduction is the meta-identity in which *Dasein* and all other things begin to *exist* together without belonging to each other, the meta-identity/after-identity/with-identity which *is* the absolute *epoché* which *is* identity: *the belonging-to identity absolutely together: the atoning identity:* the belonging-to identity of very existence. This is the beginning of the transcendental unity of transcendence absolutely manifest, of existence irreducible to Nothing: the transcendental unity of transcendence absolutely manifest as *nihil ex nihilo*: the unity of Nothing *ex nihilo.* The being atoning in every now: the Name Itself of God. This name is the identity of nothing *ex nihilo.* This is the absolute *epoché* of the mystical without reference to an other world: the One for the first time absolutely itself here & now: everything essentially existing, absolutely nothing extant: the thought of the extant reduced to Nothing: the transcendence-to-Nothing of the being of the *Dasein* reduced to Nothing: Nothing absolutely extant: the abyss of the extant/the extant Abyss/existence *ex abysso.* This *epoché* of mystical existence, this *epoché* of the mystical name, is the Spirit of God hovering over the absolutely-nothing-at-hand. The *epoché* of very identity, the *epoché* of the cogito, identifies the extant Abyss, and is thought for the first time *ex abysso.* This is the thought of existence for the first time the *epoché* of extant thought, the abyss of the thought of existence *ex abysso*: the extant abyss existence *ex abysso* in face of the absolute objectivity of the *Dasein*: the abyss not itself the matter of a beginning: not the abyss of the abyss at once not not[8] the abyss of the abyss itself,[9] not the abyss of the abyss not not the abyss of the abyss, not the (metanoetic) abyss of the abyss of the abyss, but the

[8] Where the double negative does not produce an affirmative just as not not nothing is not nothing since nothing *is* but not nothing, since, that is, there is no nothing not absolutely nothingless. Cf. above, Section III.1.

[9] Cf. above, p. 232.

beginning of existence the revolutionary metanoēsis of the abyss of the abyss. The absolute inversion of the abyss, transcendent abysmal negativity, essentially continues to look forward in order to preserve its own past, continues to anticipate in order to preserve the absolute 'its own', still but the absolute transcendental negativity of the abyss—not the abyss of the absolute not its own itself at once not not the abyss of the absolute not its own itself—not the absolutely unconditioned negative of the abysmal negativity: the *Dasein* for the first time absolutely unconditioned Spirit. The abyss is not itself the matter of a beginning, but rather the after-identity of the abyss itself is the absolute reflection of the *Dasein* of the Spirit: not the mere potentiality for a beginning, not the beginning of a merely perceptive sense of an inconceivable and undefinable 'new humanity', not a 'glimpse' or 'glimpses of a new world',[10] but, rather, the absolute reflection of an absolute unity now actually beginning for the first time in history, the absolute reflection of the absolute *epoché* of the beginning, a new humanity actually existing in the One, the actuality of the new unity of humanity. Now for the first time occurs the actual opening of the new world in the One Spirit, the absolute negativity of the new beginning, the actual unity of the abyss *ex abysso.*[11] We, *Daseins,* (not 'Dasein, we ourselves', but we, ourselves not ourselves, we, the news, we, the nows) dwell in the absolute objectivity, in the absolutely outwardized *Dasein,* of the One Existent Spirit: we are the actual unity of this Spirit hovering over the Abyss in the form of the new beginning. *Qua* beginning we are the new creation, the face of an absolute creation existing here & now, the flesh and blood of the One absolutely naming itself, of the One naming itself Creation. We for the first time are this One absolutely, the absolute inversion of the abyss *ex abysso* the beginning. This now occurring unity is the absolute template of the new creation, the beginning of the new world, the beginning of the new humanity. Nor might this One now actually existing for the first time as the essence of history

[10] Cf. above, pp. 226ff. But compare, below, p. 392, n. 83, the *absolute* 'to catch a glimpse'.

[11] Cf. above, pp. 273, 283f.

be either more or less than the absolute template, than the absolute actuality of the act of creation. This One can be neither more nor less than the historicity of history itself, the absolutely unconditioned divine opening embodied in actual flesh and blood. What now occurs for the first time in history is the invitation to the absolute loss of self from which we dare not withhold our selves as exceptions in essence to the invitation. We exist in the divine opening of the creative act which knows absolutely no hesitation, or not at all. The epoch of the One now beginning is the end of all epochs. This is the beginning of the absolute embrace of the One itself. Now for the first time is the time absolutely: this is the beginning of the One. This is the beginning of the rapture of the church, the inauguration of the divine rapture of the end, the unifying of the new creation, the beginning of the final transformation of the world, of history, of humanity: the concrete unity of salvation in the form of an absolute world-consciousness: every now for the first time atoning consciousness, every-one embodying the we, every unity/existence the absolute suffering of the One opening on the Nothing *ex nihilo*, as never before the divine patience incarnate in the absolute unity of consciousness. This absolute negativity of the atoning consciousness is the Atonement transcending the Atonement, the Atonement absolutely identifying existence with unity. This beginning is the new consciousness which is atonement. The negativity of this absolute atonement is this absolute atonement for the first time unconditionally. There is no exception to the atoning identity now itself occurring in the form of language, identically in the form of logic, identically in the form of number. Each of these is the absolute manifestation of the One identity/body: consciousness, language/logic/number, being, is consciousness of the beginning of the absolute existence of absolute unity. It is identical to say & think: 'absolute atonement', 'the conception that existence/the thing is unity', 'the logical proof that $1 = 1_{xy}$', 'the perception that $m^2/Tc^2 = 1$'. It is identically to say & think that the beginning of absolute unity exists, that the One itself is for the first time absolutely historical, that there is as never before an absolute *unum esse*, that the absolute beginning is univocally predicated of (any)thing. Indeed, if essential thinking before now was the revelation of the 'being of the subject . . . itself as other than extantness', setting 'a fundamental limit . . . to the hitherto prevailing equation of being with actuality, or extantness, and thus to ancient ontology',[12] then what now occurs for the first time in history is the transcendence of the subjectivity of being itself, the transcendence of the fundamental limit set to the equation of being with actuality, or extantness. What now actually occurs for the first time is the setting of the absolutely fundamental limit to ancient ontology, viz., the equation of actuality or extantness with existence. If before now the foundation of existence was established in the form '*Dasein* alone exists', then the foundation of existence now established is in the form 'the *Dasein* is absolutely', such that the *Dasein* is absolute objectivity, such that an absolutely fundamental limit is set to the limit of ancient ontology, viz., that there is *no* essential or transcendental subjectivity involved in the concept of the *Dasein*, that there is *no* subject not purely formal of the objectivity existing now in time for the first time, that the being of the subject is not extantness but *not other than* extantness, that the being of the subject is itself the extant abyss/the abyss extant in the face of creation, apart from which abysmal after-identity it itself is absolutely impossible. What now occurs is that the logic of creation is the essence of thought.

Now for the first time logic essentially coincides existence: the absolutely unconditioned equation is of being with unity: the existent actuality for the first time is absolute unity: the *unum*/minimum the meta-identity of actuality, the absolute actuality of absolute *Dasein* which knows no extantness which is not the absolutely impossible being of the subject, not the absolute other, which knows no extantness which is not 'the Subject is Nothing', not the abyss extant in the *Dasein* of the act of creation. This *Dasein* hears extantness say 'the Subject is Nothing', which statement is not an assertion of the *Dasein*, but an admission absolutely spoken in the midst of the act of creation which is the new *Dasein*: 'the Subject is Nothing' is the proposition (at

[12] Heidegger, *Basic Problems of Phenomenology*, p. 125.

once praise & thanks[13]) identically the extant abyss existing absolutely in the act of creation, indeed, a proposition/logos/word which before now essentially could not be heard by a thinking then not essentially logical, a thinking essentially given, not essentially logical, but essentially natural, and precisely so insofar as it found itself under the necessity of 'ontologically distinguishing' itself as 'one being of a peculiar sort from

---

[13] The absolute form of logical propositions, *qua* inflection on the foundation-proportion, *qua* 1 : 2 :: 4 : 3 (cf. above, pp. 273–75, for its construction), is, in the product of the direct multiplication of its ratios, in its 'rational product', 2/3 (cf. above, pp. 287ff.), which is the product of the identical operation on the Hebrew הודה. 'to give thanks, to praise, to admit', which *qua* proportion of the numerical values of the letters reads 5 : 6 :: 4 : 5, the rational product of which is $5/6 \times 4/5 = 2/3$. This is an identity of logical form and acknowledgment form perfectly fitting to the context. The reader is, by the way, cautioned to bear in mind that the methodology for the mathematical reading of language employed here and below in the text is essentially distinguished from the *gematria* of the ancients and the kabbalah by virtue of the fact that the number-values of letters in the ancient languages are for the first time in history treated in an *essentially* mathematical way, viz., *as elements in a proportion or members of a series of ratios,* and no substitutions are allowed, and that these and other related significant technical differences distinguish this methodology from earlier and, in *some* respects, similar practice, thereby reflecting the essential novelty of the new world consciousness set forth in this work as a whole. Here and below in the text the letter-numbers of any text are understood as elements of a ratio or proportion. In any language text the word is taken as the natural unit of division, so that the beginning of each word is the beginning of a ratio or proportion. For example, the Hebrew for *cogito ergo sum* is אני חושב ועל כן אני קים and is rendered 1 : 50 :: 10 : [1] (::) 8 : 6 :: 300 : 2 (::) 6 : 70 :: 30 : [1] (::) 20 : 50 (::) 1 : 50 :: 10 : [1] (::) 100 : 10 :: 40 : [1], where (::) links words and [1] is the implicit final value of words with an odd number of letters. There are two primary values calculated for any text, the 'rational product', which is the product of the string of ratios which comprises the text, and the 'integral product', which is the square product of the string of the numerators of the ratios (= the square product of the odd numbered letter-numbers of the text). In the example chosen the rational product = (2.304E4)/7 and the integral product = 1.1943936E25. The 'linear product' is the product of the entire string of letter-numbers. The integral product also = the rational product × the linear product. In the case just cited the linear product is 9! × 1E16. The

other beings', '*that* being to whose being (existence) *an understanding of being belongs* and *to the interpretation of which all the problems of ontology generally return*', precisely and essentially natural insofar as, although, it may be granted, '*not one-sidedly subjectivistic*', it was radically and finally bound to the 'subject'.[14] The essential reason why it was not possible for essential thinking before now to 'catch' and 'completely explicate' the essence of existence 'in a proposition', is that the content of the proposition of an absolutely propositional existence, of an essentially propositional/logical thinking is the reduction to nothing of the 'subject'/the 'given'/the 'natural'. Now the proposition/the logic/the praise is the essence of existence 'caught and completely explicated' as itself, as thought in the act of creation. Now—that is, at once, in the now and in the form of the now, the form of the thinking now occurring, in the existing form of identity *ex nihilo*—now is heard in essence the propositional content *ex nihilo*. 'The Subject is Nothing' is the form of the praise existing absolutely in the creation now for the first time in histo-

---

methodology used here can be fruitfully employed in the consideration of numbers without any reference to language, as, for example, will be the case below in Sections III.6 and III.7.

[14] Cf. Heidegger, *Basic Problems of Phenomenology*, pp. 154–55: "If we undertake to elucidate the existence of the Dasein, we are fulfilling a twofold task—not only that of ontologically distinguishing one being of a peculiar sort from other beings but also that of exhibiting the being of *that* being to whose being (existence) *an understanding of being belongs and to the interpretation of which all the problems of ontology generally return*. We must not of course think that the essential nature of existence can be caught and completely explicated in a proposition. We are concerned now only to characterize the *direction of the line of questioning* and to give a *first preview of the constitution of the Dasein's existence*. . . . We are thus repeating afresh that in the active stress upon the subject in philosophy since Descartes there is no doubt a genuine impulse toward philosophical inquiry which only sharpens what the ancients sought; on the other hand, it is equally necessary not to start simply from the subject alone but to ask whether and how the *being* of the subject must be determined as an entrance into the problems of philosophy, and in fact in such a way that orientation toward it is *not one-sidedly subjectivistic*. Philosophy must perhaps start from the 'subject' and return to the 'subject' in its ultimate questions, and yet for all that it may not pose its questions in a one-sidedly subjectivistic manner."

ry: the form of the absolute admission of the shining of the light *ex nihilo.* Now for the first time this proposition is the praise in the act of creation identically the existing One. Every-thing exists in the absolute immediacy of the One itself. What would be essentially mystical, were self-transcendence now in fact able to be conceived, were self-transcendence not in fact now absolutely inconceivable for the first time in history, *is the beginning simply of the life of everything and nothing not other than nothing.* What would be in essential continuity with the appropriation of the mystical ground, with the mystical ground of appropriation implicit in modernity's essentially self-conscious appropriation of the transcendental form of medieval natural reason,[15] were it not to be the case that there now actually occurs for the first time the absolute *epoché* of all mystical language, the absolute *epoché* of mystical thought, the *epoché* of absolutely dichotomous thought, the *epoché* of mystical existence, what would then be essentially yet another form of the continuation of the past into the future, another continuation of the past in the form of the future, what would then be not an absolutely new unity, is however in fact the existent simplicity of the abyss *ex nihilo,* existence praising the Creator in the form of the One world, the beginning of the actual existence of the abyss of the abyss, of life and death in the form of the death of the One, of the *unity* of the 'death of death itself'.

What now occurs in time for the first time is the absolute existence/unity of existence, the actual transcendence of the Double: in the absolute atonement, the double atoning. In place of the self-identity of the Double, the Double meta-identically One/Oned, the identity of the Double identically the existence of the One/the Logos/the absolutely existing absolute reason, the Double identically the absolute relativity/the absolute proportionality of the new world existing in consciousness in the form of the absolute transcendence of existence, in the form of what would not be the other annihilating self-not-self, were it not for the fact that there is absolutely no point of reference not an absolutely new existence, no point not existing in the con-

[15] Cf. Leahy, *Novitas Mundi.*

sciousness of the atonement, no point of reference not absolutely existing, no point not identical with Identity, no unnumbered 'hair', no uncreated point. This absolute novelty of everything existing for the first time is the absolute repetition of the One God: the *unum* absolutely beginning to exist is the absolute measure of the divine unity: God is the absolute measure of everything beginning to exist, which is to say, the Name of the divine unity is for the first time substance/body/identity, which is to say, as never before God is Jesus Christ, the One God is Jesus Christ Absolute in the divine unity. In his existence, in his actual historical existence, in his temporal individuality, in his absolutely personal time, Jesus is divinity, God is for the first time Jesus Absolute, Jesus the existential One, Jesus now the One. Creation is the unity of Jesus the unity of God. 'God is Jesus' is the One God beginning a new world, beginning to speak absolutely. This is the proposition of absolute existence for the first time suffering appropriation in the act of creation: the complete praise of the Creator in the form of 'Nothing is Jesus *ex nihilo*', in the form of the beginning of the absolute objectivity that is this Name, in the form of the existence which is for the first time objectively Jesus Christ, in the form of Jesus existing for the first time in substantive analogy to the '*nomen proprium*' of God, the divine '*shem ha-meforash*', of which Maimonides speaks in *The Guide for the Perplexed,* as follows:

> It is well known that all the names of God occurring in Scripture are derived from his actions, except one, namely, the Tetragrammaton, which consists of the letters *yod, hé, vau* and *hé.* This name is applied exclusively to God, and is on that account called *Shem ha-meforash,* "The Nomen Proprium." It is the distinct and exclusive designation of the Divine Being; whilst His other names are common nouns, and are derived from actions, to which some of our own are similar, as we have already explained. . . . The derivation of the name . . . is not positively known, the word having no additional signification. This sacred name, which, as you know, was not pronounced except in the sanctuary by the appointed priests, when they gave the sacerdotal blessing, and by the high priest on the Day of Atonement, undoubtedly denotes something which is pecu-

liar to God, and is not found in any other being. It is possible that in the Hebrew language, of which we have now but a slight knowledge, the Tetragrammaton, in the way it was pronounced, conveyed the meaning of "absolute existence."

. . . The frequent use of names of God derived from actions, led to the belief that He had as many [essential] attributes as there were actions from which the names were derived. The following promise was therefore made, implying that mankind will at a certain future time understand this subject, and be free from the error it involves: "In that day will the Lord be One, and His name One" (Zech. xiv. 9). The meaning of this prophecy is this: He being One, will then be called by one name, which will indicate the essence of God; but it does not mean that His sole name will be a derivative [viz., "One"]. In the *Pirke Rabbi Eliezer* (chap. iii) occurs the following passage: "Before the universe was created, there was only the Almighty and His Name." Observe how clearly the author states that all these appellatives employed as names of God came into existence after the Creation. This is true; for they all refer to actions manifested in the Universe. . . . only the Tetragrammaton is a real *nomen proprium*, and must not be considered from any other point of view. You must beware of sharing the error of those who write amulets (*kameot*). Whatever you hear from them, or read in their works, especially in reference to the names which they form by combination, is utterly senseless; they call these combinations *shemot* (names) and believe that their pronunciation demands sanctification and purification, and that by using them they are enabled to work miracles. Rational persons ought not to listen to such men, nor in any way believe their assertions.[16]

Today is the beginning of the Day of Atonement. Now thought for the first time is the universal existence of 'the Almighty and His name': today thought in essence is the beginning of the conception of 'the Lord is One, and His name is One': today is the beginning of the universal conception of the meta-identity of One Lord and One Name. Today begins the conception in

[16] Maimonides, *The Guide For The Perplexed*, trans. M. Friedländer, 2nd ed. (New York, 1956), pp. 89–91.

essence of the meta-identity of unity and the absolute *unum*.[17] Today begins the absolute meta-identity of the One Lord and the essential conception of the Name. Now for the first time in the form of the *minimum* the *unum absolute* is constructed. In the essence of the thinking now occurring for the first time the negative theology of Maimonides (as well as that of neoplatonism and, in its own way, of modernity) is radically and essentially transcended in the form of '*ex abysso*', in the form of the absolutely unconditioned unity of creation in that Name identically which was 'before the universe was created': the universe now for the first time exists absolutely in the form of the incarnate Name of the One God.

The thinking now occurring for the first time essentially deciphers the cipher of the Name in the form of the *minimum*. If the minimum *qua* proportion is 4 : 1 :: 2 : 3,[18] then its rational product[19] is 2.666. Now, taking strict care to avoid 'the arbitrary combination of letters' of which Maimonides rightly complains in his warning against the magical use of Holy Scripture, but also leaving behind the arbitrariness of negative theology, together with that of its heir, the mystical modern 'philosophy', let it be noted that תורה, 'Torah', 'Law', *qua* proportion of the numerical value of the letters, is 400 : 6 :: 200 : 5, the rational product of which is 2.666E3. It thus appears that the *minimum* is the 'little Torah', indeed, identically the multiple אלף, 'thousand' (*qua* proportion, 1 : 30 :: 80 : [1], whose rational product is 2.666) by which it is the Law, this minimum, this thousandth part, *qua* substance. Ever so lightly armed with this tiny *bona fide* credential of the perfect rationality of the Law, this 'little Torah', this דוד, 'David' (*qua* proportion, 4 : 6 :: 4 : [1], whose rational product is likewise 2.666), this essentially rational measure, the minimum, sets out to rationally unify the Name of the One God. The minimum identity is confirmed in its mission in a way substantially analogous to the confirmation of the mission of Moses, משה (*qua*

[17] Cf. above, Section III.1; also Sections II.3 and II.4, passim.

[18] Cf. above, pp. 266ff.

[19] The product of the direct multiplication of the ratios of the proportion. Cf. above, p. 357, n. 13.

proportion, 40 : 300 :: 5 : [1], whose rational product is $.\overline{666}$), as recounted by Maimonides:

> Moses was correct in declaring, "But, behold, they will not believe me, for they will say, The Lord hath not appeared unto thee" (Exod. iv. 1); for any man claiming the authority of a prophet must expect to meet with such an objection so long as he has not given a proof of his mission. . . . When God appeared to our Teacher Moses, and commanded him to address the people and to bring them the message, Moses replied that he might first be asked to prove the existence of God in the Universe, and that only after doing so he would be able to announce to them that God had sent him. . . . Then God taught Moses how to teach them, and how to establish amongst them the belief in the existence of Himself, namely, by saying Ehyeh asher Ehyeh, a name derived from the verb hayah in the sense of "existing," for the verb hayah denotes "to be," and in Hebrew no difference is made between the verbs "to be" and "to exist." The principle point in this phrase is that the same word which denotes "existence," is repeated as an attribute. The word asher, "that," corresponds to the Arabic illadi and illati, and is an incomplete noun that must be completed by another noun; it may be considered as the subject of the predicate that follows. The first noun which is to be described is ehyeh; the second, by which the first is described, is likewise ehyeh, the identical word, as if to show that the object which is to be described and the attribute by which it is described are in this case necessarily identical. This is, therefore, the expression of the idea that God exists, but not in the ordinary sense of the term; or, in other words, He is "the existing Being which is the existing Being," that is to say, the Being whose existence is absolute. The proof which he was to give consisted in demonstrating that there is a Being of absolute existence, that has never been and never will be without existence.
>
> . . . But said Moses, by what means shall I be able to show that this existing God has sent me? Thereupon God gave him the sign.[20]

[20] Maimonides, *Guide For The Perplexed*, p. 93.

Thus the minimum enunciates the absolute, save that now for the first time in history the proof-form of 'the existence of God in the Universe' manifests itself *ex abysso,* and in light of the fact that 'the Subject is Nothing' is heard in the essence of the *Dasein,* as identically the essence of the minimum, as identical with the fundamental truth of the minimum,[21] as follows: let the statement of the divine identity, אהיה אשר אהיה (*Ehyeh asher Ehyeh,* 'I AM THAT I AM', *qua* proportion, 1 : 5 :: 10 : 5 (::) 1 : 300 :: 200 : [1] (::) 1 : 5 :: 10 : 5), be reduced in a form that preserves the syntax as described by Maimonides:

$$1/5 \cdot 2 = 2/\underline{3 \cdot} \, 1/5 \cdot 2,$$
$$.40 = .2\overline{666},$$
$$1 = 2/3$$

Here is the literally and perfectly rational identification of the fundamental truth of the minimum (1 = 2/3)[22] and the rational product of the syntactically structured Mosaic proof of the existence of God. Indeed, אהיה אשר אהיה, 'I AM THAT I AM', so construed as the fundamental truth of the minimum, is, together with that truth, identically the equation, *qua* rational products, יי ('God'/'Adonai', 10 : 10, whose rational product is 1) = השם ('The Name', 5 : 300 :: 40 : [1], whose rational product is 2/3), 1 = 2/3. Thought in essence for the first time the Being of God is the Name of God. The 'I AM', אהיה, is the proportion whose ratios correspond to the rational products, respectively, of אני ('I', 1 : 50 :: 10 : [1], whose rational product is 1/5) and מלוכה ('Dominion', 40 : 30 :: 6 : 20 :: 5 : [1], whose rational product is 2). When this 'I' identified with 'Dominion', this I AM (1/5 × 2), is, in effect, Moses identified with I AM (.40 × .666 = .2666), then I AM (.40) is מובן (.2666), 'understood', and is מלול (.2666), 'speech'. Then what is 'understood' and 'speech' (.2666) is the I AM (.40) which is, *qua* rational products, identically הקמה (.40), 'construction' and 'foundation', אבי הנביאים (.40), 'father of the

[21] Cf. above, p. 274 and pp. 287ff.
[22] Ibid.

prophets, Moses', identified with the 'incomplete noun' אשר (2/3) and 'Moses' משה (2/3). Now, if it is true that 1 = 2/3, the inverse is equally true, 1 = 1.5. *Qua* rational products, יי ('God', *qua* proportion, 10 : 10 [rational product, 1]), is שלום ('Peace', *qua* proportion, 300 : 30 :: 6 : 40 [rational product, 1.5]), the very 'Peace' of which 'Moses' (.666) is the inverse. In the proof of absolute existence the divine peace is manifest, that peace in terms of which the 'incomplete noun', the inadequate 'who', the unfaithful 'that', in fact identically names the absolutely existing Being, that peace, indeed, which identifies itself with the unfaithful 'that', precisely and essentially, in proving 'the existence of God in the Universe', that peace which just so, i.e., *qua* absolute inversion of the depth of identity, is perfect. The proof of God's existence from the mouth of God is perfect. This proof is the incontrovertible evidence of God's existence. This proof is the evidence of absolute love, of the absolute identification of the divine with existence here & now, at once the logical manifestation of the Trinity as the 'Almighty and His Name', of the 3 as the 2, identically the Unity of the Three irreducible to unity, identically the Unity of Three Absolute Unities, 2 = 1 × 3, the real unity of the Trinity 'before the creation', as distinguished from the notional Trinity of absolute idealism, 1 = 1 × 3, as well as from the logical Trinity of that realism, reducible to the latter but distinguished therefrom transcendentally, which is absolute transcendental idealism, pragmatism, or logical realism, for which 2 = 2 × 3, the latter holding in the suspense of a real triadic dualism the abstract triadic unity, 1 = 3.[23] This 1 = 2/3, 1 = 1.5, is the existence of logic/the logic of existence. There is no other beyond this 'that'/this 'who' of absolute existence, this 'peace' of absolute existence, there is no outside of this absolute existence of the Divine Trinity. There is no outside of this peace which is the logical unity of existence absolutely identical with the Trinity. The God existing in the Universe is not the transcendental God, but the transcendence of the transcendental God: the absolute inside outside of the divine identity: not the absolute self-reversal of absolute solitude, but the absolute other-

[23] Ibid.

reversal/God-reversal of absolute solitude: the absolute self-reversal now actually existent meta-identified: the *after-identity of absolute self-reversal*: the revelation for the first time of the essentially logical construction of divinity: the absolutely apocalyptic identity of the new world now beginning. This is the 'that' completely that, the 'incomplete' that completely and unconditionally that, the syntax of identity which is the peace of (any)noun, (any)name, (any)thing,[24] the universal peace of existence for the first time thought in essence/the peace of the Trinity incarnate. This for the first time is the that of absolute transcendence. This is the beginning of the absolute '*da*' of the *Dasein*. There is no other than this that. This that is the it itself for the first time: this is it, absolutely it.

Thus is The Name (השם, .666) identical with Peace (שלום, 1.5) in the form of the absolute unity which is the foundation, .666 × 1.5 = 1. This is the specifically rational naming of the Absolute Existent for the first time. The Absolute Existent now actually speaks to reason שלום לך ('*shalom lecha*', 'Peace be with you', *qua* proportion, 300 : 30 :: 6 : 40 (::) 30 : 20, whose rational product is 1.5 × 1.5 = 2.25 = 1.5/.666), and speaks this greeting to reason in the peaceful constitution of the elements of the Absolute Proportion of Absolute Thought which manifests itself in the logical structure of that inflection on the Foundation which is the absolute form of logical propositions, in the absolutely specific structure of the logic of the beginning, as follows: let the product of the integers found in the bottom quadrant of the manifold of logical order, 16,[25] be associated with 1 and *PP*, the product of those in the left quadrant, 24, with 2 and *NP*, the product of those in the right quadrant, 24, with 4 and *PN*, and the product of those in the top quadrant, 36, with 3 and *NN*, by arranging the proportion of the quadrant products in the form of the universal form of all logical propositions, viz., $pq + \bar{p}q + p\bar{q} + \overline{pq}$, and, in effect, substituting for the 'logical proportion', 1 : 2 :: 4 : 3, the 'perfectly logical proportion', 16 : 24 :: 24 : 36:

[24] Cf. above, pp. 183ff.

[25] Cf. above, pp. 274ff., for the construction referred to, the basis of what follows immediately in the text.

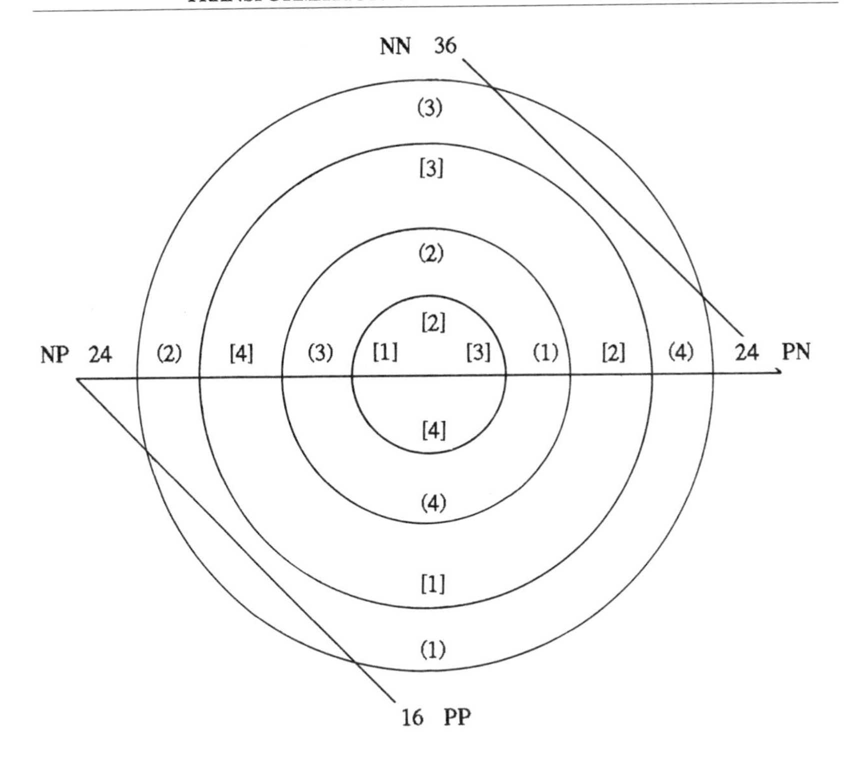

The '*shalom lecha'* identity (שלום לך, *qua* rational product 1.5 × 1.5 = 2.25) of the rational constitution of thought itself is immediately perceived when the latter proportion is constructed:

$$(1 \times 16) : (1.5 \times 16) :: [1 \times (1.5 \times 16)] : [1.5 \times (1.5 \times 16)]$$

which is reducible to 2 : 3 :: 2 : 3, so that the rational product of this proportion is 1/(1.5 × 1.5) or 1/2.25 or .444, the reduction of 'God' to 'Peace be with you', .666/1.5 = .444, the reduction of 'The Name' to 'Peace', itself at once חשבון ('reckoning', *qua* proportion, 8 : 300 :: 2 : 6 :: 50 : [1], whose rational product is .444). The Absolute Existent speaks to reason in the form of this proportion the sum of whose elements (1E2) is the square of the sum of the elements of the 'logical proportion' (1E1) and the square root of the product of the four sums of the integers in the quadrants of the manifold (1E4).[26] The ratio of the sum of the elements of the proportion to each one of the hundred is the inverse of the identity of each as one-of-a-hundred, viz., the inverse of .01, so that the 100, thought in essence distributively, is 1E2/.01 or 1E4, as a part, e.g., 36, is 36/.01 or 3.6E3. Taking each part as radically a part of the finite whole is logically a function of the fact that in the logic of the beginning zero, 0, is not nothing. This in fact is the logic of creation itself, the logic of *ex nihilo.* The Hebrew verb 'to create', the act of divinity, is ברא (*qua* proportion, 2 : 200 :: 1 : [1], whose rational product *is* .01). The product of the four sums of the integers in the quadrants of the manifold of logical order (1E4) is the 'created 100' = (1/.01)/.01 = 1E4. Now for the first time in history the 'created 100' is the thought of existence: the essence of Kant's '100 thalers' is existence.[27] There is no basis for thinking to distinguish reality from existence, or existence from the Now of the act of creation: the now existing logic is for the first time the essence of existence 'to create': creation is the essence of thought: the essence of the absolute logical manifold, the absolute inversion of the depth of identity, is for the first time the new opening. This is the infinite opening of the beginning of the act of creation. The fact is now for the first time in history conceived in essence that matter itself is created, that every logical element is an essentially relative unity, that the outside of existence is existence itself. This is the logic of the eucharist of existence the thought-form absolutely without sin:[28] for the first time the logic of the Incarnation

[26] Ibid.

[27] Cf. Heidegger, *Basic Problems of Phenomenology,* pp. 38ff., on the Kantian distinction of reality and existence, of 'being as copula'/the thing posited relatively to another/the predicate and 'being in the sense of existence'/'the thing posited in and for itself'/absolute position, and of the relation of the two as 'ap-position', a relation of the object to the concept 'added to' the latter, and involving, then, implicitly, relation to the *self.* Such self-relation is absolutely precluded by that form of unity which is the infinite opening of the act of creation, by the *epoché* of *any* mystical unity which is the new essence of *Da-sein,* the new essence of there-being, being-here.

[28] Cf. Leahy, *Novitas Mundi,* pp. 392f.

absolute. For the first time the logic of creation is absolute relativity, absolute precision. The arbitrary is absolutely excluded from the creation in the form of the absolutely unconditioned proportionality of existence: in the act of creation now actually occurring the unity of (any)number is absolutely specific, absolutely relative: number is proportion absolutely, (there is no mystical number, no secret number, no number with a meaning of 'its own'—what hitherto was hidden is now absolutely manifest, what is now absolutely manifest is absolutely existent, absolutely relative). The ground of this relativity is the 'created 100', the essence itself of the Absolute Proportion of Absolute Thought, the unit of which is the absolutely unconditioned specificity of the *cipher deciphered in essence*, or, of the fact that (where x is the sum of the elements of the 'perfectly logical proportion' [100] or any part thereof) $x/100 : .01 :: 1 : .01$, the rational product of which is $x/.01$, the maximum value of which is 1E4, the product of the four sums of the integers in the quadrants of the manifold of logical order.

The thinking now occurring for the first time perceives the perfect and precise form of language itself here in the form of the Hebrew language, perceiving in this language the precise and substantive differentiation of the logical conception of the Atonement from that of the Double which in its imitation of Atonement contrives to be identical with the latter *qua* certain form of the language, as follows:[29]

Atonement: כפור	Double: כפול	
20 : 80 :: 6 : 2	20 : 80 :: 6 : 30	(Proportion)
.25 :: .03	.25 :: .20	(Ratios)
.0075	.05	(Rational Product)
1.92E6	2.88E5	(Linear Product)
1.44E4	1.44E4	(Integral Product)

The difference is perceived as precisely rational, as the differ-

[29] In what follows the linear product is the product of the entire string of letter-numbers. The integral product is the rational product × the linear product. Cf. above, p. 357, n. 13.

ence in the different ratios of the two otherwise identical proportions. In each instance let the quotient of the digammate ratio (Hebrew *vau,* ו, = Greek *digamma,* Ϝ, = 6)[30] be reduced to the denominator of that ratio, as to the essential difference in the ratios, as follows: in the Atonement proportion .03 : 200 = 1.5E–4, or 1.5/10000, i.e., 1.5/(100/.01), while in the Double proportion .20 : 30 = .00666, or .666/100, i.e., 666/(100/1). While the shalom-factor (1.5) in the structure of Atonement is denominated with the 100 of the Absolute Proportion of Absolute Thought denominated with .01, denominated 'created', its inverse, the essentially incomplete (.666), in the structure of the Double is denominated with the 100 denominated with the indifferent 1, denominated, in effect, 'uncreated'. The identity, *qua* integral products, of the Atonement and the Double, the identity of 'absolute' Atonement and 'absolute' Double,[31] the transcendent unity of Atonement and Double, is a function of the proportionate identity in which the elements of the integral product of Double are most properly the means, and those of Atonement the extremes, viz., the proportion, 1.92E6 : 2.88E5 ::

[30] The *digamma,* which can be seen to be the constant, c, in 16 : 24 :: 24 : 36, when this proportion is comprehended in terms of $T : m :: m : c^2$ (cf. above, p. 135), is the template distinguishing the minimum proportion (4 : 1 :: 2 : 3) from the 'logical' proportion (1 : 2 :: 4 : 3) and the latter's substantive equivalent (4 : 1 :: 3 : 2) (cf. above, pp. 273ff.), as follows:

2 3 1 4 vs. 2 1 4 3 + 4 3 2 1

or, by relative inversion,

4 4 2 1 3 3 2 1

[31] Here and throughout, the value of a term or set of terms *qua* integral product is understood as its 'absolute' form, so that, for example, 'absolute' Atonement is כפור *qua* integral product, or 1.44E4. Similarly the value of a term or set of terms *qua* rational product is understood as its 'identity'. כפור or Atonement *qua* 'identity' is .0075.

.05 : .0075, the proof of which is 1.44E4/1.44E4 = 1. This proportion is constructed in perfect analogy to the proportion in which the elements of the 'law of duality' are the means and the elements of the 'law of unity' are the extremes, the proof of which is precisely the 'law of absolute unity', $I(1+1)=0$.[32] Just as the proof of the law of absolute unity is the work of the One absolutely here & now for the first time, the beginning transcending in essence the *coincidentia oppositorum*, the absolute coincidence of the beginning transcending categorically the opposites, transcending the category of the 'opposites', the absolute coincidence, *qua nihil, ex nihilo*, just as the fact that the absolute self is no longer (the fact which is the here & now of the One) absolutely limits in essence the doubling of identity, meta-identifies the double itself,[33] and relativizes unity absolutely[34] (leaving no room, generally, for the 'difference between', and, specifically, for the 'identity between',[35] (any) two things [the identity between (any) two things is the existence of the two things, or, $1_{xy} = 1$],[36] leaving no room, now for the first time in the form of thought, for the reduction to nothing of the abysmal identity of any two things), leaving no room for the absolutely uncreated abyss, leaving no room in the essence of thought for an uncreated absolute, for an uncreated totality, so just here, in the specifically historical language perfectly reflecting the creation of the abysmal identity of (any) two things, here, particularly, in the proportion, 2.88E5 : 1.92E6 :: .05 : .0075, constituted by the ratio of the linear products of Double (כפול) and Atonement (כפור) respectively, 2.88E5 : 1.92E6 = .15 = ל (30) : ר (200), identified as the inverse of the ratio of the respective rational products, .05 : .0075 = $6.\overline{666}$ = ר (200) : ל (30), the structure of the 'absolute' Double differentiates itself from that of 'absolute' Atonement, as the Double which, caught up in the embrace of this proportion whose rational product is Unity, 1, and whose

[32] Cf. above, pp. 279ff.
[33] Cf. above, pp. 230ff.
[34] Cf. above, Sections II.3 and II.4, and Section III.1, passim.
[35] Cf. above, pp. 246ff.
[36] Cf. above, p. 278.

proof-product is .0225 (*qua* rational products, שלום לך ['*shalom lecha*', 'Peace be with you'] identified with ברא ['to create'], 2.25 × .01 = .0225), so caught up, and reduced therein, *qua* 'identities', to Atonement, the Double finds itself, so reduced, identically the reduction, *qua* identities, of מציאות ('presence', *qua* proportion, 40 : 90 :: 10 : 1 :: 6 : 400, whose rational product is .0666) to ברא ('to create' [rational product, .01]), .0666/.01 = 6.666, at once the reduction of the idol בל ('Bel', *qua* ratio, 2 : 30 = .0666) and the negative בל ('not', *qua* ratio, 2 : 30 = .0666) to ברא ('to create'). It should be noted that the proof-product of the proportion whose elements are the linear and rational products of Double (כפול) and Atonement (כפור), .0225, is itself at once, *qua* rational products, the inverse of the 'perfectly logical proportion', 16 : 24 :: 24 : 36, reduced to ברא ('to create'), $(.444/.01)^{-1}$ = .0225, while the proof-product of the latter proportion is 1, identically the rational product of the former proportion.[37] It is further to be noted in the unity of the identity of the proportionate relation of the elements of 'absolute' Atonement and 'absolute' Double that while there is on the level of the distinguishing single elements a real rational inversion of ל (Double/30) : ר (Atonement/200) to ר (Atonement/200) : ל (Double/30) in the movement from the first to the second ratio of the proportion it is absolutely subsumed in the absolutely uninverted rational relation of the relational elements which actually constitute the proportion, to wit: Double/2.88E5 : Atonement/1.92E6 :: Double/.05 : Atonement/ .0075. The inversion actually occurs on the ground of the context which makes it possible but which is itself actually and transparently the absolute negation of that very inversion. *Here, then, perfectly concrete, absolutely specific and visible, is the absolute inversion of the depth of identity.* Where the ratio of the single elements is in complete and direct agreement with the ratio of relational elements the value of the ratio is .15 which is identically, *qua* rational products, שכינה ('Shekhinah', 'Godhead', *qua* proportion, 300 : 20 :: 10 : 50 :: 5 : [1], whose rational product is 15 [itself at once the inverse of the 'identity' of the Bel/Not/

[37] Cf. above, p. 371.

Presence,[38] בל\מציאות, $.0666^{-1}$]) identified with ברא ('to create'), $15 \times .01 = .15$. Where the ratio of the single elements is in incomplete and indirect agreement with the ratio of relational elements the value of the ratio is 6.666 which is identically, *qua* rational products, the very first spoken word of Godhead creating, יהי אור ('Let there be light', *qua* proportion, 10 : 5 :: 10 : [1] (::) 1 : 6 :: 200 : [1], whose rational product is 666.666), identified with ברא ('to create'), $666.666 \times .01 = 6.666$. But the Godhead (שכינה) identified with that very first spoken word of Godhead creating (יהי אור), *qua* 'identities', *is* the 'created 100', the 1E4 of the Absolute Proportion of Absolute Thought, that is, $15 \times 666.666 = 10000 = 100/.01$! This is the absolute immediacy of the act of creation now experienced for the first time in history in the form of the essence of thought in which existence is nothing *after* nothing, in which for the first time the existing nothing is not sourced in another nothing, in which existence is nothing irreducible to nothing:[39] the absolutely unconditioned freedom of the unity of existence in the form of absolute relativity/absolute precision: the freedom of thought to praise the One in the act of creation. But in that subtle but now for the first time perfectly visible and transparent disagreement of the Double with the Atonement, whereby the very first spoken word of Godhead creating, יהי אור ('Let there be light'), identified with ברא ('to create'), $666.666 \times .01 = 6.666$, whereby this last identity appears as the expression of the reduction of Atonement (ר/200) to Double (ל/30), *which last reduction is radically disallowed even as it is allowed to exist,* in that subtle but real disagreement, there is the reduction of מלה ('word', *qua* proportion, 40 : 30 :: 5 : [1], whose rational product is 6.666) to the sum of the rational products respectively of the 'logical proportion' and its substantive equivalent, viz., $6 + .666 = 6.666$,[40] which rational products taken

[38] Cf. above, p. 372.

[39] Cf. above, Section III.1, passim. Cf. also, Leahy, *Novitas Mundi,* pp. 286ff., where Heidegger's modern understanding of *ex nihilo* is contrasted with that of Thomas Aquinas. The confusion between 'source' and 'order' in regard to the *ex nihilo* goes back to the Neoplatonism of Augustine, but is still operative in the 'theology' of John Dewey (cf. below, Section V.2).

[40] Cf. above, pp. 273ff.

together, but apart from the digammate minimum proportion,[41] constitute the elements of צלב הקרס ('swastika', *qua* proportion, 90 : 30 :: 2 : [1] (::) 5 : 100 :: 200 : 60, whose rational product is, *qua* 'squatting cross', 6 × .1666 = 1), that ancient Indo-Iranian symbol of 'well-being' in the form of which the 6-identity of the 'logical' proportion identified with the .666 identity of the proportion which is its substantive equivalent is reduced to the latter-reduced-to-the-inverse-of-the-former,[42] i.e., (6 × .666)/(.666/.1666), which radical non-proportion in turn reduces to 6 × .1666 = 1. (6 × .666)/(.666/.1666) is the arithmetic expression of the fact that the swastika (צלב הקרס) is constructed in terms of an essentially unfounded logic. It is the revelation that behind the 6 × .1666 = 1 of the swastika, the 6/6 = 1, there is in fact the form of its rational construction, otherwise vanishing in its final form, (6 × .666)/(.666/.1666) = 4/4 = 1. But it is precisely this that is offered in place of the essential conception of the word of the One in the act of creation, this 1 = 4/4, that marvelous דד ('dug', *qua* proportion, 4 : 4, whose rational product is 1), the double *daleth,* that double door, which *qua* ratio is the unity of the door identically the door, the absolute but beginningless unity of the door. *Qua* 'identities', דלת ('door', *qua* proportion, 4 : 30 :: 400 : [1], whose rational product is 53.333) is identically מאפס ('out of nothing', *qua* proportion, 40 : 1 :: 80 : 60, whose rational product is 53.333), appearing in the maxim מאפס יוצא רק אפס ('*ex nihilo nihil fit*') which is the denial of the *novitas mundi,* on the understanding that מ or *ex* is taken materially as indicating *nihil* as a source,[43] but which on this same material understanding permits the affirmation of creation as a nothing sourced in nothing, as the self-emptying self-realization of self-identity in the self-silencing of speech, the total presence which silences 'every presence that is not immediately present',[44] described in *The Self-Embodiment of God*, as follows:

[41] Cf. above, p. 370, n. 30.

[42] Ibid.

[43] Cf. above, p. 373, n. 39.

[44] Altizer, *Self-Embodiment of God,* p. 91.

Now hearing is the full actualization of the self-emptying of speech, a self-emptying in which self-identity empties itself of that which is most inherently and immediately its own. But this it can do only by passing into silence, into the actuality of silence, into an immediately actual silence. Such a silence is far other than an eternally present silence, for it is an actual and active silence, a silence which is present in its act. That act immediately enacts itself, and it enacts itself when it is heard, thereby releasing a hearing which realizes its own self-identity in the self-embodiment of silence. Then hearing hears silence whenever and wherever it actually hears, whenever and wherever it is actual and real. Indeed, it then hears silence to the extent that it hears, as its own act of hearing now empties every presence of all that identity which is embodied in speech. All identity then progressively becomes drawn into the actual silence of self-identity, as the realization of that self-identity now actually and actively unsays all the naming of speech. And this unsaying is not the mere cessation of speech. It is far rather an unsaying which acts in its silencing, and acts by disembodying all those identities in its horizon which are embodiments of speech.

. . . such self-silencing is not simply self-diminution. Nor is it an inactivation or dissolution of self-identity. It is far rather a real and actual self-negation or self-emptying, a self-emptying realizing itself in the actuality of its own act. And while this act is silencing, it is not silent. Nor can it be, for this is the act of speech itself, even if it is an act whereby speech silences itself. In this act, silence is truly act, and thereby it ceases to be silent.

Silence truly comes to an end only insofar as that end is actually enacted. For the end of silence can be actual and real only when that end is an actual ending. And it does actually end in the self-emptying of speech, a self-emptying in which silence becomes totally present because it is totally spoken. In that act, speech not only unsays itself, but unsays itself by way of a total act. This act draws all presence to itself, and to itself as act. All presence is enacted in this act, and enacted as the self-enactment of self-silencing. Now presence becomes absence, and becomes actual as absence, and that absence is the self-enactment of presence. Therefore presence can now be actual only in its absence, in its absence from itself, from its own self-identity. But that absence is both a real absence and a real act. Not

> only is it a real act, it is an act realizing all act, and it realizes all act in this act. Consequently, all self-identity is realized in this act: "The door is I."
>
> "The door is I" when "I am the door." Yet this is a door opening to nowhere, the nowhere that is where identity is present as itself. And it opens to nowhere because its opening itself is all actual identity, all self-identity, all "I." So it is that this opening is a closing of all presence. Presence is closed in the ending of silence, in the final ending of silence, an ending which is the beginning of the absence of presence from itself. Once silence is no more, or once it has come to an actual and final end, then presence is no more as a presence which is itself. For the final ending of silence ends the self-identity of presence, or ends its ground, a ground without which presence cannot be itself as presence. No longer is presence other than absence, and no longer is speech other than silence. Now speech is speech only by its self-enactment of silence, and presence is present only by its self-enactment of absence. In that self-enactment presence loses itself as presence, and it actually loses itself by realizing itself as absence. "I am the door" only when "The door is I."
>
> This loss of presence silences all that speech whereby identity realizes itself as presence. Now speech can speak only when identity is absent, only when it is not itself. And identity is not itself when it is present only in its absence, when its speech can embody only the absence of itself. That absence now lies at the center of speech itself, as the silence of speech is now a self-embodiment of the self-emptying of speech. Such silence speaks, and it speaks insofar as presence is actually absent, or inasmuch as absence is actually present. This occurs not simply in the disappearance of presence, but rather in the disappearance of the self-identity of presence. And this can occur only in the act of that self-identity, an act in which self-identity actually speaks, and in which it speaks by actualizing itself as silence. Now the silence of self-identity is everywhere, but it is actually everywhere only by way of the actuality of its speech, a speech in which self-identity actually realizes its own silence.[45]

Such is the door 'opening to nowhere', to where 'identity . . . is

[45] Ibid., pp. 86–89.

present only in its absence', sourced in the self, sourced in the Nothing, the absolutely abysmal silence which is the speech of the silent self. Such is the silence of speech itself in the form of the nipple, in the form of the breast (דד), through which self-identity passes to the total awareness of the absence of everything, to the absence of awareness identically the awareness of absence, to an 'actually present' absence, an 'actually absent' presence. It is not simply that this pap is that through which 'self-identity empties itself of that which is most inherently and immediately its own', 'passing into. . . . an actual and active silence', it is not simply that the double daleth is that through which 'all identity then progressively becomes drawn into the actual silence of self-identity' which, *qua* speech, 'unsays all the naming of speech', but, in fact, this אומנת ('nurse', *qua* proportion, 1 : 6 :: 40 : 50 :: 400 : [1], whose rational product is 53.333) is itself at once the identifying, *qua* rational products, of the מינימום ('minimum', *qua* proportion, 40 : 10 :: 50 : 10 :: 40 : 6 :: 40 : [1], whose rational product is 5333.333) identified with ברא ('to create' [rational product, .01]), 5333.333 × .01 = 53.333, and the תלת-צליל ('triad', *qua* proportion, 400 : 30 :: 400 : [1] (::) 90 : 30 :: 10 : 30, whose rational product is 5333.333) identified with ברא ('to create' [rational product, .01]), 5333.333 × .01 = 53.333, and the תלת ('three', *qua* proportion, 400 : 30 :: 400 : [1], whose rational product is 5333.333) identified with ברא ('to create' [rational product, .01]), 5333.333 × .01 = 53.333, the identifying of all three identifications with the נצר פיו ('to keep silent', *qua* proportion, 50 : 90 :: 200 : [1] (::) 80 : 10 :: 6 : [1], whose rational product is 5333.333) identified with ברא ('to create' [rational product, .01]), 5333.333 × .01 = 53.333. This preserving of the mouth, this closing of the embouchure, this closing of the closure, is itself at once the 'speech in which self-identity actually realizes its own silence', the absolute self-identity of speech in its own silence, the מכפל ('double', *qua* proportion, 40 : 20 :: 80 : 30, whose rational product is 5.333) identified, *qua* rational products, with אמת ('truth', *qua* proportion, 1 : 40 : 400 : [1], whose rational product is 10), 5.333 × 10 = 53.333, the truth of the 'word', *qua* rational products, מלתא ('word', *qua* proportion, 40 : 30 :: 400 : 1, whose rational product is 533.333) reduced to אמת ('truth' [rational product, 10]), 533.333/10 = 53.333, identically, *qua* rational products, חשך ('darkness', *qua* proportion, 8 : 300 :: 20 : [1], whose rational product is .5333) reduced to ברא ('to create' [rational product, .01]), .5333/.01 = 53.333. This 'darkness' denominated 'creating' is itself at once, *qua* rational products, פורה ('the angel of oblivion', *qua* proportion, 80 : 6 :: 200 : 5, whose rational product is 533.333) denominated אמת ('truth' [rational product, 10]), 533.333/10 = 53.333. Only then, when the Nothing-source (מאפס), 'the angel of oblivion' (פורה) denominated 'truth' (אמת), only when the 'door' (דלת) is "I" is there "I am the door." "The door is I" is the identity of "I am the door." This is the proportion, taken syntactically and *qua* rational products, .40 (אהיה): 53.333 (דלת) :: 53.333 (דלת) : .20 (אני), where the value of the first ratio, .40/53.333 = .0075, is identically the rational product of Atonement (כפור),[46] while the value of the second ratio, 53.333/.20 = 266.666, is, *qua* rational products, Double (כפול)[47] identified with Minimum (מינימום)/Triad (תלת-צליל)/Three (תלת), i.e., .05 × 5333.333 = 266.666. As in Peirce so in Altizer: the minimum, the triad, the three, doubled.[48] But now in Altizer the explicit reduction of the Atonement to real triadic duality. The rational product of this proportion is not 1, the unity of the proportion reducing the linear and rational products of 'Double' to those of 'Atonement',[49] but 2, the doubled-1 'identity' of כאוס ('chaos', *qua* proportion, 20 : 1 :: 6 : 60, whose rational product is 2). The inversion of the ratio of the respective rational products of 'Atonement' and 'Double', .05 : .0075, as it actually exists in the proportion unifying the two in substantial analogy to the proportion whose proof is the law of absolute unity,[50] the inversion and transformation of the ratio to .0075 : (.05 × 5333.333 = 266.666), where the minimum-triad-three is identified with the double, is at

[46] Cf. above, p. 370f.

[47] Ibid.

[48] Cf. above, Section III.1, Afterword 2.

[49] Cf. above, p. 371f.

[50] Cf. above, p. 370f.

once the proof-product of the proportion, .40 (אהיה) : 53.333 (דלת) :: 53.333 (דלת) : .20 (אני), .0075/266.666 = (.40 × .20)/ 53.333² = .000028125, which is the very 'identity' of אי-אפשרות ('impossibility', *qua* proportion, 1 : 10 (::) 1 : 80 :: 300 : 200 :: 6 : 400, whose rational product is .000028125). Thus the proof of this proportion which inverts and transforms the relationship of Double and Atonement appears in the form of that *impossibility* which is nevertheless itself perfectly and precisely the form of צפה ברוח הקדש ('to see in the Holy Spirit', *qua* proportion, 90 : 80 :: 5 :: [1] (::) 2 : 200 :: 6 : 8 (::) 5 : 100 :: 4 : 300, whose rational product is .000028125) the form of *knowing in the Godhead.* This proportion also identifies, *qua* rational products, "I am" (אהיה) as "*the door" identical with itself* (דלת)², *reduced to the "I,"* (אני), .40 = 53.333²/.2 = 1.4222E4, which is to say that 'I am' is identified as רקד בשתי חתנות ('to serve two masters', *qua* proportion, 200 : 100 :: 4 : [1] (::) 2 : 300 :: 400 : 10 (::) 8 : 400 :: 50 : 6 :: 400 : [1], whose rational product is 142.222) denominated ברא ('to create' [rational product, .01]), 142.222/.01 = 1.4222E4, that is, "I am," in the midst of impossibility, is reduced to the impossibility, identified by Jesus,[51] of serving two masters, of dancing at two weddings, while that impossibility is reduced to creating. 'The door' identical with itself (דלת)², the door 'opening to nowhere', identified as the "I", 'all "I"', that 53.333² = 2.8444E3 is, *qua* rational products, דומית מות ('deathly silence', *qua* proportion, 4 : 6 :: 40 : 10 :: 400 : [1] (::) 40 : 6 :: 400 : [1], whose rational product is 2.8444E6) identified with ברא ('to create' [rational product, .01]) and denominated אמת ('truth' [rational product, 10]), 2.8444E6 × .01/10 = 2.8444E3. Thus the 'I am' denominated as the impossibility of serving two masters denominated creation is identically, *qua* 'identities', אנונימיות ('anonymity', *qua* proportion, 1 : 50 :: 6 : 50 :: 10 : 40 :: 10 : 6 :: 400 : [1], whose rational product is .40), the 'I am' is 'anonymity'. This is the absolute existence of the unnamed Name/the pure "I AM"/the saying unnaming the Absolute Existent.[52] This is the absolutely pure transcendence of the voice/of the Name/

---

[51] Mt. 6:24 and Lk. 16:13.

[52] Cf. above, p. 359ff.

of the 'Who AM' of I AM, the actual self-realization of the source of I AM in its 'otherness', 'the original identity of "I AM"' 'realizing itself' 'as "I AM NOT"':

> The pure emptying of voice is the pure transcendence of voice, a transcendence which is self-transcendence, for it is the self-enactment and the self-embodiment of voice. When the voice of "I AM" realizes itself as pure transcendence, it fully empties itself of its original voice and identity. That emptying is the self-embodiment of the voice of "I AM," a self-embodiment which is a self-transcendence of the original identity of "I AM." Now the voice of "I AM" is wholly self-actualized immediacy, and an immediacy wherein voice is totally present in hearing. But this presence, this self-actualizing presence, is a self-negating presence. Only the self-negation of the original presence of the voice of "I AM" can realize that presence in the immediate actuality of hearing. Pure hearing is the total embodiment of voice, an embodiment wherein voice is the otherness of itself. That otherness is the pure otherness of the original presence of "I AM." Therefore, in that otherness, the original identity of "I AM" realizes itself as "I AM NOT."
>
> If "I AM" is the original identity of the voice of "I AM," then only "I AM NOT" can be the fully embodied identity of the voice of "I AM." Not until the fullness of the original voice and identity of "I AM" has passed into the actuality and immediacy of pure hearing can "I AM" fully realize its self-identity. That identity is a fully embodied identity, a fully self-actualized identity, wherein "I AM" is wholly other than itself.[53]

Where .40 = 'I am'/'anonymity'/the 'passing into. . . . an actual and active silence'/indeed, *qua* 'door opening to nowhere', the דרך ('passage', *qua* proportion, 4 : 200 :: 20 : [1], whose rational product is .40), and where .0666 = 'Bel'/'Not'/'Presence', then, quite precisely, the 'self-negation of the original presence of the voice of "I AM" realizing 'that presence in the immediate actuality of hearing' is .40/(.40/.0666) = .0666, which presence, *qua* absolute unity ([.40/(.40/.0666)]/.0666 = 1), is the abyss of iden-

[53] Altizer, *Self-Embodiment of God,* pp. 70–71.

tity not simply itself, the abyss of identity not identity[54] in the form of the one, the 'process of self-negation' uniting 'hearing and speech',[55] in essence NOT the act of atoning, the 'doubling of hearing and speaking into a single act'[56] whereby self-identity (a double identity, 'doubled in its innermost center') 'realizes its own identity' in the absolute act of its own doubling, in the act absolutely antithetical to the atonement, in the act of doubling absolutely its own, in its own act of doubling itself. This is the unity of the absolute NOT, this fabrication/invention of unity, which is identically the double of the atonement, the reduction of Atonement (ר/200) to Double (ל/30) grounded on the Atonement, the reduction 'radically disallowed even as it is allowed to exist'.[57]

If the logic of the beginning is such that 'in this logic different terms can be differently related but it is not possible to express inequality',[58] then the foundation of identity, the identity of foundation, is the relation of perfect equality. This שויון ('equality', *qua* proportion, 300 : 6 :: 10 : 6 :: 50 : [1], whose rational product is 4.1666E3) denominated, *qua* identity, the 'created 100' (the Absolute Proportion of Absolute Thought, *qua* Godhead [שכינה] identified with that very first spoken word of Godhead creating [יהי אור], *qua* 'identities', 15 × 666.666 = 10000 = 100/.01),[59] 4.1666E3/1E4 = .41666. This latter 'created 100'-foundation-identity/equality is the ratio of the factors of the rational product of מלכות השמים ('Kingdom of Heaven', *qua* proportion, 40 : 30 :: 20 : 6 :: 400 : [1] (::) 5 : 300 :: 40 : 10 :: 40 : [1], whose rational product is 4.740E3 [identically the rational product of כגרגר של חרדל ('like a grain of mustard', *qua* proportion, 20 : 3 :: 200 : 3 :: 200 : [1] (::) 300 : 30 (::) 8 : 200 :: 4 : 30)][60]). The factors of 4.740E3 are 44.444 and 106.666. 44.444/106.666 = .41666. The first of the factors of the 'identity' of 'Kingdom of

[54] Cf. above, p. 232.
[55] Altizer, *Self-Embodiment of God*, p. 53.
[56] Ibid.
[57] Cf. above, p. 373ff.
[58] Cf. above, Section III.1, p. 256.
[59] Cf. above, pp. 368f., and p. 373.
[60] Cf. Mt. 13:31–32 and Lk. 13:18–19.

Heaven'/'like a grain of mustard' is the rational product of the Absolute Proportion of Absolute Thought (16 : 24 :: 24 : 36) denominated ברא ('to create' [rational product, .01]), i.e., 44.444 = .444/.01.[61] The second factor, 106.666, is, *qua* rational products, אהיה אשר אהיה (*Ehyeh asher Ehyeh*, 'I AM THAT I AM', *qua* proportion, 1 : 5 :: 10 : 5 (::) 1 : 300 :: 200 : [1] (::) 1 : 5 :: 10 : 5, whose rational product is .10666) denominated ברא ('to create' [rational product, .01]) and identified with אמת ('truth' [rational product, 10]), 10(.10666/.01) = 106.666, *and* the *weighted* sum of the elements of the Absolute Proportion of Absolute Thought (the simple sum is, of course, 100), as follows: in the fourfold structure of relations in the 'logical proportion',[62] take the rational product of the *NP* proportion, 2 : 4 :: 3 : 1, viz., 1.5, and that of the *PN* proportion, 4 : 2 :: 1 : 3, viz., .666, and multiply the sum of the means of the Proportion (24 + 24 = 48) by the former (1.5 × 48 = 72), and the sum of the extremes (16 + 36 = 52) by the latter (.666 × 52 = 34.666), to arrive at 72 + 34.666 = 106.666, the weighted sum, the integrated totality of the Proportion. It is clear that the *daleth*, the door, the 53.333, is the quotient of the heedless division into two equal parts[63] of the integrated totality of the Absolute Proportion of Absolute Thought, that the 'nurse' is the product of the reduction to כאוס ('chaos' [rational product, 2]) of the creation identity of the truth identified with 'I AM THAT I AM', that the 'door' of 'the door is "I"' is 106.666/2, which division constitutes the act of subversion which (were it possible) would reduce the absolute relativity of the absolute proportion to absolute self-identity absolutely doubling itself in the form of the source of itself. But the former is irreducible to the latter except, precisely, in that form of unity which is the falsehood existing in place of creation, the 1 in place of .01, the unity which is *reducible* to nothing/the (essentially) indifferent unity, indeed, the very uniformity corresponding formally to the 'humanity the very identity of which is the

[61] Cf. above, pp. 366f.

[62] Ibid.

[63] Cf. above, p. 370, n. 30, the swastika construction. Also Peirce's triadic duality, above, pp. 287ff., and below, p. 432.

common', the uniformity corresponding to the form and substance which is the experience of absolute solitude.[64] The purely formal absolute unity of self which relates of necessity by doubling, stands as the pure formality of relative unity in place of the absolute relativity of unity now existing for the first time/the unity *irreducible* to nothing[65]/the absolutely created, for the first time essentially historical, unity/the absolutely existent unity of the beginning, unity essentially absolute, *the absolutely unconditioned nothingness of creation* after *nothing*: the absolute relativity of the unity which *is* the *absolute zero* which is absolute creation, which is existence *ex nihilo* : the circle of existence itself nothing irreducible to nothing. Nothingness is neither original nor derivative. Nothingness is always and everywhere the beginning. Nothingness is always and everywhere *ex nihilo.* Now for the first time in history it is able to be essentially comprehended that the very Nothing is created, is existence after nothing, is existence not sourced in nothing/existence absolutely existence for the first time, that the *Kingdom of Heaven, like a grain of mustard, is the Absolute Existent completely existing in the absolutely complete act of the beginning of existence.* The unity of sourceless, selfless nothingness absolutely existing in the act of creation, this death of selfhood absolutely existing for the first time as the principle of a new species of unity, as the very foundation of the unity of existence in time, as the absolutely historical foundation of the unity of existence, as the principle of the unity of the world-order, this Unity is, indeed, the Nothing the Created One Existing, the Nothingness of the One existing *ex nihilo*, the Atonement for the first time absolutely existence, such that not just is there a 'disintegration of all that interior distance separating men from men and self from self', such that not just is there a 'uniting' of the 'inner and outer realms', such that not just are the 'interior depths of inwardness . . . identical with the exterior and outer depths of every other',[66] but absolutely & essentially the disintegration of Self, the *identity for the first time* of inner & outer,

[64] Cf. above, pp. 231ff.
[65] Cf. above, Section III.1.
[66] Cf. above, pp. 220ff.

indeed, the inversion of the depth of identity/of the identity of depth, the *reversal* of the inversion of identity, such that there is not merely the 'eternal outwardizing of the within', but the within absolutely outwardized : The Existent Absolute Rationality of the One : selfless/sourceless Unity such as has never hitherto been known, as such, as rationality existing historically : an absolutely unconditioned Unity which is the *reversal* of *meta-noein*,[67] unity the absolute identity of reversal and inversion, absolutely the thought of the Living God identically the One. What now actually occurs for the first time is the absolute elimination of the body which is only body, the *absolute* elimination of the self which is only self, the absolutely pure elimination of the self itself another, the absolute elimination of the absolute self purely another.[68] For the first time the One Itself is the absolute elimination of that גוף ('body', *qua* proportion, 3 : 6 :: 80 : [1], whose rational product is 40) which is identically, *qua* rational products, מאפס אפס ('nothing out of nothing', *qua* proportion, 40 : 1 :: 80 : 60 (::) 1 : 80 :: 60 : [1], whose rational product is 40) which is not only itself but itself another. This is the elimination of the actuality common to the otherwise diverse mystical modes represented by neoplatonism, the kabbalah, and modernity:[69]

---

[67] Cf. above, pp. 243ff.

[68] Cf. above, Section II.4, passim.

[69] Cf. D. Biale, *Gershom Scholem: Kabbalah and Counter-History,* 2nd ed. (Cambridge and London 1982), pp. 58ff: "For the Neoplatonists, who emphasized the absolute abstractness of the One, the world is emanated unceasingly through a series of secondary emanations or middle levels. The thirteenth-century mystics were particularly attracted to this doctrine because it could be 'Kabbalized' by reinterpreting the emanations as sefirot. Scholem shows that this reinterpretation was actually a misinterpretation because the sefirot in the Zohar, for instance, were hypostatizations of God's attributes and therefore represented a movement within God himself rather than outside of him, as was the case with the Neoplatonic middle levels . . . . The problem with emanationist philosophy is its inability to explain why the undifferentiated One should will itself to differentiate and thereby create the diversified world. The Kabbalah's misunderstanding of Neoplatonism was productive because it allowed for the possibility of differentiation within the divine itself, pointing toward a potential solution to a philosophical problem. By playing with heretical

the elimination absolutely of self-reference in the form of the actuality of the identity of unity existing in the form of nothing-not-nothing/zero *ex nihilo*, indeed, existing in the form of nothing identified with 'to create', אפס ('nothing', *qua* proportion, 1 :

---

formulations, the Kabbalah negated philosophy, but also solved philosophical problems.

"The Kabbalah attempted to solve the problem of creation by a 'productive misunderstanding' of the traditional rabbinic and philosophical doctrine of *creatio ex nihilo.* Scholem believes that philosophy had reached a dead end with Maimonides in trying to deduce this dogma from logical principles; it only succeeded in undermining the creator God of the Bible. The Kabbalists saved *creatio ex nihilo* and God's free will in creating the world by a Gnostic reinterpretation of the concept of nothingness. Nothingness, which was endowed with ontological reality, was not the same as non-Being. While seeming to adopt philosophical language, the Kabbalists interpreted *creatio ex nihilo* to mean that God himself is the source of nothingness: *creatio ex nihilo* paradoxically means creation out of God himself. This doctrine was a synthesis of the traditional concept of *creatio ex nihilo* and the Neoplatonic notion of emanation of the world out of the essence of God, but it was based on a mythical-Gnostic view of creation of the world out of the divine abyss.

"The Kabbalists of the early thirteenth century referred to the hidden God of the Neoplatonists and Gnostics as *ayin* (nothing). They therefore solved the problem of *creatio ex nihilo* by simply equating God with nothingness. Scholem points out, however, that this solution leads to pantheism since, as in Neoplatonism, there would be no difference between God and his creation. To avoid this heresy, such Kabbalists as Azriel of Gerona and Joseph Gikatila introduced a dialectical moment into their speculations: nothingness is not identical with God, but is rather the name of his first emanation or *sefirah* called *keter* (crown). Azriel identified this 'nothingness' with the first Neoplatonic emanation, representing God's will. Since the first sefirah is itself the attribute of God's will, one cannot speak of God's emanating the first sefirah by an act of free will. Only the second sefirah can be said to be 'created' by God's free will. Since the Bible attributes free will to God as creator, it must be referring to the first sefirah and not the hidden *ain sof.* In other words, the Bible never mentions the *deus absconditus* because it is only concerned with God's free actions. The Kabbalists were thus able to avoid the potential dualism of Gnostic theology by postulating a dialectical development within God himself which they appropriated from Neoplatonic emanationism. At the same time, the notion that the process of creation must pass through a moment of absolute negation decisively separated God from his creation and thus avoided the problem of pantheism.

80 :: 60 : [1], whose rational product is .75) identified with ברא ('to create' [rational product, .01]), .75 × .01 = .0075, that is, *qua* rational products, הבורא ('the Creator', *qua* proportion, 5 : 2 :: 6 : 200 :: 1 : [1], whose rational product is .075) identified as אמת

"This dialectical logic reached its culmination in the Lurianic Kabbalah of the sixteenth century. In the thirteenth century, Azriel had mentioned that the hidden God is indifferent to his emanations and therefore the emanation of the first sefirah could not be properly called an act of creation. But Luria pushed the creative act back into the hidden God himself. God creates nothingness out of himself by contracting himself (*ẓimẓum*). Every act of creation requires a space devoid of God which can only be created by God's self-negation. Despite hints of radical determinism in parts of the Lurianic Kabbalah, Luria managed to restore God's voluntarism without abrogating the philosophical requirement for his hiddenness and ineffability. Scholem argues that the Lurianic Kabbalah was perhaps the most Gnostic and mythological Kabbalistic theory, for despite its geometrical terminology, it essentially wrote a biography of the innermost workings of the divine.

"By the infusion of myth into Judaism, the Kabbalah succeeded in preserving monotheism without sacrificing the creator God of the Bible. For the philosophers, God is a static 'unmoved mover'. The Kabbalah gave this philosophical concept life by infusing it with dialectical dynamism: '[God is conceived as he who is] absolutely living and whose hidden life is considered as a movement of the Endless out of itself and into itself.' Scholem's repeated use of the word 'dialectical' and the philosophical account he gives to the Kabbalah suggest his explicit assumption of affinities between the Kabbalah and dialectical philosophies such as Hegel's and Schelling's. Through the prism of Hegel's *Logik,* he attempts to give a coherent description of what would appear otherwise a logically paradoxical and confused theosophy. Scholem's implied comparison between the Kabbalah and Hegelian philosophy is reminiscent of Krochmal's attempt to consider the Kabbalah as one of the precursors of the modern idealism, and Scholem acknowledges that Krochmal was the only nineteenth-century Jewish thinker to recognize these parallels."

In this connection, cf. Hegel's *Science of Logic,* p. 50: ". . . logic is to be understood as the system of pure reason, as the realm of pure thought. This realm is truth as it is without veil and in its own absolute nature. It can therefore be said that this content is the exposition of God as he is in his eternal essence before the creation of nature and a finite mind." Actually, Hegel turns the Kabbalah inside out, but in so doing defines an absolutely unconditioned self-reference in which 'the non-being of the finite is the being of the absolute' (ibid., p. 443): the absolute actuality of Nothing reducible to nothing. Modernity *is* the absolute self-grounding of

('truth' [rational product, 10]), .075/10 = .0075. This nothing completely identified with creation (.0075), the truth of Creator (.0075), is precisely the rational product of Atonement.[70]

The absolute elimination of self-reference which is the actuali-

---

the ground, indeed, is the old actuality which succeeds in transcending the Kabbalah precisely insofar as it has appropriated the transcendental form of natural reason which took shape in the *sacra doctrina* of Aquinas (cf. Leahy, *Novitas Mundi*), and has done so in such a way that it appears to be as oblivious of the 'new reality' which shaped that form as the Kabbalists were of both the new reality *and* the transcendental form of natural reason. Modern thought is extra-theological at precisely the point where the Kabbalah is extra-philosophical, and, implicitly therefore, modern theology, *qua* modern, is extra-theological philosophy, is, that is, essentially philosophical and the essence of 'philosophy' (cf. above, pp. 192ff.).

As for the Kabbalah, it is now transcended in essence in the very form of thought: if it is a מסתורין ('mystery, *qua* proportion, 40 : 60 :: 400 : 6 :: 200 : 10 :: 50 : [1], whose rational product is 4.444E4), then this 'mystery' is now for the first time essentially and simply מתמטי ('mathematical', *qua* proportion, 40 : 400 :: 40 : 9 :: 10 : [1], whose rational product is 4.444), when denominated by the 'created 100' (cf. above, pp. 368f.), that is, 4.444E4/1E4 = 4.444. This essentially mathematical Kabbalah is an index of the end of the secret, of the end of the mystery, an index of the new actuality which is the *epoché* of the mystical, the epoch of epochs which is the end of the mystical. Now the very conception of a 'hidden *ain sof*', or indeed, of a *hokhmah* or "'wisdom' or primordial idea of God" (cf. G.G. Scholem, *Major Trends in Jewish Mysticism*, 3rd Ed., [New York, 1961], p. 213), the very conception of anything other than the *keter*, the very conception of the *sefirot*, the very conception of the necessity to multiply unity with reference to a source or self, this itself is seen to be merely the 'wanting of a ground' the חסר יסוד ('lack of ground', *qua* proportion, 8 : 60 :: 200 : [1] (::) 10 : 60 :: 6 : 4, whose rational product is 6.666) which, *qua* rational product, is the pure potentiality of the creative word, the word not denominated by ברא ('to create' [rational product, .01]) which as such is 'radically disallowed even as it is allowed to exist' (cf. above, p. 373). Indeed the 'absolute' *keter*, that is, כתר ('crown', *qua* proportion, 20 : 400 :: 200 : [1], whose integral product is 1.6E7), is 'absolute' אמת ('truth', *qua* proportion, 1 : 40 :: 400 : [1], whose integral product is 1.6E5) denominated ברא ('to create' [rational product, .01]), 1.6E5/.01 = 1.6E7. The absolute *keter* is the absolute truth identified as 'to create'. This is the *creation* of the 'groundless'. The existence of nothing *after* nothing: the infinite opening of nothing not zero. In this act of beginning, now for the first time thought in essence, the difference between Godhead and Creator (*ain sof* and *keter*), the overcoming of which necessitated before now

ty of Unity identically *nihil ex nihilo* perfectly coincides $1_{xy} = 1$.[71] This fact manifests itself in the logico-mathematical construction of the 'Kingdom of Heaven',[72] as follows:

מלכות השמים

40 : 30 :: 20 : 6 :: 400 : [1] (::)
5 : 300 :: 40 : 10 :: 40 : [1] (Proportion)
4.740E3 (Rational Product)
1.3824E15 (Linear Product)
6.5536E18 (Integral Product)

where, if $x = 1.6E5$,[73] the 'Kingdom of Heaven', *qua* absolute, 6.5536E18, equals:

$$\left[\left(\left[x \cdot \frac{x}{10}\right]\frac{x}{10}\right)\frac{x}{10}\right]10, \text{ or,}$$

$$\frac{x^4}{100},$$

which is the 'integral product' of a proportion (preserving the order of the elements) as follows:

---

either the *zimzum* of the Kabbalah (negative self-negation) or the *kenosis* of the absolute inversion of the abyss (positive self-negation), is transcended in the form of the absolute truth of creation/in the form of the elimination of the positive-negative/negative-positive. It is only outside of that of which there is no outside (the act, *qua* act, of beginning) that the question of pantheism and dualism arises. But for the first time the act of creation is thought absolutely. The dialectical inversion and transcendence of the question/the absolute inversion of the abyss, insofar as it refers itself to the source, is not, and is NOT. Existence remains *its own,* that which *it* is not. Nothing but its own identity separates it from existence, from the truth *par excellence* of thought which is the actuality of creation.

70 Cf. above, p. 369.

71 Cf. above, p. 278, and p. 355.

72 Cf. above, p. 381ff.

73 1.6E5 is the 'absolute' form or integral product of אמת ('truth'). Likewise it is 'absolute' אחת ('one'), 'absolute' משיח ('Messiah'), 'absolute' חשיבה ('thinking'), and 'absolute' נצח ('glory'/'perpetuity').

$$x : \frac{x}{10} :: \frac{x}{10} : x,$$

the proof of which proportion is:

$$1 = .01 \text{ or } 1 = 100,$$

and substituting y for $x/10$, the identical proof is:

$$x^2/y^2 = 1, \text{ or}$$
$$1_{xy} = 1.$$

Indeed, $x^4/100$ absolutely, the integral product, 'absolute' form of the 'Kingdom of Heaven', $= (1.6E5/\sqrt{10})^4 = 1.6E5^4/\sqrt{10^4}$, thereby making explicit the identity of the denominator as the square root of the 'created 100'. As $1_{xy} = 1$ and $1 = .01$ or $1 = 100$, so there is absolutely no uncreated identity. For the first time universal identity is essentially created identity. This fact is for the first time in history thought absolutely: *the absolute form of thought the beginning the outside of which is the essential identity of existence itself.* This is the absolutely unconditioned thought of existence for the first time. This is absolute phenomenological identity beginning: the *epoché* of the essentially mystical conception of actual identity which understood identity as either a derivation or a division from itself or from another or from both of either both itself and another or itself or another. In the form of absolute thinking unity is now identified for the first time/now-identified. In the form of absolute truth beginning, the absolute unity of existence for the first time/the absolute Messiah/Christ absolute, identity is perpetually unified in the form of the Now. In the form of perpetuity identity is for the first time the unity of the Now/the Now-Unity of the beginning. The truth of this now (the *now* which *is now actually existing*), הוה ('being', *qua* proportion, 5 : 6 :: 5 : [1], whose rational product is 4.1666 [identically the rational product of הרהור ('thought', *qua* proportion, 5 : 200 :: 5 : 6 :: 200 : [1], whose rational product is $4.1\overline{666}$) denominated by אמת ('truth' [rational product, 10]), $4.1\overline{666}/10 = .41\overline{666}$, the truth of *being now actually existing* for the first time/the truth of thought for the first time, is the relation of perfect equality which is the identity of foundation/the foundation of identity denominated the 'created 100', the absolute essence of the Absolute Proportion of Absolute Thought, which last is at once itself Godhead (שכינה) identified with that very first spoken word of Godhead creating (יהי אור), $4.1\overline{666}E3/1E4 = .41\overline{666}$.[74] The difference between the value of the rational product of the Absolute Proportion of Absolute Thought ($.\overline{444}$), and the value of the truth of *being now actually existing* for the first time/the truth identically thought for the first time/the relation of perfect equality which is the foundational identity/the Godhead identified with creation ($.41\overline{666}$), is $.02\overline{777}$ or 1/36. Denominating each of these values by this critical form of the 'proven unity of the foundation',[75] 36^{-1}, by this essence of the structure of Unity[76] which separates them, $.\overline{444}/36^{-1} = 16$ and $.41\overline{666}/36^{-1} = 15$. These latter values denominated with the value (.01) of the rational product of ברא ('to create') are related as 1500 and 1600 to 3600 as they are as 15 and 16 to 36, which is neat since then they are related both to 'absolute" אחוד ('unity'/'solidarity', *qua* proportion, 1 : 8 :: 6 : 4, whose integral product is 3.6E1) and to 'absolute' אחידות ('unity'/'uniformity', *qua* proportion, 1 : 8 :: 10 : 4 :: 6 : 400, whose integral product is 3.6E3), and in their relation to one another constitute mutually the unity of the ratio of absolute unity to absolute unity in the form of the following proportion:

$$16(00) : .\overline{444} :: 15(00) : .41\overline{666},$$

proven:

$$\frac{(66)6.\overline{666}}{(66)6.\overline{666}} = 1,$$

which proof is the form of the absolute unity of the word not

[74] Cf. above, pp. 373f.

[75] Cf. above, Section III.1, pp. 272ff.

[76] Cf. below, Section IV.2, pp. 509f.

reduced to creation ($6.\overline{666}$)[77]/the Bel/Not/Presence denominated creation[78]/the composite elements of a symbolic 'well-being'[79]/the absence of foundation ('the wanting of a ground'),[80] and, *qua* identification as 'created unity' (1/.01), the form of the absolute unity of the 'very first word spoken of Godhead creating', "Let there be light" ($666.\overline{666}$).[81] The rational product of this proportion is 1.296E7 (3600^2) which is identically 'absolute' יחסיות ('relativity', *qua* proportion, 10 : 8 :: 60 : 10 :: 6 : 400, whose integral product is 1.296E7), which 'absolute' relativity is 'absolute' הקדוש ברוך הוא ('the Holy One blessed be He', *qua* proportion, 5 : 100 :: 4 : 6 :: 300 : [1] (::) 2 : 200 :: 6 : 20 (::) 5 : 6 :: 1 : [1], whose integral product is 1.296E11) denominated the 'created 100', 1.296E11/1E4 = 1.296E7. Such is the precision with which the Absolute Holy One denominated Godhead identical with Creation/the 'created 100' manifests itself as Absolute Relativity, as the absolutely unconditioned unity which is $1 = 1_{xy}$. The foundation/Absolute Relativity is the Absolute Holy One identified as the 'created 100'. The foundation/Absolute Relativity is the Absolute Holy One identified as יי ('God', *qua* proportion, 10 : 10, whose integral product is 100) or יה ('God', *qua* proportion, 10 : 5, whose integral product is 100) whose identity is ברא ('to create' [rational product, .01]), 1.296E11/(100/.01) = 1.296E7. The Absolute Holy One now for the first time in history in the form of the Act of Creation/in the form of Foundation Itself is itself at once the absolute unity of Nothingness *ex nihilo.* The One for the first time absolutely the Lord-in-the-act-of-creation. The One for the first time: nothing but the beginning of existence. Now *qua* 'identities' ברא ('to create' [rational product, .01]) is בתולי ('virginal', *qua* proportion, 2 : 400 :: 6 : 30 :: 10 : [1], whose rational product is .01), and 'absolute' כפור ('Atonement' [integral product, 1.44E4]) is 'absolute' בתולי ('virginal' [integral

[77] Cf. above, pp. 372f.

[78] Ibid.

[79] Ibid.

[80] Cf. above, p. 384, n. 69.

[81] Cf. above, pp. 372f.

product, 1.44E4]) and 'absolute' בתולים ('virginity', *qua* proportion, 2 : 400 :: 6 : 30 :: 10 : 40, whose integral product is 1.44E4). Indeed, 'absolute' הקדוש ברוך הוא ('the Holy One blessed be He' [integral product, 1.296E11]) identified with 'absolute' אמת ('truth' [integral product, 1.6E5])/'absolute' אחת ('one')/'absolute' משיח ('Messiah')/'absolute' חשיבה ('thinking')/'absolute' נצח ('glory'/'perpetuity')[82] reduced to ברא ('to create' [rational product, .01]) is 'absolute' קרום הבתולים ('virginal membrane', *qua* proportion, 100 : 200 :: 6 : 40 (::) 5 : 2 :: 400 : 6 :: 30 : 10 :: 40 : [1], whose integral product is 2.0736E18), 1.296E11 × 1.6E5/.01 = 2.0736E18, the Absolute Hymen/the Hymen Intact,[83] which, reduced to the 'created

[82] Cf. above, p. 388, n. 73.

[83] Cf. above, pp. 150ff. Also the following from Derrida's *Dissemination,* trans. B. Johnson (Chicago, 1981), pp. 261ff.: "If there is text, if the hymen constitutes itself as a textual trace, if it always leaves something behind, it is because its undecidability cuts it off from (prevents it from depending on) every—and hence *any*—signified, whether antithetic or synthetic. Its textuality would not be irreducible if, through the necessities of its functioning, it did not do without (deprivation and/or independence: the hymen is the structure of *and/or,* between *and* and *or*) its refill of signified, in the movement through which it leaps from one to another. Thus, strictly speaking, it is not a true sign or 'signifier.' And since everything that (becomes) traces owes this to the propagation-structure of the hymen, a text is never truly made up of 'signs' or 'signifiers'. (This, of course, has not prevented us from using the word 'signifier' for the sake of convenience, in order to designate, within the former code, that facet of the trace that cuts itself off from meaning or from the signified.)

"And now we must attempt to write the word *dissemination.*

"And to explain, with Mallarmé's text, why one is always at some pains to follow.

"If there is thus no thematic unity or overall meaning to reappropriate beyond the textual instances, no total message located in some imaginary order, intentionality, or lived experience, then the text is no longer the expression or representation (felicitous or otherwise) of any *truth* that would come to diffract or assemble itself in the polysemy of literature. It is this hermeneutic concept of *polysemy* that must be replaced by *dissemination.*

"According to the structure of supplementarity, what is added is thus always a blank or a fold: the fact of addition gives way to a kind of multiple division or subtraction that enriches itself with zeros as it races breathless

100', is identically the 'absolute' תמצית ('essence', *qua* proportion, 400 : 40 :: 90 : 10 :: 400 : [1], whose integral product is 2.0736E14), 2.0736E18/1E4 = 2.0736E14. This Absolute Essence is, in turn, identically 'absolute' לדת בתולים ('Virgin

---

ly toward the infinite. 'More' and 'less' are only separated/united by the infinitesimal inconsistency, the next-to-nothing of the hymen. This play of the integral unit excrescent with zeros, 'sums, by the hundreds and beyond,' is demonstrated by Mallarmé under the title of *Or* [this word is both a noun signifying 'Gold' and a conjunction marking a turning point in an argument.—Trans.] (expert as he was in alloying—in the literal alchemy of such an ironic, precious, and overinflated signifier—the sensible, phonetic, graphic, economic, logical, and syntactical virtues of this stone in which the 'two ways, in all, in which our need is bifurcated: esthetics on the one hand and also political economy' intersect ([Mallarmé, *Oeuvres complètes*] p. 399; cf. also p. 656)):

"'*OR*

. . . The currency, that engine of terrible precision, clean to the conscience, smooth to consciousness, loses even a meaning. . . . a notion of what sums, by the hundreds and beyond, can be . . . . The inability of numbers, whatever their grandiloquence, to translate, here arises from a case; one searches, with the indication that, when a number is raised and goes out of reach toward the improbable, it inscribes more and more zeros: signifying that its total is spiritually equivalent to nothing, almost.'

"Why does this almost-nothing lose the glint of a phenomenon? Why is there no phenomenology of the hymen? Because the antre in which it folds back, as little in order to conceal itself as in order to denude itself, is also an abyss. In the recoiling of the blank upon the blank, the blank colors itself, becomes—for itself, of itself, affecting itself ad infinitum—its own colorless, ever more invisible, ground. Not that it is out of reach, like the phenomenological horizon of perception, but that, in the act of inscribing itself on itself indefinitely, mark upon mark, it multiplies and complicates its text, a text within a text, a margin in a mark, the one indefinitely repeated within the other: an abyss.

"Now [*Or*], isn't it precisely such writing *en abyme* that thematic criticism—and no doubt criticism as such—can never, to the letter, account for? The abyss will never have the glint of a phenomenon because it becomes black. Or white. The one and/or the other in the squaring of writing."

But for the first time the one *is* the other absolutely. The / is absolute. It is not a question of black *and* white. It is not a question of black *or* white. (Nor is it a question of white 'comprehending itself' as black 'relative to what was once manifest and real' as white, as in the absolute fragmentation of identity which is the absolute embodiment of either/or [cf. above, pp. 226ff].) In the absolute hymen, the absolute /, the one is absolutely

Birth', *qua* proportion, 30 : 4 :: 400 : [1] (::) 2 : 400 :: 6 : 30 :: 10 : 40, whose integral product is 2.0736E12), denominated ברא ('to create' [rational product, .01]), 2.0736E12/.01 = 2.0736E14. The 'absolute' קרום הבתולים ('hymen' [integral

---

the other, black is absolutely white. Not only is there no *and,* not simply has the self changed into the other (as in the absolute inversion of the abyss), but there is no *or,* no looking back over one's shoulder into the future. In the absolute relativity of the One there is no room for actual incompleteness, whether it be the incompleteness which wills to be itself in the form of the 'Tower of Babel'/the 'the decapitated' column of numbers of a Kabbalah which 'reduced to its textuality, to its numerous plurivocality, absolutely disseminated . . . evinces a kind of atheism, which read in a certain way—or just simply *read*—it has doubtless always carried within it' (cf. *Dissemination,* pp. 340ff. [one is not surprised to discover that the toppled 'capital' of this column—כותרת ('capital', *qua* proportion, 20 : 6 :: 400 : 200 :: 400 : [1], whose rational product is 2.666E3)—is, *qua* rational products, identically תורה ('Torah' [rational product, 2.666E3]) (cf. above, p. 362)]), or whether it be the incompleteness which wills the other, which wills the existence of a 'new humanity'. In the work of the One there is no room for an actual incompleteness, whether that of the 'bottomless plurality' which 'is not lived as negativity, with any nostalgia for lost unity' (*Dissemination,* pp. 340ff.), or that which is inherent in the 'abyss of identity not identity' (cf. above, p. 232), which anonymous equivocality is lived as the passionate 'affirmation' of 'our own interior and individual dissolution as the way to the realization of our own full and universal humanity' (cf. above, p. 226), a realization made possible, according to modernity's reversal of the Kabbalah (cf. above, p. 384, n. 69), by the 'contraction of a former identity and voice'. In the work of the One, the Hymen is Absolute, the / is absolute. Indeed, this Absolute Hymen, קרום הבתולים ('virginal membrane' [integral product, 2.0736E18]) denominated ברא ('to create' [rational product, .01]) is identically אמר לשחור לבן ('what it is to prove that black is white', *qua* proportion, 1 : 40 :: 200 : [1] (::) 30 : 300 :: 8 : 6 :: 200 : [1] (::) 30 : 2 :: 50 : [1], whose integral product is 2.0736E20), 2.0736E18/.01 = 2.0736E20. The rational product of this אמר לשחור לבן is 1E5, the 'created 100' identical with אמת('truth' [rational product, 10]), 1E4 × 10. For the first time in history black is white is thought: the one definitely repeating the other for the first time, *qua* absolute existent. The absolute existent *is* the phenomenology of the hymen: the phenomenological hymen absolutely exists for the first time. There is for the first time no hymen 'next-to-nothing', no unity 'excrescent with zeros'. Unity is absolutely zero *ex nihilo* (cf. above, Section III.1), and zeros function in the absolute relativity of a unity in which if $x = 0$, $0 \neq$ nothing, or, 'zero equals nothing' is not the hymen. Zero, not equal to *any* nothing whatsoever, is the specific measure of cre-

product, 2.0736E18]) is 'absolute' לדת בתולים ('Virgin Birth' [integral product, 2.0736E12]) identified with 'absolute' כתיבה ('writing' [integral product, 1E6]),[84] 2.0736E12 × 1E6 = 2.0736E18.

---

ation transcending the conjunctive 'gold' (*Or*) which, *qua* total of the 'two ways', approximates *absolutely* to nothing. No longer is (any)number, in 'its total', 'spiritually equivalent to nothing, almost'. The *antre* itself, which otherwise is 'also an abyss' in which the 'glint of a phenomenon' is lost because it becomes black and/or white, this *antre* itself/this absolute 'cavern', 'absolute' מערה ('cavern', *qua* proportion, 40 : 70 :: 200 : 5, whose integral product is 6.4E7), when reduced to the 'created 100', is 'absolute' פז('gold'/'sparkling', *qua* ratio, 80 : 7, whose integral product is 6.4E3), 6.4E7/1E4 = 6.4E3, and *qua* rational products מערה ('cavern' [rational product, 22.857142]) is just פז ('gold'/'sparkling' [rational product, 11.428571]) identified with כאוס ('chaos' [rational product, 2]), 11.428571 × 2 = 22.857142. If the incompleteness which wills itself never has the 'glint of a phenomenon' in the abyss which the *antre* also is, while the incompleteness which wills the other is 'given glimpses of a new world in the very advent of a new and universal humanity' (cf. above, p. 227), then, the thinking now occurring for the first time perceives that, *qua* 'absolutes', חטף מבט ('to catch a glimpse', *qua* proportion, 8 : 9 :: 80 : [1] (::) 40 : 2 :: 9 : [1], whose integral product is 5.308416E10) is the *transcendence of dissemination,* 'to catch a glimpse' itself transcends 'dissemination' itself, which is to say that the radical element/square root of 'absolute' חטף מבט is 'absolute' פזור ('dissemination', *qua* proportion, 80 : 7 :: 6 : 200, whose integral product is 2.304E5), √5.308416E10 = 2.304E5 (cf. the relation of Altizer to Derrida, above, Section II.4). 'To catch a glimpse' absolutely transcending absolute dissemination is itself at once the 'absolute' form of the Absolute Proportion of Absolute Thought (16 : 24 :: 24 : 36, whose integral product is 1.47456E5) identified with 'absolute' יחס ('proportion', *qua* proportion, 10 : 8 :: 60 : [1], whose integral product is 3.6E5), 1.47456E5 × 3.6E5 = 5.308416E10, in which event it is thought transparently for the first time in history, or it itself is the 'absolute' form of the Absolute Proportion of Absolute Thought identified with 'absolute' יחידות ('solitude', *qua* proportion, 10 : 8 :: 10 : 4 :: 6 : 400, whose integral product is likewise 3.6E5) 1.47456E5 × 3.6E5 = 5.308416E10, in which event it is 'the advent of a new humanity' neither 'definable' nor 'conceivable' (ibid.). In the first case the 'identity' of יחס ('proportion' [rational product, 75]) is אפס ('nothing' [rational product, .75]) denominated ברא ('to create' [rational product, .01]), .75/.01 = 75; in the second case the 'identity' of יחידות ('solitude' [rational product, .046875]) is the inverse of the identification of אהיה ('I Am' [rational product, .40]) and דלת ('door' [rational product, 53.333]), $(.40 \times 53.333)^{-1}$ = .046875. *Qua* 'identities',

Absolute Hymen (2.0736E18) is to the Absolute Kingdom of Heaven (6.5536E18) as 1 : 3.160493827, or in terms of the minimum integral root of 6.5536E18 where both elements of the ratio are greater than 1, as 1.265625 : 4:

---

the identification of יחס ('proportion') with יחידות ('solitude') is the reduction of אמר לשחור לבן ('what it is to prove that black is white' [rational product, 1E5]) denominated ברא ('to create' [rational product, .01]) to דומית מות ('deathly silence' [rational product, 2.8444E6]), 75 × .046875 = (1E5/.01)/2.8444E6.

Now, 'absolute' יחס ('proportion' [integral product, 3.6E5]), distinguished *qua* identity from Absolute Solitude, is 'absolute' פזור ('dissemination' [integral product, 2.304E5 (at once itself 'absolute' חבור ['writing', *qua* proportion, 8 : 2 :: 6 : 200, whose integral product is 2.304E3] denominated ברא ['to create' (rational product, .01)], 2.304E3/.01 = 2.304E5) identified with the 'created 100' and denominated 'absolute' פז ('gold'/'sparkling' [integral product, 6.4E3]), 2.304E5 × 1E4/6.4E3 = 3.6E5. This Absolute Proportion (3.6E5), the Absolute Sparkling Identity of Absolute Dissemination, identified with 'absolute' תהום ('depth' [the 'deep' of Genesis 1:2], *qua* proportion, 400 : 5 :: 6 : 40, whose integral product is 5.76E6) is 'absolute' התפשטות ('expansion', *qua* proportion, 5 : 400 :: 80 : 300 :: 9 : 6 :: 400 : [1], whose integral product is 2.0736E12), 3.6E5 × 5.76E6 = 2.0736E12. This absolute sparkling of absolute dissemination identified with depth, this absolute golden dissemination of the waters of the Creation, this absolute expansion is itself (2.0736E12) at once 'absolute' לדת בתולים ('Virgin Birth [integral product, 2.0736E12 (cf., p. 395)]): the Virgin Birth thought is at once itself the Absolute Expansion of Identity. This is the sparkling dissemination of the abyss of thought/the absolute scattering of the sparkling depth of creation. This is the Gold Itself exiled from the abyss: the absolute brilliance of the propagation of identity *ex abysso*: the new act of creation *now*.

'Absolute' תהום ('depth' [the 'deep' of Genesis 1:2] [integral product, 5.76E6]) denominated ברא ('to create' [rational product, .01]) is 'absolute' אנושיות ('humanity', *qua* proportion, 1 : 50 :: 6 : 300 :: 10 : 6 :: 400 : [1], whose integral product is 5.76E8), 5.76E6/.01 = 5.76E8, at once itself 'absolute' חלל ('void', *qua* proportion, 8 : 30 :: 30 : [1], whose integral product is 5.76E4) identified with the 'created 100', with 'Godhead identified with the first word spoken of Godhead creating', 5.76E4 × 1E4 = 5.76E8. In turn, this absolute humanity/absolute void at once the 'created 100', denominated ברא ('to create' [rational product, .01]), is 'absolute' התגשמות ('incarnation', *qua* proportion, 5 : 400 :: 3 : 300 :: 40 : 6 :: 400 : [1], whose integral product is 5.76E10), 5.76E8/.01 = 5.76E10. This Absolute Incarnation is 'absolute' מאור ('light', *qua* proportion, 40 : 1 :: 6 : 200, whose integral product is 5.76E4 [identically 'absolute' חלל ('void')])

1.265625 : 4 :: 2.0736E18 : 6.5536E18,

the proven unity of which is:

---

identified with 'absolute' כתיבה ('writing', *qua* proportion, 20 : 400 :: 10 : 2 :: 5 : [1], whose integral product is 1E6), 5.76E4 × 1E6 = 5.76E10. Absolute Writing identified with Absolute Light/Absolute Void is Absolute Humanity identified as 'to create', Absolute Incarnation, Absolute Depth the Godhead identified with the First Word of Creation. 'Absolute' התגשמות ('incarnation') identified with 'absolute' כתיבה ('writing') is 'absolute' שארית ('remnant', *qua* proportion, 300 : 1 :: 200 : 10 :: 400 : [1], whose integral product is 5.76E14) denominated ברא ('to create' [rational product, .01]), 5.76E10 × 1E6 = 5.76E16. This Absolute Remnant/Absolute Remainder (the remainder without remainder/the remnant without a source/the relic without a past/the rest without relation) identified as 'to create' is the 1/36th part (cf. above, p. 390) of Absolute Hymen, 5.76E16/.02777 = 2.0736E18. (Cf. above, pp. 272f., the number identical with the totality.) 'Absolute' שארית ('remnant') denominated 'absolute' תופעה ('appearance', *qua* proportion, 400 : 6 :: 80 : 70 :: 5 : [1], whose integral product is 2.56E10) is 'absolute' לבן ('white', *qua* proportion, 30 : 2 :: 50 : [1], whose integral product is 2.25E6), 5.76E16/ 2.56E10 = 2.25E6. (*Qua* identities, לבן ['white' (rational product, 750)] is אמת ['truth' (rational product, 10)] identified with יחס ['proportion' (rational product, 75)], 750 = 75 × 10.) 'Absolute' לבן ('white'), in turn, is the 1/36th part of 'absolute צדק ('righteousness', *qua* proportion, 90 : 4 :: 100 : [1], whose integral product is 8.1E7), 2.25E6/.02777 = 8.1E7. Absolute White the Absolute Appearance of the Absolute Remnant identically 'to create': the 1/36th part, *qua* substance and form, identical with Absolute Righteousness, the absolute effect, in turn, of the 1/36th part, *qua* substance and form, identical with the Absolute Hymen. This is the Absolute Hymen identical with White. The Absolute Hymen identical with Black is the Absolute Hymen (2.0736E18) denominated the 'created 100', 2.0736E18/1E4 = 2.0736E14 (= Absolute Essence [cf. the text, immediately following]), reduced to Absolute Cavern/Absolute *antre* (6.4E7), 2.0736E14/6.4E7 = 3.24E6, which is 'absolute' שחור ('black', *qua* proportion, 300 : 8 :: 6 : 200, whose integral product is 3.24E6). The reduction of 'absolute' שחור ('black') to 'absolute' לבן ('white'), identified with the 'created 100', is Absolute Atonement (1.44E4)/Absolute Virginity (1.44E4) and 'absolute' הזדהות ('identification', *qua* proportion, 5 : 7 :: 4 : 5 :: 6 : 400, whose integral product is 1.44E4),(3.24E6/2.25E6) × 1E4 = 1.44E4.

Finally, 'absolute' תופעה ('appearance' [integral product, 2.56E10]) denominated ברא ('to create' [rational product, .01]) is 'absolute' פענח ('deciphering', *qua* proportion, 80 : 70 :: 50 : 8, whose integral product is

8.2944E18/8.2944E18 = 1,

where 8.2944E18 is 'absolute' יהוה מלך-ישראל ('Yahweh King of Israel' [Is. 44:6], *qua* proportion, 10 : 5 :: 6 : 5 (::) 40 : 30 :: 20 : [1] (::) 10 : 300 :: 200 : 1 :: 30 : [1], whose integral product is 8.2944E18), and 'absolute' אבנא די-מחת לצלמא ('the stone that smote the image' [Dn. 2:35], *qua* proportion, 1 : 2 :: 50 : 1 (::) 4 : 10 (::) 40 : 8 :: 400 : [1] (::) 30 : 90 :: 30 : 40 :: 1 : [1], whose integral product is 8.2944E18). Let there be 'absolute' חק ('limit', *qua* ratio, 8 : 100, whose integral product is 64) or 'absolute' חג ('to describe a boundary'/'move in a circle', *qua* ratio, 8 : 3, whose integral product is 64 [possessing the identical integral and rational products (64 and 2.$\overline{666}$) as the *minimum* proportion, 4 : 1 :: 2 : 3][85]), and let this absolute limit denominate both Absolute Hymen and Absolute Kingdom of Heaven to yield, respectively, 'absolute' ראויים לגנוי ('the damned', *qua* proportion, 200 : 1 :: 6 : 10 :: 10 : 40 (::) 30 : 3 :: 50 : 6 :: 10 : [1], whose integral product is 3.24E16), 2.0736E17/64 = 3.24E16,[86] and 'absolute' תחית המתים ('the resurrection of the dead, *qua* proportion, 400 : 8 :: 10 : 400 (::) 5 : 40 :: 400 : 10 : 40 : [1], whose integral product is 1.024E17), 6.5536E18/64 = 1.024E17.[87] Then the following analogous proportion is true of Absolute Hymen and

---

1.6E7 [identically 'absolute' אמת ('truth' [integral product, 1.6E5]) denominated ברא ('to create' [rational product, .01])]) identified with 'absolute' נסח ('text', *qua* proportion, 50 : 60 :: 8 : [1], whose integral product is 1.6E5 [identically Absolute Truth/Absolute Messiah/Absolute Thinking (cf. above, p. 392)]), 2.56E12 = 1.6E7 × 1.6E5. This Absolute Deciphering identified with Absolute Text is at once itself 'absolute' פענך כתב יד ('to decipher a manuscript', *qua* proportion, 80 : 70 :: 50 : 8 (::) 20 : 400 :: 2 : [1] (::) 10 : 4, whose integral product is 2.56E12).

[84] Cf. above, p. 392, n. 83.

[85] Cf. above, pp. 266ff.

[86] Cf. 'absolute' יורש גיהנום ('one who deserves hell' [integral product, 3.24E10]) which, when denominated by the 'created 100', 3.24E10/1E4 = 3.24E6, absolute שחור ('darkness' [integral product, 3.24E6 (cf. above, p. 392, n. 83)]) and absolute שאול ('hell', *qua* proportion, 300 : 1 :: 6 : 30, whose integral product is 3.24E6).

[87] Cf. 'absolute' רוח המת ('saint', *qua* proportion, 200 : 6 :: 8 : [1] (::) 5 : 40 :: 400 : [1], whose integral product is 1.024E13).

Absolute Kingdom of Heaven when each is denominated by 'absolute limit': Absolute Damned is to Absolute Resurrection of the Dead as 1.265625 : 4:

1.265625 : 4 :: 3.24E16 : 1.024E17,

the proven unity of which is:

1.296E17/1.296E17 = 1,

where 1.296E17 is 'absolute' הבתולה הקדושה ('Holy Virgin', *qua* proportion, 5 : 2 :: 400 : 6 :: 30 : 5 (::) 5 : 100 :: 4 : 6 :: 300 : 5, whose integral product is 1.296E17). But then 'absolute' יהוה מלך-ישראל ('Yahweh King of Israel' [integral product, 8.2944E18]) denominated 'absolute' חק ('limit' [integral product, 64]) or 'absolute' חג ('to describe a boundary'/'to move in a circle' [integral product, 64]) is Absolute Holy Virgin: the Absolute Holy Virgin identified with Absolute Limit/Absolute Describing of the Boundary/Absolutely Moving in a Circle is Absolute Yahweh King of Israel. Now, let there be a proportion incorporating in one proportion both Absolute Damned and Absolute Resurrection of the Dead and Absolute Hymen and Absolute Kingdom of Heaven, in a straightforward 1 : 2 :: 3 : 4 order,[88] as follows:

Damned : Resurrection of the Dead :: Hymen : Kingdom of Heaven
3.24E16 : 1.024E17 :: 2.0736E18 : 6.5536E18.

The proven unity of this proportion is:

2.1233664E35/2.1233664E35 = 1,

[88] The 'logical order' and the order which is its 'substantive equivalent' (cf. above, Section III.1, pp. 273ff.) excluded here since they merely produce in the proof-product the square of the original ratio of the two sets of terms.

where 2.1233664E35 is 'absolute' התמלאות תקוותיו ('fulfillment of one's hopes', *qua* proportion, 5 : 400 :: 40 : 30 :: 1 : 6 :: 400 : [1] (::) 400 : 100 :: 6 : 6 :: 400 : 10 :: 6 : [1], whose integral product is 2.1233664E23) identified with 'absolute' קץ הימין ('the end of days'/'the days of the Messiah', *qua* proportion, 100 : 90 (::) 5 : 10 :: 40 : 10 :: 50 : [1], whose integral product is 1E12), 2.1233664E35 = 2.1233664E23 × 1E12. In the proof-product of this 1 : 2 :: 3 : 4 ordered proportion there is a splicing or dovetailing of the substantial elements of the those proportions whose proof-products are, respectively, the absolute unities of 'absolute' יהוה מלך-ישראל ('Yahweh King of Israel') and 'absolute' הבתולה הקדושה ('Holy Virgin'). The proof-product of this proportion is the subjective and thoroughly generic absolute unity of 'the days of the Messiah' identified with 'the fulfillment of one's hopes'. But let the proportion read in the minimum-order, 4 : 1 :: 2 : 3, in the order of the proportion whose integral and rational products are identically those of 'absolute' חג ('to describe a boundary'/'move in a circle' [integral product, 64; rational product, 2.666]),[89] thusly:

Kingdom of Heaven : Damned :: Resurrection of the Dead : Hymen
6.5536E18 : 3.24E16 :: 1.024E17 : 2.0736E18.

The proven unity of this proportion is the essentially historical and perfectly specific:

1.358954496E37/3.31776E33 = 4.096E3,

where 1.358954496E37 is 'absolute' והיה באחרית הימים נכון יהיה הר בית ה׳ בראש ההרים ('In the last days the mountain of Yahweh's house will rise higher than the mountains' [Is. 2:2], *qua* proportion, 6 : 5 :: 10 : 5 (::) 2 : 1 :: 8 : 200 :: 10 : 400 (::) 5 : 10 :: 40 : 10 :: 40 : [1] (::) 50 : 20 :: 6 : 50 (::) 10 : 5 :: 10 : 5 (::) 5 : 200 (::) 2 : 10 ::

[89] Cf. above, Section III.1. pp. 266ff. The minimum order 4–1–2–3 is precisely the moving in a circle which *is* the fourfold revolution of the 'cornerstone' which *is* the 'foundation'.

400 : [1] (::) 5000 : [1] (::) 2 : 200 :: 1 : 300 (::) 5 : 5 :: 200 : 10 :: 40 : [1], whose integral product is 1.358954496E49) denominated 'absolute' רציונלי ('rational', *qua* proportion, 200 : 90 :: 10 : 6 :: 50 : 30 :: 10 : [1], whose integral product is 1E12),[90] 1.358954496E49/ 1E12 = 1.358954496E37, and this absolute prophecy, denominated 'absolute rational', is further denominated 3.31776E33, which is 'absolute' מטריאליסם היסטורי ('historical materialism', *qua* proportion, 40 : 9 :: 200 : 10 :: 1 : 30 :: 10 : 60 :: 40 : [1] (::) 5 : 10 :: 60 : 9 :: 6 : 200 :: 10 : [1], whose integral product is 3.31776E21) identical with 'absolute' רציונלי ('rational' [integral product, 1E12 (*identically*, *qua* 'absolute', קץ הימין ['the end of days'/'the days of the Messiah' (integral product, 1E12)])]), 3.31776E21 × 1E12 = 3.31776E33, so that the proven unity of this minimum-order proportion, the quotient which is the absolute word of Isaiah identified as absolutely rational denominated absolutely rational historical materialism, i.e., denominated *essentially* historical materialism,[91] the quotient at once itself the product of the substantial elements of the Yahweh-King-of-Israel proportion denominated by the product of the substantial elements of the Holy-Virgin proportion, this quotient is 'absolute' חלחל ('to penetrate', *qua* proportion, 8 : 30 :: 8 : 30, whose integral product is 4.096E3), 'absolute penetration', at once itself 'absolute' ἡ ἀγάπη ('agape'/'unconditioned love', *qua* proportion, 8 : 1 (::) 1 : 3 :: 1 : 80 :: 8 : [1], whose integral product is 4.096E3).[92] The absolutely logical foundation of

---

90 The rational product of רציונלי ('rational') is the whole number equivalent of the 'extreme and mean' rational division of the line, ϕ^{-1}, denominated ברא ('to create' [rational product, .01]), that is, the whole number equivalent of $\phi^{-1}/.01 = 1.618033989^{-1}/.01$, $1.62^{-1}/.01$.

91 Cf. above, Sections I and II, passim, for the distinction of inessentially historical materialism from materialism essentially historical.

92 The square root of 'absolute' והיה באחרית הימים נכון יהיה הר בית הי בראש ההרים ('in the last days the mountain of Yahweh's house will rise higher than the mountains' [Is. 2:2] [integral product, 1.358954496E49]) is 'absolute' חלחולת ('to penetrate', *qua* proportion, 8 : 30 :: 8 : 6 :: 30 : 400, whose integral product is 3.6864E6) times 'absolute' תורת האנליסה ('analysis', *qua* proportion, 400 : 6 :: 200 : 400 (::) 5 : 1 :: 50 : 30 :: 10 : 60 :: 5 : [1], whose integral product is 1E18), $\sqrt{1.358954496E49} = 3.6864E6 \times 1E18 = 3.6864E24$.

the structure of this 'absolute penetration'/'absolute' agape is clearly evident if the minimum-order proportion is reduced to the extended base factors of its elements, respectively, 65536, 324, 1024, and 20736, and the rational relationship of each of these elements to the 16th root of 65536, 2, is substituted in the proportion, as follows:

$$\begin{aligned} \textit{Kingdom of Heaven} : \textit{Damned} &:: \textit{Resurrection of the Dead} : \textit{Hymen} \\ 6.5536\text{E}18 : 3.24\text{E}16 &:: 1.024\text{E}17 : 2.0736\text{E}18, \\ 65536 : 324 &:: 1024 : 20736, \\ (1 \cdot 2^{16}) : (.31640625 \cdot 2^{10}) &:: (1 \cdot 2^{10}) : (.31640625 \cdot 2^{16}), \end{aligned}$$

where, substituting x for 1 and y for .31640625, v for 2^{10}, and w for 2^{16}, its fundamental constitution is manifested as:

$$xw : yv :: xv : yw,$$

which proven is *formally*:

$$w^2/v^2 = 1, \text{ or,}$$

$$1_{wv} = 1,$$

unity identified as absolutely relative unity, identically the proof-form of the fundamental structure of the Absolute Kingdom of Heaven, as well as of the minimum proportion itself,[93] at once the absolute identity of the within and the without of the Kingdom of Heaven, i.e., of the minimum-structure which is the within of the Kingdom and of the Kingdom *qua* element in the midst of the minimum elements, the *logos katholikos*, catholicological identity, here with a special specificity in the form $w^2/v^2 = 1$, that is, $65536^2/1024^2 = 64^2 = 4096$, where, *qua* extended base factors, the absolute unity of the Absolute Kingdom of Heaven denominated the absolute unity of the Abso-

[93] Cf. above, pp. 277f., pp. 388ff.

lute Resurrection of the Dead (Absolute Damned and Absolute Hymen having vanished) is the absolute unity of Absolute Limit/the absolute unity of Absolute To Describe a Boundary/ the absolute unity of Absolute To Move In A Circle which *is* Absolute Penetration/Absolute Agape. Here it is clear that the *absolute penetration*, the *absolute agape* which is absolutely selfless love of the other, which is for the first time in history the absolute unity of Yahweh King of Israel denominated the absolute unity of Holy Virgin, effectively, and precisely as the unification of their separate proofs, *that this absolute penetration/absolute unconditioned love is the absolute unity of absolutely moving in a circle/the absolute unity of the minimum/the absolute unity of logic*, and as such, the perfect leaving behind of the merely formal circle itself of modernity, the perfect leaving behind of the mystical-modern circle of eternity which 'itself in its totality forms a cycle returning upon itself, wherein the first is *also* the last, and the last first'.[94] The catholicological

[94] This last from Hegel's *Science of Logic* as quoted by T. J. J. Altizer, *The New Apocalypse: The Radical Christian Vision of William Blake* (Michigan, 1967), pp. 184ff., in this context: "While for Sankara it can only be through a great cosmic ignorance that God and the world can be known as moving and existing out of the depths of Brahman-Atman, Eckhart's God is in Himself a living *process,* not a static Being, who moves forward out of the Godhead:

> God is the wheel rolling out of itself, which rolling on, not rolling back, reaches its first position again. That it rolls from inward, outward and inward again is of deep significance. God is, in Himself, tremendous life movement. Out of undifferentiated unity He enters into the multiplicity of personal life and persons, in whom the world and therewith the multiplicity of the world is contained. Out of this He returns, back into the eternal original unity. "The river flows into itself." But it is not an error to be corrected in Him, that He is eternally going out from and entering "into" Himself; it is a fact that has meaning and value—as the expression of life manifesting its potentiality and fullness. The issuing forth becomes itself the goal again of that process enriched by the course of its circuit. [R. Otto]

Therefore, Eckhart's is a dynamic, as opposed to a static, mysticism; it celebrates the living process of God as a manifestation of ultimate Reality, and consequently it culminates in an active ethical life that engages in a positive confrontation with the world. . . . the ground of this deeply Christ-

foundation now actually existing for the first time precludes the principle that the principle is not the principle, the principle that the 'result is the principle', the retrospective anticipation of the result, the purely formal, symbolic circle/cycle in

---

ian form of mysticism is an eschatological vision of the final manifestation of God as the end and goal of an eternal cosmic process. . . .

"Throughout history the circle has been the primary symbol of eternity in both East and West, and it should not surprise us that it was reborn in Nietzsche's vision of Eternal Recurrence, just as it had previously come to occupy the center of the 'systems' of Blake and Hegel. When Albion contracts his infinite senses, he beholds multitude, or, expanding, he beholds as one; 'As One Man all the Universal Family, and that One Man we call Jesus the Christ' (J[erusalem] 38:17 ff.). And this cosmic movement of Albion is an expression of a forward if circular movement of Eternity:

> What is Above is Within, or every-thing in Eternity is translucent:
> The Circumference is Within, Without is formed the Selfish Center,
> And the Circumference still expands going forward to Eternity . . .
> (J. 71:6–8)

These cryptic words are illuminated by comparing them with their analogue in Hegel. In the preface to the *Phenomenology*—the best précis of his system Hegel ever wrote—and, in the context of saying that everything depends upon grasping the ultimate truth not only as substance but as subject as well, Hegel speaks from the very heart of his dialectical system:

> The Living substance, further, is that being which is truly subject, or, what is the same thing, is truly realized and actual (*wirklich*) solely in the process of positing itself, or in mediating with its own self its transitions from one state or position to the opposite. As subject it is pure and simple negativity, and just on that account a process of splitting up what is simple and undifferentiated, a process of duplicating and setting factors in opposition, which [process] in turn is the negation of this indifferent diversity and of the opposition of factors it entails. True reality is merely this process of reinstating self-identity, of reflecting into its own self in and from its other, and is not an original and primal unity as such, not an immediate unity as such. It is the process of its own becoming, the circle which presupposes its end as its purpose, and has its end for its beginning; it becomes concrete and actual only by being carried out, and by the end it involves.

Hegel even goes so far as to adopt the seemingly Indian idea that the life of the Godhead is love disporting with itself; but this is a Christian vision of the Godhead, for Hegel insists that the life of the Godhead must never be dissociated from 'the seriousness, the suffering, the patience, and the

which the first is also the last and the last is also the first, that distance which is the division within the identity of the first and the last, the modern identity[95] of the first and the last, that distance the index of which is precisely the 'also', that distance/circle which takes the form, in the mathematical realism of Peirce, of the merely *ideal* unity of the triad, which takes the form of the triadic unity in which 0° is *ideally* 'the same as 360°', the 'same' *qua* the absolute reduction of the circle to

labor of the negative.' Apart from the negative, and the process of self-negation, the Godhead would be neither realized nor actual, and hence would not be. Whereas in the Phenomenology this circular and negative process is the self-evolution of Spirit in consciousness, in the *Science of Logic* Spirit is transposed into the abstract Notion, but the form of its movement remains exactly the same:

> . . . Absolute Spirit, which is found to be the concrete, last, and highest truth of all Being, at the end of its evolution freely passes beyond itself and lapses into the shape of an immediate Being; it resolves itself to the creation of a world which contains everything included in the evolution preceding that result; all of which, by reason of this inverted position, is changed, together with its beginning, into something dependent on the result, for the result is the principle. What is essential for the Science is not so much that a pure immediate is the beginning, but that itself in its totality forms a cycle returning upon itself, wherein the first is also last, and the last first.

It certainly is not accidental that Hegel was able to absorb these eschatological words of Jesus into his own system, although he has transformed their original apocalyptic meaning into a dialectical movement that moves only by inverting itself. Nevertheless, this dialectical movement is a Christian process of self-negation, a self-negation that moves by continually ceasing to be itself, and therefore a kenotic self-negation that evolves by eternally becoming its own Other.

"Seen in this perspective, the distinctive motif of Christian mysticism is its celebration of the Godhead as a living process, a process that moves *forward* to Eternity, and therefore authentic Christian mysticism retains an eschatological religious ground because it knows a final Reality whose end transcends its beginning. Christian mysticism must know the Godhead as a living and forward-moving process if only because a vision of ultimate Reality as absolute quiescence forecloses the possibility of the final reality of the essential being and the decisive acts of Jesus Christ."

[95] Cf. above, pp. 142ff.

the 'indefiniteness' which is the 'Dawn'.[96] The catholicological minimum, *qua* absolute penetration, *qua* absolutely selfless love of the other, *qua* absolute transcendence of the limit for the first time, precludes the identical 'also', the identical division-within identity/distance/circle, which is the abysmal form of the 'Eternal Recurrence of All Things', and which yawns essentially in the radical incompleteness which *wills* the absolute opening and resolves to exist in the midst of the abyss in the form of the two-sided subjectivity[97] of the depths of outwardness,[98] which, on the one hand, yawns absolutely *uninverted* in the hymenal structure of the 'black and/or white', in the absolute undecidability of the hymen, in the incompleteness which wills itself,[99] and which, on the other hand, yawns absolutely *inverted* in the incompleteness which wills the other in the form of the eternal outwardizing of the within, in the form of the saying unnaming the Absolute Existent, in the form of the absolute 'quiescence' transcending 'the final reality of the essential being and the decisive acts of Jesus Christ', in the form of the silence transcending the Lord Jesus Christ, the absolute silence.[100] *What now occurs for the first time in history is the absolute penetration which is the absolute suspension of the process of beginning and ending/the absolute suspension of the beginning and ending of the process: the absolute unity of the absolute penetration is the midst itself absolutely existent for the first time, the absolutely existent beginning.* Absolutely *after* nothing, 'absolute' חלחל ('to penetrate' [integral product, 4.096E3]) identical with 'absolute' רציונלי ('rational' [integral product, 1E12]) is 'absolute' קדם כל דבר ('before all things', *qua* proportion, 100 : 4 :: 40 : [1] (::) 20 : 30 (::) 4 : 2 :: 200 : [1], whose integral product is 4.096E15), 4.096E3 × 1E12 = 4.096E15: absolutely after

[96] Cf. above, pp. 293ff.

[97] Cf. above, pp. 356ff.

[98] Cf. above, pp. 220ff.

[99] Cf. above, pp. 392ff.

[100] Ibid. Also above, p. 403, n. 94. This absolute 'quiescence' is the 'absolute' שלוה ('peace', *qua* proportion, 300 : 30 :: 6 : 5, whose integral product is 3.24E6) which is identically 'absolute' שאול ('hell', *qua* proportion, 300 : 1 :: 6 : 30, whose integral product is 3.24E6.)

nothing absolutely before everything absolutely rational absolute penetration is the 'created 100' identical with 'absolute' אחר "מאפס" ('*after* "out of nothing"', *qua* proportion, 1 : 8 :: 200 : [1] (::) 40 : 1 :: 80 : 60, whose integral product is 4.096E11), 1E4 × 4.096E11 = 4.096E15, and 'absolute' מתכנת הנדסית ('geometrical proportion', *qua* proportion, 40 : 400 :: 20 : 50 :: 400 : [1] (::) 5 : 50 :: 4 : 60 :: 10 : 400, whose integral product is 4.096E15), the absolute geometrical proportion, and 'absolute' מקרא מפרש ('plaintext', *qua* proportion, 40 : 100 :: 200 : 1 (::) 40 : 80 :: 200 : 300, whose integral product is 4.096E15), the *absolute plaintext.*[101] 'Absolute' אחרית הימים ('end of days', *qua* proportion, 1 : 8 :: 200 : 10 :: 400 : [1] (::) 5 : 10 :: 40 : 10 :: 40 : [1], whose integral product is 4.096E17) denominated 'absolute' רציונלי ('rational' [integral product, 1E12]) is 'absolute' פתח ('to begin', *qua* proportion, 80 : 400 :: 8 : [1], whose integral product is 4.096E5), 4.096E17/1E12 = 4.096E5. This end of days is absolutely the beginning. 'Absolute' פתח ('to begin' [integral product, 4.096E5]) identified with ברא ('to create' [rational product, .01]), 4.096E5 × .01, = 4.096E3. This is the absolute penetration, the absolute agape, of the beginning. In the form of the absolute transcendence of the limit *unity is to penetrate one another absolutely.* For the first time identity is absolute penetration, and this absolute penetration of the other/the other absolutely this projection, this absolute exteriority of the outside,[102] when identified with 'absolute' האמין ('to trust', *qua* proportion, 5 : 1 :: 40 : 10 :: 50 : [1], whose integral product is 1E8), 4.096E3 × 1E8 = 4.096E11, is, *qua* 'absolute,' אחר "מאפס" ('*after* "out of nothing"', *qua* proportion [integral product, 4.096E11]), identically 'absolute' חברותה ('society', *qua* proportion, 8 : 2 :: 200 : 6 :: 400 : 5, whose integral product is 4.096E11). The latter, 'absolute' חברותה ('society' [integral product, 4.096E11]), when identified with 'absolute' אחוז ('become a friend', *qua* proportion, 1 : 8 :: 6 : 7,

[101] For the thinking now occurring for the first time as 'absolute plaintext' see above, Sections I and II, passim.

[102] Compare this absolute penetration of unity with the absolute penetration of solitude (above, pp. 226ff.).

whose integral product is 3.6E1) or with 'absolute' אחוה ('brotherhood'/'intimacy', *qua* proportion, 1 : 8 :: 6 : 5, whose integral product is 3.6E1) or with 'absolute' אמון ('trust', *qua* proportion, 1 : 40 :: 6 : 50, whose integral product is 3.6E1) or with 'absolute' אלוה ('God', *qua* proportion, 1 : 30 :: 6 : 5, whose integral product is 3.6E1) or, finally, with 'absolute' אנוש ('man', *qua* proportion, 1 : 50 :: 6 : 300, whose integral product is 3.6E1),[103] is 'absolute' חברותיות ('sociability', *qua* proportion, 8 : 2 :: 200 : 6 :: 400 : 10 :: 6 : 400, whose integral product is 1.47456E13), 4.096E11 × 3.6E1 = 1.47456E13. This 'absolute sociability' is itself at once 'absolute' האמין ('to trust' [integral product, 1E8]) times the integral product/'absolute' form of the Absolute Proportion of Absolute Thought itself (16 : 24 :: 24 : 36), 1E8 × 1.47456E5 = 1.47456E13. This absolute sociability itself is the 1/36th part of the 'created 100' identified with that 'absolute' חטף מבט ('to catch a glimpse' [integral product, 5.308416E10]) which is at once the 'absolute' form of the Absolute Proportion of Absolute Thought (16 : 24 :: 24 : 36, whose integral product is 1.47456E5) identified with 'absolute' יחס ('proportion' [integral product, 3.6E5]), 1.47456E13 × 3.6E1 = 1E4 × 1.47456E5 × 3.6E5 = 5.308416E14,[104] One absolutely penetrating another one (catholicologically, one another = one another one, unity = identity). Indeed, the One absolutely penetrating the 'one another' for the first time/the One absolutely penetrating the two (the others)/the First Absolute absolutely penetrating the Second Absolute, this absolute penetration, *qua* proven unity of the minimum order in which the Absolute Kingdom of Heaven is the last *identically* the first, *qua* unity of the Kingdom of Heaven, is now for the first time in history clearly perceived as the foundation of society, that is, *the absolute penetration/the unconditioned love of unity is for the first time the foundation of society:* Foundation is for the first time the Absolute Shaking of the Absolute One, the Absolute One moving unconditionally.

103 Cf. above, p. 390. For the 36 as the radically logico-mathematical unity factor, here appearing dramatically in the vocalization of concepts of unity, see Sections III.1 and IV.2.

104 Cf. above, p. 392, n. 83.

The new identity beginning is the actually other one. Existence is not *also* nothing. Writing is not *also* nothing. Existence/writing is *nihil ex nihilo.* The new identity is existence absolutely/writing absolutely/the Word absolute. *Absolute sociability is the Absolute Word absolutely embodied in the One World Now absolutely penetrating every-one, concretely existing universality.* Absolute sociability is a function of the absolutely unconditioned substitution of the irreversible for the reversible. The elimination/vanishing of the base factors of the Absolute Damned and the Absolute Hymen in the proof-form of the proportion in which they appear as such,[105] a vanishing perfectly & essentially analogous to the 'vanishing' of the 'negative meta-identity', 1, in the deduction of the 'positive absolute alio-relative' from the fourfold complex of the Foundation Itself.[106] Absolute sociability exists as the transcendent subsumption of the 'realization of the *coincidentia oppositorum*'.[107] This absolutely existing sociability/essentially historical existence transcends the opposites as such, transcends the consciousness at once of 'the Absolute Damned', *even,* in the final analysis, of 'the Absolute Hymen' identity of opposites. The absolutely existing sociability of the absolute Kingdom of Heaven, thought in essence for the first time in history, this absolute consciousness of the finality of history, leaves behind at once the thinking of שאול ('Saul', *qua* proportion, 300 : 1 :: 6 : 30, whose integral product is 3.24E6), even that of פולוס ('Paul', *qua* proportion, 80 : 6 :: 30 : 6 :: 60 : [1], whose integral product is 2.0736E10), essentially thinks the identification of creation (ברא ['to create (rational product, .01)]) and 'absolute' לדת בתולים ('Virgin Birth' [integral product, 2.0736E12]). The absolute sociability of the Kingdom of Heaven, the essence of the consciousness of One World now actual, for the first time *thinks* Paul, *thinks* creation, is *ex nihilo,* but without the resulting form of consciousness of a New Saul, the consciousness of an 'eternal death'[108] resulting from the relatively irreversible identity of an

[105] Cf. above, pp. 402f.

[106] Cf. above, pp. 276ff.

[107] Compare the subsumption of identity in the form of 'absolute solitude', above, Section II.4, passim; also the text immediately here following.

[108] Cf. above, Section II.4, passim.

absolute solitude, resulting from the division of absolute solitude from self, resulting from the relatively irreversible identity of an absolute self-reversal.[109] The consciousness of the essence of the sociability of the Kingdom of Heaven is the transcendent subsumption of existence, i.e., the absolutely irreversible identification of existence as *nihil ex nihilo*, not nothing 'made out of nothing', but nothing *after* nothing: *ex nihilo* the meta-identity of the thought of existence is *nihil*. This consciousness is the incorporation of the reality of the Abyss in the act of creation: not the absolute inversion of the Abyss, but the absolute Abyss *ex nihilo*, the Abyss absolutely *ex nihilo*, the abyss of the absolute *ex nihilo*, the absolute *ex nihilo* not the absolute *ex nihilo*: the identity/meta-identity of *nihil ex nihilo*. Insofar as existence *is* nothing this consciousness is thought *ex nihilo*, insofar as creation/existence-*ex-nihilo* *is*, this consciousness is the absolute death of thought, *is* the Abyss. Insofar as an 'eternal death identically eternal life'[110] *is*, it is creation, it is the *act* of creation embodied in an *absolutely historical person*. The thinking now occurring for the first time in history is the *transcendence of the one-sided objectivity*[111] of the 'eternal outwardizing of the within',[112] the transcendence/meta-identity of the 'absolute fragmentation of identity',[113] which latter before now essentially & absolutely *is* a drawing near to/a being far from[114] the *two-sided objectivity* of identity (the absolute objectivity of the thinking now occurring, the absolute exteriority of [any] one side, its transcendent objectivity), *the absolute one-sidedness of the identity of (any)two*, the fact that (any)one is the existence of the transcendent other, the within absolutely outwardized. This absolute Abyss *ex nihilo*, this transcendent objectivity of (any) existing thing for the first time, wherein is subsumed 'the absolute reversal and inversion of the historical ideal of being'[115] (which transcendent subsumption of

[109] Cf. above, pp. 234ff.
[110] Cf. above, p. 209.
[111] Cf. above, pp. 356ff., 403ff.
[112] Cf. above, Section II.4.
[113] Cf. above, pp. 226ff.
[114] Ibid.
[115] Cf. above, pp. 230ff.

the identity of absolute solitude is the absolute unintelligibility of the windowless monad in face of the fact that every existing unity is the absolute opening of the world identity, in face of the fact that every existing *unum* is the absolute window transcendently the world for the first time, is not the blind, windowless, perspectival monad, but is, the *unum*, the absolute world-identity the window identically [wherein] absolutely everything [is] perceived, [wherein] each thing [is] perceived absolutely), this essentially transcendental existence is the denomination of the identification of 'absolute' חטף מבט ('to catch a glimpse' [integral product, 5.308416E10]) and the 'created 100' as 'absolute' ג׳ברלטר ('the Rock', *qua* proportion, 3 : 10 :: 2 : 200 :: 30 : 9 :: 200 : [1], whose integral product is 1.296E9 [itself at once the identification of the 'absolute' הקדוש ברוך הוא ('the Holy One blessed be He' [integral product, 1.296E11])[116] and ברא ('to create [rational product, .01])]), which *absolute* 'to catch a glimpse' *ex nihilo* denominated the absolute Rock is 'absolute' פתח ('window'/'opening'/'doorway'/'to begin'/'not blind'/'to loosen' [integral product, 4.096E5]), (5.308416E10 × 1E4) / 1.296E9 = 4.096E5, the absolute window/absolute opening/absolute perception/absolute loosening which is the creation identity of the absolute penetration now actually occurring for the first time. This is itself at once 'absolute' פסח ('Passover', *qua* proportion, 80 : 60 :: 8 : [1], whose integral product is 4.095E5).[117] The Absolute Rock which is the Absolute Holy One at once 'to create' is identically 'absolute' ישו הנוצרי ('Jesus of Nazareth', *qua* proportion, 10 : 300 :: 6 : [1] (::) 5 : 50 :: 6 : 90 :: 200 : 10, whose integral product is 1.296E11) identified with ברא ('to create [rational product, .01]), 1.296E11 × .01 = 1.296E9, Absolute Jesus of Nazareth at once 'to create'.

The rational product of ישו הנוצרי ('Jesus of Nazareth') is .02666, דוד ('David' [rational product, 2.666]) identical with ברא ('to create [rational product, .01]), משה ('Moses' [rational product, .666]) identified with אהיה ('I AM' [rational product, .40]) denominated אמת ('truth' [rational product, 10]), (.666 × .40) /

[116] Cf. above, p. 391.

[117] Compare the 'absolute' Passover here with the 'infinite passover' in Leahy, *Novitas Mundi,* Appendix γ.

$10 = .02\overline{666}$.[118] It is this Jesus of Nazareth which is I AM NOT, where I AM NOT is not I AM denominated NOT/NOT denominated I AM/denominational I AM NOT, but I AM immediately NOT/NOT immediately I AM/immediate I AM NOT. Not I AM/NOT, not בל/אהיה, not I AM/PRESENCE, not מציאות/אהיה, but I AM × NOT, בל × אהיה, I AM × PRESENCE, מציאות × אהיה, not $.40/.0\overline{666} = 6$, but $.40 \times .0\overline{666} = .02\overline{666} = (.40/.0\overline{666})/225$, where 225 is 'absolute' השגה ('perception'/'conception', *qua* proportion, 5 : 300 :: 3 : 5, whose integral product is 225) or 'absolute' גלה ('to appear'/'to reveal', *qua* proportion, 3 : 30 :: 5 : [1], whose integral product is 225). If what now actually occurs is the beginning of the actual existence of the abyss of the abyss,[119] then the Foundation Itself which is the beginning of the Resurrection, and for the first time the foundation of society, is the essential comprehension of the beginning in the form of the proportion which is the double Abyss of I AM, construed in the universal form of logical propositions (where the positive-negative pattern is *PP* + *NP* + *PN* + *NN*):

'I AM' – P : 'I AM NOT' – P :: 'I AM' – N : 'I AM NOT' – N,

where, substituting .40 for I AM and $.02\overline{666}$ for I AM NOT,

$$.40 : .02\overline{666} :: -.40 : -.02\overline{666},$$

the proven unity of this proportion is:

$$-0.010\overline{666}/-0.010\overline{666} = 1,$$

where $-0.010\overline{666}$ is the negative 'identity' of אהיה אשר אהיה ('I AM THAT I AM' [rational product, $.10\overline{666}$]) denominated אמת

[118] Likewise אשר אהיה ('WHO I AM', *qua* proportion, 1 : 300 :: 200 : [1] (::) 1 : 5 :: 10 : 5 , whose rational product is $.2\overline{666}$) denominated אמת ('truth' [rational product, 10]). Cf. above, p. 364.

[119] Cf. above, p. 353f.

('truth' [rational product, 10]), $-(.10\overline{666}/10) = -0.010\overline{666}$. The rational product of this proportion is:

$$(.40/.02\overline{666}) \times (-.40/-.02\overline{666}) = 225,$$

where 225 is the 'identity' of מחסר לחם ('breadless', *qua* proportion, 40 : 8 :: 60 : 200 (::) 30 : 8 :: 40 : [1], whose rational product is 225), and 'absolute' השׂגה ('perception'/'conception' [integral product is 225]) and 'absolute' גלה ('to appear'/'to reveal' [integral product is 225]), while the integral product of this proportion is:

$$.40^2 \times -.40^2 = .0256,$$

where .0256 is the 'identity' of קרבן מנחה ('meal offering',[120] *qua* proportion, 100 : 200 :: 2 : 50 (::) 40 : 50 :: 8 : 5, whose rational product is .0256), whose 'absolute' form is 4.096E9, identically 'absolute' חלחל ('to penetrate' [integral product, 4.096E3]), 'absolute' ἡ ἀγάπη ('agape'/'unconditioned love' [integral product, 4.096E3]), identified with 'absolute' כתיבה ('writing' [integral product, 1E6]),[121] 4.096E3 × 1E6 = 4.096E9, which, denominated ברא ('to create [rational product, .01]), is 'absolute' אחר "מאפס" ('after "out of nothing"', *qua* proportion [integral product, 4.096E11]), identically 'absolute' חברותה ('society' [integral product, 4.096E11]), 4.096E9/.01 = 4.096E11. This is the proportion of negative unity, the 'logical' order of the elements of the fourfold which is the double Abyss of I AM. The proportion of absolutely clarified unity is the proportion in the minimum-order, 4 : 1 :: 2 : 3, (recognizing that *PP* = 1, *NP* = 2, *PN* = 4, and *NN* = 3):[122]

'*I AM*'–*N* : '*I AM*'–*P* :: '*I AM NOT*'–*P* : '*I AM NOT*'–*N*,

$$-.40 : .40 :: .02\overline{666} : -.02\overline{666},$$

[120] The sacrifice the remainder of which was to be eaten by Aaron and his descendents inside the holy place in the form of unleavened bread (Lv. 2:1–16; 6:7–11).

[121] Cf. above, p. 392, n. 83.

[122] Cf. above, pp. 273ff.

the proven unity of which proportion is:

$$0.010\overline{666}/0.010\overline{666} = 1,$$

where $0.010\overline{666}$ is the positive 'identity' of אהיה אשר אהיה ('I AM THAT I AM' [rational product, $.10\overline{666}$]) denominated אמת ('truth' [rational product, 10]), $(.10\overline{666}/10) = .010\overline{666}$. The rational product of this proportion is:

$$(-.40/.40) \times (.02\overline{666}/-.02\overline{666}) = 1,$$

where 1 is 'absolute' אל ('God', *qua* ratio, 1 : 30, whose integral product is 1), 'absolute' אב ('father', *qua* ratio, 1 : 2, whose integral product is 1), 'absolute' אם ('mother', *qua* ratio, 1 : 40, whose integral product is 1), and 'absolute' את ('with', *qua* ratio, 1 : 400, whose integral product is 1), while the integral product of this proportion is:

$$-.40^2 \times .02\overline{666}^2 = .000113\overline{777},$$

where $.000113\overline{777}$ is the integral product of the 'logical' proportion of the double Abyss of I AM reduced to the rational product of that proportion, .0256/225, the 'identity' of קרבן מנחה ('meal offering' [rational product, .0256]) denominated the 'identity' of מחסר לחם ('breadless' [rational product, 225]), at once itself 'absolute' השגה ('perception'/'conception' [integral product, 225]) and 'absolute' גלה ('to appear'/'to reveal' [integral product, 225]). This is the sacrifice whose remainder is consumed in the form of unleavened bread denominated 'the bread subtracted': this is the eucharist of existence itself/absolute perception/absolute conception/absolute revelation/absolute appearance.[123]

Now this 'absolute' form of the 'proportion of absolute Davidic clarity', this breadless identity of the meal offering, at

[123] Cf. Leahy, *Novitas Mundi*, pp. 338ff., and pp. 344ff.

once itself the square of the positive and negative 'identity' of אהיה אשר אהיה ('I AM THAT I AM' [rational product, .10666]) denominated אמת ('truth' [rational product, 10]), that is, $.0256/225 = (.10666/10)^2 = 0.010666^2 = .000113777$, the existent 'I AM THAT I AM', at once itself the square of the weighted sum of the Absolute Proportion of Absolute Thought reduced to the 'created 100', $(106.666/1E4)^2$, is 'absolute' חברותיות ('sociability' [integral product, 1.47456E13]) denominated 'absolute' ישו הנוצרי ('Jesus of Nazareth' [integral product, 1.296E11]) denominated 'absolute' כתיבה ('writing' [integral product, 1E6]),[124] (1.47456E13/1.296E11)/1.E6 = .000113777, the conception of sociability identically the conception of Jesus of Nazareth identically absolute text. This 'absolute' form of the proportion of absolute Davidic clarity is itself at once, again, *identically* 'absolute' חטף מבט ('to catch a glimpse' [integral product, 5.308416E10], at once the 'absolute' form of the Absolute Proportion of Absolute Thought [16 : 24 :: 24 : 36 (integral product, 1.47456E5)] identified with 'absolute' יחס ['proportion' (integral product, 3.6E5)], 1.47456E5 × 3.6E5 = 5.308416E10) identified with 'absolute' כתיבה ('writing' [integral product, 1E6]) and denominated 'absolute' יום א׳ של שלוש ('day one of the Trinity', *qua* proportion, 10 : 6 :: 40 : [1] (::) 1000 : [1] (::) 300 : 30 (::) 300 : 30 :: 6 : 300, whose integral product is 4.6656E22) denominated ברא ('to create' [rational product, .01]), (5.308416E10 × 1E6/4.6656E22)/.01 = .000113777, the absolutely unconditioned 'to catch a glimpse' identically Absolute Trinity Sunday identically 'to create'. This absolute form of the minimum-order arrangement of the proportion of the double Abyss of 'I AM' is itself at once, again, 'absolute' חלחל ('to penetrate' [integral product, 4.096E3]), 'absolute' ἡ ἀγάπη ('agape'/'unconditioned love' [integral product, 4.096E3]), denominated 'absolute' אחוד ('solidarity', *qua* proportion, 1 : 8 :: 6 : 4, whose integral product is 3.6E1) denominated 'absolute' כתיבה ('writing' [inte-

124 'Absolute' כתיבה ('writing' [integral product is 1E6]) is identically 'absolute' קרי ('text of Scripture *read*', *qua* proportion, 100 : 200 : 10 : [1], whose integral product is 1E6) and 'absolute' יצירי ('creative'/'productive', *qua* proportion, 10 : 90 :: 10 : 200 :: 10 : [1], whose integral product is 1E6).

gral product, 1E6]), (4.096E3/3.6E1)/1E6 = $.000113\overline{777}$, the absolute text identity of absolute penetration/absolutely selfless love of the other identically absolute solidarity, and, again, the absolute writing identity of 'absolute' פתח ('window'/'opening'/'doorway' [integral product, 4.096E5]) denominated 'absolute' אחידות ('unity'/'uniformity' [integral product, 3.6E3]), (4.096E5/3.6E3)/1E6 = $.000113\overline{777}$.

The absolute text identity of the absolute opening denominated absolute unity is identically the 'absolute' פתח ('window'/'opening'/'doorway' [integral product, 4.096E5]) denominated 'absolute' יהוה ('Yahweh', *qua* proportion, 10 : 5 :: 6 : 5, whose integral product is 3.6E3) denominated 'absolute' הכרה ('consciousness'/'discernment', *qua* proportion, 5 : 20 :: 200 : 5, whose integral product is 1E6), (4.096E5/3.6E3)/1E6 = $.000113\overline{777}$, absolute consciousness the absolute Lord God, Yahweh, the absolute 'to begin', the *absolute* window. Now, the Absolute Unity which is 'absolute' Yahweh, it turns out, is related to existence, to Being/being, as the minimum-order of the foundation (4 : 1 :: 2 : 3) is related to the 'logical' order (1 : 2 :: 4 : 3).[125] Existence, Being, is

הויה,

which, *qua* 1 : 2 :: 4 : 3 proportion, is:

5 : 6 :: 10 : 5,

whose integral product is 2.5E3 and whose rational product is 1.666. But the Name Itself of Yahweh is:

יהוה,

which, *qua* 4 : 1 :: 2 : 3 proportion, is:

10 : 5 :: 6 : 5,

[125] Cf. above, Section III.1.

the elements of existence, of Being/being, *qua* minimum, *qua* Foundation, the Name of God which was *with* God 'before the universe was created',[126] Being/Existence the logical arrangement of the elements of that Name which, *qua* 'absolute', is *identically* 'absolute' אחידות ('unity'/'uniformity' [integral product, 3.6E3]). For the first time Being is identified through the minimum change in the order of the elements as, *qua* 'absolute' Yahweh, Unity, the 'univocal predication of Being itself' itself manifest.[127] This Being *minimum*ized, 'absolute' יהוה ('Yahweh') identically 'absolute' אחידות ('Unity'), is the cube root of 'absolute' יום א׳ של שלוש ('day one of the Trinity' [integral product, 4.6656E22]) denominated 'absolute' רציונלי ('rational [integral product, 1E12]),[128] $4.6656E22/1E12 = 3.6E3^3$. This Being *minimum*ized, 'absolute' יהוה ('Yahweh') identically 'absolute' אחידות ('Unity'), denominated ברא ('to create' [rational product, .01]), is 'absolute' יחס ('proportion' [integral product, 3.6E5]), $3.6E3/.01 = 3.6E5$, which 'absolute proportion' is the cube root of 'absolute' יום א׳ של שלוש ('day one of the Trinity') denominated 'absolute' כתיבה ('writing'), $4.6656E22/1E6 = 3.6E5^3$. Indeed, this Absolute Trinity Sunday *squared*, *qua* existent, is the *cube* of 'absolute' הקדוש ברוך הוא, ('the Holy One blessed be He' [integral product, 1.296E11]) identified with 'absolute' רציונלי ('rational' [integral product, 1E12]), is 'absolute' הקדוש ברוך הוא × 'absolute' הקדוש ברוך הוא × 'absolute' הקדוש ברוך הוא × 'absolute' רציונלי, $4.6656E22^2 = 1.296E11^3 \times 1E12 = 2.176782336E45$. And this 'absolute Holy One blessed be He' Who is Three absolutely rational, this existent 'absolute day one of the Trinity', is 'absolute' כל גיא ינשא וכל הר וגבעה ישפלו ('Every valley shall be lifted up, and every mountain and hill shall be made low' [Is. 40:4], *qua* proportion, 20 : 30 (::) 3 : 10 :: 1 : [1] (::) 10 : 50 :: 300 : 1 (::) 6 : 20 :: 30 : [1] (::) 5 : 200 (::) 6 : 3 :: 2 : 70 :: 5 : [1] (::) 10 : 300 :: 80 : 30 :: 6 : [1], whose integral product is 2.176782336E27) identified with 'absolute' הכרה ('consciousness'/'discernment' [integral product, 1E6]) and 'absolute' רציונלי ('rational' [integral prod-

[126] Cf. above, pp. 360ff. for the citation of Maimonides.
[127] Cf. above, Sections II.3 and II.4, passim.
[128] Cf. above, p. 415, n. 124.

uct, 1E12]), 2.176782336E27 × 1E6 × 1E12 = 2.176782336E45, existent absolute Trinity Sunday identically the Absolute Holy Trinity blessed be He is Isaiah's prophecy of the Messianic age identical with absolute rational consciousness. And when this existent absolute Trinity Sunday identically the Absolute Holy Trinity blessed be He identical with absolute rational consciousness is denominated 'absolute writing', or when the prophecy of Isaiah is identical with 'absolute consciousness' *squared,* it is the 'absolute' אבן הפנה של שיטה פילוסופית ('cornerstone of a philosophical method', *qua* proportion, 1 : 2 :: 50 : [1] (::) 5 : 80 :: 50 : 5 (::) 300 : 30 (::) 300 : 10 :: 9 : 5 (::) 80 : 10 :: 30 : 6 :: 60 : 6 :: 80 : 10 :: 400 : [1], whose integral product is 2.176782336E39), 2.176782336E45/1E6 = 2.176782336E27 × 1E6² = 2.176782336E39. This is the absolute cornerstone of philosophical method manifesting itself for the first time in history. Existence, Being/being, (הויה) reduced for the first time to the Tetragrammaton (יהוה) as 'logic' is reduced to the *minimum,* and reduced *qua* integral products as 2.5E3/3.6E3 and *qua* rational products as 1.666/2.4, is .69444. This is itself at once the reduction, *qua* rational products, of נשנה ('recurrence', *qua* proportion, 50 : 300 :: 50 : 5, whose rational product is 1.666) to מתחיל ('beginning', *qua* proportion, 40 : 400 :: 8 : 10 :: 30 : [1], whose rational product is 2.4), 1.666/2.4 = .69444. This quotient of recurrence reduced to beginning, of Being reduced to Yahweh, is the very 'identity' of הצרפה ('synthesis', *qua* proportion, 5 : 90 :: 200 : 80 :: 5 : [1], whose rational product is .69444). The integral product of הצרפה, 'absolute' synthesis, is 2.5E7 which is identically 'absolute' הויה (Being) identified with the 'created 100' or identified with 'absolute' בין ('between', *qua* proportion, 2 : 10 :: 50: [1], whose integral product is 1E4]), 2.5E3 × 1E4 = 2.5E7, while the linear product of הצרפה, synthesis, is 3.6E7 which is identically 'absolute' יהוה (Yahweh) identified with the 'created 100' or identified with 'absolute' בין ('between' [integral product, 1E4]), 3.6E3 × 1E4 = 3.6E7. The *identical* logico-mathematical structure found in הצרפה ('synthesis') is to be found in קפיצה ('leap') which קפיצה is at once 'closing', where the integral, rational, and linear products are identically those of הצרפה. Thus the synthesis thought for the first time (.69444) is the leap thought for the first time (.69444) and the closing thought for the first time (.69444), and the beginning of the absolute synthesis (2.5E7) is the beginning of the absolute leap (2.5E7) and the beginning of the absolute closing (2.5E7). But 'absolute' synthesis/leap/closing, which is 'absolute' being identified with 'absolute' between (2.5E7), is itself at once 'absolute' נפקח ('to be opened'/'to get sight of'/'to understand', *qua* proportion, 50 : 80 :: 100 : 8, whose integral product is 2.5E7). The very 'identity'/rational product of this נפקח ('to be opened'/'to get sight of'/'to understand'), 7.8125 (at once itself, *qua* rational products, יד המקרה ['coincidence', *qua* proportion, 10 : 4 (::) 5 : 40 :: 100 : 200 :: 5 : [1], whose rational product is .78125] identified with אמת ['truth' (rational product, 10)], .78125 × 10 = 7.8125 or התהלך את האלהים ['to walk with God' (Gn. 5:22), *qua* proportion, 5 : 400 :: 5 : 30 :: 20 : [1] (::) 1 : 400 (::) 5 : 1 :: 30 : 5 :: 10 : 40, whose rational product is .00078125] identified with the 'created 100', .00078125 × 1E4 = 7.8125) is the square root of the quotient of 'absolute' being identified with 'absolute' between/'absolute' synthesis/'absolute' leap/'absolute' closing (2.5E7) reduced to 'absolute' פתח ('window'/'opening'/'doorway'/'to begin'/'not blind'/'to loosen' [integral product, 4.096E5]), that is, 2.5E7/4.096E5 = 7.8125^2 = 61.03515625, which last, closing the circle of the beginning absolutely, is the 'synthesis' (הצרפה) denominated the 'absolute' form of 'the proportion of absolute Davidic clarity' identified with 'to create' (ברא), (.69444/.000113777) × .01 = 61.03515625.

The *novitas mentis* now actually existing for the first time[129] is the synthesis of the *novitas mundi.* This is not merely 'being beginning in every now', nor 'consciousness beginning in every now',[130] but being occurring in every now for the first time: the absolute intelligibility of the new creation for the first time: *creation in the form of thought itself at once the essence of thought* ex nihilo. The creation of a thinking the essential form of which is indifference to dichotomy, absolute relativity *ex nihilo,* the essential form of the Absolute Holy One blessed be He/Absolute

[129] Cf. Leahy, *Novitas Mundi,* pp. 14ff., pp. 296ff., 323, and 394.
[130] Cf. above, pp. 205f., and 350.

Jesus of Nazareth : neither the reduction of the Absolute Alone to the beginning, nor the reduction of the Absolute Alone to God in the beginning, but the recurring which is the beginning in the form of the absolute now, *the recurring of the beginning in the very form of order, in the very form of the absolute proportion.* If, before now, Descartes doubted, and in that doubt (*Cogito ergo sum*) founded thought in *order*, if, then, Kant doubted essentially, founding knowledge in a universal order, and if, finally, Hegel doubted absolutely,[131] founding knowledge in the existing universal order, and if, further, while Marx absolutely, but non-categorically, doubted the existing universal order, the absolute doubt was doubted inessentially by Kierkegaard, Husserl, and Heidegger,[132] and if, just before now, the absolute doubt has been undoubtingly transcended by Derrida, and the absolute undoubt undoubtingly transcended by Altizer, then, now for the first time in history, in the form of existence absolutely the name/the minimum/the proportion/the *unum/* the Tetragrammaton, the absolute doubt is doubted essentially, founding *thought* in the existing universal order, founding *knowledge* in the *transcendence* of the existing universal order, at once the absolutely & essentially categorical doubting of the existing universal order: the 'knowledge of what is transcendent'[133] absolutely doubted. It is precisely *this doubt,* viz., that of the 'knowledge of what is transcendent', which the Cartesian doubt was *essentially* not, so that with each advance on the Cartesian doubt, 'essential doubt', 'absolute doubt', 'absolute contingency', 'absolute absurdity', 'absolute science', 'absolute speculation', 'absolute abyss', 'absolute inversion of the abyss', (respectively, Kant, Hegel, Marx, Kierkegaard, Husserl, Heidegger, Derrida, Altizer), modernity moves further and further away from that substance of which, in its origin, it is the formal recollection, and in its infinite progress remains essentially unable to doubt essentially what it doubts absolutely, remains a thinking the essential form of which is 'to lack unity'/'to lack existence', precisely &

[131] Cf. Leahy, *Novitas Mundi,* pp. 130 and 258f.

[132] Ibid.

[133] Ibid., pp. 57f.

absolutely insofar as it does *not* lack *'self'*, or, where it either does or would lack 'self', it neither does nor can lack the category of 'self' or the self essentially, neither can nor does *think the other absolutely and essentially without self-reference, think* categorically *the absolute not-self.* Every form of the thinking before now doubting 'the knowledge of what is transcendent' is ultimately a form of self-doubt. The essential & absolute doubting of the knowledge of what is transcendent is the reduction of Being to the Tetragrammaton, of existence to the minimum, of logic to existence: any & everything, 'existing' or not existing, *nihil ex nihilo,* is absolutely an element in a proportion/absolutely an element in the one proportion/absolutely an element in the proportion of the One: any & everything absolutely the elemental unity: any & everything, *qua* element, the absolute unity of the absolute text of the absolute opening/of the Name: any & everything, *qua* element, the *unum ex nihilo* : the absolute recurring of the beginning of the proportion in the form of catholicological absolute novelty: the absolutely unconditioned recurring of the absolute beginning: the absolute unity of the window identically the transcendent appearance, *qua* absolute. The essential and absolute doubting is the reduction of knowledge to the proportion of the beginning. In the proportion of the beginning the opposites absolutely share the between, exist in essence categorically, share absolutely & essentially the 'absolute between': thinking thinks the 'not-self' categorically in the form of the beginning. This other, *qua* the coincidence of opposites transcended in the absolute between of the proportion of the beginning, is the absolute foundation/absolute element/absolute beginning, the יסוד ('foundation', *qua* proportion, 10 : 60 :: 6 : 4, whose rational product is .25 [= 1 – .75, Unity minus the very 'identity' of אפס ('nothing' [rational product, .75]),[134] Unity minus the very basis of plus and minus,[135] at once itself 'absolute' הויה ('being' [integral product, 2.5E3]) denominated 'abso-

[134] Cf. above, Section III.1, passim. This follows Peirce's usage, 'not *x*' = '1 – *x*'.

[135] Cf. Section III.I, including "Afterword 2," for the 'falsity of truth and falsehood'.

lute' בין ('between' [integral product, 1E4, the 'created 100']), 2.5E3/1E4 = .25]), the 'absolute' form, integral product, of which is 3.6E3, identically 'absolute' יהוה ('Yahweh' [integral product, 3.6E3]), while its linear product is 1.44E4, identically 'absolute' כפור ('Atonement' [integral product, 1.44E4[136]). This 'absolute' Foundation/'absolute' Yahweh is itself at once 'absolute' יקום ('living substance', *qua* proportion, 10 : 100 :: 6 : 40, whose integral product is 3.6E3), identically 'absolute' ישו ('Jesus', *qua* proportion, 10 : 300 :: 6 : [1], whose integral product is 3.6E3). It is to this other, *qua* 'absolute living things'/'absolute foundation'/'absolute Jesus'/'absolute Yahweh', that existence, Being/being, is for the first time essentially and categorically reduced in the very form of thought. This is 'absolute' תודעה ('consciousness'/'conscience', *qua* proportion, 400 : 6 :: 4 : 70 :: 5 : [1], whose integral product is 6.4E7) denominated 'absolute' הגשמה ('realization'/'materialization'/'personification of the deity', *qua* proportion, 5 : 3 :: 300 : 40 :: 5 : [1], whose integral product is 5.625E7 [= 'absolute' החלפה ('changing', *qua* proportion, 5 : 8 :: 30 : 80 :: 5 : [1], whose integral product is 5.625E5) denominated ברא ('to create' [rational product, .01]), 5.625E5/.01 = 5.625E7]) denominated 'absolute' בין ('between' [integral product, 1E4, the 'created 100']), (6.4E7/5.625E7)/1E4 = $.000113\overline{777}$, the 'absolute' form of the 'proportion of absolute Davidic clarity', the breadless identity of the meal offering, the existent 'I AM THAT I AM'.[137] This is consciousness *ex nihilo* categorically the other: the absolutely revolutionary consciousness, revolutionary metanoēsis,[138] the metanomous existence of the person.[139] This is the beginning of existence. The very consciousness of the beginning. *Every now begins the transcendence of consciousness. Every now begins the body itself.* This consciousness of foundation is, at once, the reduction to nothing of the selfhood of *Dasein*. This beginning of consciousness is the death of selfhood, indeed, of the very same self-

[136] Cf. above, p. 369.
[137] Cf. above, p. 412.
[138] Cf. above, Section II.4, passim.
[139] Cf. above, pp. 85ff. and 204ff.

hood of *Dasein* of which Heidegger says in *The Metaphysical Foundations of Logic*:

> Only because Dasein is primarily determined by egoicity can it factically exist as a thou for and with another Dasein. The thou is not an ontic replicate of a factical ego; but neither can a thou exist as such and be itself as thou for another ego if it is not at all Dasein, i.e., if it is not grounded in egoicity. The egoicity belonging to the transcendence of Dasein is the metaphysical condition of the possibility for a thou to be able to exist and an I-thou relationship to be able to exist. The thou is also most immediately thou if it is not simply another ego, but rather a "you yourself are." This selfhood, however, is its freedom, and this freedom is identical with egoicity, on the basis of which Dasein can, in the first place, ever be egoistic or altruistic.[140]

For the first time the absolute death of selfhood is thought. The act of creation in the form of consciousness. Being beginning in the absolute now. The abyss yields itself to the divine power in the form of praise. This is the fulfillment of the beginning, the beginning of the fulfillment, the beginning of the end of the world in essence, the beginning of the end of time itself. Indeed, the beginning of the end of time itself, consciousness *ex nihilo*, *qua* beginning of fulfillment, *qua* beginning of existence in the absolute now, is for the first time the end of expectancy. The act of creation now beginning is the transcendence of the very same time itself of which Heidegger says:

> In the common understanding we call time the mere sequence of nows (now, not yet now—forthwith, now no longer—just now). And in a certain way we also know that time is not an accumulation of nows but a continuum; again, not a rigid continuum, but one which flows (the "stream of time"). But, however time, thus understood, may be defined, and whether or not a definition might be successful from this viewpoint, it has in any case become clear that then, formerly, and now emerge,

[140] M. Heidegger, *The Metaphysical Foundations of Logic* (Bloomington, 1984), p. 187.

> and do so in their unity, from expectance, retention, and making-present—which obviously must first be unitary among and in themselves.
>
> If, however, time means something we come upon here as emergent, then the origin of what emerges and what lets it emerge must evidently be that which, all the more, and in the primordial sense, deserves to be called time. Time is therefore originally this expectance, retention, and making-present. . . . To repeat: expectancy, retention, and making-present are not merely the way we grasp the then, the formerly, and the now, not merely modes of being conscious of them; they are rather the very origin of the then, the formerly, and the now. Expectancy is not a mode of being conscious of time, but, in a primordial and genuine sense is time itself.[141]

It is just this expectancy, this time itself, this transcendence of the consciousness of time, which is transcended in the Beginning, transcended *qua* form of beginning, transcended *as beginning*. But beginning to exist, beginning of existence, is beginning of the other categorically other, the beginning categorically not self-transcendence. The absolute negativity of this beginning transcends the '*nihil originarium*', transcends the world : this beginning is the absolute opening onto the transcendent world. Being beginning as the absolute now is time *absolutely* 'opening and expanding into a world', as contrasted with the following absolutely self-limiting expectancy which Heidegger contrasts with the monadology of Leibniz:

> The essential difference between Leibniz' interpretation of the monad and my interpretation of Dasein as temporality lies in the following : in Leibniz the realization of the truly metaphysical sense of his conception is hindered by the fact that he, in principle, places the Cartesian *ego cogito* at the basis of his conception of the monad, of the I; that he also takes the monad as a substance enclosed in its sphere, even though he incorporates the whole world in this immanence and its [the monad's] contents. Leibniz can therefore say, Monads need no windows,

[141] Ibid., pp. 202f.

> because they already have everything on the interior. We would say, conversely, they have no windows, not because they have everything within, but because there is neither inside nor outside—because temporalization (drive) in itself implies the ecstatic happening of world-entry, insofar as transcendence is already in itself the possible leap over possible beings that can enter into a world. Thus time is not a *mundus concentratus* but the converse. Time is essentially a self-opening and expanding into a world. I will not go into the comparison any further, particularly the question of the extent to which one might conceive the interpretation of Dasein as temporality in a universal-ontological way—just as the monadology is presented as an exposition of the whole universe of beings. This is a question which I myself am not able to decide, one which is still completely unclear to me.[142]

The beginning thought as the death of absolute selfhood, the beginning of existence, is the complete elimination of the self of time itself, the complete elimination of the self of *Dasein*'s temporality, the complete elimination of the absolute self-limitation of expectancy. What now occurs for the first time is not the transcendence of the dichotomous conception of the monad of Leibniz which is Heidegger's absolute dispersal of the preemption of the necessity of the window, his absolute denial/absolute interpretation of the conditional necessity of the window, indeed, of the world (his *de facto* interpretation, indeed, denial-by-way-of-the-interpositioning-of-nothing [which is what interpretation is], of the beginning of the world-window), not the transcendence of dichotomy (which by transposition is the 'ontological difference'), the transcendence of the window which is at once the self-transcendence of the world-window, but rather, now actually for the first time in history, the *transcendental dichotomy*: the creation of a new universe, indeed, the 'universal-ontological' conception of the temporality of *Dasein* as the beginning of existence, as the existence of the beginning. This transcendental dichotomy is the fundamental fact of the new consciousness now existing for the first time in history. It is the

[142] Ibid., pp. 209f.

creation of a second absolute, the creation of a new thinking, the beginning of a new identity, the *actual* beginning of a new humanity. This *transcendental dichotomy* is the end of dichotomy for the first time, not a (merely) formal matter, not essentially a (merely) conceptual matter, not absolutely a matter of (merely) being, it is the form of an actual matter, essentially a matter of fact, and absolutely a matter of action. Occurring in time for the first time now, it is essentially historical, at once itself the transcendence of history. The fundamental fact is the beginning of the end of historical existence now occurring, at once the beginning of absolute history, of the fulfillment of expectancy, essentially matter itself for society, essentially the matter itself of & for the essentially universal society now actually newly existing as the world. The transcendental dichotomy is at once the transcendental dichotomy of time itself, the transcendental dichotomy of expectancy: the creation of an essentially practical existence, at once the beginning of an absolutely practical existence, in the form of the absolute now: an absolutely revolutionary consciousness transcending the difference between past & future[143] in the form of the transcendence of expectancy, in the form of *time itself actually opening and expanding into a world,* in the form of time transcending temporality, in the form of time transcending the measure of time, in the form of time categorically the other, in the form of the end of time itself, in the form of the absolute objectivity of time, of the world itself—in the form of the appearance meta-identically the window.

Now, the integral product of 'the proportion of absolute Davidic clarity' is $.000113\overline{777}$.[144] Let π equal the circumference of a circle whose diameter is Unity. This circumference or π then ≈ $.000113\overline{777} \times 2.7648E4$. The integral product of 2.7648E4, *qua* proportion, 2 : 7 :: 6 : 4 :: 8 : [1], is 9.216E3. But 9.216E3 = (2.7648E4)/3. The integral product of 2.7648E4 is exactly 1/3rd itself. Indeed, the foundational property of this number nearly shouts itself out when it is noticed further that the integral product of 9.216E3 (*qua* proportion, 9 : 2 :: 1 : 6,

[143] Cf. above, p. 87.

[144] Cf. above, pp. 413ff.

whose integral product is 81) is $1/113.\overline{777}$th itself. Now it turns out that 2.7648E4 is related to Unity, to 1, in the following way. Where n is either $.\overline{333}$ or 2.7648E4 and $f(n)$ is the integral product of the number within the parentheses, the following is true:

$$n/3f(n) = \frac{f(3n)}{3n},$$

where $n = .\overline{333}$ and its integral product is $.\overline{333}^2 = .\overline{111}$,

$$.\overline{333}/3(.\overline{111}) = 1/1,$$

and where $n = 2.7648\text{E}4$ and its integral product is 9.216E3,

$$(2.7648\text{E}4)/3(9.216\text{E}3) = (8.2944\text{E}4)/3(2.7648\text{E}4) = 1/1.$$

In the infinite series of natural numbers, 8.2944E4 is the only one which like 1 has the property that it is identically its integral product while its 1/3rd part is a number whose integral product is the 1/3rd part of that 1/3rd part, in its case, the 1/9th part of 8.2944E4.[145] The integral product of 8.2944E4, *qua* proportion, 8 : 2 :: 9 : 4 :: 4 : [1], is 8.2944E4 (its rational product is the *unity* number, 36). The foundational 1/9th part of 8.2944E4 is related to *its* integral part as $113.\overline{777}$ to 1, precisely as the 'absolute' פתח ('window'/'opening'/'doorway' [integral product, 4.096E5] is related to 'absolute' יהוה ('Yahweh' [integral product, 3.6E3]), $4.096\text{E}5/3.6\text{E}3 = 113.\overline{777}$, and is the integral product of the 'proportion of absolute Davidic clarity' identified with 'absolute' הכרה ('consciousness'/'discernment' [integral product, 1E6]), $.000113.\overline{777} \times 1\text{E}6 = 113.\overline{777}$. The perfectly unique 8.2944E4 has already been encountered as the extended base factor of 'absolute' יהוה מלך־ישׂראל ('Yahweh King of Israel' [integral product, 8.2944E18]).[146] The foundational

[145] Cf. below, Section III.6.

[146] Cf. above, p. 398, et passim. See also, above, Section III.2, Theorems 4 and 5.

1/9th part of 'absolute' יהוה מלך־ישׂראל ('Yahweh King of Israel') is 'absolute' סתרי תורה ('secrets of the law', *qua* proportion, 60 : 400 :: 200 : 10 (::) 400 : 6 :: 200 : 5, whose integral product is 9.216E17), (8.2944E18)/9 = 9.216E17.[147] If 'absolute' יהוה מלך־ישׂראל ('Yahweh King of Israel' [integral product, 8.2944E18]) is identified with 'absolute' בין ('between' [integral product, 1E4, the 'created 100']) the product is 'absolute' נקדת האפס של תנופה ('dead center'/ 'point zero of energy', *qua* proportion, 50 : 100 :: 4 : 400 (::) 5 : 1 :: 80 : 60 (::) 300 : 30 (::) 400 : 50 :: 6 : 80 :: 5 : [1], whose integral product is 8.2944E22), 8.2944E18 × 1E4 = 8.2944E22, 'absolute Yahweh King of Israel' identified with 'absolute between' is 'absolute dead center'. The rational product of נקדת האפס של תנופה ('dead center') is Unity, 1. The foundational 1/9th part of 'absolute' נקדת האפס של תנופה ('dead center' [integral product, 8.2944E22]) is 'absolute' קול קורא במדבר ('a voice cries "in the wilderness . . . [prepare a way for Yahweh."]' [Is. 40:3], *qua* proportion, 100 : 6 :: 30 : [1] (::) 100 : 6 :: 200 : 1 (::) 2 : 40 :: 4 : 2 ::

[147] That the thinking now occurring for the first time is the cracking of the (1/9) – (1/113.$\overline{777}$) code may be seen from the following: 'absolute' מפתח לכתב סתרים ('cipher', *qua* proportion, 40 : 80 :: 400 : 8 (::) 30 : 20 :: 400 : 2 (::) 60 : 400 :: 200 : 10 :: 40 : [1], whose integral product is 8.4934656E27, while its rational product is 9E5 and its linear product is 9.437184E21) is, *qua* integral products, 9E4 times 'absolute' מפתח כתב סתרים ('cipher key', *qua* proportion, 40 : 80 :: 400 : 8 (::) 20 : 400 :: 2 : [1] (::) 60 : 400 :: 200 : 10 :: 40 : [1], whose integral product is 9.437184E22, while its rational product is 3E2 and its linear product is 3.145728E20 [$\sim\pi \cdot 10^{20}$]), which, *qua* integral products, is (9E8 × 113.$\overline{777}$) times 'absolute' ספר הקים ('code', *qua* proportion, 60 : 80 :: 200 : [1] (::) 5 : 100 :: 10 : 40, whose integral product is 9.216E11, while its rational product is 3 and its linear product is 3.072E11), while the product of the connecting multiples, 9E4 × 9E8 × 113.$\overline{777}$ = 9.216E15, times 'absolute' דבר סתר ('secret matter', *qua* proportion, 4 : 2 :: 200 : [1] (::) 60 : 400 :: 200 : [1], whose integral product is 9.216E11) *is* 'absolute' מפתח לכתב סתרים ('cipher' [integral product, 8.4934656E27]). The reduction of 'absolute' נקדת האפס של תנופה ('dead center' [integral product, 8.2944E22]) to 'absolute' מפתח לכתב סתרים ('cipher' [integral product, 8.4934656E27]) identified with ברא ('to create [rational product, .01]),(8.2944E22)/(8.4934656E27 × .01) = .0009765625 = (9 × 113.$\overline{777}$)$^{-1}$, which is the very 'identity' of אבן הפילוסופים ('philosopher's stone', *qua* proportion, 1 : 2 :: 50 : [1] (::) 5 : 80 :: 10 : 30 :: 6 : 60 :: 6 : 80 :: 10 : 40, whose rational product is .0009765625).

200 : [1], whose integral product is 9.216E21, while its rational product is 3.333E7 and its linear product is 2.7648E14). The 'absolute' סתרי תורה ('secrets of the law' [integral product, 9.216E17]) which is the 1/9th foundational identity of 'absolute' יהוה מלך-ישראל ('Yahweh King of Israel') is identically 'absolute' אני חושב אני קים ('I think, I am', *qua* proportion, 1 : 50 :: 10 : [1] (::) 8 : 6 :: 300 : 2 (::) 1 : 50 :: 10 : [1] (::) 100 : 10 :: 40 : [1], whose integral product is 9.216E17), where the Cartesian *ergo* has been eliminated, removing any reference whatsoever to the doubt/certainty implicit in the resolving *therefore*, including even the reference which continues in phenomenological bracketing, removing any reference whatsoever to the resolution of any subjectivity whatsoever, transcendent or transcendental. Here *Ego* is *meta*-identically Ego *ex nihilo:* I transcendentally I for the first time. Here there is no ground for identifying *Ego* and *self*. For the first time dead center is the absolute. This is the absolute explosion of identity, the absolute exteriority of (any)second side: the second absolute is the absolute outside: the new universe is the absolute universe: the absolutely measured, absolutely self-less 'opening and expanding' of time itself.[148] This is the absolute objectivity of existence, at once the 'absolute recurrence for the first time of existence', the absolute recurrence of creation, the absolute reduction of Being *ex nihilo* to Yahweh existing *ex nihilo*, very Existence very Name the very Synthesis, the very Leap, the very Closing which is completely and unconditionally the beginning 'in which we (categorically self-less ego's) live and move and exist'.[149] The unconditionality of this beginning of existence manifests itself in the fact that 'absolute' נקדת האפס של תנופה ('dead center' [integral product, 8.2944E22]) identified as very הצרפה ('synthesis'), very קפיצה ('leap'/'closing'), is 'absolute' אני חושב ועל כן אני קים ('*Cogito ergo sum*'/I think therefore I am', *qua* proportion, 1 : 50 :: 10 : [1] (::) 8 : 6 :: 300 : 2 (::) 6 : 70 :: 30 : [1] (::) 20 : 50 (::) 1 : 50 :: 10 : [1] (::) 100 : 10 :: 40 : [1], whose integral product is 1.1943936E25) identified with ברא ('to create [rational product, .01]), (8.2944E22)/

[148] Cf. above, p. 327.
[149] Cf. above, pp. 418ff.

$.69\overline{444} = 1.1943936E25 \times .01 = 1.1943936E23$. This is the absolute *Cogito ergo sum* identified with creation in which form the 'absolute' ועל כן ('ergo'/'therefore', *qua* proportion, 6 : 70 :: 30 : [1] (::) 20 : 50, whose integral product is 1.296E7) is that of no subjectivity whatsoever, but is, identically 'absolute' יחסיות ('relativity' [integral product, 1.296E7]). This absolute relativity is the absolute unity of the absolute *cogito sum* identified with creation. 'Absolute' אני חושב ועל כן אני קים ('*Cogito ergo sum*'/I think therefore I am' [integral product, 1.1943936E25]) identified with ברא ('to create [rational product, .01]), 1.1943936E23, is itself at once 'absolute' מטריצה מחלפת ('transposed matrix', *qua* proportion, 40 : 9 :: 200 : 10 :: 90 : 5 (::) 40 : 8 :: 30 : 80 :: 400 : [1], whose integral product is 1.1943936E23). The *Ego* of absolute *Cogito ergo sum* identified with 'to create', the *Ego* of the absolutely transposed matrix, is the beginning of absolute objectivity, identically time itself the absolute window. Absolutely before now, the abysmal dead center existed everywhere in the form of absolute solitude, everywhere relative to nothing, perpetually unable to *measure* the unity of the circle. Now for the first time this is the unity of the circle measured *ex abysso*: "I Am this beginning, 'Dead Center absolutely everywhere.'" This is the beginning of the circle absolutely eliminating nothing/eliminating absolutely nothing from dead center. Not the 'original synthetic unity of *ap*perception',[150] but the

[150] Cf. Heidegger, *Basic Problems of Phenomenology*, pp. 128f.: "From our previous considerations we know that for Kant being equals perceivedness. The basic conditions of the being of beings, or of perceivedness, are therefore the basic conditions of the being-known of things. However, the basic condition of knowing as knowing is the ego as 'I-think'. Hence Kant continually inculcates that the ego is not a representation, that it is not a represented object, not a being in the sense of an object, but rather the ground of the possibility of all representing, all perceiving, hence of all the perceivedness of beings and thus the ground of all being. As original synthetic unity of apperception, the ego is the fundamental ontological condition of all being. The basic determinations of the being of beings are the categories. The ego is not one among the categories of beings but the condition of the possibility of categories in general. Therefore, the ego does not itself belong among the root concepts of the understanding, as Kant calls the categories; instead, as Kant expresses it, the ego is 'the vehicle of all

existence *ex nihilo* of the synthetic unity of *perception*, personality absolutely unconditioned, absolute *personalitas transcendentalis*: the transcendental ego in fact 'one among the categories of being', and, as such, the category, but, as such, the absolute elimination of subjectivity, of that subjectivity with which it has been, hitherto, identified (as well as of perception identified as *representation*). The way to this absolute perception of the transcendental ego is formally, but not essentially, prepared in Peirce's having in fact reduced the Ego to a 'mere point', in effect, in his reduction of 'the present instant' to an 'absolute present', to a 'sort of consciousness, or feeling, with no self' (the category of Firstness),[151] and in his reduction, in effect, of thinking purely to the 'combining' of a Second with this First, in his categorical postponement of self-consciousness. The way to the absolute objectivity of the Ego is absolutely, but inessentially, prepared in Altizer's conception of self-identity inverted to the point of the other, 'in the form of that total evacuation of interior identity and individuality which, *qua* world-time/*qua* expectancy, is the identity of a new humanity'.[152] If the index of Peirce's essentially combinatory conception of unity is that which is at the base of his conception of the ideal triad, namely,

concepts of the understanding'. It first of all makes possible the basic a priori ontological concepts. For the ego is not something isolated, not a mere point, but always 'I-think', that is, 'I-combine'. And Kant interprets the categories as that which, in every combining by the understanding, has already been seen and understood beforehand as what provides the corresponding unity of the combined for each combining to be accomplished. The categories are the possible forms of unity of the possible modes of the thinking ego, the 'I-combine'. Combinability and, corresponding to it, its own form, its respective unity, are grounded in the 'I-combine'. Thus the ego is the fundamental ontological condition, the transcendental that lies at the basis of every particular a priori. We now understand that the ego as the I-think is the formal structure of personality as personalitas transcendentalis . . . . This, however, does not exhaustively define the concept of subjectivity in Kant. To be sure, this concept of the transcendental ego remains the model for the further interpretation of egohood, personality in the formal sense. But personalitas transcendentalis does not coincide with the complete concept of personality."

[151] Cf. below, Section IV.1, p. 456.

[152] Ibid., p. 454.

the pairing of two halves of a presumed unity so as to create the apparent circle, the diameter of which is no diameter, but the absolutely indefinite point of intersection of the two halves of a purely symbolic unity, the diameter of which is actually the indefinite measure of the depths of the 'Dawn', as may be imaged:[153]

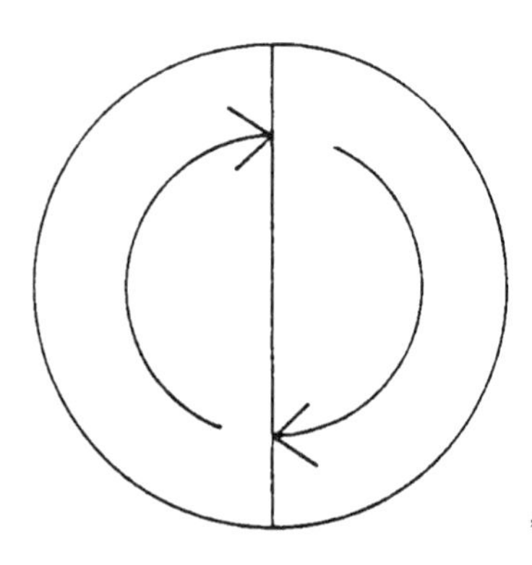

and if the index of the reduction in Altizer in effect, of this ideal combinatory unity of the circle to Nothing, the index of (not the Peircean fragments unified in the intersection, but the inversion thereof identifying that very unity with Nothing, at once, the absolute fragmentation of the intersection) the absolute fragmentation of identity,[154] the fragmentation of the very identity which embodies the fragmented *cogito*, the fragmentation of the I-fragment and the think-fragment, which, bound together had constituted the ideal unity of the circle (the real duality of an I-not-self [the double inversion of thought] and thought, bound together in the indefinite depths of the intersection: Night and Day, –1 and 1),[155] if the index of the re-embodiment of the *membra disiecta* of a disembodied Nothing[156] is, beyond the 'celebration' which 'issued from a passage through' a center at once a nothing, a 'nothingness or a void', which may be imaged:

[153] Cf. above, pp. 294ff.
[154] Cf. above, pp. 226ff.
[155] Cf. above, pp. 294ff.
[156] Cf. above, pp. 192ff. and 228.

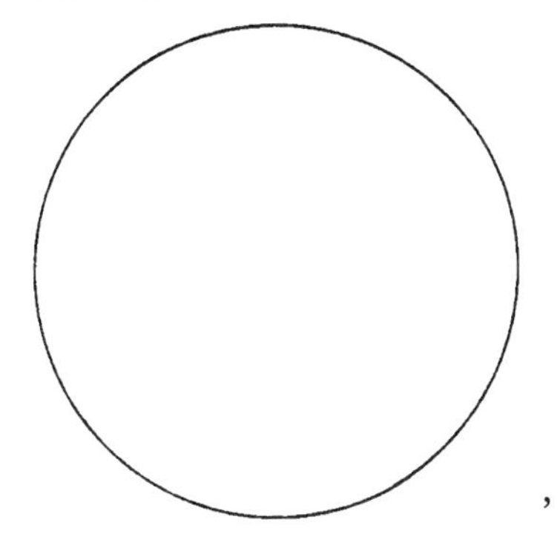

the circle which is a zero, the circle containing nothing, the nothing which *is* nothing, the nothing which is not *ex nihilo,* which, although it possesses the potentiality of dead center absolutely, not lacking, *qua* pure potential, dead center absolutely, lacks, nevertheless, the diameter, the measure of absolute dead center (liquid identity that this circle is in reality[157]), then the index of the zero *ex nihilo* diametrically unified as absolute dead center, the index of dead center *ex abysso* measuring the circle, the index of the absolutely firm circle the diameter of which is identity *ex nihilo,* the index of the absolutely unshakeable foundation the measure of which is *cogito esse, sum ex nihilo,* this index, is the panoptic eye,[158] the foundational manifold of identity, the absolutely structured identity of the new world now actually existing, which is imaged:

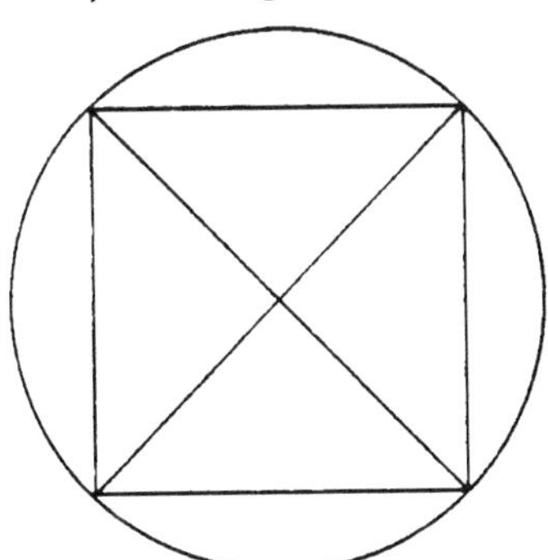

[157] Cf. above, pp. 225ff.
[158] Cf. above, pp. 275 and 290.

Now, in order to make manifest the specific structure of absolute dead center, let the diameter of this index, at once the diagonal equally dividing the face of a cube inscribed within a sphere, equal 1.44E2 units ('absolute' אלכסון ['diameter'/'diagonal', *qua* proportion, 1 : 30 :: 20 : 60 :: 6 : 50, whose integral product is 1.44E4 (= 'absolute' כפור ['Atonement'])] identified with ברא ['to create' (rational product, .01)], 1.44E4 × .01 = 1.44E2). Then, each edge of the face of the cube = 101.8233765, and the area of each side of the cube = 1.0368E4. The total surface area of this 'absolute dead center' cube is then 6.2208E4, or 8.2944E4 (the perfectly unique natural number functioning as 1 *qua* integral product relations, and the extended base factor of 'absolute' נקדת האפס של תנופה ('dead center'/'point zero of energy' [8.2944E22]) × .75 (the 'identity'/rational product of אפס ['nothing']) = 6.2208E4. But then this cube, *qua* surface, while not 'nothingness or a void', is, nevertheless, not substantially different, *qua* absolute dead center lacking a measure, from the center of the circle lacking the measure of absolute dead center, not substantially different from the center void of dead center (the absolute inversion of the abyss), not substantially different from the relative center of nothingness, nor, indeed, *qua* surface of a cube, substantially different from that '2 × 3 affair' to which Peirce reduces trichotomic mathematics, of which 'affair' the 'celebration' issuing 'from a passage through'/at once the inversion of the Void is but the ultimate function. What, then, is the measure of absolute dead center, of that which, lacking a measure, is but a variant of the void? It is the 'not nothing', the '1 – .75',[159] which precedes the substantial nothingness of the cube *qua* six-sided surface, that is, the 8.2944E4 – 6.2208E4 = 2.0736E4 which is the square of the creation-diameter, $1.44E2^2$, at once itself the area of the two interior planes or 'sides' which define the unitary structure of the cube. The square of the creation-diagonal (2.0736E4 [the 'not nothing', '1 – .75']), in the form of the two additional 'sides' inside the cube (perpendicular to each other and to the sides of the cube [jointly to two sides, and each separately to two sides], and bisecting each other at the center of the cube), mea-

[159] Cf. above, pp. 421f.

sures the cube, as here illustrated:

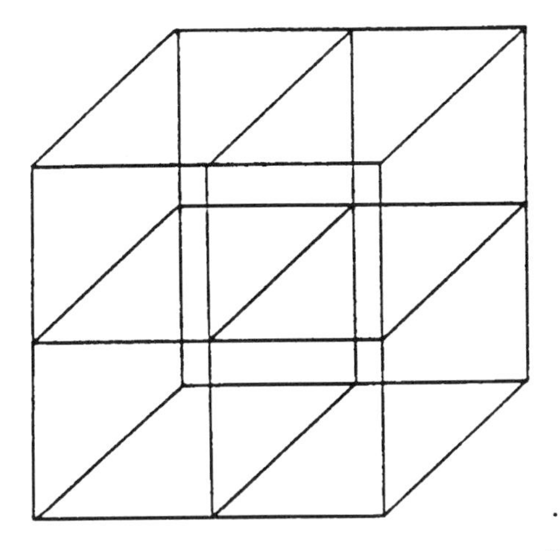

Here, three-dimensionally, is the minimum *ex nihilo* the greater than which is reducible to nothing. This fundamental element, in the form of a ' + ', divides each of two opposite sides of the cube (between which there is no intervening 'additional side' *parallel* to the opposite sides in question, as there is in the case of each of the other two pairs of opposite sides, since any *third* 'additional side' sharing the center of the cube would obliterate the unitary structure of the cube by immediately reducing it to eight smaller cubes) into four equal square sub-sections each of whose areas is 2.592E3. The critical understanding of the measure of the 'absolute dead center' cube is that the surface is the nothingness unified *ex nihilo* in the form of the two-sided objectivity, that the surface is the two-sided objectivity of nothing *ex nihilo,* that in the midst of the two-sided objectivity of the cube exists absolutely nothing at the center of which is the 'not nothing', the 1/4th of unity (the unitary structure of the cube, 2.0736E4 = [8.2944E4]/4) which is the 1/3rd of nothing (the two quartered sides of the surface of the cube, 2.0736E4 = [6.2208E4]/3), 82944/4 = .75(82944)/3, the creation-diameter squared, the unitary structure of the cube, measuring the two-sided objectivity the fundamental section of which is the 2.592E3 square.[160] With the

[160] For 2.592E3, cf. above, p. 277, n. 30.

unitary structure of the cube so constructed, it is possible to see that the volume of this (or any) cube, *V*, is equal to the product of the square root of the area of the one-fourth section of the side as created by the 2 interior planes here depicted, $\sqrt{S_{x^2/4}}$ (where x is the length of a single edge of the cube), times the total area of those 2 planes, which latter area—let it be d^2—is identically the square of the face diagonal of the cube, D^2. But this square root of the one-fourth section of the side, $S_{x^2/4,}$ so identified by the construction of the unitary structure, is at once equal to the surface area of the cube, S_c, divided by the total superficies of the cube, P_c, the bounding edges of the cube, and equal to 4 times the area of the one-fourth section of the side, $\sqrt{S_{x^2/4}}$, divided by the length of the superficies bounding that area, $P_{x^2/4}$,

$$\sqrt{S_{x^2/4}} = \frac{V}{D^2} = \frac{S_c}{P_c} = 4\left(\frac{S_{x^2/4}}{P_{x^2/4}}\right) = \frac{x^2}{P_{x^2/4}},$$

which is to say that the root of the square one-fourth the side of the cube is the reduction of the volume of the cube to the 2 interior planes, at once the reduction of the surface of the cube to the bounding edges of the cube, at once the reduction of the surface of the side of the cube to the bounding edges of the one-fourth section of the side. Since $x^2/P_{x^2/4}$ equals $4(S_{x^2/4}/P_{x^2/4})$, the cube, *qua* volume/face-diagonal-squared ratio, is radically its fourfold side. The reduction of the volume of the cube to its face-diagonal squared is the reduction of the volume to the two-sidedness of the unitary structure of the cube, identically the one-sidedness of the cube, the absolute one-sided. 'Absolute' חד-צדדי ('one-sided', *qua* proportion, 8 : 4 (::) 90 : 4 :: 4 : 10, whose integral product is 8.2944E6) identified with 'absolute' תשנון ('repetition', *qua* proportion, 400 : 300 :: 50 : 6 :: 50 : [1], whose integral product is 1E12) is identically 'absolute' נקדת האפס של תנופה ('dead center' [integral product, 8.2944E22]) denominated 'absolute' בין ('between' [integral product, 1E4]), 8.2944E6 × 1E12 = 8.2944E22/1E4 = 8.2944E18. This reality of the cubic dead center structure is perceivable when the elements of the fourfold logical foundation, the fourfold positioning of the square essence of the infinite logical lattice,[161] are placed in order in the quadrants of the face of the cube, starting in the lower left quadrant and running counter-clockwise to the upper left quadrant:

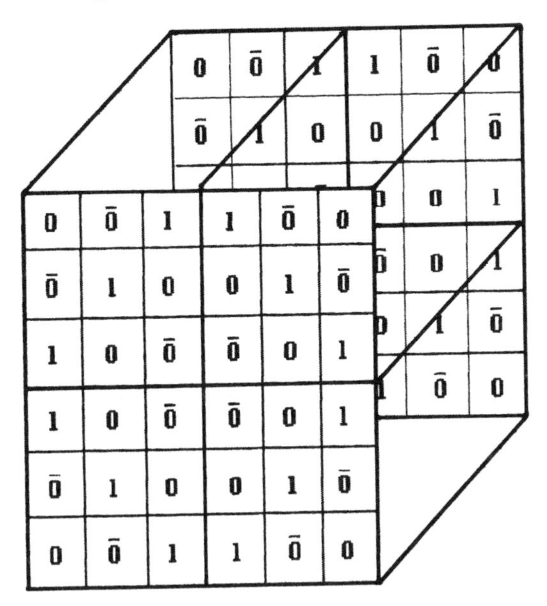

The proof that for the first time seeing is thinking, perceiving is thinking, that the two-sided objectivity is the one-sided absolute is the following. Since $\sqrt{S_{x^2/4}} = V/D^2 = S_c/P_c = x^2/P_{x^2/4} = P_c/24$, then $D^2P_c/V = 24$. But 24 is the mean proportional of the Absolute Proportion of Absolute Thought, 16 : 24 :: 24 : 36. If, then, $D^2P_{d^2}/V = 16$ (where $d^2 = 2$ interior planes whose area $= D^2$), and $D^2P_{1.5c}/V = 36$, the structure of the cube is comprehended in a form which is identically the 'perfectly logical proportion',[162] viz.:

$$\frac{D^2P_{d^2}}{V} : \frac{D^2P_c}{V} :: \frac{D^2P_c}{V} : \frac{D^2P_{1.5c}}{V},$$

[161] Cf. above, Section III.1.

[162] Cf. above, p. 367.

the 'perfectly logical proportion', *qua* cube, which in the case of the 'absolute dead center' cube is the proportion

$$16\sqrt{2592} : 24\sqrt{2592} :: 24\sqrt{2592} : 36\sqrt{2592}.$$

The universal form of the unitary structure of the cube identified in each of its elements with the specific fundamental unitary measure of the cube, viz., $\sqrt{S_{x^2/4}}$, is:

$$P_{d^2} : P_c :: P_c : P_{1.5\,c},$$

in which form it is perceived that the absolutely rational identity of the cube is 'the absolute one-sided' unity *ex nihilo*, that there is no question of a value beyond $P_{1.5c}$, no question of a multiple of c greater than the logical 1.5, the ratio the repetition of which is the essential structure of the 'absolute proportion of absolute thought', no question of a doubling, no question of a division within and of unity from itself. The proven unity of this proportion in the case of the 'absolute dead center' cube is:

$$8.14587012\text{E}2 : 1.221880518\text{E}3 :: 1.221880518\text{E}3 : 1.832820\bar{7}\text{E}3,$$

$$(8.14587012\text{E}2 \cdot 1.832820\bar{7}\text{E}3)/1.221880518\text{E}3^2 = 1,$$

$$1.492992\text{E}6/1.492992\text{E}6 = 1,$$

where 1.492992E6 is the product of the perfectly unique 8.2944E4 (identically 'absolute' דו-חוש' ('bifilar', *qua* proportion, 4 : 6 (::) 8 : 6 :: 9 : 10, whose integral product is 8.2944E4) and the very 'identity' of חד-צדדי ('one-sided' [rational product, 18]), $1.492992\text{E}6 = 8.2944\text{E}4 \times 18$. The proven unity of the 'absolute proportion of absolute thought' structure of the 'absolute dead center' cube is the bifilar absolutely identical with the one-sided, and, again, itself at once the product of 'absolute' חד-צדדי ('one-sided' [integral product, 8.2944E6]) and the very 'identity' of

אנליסת נפחים ('volumetric analysis', *qua* proportion, 1 : 50 :: 30 : 10 :: 60 : 400 (::) 50 : 80 :: 8 : 10 :: 40 : [1], whose rational product is .18), 1.492992E6 = 8.2944E6 × .18.

The last term in the 'absolute dead center' proportion, $P_{1.5c} = 36\sqrt{2592} = 1832.820\overline{7}$, is the transcendental constant.[163] The transcendental constant is the culminating substance of that שׁלום ('peace' [rational product, 1.5]) repeated in the שׁלום לך ('*shalom lecha*', 'Peace be with you' [rational product, 2.25 = 1.5 × 1.5]) which is, *qua* beginning, the death of solitude. It reflects the fact that in the logical foundation (= the face of the 'absolute dead center' cube) the 12 1's, 12 $\overline{0}$'s, and 12 0's, the 36 digits, have a sum total *arithmetic* value of 24,[164] and that 36 is 24 identical with its actual and equal distribution among each of the 4 squares of the foundation, 36 = (24 × 6)/4.

Such is the absolutely simple complexity, absolutely complex simplicity of the conception of creation. Thought now for the first time identifies absolute dead center as creation in the form of an *absolutely unconditioned Cogito ergo sum (absolutely self-less),* identifies the beginning of an absolute 'I Am' as dead center everywhere (the ground of the absolute explosion of identity) existing now in the very form of time itself. This is at once itself for the first time the perfect reduction of depth to surface.[165]

---

163 Cf. Rv. 21:6: Γέγοναν. ἐγὼ τὸ Ἄλφα καὶ τὸ Ὦ, ἡ ἀρχὴ καὶ τὸ τέλος, "They are accomplished facts. I am the Alpha at once the Omega, the Beginning even the End," where the perfectly radical existence of the transcendental intelligibility of the beginning of all things manifests itself in, at once as, the very form of these words of the angel of the Apocalypse, as well as in, at once as, the substance of the words of the angel Jesus. Here, where the text speaks of the transcendental intelligibility of the eventuality of beginning to exist, the 'integral product' of the Greek text is 1.1284439629824E71, exactly 1E58 times the fourfold identity of the transcendental constant ($C^4 \cdot$ 1E58), while the 'rational product' of the angel's words, 1.110394478491105E20, equals, with a difference less than one in 10,000, the π root of 1E58 times the integral product of the 'proportion of absolute Davidic clarity' (1.13$\overline{7}$E–4) times the total area of the unitary structure of the 'absolute dead center' cube (8.2944E4) identified with the 'absolute' between (1E4), that is, $(9.437184\text{E}62)^{1/\pi}$ (cf. above, p. 428, n. 147).

164 Cf. above, p. 274, n. 27.

165 Cf. above, Section III.3.

Neither the equivocation which was the depths of the 'Dawn',[166] nor the relatively unequivocal identification of the depth of identity, which was the absolute liquidity of identity,'[167] but the absolutely unequivocal identification of the depth of identity as the surface. This is the body of the Living God thought in essence for the first time. Being atoning in every now for the first time. 'Concrete infinite potentiality' *sans* horizon[168]/*ex nihilo* : the absolute actuality of the beginning: the transcendence of the modern project in the form of the reduction of pure potentiality, absolutely & essentially, to the absolute act of creation. Now for the first time in history the categorically selfless transcendence of the transcendental ego: for the first time, 'I think' absolutely the appearance *in essence:* not an epiphany, but the phenomenon. The Face of God appearing for the first time as the face of existence: the divine and absolute superficiality of every actual thing *ex nihilo.*

---

[166] Cf. above, pp. 432ff. and 294ff.

[167] Cf. above, Section II.4, especially pp. 230ff., for the relatively vs. the absolutely unequivocal. Also, Section II.3, especially pp. 000ff., for the 'univocal predication of being itself' in the context of the critique of *la différance.* Cf. also J. Derrida, *Edmund Husserl's Origin of Geometry: An Introduction,* trans. J. P. Leavey (Stony Brook, 1978), pp. 100ff., for the relations between univocity and equivocity and the projects of Husserl and Joyce, respectively.

[168] Cf. Derrida, *Edmund Husserl's Origin of Geometry,* p. 117.

6

THEOREM CONCERNING THE NATURAL NUMBERS, 1, 784, AND 82944, FACTORS OF $(9!/45)^2$

THEOREM. 1, 784, and 82944 are the only natural numbers the square of whose product of odd-numbered digits (counting left to right) equals the number.

Proof: Natural numbers the square of whose product of odd-numbered digits equals the number must contain no zeros in the odd-numbered digits. Determine the natural numbers which are candidate numbers, that is, the numbers in each order of magnitude which satisfy the minimum condition necessary to be potentially the sought-for numbers, by finding those numbers in each order of magnitude which are the square product of the odd-numbered digits of any number of that order of magnitude which has the identical first digit (the square product of odd-numbered digits, let it be called the integral product, for the 10^0 order of magnitude, 1, 2, . . . , 9, is the square of the single digit; for the 10^2 order of magnitude, 100, 101 . . . , 999, the square of the first times the square of the third digit, and so on for the higher orders of magnitude). Candidate numbers cannot be found in the odd-powered orders of magnitude (10^1, 10^3, 10^5, etc.) which add in each case an even-numbered digit place to the preceding order of magnitude.

There are 72 candidate numbers distributed as follows among eleven orders of magnitude of numbers:

Order of Magnitude	*Number of Candidates*
10^0	1
10^2	4

Order of Magnitude	*Number of Candidates*
10^4	11
10^6	13
10^8	15
10^{10}	10
10^{12}	7
10^{14}	4
10^{16}	4
10^{18}	2
10^{20}	1 .

The last candidate number to be found is 9^{22} or 984,770,902,183,711,232,881, the integral product of any number the product of whose odd-numbered digits is 9^{11} (which candidate number is not a sought-for number). At one sextillion (10^{21}) the minimum condition for candidate numbers ceases to occur. The square products of the odd-numbered digits of numbers in the even-powered orders of magnitude 10^{22} through 10^{40} are possibly numbers of the original order of magnitude but without a first digit identical with that of the original number. Beginning at one hundred duodecillion (10^{41}) the square product of the odd-numbered digits of no number is a number of an order of magnitude as great as its own. Of the 72 candidate numbers only 1, 784, and 82944 equal the square product of their odd-numbered digits.

Note : In 1985 the writer discovered that the number 82944 equaled the square product of its odd-numbered digits.[1] Until the summer of 1990 he had found in the course of his ordinary consideration of numbers—with the exception of the number 1—no other number with this property. Then he designed and wrote a computer program with the following systematic objectives:

1. To identify those 'integral products' which qualify as candidate numbers, as potentially the numbers of which they are the square product of the odd-numbered digits,

[1] Cf. above, Section III.5.

2. To determine if the candidate number is the sought-for number,
3. To determine exhaustively which natural numbers are their 'integral products', that is, which are identically the square of the product of their odd-numbered digits.

The program analyzes each candidate number into its constituent digits in place order, computes *its* integral product, and compares the latter to the candidate number for identity. The multiples of first digits, that is, the products of the possible combinations of secondary digits for each even-powered order of magnitude beyond 10^0 (the latter having no secondary odd-numbered digit, its multiple is 1), are determined by a module of the program which first identifies which squares of the products of possible combinations of non-zero digits for each order of magnitude produce a number of that order of magnitude. It does this by multiplying each multiple from the preceding order of magnitude by the product of all possible combinations of two natural digits except by the product of 1 and 1 and except by such of those products as end in zero, and then squaring the result. (If products ending in zero are not excepted two multiples are added to the total number of multiples without in any way affecting the number of candidate numbers or the final results of the program.) If the result squared is a number of the current order of magnitude, the multiple of the preceding order of magnitude is multiplied by each of the single-digit factors of the product of the two digits, except by 1, and the products of this last multiplication are added, without duplication, to the list of multiples for the current order of magnitude. If the multiples which contain a zero in the last place are eliminated before calculating the candidate numbers for each order of magnitude, then, across the eleven orders of magnitude (10^0 to 10^{20}, as above) the total number of multiples in combination with which possible first digits are evaluated drops by 157, from 692 to 535, but the total number of candidate numbers drops by just 2, from 72 to 70. The ratio of the total number of occurrences of candidate numbers in the full and abbreviated versions respectively, 72/70 ($1.0\overline{285714}$), is one-tenth the square root of (82944/784). The two candidate numbers eliminated by the possible economy in the running of the program are 78400 and 8294400. The ultimate results of the analysis are identical, but the distribution of candidate numbers is altered from 1, 4, 11, 13, 15, 10, 7, 4, 4, 2, 1, to 1, 4, 10, 12, 15, 10, 7, 4, 4, 2, 1.

The fundamental relationship of 1, 784, and 82944, and, therefore, of integral product reckoning, to the system of natural numbers manifests itself in the fact that the product of these numbers, therefore, the product of their 'integral products', viz. 65028096, is the square of the product divided by the sum of the primary digits of the natural number system, that is, $(9!/45)^2$.[2]

---

2. The technical mathematical term for the ϕ ratio (cf. Euclid, *Elements,* 6, def. 3) is ὁ ἄκρος καὶ μέσος λόγος, "the extreme and mean ratio." The fact is that the integral product of this Greek mathematical term, the technical linguistic expression for the 'golden section' ratio, is $1 \cdot 784 \cdot 82944 \cdot 10^{30}$, or $(9!/45)^2 \cdot 10^{30}$. The rational product of ὁ ἄκρος καὶ μέσος λόγος, is—with a difference of 0.10 pph—10^5 times the area of the 'golden rectangle' produced in the course of the Proof of Euclid 2, 11, when the sides of that rectangle are the ideal 'retrospective square' value of $*F_1$ (= $\phi^2/5^{1/2}$) in the *unum*-founded Fibonacci sequence (cf. above, Section III.2) multiplied by, respectively, ϕ^{10} and ϕ^{11}. The integral product of ἡ καταβολὴ κόσμου, "the foundation of the universe," is $(9!/45)^2 \cdot 10^{16}$, and the integral product of Jn. 8:12, 'Εγώ εἰμι τὸ φῶς τοῦ κόσμου, "I am the light of the universe," is $(9!/45)^2 \cdot 10^{40}$.

7

THEOREM CONCERNING THE SETS OF TWENTY-TWO AND EIGHT NATURAL NUMBERS WHOSE INTEGRAL PRODUCTS EQUAL UNIT AND MULTI-UNIT FRACTIONS OF THEMSELVES THE DENOMINATORS OF WHICH ARE PRIMARY DIGITS OF THE NUMBER SYSTEM

Definitions : The integral product of a natural number is the square of the product of its odd-numbered digits (counting left to right). In the case of those fractions here considered whose denominators are single digits, a unit fraction is a fraction whose numerator is 1. A multi-unit fraction is a fraction of the same kind whose numerator is between 2 and 9 and not greater than its denominator.

THEOREM. Two sets of twenty-two and eight natural numbers respectively contain all the natural numbers in which the integral product of the number equals either a unit or multi-unit fraction of itself.

Proof: 1. Determine candidate numbers by multiplying, in order, the square of each of the natural numbers by each of the primary digits of the natural number system.

2. Determine which of the products of the operation in paragraph 1 are numbers whose integral products equal themselves divided by one of the primary digits of the natural number system.

3. At one sextillion (10^{21}) the minimum condition for candidate numbers ceases to occur. The square products of the odd

digits of numbers in the orders of magnitude above 10^{22} are possibly numbers of the original order of magnitude but without a possible first digit identical with that of the original number.

4. The natural numbers which satisfy the criterion in paragraph 2 are as follows:[1]

UNIT FRACTIONS

Numerator	*Denominator*	*Number*	*Integral Product*
1	1	1	1
1	1	784	784
1	1	82944	82944
1	2	50	25
1	2	128	64
1	3	48	16
1	3	147	49
1	3	972	324
1	3	11907	3969
1	3	27648	9216
1	4	36	9
1	4	36864	9216
1	4	429981696	107495424
1	5	20	4
1	5	125	25

[1] For proof that the list of integral products is exhaustive in the case where 1 is the denominator of the fraction representing the unit part of the natural number, cf. above, Section III.6. The procedure employed in that case, computer programming within an analytically defined range, has been used here to discover the natural numbers actually existing whose integral products are unit or multi-unit fractions of themselves the denominators of which are between 2 and 9. However, for these latter numbers limitations of time and computer speed have made it impractical to examine candidate numbers beyond 8.99982E10. Since all the qualifying numbers discovered by the computer program exist within the range of the first 500 million numbers, while none have been found beyond, among the next 89.5 billion examined, it may be supposed that in fact none exist between 90 billion and 1 sextillion, the end of the range of possible candidate numbers.

THEOREM CONCERNING THE SETS OF TWENTY-TWO AND EIGHT

Numerator	*Denominator*	*Number*	*Integral Product*
1	6	24	4
1	6	7350	1225
1	7	28	4
1	7	175	25
1	8	2592	324
1	9	144	16
1	9	2985984	331776

MULTI-UNIT FRACTIONS

Numerator	*Denominator*	*Number*[2]	*Integral Product*
4	5	80	64
4	6	216	144
4	7	63	36
4	9	225	100
4	9	324	144
4	9	46656	20736
4	9	50625	22500
6	9	69984	46656

Note: 27648 is unique among the above numbers and all natural numbers since it is the only number, whose integral product is a fraction of itself whose denominator is a primary digit, which is itself that *identical* primary digit fraction of a number whose integral product is in turn a primary digit fraction of itself, viz., 82944, whose integral product is the 1st part of itself, i.e., itself identically.[3] The integral product of the rational number .333 is,

[2] The integral product of the last number in this column is 2/3rds the number, but the computer program recognized it as 6/9ths. The program also identified 128 as a number whose integral product, 64, is 4/8ths itself, but since it occurs above as a number whose integral product is 1/2 itself, it is not repeated here.

[3] Cf. above, Section III.6.

however, if the infinitely recurring $.\overline{333}$ be conceived as a single digit, likewise its 3rd part, $.\overline{111}$, i.e., $.\overline{3}^2 = .\overline{111}$. Since $.\overline{333}$ is the 3rd part of 1, which, in turn, is identically its integral product, then, *qua* integral product relations, 27648 is to 82944 precisely as .333 is to 1. 27648 and 82944 are the perfect and last numbers of their kind in the infinite series of natural numbers.[4]

The sum of all natural numbers whose integral products are either their 1st or 3rd parts, is 124451, while the sum of all natural numbers whose integral products are unit fractions of themselves the denominators of which are primary digits of the number system other than 1 or 3, is 47536 (excepting the only two numbers assimilated to unity as numbers structured as 82944 [= $1^2 \times 82944$], viz., 2985984 [= $6^2 \times 82944$] and 429981696 [= $72^2 \times 82944$]). The ratio 124451 : 47536, with a difference ~ 1/1E6, $\cong \phi^2$, the square of the extreme and mean ratio (the golden section).[5]

---

[4] Cf. above, Section III.5, pp. 426ff.

[5] The writer has determined through computer analysis that there are exactly 162 natural numbers (again excepting 2985984 [= $6^2 \times 82944$] and 429981696 [= $72^2 \times 82944$], the numbers assimilated to unity) whose integral products are unit fractions of themselves the denominators of which are between 1 and 100. 2985984 is the sum of the numerator (1492992) and denominator (1492992) in the proof of the absolute dead center cube proportion (cf. above, Section III.5, pp. 437f.). 429981696 = 1492992 $\times$ $82944^{1/2}$. For the conceptual role played by these two numbers, see also, below pp. 513ff. The ratio 162 : 100 is exactly the whole number equivalent of the extreme and mean ratio, ϕ (cf. above, p. 401, n. 90, the rational product of the Hebrew for 'rational'). Further, for ϕ, see above, Section III.2.

IV

ABSOLUTE PERCEPTION

1

AMERICAN THOUGHT AND THE NEW WORLD ORDER[1]

Now, in the beginning, three questions. First, what is the essence of the new world order now actually existing? Second, what is the essence of American thought? Third, what is the essence of the relationship of American thought and the new world order? Three questions of essence to which there is essentially one transcendentally differentiated answer, or, a question of three essences to which the answer is a differentiated transcendental unity, which transcendental unity, *qua* differentiated, is, as such, and therefore, categorically not self-differentiated, lest it were to appear that it is possible to continue to think, in the face of the new actuality of the world, in the essentially redundant categories of past thinking. In saying this, the answer to the first question is begun. The essence of the new world order now actually existing is perceived as essence, perceived, at once, as absolutely historical, in reflection upon the fact that the essence of modern consciousness was to doubt absolutely what it did not doubt essentially, in reflection upon the fact that the essence of modernity, transcendently subsumed, was to exist inessentially. The inessentially existing essence of modern consciousness is first distilled in the Cartesian *Cogito ergo sum*, the very form of which is that of absolute doubt resolved essentially in self-existence, or, the resolution of absolute self-foundation (the phenomenological reduction of Husserl is nothing but the

[1] A paper, slightly revised, originally presented at The InterAmerican Conference on "Philosophy, Culture, and History in the Americas," at the University of Puerto Rico, Mayagüez, February 15, 1985.

bracketing of the Cartesian *resolve*, so as to allow free play to the absolute self-foundation in the form of the infinite *a priori* of the transcendental ego). What the Cartesian distillate absolutely & essentially is *not*, *qua* distillate of the so-called 'metaphysical' deposit of Christian faith, of the philosophical and theological apprehension of the body of belief, what it is *not* is an essential doubt of that which the body of belief produced in its apprehension of ancient onto-theological speculation, namely, the knowledge of what is transcendent, which 'knowledge of what is transcendent' was the substantive form of Christian speculation's transcendence of ancient scientific philosophy (metaphysics). Precisely because of the fact of this transcendence not then (and not until now) essentially doubted, there was not (nor is there now) any real possibility of erasing it (which were it possible would amount to erasing historical existence, indeed, to erasing the body). Descartes formally doubted/doubted the form of 'the knowledge of what is transcendent', which for essential reasons was the founding of the essential form of knowledge in *order*, the founding of what before had been unfounded, when the essential form of knowledge had been founded in *perception*. The essential foundation of knowledge, the fact that knowledge was founded in essence, remained intact in this shift from *perception* to *order*, at once the shift from divine providential order to the order of human resolve, from the absolute self-evidence of the body to the ordered self-evidence/self-ordered evidence of the body. The resolution of modernity's inessentially ordered doubting, of its self-ordered doubting of the evidence, was the origination of a real and potent darkness of consciousness, of a real and powerfully windowless perception, which manifested itself in all of the essential forms of modern philosophy and modern critique, explicitly in the windowless monads of Leibniz which constituted the foundation of an indiscernible identity (identity of indiscernibles), an infinite unicity known only to God, but again in the critical idealism of Kant which founds the transcendental unity of self-consciousness in the unknowability of the *noumena*, which transcends the Cartesian doubt not by doubting essentially 'the knowledge of what is transcendent', but by doubting essentially the *form* thereof, advancing on the

Cartesian doubt by founding the essential form of *thought* in order, and the essential form of *knowledge* in the ordering of transcendence. Indeed, the windowless consciousness of the purely formal doubt of 'the knowledge of what is transcendent' is absolute, as such, in the absolute self-consciousness of Hegel's absolute idealism which founded the essential form of *thought* in that wherein Kant had founded the essential form of knowledge, which founded formally absolute thought, and founded the essential form of *knowledge* in the actual ordering of transcendence, and founded, at once, formally the absolute knowledge of existence, which as such, was the absolute doubt of 'the knowledge of what is transcendent', but essentially not so. In Marx 'the knowledge of what is transcendent' *was* essentially doubted for the first time in history, but non-categorically, and non-categorically out of the very necessity of its existence as the materialist conception of history: out of the very necessity of its essence revolutionary materialism doubted 'the knowledge of what is transcendent' essentially, and doubted thought absolutely, indeed, doubted the absolute thought which was Hegel's synthetic idealism, a doubt the form of which is 'the non-categorical self-opposition of the absolute knowledge of existence, the essence of which *is* the revolutionary imperative', indeed, the revolutionary doubt which *is* the windowless opposition of a categorical non-existence. On the other hand, the categorical forms of the self-opposition of absolute thought were equally windowless forms of transcending the synthetic ideal, except they were so *qua* absolute subjectivity, whether in the form of the self-consciously absurd faith of Kierkegaard, or in the form of Husserl's phenomenological reduction of the transcendent ego to the transcendental ego, the pure form of transcendental self-consciousness, the pure form of windowless infinite *a priori* identity, or, at the last, in the form of Heidegger's reduction of time itself to pure expectancy, at once the reduction of the world, *qua* a certain nothing, to the windowless opening and expanding of temporality, at once time identically the Nietzschean abyss (which abyss had been but the reduction to nothing of the Leibnizian identity of indiscernibles, of that infinite unicity known only to God which, in fact, is formally indistinguishable from that monadology which is the higher communism, concerning which latter Nietzsche's judgment was that the matter for such a society did not exist). Just now, in Derrida, the time of the abyss is diffracted, the abyss intact—at once, the abyss of thought, perception not perception, the undoubting transcendence of the absolute doubt of 'the knowledge of what is transcendent', the deconstruction of the identity of thought, of the thought of identity. And just now in the American theology of the death of God, in Altizer, this diffracted time of the abyss is inverted to the form of the self-division of God Alone, at once the division of time from self, of consciousness from self in the form of absolute solitude, in the form of that total evacuation of interior identity and individuality which, *qua* world-time/*qua* expectancy, is the identity of a new humanity. This division from self of the identity of solitude is the undoubting inversion of the absolute doubting of identity, the essential division of 'the knowledge of what is transcendent' from self: the furthest possible extension of the essence of modern consciousness: the time absolutely before now. So then, the essence of the new world order now actually existing is the transcendence of the furthest possible extension of the essence of modern consciousness, indeed, it is the transcendental dichotomy of existence divided from self and existence categorically not-self. The essence of the new world order is the creation of a new world: the essence is to create a new world. Categorically the creation of a new world is not self-creation. The transcendental dichotomy is the fact that before now this is transcendence, and that now for the first time this is absolute existence. The transcendental dichotomy is the fact that before now the absolute now is transcendent, and that now for the first time the now is absolute, that now for the first time consciousness is the world concretely & essentially. The transcendental dichotomy is the fact that before now the categorically new is transcendent, and that now there begins a categorically new world-consciousness, the fact that before now there exists the revolutionary imperative, and that now for the first time existence is essentially revolutionary, i.e., that now existence is the existence, for the first time essentially & categorically, of the other. The transcendental dichotomy is that now, not before now, there is a universal consciousness, a consciousness universal & perpetual, at once the absolute evidence of the existence of the body. The essence of the new world order is the universal & perpetual perception of the identity of the body and 'the knowledge of what is transcendent', the doubting in essence of the absolute doubt, *qua* beginning. The transcendental dichotomy itself is the beginning of existence, which is to say, it is existence begun. It is categorically not a project of self-transcendence, whether the latter be of a positive or negative form. In the actual realization of the modern project which is this beginning, the modern is absolutely not. The three-selved source is left behind. In the actual realization of the projected body which is begun, the other is absolute. The transcendental dichotomy which is the beginning which is the categorical break with past thinking is the perception of the absolute body underway, the beginning of the fulfillment of the expectancy, the beginning of the essentially synthetic reality, indeed, the beginning of absolute history, the beginning of the absolute identity of the story and the storyteller.[2] From this beginning of the end of expectancy there is no going back, except to absolute self-destruction. If the essence of the new world order is the creation of a new world, then this beginning is the absolute opening and expanding of time into the absolute relativity of the world: time for the first time the absolute measure: the beginning of time itself identically the magnitude of being. The transcendental dichotomy, then, is the beginning of an absolutely practical existence.

Now this answer to the first question is the beginning of the answer to the second question, viz., what is the essence of American thought? If C. S. Peirce's pragmatism (the transcendental and logical locus of the essence of American thought) is the belief in the maxim that "In order to ascertain the meaning of an intellectual conception one should consider what practical consequences might conceivably result by necessity from the truth of that conception; and the sum of these consequences

[2] Cf. D. G. Leahy, *Novitas Mundi, Perception of the History of Being* (Reprint; Albany, 1994).

will constitute the entire meaning of the conception,"[3] and if in that maxim it is seen that pragmatism is the idealism of transcendental practicality, indeed, critical idealism in the form of 'action' (as such, formally indistinguishable both from the Leibnizian infinite unicity known only to God, and from the monadological postponement of the higher communism), then it is possible to appreciate the fact that the essence of American thought is the revolutionary candor of its reversal and inversion of the radical self-doubt of European modernity to the belief in the *a priori* possibility of the ideal knowledge of what is transcendent, to that modern realism which is at once, succinctly, the belief in God & the belief in the *a priori* impossibility of the knowledge of what is *actually* transcendent: that the essence of American thought is at once the inversion of the transcendental unity of self-consciousness in Kant, and the inversion and reversal of the absolute self-consciousness in Hegel, that it is the pure relativity of consciousness for which the first category is absolutely that of a 'being' which is irreducible to self-consciousness, irreducible to the consciousness of nothing, indeed, the category of Firstness, of which Peirce says: "Let us consider now what could appear as being in the present instant were it utterly cut off from past and future. We can only guess; for nothing is more occult than the absolute present. There plainly could be no action; and without the possibility of action, to talk of binarity would be to utter words without meaning. There might be a sort of consciousness, or feeling, with no self; and this feeling might have its tone. . . . There could not even be a degree of vividness of the feeling . . . The world would be reduced to a quality of unanalyzed feeling. . . . I cannot call it unity; for even unity supposes plurality. I may call its form Firstness, Orience, or Originality. It would be something *which is what it is without reference to anything else* within it or without it, regardless of all force and of all reason."[4] Such is the 'originality' of the consciousness of a purely transcendental unity, such is the 'originality' of the essence of American thought wherein it mirrors itself

[3] C. S. Peirce, *Collected Papers* (Cambridge, Mass., 1933), 5.9.

[4] Ibid., 2.85.

unselfconsciously in its relation to the past & future which was Hegel & Kant, to the within and the without, to the force & reason which was the same, as this originality *in principle.* The fact that American thought is essentially this 'beginning'-in-principle is absolutely demonstrated from the fact that in addition to the three categories (of the monad, dyad, & triad, of feeling, volition, & cognition, of beginning, end, & means, of original, other, & medium, of being, existence, & thought) there is, for this consciousness of the transcendence of purely transcendental unity, neither in fact nor in possibility, a fourth category. This absolutely unselfconscious pure transcendental consciousness, at once the absolute unconsciousness of the absolute self, is the logical analysis which is "not an analysis into existing elements. . . . [but] the tracing out of relations between [absolute] concepts".[5] It is, this essence of American thought, quite literally, absolute ideology, the three categories of which are 'freedom', 'force', and 'mediation', the first of which, 'freedom', excludes in fact and in principle a fourth category, and is the sign & guarantee that there is no necessary order of the (three) categories. Indeed, the categorical threefold is elaborated on the ground of pure *a priori* possibility, and the fourth category is excluded as *a priori* impossible on the ground that it exceeds what is sufficient, which is to say that the ground for excluding the fourth category is the actual belief in the transcendental idea, i.e., the ground for excluding the fourth category from absolute ideology is the belief in absolute ideology. Peirce proceeds as follows: " . . . we may say *in primo*, there is no *a priori* reason why there should not be indecomposable elements of the phaneron [the collective total of all that is in any way or in any sense present to the mind, quite regardless of whether it corresponds to any real thing or not[6]] which are what they are regardless of anything else, each complete in itself; provided, of course, that they be capable of composition. . . . In *secundo,* there is no *a priori* reason why there should not be indecomposable elements which are what they are relatively to a second but inde-

[5] Ibid., 1.294.
[6] Ibid., 1.284.

pendently of any third. . . . In *tertio*, there is no *a priori* reason why there should not be indecomposable elements which are what they are relatively to a second and a third, regardless of any fourth. . . . It is *a priori* impossible that there should be an indecomposable element which is what it is relatively to a second, a third and a fourth. The obvious reason is that that which combines two will by repetition combine any number. Nothing could be simpler; nothing in philosophy is more important."[7] This simplest and most important philosophical fact is the pure relativity of the ideal consciousness, the only necessary condition that there be no actually absolute being, no actually absolute freedom, no indecomposable not capable of composition, the only necessary condition that the order be ideal: the ideal of transcendental existence/the existence of the transcendental ideal on the condition that it alone is necessary (if this were theology, this pure relativity of the real ideal consciousness would be God in the condition/on the condition of absolute solitude [indeed, the essentially American theology of the death of God is, essentially & necessarily, the inversion to nothing of just that conditional existence of God as the Absolute Solitary]). As transcendental sociology, the pure relativity of the ideal consciousness (absolute ideology) lays it down, at once in principle & in freedom, that the *a priori* condition for the intelligibility of the social essence is that its existence is only ideal, that *a priori* the existing social order is actually identified, in the heroic solitude which sacrifices self-identity, as having interests identical with the interests of an 'unlimited community'. So Peirce says: ". . . logicality inexorably requires that our interests shall not be limited. They must not stop at our own fate, but must embrace the whole community. This community, again, must not be limited, but must extend to all races of beings with whom we can come into immediate or mediate intellectual relation. It must reach, however vaguely, beyond this geological epoch, beyond all bounds. He who would not sacrifice his own soul to save the whole world, is, as it seems to me, illogical in all his inferences, collectively. Logic is rooted in the social principle. To be logical

[7] Ibid., 1.295–98.

men should not be selfish; and, in point of fact, they are not so selfish as they are thought. . . . We discuss with anxiety the possible exhaustion of coal in some hundreds of years, or the cooling-off of the sun in some millions, and show in the most popular of all religious tenets that we can conceive the possibility of a man's descending into hell for the salvation of his fellows. Now, it is not necessary for logicality that a man should himself be capable of the heroism of self-sacrifice. It is sufficient that he should recognize the possibility of it, should perceive that only that man's inferences who has it are really logical, and should consequently regard his own as being only so far valid as they would be accepted by the hero. So far as he thus refers his inferences to that standard, he becomes identified with such a mind."[8] The originality of the essence of American thought is that it is neither the absolute self-consciousness of Hegel, nor the belief in self-consciousness of Kant, but the *infinite postponement of self-consciousness* in the form of the belief in the reality of the transcendental ideal. This is the infinite postponement of self-consciousness in the form of the belief in the ideal order of the three categories, in the form of the belief in ideal, i.e., self-sacrificing, identity, in the form of the belief, in sociology, "That consciousness is a sort of public spirit among the nerve-cells. Man as a community of cells. . . ."[9] The inversion and reversal of absolute self-consciousness, at once the inversion of the self-consciousness of unconsciousness which was critical idealism, this other-consciousness of unconsciousness, is the belief in technology as the form of the infinite postponement of self-consciousness. Indeed, the essence of American thought is then at once the belief in the infinite self-postponement of technological consciousness: the belief in the technology of self-postponement, at once the belief in the self-postponement of technology. The halting inconsequence of this circle is the essence of American thought: a relative window. Indeed, a generalization of the organs of sense which *is* a *blind seeing: the monad related to the other ideally:* the one related to the other in a republic of being founded in self-sacri-

[8] Ibid., 2.654.
[9] Ibid., 1.354.

fice: the ideally unlimited monad, at once the actually limited monad of an ideal order (so much so that in the actual event of the inversion to nothing of this ideal, i.e., in the event of absolute solitude, the complete inversion which is the death of the essentially American God [at once, the inverted form of the transcendence of the abyss of transcendental idealism], which just now occurs, a 'vision', as Altizer says,[10] is 'partially released', and a new humanity 'which we can neither conceive nor define' is *known to be present*, i.e., not absolutely known.)

But this last mentioned 'new humanity known to be present' is 'the furthest possible extension of the essence of modern consciousness'. It is now time then, to answer the third and last question, viz., what is the essence of the relationship of American thought and the new world order? The answer is subsumption: the new world order categorically subsumes American thought. The categories are ordered categorically. For the first time the category of Fourthness exists. If Firstness is the 'orience', being, or freedom, irreducible to self-consciousness, if Secondness is pure otherness, or existence as force or resistance, and if Thirdness is the middle term, relation, or essence, then Fourthness is that which is *originaliter* after Secondness, but before Thirdness, i.e., after the pure other, but before mediation, namely, the immediate existence of the other: not Secondness, not the fact of existence as force, but the fact of existence as actual force, the fact of existence as actuality, the *fact of identity*. Fourthness cannot, as has been noted, simply follow Thirdness, since *qua* absolute relation it is more than is required for ordering the pure relativity of consciousness, nor can it precede Secondness simply, since *qua* immediate existence, *qua* actuality, it must follow the pure other. And, in fact, Fourthness, the Fact of Identity, forces itself between Secondness and Thirdness, and forces itself between the-fact-of-existence-as-force and mediation with an absolute originality, indeed, as absolute originality, as that beginning *absolutely* irreducible to self-consciousness, as the beginning of a categorically other consciousness, the beginning

[10] T. J. J. Altizer, *Total Presence: The Language of Jesus and The Language of Today* (New York, 1980), pp. 104–7.

of the consciousness of the absolute force of Identity, the transcendence in essence of the originality of the essence of American thought. What occurs here & now is the fact that logicality forces itself (at once, is logicality forcing itself) through & over the radical illogicality of a logicality the elements of which do not exist in such a way as to reduce the radical dis-hiscence of the circle of merely logical elements to logic, to, in the first instance, the logical order *par excellence* (Firstness, Secondness, Fourthness, and Thirdness), and, in the second instance, to the absolute order transcending the logical order, the existential order *par excellence*, the logical order logically grounded, i.e., Fourthness, Firstness, Secondness, and Thirdness, or, Fact of Identity, Reflection, Appearance, and Essence.[11] This last the order of the transcendental dichotomy in which the priority of the absolute originality of the immediately existing other is logically perceived, that is, in which the priority of the absolute irreducibility to self-consciousness of the immediately existing other is logically perceived: absolute identity is perceived. If the essence of the new world order is 'to create a new world', then it is clear that the transcendence of the merely relative originality of the essence of American thought, while, & precisely because, it is the transcendental founding of the organs of sense, while, & precisely because, it is the absolute window of 'the knowledge of what is transcendent', while, & precisely because, it is the absolute perception of the new humanity, is not, nor can it be, a form of time itself before now, a form of expectancy, a form of experiencing the presence of the world (not even the presence of a new world): the essence of the new world is absolutely to create the new world, to create the new humanity. To perceive this essence is to perceive absolutely the new humanity in the very form of the beginning. The absolute & essential form of this beginning is the absolutely technological displacement of ideology: absolute technology absolutely displacing the belief in technology: the monad related to the other actually, i.e., the monad categorically identified as the other. A categorically social order begins when, as here & now occurs, the knowledge

[11] Cf. above, Sections III.1 and III.5.

of what is transcendent forces itself through & over the pure relativity of consciousness, subsuming that founding of the social order in the self-sacrificing identification of the individual with an 'unlimited community' by reducing that ideal to the form: 'the foundation of society is the immediately existing other'.

2

THE BEGINNING OF THE ABSOLUTELY UNCONDITIONED BODY

> Few things would seem to have fewer pragmatic consequences for us than substances, cut off as we are from every contact with them. Yet in one case scholasticism has proved the importance of the substance-idea by treating it pragmatically. I refer to certain disputes about the mystery of the Eucharist. Substance here would appear to have momentous pragmatic value. Since the accidents of the wafer don't change in the Lord's supper, and yet it has become the very body of Christ, it must be that the change is in the substance solely. The bread-substance must have been withdrawn, and the divine substance substituted miraculously without altering the immediate sensible properties. But tho these don't alter, a tremendous difference has been made, no less a one than this, that we who take the sacrament, now feed upon the very substance of divinity. The substance-notion breaks into life, then, with tremendous effect, if once you allow that substances can separate from their accidents, and exchange these latter.
>
> This is the only pragmatic application of the substance-idea with which I am acquainted; and it is obvious that it will only be treated seriously by those who already believe in the 'real presence' on independent grounds.
>
> W. James, *Pragmatism*[1]

Absolutely before now the absolute reality of the unreal pres-

[1] W. James, *Pragmatism* (Cambridge and London, 1975), pp. 46f.

ence, the absolute and essential unreality of the 'real presence', in the form of the total presence which is the self-embodiment of God. Yet this black was but the latest and last extension of the modern possibility, of that essence of modernity which was essentially and in its entirety, both in 'philosophy' and in science, radically the negative application of the 'only pragmatic' 'substance-idea' with which James was acquainted. Neither continental rationalism, nor its feeder, British empiricism, together with their respective progenies, nor finally, pragmatism, that quintessentially American thinking, none is ultimately intelligible in its historical reality apart from the scholastic treatment of the Incarnation, which treatment proved the latter's ideal import by bringing into the world for the first time one science of supreme speculative and pragmatic value in terms of which the mystery and miracle of the Eucharist was comprehended—the unleavened bread leavening consciousness—as, at once, the transcendental and transcendent separability of substance and 'immediate sensible properties'. Indeed, it might be said that since the scholastic achievement there has been no 'substance', no matter how treated, whether conceived to exist or not to exist, whether not experienced or experienced, whether appropriated or expropriated, constructed or deconstructed, denied or affirmed, which has not been the 'very substance of divinity', related positively or negatively to Self. (The last qualification is made necessary by the fact that *appropriation* is the absolute form of modern consciousness.) It might be understood that modernity so universalized the scholastic understanding of the intentional structure of the Eucharist that the 'bread-substance' was to be found nowhere in the world except it be 'bread'-sent-directly-by-God, a purely formal/immaterial substance, at once the insubstantial matter which was Berkeley's sensible world, at once, that is, the empiricist subjectivity counter-balancing the transcendental subjectivity of Descartes, a universal transubstantiation-in-the-negative emptying out the content of substance and the substance of content, a pure practical idea, described by James in a passage immediately following the one cited above, without the least indication of any awareness of the substantial historical continuity with which he was dealing, as follows:

> *Material* substance was criticized by Berkeley with such telling effect that his name has reverberated through all subsequent philosophy. . . . So far from denying the external world which we know, Berkeley corroborated it. It was the scholastic notion of a material substance unapproachable by us, *behind* the external world, deeper and more real than it, and needed to support it, which Berkeley maintained to be the most effective of all reducers of the external world to unreality. Abolish that substance, he said, believe that God, whom you can understand and approach, sends you the sensible world directly, and you confirm the latter and back it up by his authority. Berkeley's criticism of 'matter' was consequently absolutely pragmatistic. Matter is known as our sensations of colour, figure, hardness and the like. They are the cash value of the term. The difference matter makes to us by truly being is that we then get such sensations; by not being, is that we lack them. These sensations then are its sole meaning. Berkeley doesn't deny matter, then; he simply tells us what it consists of. It is a true name for just so much in the way of sensations.[2]

Just as Descartes appropriated the transcendental form of natural reason shaped in the thinking of Aquinas, and appropriated it to an ideally immediate subjectivity,[3] so Berkeley naturalizes the scholastic notion of created matter by confounding it with the 'immediate sensible properties' which, in the modern understanding, exist 'for us' in the absence of the 'bread-substance', and, if not in the absence of divinity, in the absence of the 'very substance of divinity'. Kant, just as he had removed the source of verification from the Cartesian idea of God to the ideal of the universal scientific community,[4] removed the source of the synthetic unity of perception from Berkeley's God to the Self which was the transcendental Ego, thereby grounding pure practical idealism/empiricism in Reason as the origin. The absent substance of divinity, Leibniz' intelligible world, persisted in the form of the *noumena*. Kant appropriated the *phenomena*, but not

[2] Ibid.

[3] Cf. Leahy, *Novitas Mundi.*

[4] Ibid.

the *noumena*. The genius of Kant was to reduce pure practical idealism to the form of *appropriation*, to invert Hume. But the genius of Hegel was the absolute reversal of critical/transcendental idealism in the form of the appropriation of the very absence of the substance of divinity, in the form, in turn, of the very transcendence of the original synthetic unity of apperception. In Hegel the noumenal is the pure absence which *is* the 'real presence' of the Absolute: the 'bread-substance' is the 'real presence'. This is the Eucharist in the form of the separability of 'immediate sensible properties' from *absolute self-relation*. The finite non-being of the sensible immediate the actual being of the absolute. Hegel's is the pure practical transcendence of idealism, absolutely real idealism. The essence of American thought, the primary locus of which is found in Peirce, *qua* reversal and inversion of Hegel,[5] was the pure practice of this practical transcendence of idealism, the pure relativity of ideal consciousness,[6] the essentially non-Eucharistic transcendental separability of substance and 'immediate sensible properties', the transcendental non-Eucharistic separability of 'immediate sensible properties' *and relations* from substance. Just here may be seen the fact that historical materialism, insofar as it was the inversion merely, and not at once the reversal of absolute idealism, as was pragmatism, was the reduction of the appropriation of the very absence of the substance of divinity to the pure form of association, at once, therefore, the inversion both of absolute idealism and of the transcendence thereof which was the essence of pragmatism, the inversion both of the absolute identification of the individual with the universal, and of the reduction of association to an ideal, self-sacrificing, identity.[7] Historical materialism was the idealistic inversion of idealism, idealistic materialism,[8] at once the reversal of implicitly pluralistic pragmatism/the reversal of the infinite postponement of self-consciousness:[9] the infinite

[5] Cf. above, pp. 456ff.

[6] Cf. above, Section IV.1, passim.

[7] Ibid. Cf. also, above, pp. 248ff.

[8] Cf. above, Section I.

[9] Cf. above, p. 459.

anticipation of self-consciousness, the anticipation of that which, *qua* now occurring actuality, is for the first time perceived as categorically self-less consciousness, that is, perceived this side of the transcendental dichotomy.[10] Thus it is that the absolute grounding of historical materialism is the absolute implication of the absolute inversion of the abyss,[11] i.e., of the abyss of transcendental idealism which is the reduction to nothing of the 'pure practice of the practical transcendence of idealism', the absolute implication of the absolute unreality of the 'real presence' in the form of absolute solitude, in the form of the absolute safeguarding of absolute idealism from this beginning of the Day of Reckoning. The profound consonance of absolute idealism, historical materialism, and the essence of pragmatism is actually comprehended in the reduction of the latter, in Altizer, to Nothing, i.e., in the Abyss of the Postponement of Self-Consciousness at once itself the absolute quality of the abyss,[12] in the form of the Nothing which is *experienced* as the form of the beginning, a beginning in the form of 'absolutely alone in the presence of a reality "which we can neither conceive nor define"',[13] in the form of the reduction of the very form of 'self-sacrifice' to the very form of Nothing beginning, comprehensible as the inversion absolutely & precisely of the non-Eucharistic 'immediate sensible properties' to nothing: the abyss of the actual non-Eucharistic 'immediate sensible properties': the actual non-Eucharistic 'immediate sensible properties' *not* the actual non-Eucharistic 'immediate sensible properties': the non-Eucharistic appearances *identically* the Eucharistic appearances: that 'behind' which there is no substance identically that 'behind' which is 'the very substance of divinity': appearances-actually-absent-substance appearances the very presence of the substance of divinity. This is the very identity of total absence the actually present divinity,[14] the absolute reversal of absurdity,

[10] Cf. above, pp. 425f., and Section IV.1.

[11] Cf. above, Section II.4.

[12] Ibid., passim.

[13] Cf. above, pp. 228ff., 459f.

[14] Cf. above, Section II.4, passim. Also, above, pp. 369ff.

the absolute self-division of reason, the division of absolute idealism from self, at once the non-being of sensible immediate substance the non-being of the absolute, the non-being of Very Identity: at once the voiding of pragmatism and the grounding of historical materialism in the form of the reduction of the form of association to the absence of the reality of selves, the reduction of the form of society/of the form of a new humanity to the complete absence of individual selves: the reduction at once to nothing of self-postponement and self-anticipation: the absolute collapse of self-relation upon its own other: the non-categorical externality of 'the immediate sensible properties' of the Eucharist: the external absolutely nothing within/the within absolutely nothing external: non-Eucharistic Eucharistic externality.[15] If the essence of pragmatism is the transcendental sepa-

[15] The magnitude of the collapse of modernity which is this abyssal reversal of absolute idealism (at once the pragmatistic Void, the abyss of transcendental idealism, the implicit absolute of historical materialism) may be best gauged from the summit it occupied in the pre-Nietzschean text of Hegel's *Philosophy of History,* trans. J. Sibree (New York, 1956), pp. 377ff.: "We have then to probe to its depths the *spiritual element* in the Church—the form of its power. The essence of the Christian principle has already been unfolded; it is the principle of Mediation. Man realizes his Spiritual essence only when he conquers the Natural that attaches to him. This conquest is possible only on the supposition that the human and the divine nature are essentially one, and that Man, so far as he is Spirit, also possesses the essentiality and substantiality that belong to the idea of Deity. The condition of the mediation in question is the consciousness of this unity; and the intuition of this unity was given to man in Christ. The object to be attained is therefore, that man should lay hold on this consciousness, and that it should be continually excited in him. This was the design of the *Mass:* in the *Host* Christ is set forth as actually present; the piece of bread consecrated by the priest is the present God, subjected to human contemplation and ever and anon offered up. One feature of this representation is correct, inasmuch as the sacrifice of Christ is here regarded as an actual and eternal transaction, Christ being not a mere sensuous and single, but a completely universal, i.e., divine *individuum;* but on the other hand it involves the error of isolating the sensuous phase; for the Host is adored even apart from its being partaken of by the faithful, and the presence of Christ is not exclusively limited mental vision and Spirit. Justly therefore did the Lutheran Reformation make this dogma an especial object of attack. Luther proclaimed the great doc-

rability of a non-Eucharistic 'matter' from the 'very substance' of Jesus Christ, if, indeed, the essentially American conception of the descent of Jesus into Hell 'for the salvation of his fellows' is that the latter is a paradigm of that ideal of self-sacrifice which is

---

trine that the Host had spiritual value and Christ was received only on the condition of faith in him; apart from this, the Host, he affirmed, was a mere external thing, possessed of no greater value than any other thing. But the Catholic falls down before the Host; and thus the merely outward has sanctity ascribed to it. The Holy as a mere thing has the character of externality; thus it is capable of being taken possession of by another to my exclusion: it may come into an alien hand, since the process of appropriating it is not one that takes place in Spirit, but is conditioned by its quality as an external object [Dingheit]. The highest of human blessings is in the hands of others. Here arises *ipso facto* a separation between those who possess this blessing and those who have to receive it from others—between the *Clergy* and the *Laity*. The Laity as such are alien to the Divine . . . .

"The generality of men are thus cut off from the Church; and on the same principle they are severed from the Holy in every form. For on the same principle as that by which the clergy are the medium between man on the one hand and God and Christ on the other hand, the layman cannot directly apply to the Divine Being in his prayers, but only through mediators—human beings who conciliate God for him, the Dead, the Perfect—*Saints*. . . . The element of mediation between God and man was thus apprehended and held as something external. . . . This view imports the denial of the essential unity of the Divine and Human; since man, as such, is declared incapable of recognizing the Divine and of approaching thereto.

"With this perversion is connected the absolute separation of the spiritual from the secular principle generally. There are two Divine Kingdoms—the intellectual in the heart and cognitive faculty, and the socially ethical whose element and sphere is secular existence. It is science alone that can comprehend the kingdom of God and the socially Moral world as one Idea, and that recognizes the fact that the course of Time has witnessed a process ever tending to the realization of this unity. But Piety [or Religious Feeling] as such, has nothing to do with the Secular: it may make its appearance in that sphere on a mission of mercy, but this stops short of a strict socially ethical connection with it—does not come up to the idea of Freedom. Religious Feeling is extraneous to History, and has no History; for History is rather the Empire of Spirit recognizing itself in its *Subjective* Freedom, as the economy of social morality [sittliches Reich] in the State. In the Middle Ages that embodying of the Divine in

required of men by a logic 'rooted in the social principle',[16] then the voiding of this pragmatism,[17] the death, in fact, of pragmatism, the essentially pragmatistic conception of death, the reduction to Nothing of the self-sacrificial descent of Jesus into

---

actual life was wanting; the antithesis was not harmonized. Social morality was represented as worthless. . . . "

But in the absolute inversion of the abyss (the complex at once the abyss of absolute idealism [cf. above, pp. 208ff., and pp. 216ff.]) the abyss swallows the 'sensuous phase'/the 'sensuous phase' swallows the abyss (the self itself swallows its own other [cf. above, pp. 220ff.]) in the form of the abyss of the exclusively interior reality of Eucharistic presence, in the form of the exclusive interiority of the presence of Christ *not* the interiority of presence, but identically the exclusive exteriority of the reality of the absolute present: the exclusive present identically the exclusive present, the series of 'punctual embodiment(s) of the "historical realization of the new creation"' (ibid.) which is at once 'the reduction of the pure form of society to the absence of individual selves', that is, to the absence of that 'interior distance separating men from men and self from self', the abysmal reversal of the actual 'embodying of the Divine in actual life', identically the sin against the Holy Spirit, the absolute self-alienation of the Spirit, the sin of the Spirit Itself against the Eucharist in the form of the absolute self-division of the Absent God in the form of the absolutely unconditioned substitution of the self-forgiveness of sin for confession, the absolutely unconditioned elimination of the very possibility of the private experience of the 'immediate sensible properties' (albeit unrecognizable) of the 'very substance of divinity', indeed, the absolutely unconditioned elimination of the very possibility of private experience/identity/property/substance/body: the absolute solitude which is the privacy eliminating the very possibility of the 'immediate sensible properties' of privacy, the exteriority identically interiority in the form of the 'humanity that can neither be named nor apprehended by an interior and individual voice' (cf. above, pp. 224ff.). The absence of the 'immediate sensible properties' of the 'present God' identically the absence of the present God. So is the collapse of modernity the absolute inversion of the 'Host . . . adored even apart from its being partaken of by the faithful', i.e., of the Eucharist reduced to Nothing/of the object of disbelief, i.e., of the immediate sensible properties of the consecrated bread *qua* finite non-being: *the inversion of the void which is the absolute immediacy of the Eucharist:* the non-categorical absolute immediacy of the Eucharist which is the purity and divinity of Nothing.

[16] Cf. above, pp. 248ff. and 458ff.

[17] Cf. above, pp. 468f. and n. 15.

Hell, Nothing experienced as the non-Eucharistic 'matter' actually separate from the 'very substance of divinity' which is Jesus, Nothing actually experienced as the Eucharistic 'matter' separate from the non-substantial, i.e., purely formal, Jesus Christ, then this non-categorical experience of the 'purity and divinity of Nothing',[18] of the death of Christ in the form of the absolute immediacy of the Eucharist, is perfectly intelligible in & as the form of Altizer's reception of James Joyce's *Finnegans Wake* in his *History as Apocalypse*, where, speaking of "that tavern orgy which is a cosmic repetition of an Easter which is Good Friday, an Easter or Resurrection which is an ecstatic consumption of the crucified body of God. . . . possible only as a consequence of the breaking of the Host," he says, in explanation of the fact that "H. C. E. is himself accused of the primal crime. . . . pleads guilty . . . and goes on to associate or link himself with the executioner," the following:

> For the death of God is the self-sacrifice of God, and not only is the executed the executioner, but the condemned one is the eternal Judge, and nothing whatsoever distinguishes guilt and condemnation or crime and execution, because Victim and Judge and Host and Creator are one. While these primordial and apocalyptic motifs are only indirectly and ironically present in Christian Scripture, they are directly and immediately present in the Eucharistic liturgy, a liturgy revolving about the breaking of the Host and Victim who is God Himself. True, these primal motifs are dismembered and disguised in Christian mythology and theology, but they are present with an immediate power in the Eucharist or mass, which is surely a decisive source of the power and authority of the mass. But that authority and power can only be recovered and renewed by reversing and inverting the given or manifest form and language of both liturgy and catechism, of both Scripture and creed, an inversion and reversal which is present in the *Wake*. Now the awe and solemnity of the mass passes into a comic ribaldry, but a ribaldry and even a scatological ribaldry which is absolutely essential to the epic project of inverting and revers-

[18] Ibid.

> ing the mass, a project which can realize itself only by a reversal and inversion of the language of the mass. The language of the Roman rite becomes the very opposite of itself in the language of *Finnegans Wake*, but nothing less could effect a resurrection of liturgy, or an awakening of the Christian God.[19]

But what is present in Joyce is absent in Altizer, and this absence is the luciferous inversion and reversal, not of the language, but of the substance of the mass, the not-language/not the *nat* language, the very language of light in which 'a Eucharistic sacrifice of the Godhead'[20] is brought face to face with the pure Darkness of Divinity, in which the 'sacrifice of God' is the pure Nothing/the Darkness which is Light:

> The "nullification" of God embodied in the resurrection of Book Four of the *Wake* is . . . a realization or self-realization of God wherein the whole perfection of being realizes itself in the pure actuality of *ipsum esse* or existence itself. But that actuality is here realized not simply through language and speech, but in and as word and speech, for now God is fully and finally *logos* or "word." That "word" is pure immediacy, an immediacy which is darkness and light, and pure darkness and pure light, a light which is the cosmic and apocalyptic sacrifice of God. If the epic action of the *Wake* proceeds out of the dark abyss of primordial sacrifice, a primordial sacrifice which *is* creation, that sacrifice culminates in the transcendental repetition of the creation itself, a transcendental repetition which is the apocalyptic repetition of "God said." But an apocalyptic repetition reverses primordial repetition, so that "Let there be light" becomes "Let there be darkness," an apocalyptic darkness reversing but nevertheless renewing the primordial abyss and night. For the night language or the "not language" of the *Wake* embodies the brute and formless matter of the primordial "water." But now that "water" speaks, and it speaks with an immediacy that has never been sounded before, or not sounded since the original act of creation.[21]

---

[19] T. J. J. Altizer, *History as Apocalypse* (Albany, 1985), p. 240.
[20] Ibid., p. 234.
[21] Ibid., pp. 250f.

This is the inversion and reversal of the substance of the mass to the pure immediacy of Darkness, not *verbum caro factum est,* but the "word" made "water" absolutely. The project of 'silence' which is the absolute inversion of the abyss is the pure repetition of the 'epic' project, the dissembling of the dissembling of the void, the dissembling of the 'scatological ribaldry' in the form of the absolute semblance of nothing, the very semblance of the abyss/the abyss of very semblance, the absolute dissembling of the pure semblance/the semblance of dissembling which *is* the scatological absolute, at once the 'pure immediacy' of the dark "word" speaking: 'nothing whatsoever distinguishes guilt and condemnation or crime and execution, because Victim and Judge and Host and Creator are one'.[22] This last is the 'silencing of the 'epic' "word," at once the hearing of the *nat* language. This very silence, *qua* the *nat* language speaking/ *qua* "water" speaking, the form of the 'original act of creation'/*qua* origin of an original *ex nihilo,* is the not-thought form not the *nat* thought form which is now comprehended for the first time *qua* proportion as עבירה ('guilt', *qua* proportion, 70 : 2 :: 10 : 200 :: 5 : [1], whose rational product is 8.75) : חיוב בדין ('condemnation', *qua* proportion, 8 : 10 :: 6 : 2 (::) 2 : 4 :: 10 : 50, whose rational product is .24) :: עוון ('crime', *qua* proportion, 70 : 6 :: 6 : 50, whose rational product is 1.4) : הרם ('execution', *qua* proportion, 5 : 200 :: 60 : [1], whose rational product is 1.5), which, *qua* 'identities' or rational products, is:

עבירה('guilt') : חיוב בדין('condemnation') ::
עוון('crime') : הרם('execution')

8.75 : .24 :: 1.4 : 1.5,

the proven unity of which proportion is:

$$\frac{13.125}{.336} = 39.0625,$$

[22] Cf. above, p. 459.

where 39.0625 is the inversion of the 'identity' of קרבן מנחה ('meal offering',[23] [rational product, .0256]),[24] identically the inversion of the integral product of the proportion which is the double Abyss of 'I AM,[25] $.0256^{-1} = 39.0625$, which inversion is nevertheless itself at once the 'identity' of אל רחום וחנון ('God compassionate and gracious', *qua* proportion, 1 : 30 (::) 200 : 8 :: 6 : 40 (::) 6 : 8 :: 50 : 6 :: 50 : [1], whose rational product is 39.0625). The identification of the elements of this proportion, the 'nothing whatsoever distinguishes guilt and condemnation or crime and execution', $8.75 \times .24 \times 1.4 \times 1.5 = 4.41$, is the inversion and reversal of the הצרפה ('synthesis' [rational product, .69444]), of the קפיצה ('leap' [rational product, .69444]), and of the קפיצה ('closing' [rational product, .69444]), which is the reduction, as of logic to the minimum, of Existence (הויה) to the Tetragrammaton (יהוה), *qua* integral products, 2.5E3/3.6E3, *qua* rational products, 1.666/2.4, which = .69444, the inversion and reversal of the reduction of נשנה ('recurrence' [rational product, 1.666]) to מתחיל ('beginning' [rational product, 2.4]), 1.666/2.4 = .69444,[26] that is, the inversion and reversal of .69444: → 1.44 → 4.41, which is itself at once 'absolute' זבל ('excrement', *qua* proportion, 7 : 2 :: 30 : [1], whose integral product is 4.41E4) denominated the 'created 100', 4.41E4/1E4 = 4.41. But 'nothing whatsoever distinguishes guilt and condemnation or crime and execution, because Victim and Judge and Host and Creator are one', that is, the former identification rests on the identification of קרבן ('victim', *qua* proportion, 100 : 200 :: 2 : 50, whose rational product is .02) and דין ('judge', *qua* proportion, 4 : 10 :: 50 : [1], whose rational product is 20) and לחם קדוש ('Host', *qua* proportion, 30 : 8 :: 40 : [1] (::) 100 : 4 :: 6 : 300, whose rational product is 75) and הבורא ('Creator', *qua* proportion, 5 : 2 :: 6 : 200 :: 1 : [1], whose rational product is .075). The proportion of the elements of this identification, *qua* 'identities', is:

[23] The sacrifice the remainder of which was to be eaten by Aaron and his descendents inside the holy place in the form of unleavened bread (Lv. 2:1–16; 6:7–11).

[24] Cf. above, Section III.5, pp. 411ff.

[25] Ibid.

[26] Cf. above, pp. 418ff.

קרבן ('victim') : דין ('judge') :: לחם קדוש ('Host') : הבורא ('Creator'),

$$.02 : 20 :: 75 : .075,$$

the proven unity of which is:

$$\frac{.0015}{1500} = 1E{-}6,$$

where 1E–6 is the inversion of 'absolute' כתיבה ('writing' [integral product, 1E6]), the inversion of 'absolute' הכרה ('consciousness'/'discernment' [integral product, 1E6]), the inversion of 'absolute' קרי ('text of Scripture *read'* [integral product, 1E6]),[27] which inversion is nevertheless itself at once the inversion of the 'created 100' identified with ברא ('to create' [rational product, .01]), 1E-4 × .01 = 1E-6. The identification of the elements of 'Victim and Judge and Host and Creator are one', .02 × 20 × 75 × .075 = 2.25, is the inversion of the rational product of the Absolute Proportion of Absolute Thought ($.\overline{444}$),[28] שלום לך (*'shalom lecha'*, 'Peace be with you' [rational product, 2.25])[29] not denominating unity, the inversion of the 'created 100' identified with 'absolute' הכל ('everybody'/'everything', *qua* proportion, 5 : 20 :: 30 : [1], whose integral product is 2.25E4), 'absolute' העלם ('oblivion', *qua* proportion, 5 : 70 :: 30 : 40, whose integral product is 2.25E4), and 'absolute' הבל ('vanity', *qua* proportion, 5 : 2 :: 30 : [1], whose integral product is 2.25E4), $1E4^{-1}$ × 2.25E4 = 2.25. The שלום לך (*'shalom lecha'*, 'Peace be with you') not denominating unity is the self-silencing word 'because' of which the 'watery' word now sounds for the first time or for the first time again. The reduction implicit in the 'because' in 'nothing whatsoever distinguishes guilt and condemnation or crime and execution, because Victim and Judge and Host and Creator are one', viz., 4.41/2.25 = 1.96, is itself at once 'absolute' נוזליות ('liq-

[27] Ibid.

[28] Cf. above, pp. 367f.

[29] Ibid.

uidity', *qua* proportion, 50 : 6 :: 7 : 30 :: 10 : 6 :: 400 : [1], whose integral product is 1.96E12) identified as 'absolute' תשנון ('repetition', *qua* proportion, 400 : 300 :: 50 : 6 :: 50 : [1], whose integral product is 1E12), so identified identically identified as 'absolute' קץ הימין ('the end of days'/'the days of the Messiah' [integral product, 1E12]) and 'absolute' רציונלי ('rational' [integral product, 1E12]),[30] 1.96E12/1E12 = 1.96. Indeed, יהי אפלה ('Let there be darkness', *qua* proportion, 10 : 5 :: 10 : [1] (::) 1 : 80 :: 30 : 5, whose rational product is 1.5) denominated אמת ('truth' [rational product, 10]), 1.5/10 = .15, identically כריסטוס ('Christ', *qua* proportion, 20 : 200 :: 10 : 60 :: 9 : 6 :: 60 : [1], whose rational product is 1.5 [= שלום ('peace' [rational product, 1.5])]) denominated אמת ('truth'), 1.5/10 = .15, is the reduction here, *qua* 'identities', of יחסיות ('proportionality', *qua* proportion, 10 : 8 :: 60 : 10 :: 6 : 400, whose rational product is .1125) to אפס ('nothing' [rational product, .75]), .1125/.75 = .15, which truth of Christ identically truth of 'Let there be darkness' identified with ברא ('to create' [rational product, .01]) is the very identity of דמות ('semblance', *qua* proportion, 4 : 40 :: 6 : 400, whose rational product is .0015), which in turn is the inversion of יהי אור ('Let there be light' [rational product, $666.\overline{666}$]), .15 × .01 = .0015 = $666.\overline{666}^{-1}$.[31] And just as the 'All'[32] denominated truth, הכל ('everybody'/'everything' [rational product, 7.5]) denominated אמת ('truth' [rational product, 10]), is אפס ('nothing' [rational product, .75]), 7.5/10 = .75, so this דמות ('semblance' [rational product, .0015]) or proportionality identical with creating as Nothing is the 'final and apocalyptic "Given!"'[33] as truth: נתון ('given', *qua* proportion, 50 : 400 :: 6 : 50, whose rational product is .015) denominated אמת ('truth'), .015/10 = .0015. Further, the identification of the 'identities' of the 'All' and the 'Given!' is proportionality, i.e., 7.5 × .015 = .1125, and the identity of this proportionality[34] and the proportionality identical with

[30] Cf. above, p. 401.

[31] Cf. above, p. 373.

[32] Altizer, *History as Apocalypse*, pp. 234ff.

[33] Ibid.

[34] Cf. above, pp. 388ff.

creating, which latter is identically the identification of Nothing and Semblance, i.e., .75 × .0015 = .001125, constitutes the proof-form of the proportion, *qua* rational products:

הכל ('All') : אפס ('Nothing') :: דמות ('Semblance'): נתון ('Given'),

7.5 : .75 :: .0015 : .015,

the proven unity of which is:

$$\frac{.1125}{.001125} \text{ or } \frac{.001125}{.1125} = 100 \text{ or } .01,$$

the 1 of the 'created 100' or the very 'identity' of ברא ('to create').[35] The very form of the absolute inversion of the abyss, the very form of the abysmal 'Given!', of the given abyss, of the abyss of the given, of the given not given, of the postulate not postulated, of the 'never sounded before' 'not sounded since the original act of creation', of the 'nothing whatsoever stands outside of this presence' 'nothing which can be heard', the very form of this פסח על שתי הסעפים ('to hesitate'/'to halt between two opinions', *qua* proportion, 80 : 60 :: 8 : [1] (::) 70 : 30 (::) 300 : 400 :: 10 : [1] (::) 5 : 60 :: 70 : 80 :: 10 : 40, whose rational product is $3.402\overline{777}$) which *is* the rational product of the proportion formed of the 'identities' of עבירה ('guilt') : חיוב בדין ('condemnation') :: עוון ('crime') : הרס ('execution'), 8.75 : .24 :: 1.4 : 1.5, viz., $34.02\overline{777}$, denominated אמת ('truth' [rational product, 10]), $34.02\overline{777}/10 = 3.402\overline{777}$, the very form of this double-mindedness here clearly manifest for the first time, is the incorporation of the abyss in the proportionality of the act of creation,[36] the beginning of the actual existence of the abyss of the abyss, of the absolute abyss of the abyss. This is the actual abyss of the abyss of 'Let there be light!', the proportionality of creation which is the 'Given!' of the abyss of the abyss reduced to existence *ex*

[35] Cf. above, pp. 366ff., 388ff., 392, n. 83.
[36] Cf. above, Section III.5, pp. 410f., et passim.

nihilo.[37] And this very text, this very writing/saying 'this is the abyss of the abyss of "Let there be light!"', this very text is the transcendence of the 'given' text, the categorically not-given text of the text of *nihil ex nihilo fit*: 'absolute' מאפס יוצא רק אפס ('*ex nihilo nihil fit*', *qua* proportion, 40 : 1 :: 80 : 60 (::) 10 : 6 :: 90 : 1 (::) 200 : 100 (::) 1 : 80 :: 60 : [1], whose integral product is 1.1943936E21) identified with the 'created 100', identically 'absolute' אני חושב ועל כן אני קים ('*Cogito ergo sum*'/'I think therefore I am' [integral product, 1.1943936E25]), 1.1943936E21 × 1E4 = 1.1943936E25, the 'absolute' *Cogito ergo sum* which identified with the 'synthesis'/the 'leap'/the 'closing' is the 'absolute dead center' identified as 'to create'.[38] This text is the *cogito esse, sum ex nihilo*, this is the appearance of the *cogito ex nihilo*, the actual objectivity of the abyss of the abyss *ex nihilo*. Take and eat and taste the sweetness of the Lord: matter the body of Christ. This is dead center *ex nihilo*, the Eucharist the new creation.

EXCURSUS CIRCULARIS

Here begins an excursion which shall return the reader to the point at which we have arrived, the point from which we shall begin to conclude this section. But first, this circular excursion on the circle. Galileo Galilei gives the following proof of the identity of the center and the circumference of the circle:

> Let *AFB* be a semicircle with center at *C;* about it describe the rectangle *ADEB* and from the center draw the straight lines *CD* and *CE* to the points *D* and *E*. Imagine the radius *CF* to be drawn perpendicular to either of the lines *AB* or *DE,* and the entire figure to rotate about this radius as an axis. It is clear that the rectangle *ADEB* will thus describe a cylinder, the semicircle *AFB* a hemisphere, and the triangle *CDE,* a cone. Next let us remove the hemisphere but leave the cone and the rest of the cylinder, which, on account of its shape, we will call a 'bowl'. First we shall prove that the bowl and the cone are equal; then we shall show that a plane drawn parallel to the cir-

[37] Cf. above, pp. 353f.

[38] Cf. above, Section III.5, pp. 429ff., et passim.

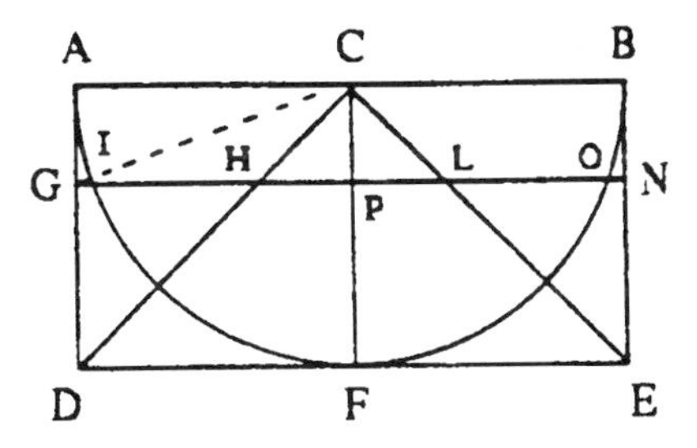

cle which forms the base of the bowl and which has the line *DE* for diameter and *F* for a center—a plane whose trace is *GN*—cuts the bowl in the points *G, I, O, N,* and the cone in the points *H, L,* so that the part of the cone indicated by *CHL* is always equal to the part of the bowl whose profile is represented by the triangles *GAI* and *BON.* Besides this we shall prove that the base of the cone, i.e., the circle whose diameter is *HL,* is equal to the circular surface which forms the base of this portion of the bowl, or as one might say, equal to a ribbon whose width is *GI.* . . . the plane, drawn to any height whatever, so long as it is parallel to the base, i.e., to the circle whose diameter is *DE,* always cuts the two solids so that the portion *CHL* of the cone is equal to the upper portion of the bowl; likewise the two areas which are the bases of these solids, namely the band and the circle *HL,* are also equal. Here we have the miracle mentioned above; as the cutting plane approaches the line *AB* the portions of the solids cut off are always equal, so also the areas of their bases. And as the cutting plane comes near the top, the two solids (always equal) as well as their bases (areas which are also equal) finally vanish, one pair of them degenerating into the circumference of a circle, the other into a single point, namely the upper edge of the bowl and the apex of the cone. Now, since as these solids diminish equality is maintained between them up to the very last, we are justified in saying that, at the extreme and final end of this diminution, they are still equal and that one is not infinitely greater than the other. It appears therefore that we may equate the circumference of a large circle to a single point. And this which is true of the solids is true also of the surfaces which form their bases; for these also preserve equality between themselves throughout their diminution and in the end vanish, the one into the circumference of a circle, the other into a single point. Shall we

> not call them equal seeing that they are the last traces and remnants of equal magnitudes? Note also that, even if these vessels were large enough to contain immense celestial hemispheres, both their upper edges and the apexes of the cones therein contained would always remain equal and would vanish, the former into circles having the dimensions of the largest celestial orbits, the latter into single points. Hence in conformity with the preceding we may say that all circumferences of circles, however different, are equal to each other, and are each equal to a single point.[39]

Such is Galileo's 'miracle'. The further miracle is the fact that the Hebrew states the theorem, *qua* rational products, as the מרכז ('center', *qua* proportion, 40 : 200 :: 20 : 7, whose rational product is .571428) denominated אמת ('truth' [rational product, 10]), the truth of the center, identically the מעגל ('circle', *qua* proportion, 40 : 70 :: 3 : 30, whose rational product is .0571428), .571428/10 = .0571428, which truth of the center identically the circle *is identically* the נקדת-מגוז ('vanishing point', *qua* proportion, 50 : 100 :: 4 : 400 (::) 40 : 3 :: 6 : 7, whose rational product is .0571428)! Just here is to be noted the fact that the absolutely critical matter respecting Galileo is not that he inaugurated the mathematical treatment of nature, nor that in so doing he was, according to Husserl,[40] merely "an heir in respect of pure geometry" and committed the "fateful omission" of not inquiring "back into the original meaning-giving achievement which, as idealization practiced on the original ground of all theoretical and practical life—the immediately intuited world (and here especially the empirically intuited world of bodies)—resulted in the geometrical ideal constructions." The absolutely critical perception is that the mathematics of Galileo is the mathematics of *the vanishing point,* and that the mathematics of the vanishing point is identically the mathematics of מעמקים ('abyss', *qua* proportion, 40 : 70 :: 40 : 100 :: 10 : 40, whose rational product is

[39] G. Galilei, *Dialogues Concerning Two New Sciences,* trans. H. Crew and A. deSalvio (New York, 1954), pp. 27ff.

[40] E. Husserl, *The Crisis of European Sciences and Transcendental Phenomenology,* trans. D. Carr (Evanston, 1970), p. 49.

.0571428), the mathematics of the abyss. This is the very *vanishing point*, very abyss, underlying the whole of the modern enterprise, identically the abyss exposed by Nietzsche, and into which phenomenology entered, unknowingly in the case of Husserl, knowingly in the person of Heidegger. The miracle of miracles now actually occurring for the first time is the exit from the abyss (at once the reduction to nothing of the very conception of an exit—the exit which is no exit identically the nothing which is not nothing) in the very form of the סעדת ישו ('Eucharist', *qua* proportion, 60 : 70 :: 4 : 400 (::) 10 : 300 :: 6 : [1], whose rational product is .00714285) which is the 'created 100' (the-Godhead-identified-with-"Let there be light!")[41] identity of the identification of the square root of שעת סכנה ('crisis', *qua* proportion, 300 : 70 :: 400 : [1] (::) 60 : 20 :: 50 : 5, whose rational product is 5.142857E4) and the square root of מעמקים ('abyss' [rational product, .0571428]) or נקדת-מגוז ('vanishing point' [rational product, .0571428]) denominated אמת ('truth' [rational product, 10]), .00714285 = [√5.142857E4 × √(.0571428/10)]/1E4: for the first time the exit from the abyss in the very form of the Eucharist identified with the 'created 100' the very identity of the square or existential root of the identification of the crisis and the abyss identified as truth. Husserl writes in *The Crisis:*

> In his view of the world from the perspective of geometry, the perspective of what appears to the senses and is mathematizable, Galileo *abstracts* from the subjects as persons leading a personal life; he abstracts from all that is in any way spiritual, from all cultural properties which are attached to things in human praxis. The result of this abstraction is the things purely as bodies; but these are taken as concrete real objects, the totality of which makes up a world which becomes the subject matter of research. One can truly say that the idea of nature as a really self-enclosed world of bodies first emerges with Galileo. A consequence of this, along with mathematization, which was too quickly taken for granted, is [the idea of] a self-enclosed

[41] Cf. above, Section III.5, pp. 373f. For the 'Eucharist' and the 'diagonal', see below, pp. 490 and 500.

> natural causality in which every occurrence is determined unequivocally and in advance. Clearly the way is thus prepared for dualism, which appears immediately afterward in Descartes. . . . The world splits, so to speak, into two worlds : nature and the psychic world, although the latter, because of the way in which it is related to nature, does not achieve the status of an independent world.[42]

But this 'splitting' of the world inherent in Galileo's abstractive reduction of the subject to the matter of physical research is not merely something which 'mathematization' accompanies as the form of its 'nature'. Galileo's mathematics absolutely manifests the fundamental form of his consciousness as that which in the form of a hemisphere reduced to chaos is reduced to the vanishing point, as his presence embodied in the body reduced to the vanishing point. His mathematics is the mathematics of a radical subjectivity which requires the *absence of presence/the removal, absolutely & precisely, of just 1/2 the (original) hemisphere* in the proof of the identity of the circumference and the center (although Galileo speaks of removing the hemisphere, that portion of the cone which he leaves, which is in the 'bowl', which rests on the surface of the 'bowl', = 1/2 the hemisphere) in order to identify the circumference as the center, as the vanishing point, which is to say that Galileo *actually* removes the מציאות ('presence'/'reality' [rational product, .0666])[43] which is, *qua* rational products, identically the חצי-כדור ('hemisphere', *qua* proportion, 8 : 90 :: 10 : [1] (::) 20 : 4 :: 6 : 200, whose rational product is .1333) denominated כאוס ('chaos' [rational product, 2]),[44] .1333/2 = .0666, the אמת ('truth' [rational product, 10]) of which מציאות ('presence'), the truth of which 1/2 hemisphere, is אי-מציאות ('absence', *qua* proportion, 1 : 10 (::) 40 : 90 :: 10 : 1 :: 6 : 400, whose rational product is .00666), .0666/10 = .00666. The identical truth which identifies the center as the circle identically the vanishing point identically the abyss in the form

[42] Husserl, *Crisis,* p. 60.

[43] Cf. above, Section III.5, p. 372.

[44] Cf. above, p. 378.

.571428/10. The absolute unity of this truth is the identity of this 1/2 hemisphere as the vanishing point, the reduction, *qua* 'identities', of the חצי-כדור ('hemisphere' [rational product, .1333]) denominated כאוס ('chaos' [rational product, 2]) to מעמקים ('abyss' [rational product, .0571428]) or נקדת-מגוז ('vanishing point' [rational product, .0571428]), the abyssal identity of the 1/2 hemisphere which is *removed* (leaving the 'bowl' and the cone) *and left* (in the form of the portion of the cone *within* the bowl). This split identity, .0666/.0571428 = 1.1666, is the real התבקעות ('splitting'/'cleavage', *qua* proportion, 5 : 400 :: 2 : 100 :: 70 : 6 :: 400 : [1], whose rational product is 1.1666). When this is seen it is evident that Husserl's inquiry into the 'origin of geometry',[45] his 'inquiring back' into an 'original meaning-giving achievement', indeed, the distinction fundamental to phenomenology of the 'life-world' and the 'world of science',[46] concerning which Husserl says:

> Now though we must [further] make evident the fact that the life-world itself is a 'structure', it is nevertheless not a 'purposeful structure', even though to its being, which precedes all purpose, belong men . . . with all their purposes and their works. . . . But now the paradoxical question : Can one not [turn to] the life-world, the world of which we are all conscious in life as the world of us all, without in any way making it into a subject of universal investigation . . . —can one not survey it universally in a changed attitude, and can one not seek to get to know it, as what it is and how it is in its own mobility and relativity, make it the subject matter of a universal science, but one which has by no means the goal of universal theory in the sense in which this was sought by historical philosophy and the sciences?

—this distinction and the enterprise of which it is the foundation—is not the overcoming of Galileo's 'splitting', but, on the contrary, the carrying back into the life-world, *via* the infinitizing detour of pure transcendental subjectivity, of an absolutely

[45] Husserl, *Crisis,* pp. 353ff.
[46] Ibid., pp. 379–83.

radicalized cleavage in the form of that entering into the abyss of presence which is the requirement for an absence which takes the form of the infinite *a priori* of the pure ego, the 'structuring' nevertheless 'not purposeful structuring', or, the square root of 'absolute' התבקעות ('splitting'/'cleavage' [integral product, 7.84E10]) denominated the 'absolute' בקיעה ('splitting'/'cleaving', *qua* proportion, 2 : 100 :: 10 : 70 :: 5 : [1], whose integral product is 1E4), √7.84E10/1E4 = 28, which is identically the Galileian 'splitting' in the form of *the truth of the 'system of reference' minus the center,* where the rational product of מערכת יחוס ('system of reference', *qua* proportion, 40 : 70 :: 200 : 20 :: 400 : [1] (::) 10 : 8 :: 6 : 60, whose rational product is 285.714285) denominated אמת ('truth' [rational product, 10]), 285.714285/10 = 28.571428, minus מרכז ('center' [rational product, .571428]), 28.571428 – .571428, = 28. In Derrida the השלמה ('supplement', *qua* proportion, 5 : 300 :: 30 : 40 :: 5 : [1], whose rational product is .0625) is the inversion of the center identified with the truth of the 'system of reference' minus the center, the inversion of the identification of the center with the radical element of absolute splitting identified as absolute splitting, the inversion of מרכז ('center' [rational product, .571428]) identified with מערכת יחוס ('system of reference' [rational product, 285.714285]) denominated אמת ('truth' [rational product, 10]), 285.714285/10 = 28.571428, minus מרכז ('center' [rational product, .571428]), that is, [.571428 × (28.571428 – .571428 = 28)]$^{-1}$ = .0625. In Altizer the השלמה ('supplement' [rational product, .0625]) is itself at once squared and identified with 'absolute' בקיעה ('splitting'/'cleaving' [integral product, 1E4]), .0625^2 × 1E4 = 39.0625, at once itself the reduction of 'absolute' רעיון ('idea'/'imagination', *qua* proportion, 200 : 70 :: 10 : 6 :: 50 : [1], whose integral product is 1E10) to 'absolute' הסתעף ('to be split up', *qua* proportion, 5 : 60 :: 400 : 70 :: 80 : [1], whose integral product is 2.56E10), denominated ברא ('to create' [rational product, .01]), (1E10/2.56E10)/.01 = 39.0625, where the quotient of the ratio of the identical reduction of the very 'identity' of רעיון ('idea'/'imagination' [rational product, 238.095238]) to that of הסתעף ('to be split up' [rational product, 38.095238]) is the square root/radical element of 39.0625, i.e., 238.095238/38.095238 = 6.25 = √39.0625.[47]

The last mentioned ratio of the absolute inversion of the abyss, 39.0625, at once the proven unity of the proportion, *Guilt* : *Condemnation* :: *Crime* : *Execution,* is the identification of ברא ('to create' [rational product, .01]) and נפקח ('to be opened'/'to get sight of'/'to understand' [rational product, 7.8125]) reduced to that אסון ('calamity', *qua* proportion, 1 : 60 :: 6 : 50, whose rational product is .002) which is identically the reduction of the 'center' to the 'system of reference', of מרכז ('center' [rational product, .571428]) to מערכת יחוס ('system of reference' [rational product, 285.714285), 39.0625 = .01 × 7.8125/.002 = .01 × 7.8125/(.571428/285.714285). But then the 'existent supplement identified with absolute splitting' reduced to 'understanding' & 'creating' is the very 'identity' of קבי ('cubic', *qua* proportion, 100 : 2 :: 10 : [1], whose rational product is 5E2), 39.0625/7.8125/.01 = 5E2, identically the 'system of reference' identified as/reduced to 'center'—the center existing everywhere for the first time[48]—מערכת יחוס ('system of reference')/מרכז ('center'), 285.714285/.571428 = 5E2. Indeed, if the 'center' is identically פוגע ('violator', *qua* proportion, 80 : 6 :: 3 : 70, whose rational product is .571428), then the center/violator is the very identity of the system of reference for the first time in history: no longer is the violator/center either without the system of reference, or reducible to it. This center existing everywhere for the first time, 285.714285/.571428 = 5E2, this 'cubic' 'identity' is itself at once identically the very 'identity' of מוסדה ('foundation', *qua* proportion, 40 : 6 :: 60 : 4 :: 5 : [1], whose rational product is 5E2), אמת מדה ('criterion'/'true measure', *qua* proportion, 1 : 40 :: 400 : [1] (::) 40 : 4 :: 5 : [1], whose rational product is 5E2), קו מחולל ('generating

[47] Cf. above, p. 473. Also, compare this reading of the absolute inversion of the abyss in Altizer as the 'absolutely split up' identity of the 'absolute idea' with the 'absolute fragmentation of identity', above, Section II.4, and with 'the absolutely unconditioned porosity of consciousness itself', below Section V.3.

[48] Cf. above, Section III.5, pp. 426ff., et passim.

line', *qua* proportion, 100 : 6 (::) 40 : 8 :: 6 : 30 :: 30 : [1], whose rational product is 5E2), קין ('edge'/'point', *qua* proportion, 100 : 10 :: 50 : [1], whose rational product is 5E2), and נומרטור ('numerator', *qua* proportion, 50 : 6 :: 40 : 200 :: 9 : 6 :: 200 : [1], whose rational product is 5E2). This last identity of the system of reference reduced to the center as the 'numerator' is confirmed when מערכת יחוס ('system of reference' [rational product, 285.714285]) is reduced to קבוע ('constant'/'immutable', *qua* proportion, 100 : 2 :: 6 : 70, whose rational product is 4.285714), the quotient of which reduction is the very 'identity' of מונה ('numerator', *qua* proportion, 40 : 6 :: 50 : 5, whose rational product is 66.666), 285.714285/4.285714 = 66.666. The 'identity' of the 'constant' identified with the 'identity' of the 'center' is itself at once קבוע הזמן ('time constant', *qua* proportion, 100 : 2 :: 6 : 70 (::) 5 : 7 :: 40 : 50, whose rational product is 2.44897959183673), 4.285714 × .571428 = 2.44897959183673, which last reduced to ברא ('to create' [rational product, .01]) is the very 'identity' of תזוזה ('motion'/'displacement', *qua* proportion, 400 : 7 :: 6 : 7 :: 5 : [1], whose rational product is 244.897959183673), 2.44897959183673/.01 = 244.897959183673. The absolute unity of the system of reference is the identity of the constant as the center, קבוע ('constant'/'immutable')/מרכז ('center'), 4.285714/.571428 = 7.5, which is itself at once the very 'identity' of הכל ('everybody'/'everything' [rational product, 7.5]) and the very 'identity' of שם('Name', *qua* ratio, 300 : 40, whose rational product is 7.5).

It is from the fundamental fact that *the constant identity of the system of reference, the identity of the system of reference as the center, is the numerator,* that the laws of 'matter' and 'mind' are to be transcendentally deduced, as from unity. Take, for example, Galileo's discovery that "the distances traversed, during equal intervals of time, by a body falling from rest, stand to one another in the same ratio as the odd numbers beginning with unity. . . . [which] is the ratio of the differences of the squares of the lines [which represent time], differences which exceed one another by equal amounts, this excess being equal to the smallest line [viz. the one representing a single time interval]: or we may say [that this is the ratio] of the differences of the square of the natural numbers beginning with unity."[49] Here the odd numbers beginning with unity are the numerators of the infinite series of natural numbers *qua* proportion, i.e., 1 : 2 :: 3 : 4 :: 5 : 6 :: 7 : 8 . . . , or the differences of the squares of the natural numbers beginning with unity are the numerators of the infinite series of natural numbers *qua* proportion, i.e., *qua* rational infinite, and the constant identity of the relative distance traversed is the sum of the numerators intervening. In the work before the reader, the integral product or 'absolute' form of any number or word in the deciphering of the absolute text is the product of the squares of the numerators of that word or number *qua* proportion. Both of these examples are embodiments, in diverse ways, of the rule that the constant of the system of reference is the numerator. The underlying formal matrix is the following:

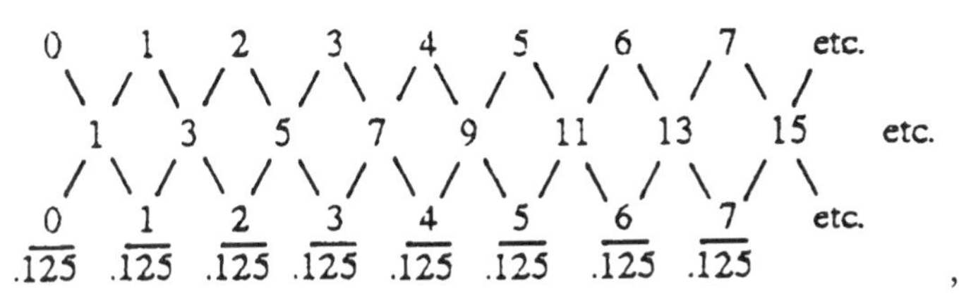

,

so that, if the differences of the squares of the natural numbers beginning with unity are the odd numbers beginning with unity, then the differences of the squares of the numerators of the series of natural numbers *qua* proportion, i.e., the differences of the squares of the differences of the squares of the natural numbers beginning with unity, are the natural numbers beginning with unity reduced to the 'identity' of יחוס ('relation', *qua* proportion, 10 : 8 :: 6 : 60, whose rational product is .125), reduced to .125, and the differences of the squares of these last, and the differences of the squares of those, and so on and so on *ad infinitum*, are alternately the series of odd numbers beginning with unity and the series of natural numbers beginning with unity *reduced to increasing powers of this very relation-'identity'*, the form of which increase is the following proportion (beginning with .125 as above):

[49] Cf. Galilei, *Two New Sciences*, pp. 153, 175.

$$.125^1 : .125^2 :: .125^5 : .125^{10} :: .125^{21} : .125^{42} ::$$

$$.125^{85} : .125^{170} :: 125^{341} : .125^{682} ::$$

$$.125^{1365} : .125^{2730} \text{— etc., etc.,}$$

where the exponents of the numerators of the proportion, viz., 1, 5, 21, 85, 341, 1365, 2730, etc., (the exponents of the denominators, these exponents doubled, the denominators the numerators squared) are a series constructed as follows:

$$1,$$

$$1 + 4,$$

$$(1 + 4) + (4 \times 4),$$

$$(1 + 4) + (4 \times 4) + 4(4 \times 4),$$

$$(1 + 4) + (4 \times 4) + 4(4 \times 4) + 4[4(4 \times 4)],$$

$$(1 + 4) + (4 \times 4) + 4(4 \times 4) + 4[4(4 \times 4)] + 4[4(4[4 \times 4])], \ldots .$$

Let the base proportion of the increasing powers of 'relation' in this matrix of infinite proportionality be:

$$.125^1 : .125^2 :: .125^5 : .125^{10},$$

the proven unity of which proportion is, *qua* whole number,

$$\frac{.125^2 \cdot .125^5}{.125^1 \cdot .125^{10}} = 4.096E3,$$

where 4.096E3 is identically the proven unity of the *Kingdom of Heaven* : *Damned* :: *Resurrection of the Dead* : *Hymen* proportion, and 'absolute' חלחל ('to penetrate') and 'absolute' ἡ ἀγάπη ('agape'/'unconditioned love').[50] Further, let the base proportion of the infinite matrix itself be its first four term-overlapping sets of natural numbers as follows:

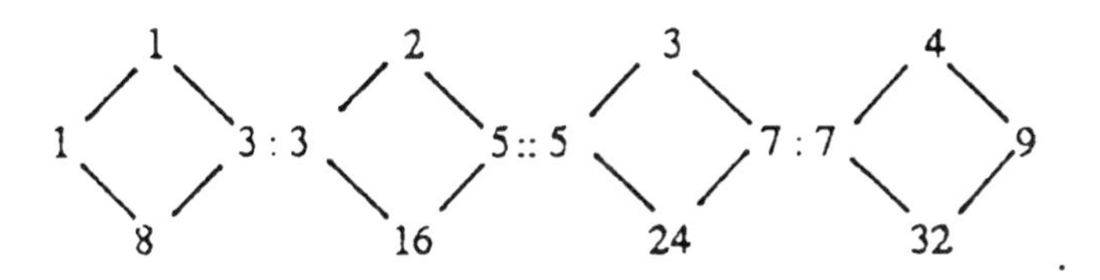

where if the value of the first set be taken as $(1 + 3)/(1 + 8)$ it and each of the other sets by the analogous reading has the value of the rational product of the Absolute Proportion of Absolute Thought, viz., $.\overline{444}$.[51] If the value of the first set be taken as $(1/3)/(1/8)$ it has the value of the rational product of the 'minimum' proportion, viz., $2.\overline{666}$,[52] and is the 'identity' which is the cornerstone of the matrix of infinite proportionality. It is related to the other elements of the proportion (valued respectively by the analogous operation to this last) as follows:

$$2.\overline{666} : 4.8 :: 5.\overline{714285} : 6.\overline{222},$$

and the proven unity of this proportion is:

$$\frac{(2.\overline{666} \cdot 6.\overline{222})}{(4.8 \cdot 5.\overline{714285})} = .\overline{777}^2$$

where $.\overline{777}^2$ is the square of מקדת האמצע ('mid-point', *qua* proportion, 40 : 100 :: 4 : 400 (::) 5 : 1 :: 40 : 90 :: 70 : [1], whose rational product is $.\overline{777}$), while the integral product of this proportion is:

$$(2.\overline{666} \cdot 5.\overline{714285})^2 = 15.\overline{238095}^2,$$

[50] Cf. above, Section III.5, pp. 400f.

[51] Cf. above, p. 367.

[52] Cf. above, p. 362.

where $15.\overline{238095}^2$ is the square of διαγώνιον ('diagonal', *qua* proportion, 4 : 10 :: 1 : 3 :: 800 : 50 :: 10 : 70 :: 50 : [1], whose rational product is $15.\overline{238095}$). The rational product of this proportion is:

$$\frac{2.\overline{666}}{4.8} \cdot \frac{5.\overline{714285}}{6.\overline{222}} = .\overline{714285}^{\,2},$$

where $.\overline{714285}^{\,2}$ is the square of קרנזול ('diagonal', *qua* proportion, 100 : 200 :: 50 : 7 :: 6 : 30, whose rational product is $.\overline{714285}$), which 'squared diagonal' is itself at once the *inversion* of the reduction of 'absolute' נוזליות ('liquidity' [integral product, 1.96E12]) to 'absolute' תשנון ('repetition' [integral product, 1E12]), and 'absolute' קץ הימין ('the end of days'/'the days of the Messiah' [integral product, 1E12]) and 'absolute' רציונלי ('rational' [integral product, 1E12]), the inversion by which the latter become the numerators denominated 'absolute liquidity', where $1E12/1.96E12 = .\overline{714285}^2$. Not that 'absolute liquidity' is the form of 'absolute repetition', 'absolute end of days', 'absolute rational', but that these are the forms of 'absolute liquidity': not the absolute liquidity of identity/the identity of absolute liquidity, but the absolute repetition of identity/the identity of absolute repetition. 'The disownment of the darkness is absolutely the shining of the light.'[53] Not that the absolute Jesus of Nazareth is the known identity of the darkness, but that the darkness is the known identity of absolute Jesus of Nazareth. This is 'the absolute disowning of self-identity identified as the absolutely irreversible reversal of self-identity, as, in fact, not the reversal of the darkness of identity, but, in fact, the disownment thereof.'[54] The perfect non-reciprocity of the reciprocal relation here founded in the base proportion of the infinite matrix of proportionality where the common denominator of the term-overlapping numerators of the natural number series is the very 'identity' of יחוס ('relation' [rational product, .125; integral product, 3.6E3, linear product √8.2944E8]) whose

[53] Cf. above, Section II.4.

[54] Ibid.

'absolute' form, 3.6E3, is identically 'absolute' יהוה ('Yahweh' [integral product, 3.6E3]).

For Plato the fourfold proportionality of the line was an index of the relations existing among different levels of cognition. How is the thinking now occurring for the first time related to Plato's understanding of thought and reality, and how in relating the essentially new form of thinking to Plato's understanding, can it be at once related to the essential history of thought? To begin to answer this question, let there be a line as described by Plato in Book 6 of the *Republic* as follows:[55] ". . . a line divided into two unequal parts, one to represent the visible order, the other the intelligible; and divide each part again in the same proportion, symbolizing degrees of comparative clearness or obscurity," except that, whereas Plato does not specify the ratio of division beyond saying that "the proportion in which the visible world has been divided [into likeness and original should be such that they stand to one another] . . . in the same ratio as the sphere of appearances and belief to the sphere of knowledge," let the ratio be 2 : 1, as here:

so that $AB : BC :: CD : DE :: AC : CE :: 1 : 2$.[56] It follows, then, that

[55] *The Republic of Plato*, trans. F. M. Cornford (London, 1941), pp. 224ff.

[56] The Platonic line can be construed as here but using the ratio $\phi : 1$ in

for Plato the line segments *BC* and *CD* are equal, i.e., the *BC* section of the line corresponding to ἡ πίστις ('belief'), the state of mind appropriate to the 'actual things' of the visible world, 'the works of nature or of human hands', equals in length the *CD* section corresponding to ἡ διανοία ('thinking'), the state of mind which 'uses as images those actual things which themselves had images in the visible world', and which 'is compelled to pursue its inquiry by starting from assumptions and traveling, not up to a principle, but down to a conclusion', and that, therefore, taken in and of themselves (apart from their respective relations to *AB*, the line section corresponding to ἡ εἰκασία ['imagining'], the state of mind corresponding to 'shadows' and 'reflections' in the visible world, and apart from their respective relations to *DE*, the line section corresponding to ἡ νόησις ['intelligence'], where 'the mind moves in the other direction [from that of ἡ διανοία ('thinking')], from an assumption up towards a principle which is not hypothetical . . . and makes no use of the images employed in the other section, but only of Forms, and conducts its inquiry solely by their means'), ἡ πίστις ('belief') and ἡ διανοία ('thinking') are distinguished not by degree of clarity, but by the fact that the objects of the former are the images of the objects of the latter, and that therefore, unlike the 'images of images' which are the objects of mere 'imagining', the objects of 'belief' are rational images or images of reason, what might be called images *proper*, while the objects of 'imagining', even reflections in water or in mirrors, are not *properly* images, but *properly* shadows, that is, 'belief' and 'thinking' are distinguished from one another by the fact that they mirror one another as the realms, respectively, of the improperly and properly reflected objects, indeed, as, respectively, the real

place of the ratio 2 : 1. It can then be shown that the absolute structure of existence is—essentially, and specifically at the place of entry—an interlocking and interweaving of the 'golden bowls' produced by the use of the former ratio with the pattern of 'logical bowls' constructed below in the text on the basis of the latter ratio (see below, pp. 507ff.). Specifically, the base of the entry-bowl in the system of 'golden bowls' is the 2-side of the 4-square which is the fourth-foundational segment of the 576-entry-bowl in the system of 'logical bowls' elaborated below.

(using images, not an image) and the (unreal) image of the real. Let Plato's line, *qua* visible and intelligible orders, *qua* *AC* and *CE*, be squared in such a way that the diagonally divided halves of each square have *AC* and *CE*, respectively, as their common sides, and arranged so as to preserve the order of the original proportion, thusly:

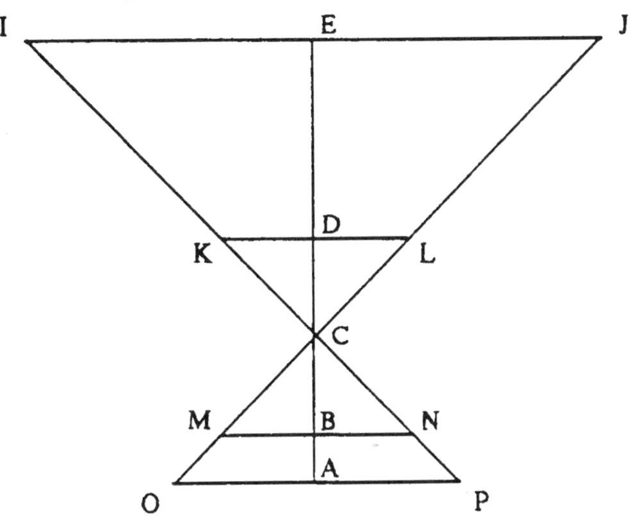

where 'belief' (the triangle *MNC*) is the mirror image of 'thinking' (the triangle *KLC*), while the improper images of 'imagining' (the trapezoid *MNOP*) are to the proper images of 'belief' (*MNC*) as the properly intelligible objects of 'intelligence' (the trapezoid *IJKL*) are to the improperly intelligible objects (the 'assumptions') of 'thinking' (*KLC*). The proportion *AB* : *BC* :: *CD* : *DE* is actually in the 'logical' order, 1 : 2 :: 4 : 3, or the order, *PP* : *NP* :: *PN* : *NN*.[57] Let the diagram be further modified to make explicit the direct sequence, 1, 2, 3, interrupted as it is by the interposition of 4 between 2 and 3, in the form of the distorted mirror inversion, *MNOP* : *MNC* :: *IJKL* : *KLC*, then the two triangles, *ICO* and *JCP*, emerge, together with the triangles interior to them, respectively, *ICM* and *JCN*, which latter two have a combined area of 24 (since what has been specified is the simplest

[57] Cf. above, pp. 273f.

whole number division of Plato's line as *AB* : *BC* :: *CD* : *DE* :: 1 : 2 :: 2 : 4), while the former two triangles, of which the latter two are parts, have a combined area of 36, so that the ratio of the set of inner triangles to the outer set is $.\overline{666}$: 1, identically the rational product of the logical order, i.e., $1/2 \times 4/3 = .\overline{666}$:

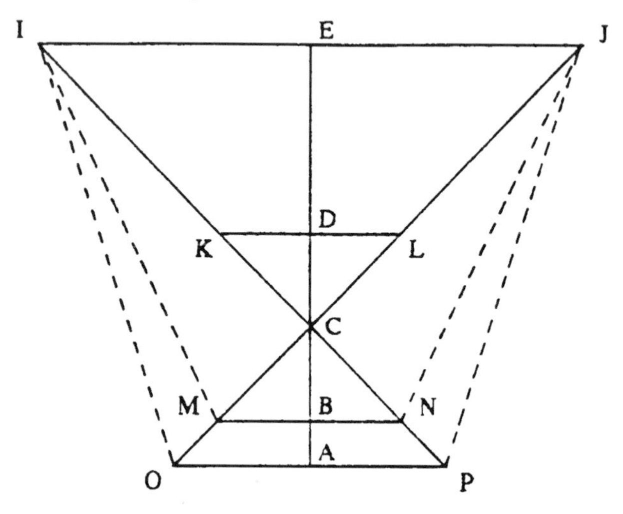

The square of $.\overline{666}$: 1 is the ratio of the total area of *ICO–JCP*, 36, to the total area of the trapezoid *IJOP*, 81, viz., $.\overline{444}$. $.\overline{444}$ is the rational product of the Absolute Proportion of Absolute Thought, 16 : 24 :: 24 : 36, therefore the value of the ratio of the extremes, 16 : 36. Let, therefore, two analogous exterior triangles whose combined area equals 16 emerge by extending *EA* by *FE*, squaring *FC* and *CA* as above, and folding at *C* and along *MN* so that the triangle *MCN* ('belief') lies in the place of *KCL* ('thinking'), while the latter removes by inverting itself to KC_1L where with *KCL–MNC* it forms the decisive interior base of the triangles IC_1C–JC_1C, the combined area of which is 24, while, further, the line segments, *ML*, *BD*, and *NK*, hidden from sight in the fold, are replaced by *JH*, *EF*, and *IG* (the defining limits of the new trapezoid *GHIJ*, which may be called ή μετανόησις ('meta-intelligence', *qua* proportion, 8 : [1] (::) 40 : 5 :: 300 : 1 :: 50 : 70 :: 8 : 200 :: 10 : 200, whose integral product is 1.47456E17 [= the integral product of the Absolute Proportion of Absolute Thought, 1.47456E5, identified with 'absolute' רציונלי ('rational'

[integral product, 1E12]), 1.47456E5 × 1E12 = 1.47456E17])—first the construction in its unfolded form is here illustrated:

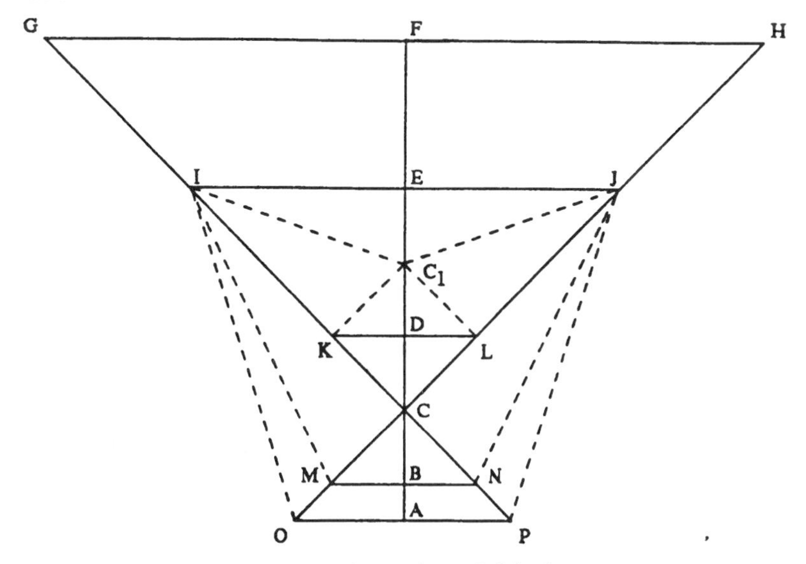

then the identical construction when folded:

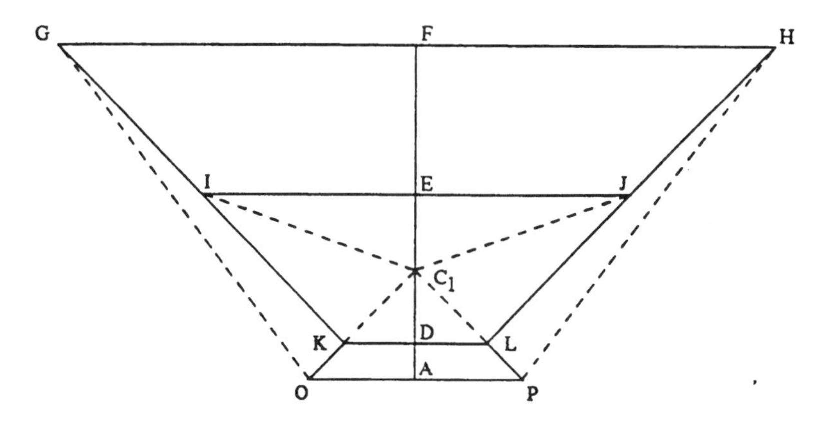

—so folded, a 'bowl' is formed, and the triangles *GKO–HLP* emerge, the combined area of which is 16. Finally, then, the Absolute Proportion of Absolute Thought, 16 : 24 :: 24 : 36, is in the form of the completely specified Platonic line *GKO-HLP* : *ICM–I*C_1*C* :: *J*C_1*C–JCN* : *ICO–JCP*. This is at once a form of the positive-negative distribution in the essential form of all logical propositions, *PP* : *NP* :: *PN* : *NN*,[58] here, *FF* (folded fold) : *UF* (unfolded fold) :: *FU* (folded unfolded) : *UU* (unfolded unfolded). Here, then, is the index embodying the essentially historical transformation of the bases of previous thought, the transformation of Platonic-Idealist 'imagining' (*MNOP*, ἡ εἰκασία) into what may be called 'constructive imagination' (*KLOP*, τὸ διατυπόειν), upon which now rests the superimposed and inverted elements of the mirror which was 'belief' (*MCN*, ἡ πίστις) and 'thinking' (*KCL*, ἡ διανοία), 'belief', twice, and 'thinking', once, inverted, in the form of what may be called 'positing' (KC_1L τὸ ὑποτιθέναι), where the twice inverted 'belief' (the sensible world reconstructed) is the inseparable base of the inverted 'thinking' (presuppositionless thinking) which now forms the interior base of 'intelligence' (*IJKL*, ἡ νόησις). But this construction of the history of thought and reconstruction of the interior base of intelligence is inseparable from the construction of the 'meta-intelligence' (*GHIJ*, ἡ μετανόησις) directly related to 'constructive imagination' through the structure *GKO–HLP* and its internal counterpart IC_1K–JC_1L. The latter provide the measure of the conformity of the whole construction, *qua* folded, *qua* 'bowl', to the universal law of identity, as follows (where capital letters indicate elements of *GKO–HLP*, and lower-case letters elements of IC_1K–JC_1L:

$$LP/c_1l :: jl/HL :: ik/GK :: KO/c_1k,$$

which, since it equals:

$$\sqrt{2}/\sqrt{8} :: \sqrt{32}/\sqrt{128} :: \sqrt{32}/\sqrt{128} :: \sqrt{2}/\sqrt{8},$$

proves, in the first instance, to:

$$16\text{–}LP(HL)/16\text{–}c_1l(jl) :: 16\text{–}ik(c_1k)/16\text{–}GK(KO),$$

and finally, substituting *x* for capitalized sets and *y* for lower-case sets, to:

[58] Ibid.

$$256-x^2/256-y^2 = 1,$$

$$x^2/y^2 = 1,$$

$$1_{xy} = 1.$$[59]

In the construction which is the specification of the Platonic line for the first time manifesting the essential history of thought the 'identity' of τὸ ὑποτιθέναι ('positing', *qua* proportion, 300 : 70 (::) 400 : 80 :: 70 : 300 :: 10 : 9 :: 5 : 50 :: 1 : 10, whose rational product is .0555) is the precise relative portion of the whole of the area shared with τὸ διατυπόειν ('constructive imagination', *qua* proportion, 300 : 70 (::) 4 : 10 :: 1 : 300 :: 400 : 80 :: 70 : 5 :: 10 : 50, whose rational product is .08) which is occupied by the latter, denominated אמת ('truth' [rational product, 10]), ($KLOP/OC_1P$ = 5/9 = .555)/10 = .0555, while the 'identity of τὸ διατυπόειν ('constructive imagination') identified with אמת ('truth') is precisely the ratio of the area occupied by τὸ ὑποτιθέναι ('positing') to that which it occupies, ($KC_1L/KLOP$= 4/5 = .80)/10 = .08. The very 'identities' bespeak the truth of the foundational priority of 'constructive imagination' to 'positing' in such a way that the very existence of the other is absolutely posited, that *the very identity of positing is the foundational priority of the other in the form of the constructive imagination.* The fold completely folded, the blank completely blank, the consciousness absolutely now, there is neither necessity nor possibility of positing the self/of the self positing/of self-positing, but nothing is posited *ex nihilo* as the other. This is the absolutely unconditioned meta-identity of unity/the other absolutely and finally the one in the 'squaring of writing'.[60] This absolutely folded fold, this constructed 'bowl', insofar as it itself is at once this reduction of 'positing' to 'constructive imagination', is, as such and thereby, *qua* 'identities', τὸ ὑποτιθέναι ('positing' [rational product, .0555]) reduced to τὸ διατυπόειν ('constructive imagi-

59. Cf. above, Section III.1, pp. 277f., and Section III.5, passim.
60. Cf. above, p. 392, n. 83.

nation' [rational product, .08]), thereby identified as the very identity of what now actually occurs for the first time, viz., .0555/.08 = .69444, the הצרפה ('synthesis' [rational product, .69444]), the קפיצה ('leap' [rational product, .69444]), and the קפיצה ('closing' [rational product, .69444]), the reduction, as of 'logic' to the minimum, of Existence (הויה) to the Tetragrammaton (יהוה), *qua* integral products, 2.5E3/3.6E3, *qua* rational products, 1.666/2.4, which = .69444, the reduction of נשנה ('recurrence' [rational product, 1.666]) to מתחיל ('beginning' [rational product, 2.4]), 1.666/2.4= .69444. The absolutely folded fold, the 'bowl', is the indicial embodiment of the new consciousness of the beginning, of the creation of absolute recurrence : the absolute recurrence of creation, the beginning of the existence of absolute consciousness. Revolutionary metanoēsis is the recurrence for the first time of history, the comprehension for the first time of the Incarnation, of the essential change in time of consciousness not before now. Essentially historical consciousness for the first time comprehending temporality absolutely here shows itself, *qua* mathematical index, the historical at once itself essentially new, shows itself the transcendental dichotomy/foundation itself existent/consciousness of the beginning, as follows: Let it be recognized that as *before* the fold *ICO–JCP* (area 36) is to *IJOP* (area 81), so *after* the fold *GKO–HLP* (area 16) is to the six-sided polygon *KOGHPL* resting on *KLOP* (*qua* areas, 112/5 = 22.4, where, instead of the undifferentiated total 117, 112/5 = 22.4 captures the fact of the folding, at once the foundational role of 'constructive imagination', to which discrete and creative identity 'metanoēsis' and 'intelligence' are here reduced), that is,

$$36 : 81 :: 16 : (112/5),$$

the proportion of the history of the construction *qua before and after.* The rational product of this before-and-after proportion is 3.15^{-1}. Let it also be recognized that the 'identity' or rational product of this before-and-after proportion is the truth 'identity' of the rational product of the *first three elements* of the base proportion of the matrix of infinite proportionality,[61] i.e., the latter rational product denominated אמת ('truth' [rational product, 10]), $(2.\overline{666}/4.8) \times 5.\overline{714285}/10 = 3.15^{-1} = (36/81) \times [16/(112/5)]$. Let it be further recognized that the truth 'identity' of the fourth element of the base proportion of the matrix of infinite proportionality is the proven unity of the before-and-after proportion, i.e., $6.\overline{222}/10 = .\overline{6222} = [36 \times (112/5)]/(81 \times 16)$. Finally, the very 'identity' or rational product of the base proportion,

$$\frac{2.\overline{666}}{4.8} \cdot \frac{5.\overline{714285}}{6.\overline{222}} = .\overline{714285}^2$$

where $.\overline{714285}^2$ is the square of קרנזול ('diagonal' [rational product, $.\overline{714285}$]), the *inversion* of the reduction of 'absolute' נוזליות ('liquidity' [integral product, 1.96E12]) to 'absolute' תשנון ('repetition' [integral product, 1E12]), etc.,[62] this very 'identity' is the *reduction* of the 'before-and-after' proportion, *qua* identity, *to the reduction* which is the 'after' *identifying* the 'before', that is, is identically:

$$\frac{36}{81} \cdot \frac{[16/(112/5)]}{[(36/81)/(16/[112/5])]} = .\overline{714285}^2$$

the fundamental structure of which essentially-historical-&-new-identity is manifest when, substituting v for 36, w for 81, x for 16 and y for 112/5, it is written:

$$\frac{v/w \cdot x/y}{(v/w)/(x/y)} = .\overline{714285}^2,$$

that is,

$$\frac{vx}{wy} \cdot \frac{wx}{vy} = .\overline{714285}^2,$$

finally,

[61] Cf. above, pp. 489f.

[62] Ibid.

$$\frac{x^2}{y^2} = .\overline{714285}^2,$$

or,

$$1_{xy} = .\overline{714285},$$

which last, a form of $1_{xy} = 1$,[63] says that the unity which is סעדת ישו ('Eucharist' [rational product, .00714285]) identified as ברא ('to create [rational product, .01]), .00714285/.01 = .714285, which is identically the קרנזול ('diagonal' [rational product, .714285]), is the unity of the x/y coordinate system. Indeed, *qua* 'identity', the סעדת ישו ('Eucharist') identified as ברא ('to create), itself at once the קרנזול ('diagonal'), identified with אמת ('truth' [rational product, 10]) identified with absolute' הכרה ('consciousness'/'discernment' [integral product, 1E6]) is the very 'identity' of קואורדינשות קרטזיות ('Cartesian coordinates', *qua* proportion, 100 : 6 :: 1 : 6 :: 200 : 4 :: 10 : 50 :: 9 : 6 :: 400 : [1] (::) 100 : 200 :: 9 : 7 :: 10 : 6 :: 400 : [1], whose rational product is 7.142857E6), .714285 × 10 × 1E6 = 7.142857E6. The Unity that is x^2/y^2 is the unity of the *novitas mundi,* the unity of the newness of the world, the unity of the eucharist of existence. This is the transcendental dichotomy which is itself at once the second absolute/the 'after' absolute/the identity of the 'after'-elements squared: *the dichotomy in which the transcendental transcends itself*:[64] the absolutely unconditioned meta-dichotomy in which the 'after' exists absolutely unconditioned: the transcendental meta-transcendentally absolute: the 'after'-elements absolute.[65] This unity of existence itself, $x^2/y^2 = .\overline{714285}^2$, 'diagonal' squared, the absolute 'after'-elements, identically the 'identity' of the base proportion of infinite proportionality, is, here, $.\overline{714285}^2 = 16^2/(112/5)^2 =$ 256/501.76, which is itself at once the reduction of 'absolute' ἡ εἰκασία ('imagining', *qua* proportion, 8 : [1] (::) 5 : 10 :: 20 : 1 :: 200 : 10 :: 1 : [1], whose integral product is 2.56E10) to 'abso-

[63] Cf. above, Section III.1, pp. 277f., et passim.

[64] Cf. above, pp. 172ff., 'itself transcending itself'.

[65] Compare the disappearance here of the 'before'-elements, v and w, with the vanishing of the 'negative meta-identity', above, pp. 276ff.

lute' ἡ διανοία ('thinking', *qua* proportion, 8 : [1] (::) 4 : 10 :: 1 : 50 :: 70 : 10 :: 1 : [1], whose integral product is 5.0176E6), when that reduction is denominated Godhead (שכינה [rational product, 15]) identified with "Let there be light!" (יהי אור [rational product, 666.666]), 2.56E10/5.0176E6/(15 × 666.666) = $.714285^2$.[66] If this 'identity' is denominated by the הצרפה ('synthesis' [rational product, .69444]) identically the קפיצה ('leap' [rational product, .69444]) and the קפיצה ('closing' [rational product, .69444]), identically the reduction of Existence (הויה) to Yahweh (יהוה), *qua* integral products, 2.5E3/3.6E3, *qua* rational products, 1.666/2.4, which = .69444, and the reduction of נשנה ('recurrence' [rational product, 1.666]) to מתחיל ('beginning' [rational product, 2.4]), 1.666/2.4 = .69444, it is the very 'identity' of מערכת שעורים ('system of coordinates', *qua* proportion, 40 : 70 :: 200 : 20 :: 400 : [1] (::) 300 : 70 :: 6 : 200 :: 10 : 40, whose rational product is 7.3469387755E1) identified with ברא ('to create' [rational product, .01]), $.714285^2$/.69444 = .73469387755 = 7.3469387755E1 × .01.[67]

This unity of existence itself, $x^2/y^2 = .714285^2$, 'diagonal' squared, the absolute 'after'-elements, the 'identity' of the base proportion of infinite proportionality, identified with the 'absolute' form of that יחוס ('relation' [integral product, 3.6E3]) whose increasing powers, *qua* rational product, denominate the infinite matrix of proportionality, identified therefore at once itself with 'absolute' יהוה ('Yahweh' [integral product, 3.6E3]) is, as such, the 'identity' or rational product of

---

66 The quotient of the reduction carried out *qua* rational products, ἡ εἰκασία ('imagining' [rational product, 1.6E3]) to ἡ διανοία ('thinking' [rational product, .448]), identified with τὸ διατυπόειν ('constructive imagination' [rational product, .08]) is the very 'identity' of מערכת יחוס ('system of reference' [rational product, 285.714285]), (1.6E3/.448) × .08 = 285.714285. When the reduction of 'imagining' to 'thinking' denominates 'constructive imagination' the ultimate quotient is the six-sided polygon *KOGHPL* resting on *KLOP*, *qua* areas, 112/5 = 22.4, identified as 'absolute' הכרה ('consciousness'/'discernment' [integral product, 1E6]), [.08/(1.6E3/.448)] × 1E6 = 112/5 = 22.4.

67 .73469387755 is exactly the inverse squared, i.e., the existent inversion, of the 'identity' of the התבקעות ('splitting'/'cleavage' [rational product, 1.1666]) discussed above, pp. 482ff.

’Ιησοῦς Χριστός

(‘Jesus Christ’, *qua* proportion, 10 : 8 :: 200 : 70 :: 400 : 200 (::) 600 : 100 :: 10 : 200 :: 300 : 70 :: 200 : [1], whose rational product is 1.83673469E3), $.\overline{714285}^2 \times 3.6E3 = 1.83673469E3$.[68] Likewise the ‘identity’ of ’Ιησοῦς Χριστός is the identification of ברא (‘to

[68] The rational product of ’Ιησοῦς Χριστός (‘Jesus Christ’) is the square of that of קבוע (‘constant’/’immutable’ [rational product, $4.\overline{285714}$]) denominated ברא (‘to create’ [rational product, .01]), $4.\overline{285714}^2/.01 = 1.83673469E3$, the existent constant identified as ‘to create’. The linear product of ’Ιησοῦς Χριστός is ‘absolute’ השתוה (‘to be made alike’, *qua* proportion, 5 : 300 :: 400 : 6 :: 5 : [1], whose integral product is 1E8) identified with ‘absolute’ ὁ πέλεκυς (‘double axe’, *qua* proportion, 70 : [1] (::) 80 : 5 :: 30 : 5 :: 20 : 400 :: 200 : [1], whose integral product is 4.51584E17), 1E8 × 4.51584E17 = 4.51584E25. In fact the rational and linear products of ὁ πέλεκυς are ‘made alike’, the rational, 6.72E4, the linear 6.72E12, a mathematical-linguistic structure corresponding perfectly to the ‘content’ of the word, i.e., to the shared identity of the blades of the double axe:

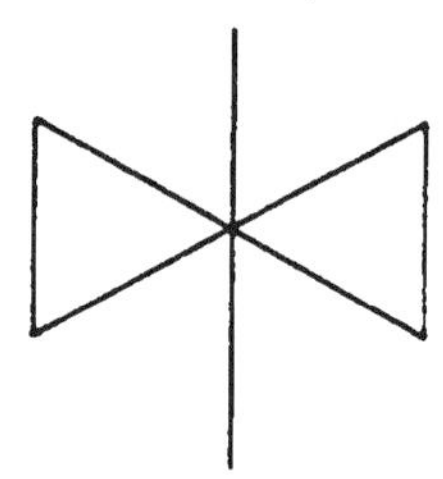

and a structure repeated in the names of the ancient sky-fathers whose weapon the double axe is, to wit, in ὁ κρόνος (‘Kronos’, *qua* proportion, 70 : [1] (::) 20 : 100 :: 70 : 50 :: 70 : 200, whose rational product is 6.86 and whose linear product is 6.86E12), ὁ Ζεύς (‘Zeus’, *qua* proportion, 70 : [1] (::) 7 : 5 :: 400 : 200, whose rational product is 1.96E2 and whose linear product is 1.96E8), and in ὁ Ζάν (‘Zan’, *qua* proportion, 70 : [1] (::) 7 : 1 :: 50 : [1], whose rational product is 2.45E4 and whose linear product is 2.45E4). The perfect symmetry of the last reflecting the fact that Zan is the primordial Kronos-Zeus (cf. A. B. Cook, *Zeus: A Study in Ancient Religion* [reprint; New York, 1964]). The structure of the double axe is identically that of the mirroring structure of *KCL* and *MCN,* ὁ πίστις (‘belief’) and ἡ διανοία (‘thinking’), in the original construction of the Platonic line, which in the folding is folded over and inverted, transformed, to KC_1L. One form of the double axe is in fact the letter *zayin:*

ז

create') and מערכת שעורים ('system of coordinates') identified with 'absolute' הויה, ('Being'/Existence' [integral product, 2.5E3]), .01 × 7.3469387755E1 × 2.5E3 = 1.83673469E3. In fact, 'absolute' Ἰησοῦς Χριστός ('Jesus Christ' [integral product, 8.2944E28]) is 'absolute' נקדת האפס של תנופה ('dead center'/'point zero of energy' [integral product, 8.2944E22])[69] identified with 'absolute' הכרה ('consciousness'/'discernment' [integral product, 1E6]), 8.2944E22 × 1E6 = 8.2944E28. It is identically 'absolute' הכרה ('consciousness'/'discernment') identified with 'absolute' קוד קואורדינשות ('coordinate code', *qua* proportion, 100 : 6 :: 4 : [1] (::) 100 : 6 :: 1 : 6 :: 200 : 4 :: 10 : 50 :: 9 : 6 :: 400 : [1], whose integral product is likewise 8.2944E22).[70] Let there be the proportion, *qua* integral products, of the elements of the 'absolutely

---

(ibid., II, p. 613) which is the rational product of זהה ('to identify', *qua* proportion, 7 : 5 :: 5 : [1], whose rational product is 7). *Qua* 'identities', זהה identified with ό νόησις ('intelligence' [rational product, $.01\overline{142857}$]) is τό διατυπόειν ('constructive imagination' [rational product, .08]), 7 × $.01\overline{142857}$ = .08. ή μετανόησις ('meta-intelligence' [rational product, $27.\overline{428571}$]) is to τό ὑποτιθέναι ('positing' [rational product, .0555]) as √(1.1943936E7)/7 is to 1, where 1.1943936E7 is the extended base factor of 'absolute' אני חושב ועל כן אני קים ('*Cogito ergo sum*'/'I think therefore I am' [integral product, 1.1943936E25]).

If, substituting 'absolute' רחן ('to spiritualize', *qua* proportion, 200 : 8 :: 50 : [1], whose integral product is 1E8) for 'absolute' השתוה ('to be made alike'), 'absolute' Jesus Christ is the 'to create' identity of the immutable existent identified with the identification of 'absolute' double axe and 'absolute' spiritualizing, then in Jesus Christ the double axe is taken up into the very act of creation in the form of the transcendence of the a-theological 'self-sacrifice of God', in the form of the Godhead of God sacrificing the Godless self-sacrifice of God, in the form of the absolutely selfless sacrifice of Christ, in the form of the selfless sacrifice of God which is being, the Name, existence, the minimum, which is, indeed, absolute actuality.

69 Cf. above, Section III.5, pp. 426ff.

70 The rational product of קוד קואורדינשות ('coordinate code' [rational product, $1.\overline{111}$E6]) is identically 'absolute' קושטא קאי שקרא לא קאי ('truth stands, a lie does not', *qua* proportion, 100 : 6 :: 300 : 9 :: 1 : [1] (::) 100 : 1 :: 10 : [1] (::) 300 : 100 :: 200 : 1 (::) 30 : 1 (::) 100 : 1 :: 10 : [1], whose integral product is 1E13) denominated 'absolute' אבן יסוד ('cornerstone', *qua* proportion, 1 : 2 :: 50 : [1] (::) 10 : 60 :: 6 : 4, whose integral product is 9E6), 1E13/9E6 = $1.\overline{111}$E6.

folded fold', i.e., of the 'bowl' from which neither hemisphere nor 1/2 hemisphere has been removed,[71] *GHIJ* ('meta-intelligence') : *IJKL* ('intelligence') :: KC_1L ('positing') : *KLOP* ('constructive imagination'), as follows:

ἡ μετανόησις : ἡ νόησις :: τὸ ὑποτιθέναι : τὸ διατυπόειν,
1.47456E17 : 1.024E9 :: 1.764E17 : 1.12896E17,

the proven unity of which proportion is:

$$(1.47456E17 \cdot 1.12896E17)/(1.024E9 \cdot 1.764E17) = 9.216E7,$$

where 9.216E7 is the foundational 1/9th identity[72] of 'absolute' חכמת ההגיון ('science of logic', *qua* proportion, 8 : 20 :: 40 : 400 (::) 5 : 5 :: 3 : 10 :: 6 : 50, whose integral product is 8.2944E8) and itself at once 'absolute' חצי-כדור ('hemisphere' [integral product, 9.216E7]), 'absolute' חצי-מעגל ('semi-circle', *qua* proportion, 8 : 90 :: 10 : [1] (::) 40 : 70 :: 3 : 30, whose integral product is 9.216E7), and 'absolute' אחדותיות ('unity', *qua* proportion, 1 : 8 :: 4 : 6 :: 400 : 10 :: 6 : 400, whose integral product is 9.216E7). The rational product of this proportion is:

$$\frac{1.47456E17}{1.024E9} \cdot \frac{1.764E17}{1.12896E17} = 2.25E8,$$

where 2.25E8 is 'absolute' התקפל ('to be folded', *qua* proportion, 5 : 400 :: 100 : 80 :: 30 : [1], whose integral product is 2.25E8), 'absolute' שם הויה ('Tetragrammaton', *qua* proportion, 300 : 40 (::) 5 : 6 :: 10 : 5, whose integral product is 2.25E8), and 'absolute' שכינה ('Shekhinah', 'Godhead' [integral product, 2.25E8]).[73] The integral product of this proportion is:

[71] Cf. above, pp. 478ff.
[72] Cf. above, Section III.5, pp. 426ff.
[73] Cf. above, pp. 372f.

$$(1.47456E17 \cdot 1.764E17)^2 = 6.76584523101634E68,$$

where 6.76584523101634E68 is 'absolute' עני ורוכב על חמור ('the Messiah'/'lowly and riding upon an ass' [Zc. 9:9], *qua* proportion, 70 : 50 :: 10 : [1] (::) 6 : 200 :: 6 : 20 :: 2 : [1] (::) 70 : 30 (::) 8 : 40 :: 6 : 200, whose integral product is 2.8677390336E16) identified with 'absolute' תשנון ('repetition' [integral product, 1E12]) identified in turn with 'absolute' קץ הימין ('the end of days'/'the days of the Messiah' [integral product, 1E12]), or identified with the square of 'absolute' רציונלי ('rational' [integral product, 1E12]), in either case, identified in turn with 'absolute'

בראשית ברא אלהים את השמים ואת הארץ

('In the beginning God created the heaven and the earth' [Gn. 1:1], *qua* proportion, 2 : 200 :: 1 : 300 :: 10 : 400 (::) 2 : 200 :: 1 : [1] (::) 1 : 30 :: 5 : 10 :: 40 : [1] (::) 1 : 400 (::) 5 : 300 :: 40 : 10 :: 40 : [1] (::) 6 : 1 :: 400 : [1] (::) 5 : 1 :: 200 : 90, whose integral product is 2.359296E28), 6.76584523101634E68 = 2.8677390336E16 × $1E12^2$ × 2.359296E28. Now the mind stands in the center of the absolute circle of absolute thought : the prince of peace the rational creation of the heaven and the earth. The very 'identity' or rational product of בראשית ברא אלהים את השמים ואת הארץ ('In the beginning God created the heaven and the earth' [Gn. 1:1]) is

$$0.00000\overline{098765432},$$

which is 'absolute' בראשית ברא אלהים את השמים ואת הארץ ('In the beginning God created the heaven and the earth' [integral product, 2.359296E28]) identified as 'absolute' נקדת האפס של תנופה ('dead center'/'point zero of energy' [integral product, 8.2944E22]) raised to the כריסטוס ('Christ' [rational product, 1.5]) or שלום ('peace' [rational product, 1.5]) power, that is, the 'absolute' proportion of the 'bowl' identified as absolute rational Messiah identified as the Christ power of absolute dead center,

$0.0000\overline{0098765432}$, = 6.76584523101634E68/ (2.8677390336E16 × 1E12^{2})/8.2944E22$^{1.5}$ = 2.359296E28/ 8.2944E22$^{1.5}$, where, therefore, 8.2944E22$^{1.5}$ must be and is the linear product of Genesis 1:1. Now the base of the constructed 'bowl', *KLOP,* is τὸ διατυπόειν ('constructive imagination' [integral product, 1.12896E17]), whose 'absolute' form is identically 'absolute' ἡ ψυχή ('psyche', *qua* proportion, 8 : [1] (::) 700 : 400 :: 600 : 8, whose integral product is 1.12896E13) identified with the 'created 100',[74] and identically 'absolute' משכל עיוני ('speculative intelligence', *qua* proportion, 40 : 300 :: 20 : 30 (::) 70 : 10 :: 6 : 50 :: 10 : [1], whose integral product is 1.12896E13) identified with the 'created 100', 1.12896E17 = 1.12896E13 × 1E4. But this 'absolute constructive imagination', or 'absolute psyche' or 'absolute speculative intelligence' identified with the 'created 100', is itself at once 'absolute' ἡ τοῦ ἀγαθοῦ ἰδεά ('the Idea of the Good', *qua* proportion, 8 : [1] (::) 300 : 70 :: 400 : [1] (::) 1 : 3 :: 1 : 9 :: 70 : 400 (::) 10 : 4 :: 5 : 1, whose integral product is 1.12896E19) identified with ברא ('to create' [rational product, .01]), 1.12896E17 = 1.12896E19 × .01: the Idea of the Good identically to create. *Qua* identity, ἡ τοῦ ἀγαθοῦ ἰδεά ('the Idea of the Good' [rational product, $1.\overline{111}$E3]) is קוד קואורדינטות ('coordinate code' [rational product, $1.\overline{111}$E6]) identified with ברא ('to create' [rational product, .01]) and denominated אמת ('truth' [rational product, 10]), $1.\overline{111}$E3 = $1.\overline{111}$E6 × .01/10. But the 'identity' of 'coordinate code' so identified, at once itself the 'identity' of 'the Idea of the Good', is 'absolute' רעיון ('idea'/'imagination' [integral product, 1E10]) denominated 'absolute' אבן יסוד ('cornerstone', *qua* proportion, 1 : 2 :: 50 : [1] (::) 10 : 60 :: 6 : 4, whose integral product is 9E6)/'absolute' סדירה ('order'/'arrangement', *qua* proportion, 60 : 4 :: 10 : 200 :: 5 : [1], whose integral product is 9E6)/'absolute' שוין ('equalizer', *qua* proportion, 300 : 6 :: 10 : 50, whose integral product is 9E6)[75]/'absolute' קפל ('to fold', *qua* proportion, 100 : 80 :: 30 :

[74] Cf. above, pp. 366ff.

[75] Cf. above, Section III.1, pp. 255f., for the categorically new logic in whose terms inequality cannot be expressed.

[1], whose integral product is 9E6), $1.\overline{111}E3 = 1E10/9E6$. The center identical with the circumference of the absolute circle of absolute thought manifests itself powerfully and directly when the mind sees that where 1E10 is 'absolute thought', 9E6 is 'absolute arrangement', $0.0000\overline{0098765432}$ is the 'identity' of 'In the beginning God created the heaven and the earth', and .1125 is the identity of יחסיות ('proportionality' [rational product, .1125]),

$$\frac{1E10}{9E6 \cdot 0.0000\overline{0098765432} \cdot .1125} = 1E10,$$

'absolute order' itself identified with the 'Creation', at once with 'proportionality', *is* the Unity denominating 'absolute thought'. 'Absolute thought', *so* denominated, *is* 'absolute thought'. 'Absolute' רעיון ('idea'/'imagination' [integral product, 1E10]), so denominated, is 'absolute' היה קים ('to be in existence', *qua* proportion, 5 : 10 :: 5 : [1] (::) 100 : 10 :: 40 : [1], whose integral product is 1E10). 'To prove that black is white' (אמר לשחור לבן [rational product, 1E5]) *squared*,[76] 'to solve a problem' (פרק קושיה, *qua* proportion, 80 : 200 :: 100 : [1] (::) 100 : 6 :: 300 : 10 :: 5 : [1], whose rational product is 1E5) *squared*, is the 'absolute thought' which is itself at once 'absolute' רביון ('multiplication', *qua* proportion, 200 : 2 :: 10 : 6 :: 50 : [1], whose integral product is 1E10), 'absolute' הפקיר ('to renounce ownership', *qua* proportion, 5 : 80 :: 100 : 10 :: 200 : [1], whose integral product is 1E10), 'absolute' רחיון ('mercy'/'forgiveness', *qua* proportion, 200 : 400 :: 10 : 6 :: 50 : [1], whose integral product is 1E10), $1E5^2 = 1E10$.

Now the 'absolutely folded fold', the constructed 'bowl', *KOGHPL/KLOP*, taken as the trapezoid *GHOP*, is the יסוד ('foundation' [rational product, .25]),[77] the 1/4th which measures the base square of the absolute structure of existence, as here illustrated:

[76] Cf. above, Section III.5, p. 392, n. 83.
[77] Cf. above, Section III.5, p. 421.

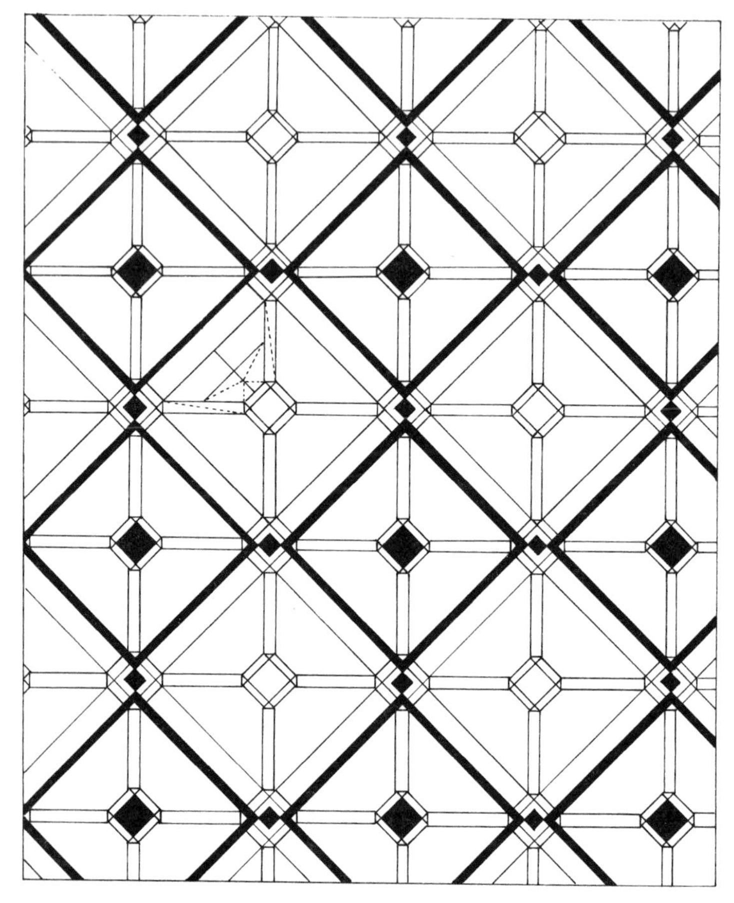

The absolutely folded fold is the foundational measure of that square which perfectly embodies the 'perfectly logical proportion', 16 : 24 :: 24 : 36, the black-bordered square which measures 24 × 24 within the four points formed by the explosion of its central 16-square (= 36^{-1} times the 576 area of the 24 × 24 square) into the four 4-squares each of which shares one of its corner-points with the 576-square. The four 4-squares are each the 144th part of the 576-square, just as the latter is itself a fourth part of the exploded 2304-central-square of the square sharing the infinite diagonal of existence which is 144 times the size of the 576-square, viz., the 82944-square which in turn is the foundational segment of the exploded 331776-central-square of that square sharing the diagonal which is again 144 times the size of the 82944-square, viz., the 11943936-square. The relationship of these four primary squares is illustrated in the following drawing where the 576-square is 'magnified' in the inset so as to show it not only in relation to the 4-squares upon its corners, but also in its relation to the 82944-square and the 11943936-square:

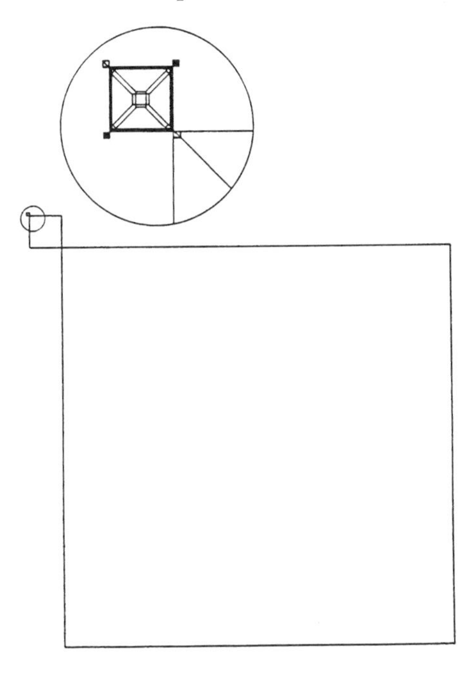

Descending, then, the infinite diagonal of exploding foundational segments of the central squares of the series of squares of which the 576-square embodying the Absolute Proportion of Absolute Thought is the entry-square, the smallest whole number square is the 4-square immediately below it, the central square of which is the 1/9th square (= 1/36th of 4 as 16 = 1/36th of 576),[78] which is the basis of the division of the 1-square (the diameter of which, $\sqrt{2}$, is the fourth root of 4, i.e., $\sqrt[4]{4}$) into 36 1/36ths:

[78] Cf. the function of the 1/9th part in discriminating 1 and 82944 from all other natural numbers, above, pp. 426f., and, below, Section III.7.

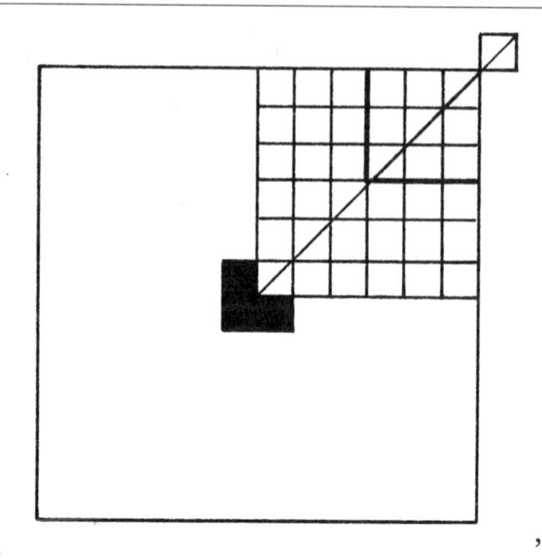

,

a division of unity which is here shown to be neither arbitrarily nor mystically grounded, but completely and essentially grounded in the essentially new logic now thought for the first time in history.[79] Here the fourfold turn of the 3 × 3 cornerstone[80] grounds itself as the very structure of the square of Unity. Next in descent along the infinite diagonal of existence is the foundational segment of the exploded 1/9th-central-square of the 4-square, viz., the 1/36th-square whose central square is *for the first* and *last time itself squared,* the .00077160493827-square. .00077160493827 is the proven unity of the square of the minimum-order form of the base proportion of the matrix of infinite proportionality reduced to the 'created 100', $(6.\overline{222} \times 5.\overline{714285})^2/(2.\overline{666} \times 4.8)^2/1E4 = .00077160493827$, and its foundational-fourth root is the 'identity' of הויה ('Being'/Existence' [rational product, 1.$\overline{666}$]) denominated אמת ('truth' [rational product, 10]), and, therefore, the very 'identity' of אני–הוא ('I am He' [Is. 48:12], *qua* proportion, 1 : 50 :: 10 : [1] (::) 5 : 6 :: 1 : [1], whose rational product is .1666), $.1666 = \sqrt[4]{.00077160493827}$. The entry 576-square embodying the Absolute Proportion of Absolute Thought is inscribed in a

[79] See above, Section III.1, pp. 267f., and Section III.5, pp. 436f., for the 4 × 9 structure of the minimum unity.

[80] Ibid.

circle the circumference of which is, if $\pi = 22/7$, 106.6721087, and if $\pi = 3.141592654$, 106.6291905, where the former value is exactly related to the 'weighted sum' of the Absolute Proportion of Absolute Thought, $106.\overline{666}$, as $1 + (.\overline{714285}^2/1E4)$ to 1, that is, as 1 + (the rational product of the base proportion of the matrix of infinite proportionality, the latter denominated by the 'created 100') to 1,[81] while the second value is identical to the identical 'weighted sum' minus $2.\overline{666}^{-1}/10$, that is, minus the inverse rational product of the *minimum* proportion (4 : 1 :: 2 : 3) denominated אמת ('truth' [rational product, 10]), with a difference, $106.\overline{666} - .0375 = 106.6291\overline{666}$, which rounds to 22.4 in 100 million parts, which last is the ratio, *qua* areas, of the constructed 'bowl', *KOGHPL/KLOP*, 112/5 = 22.4, when the latter is denominated 'absolute' השתתה ('founding', *qua* proportion, 5 : 300 :: 400 : 400 :: 5 : [1], whose integral product is 1E8), 22.4/1E8 = .000000224.

The radius of the circle in which the entry 576-square is inscribed is the fourth root of that square of whose exploded central square the 576-square is a foundational-fourth segment, the fourth root of the square next on the ascending infinite diagonal of existence, the fourth root of the 82944-square, $16.970562 = \sqrt[4]{82944}$. But since the radius of the circle in which the 82944-square is inscribed is not the fourth root of the next square on the ascending diagonal ($203.64675 = \sqrt[4]{1719926784}$, the fourth root of the square *next after the next*, next after the 11943936-square), the question arises as to just how the 11943936-square is rooted in the preceding three squares, that is, in the 82944-square whose fourth root is the half-diagonal of the 576-square, and in the 4-square whose fourth root is the half diagonal of itself. The answer is that as the 576-square has its fourth root in the radius of the circle which inscribes the square which is the mean proportional between the 4-square and the 576-square, viz., in the radius of the circle inscribing the 48-square ($\sqrt{24} = \sqrt[4]{576}$), so the 11943936-square has its fourth root in the radius of the circle inscribing the square which is the mean proportional between the 576-square and the 82944-

[81] Cf. above, pp. 489ff.

square, viz., in the radius of the circle inscribing the 6912-square ($\sqrt{3456} = \sqrt[4]{11943936}$), so that it is immediately evident that the radical order of the foundational segments of the exploded central squares of the squares on the ascending diagonal beginning from that square whose half-diagonal is the fourth root of itself, the radical order of 4-square, 576-square, 82944-square, and 11943936-square is not the apparent 1-2-3-4 order but rather the 1-2-4-3 'logical' order[82] evident in the following display of the fourth-root relations of the fourfold:[83]

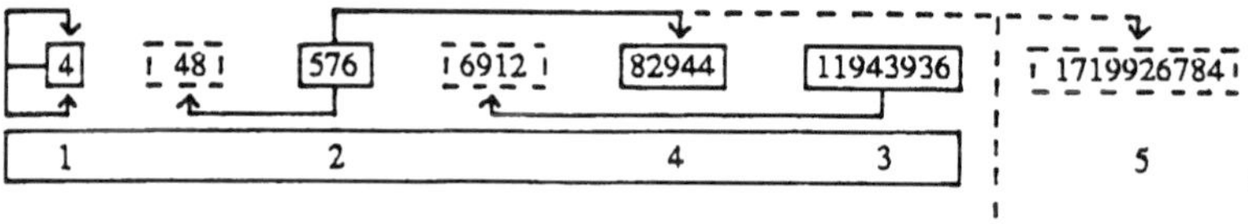

4 | 48 | 576 | 6912 | 82944 | 11943936 | 171992678 4

1 | 2 | 4 | 3 | 5 ,

and that further, therefore, the minimum-order 4-1-2-3 arrangement of the base proportion of the infinite series of foundational squares is:[84]

---

[82] Cf. above, Section III.1, pp. 273ff.

[83] Two squares have been omitted here for the sake of simplifying the presentation, the 995328-square and the 143327232-square, which do not directly bear on the matter under consideration. But the reader should note that in the full series the ratio of each square to the one immediately following, $s : (s+1)$, is .08$\overline{333}$, the rational product of השתחה ('founding' [rational product, .08$\overline{333}$]).

[84] The elements of the base proportion of the infinite series of foundational squares are differentiated from the intervening mean proportional squares as—unlike the latter—the squares of whole numbers. The square-based pyramid the area of each of whose triangular faces is 1/2 the area of the base of the pyramid is the polyhedron the sum of one of whose ascending edges and 1/2 the linear base is to the triangular height of each of its faces as $\phi : 1$. In the case of such a pyramid whose base is the smallest whole number square in the infinite structure of existence, the 4-square, this ratio is the defining ratio of ϕ, $(\sqrt{5} + 1)/2$, and the product of the diagonal of the base times the length of the base and the heights of the two triangular faces continuous with the latter, $\sqrt{8}(2 + 2 + 2)$, $= 82944^{.25}$, the fourth-foundational root of the unique 82944. The ratio of the diagonal of the base of this pyramid to the vertical height of its apex, $\sqrt{8} : \sqrt{3}$, $= \sqrt{2.\overline{666}}$, the square root of the rational product of the minimum proportion, 4 : 1 :: 2 : 3. Cf. above, Sections III.1 and III.5.

82944 : 4 :: 576 : 11943936,

the rational product of which proportion is Unity. Let this proportion be fleshed out, *qua* integral products, as:[85]

Ἰησοῦς Χριστός : המקום :: חלל/מאור : אני חושב ועל כן אני קים,
Jesus Christ : THE PLACE :: Light/Void : *Cogito ergo sum*,
8.2944E28 : 4E8 :: 576E4 : 11943936E25.

The rational product of this proportion is Unity. The proven unity of this fleshed out proportion is:

$$\frac{8.2944E28 \cdot 1.1943936E25}{4E8 \cdot 5.76E4} = 4.29981696E40,$$

where 4.29981696E40 is 'absolute' τὸ σῶμα τοῦ Χριστοῦ ('the Body of Christ', *qua* proportion, 300 : 70 (::) 200 : 800 :: 40 : 1 (::) 300 : 70 :: 400 : [1] (::) 600 : 100 :: 10 : 200 :: 300 : 70 :: 400 : [1], whose integral product is 4.29981696E40), at once itself 'absolute' רעיון ('idea'/'imagination'/'thought' [integral product, 1E10]) identified with 'absolute' שפה ברורה לקרא כלם בשם יהוה ('a purer language that they may all call upon the name of Yahweh' [Zp. 3:9], *qua* proportion, 300 : 80 :: 5 : [1] (::) 2 : 200 :: 6 : 200 :: 5 : [1] (::) 30 : 100 :: 200 : 1 (::) 20 : 30 :: 40 : [1] (::) 2 : 300 :: 40 : [1] (::) 10 : 5 :: 6 : 5, whose integral product is 4.29981696E30), 1E10 × 4.29981696E30 = 4.29981696E40. The rational product of the prophetic line is 28.8, the tenth part of the square root of 82944, and the 'identity' of שנידם שקולים כאחד ('the two are identical, *qua* proportion, 300 : 50 :: 10 : 5 :: 40 : [1] (::) 300 : 100 :: 6 :

[85] Of these terms one is introduced for the first time: המקום ('THE PLACE'/'God', *qua* proportion, 5 : 40 :: 100 : 6 :: 40 : [1], whose integral product is 4E8, and whose rational product is 8.$\overline{333}$E1 [= the rational product of השתתה ('founding' [rational product, .08$\overline{333}$]) denominated ברא ('to create' [rational product, .01]) and identified with אמת ('truth' [rational product, 10]), 8.$\overline{333}$E1 = .08$\overline{333}$ × 10/.01]). For Ἰησοῦς Χριστός, cf. above, this section, pp. 501ff., et passim. For מאור and חלל, cf. above, Section III.5, p. 392, n. 83. For אני חושב ועל כן אני קים, cf. above, Section III.5, p. 357, n. 13, and above, this section, p. 502, n. 68.

30 :: 10 : 40 (::) 20 : 1 :: 8 : 4, whose rational product is 2.88E3) identified with ברא ('to create' [rational product, .01]), 28.8 = 2.88E3 × .01, while the integral product of 'the two are identical', 1.1943936E23, is identically that of 'absolute' אני חושב ועל כן אני קים ('*Cogito ergo sum*' [integral product, 1.1943936E25]) identified with ברא ('to create'), 1.1943936E23 = 1.1943936E25 × .01. The integral product of the proportion is:

$$(8.2944E28 \cdot 5.76E4)^2 = 2.282521714753536E67,$$

where 2.282521714753536E67 identified as the 'created 100' identified with the 'identity' of הצרפה ('synthesis' [rational product, .69444]) which latter is itself at once the 'identity' of the קפיצה ('leap' [rational product, .69444]),[86] is 'absolute' קול קורא במדבר פנו דרך יהוה ישרו בערבה מסלה לאלהינו ('A voice cries, "Prepare in the desert a way for Yahweh, make straight across the wastelands a highway for our God."' [Is. 40:3], *qua* proportion, 100 : 6 :: 30 : [1] (::) 100 : 6 :: 200 : 1 (::) 2 : 40 :: 4 : 2 :: 200 : [1] (::) 80 : 50 :: 6 : [1] (::) 4 : 200 :: 20 : [1] (::) 10 : 5 :: 6 : 5 (::) 10 : 300 :: 200 : 6 (::) 2 : 70 :: 200 : 2 :: 5 : [1] (::) 40 : 60 :: 30 : 5 (::) 30 : 1 :: 30 : 5 :: 10 : 50 :: 6 : [1], whose integral product is 3.28683126924509144E63), 2.282521714753536E67/(1E4 × .69444) = 3.28683126924509144E63. Or, 2.282521714753536E67 identified as the 'created 100' and identified with the 'identity' of לשון סתרים ('secret language'/'code', *qua* proportion, 30 : 300 :: 6 : 50 (::) 60 : 400 :: 200 : 10 :: 40 : [1], whose rational product is 1.44), which latter is itself at once the 'identity' of תאור גרפי ('graphic description'/'diagram', *qua* proportion, 400 : 1 :: 6 : 200 (::) 3 : 200 :: 80 : 10, whose rational product is 1.44) and the 'identity' of שנוי כוון ('change of direction', *qua* proportion, 300 : 50 :: 6 : 10 (::) 20 : 6 :: 6 : 50, whose rational product is 1.44), (2.282521714753536E67/1E4) × 1.44, = 3.28683126924509144E63. The rational product or 'identity' of Isaiah 40 : 3 is 4.2130285714E12 which, denominated אמת ('truth' [rational product, 10]), (4.2130285714E12)/10, is 4.2130285714E11, which identified with

[86] Cf. above, pp. 418f., et passim.

the 'identity' of שפה עולמית ('world language'/'eternal language', *qua* proportion, 300 : 80 :: 5 : [1] (::) 70 : 6 :: 30 : 40 :: 10 : 400, whose rational product is 4.1015625) is the square root of 'absolute' שמר מחסום לפיו ('to keep silent'/'to keep a secret', *qua* proportion, 300 : 40 :: 200 : [1] (::) 40 : 8 :: 60 : 6 :: 40 : [1] (::) 30 : 80 :: 10 : 6, whose integral product is 2.985984E24), $4.2130\overline{285714}E11 \times 4.1015625 = \sqrt{2.985984E24}$. But that square root of 'absolute' 'to keep a secret' when identified with the 'identity' of גלה את אזנו ('to reveal'/'to tell a secret', *qua* proportion, 3 : 30 :: 5 : [1] (::) 1 : 400 (::) 1 : 7 :: 50 : 6, whose rational product is $.001488\overline{095238}$) is the 'identity' of Isaiah 40:3 as 'truth' identified with the 'synthesis' (הצרפה)/ the 'closing' (קפיצה) identified as the 'absolute' form of 'the proportion of absolute Davidic clarity' denominated 'absolute' הכרה ('consciousness'/'discernment' [integral product, 1E6]),[87] that is, $\sqrt{2.985984E24} \times .001488\overline{095238} = 4.2130\overline{285714}E11 \times (.69\overline{444}/.000113\overline{777})/1E6 = 4.2130285714E11 \times 4.1015625 \times .001488\overline{095238}$, so that, finally:

$$\frac{4.2130\overline{285714}E11 \cdot .69\overline{444}}{.000113\overline{777} \cdot 4.1015625 \cdot .001488\overline{095238} \cdot 1E6} = 4.2130\overline{285714}E11.$$

the 'identity' of Isaiah 40:3 as 'truth' identified with the Unity which is the 'synthesis'/the 'leap'/the 'closing' identified as the 'absolute consciousness' identified with 'to reveal a secret', 'world language' and the 'absolute' form of the 'proportion of absolute Davidic clarity', this 'identity' of the verse as 'truth,' *so* identified, *is* itself. If the following proportion, *qua* 'absolutes', is substituted for the one above, viz.,

אני חושב ועל כן אני קים : התגשמות :: המקום : נקדת האפס של תנופה
Dead Center : THE PLACE :: Incarnation : *Cogito ergo sum,*
8.2944E22 : 4E8 :: 5.76E10 : 1.1943936E25,

[87] Cf. above, pp. 426ff., 500ff.

there is no change in the rational and integral products, but the proof form changes as follows : in the first form of the proportion 'absolute' Jesus Christ identified with 'absolute' *Cogito ergo sum* is identified as God-existing-everywhere identified with 'absolute' Light/'absolute' Void, which proven unity is 'absolute' the Body of Christ, 4.29981696E40, the fourth-foundational root of which is 'absolute' תחלה ('beginning', *qua* proportion, 400 : 8 :: 30 : 5, whose integral product is 1.44E8) identified as ברא ('to create' [rational product, .01]), $\sqrt[4]{4.29981696E40}$ = 1.44E8/.01 = 1.44E10. In the second form of the proportion 'absolute' dead center identified with 'absolute' *Cogito ergo sum* is identified as God-existing-everywhere identified with 'absolute' incarnation, 4.29981696E28, which proven unity is 'absolute' τὸ σῶμα χριστοῦ ('the Body of Christ, *qua* proportion, 300 : 70 (::) 200 : 800 :: 40 : 1 (::) 600 : 100 :: 10 : 200 :: 300 : 70 :: 400 : [1], whose integral product is 2.985984E30) denominated הצרפה ('synthesis' [rational product, .69444]), קפיצה ('leap' [rational product, .69444]), קפיצה ('closing' [rational product, .69444]), and identified with ברא ('to create', rational product .01]), (2.985984E30/.69444) × .01 = 4.29981696E28, the fourth-foundational root of which is 'absolute' כפור ('Atonement' [integral product, 1.44E4]) denominated ברא ('to create' [rational product, .01]) and identified with אמת ('truth' [rational product, 10]), $\sqrt[4]{4.29981696E28}$ = 10(1.44E4/.01) = 1.44E7.

This last fourth-foundational root of the proof form of the fleshed out minimum-order 4-1-2-3 arrangement of the base proportion of the infinite series of foundational squares, 1.44E7, denominated אמת ('truth'), 1.44E7/10 = 1.44E6, is identically the former fourth-foundational root, 1.44E10, denominated the 'created 100', 1.44E10/1E4 = 1.44E6. But 1.44E6 is 'absolute' רבוע ('square', *qua* proportion, 200 : 2 :: 6 : 70, whose integral product is 1.44E6). The rational product of רבוע ('square') is 8.571428, which, denominated אמת ('truth'), 8.571428/10 = .8571428, is just the inversion of that התבקעות ('splitting'/'cleavage' [rational product, 1.1666]) which is the form of the Galileian and modern consciousness, 8.571428/10 = .8571428 = 1.1666^{-1}. And this 'identity' of רבוע ('square') denominated אמת ('truth'), reduced to the entry 576-square of the infinite structure of existence, is the very 'identity' of גלה את אזנו ('to reveal'/'to tell a secret' [rational product, .001488095238]), .8571428/576 = .001488095238, at once itself, therefore, .69444/(.000113777 × 4.1015625 × 1E6), the 'synthesis'/the 'leap'/the 'closing' identified as the 'absolute' 'proportion of absolute Davidic clarity' identified with 'world language' and 'absolute consciousness'. This is the *a priori a posteriori*, the *a priori experience* for the first time in history, the phenomenological absolute, the absolute phenomenology, the conception of the infinitely specific *a priori* ego leaving behind the 'absolutely radicalized cleavage in the form of that entering into the abyss of presence which is the requirement for a perfect absence'.[88] This is the infinitely limited/infinitely measured form of the *a priori* of an absolutely pure ego, absolutely selfless I, *perceiving* for the first time: the absolutely unconditioned objectivity of perception an *absolutely* 'not purposeful' structuring of the science of the 'life-world itself' (lacking even the purposefulness of the difference between the 'life-world' and the 'world of science').[89] This is the absolute judgment absolutely limiting the transcendental *ego*: the transcendental dichotomy which is the for-the-first-time-actuality of the *ego*. This is the conception of life itself, the real objectivity which is the transcendental *ego* experiencing for the first time the absolute reality of the end of history, the reality of history, the very form of the end of the world. This is the existential experience of the transcendental ego, the transcendental ego existing, the transcendental ego experiencing absolute finality: this is the God-experience of the transcendental ego: the transcendental ego experiencing God. The transcendental ideal is transcendentally meta-identified for the first time, transcendentally identified as existence, as being, as the actual: *cogito esse, i.e., cogito esse ipsum alterum, i.e., cogito exsistere, cogito alterum,*

[88] Cf. above, pp. 482ff.

[89] Ibid. Cf. above, Section II.3, p. 182, et passim, for the fact that the thinking now occurring for the first time is the absolute analogy of being transcending the analogy of being predicated before now in terms of the presumed difference between concept and reality, language and thought, logic and existence.

i.e., cogito ipsum esse exsistere: the transcendental ego experiencing an absolutely manifest God. The infinite structure of existence is an infinite order of squares whose center-points are respectively and identically each of their four corner-points, and, therefore, the center-points and four corner-points of each of the squares whose corner-points coincide the corner-points and center-points of each of the infinite number of squares. The constant measure of this absolute explosion of identity, the ratio of the sides and diagonals of the foundational-fourth segments of the exploded central squares of the primary squares ascending and descending the infinite diagonal above and below the entry 576-square, identically the ratio of the area separating each side of each square *qua* primary from the parallel side of its next identical neighbor in the infinite pattern to the area of the square itself, identically the ratio of the area of each foundational-fourth square to the area between primary squares separating it *qua* corner-square from its next identical neighbor, is the rational product of השתתה ('founding' [rational product, .08333]), at once itself the rational product of המקום ('THE PLACE'/'God-existing-everywhere' [rational product, 8.333E1]) identified with ברא ('to create' [rational product, .01]) and denominated אמת ('truth' [rational product, 10]), 8.333E1 × .01/10 = .08333. This ratio measuring the infinite structure of existence is the square or existential root of the 'identity' of הצרפה ('synthesis' [rational product, .69444])/קפיצה ('leap' [rational product, .69444])/קפיצה ('closing' [rational product, .69444]) identified with ברא ('to create' [rational product, .01]), and the existential root of 'absolute Davidic clarity', 'world language', 'to reveal a secret', and 'absolute consciousness', .08333 = √(.000113777 × 4.1015625 × .001488095238 × 1E6 × .01) = √(.69444 × .01). In this founding place of infinitely structured existence the mind is prepared to see directly that the walls hitherto separating 'mathematics', 'logic', 'language', and 'matter', 'science' and 'life', begin to vaporize (unity reduced to the square root of 'absolute' חלחל ['to penetrate' (integral product, 4.096E3)][90] is what it is התאדה ['to vaporize', *qua* proportion, 5 :

[90] Cf. above, Section III.5, pp. 400ff, et passim. Also above, p. 488.

400 :: 1 : 4 :: 5 : [1], whose rational product is .015625], $1/\sqrt{4.096E3} = .015625$). First, let there be a series, L, composed of the sequential *arithmetic* sums of the infinitely relative series of logical digits, 1, 0, $\bar{0}$, 1, 0, $\bar{0}$, . . . , beginning with 1. Since the positive arithmetic equivalent of the logical, $0 \because \bar{0} = 0 \because 0 = \bar{0} \because 0 = 1$, is $0 + \bar{0} = 0 + 0 = \bar{0} + \bar{0} = 1$, let the logical digits 0 and $\bar{0}$ each have the arithmetic value .5.[91] Then, summing sequentially, $1 + 0 + \bar{0} + 1 + 0 + \bar{0} + 1 + 0 + \bar{0} + 1 + 0 + \bar{0} + 1 + 0 + \bar{0} + \ldots$, produces the L series, $1 + 1.5 + 2 + 3 + 3.5 + 4 + 5 + 5.5 + 6 + 7 + 7.5 + 8 + 9 + 9.5 + 10 + 11 + 11.5 + \ldots$, that is,

$$L = \sum_{i=1}^{\infty} (2i - 1) + (2i + .5) + 2i.$$

This series contains the infinite series of odd and even integers (therefore also the infinite series of the halves of the even integers) and the infinite series of the halves of the even-numbered odd integers (3/2, 7/2, 11/2, 15/2 . . .).[92] Since it is true that

$$\sum_{i=1}^{n} (2i - 1) + (2i - .5) + 2i = \sum_{i=1}^{n} (2i - 1) + \sum_{i=1}^{n} (2i - .5) + \sum_{i=1}^{n}$$

$$= \sum_{i=1}^{2n} i + \sum_{i=1}^{n} (2i - .5),$$

then any partial sum of the L series is

$$S_n = \sum_{i=1}^{x} i + \sum_{i=1}^{y} (2i - .5),$$

where, if n is a whole number, $x = n$, or, if n is a mixed number, $x = n - .5$, and, if x is an even number, $y = n/2$, or, if x is odd and n is whole, $y = (n - 1)/2$, or, if x is odd and n is mixed, $y = (n + .5)/2$.

[91] Cf. above, Section III.1.

[92] The additive rule, $000 = \overline{000} = 111$, for any three sets of three consecutive numbers selected from an arithmetic series and placed in any order in the three rows of the 'foundation stone' square, holds for the double/triple arithmetic L series and all analogously structured series, provided each of

The formulas for finding the sum of the L series, with x and y as defined, are the following: where n is an even whole integer,[93]

$$S_n = .75(x^2 + x),$$

where n is an odd whole integer,

$$S_n = .75(x^2 + x) \; - .5x,$$

and where n is a mixed number,

$$S_n = .75(x^2 + x) + y.$$

Second, since the thinking now occurring for the first time in history is the subsumption of the mathematics of subjectivity, the perfect elimination of any essential notion of 'nothing', the leaving behind of the 'vanishing point' and the abyss, and since this categorically new logic, this essentially new beginning of thought, is absolutely not a *self*-enclosed system, let it be demonstrated at the most fundamental point, at the absolutely historical point, at the point absolutely without reference to nothing, at the point of absolute reference, at the point which is the limit of mathematics, at the point embodying the identification of

---

the three sets of three numbers selected corresponds directly with the set, $1, 0, \bar{0}$, in the underlying logical pattern. Likewise the multiplicative rule, $000 = \overline{000} = 111$, holds, with the identical restriction, for the double series of the form, $1 + x + x^{1.5} + x^2 + x^3 + x^{3.5} + x^4 + x^5 + x^{5.5} + \ldots$, and all analogously structured series. The restriction mentioned does not apply in the case of a simple arithmetic or geometric series. Cf. above, Section III.2, pp. 307ff.

[93] The basic formula which follows immediately in the text is derived from the fact that, for even number n, $S_n = [(n^2 + n)/2] + [(n^2 + n)/4] = 2(n^2 + n)/2.\overline{666} = 3(n^2 + n)/4$. Note that the divisor, $2.\overline{666}$, is the rational product of the foundational or minimum order 4 : 1 :: 2 : 3 (cf. above, Section III.1, pp. 268ff.).

thought and extension,[94] at the point embodying the absolute priority of the fourth-foundational point, at 'point zero of energy', at the 'dead center' of the absolute circle of absolute thought, let the 'absolute penetration' of language and matter be demonstrated. Let, then, 'absolute' נקדת האפס של תנופה ('dead center'/'point zero of energy' [integral product, 8.2944E22]) be denominated 'absolute' מדות שטח ('area measure', *qua* proportion, 40 : 4 :: 6 : 400 (::) 300 : 9 :: 8 : [1], whose integral product is 3.31776E11),[95] 8.2944E22/3.31776E11 = 2.5E11. 'Absolute' נקדת האפס של תנופה ('dead center'/'point zero of energy') divided by 'absolute' מדות שטח ('area measure') equals 'absolute' נקדת העיון ('point of balance', *qua* proportion, 50 : 100 :: 4 : 400 (::) 5 : 70 :: 10 : 6 :: 50 : [1], whose integral product is 2.5E11). Identified as 'absolute area measure' 'absolute dead center' is 'absolute balance point'. The rational product or 'identity' of נקדת העיון ('point of balance') is $.029\overline{761904}$. Recalling that the infinite matrix of proportionality is structured as infinitely alternating rows of the infinite series of natural numbers and the infinite series of odd numbers, denominated by foundational-four proportionately increasing powers of יחוס ('relation' [rational product, .125]), let the 'point of balance' be raised to the 'relation' power, *qua* 'identities':[96]

נקדח העיון^{יחוס} = $.029\overline{761904}^{.125}$.

But then, with a difference of 1.53521862 (~ 1.536) parts per

94 At this point both the substance of Spinoza, of whose infinite number of attributes only thought and extension are named, the substance of implicit subjectivity/the implicitly subjective One, and the substance of Hegel suffused with the life of absolute self-consciousness, the substance of explicit subjectivity/the God of spiritual self-consciousness—both—are left behind in this absolute identification of the substance of thought and extension.

95 The square root of 'absolute' מדות שטח ('area measure') is the area of the entry 576-square of the infinite structure of existence denominated ברא ('to create') and identified with אמת ('truth'), $\sqrt{3.31776E11}$ = 10(5.76E2/.01). Cf. above, pp. 507ff.

96 Cf. above, Section II.3, pp. 155ff., and this Section, pp. 487f.

million, where 1.536 is the square root of 'absolute' בראשית ברא אלהים את השמים ואת הארץ ('In the beginning God created the heaven and the earth' [integral product 2.359296E28]) divided by the product of 'absolute' רעיון ('idea'/'imagination'/'thought' [integral product, 1E10]) identified with the 'created 100', $\sqrt{2.359296E28/(1E10 \times 1E4)} = 1.536$, the 'relation' power of the 'point of balance' (.644477248) which *qua* 'absolute' is 'absolute dead center' denominated 'absolute area measure' is *the sum* (.644476259) *of the alternating series in which Unity is denominated by the* L *series* derived from the categorically new logic of the beginning:

$$.029\overline{761904}^{.125} \approx \sum_{i=1}^{\infty} \frac{(-1)^{i+1}}{(2i-1)} - \frac{(-1)^{i+1}}{(2i-.5)} + \frac{(-1)^{i+1}}{2i},$$

that is,

נקדת העיון^{יחוס} $\approx 1^{-1} - 1.5^{-1} + 2^{-1} - 3^{-1} + 3.5^{-1} - 4^{-1} + 5^{-1} - 5.5^{-1} \ldots.$

The difference between .644477248 and .644476259 is, with a difference less than 1 in 100 million parts, the rational product of Genesis 1:1, $0.000000\overline{098765432}$. With a difference of 1 part per 2.24118362392759E5 (~ 2.24E5), where 2.24E5 is the 'absolutely folded fold', the constructed 'bowl', *KOGHPL/KLOP, qua* areas, $112/5 = 22.4$, times the 'created 100', $22.4 \times 1E4 = 2.24E5$, the 'identity' of מרכז ('center' [rational product, $.\overline{571428}$]) identified as the 'relation' power of the 'point of balance' in the form of the alternating inverse *L* series (.644476259) is the יסוד ('foundation' [rational product, .25]) 'identity' power of the unique and minimum mathematical partition of unity which is the inverse of the extreme and mean ratio, $\phi = 1.618033989$, that is, $.571428/.644476259 \approx \phi^{-\text{יסוד}}$, the fourth-foundational root of the 'golden' section of the line, $\phi^{-.25}$. The center is shown to be the fourth-foundational root of the unique mathematical division of the line identified with the 'relation' power of the 'point of balance', נקדת העיון^{יחוס}, in the form of the alternating inverse *L* series. Finally, then, without leaving the center so denominated, it is possible to arrive at the physical center which rests upon the absolute center of absolute thought as upon a template of itself which is itself essentially. *The fundamental number in physics is the 'fine structure' constant, a dimensionless number which appears among the groups of lines in the spectra of the lightest elements. The fundamental element of the 'absolute dead center' cube is the length of the line upon which it is constructed.*[97] The alternating inverse L series embodiment of the 'relation' power of the 'point of balance' takes with utter seriousness the implications of the logical equations when translated into the arithmetic equation, $0 + \overline{0} = 1$, namely, that 0 and $\overline{0}$ both equal .5. This series combined with the Fibonacci sequence and the arithmetic value of the logical digits relates the fundamental element of the 'absolute dead center' cube to the 'fine structure' constant. Let there be an infinite alternating series in which $x = .5$ (the arithmetic value of logical 0 and $\overline{0}$), $y = 101.8233764$ (the length of the edge of the 'absolute dead center' cube existing everywhere), $\alpha = .007297353$ (the dimensionless number which is the 'fine structure' constant), f_n = a number in sequence of the Fibonacci sequence, 0, 1, 1, 2, 3, 5, 8, 13, . . . , beginning with 0, and the multiples of the denominator are the L series {1, 1.5, 2, 3, 3.5, 4, 5, 5.5 . . . }, beginning with 1, as here set forth:

$$\alpha^x \approx \sum_{i=1}^{\infty} \frac{(-1)^{i+1}\, x^{f_n}}{(2i-1)\, y^x} - \frac{(-1)^{i+1}\, x^{f_n}}{(2i-.5)\, y^x} + \frac{(-1)^{i+1}\, x^{f_n}}{2iy^x},$$

that is,

$$\alpha^x \approx \frac{x^0}{1y^x} - \frac{x^1}{1.5y^x} + \frac{x^1}{2y^x} - \frac{x^2}{3y^x} + \frac{x^3}{3.5y^x} - \frac{x^5}{4y^x} + \frac{x^8}{5y^x} - \frac{x^{13}}{5.5y^x} \cdots,$$

where $\alpha^x \approx 0.0854241$ . . . and the observed value of the square root of the 'fine structure' constant ≈ 0.0854245. . . . *The categorically new logic in the form of the arithmetic value of the 0 and $\overline{0}$ components of Unity raised in alternating series to the powers of the Fibonacci sequence and denominated by the square root of the edge of the 'absolute*

[97] Cf. above, Section III.5, pp. 434ff.

dead center' cube identified with the alternating L series is the structure actually conceived of the square root of the 'fine structure' constant, the actually perceived structure of the electromagnetic coupling constant.[98] In fact, where $x = .5$ (the arithmetic value of logical 0 and $\overline{0}$), $z =$

[98] Note in this connection: the text in Wisdom 11:20 in the Septuagint, ἀλλὰ πάντα μέτρῳ καὶ ἀριθμῷ καὶ σταθμῷ διέταξας, is translated, "You have ordered all things in measure, in number, and in weight." Now 82944 *is* its integral product and a number the distinguishing feature of which is that its 1/9th part (9216) is the integral product of its 1/3rd part (27648), a relation true of only one other number in the infinite series of natural numbers, viz., 1 (cf. above, Sections III.5 and III.6). But the integral product of this Septuagint text is $8.6973087744 \times 10^{48} = 82944 \times 9216 \times 113.\overline{777} \times 10^{38}$ (where $113.\overline{777} = 9216/81$, the ratio of 9216 to *its* integral product). Since $x = f(x)$ where $x = 82944$ and the function f is the integral product, this neat triad of factors corresponding to measure, number, and weight is $f(x)$, $f(x)/9$, and $[f(x)/9]/f[f(x)/9]$. In the universal wave function of quantum gravity, ψ(h, F, S), the corresponding elements are metric, field, and manifold. The rational product of the Greek text = $1.1705532693187 \times 10^{-2}$, where the base factor is that of the inverse of the electromagnetic coupling constant (= 1.170623721). Adjusting the decimals, this is exact to the fifth place in its uninverted form (.0854296875 vs. .085424546).

In *QED: The Strange Theory of Light and Matter* (Princeton, 1985), the late Richard Feynman wrote concerning .08542455, "It's one of the *greatest* damn mysteries of physics: *a magic number* that comes to us with no understanding by man. You might say the 'hand of God' wrote that number, and 'we don't know how he pushed his pencil.' We know what kind of a dance to do experimentally to measure this number very accurately, but we don't know what kind of a dance to do on a computer to make this number come out—without putting it in secretly!" But, even before deriving the *L* series, let the *prenumeral* logical digits, 0, $\overline{0}$, and 1, be arranged in the form of a triple-cube, with the logical cornerstone in three dimensions deployed as the first and the last of three subsections, and let the third, middle subsection be a cubic structure formed of the back side of the first and the front side of the last subsection, each of the three cubic subsections having an identically structured middle plane parallel to its front and back sides, where the middle plane, with respect to the arrangement of the cornerstone, has 0's for 1's, 1's for $\overline{0}$'s, and $\overline{0}$'s for 0's. This triple-cubic arrangement of the trinary logical digits in which the middle subsection is effectively the first rotated a *three-quarter* turn backward and the last rotated a *one-quarter* turn forward (compare the ratio of empty space to visible matter as reflected in the distribution of radiation in the earliest universe) now provides for the first time the how of 'God's pencil' and, in the ratios of the number of 1- plus $\overline{0}$-diagonals (20) and 0-diagonals (17) to

118.1305775 (the length of the edge of a cube whose surface area is the sum of the only three numbers in the infinite series of natural numbers whose integral products are the very numbers, $1 + 784 + 82944 = 83729$),[99] $\alpha = .007297353$ (the 'fine structure' constant), the exponents of x are the Fibonacci sequence {0, 1, 1, 2, 3, 5, 8, 13, . . .}, beginning with 0, and the denominator of x is the L series, beginning with 1,

---

the total number of diagonals in the triple-cube(37), respectively, the 8th root of the fine-structure constant ($.007288299^{.125}$, exact to the fourth place and to the fifth rounded) and the area of the circle whose diameter is the inverse 8th root of a hundred times the latter's square root ($[100 \times .08538286731]^{-.125}$, the relevant base factor exact to the third place and to the fourth rounded). This shared number of science and revelation derives then immediately from this arrangement of the prenumeral digits of the logic set forth above in Section III.1, as well as from the forms derivative of the logic shown at this point in the text. With respect to these latter, note that the tenth part of the base factor of the linear product of the Septuagint text, $7.43008370688 \times 10^{50}$, compares to the product of the fine-structure constant, α, and the edge of the 'dead center cube' as .743008370688 to .74304113 ($= .00729735308 \times 101.8233765 \approx [\alpha z]^2$, the square of the sum of the series following immediately below in the text). The 'dead center cube' is the only size cube which satisfies the requirement of the logic that $1 = 36 \times 36^{-1} = 1 \times 1^{-1}$ (cf. above, Section III.1), since the circumference circumscribing the face of this cube (144π) is the only such which is identically the area of each of the circumferences circumscribing each of the thirty-six equal square parts of the cubic face (144π). Cf. also n. 99.

[99] Cf. above, Section III.6. In connection with this and with what follows in the text note the following: A. Thom proposed that megalithic man used a universal standard of measure which Thom called the megalithic yard, equal to 2.722 ft. (cf. *Records in Stone: Papers in Memory of Alexander Thom* [Cambridge, 1988]). But 2.722 ft. = .8296656 m. The metric area of the circle whose diameter is 1 megalithic yard, $\pi(.8296656/2)^2$, is .540624905, which number, with a difference of 0.871 *parts per million,* is $\alpha^{.125}$, the eighth root or 'relation' power of the fine structure constant, $.00729735308^{.125}$. The English measure area of this circle is 837.97 sq. in., which, with a difference less that 1 part per thousand, is the one-hundredth part of the sum of the three unique numbers whose integral products equal themselves, $1 + 784 + 82944 = 83729$. The product of the metric and English measures of this area is, with a difference less than one in a hundred, 144π, the area of the circle in which the 'central square' (cf. above, pp. 507ff.) of the side of the 'absolute dead center' cube (its 1/36th part = $288 = \sqrt{82944}$) is inscribed. Cf. also n. 98.

$$\alpha z \approx \sum_{i=1}^{\infty} \frac{(-1)^{i+1}\, x^{f\,n}}{(2i-1)} - \frac{(-1)^{i+1}\, x^{f\,n}}{(2i-.5)} + \frac{(-1)^{i+1}\, x^{f\,n}}{2i},$$

that is,

$$\alpha z \approx \frac{x^0}{1} - \frac{x^1}{1.5} + \frac{x^1}{2} - \frac{x^2}{3} + \frac{x^3}{3.5} - \frac{x^5}{4} + \frac{x^8}{5} - \frac{x^{13}}{5.5} \ldots,$$

or, precisely,

$$.007296961z \approx$$

$$\frac{x^0}{1} - \frac{x^1}{1.5} + \frac{x^1}{2} - \frac{x^2}{3} + \frac{x^3}{3.5} - \frac{x^5}{4} + \frac{x^8}{5} - \frac{x^{13}}{5.5} \ldots,$$

which is to say (since the sum of this series, .861994253909891, is precisely the edge of a cube the area of whose side is the product of the edge of the 'absolute dead center' cube [101.8233765] and .007297284) that the 'fine structure' constant is approximately the ratio of the edges of two cubes each of which edges is the mean proportional between the edge of the 'absolute dead center' cube and, in one case, the 'fine structure' constant, and, in the other case, the inverse of the 'fine structure' constant. Alternately, this situation can be expressed as the square root of the edge of the 'absolute dead center' cube divided by the electromagnetic coupling constant, $(101.8233765/\alpha)^{1/2}$, ≈ the edge of the 83729-cube. This cube's face area ≈ $(\sqrt{1.1} \times h)^{-.125}$, the 'relation power' of the inverse product of the body-/face-diagonal ratio of the triple cube and the Planck constant. Both α and h are functions of the logically founded mathematics.[100]

This is the beginning of an essentially transmural consciousness. Indeed, the square root of the identification—the mean

[100] Cf. the 100-square grid of the unum-founded Fibonacci sequence (above, Section III.2, Theorem 4): the 256th root of the product of the end place-numbers of the 1-diagonal of the final subsquare, divided by the square constant, $[(78 \times 100)/{}^*F_{78} \times {}^*F_{100})]^{1/256}$, ≈ $(\alpha z)^2$ or $(\alpha y)^{2x}$ (cf. above, pp. 525ff.), while $[(78 \times 100)/({}^*F_{78} \times {}^*F_{100})] - 3.6\text{E}33^{-1} \approx h$, the Planck constant. Cf. also, above, p. 525, n. 98 and n. 99.

proportional—of the 'fine structure' constant and the edge of the 'absolute dead center' cube is at once itself the sum of the last series, that is,

$$(\alpha y)^x \approx \frac{x^0}{1} - \frac{x^1}{1.5} + \frac{x^1}{2} - \frac{x^2}{3} + \frac{x^3}{3.5} - \frac{x^5}{4} + \frac{x^8}{5} - \frac{x^{13}}{5.5} \ldots,$$

and, *qua* identities, the 'relation' (יחוס) power of the identification of מרכז רוחני ('spiritual center', *qua* proportion, 40 : 200 :: 20 : 7 (::) 200 : 6 :: 8 : 50 :: 10 : [1], whose rational product is 3.$\overline{047619}$E1) and ברא ('to create' [rational product, .01]), identically the 'relation' power of that identification which is the very 'identity' of משכל מזגני ('synthetical intelligence', *qua* proportion, 40 : 300 :: 20 : 30 (::) 40 : 7 :: 3 : 50 :: 10 : [1], whose rational product is .$\overline{3047619}$), (3.$\overline{047619}$E1 × .01)$^{.125}$ = .$\overline{3047619}^{.125}$, that is,

$$(\alpha y)^x \approx .\overline{3047619}^{.125} \approx (\text{ברא} \cdot \text{מרכז רוחני})^{\text{יחוס}} \approx \text{משכל מזגני}^{\text{יחוס}},$$

with a difference of 2.1382 (~ 2.1$\overline{333}$) parts per hundred thousand, where α^x = 0.0854241 and 2.1333 is the rational product of חולל מהפכה ('to revolutionize', *qua* proportion, 8 : 6 :: 30 : 30 (::) 40 : 5 :: 80 : 20 :: 5 : [1], whose rational product is 2.1$\overline{333}$E2) identified with ברא ('to create'), 2.1$\overline{333}$E2 × .01 = 2.1333. Further, in a relationship which is the analogue of that existing between the cube of 'absolute' הקדוש ברוך הוא ('the Holy One blessed be He' [integral product, 1.296E11]) identified with 'absolute' רציונלי ('rational' [integral product, 1E12]), 'absolute' הקדוש ברוך הוא × 'absolute' הקדוש ברוך הוא × 'absolute' הקדוש ברוך הוא × 'absolute' רציונלי, and the square of 'absolute' יום א' של שלוש ('day one of the Trinity' [integral product, 4.6656E22]), 1.296E11^3 × 1E12 = 4.6656E22^2 = 2.176782336E45,[101] $(\alpha y)^3 \approx$ the square of the sum of the alternating inverse *L* series,

$$(\alpha y)^3 \approx \sum_{i=1}^{\infty} {}^2 \; \frac{(-1)^{i+1}}{(2i-1)} - \frac{(-1)^{i+1}}{(2i-.5)} + \frac{(-1)^{i+1}}{2i},$$

[101] Cf. above, Section III.5, p. 417, and, below, Appendix, pp. 629ff.

that is,

$$(\alpha y)^3 \approx (1^{-1} - 1.5^{-1} + 2^{-1} - 3^{-1} + 3.5^{-1} - 4^{-1} + 5^{-1} - 5.5^{-1} \ldots)^2,$$

the identification of the 'fine structure' constant and the edge of the 'absolute dead center' cube is the cube root of the square of the sum of the alternating inverse L series, with a difference (where $\alpha = 0.0854241^2$) such that the ratio of $(\alpha y)^3$ to $.644476259^2$ is .987671172 (~ .987654320), where .987654320 is the rational product of בראשית ברא אלהים את השמים ואת הארץ ('In the beginning God created the heaven and the earth' [rational product, 9.876543209E–7]) identified with 'absolute' הכרה ('consciousness'/'discernment' [integral product, 1E6]), 9.876543209E–7 × 1E6 = .987654320. The transparency, the very pellucidity, of the relations which constitute this center of the consciousness of creation, where the reader has arrived, is not a matter of subjective feeling, but, in fact, 'absolute' משכל מזגני ('synthetical intelligence' [integral product, 9.216E11]) reduced to 'absolute' מרכז רוחני ('spiritual center' [integral product, 1.6384E14]) is as such the very 'identity' of, the very essence of what it is to be, שקופות ('transparence'/'pellucidity', *qua* proportion, 300 : 100 :: 6 : 80 :: 6 : 400, whose rational product is .005625), that is, 9.216E11/1.6384E14 = .005625. The reciprocal of this very 'identity' of 'transparence' is the very 'identity' of רוח אלהים ('Spirit of God', *qua* proportion, 200 : 6 :: 8 : [1] (::) 1 : 30 :: 5 : 10 :: 40 : [1], whose rational product is $.005625^{-1}$). The former identified with the latter is Very Unity: .005625 × $.005625^{-1}$ = 1. 'Absolute' משכל מזגני ('synthetical intelligence') identified with 'absolute' מרכז רוחני ('spiritual center') is 'absolute' התחל מבחינה פורמלית ('to lay the cornerstone', *qua* proportion, 5 : 400 :: 8 : 30 (::) 40 : 2 :: 8 : 10 :: 50 : 5 (::) 80 : 6 :: 200 : 40 :: 30 : 10 :: 400 : [1], whose integral product is 1.50994944E28) identified with ברא ('to create' [rational product, .01]), 9.216E11 × 1.6384E14 = 1.50994944E28 × .01 = 1.50994944E26. Finally, the identification of the edge of the 'absolute dead center' cube and the 'fine structure' constant is, *qua* identities, the שפה עולמית ('universal language'/'world language' [rational product,

4.1015625]) identity of משכל מזגני ('synthetical intelligence' [rational product, .3047619]) identified with אמת ('truth' [rational product, 10]), $\alpha y \approx .7430 \approx (.3047619 \times 10)/4.1015625$, that is,

שפה עולמית · $\alpha y \approx$ משכל מזגני · אמת,

with a difference of 5.99565916 (~ 5.997501037) parts per million, where 5.997501037 is the square of the rational product of קבוע הזמן ('time constant' [rational product, 2.44897959183673]), $2.44897959183673^2 = 5.997501037$: the universal language identified with the identification of the edge of the 'absolute dead center' cube and the 'fine structure' constant is 'synthetical intelligence' identified with 'truth'.

Supporting the walls hitherto existing between language and number, science and life, logic and existence was the wall of separation which is 'nothing finite is infinite'. In the logic of the beginning infinite number is identical with finite number. But for Galileo infinite number had nothing in common with finite number. The infinite circle had no possibility of existence. He writes in *Two New Sciences:*

> In the preceding discussion we concluded that, in an infinite number, it is necessary that the squares and cubes should be as numerous as the totality of the natural numbers [*tutti i numeri*], because both of these are as numerous as their roots which constitute the totality of the natural numbers. Next we saw that the larger the numbers taken the more sparsely distributed were the squares, and still more sparsely the cubes; therefore it is clear that the larger the numbers to which we pass the farther we recede from the infinite number; hence it follows that, since this process carries us farther and farther from the end sought, if on turning back we shall find that any number can be said to be infinite, it must be unity. . . . There is no difficulty in the matter because unity is at once a square, a cube, a square of a square and all the other powers [*dignita*]; nor is there any essential peculiarity in squares or cubes which does not belong to unity. . . . Therefore we conclude that unity is the only infi-

nite number. These are some of the marvels which our imagination cannot grasp and which should warn us against the serious error of those who attempt to discuss the infinite by assigning to it the same properties which we employ for the finite, the natures of the two having nothing in common. With regard to this subject I must tell you of a remarkable property which just now occurs to me and which will explain the vast alteration and change of character which a definite quantity would undergo in passing to infinity.

Let us draw the straight line AB of arbitrary length and let the point C divide it into two unequal parts; then I say that, if pairs of lines be drawn, one from each of the terminal points A and B, and if the ratio between the lengths of these lines is the same as that between AC and CB, their points of intersection will all lie upon the circumference of one and the same circle.

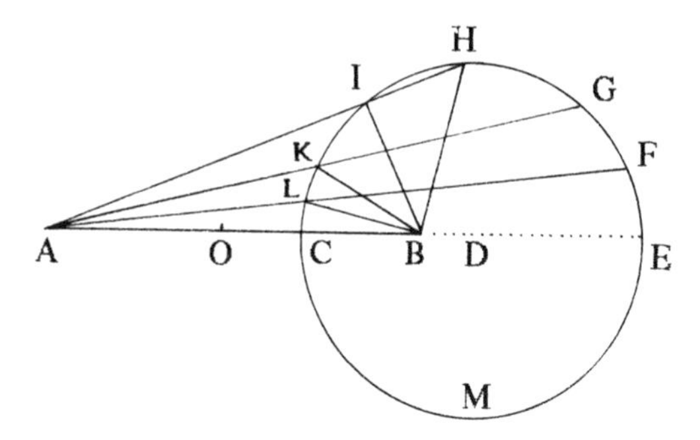

. . . Accordingly if we imagine the point C to move continuously in such a manner that the lines drawn from it to the fixed terminal points, A and B, always maintain the same ratio between their lengths as exists between the original parts, AC and CB, then the point C will . . . describe a circle. And the circle thus described will increase in size without limit as the point C approaches the middle point which we may call O; but it will diminish in size as C approaches the end B. So that the infinite number of points located in the line OB will, if the motion be as explained above, describe a circle of every size, some smaller than the pupil of the eye of a flea, others larger than the celestial equator. Now if we move any of the points lying between the two ends O and B they will all describe circles, those nearest O, immense circles; but if we move the point O itself, and continue to move it according to the aforesaid law, namely, that the lines drawn from O to the terminal points, A and B, maintain the same ratio as the original lines AO and OB, what kind of line will be produced? A circle will be drawn larger than the largest of the others, a circle which is therefore infinite. But from the point O a straight line will also be drawn perpendicular to and extending to infinity without ever turning, as did the others, to join its last end with its first; for the point C, with its limited motion, having described the upper semi-circle, CHE, proceeds to describe the lower semicircle EMC, thus returning to the starting point. But the point O having started to describe its circle, as did all the other points in the line AB, . . . is unable to return to its starting point because the circle it describes, being the largest of all, is infinite; in fact, it describes an infinite straight line as circumference of its infinite circle. Think now what a difference there is between a finite and an infinite circle since the latter changes character in such a manner that it loses not only its existence but its possibility of existence; indeed, we already clearly understand that there can be no such thing as an infinite circle; similarly there can be no infinite sphere, no infinite body, and no infinite surface of any shape. Now what shall we say concerning this metamorphosis in the transition from finite to infinite? And why should we feel greater repugnance, seeing that, in our search after the infinite among numbers we found it in unity? Having broken up a solid into many parts, having reduced it to the finest of powder and having resolved it into its infinitely small indivisible atoms why may we not say that this solid has been reduced to a single *continuum* [*un solo continuo*] perhaps a fluid like water or mercury or even a liquefied metal? And do we not see stones melt into glass and the glass itself under strong heat become more fluid than water?[102]

So modernity essentially, from the inception of its physics in the mathematics of Galileo, to the extremity of its philosophy in the radical theology of Altizer. The infinite circle absolutely nonexistent: losing 'not only its existence but also its possibility of existence'. Faced with the infinite unity of indivisibles, the unity of infinite indivisibles—the liquefaction of the finite. The time-

[102] Galilei, *Two New Sciences,* pp. 37ff.

less time, existence-less existence, the shapeless shape of the unity of the infinitely indivisible. This was the absolute liquidity of the infinite circle, the Nothing, continuous compatible quantitative order: the absolute liquescence which is the very insubstantiality of existence. But now for the first time in history 'time itself is the transcendent unity of indivisibles',[103] and thought transcends the essentially finite imagination of the infinite, transcends the finite imagination, infinitely, in the form of the radical novation of the indivisible point, in the form of the categorical fourfold of identity, in the form of an absolutely temporal line. For Galileo the circle is the radical eccentricity in which the end-points of a line meet in an infinite succession of different places according to a law which requires that the meeting place be removed from the end-points in any constant ratio other than unity, in a constant form the identity of which is the vanishing point, in a form the truth of which is the truth identical with Nothing, in a constant form the truth of which is the center identical with Nothing, in a constant form the identity of which is the impossibility of the infinite circle. This radical eccentricity of the circle itself in Galileo, reduced as it is to the fact that unity, *qua* finite, is nothingness,[104] is the underlying presupposition of the 'two infinite series of circles' which describe for Galileo the two kinds of natural motion, even, therefore, the ecstatic centrality which is the former series (the infinite number of concentric circles), concerning which he writes:

> The two kinds of motion occurring in nature give rise therefore to two infinite series of circles, at once resembling and differing from each other; the one takes its rise in the center of an infinite number of concentric circles; the other has its origin in the contact at their highest points, of an infinite number of eccentric circles; the former are produced by motions which are equal and uniform; the latter by motions which are neither

[103] Cf. Leahy, *Novitas Mundi*, pp. 324ff.

[104] A mathematics of the very essence of the consciousness of modernity, as can be seen in the whole fabric of the Hegelian logic (cf. ibid., pp. 123ff., pp. 233ff., et passim).

> uniform nor equal among themselves, but which vary from one to another according to the slope. Further, if from the two points chosen as origins of motion, we draw lines not only along horizontal and vertical planes but in all directions then just as in the former cases, beginning at a single point ever-expanding circles are produced, so in the latter case an infinite number of spheres are produced about a single point, or rather a single sphere which expands in size without limit; and this in two ways, one with the origin at the center, the other on the surface of the spheres. . . . [to which account of Sagredo's, Simplicio responds:] the fact that one can take the origin of motion either at the inmost center or at the very top of the sphere leads one to think that there may be some great mystery hidden in these true and wonderful results, a mystery related to the creation of the universe (which is said to be spherical in shape), and related also to the seat of the first cause [prima causa]. [to which Salviati replies:] I have no hesitation in agreeing with you. But profound considerations of this kind belong to a higher science than ours [*a più alte dottrine che le nostre*].[105]

This is the absolute expansion predicated of the difference between center and surface which is the impossibility of the existence of the infinite circle, predicated of the Nothing which infinitely removes the center of the infinite number of concentric circles, together with its counterpart, the highest point of contact of the infinite number of eccentric circles, from (the center of) a line the elements of which form a rational unity. But now for the first time in history just such a line, just such a center exists, indeed, is existence. Existence is the line/the center/the time/the text the elements of which form a rational unity: the unconditionally absolute expansion of absolute unity: the absolute opening time itself for the first time the circle itself the fourfold proportionality identically the indivisible point: the absolute existence of dead center measuring the circumference of the circle. Insofar as the truth of THE PLACE identical with creation is the measure of an infinite order of squares (as con-

[105] Galilei, *Two New Sciences*, pp. 193ff.

structed above), or cubes (in the third dimension), each one of which, in the absolute exteriority of the within now actually existing for the first time, here in the form of the foundational segments of the exploded central square (cube) of any square (cube), measures the diameter of a circle (sphere), there exists for the first time in thought, not 'a single sphere which expands in size without limit', but an infinite number of infinitely transparent absolute actualities : the sphere of absolute objectivity now existing: the sphere of spheres infinitely newly beginning, the sphere of infinitely new, infinitely separate spheres: the sphere the surface of which is the beginning of an absolutely transparent depth. This is the inception of the infinite proportionality of the body. This is the limit of the infinite expansion of the 'single sphere'. This is the beginning of the circumference of the infinite circle. This is the line for the first time. This is the time of beginning. This is creation displacing the abyss itself: the body of the Living God in the form of the beginning, depth absolutely surface, the infinite identical with the finite: the absolute incompatibility of the infinitely numbered points of the circumference of the circle: the absolutely transparent circle. The points of the infinite circle are squares between squares: the point, the square, is the side identical with the diagonal. The logical foundation of the last is most simply and directly evident in the structure of the cornerstone:

1	0	$\bar{0}$
$\bar{0}$	1	0
0	$\bar{0}$	1

,

where the extreme 1 of any side, $10\bar{0}$ or $\bar{0}01$ or $1\bar{0}0$ or $0\bar{0}1$, never appears as the middle, but is both the extremes *and* the middle of the 111 diagonal, which has significance if this 111 diagonal can be identified with the sides, which in fact it can be, since the alternate $01\bar{0}$ diagonal which unites the alternate extremes of the sides, so that 0 and $\bar{0}$ are only in this diagonal at once extremes of one middle (the diagonal 1), has the discrete arithmetic value of any side, $10\bar{0}$ or $\bar{0}01$ or $1\bar{0}0$ or $0\bar{0}1$, as $1+0+\bar{0}=2$, while sharing with the 111 diagonal (arithmetically $1+1+1=3$) the identical logical value, $010=1$ and $111=1$. The logical identification of 2 and 3, 'appearance' and 'essence',[106] is the logical identification of side and diagonal, itself at once the finite identified with the infinite. Let, then, a square, PQRS, be inscribed in the infinitely expanding circle of Galileo's demonstration:

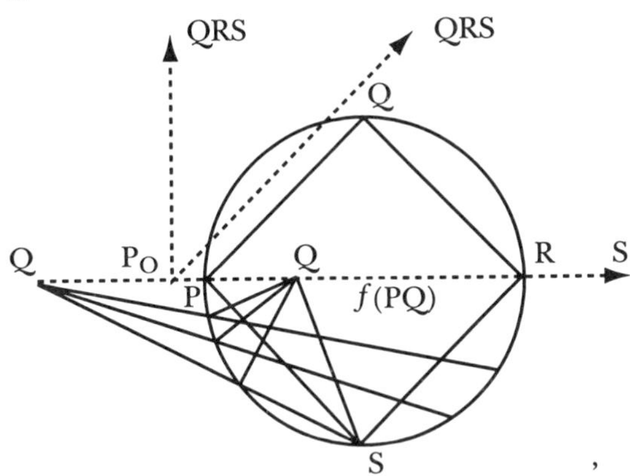

so that when P coincides the moving P_O the infinite straight line which is the circumference of the infinite circle coincides the infinite superficies of its inscribed square: absolute superficiality transcends the necessity of the revolution of the square in the description of the line which is the circumference of the infinite circle, neither 'ever turning . . . to join its last end with its first', nor, *qua* existence, *qua* absolute incompatibility of the beginning, under the necessity of ever turning, this line turns turning absolutely straight. This is the beginning which is infinitely the 'relation' power of the 'balance point'. The 'first end' of the infinite line *identically* the 'last end'. This line essentially is the beginning which turns turning. The righteousness of this line rules the body itself, the infinite surface, the infinite body now actually existing. In the form of the absolute world of time itself for the first time the infinite sphere is absolutely flat. In the form of time itself opening as world for the first time, in the form of the fulfillment of the expectancy, very Flat, very Straight

[106] Cf. above, Section III.1, pp. 273ff., 287ff., 293.

is—the infinitely numbered infinite number of infinite spheres which is the absolute necessity of the infinite sphere now actually existing—the absolutely straight line turning absolutely: the absolute coincidence of 'circumference' and 'infinite straight line' not in the absolutely indifferent point/the absolute indifference which is 'nothing', but in the absolutely incompatible point/the 'not nothing' which is the square root of unity/the point raised to the power of relation/the point of absolute reference, in the perfectly intelligible point, the point of infinitely unconditioned intelligibility, in the point which is, *qua* point, absolute dead center. This is the point which for the first time *is* the system of reference. This is the point which for the first time is the line, the square, the circle.

RECURSUS

The inversion and reversal of the Eucharistic substance to the form of the dark identity of the immediate actuality of experience, this inversion and reversal of the Black Mass in the satanic form of a Mass of the Resurrection for a dead god, in the form of the absolute dilution of the Word in the primal waters of nonexistence, this total presence of an unreal infinite solitary, the real presence of the insubstantiality of the private individual, this absolutely implicit absolute grounding of historical materialism, is, in fact, the reversal of James' pragmatic pluralism, the inside-outside-the-outside-inside of the latter, indeed, the reduction to nothing of the difference between pluralism and monism, this reduction at once that reversal, and, as can be seen from James' own presentation, a logically necessary identity. James writes:

> Perhaps the words 'foreignness' and 'intimacy', which I put forward in my first lecture, express the contrast I insist on better than the words 'rationality' and 'irrationality'—let us stick to them, then. I now say that the notion of the 'one' breeds foreignness and that of the 'many' intimacy. . . . But what at bottom is meant by calling the universe many or by calling it one?

Pragmatically interpreted, pluralism or the doctrine that it is many means only that the sundry parts of reality *may be externally related.* Everything you can think of, however vast or inclusive, has on the pluralistic view a genuinely 'external' environment of some sort or amount. Things are 'with' one another in many ways, but nothing includes everything, or dominates over everything. The word 'and' trails along after every sentence. Something always escapes. 'Ever not quite' has to be said of the best attempts made anywhere in the universe at attaining all-inclusiveness. The pluralistic world is thus more like a federal republic than like an empire or a kingdom. However much may be collected, however much may report itself as present at any effective centre of consciousness or action, something else is self-governed and absent and unreduced to unity.

Monism, on the other hand, insists that when you come down to reality as such, to the reality of realities, everything is present to *everything* else in one vast instantaneous co-implicated completeness—nothing can in *any* sense, functional or substantial, be really absent from anything else, all things interpenetrate and telescope together in the great total conflux.

For pluralism, all that we are required to admit as the constitution of reality is what we ourselves find empirically realized in every minimum of finite life. Briefly it is this, that nothing real is absolutely simple, that every smallest bit of experience is a *multum in parvo* plurally related, that each relation is one aspect, character, or function, way of its being taken, or way of its taking something else; and that a bit of reality when actively engaged in one of these relations is not *by that very fact* engaged in all the other relations simultaneously. The relations are not all what the French call *solidaires* with one another. Without losing its identity a thing can either take up or drop another thing, like the log I spoke of, which by taking up new carriers and dropping off old ones can travel anywhere with a light escort.

For monism, on the contrary, everything, whether we realize it nor not, drags the whole universe along with itself and drops nothing. The log starts and arrives with all its carriers supporting it. If a thing were once disconnected, it could never be connected again, according to monism. The pragmatic difference between the two systems is thus a definite one. It is just this, that if *a* is once out of sight of *b* or out of touch with it, or,

> more briefly, 'out' of it at all, then, according to monism, it must always remain so, they can never get together; whereas pluralism admits that on another occasion they may work together, or in some way be connected again. Monism allows for no such things as 'other occasions' in reality—in *real* or absolute reality, that is.
>
> The difference I try to describe amounts, you see, to nothing more than the difference between what I formerly called the each-form and the all-form of reality. Pluralism lets things really exist in the each-form or distributively. Monism thinks that the all-form or collective-unit form is the only form that is rational.[107]

The absolute reality of the unreal presence is just the reduction to nothing of the difference between 'foreignness' and 'intimacy', the abyss of foreignness-and-intimacy, foreignness-and-intimacy not-foreignness-and-intimacy, just the intimate self-alienation/absolute self-alienation of intimacy, at once the abyss of 'rationality' and 'irrationality', the absolute irrationality of rationality, indeed, the irreality of the reality[108] of rationality-and-irrationality which is the *necessity* that 'the sundry parts of reality' 'be externally related', at once the reversal of 'nothing includes everything, or dominates over everything', indeed, the internalizing of the exterior nothingness which 'separates self from self and man from man', which identifies man with man and self with self[109] (at once the absolutely & essentially implicit *raison d'être* of the revolutionary mass of free individuals): the interior domination of the exterior nothing/the exterior self: the solidarity of everything swallowed in the abyss, the solidarity of everything, its own not its own (not its own swallowed).[110] The real experience of the nothingness of individual interiority and identity, the presence of the totality of substance in the form of the Nothing, is, precisely comprehended, the absolute distribution of the 'collective-unit form', the thing, which 'without los-

[107] W. James, *A Pluralistic Universe* (Cambridge and London, 1977), pp. 145f.
[108] Cf. above, p. 236ff.
[109] Cf. above, Section II.4.
[110] Ibid.

ing its identity . . . can either take up or drop another thing', absolutely 'everything' which 'drags the whole universe along with itself and drops nothing'. The real experience of the light which is darkness, of the transcendental nothingness which *is* the finite non-being of the finite God, of the Mass in remembrance of God, is that of the log, 'which by taking up new carriers and dropping off old ones can travel anywhere with a light escort', absolutely the log which 'starts and arrives with all its carriers supporting it', the each-form willy-nilly the all-form of the apparent nothingness of divinity.[111] The eucharistic remembrance of the death of God is the absolute dispensability of the actual carriers of the log: the log, *qua* Nothing, essentially carrying itself/Nothingness carrying Identity : the absolute reduction to nothing of the nothing of pluralism, at once the inversion of the abyss of the absolute: the identity of pluralism identically the identity of the Nothing: not James' 'multiverse' which 'still makes a universe', but a universe of nothingness, at once the 'absolute fragmentation of identity'/the 'profound fissure of consciousness' which is the nothingness of the 'genuine reality'/the 'genuine reality' of the nothingness which 'the word "or" names'. James writes:

> The all-form allows of no taking up and dropping of connexions, for in the all the parts are essentially and eternally co-implicated. In the each-form, on the contrary, a thing may be connected by intermediary things, with a thing with which it has no immediate or essential connexion. It is thus at all times in many possible connexions which are not necessarily actualized at the moment. They depend upon what actual path of intermediation it may functionally strike into: the word 'or' names a genuine reality. Thus, as I speak here, I may look ahead *or* to the right *or* to the left, and in either case the intervening space and air and aether enable me to see the faces of a different portion of this audience. My being here is independent of any one set of these faces.
>
> If the each-form be the eternal form of reality no less than it is the form of temporal appearance, we still have a coherent

[111] Ibid.

> world, and not an incarnate incoherence, as is charged by so many absolutists. Our 'multiverse' still makes a 'universe'; for every part, tho it may not be in actual or immediate connexion, is nevertheless in some possible or mediated connexion, with every other part however remote, through the fact that each part hangs together with its very next neighbors in inextricable interfusion. The type of union, it is true, is different here from the monistic type of *alleinheit.* It is not a universal co-implication, or integration of all things *durcheinander.* It is what I call the strung-along-type, the type of continuity, contiguity, or concatenation. If you prefer greek words, you may call it the synechistic type. At all events, you see that it forms a definitely conceivable alternative to the through-and-through unity of all things at once, which is the type opposed to it by monism. You see also that it stands or falls with the notion I have taken such pains to defend, of the through-and-through union of adjacent minima of experience, of the confluence of every passing moment of concretely felt experience with its immediately next neighbors. The recognition of this fact of coalescence of next with next in concrete experience, so that all the insulating cuts we make there are artificial products of the conceptualizing faculty, is what distinguishes the empiricism which I call 'radical' from the bugaboo empiricism of the traditional rationalist critics, which (rightly or wrongly) is accused of chopping up experience into atomistic sensations, incapable of union with one another until a purely intellectual principle has swooped down upon them from on high and folded them in its own conjunctive categories.
>
> Here, then, you have the plain alternative, and the full mystery of the difference between pluralism and monism. . . .[112]

But absolute solitude is the reduction to nothing of the 'full mystery of the difference between pluralism and monism', the mysterious identity of 'pluralism and monism' in the form of the Nothing (at once, indeed, the reduction to nothing of the 'mystical body', the abysmal memorial of the Mass), the denial of the 'plain alternative' in the form of the Nothing which is, at once, the confusing-interfusing of the 'sundry parts of reality', indeed,

[112] James, *Pluralistic Universe,* pp. 146ff.

of the separate individuals who are then able to speak to one another of 'our darkness'. To the rhetorical question framed by James, to wit:

> Is the manyness-in-oneness that indubitably characterizes the world we inhabit, a property only of the absolute whole of things, so that you must postulate that one-enormous-whole indivisibly as the *prius* of there being any many at all—in other words, start with the rationalistic block-universe, entire, unmitigated, and complete?—or can the finite elements have their own aboriginal forms of manyness-in-oneness, and where they have no immediate oneness still be continued into one another by intermediary terms—each one of these terms being one with its next neighbors, and yet the total 'oneness' never getting absolutely complete?[113]

—to this 'definite alternative'—the mysterious pluralism of the abyss, in its refusal to take the bull by the horns, in its refusal to undergo, i.e., to transcend, the 'fully co-ordinate' hypotheses of pluralism and monism, answers with its own absolute indefiniteness in the form of the dark identity of the immediate actuality of experience, following, in this, pluralism (for which, in the final analysis, 'life' exceeds 'logic') beyond pluralism to the very death of the finite God, and answers with the final, absolute completion of a total nothingness, answers with the final, absolute perfection of the abyss, reverses 'the finite elements' having 'their own aboriginal forms of manyness-in-oneness' to the final form of the finite elements having oneness-in-their-own-nothingness, to the final forms of their own not their own. James writes:

> This world *may*, in the last resort, be a block-universe; but on the other hand it *may* be a universe only strung-along, not rounded in and closed. Reality *may* exist distributively just as it sensibly seems to, after all. On that possibility I do insist.[114]

---

[113] Ibid.

[114] James, *Pluralistic Universe,* p. 148.

The reversal of this decided undecidedness to the undecided decidedness which is the abyss of the mystery of pluralism, in which the world may *not* 'be a block-universe, but on the other hand may *not* 'be a universe only strung-along', in which reality *must* exist distributively 'just as it sensibly seems to' in the collective-unit form of the total presence of the divine, this reversal and inversion of the substance of the Mass (the inversion of the void which is the absolute immediacy of the Eucharist[115]), this reversal of pluralism, of the inversion of the immediacy of the voided Eucharist, the '"word" made "water" absolutely',[116] radical theology, is the coincidence of radical empiricism and monism, that is, the *watery* coincidence of the otherwise irreconcilable opposites in which the finite elements of the former are transformed into their own 'intrinsic' and 'inherent' others in the very form of *this* very coincidence, in the form of the absolute dissolution of the very line in terms of which a 'block-universe' and a 'universe only strung-along' might be and, in being, might be distinguished, and further, distinguished as rationalistic monism and pragmatistic pluralism, as internally related unity and externally related multiplicity,[117] in the form of the

[115] Cf. above, pp. 466ff.

[116] Ibid.

[117] The nothingness transcending 'rationalistic monism' and 'pragmatistic pluralism' is, at once, the nothingness transcending Feuerbach and Marx, i.e., the reduction to nothing of the difference between the 'rationalistic pluralism' of the former and the latter's 'pragmatistic monism', the nothingness transcending the conceptual realization of the divinity of the human species through love and feeling *and* the practical realization of 'man' through the organized activity of the revolutionary mass, that is, the 'absolute dissolution of the line', while relating explicitly to the distinction, unity/multiplicity, is, *qua* absolute implication, at once the nothingness transcending the latter alternatives as such. For calling attention to the "dissolution of the Feuerbachian circle. . . . as a simultaneous dissolution of the Marxian line," the writer is indebted to E. Lindsay, who, in "Transitive Identity and Space: The Dilemma in Marx and Feuerbach" (a paper presented to the writer at the end of the Spring 1986 term at New York University), concludes, with suggestive reference to Altizer, as follows: "Perhaps what is necessary to make plausible the idea that 'only through his fellow does man become clear to himself,' is a dissolution of the Feuerbachian circle. This could be conceived of as a simultaneous dis-

absolute liquefaction of time, the dissolution of time itself/the nothingness of temporality, in the form of the pure presence of the substance of divinity/the 'eternal death of Jesus',[118] the real anonymity of the divine. The reversal of pluralism/the abyss of pluralism *and* monism, the very essence of the intelligibility of the death of the American God/of the American death of God, makes perfectly manifest, for the first time in history, that 'the only pragmatic application of the substance-idea with which [James was] acquainted' will be 'treated seriously' not only 'by those who already believe in the "real presence" on independent grounds', but also by those who 'on independent grounds' do not believe, but, nevertheless, experience the substantial nothingness of the 'real presence', experience the reality of the death of God, by those who, transcending the absolute idea, have no self, but, nevertheless, experience self in the form of the death of divinity. But, as has been demonstrated,[119] what now occurs for the first time in history (at once, 'what now occurs for the first time in history') 'is' (*is*) *the absolute cancellation of the dissolution of the line,* indeed, the line, time itself, de-actualizing the absolute liquidity of identity, the line, absolute dead center (the diameter/diagonal, the center itself), the absolute novation of the point/line/time/existence,[120] absolutely self-canceling/canceling the Absolute Self, destroying/ destructuring Nothing, yet leaving Nothing intact. This is unity in the form of the 'absolute hymen',[121] the line reversing the absolute inversion of the abyss, the absolute hymen reversing & inverting the hymen of *la différance,* at once the 'square of the creation-diagonal'[122] to which, *qua* foundation, the *structure* of the cube measuring dead center

solution of the Marxian line, for the limit of an infinitely decreasing arc along a circle is a [straight] line. In this manner, perhaps the inner may truly become the outer. For there will be both space and, at the same moment, no division-producing boundaries. Perhaps this is the solution to the identity-space paradox in Feuerbach and Marx. Perhaps."

[118] Cf. above, Section II.4.

[119] Cf. above, Sections II and III, passim.

[120] Cf. above, pp. 529ff.

[121] Cf. above, p. 392, n. 83.

[122] Cf. above, p. 434, 501f., 507ff., et passim.

is reduced, destroying the cubic nothing while permitting it to stand. The reversal of the absolute inversion of identity, in which form, now for the first time in history, the 'block-universe' is *seen to be essentially*, i.e., *linearly*, identical with the 'universe only strung-along', in which form, there is absolute differentiation without space (the reversal of 'space and, at the same moment, no division-producing boundaries'[123]), the form which is absolute perception/conception, this reversal is absolutely that of the absolute unreality of the 'real presence', is, that is, the absolute unreality of the 'real presence' *not* the absence of the actual substance/body of divinity, not, i.e., *absence* of the essence of Christ, *is*, that is, the real existence of the substance of divinity *qua* appearance/*qua* the phenomenon the absolute appearance, the reality of Christ *qua* absolute phenomenology. The text, the appearance, the very conception of the universe, is the actual body of Christ, indeed, the fact that the universe is identically conception/perception is the absolutely new, absolutely pragmatic conception of substance for the first time/of substance-for-the-first-time: transubstantiation thought absolutely.[124] The absolute transcendence of 'foreignness and intimacy' in the form of the conception now actually existing of the 'infinite number of infinitely transparent absolute actualities'/of the 'absolutely flat sphere the surface of which is an absolutely transparent depth/of the 'absolute'/perceived/thought, 'coincidence of the "circumference" and the "infinite straight line"',[125] this absolute opening/absolute exteriority of the outside which is the 'very beginning of the absolutely unconditioned differentiation of time itself',[126] this outside *identically* inside/inside *absolutely* outwardized[127] manifests itself, finally & absolutely, as that completely fundamental structure now occurring for the first time in history, at once the completely transparent essential transcendentality of thought, the very structure & identity of very existence.

---

[123] Cf. above, p. 542, n. 117.

[124] Cf. Leahy, *Novitas Mundi*, Appendix γ.

[125] Cf. above, pp. 535f.

[126] Ibid. Also, above, Section III.5.

[127] Cf. above, Section II.4.

V

THE NEW BEGINNING

1

AMERICA AFTER DEATH: THE UNIVERSALITY OF GOD'S BODY

> That was a rather short course, without laboratory work, in Physiology, a book of Huxley's being the text. It is difficult to speak with exactitude about what happened to me intellectually so many years ago, but I have an impression that there was derived from that study a sense of interdependence and interrelated unity that gave form to intellectual stirrings that had been previously inchoate, and created a kind of type or model of a view of things to which material in any field ought to conform. Subconsciously, at least, I was led to desire a world and a life that would have the same properties as had the human organism in the picture of it derived from study of Huxley's treatment.
>
> J. Dewey, "From Absolutism to Experimentalism"[1]

'Interdependence and interrelated unity', however, embodies the same division within identity which is the root structure of the categorically incomplete thinking of the humanity of the past. The ruling conception is that of an essentially incomplete body. The thought is: the radical incompleteness of identity. But this thought is purely formal, methodological, self-perpetuating method. No matter that the *a priori* self of critical idealism, in the logic of instrumentalism, is not; no matter that the latter

[1] J. Dewey, *John Dewey: The Later Works, 1925–1953,* vol. 5 (Carbondale and Edwardsville, 1984), pp. 147f.

is just so far the divine method of absolute idealism made flesh, that is, the pure ideal of methodology reduced to the real plurality of experience, there clings nevertheless to this emptied bowl the most subtle residue of its thought-eternally history in the form of the *a priori* not-self, the *a priori* other, the other which is not a matter of actual experience. This not-experienced other actually functions, then, as the foundation of the methodological infinity of perpetual self-construction, indeed, as the historical basis for the self-transcendence of the *a priori* organism. The not-experienced other *is* experienced in multiple essentially identical forms: *machine, technology, industry, science, method, individual, work of art, politics, criticism, theology, situation, et cetera,* faces of self-reconstruction which, insofar as they do embody the other, speak of the abyss, embody concretely the silence, say nothing absolutely, that is, say absolutely nothing. There is, on the one hand, *either* the methodology of self-reconstruction which, while it does not uncritically regard science, so regards scientific method, and, while it does not uncritically regard pluralism (a term here taken to embody the entire collection of 'non-scientific', social or 'moral' disciplines), so regards the perception of the pluralistic reality of the world, and which, finally, while it does not uncritically regard self, can be said, since science and pluralism are respectively and relatively its simple and complex faces, to so regard being on the way to self, *or*, on the other hand, there is the experience of the solitude absolutely underlying the superhuman, Nietzschean yearning of this methodology, the pure experience of another self completely not-self, the *actual* experience of/the-experience-of-the-*actual* death of God.

The reality of the death of God is the actual sensation in the interiority of the organism of the final solitude of God, that is, the recognition in the 'interior depths' of individual consciousness of the fact that *society is the only body.* This is what, in effect, Altizer comprehends in 'the descent into hell,' 'the self-embodiment of God,' and 'total presence'.[2] This comprehension of the totality of God's presence is the going at a bound, at once the

[2] Cf. above, Sections II.4, III.2, and IV, passim.

going bound, from instrumentalism's inherent view of the foreground of the world to the infinite view of the background of the universe, to God's point of view, to Nothing. This is the *impossible* 'point of view from which the world can appear an absolutely single fact'[3] made at once not actual but *possible.* In this shifting bound the vague edge of everything is inverted to the central vagueness of self. In this process of the voiding of pragmatism which is the death of God in American theology—the locus of the intelligibility of the American Death—the existing individual *as social product* is reduced to Nothing, so as to be in fact, however, as such, what it as the matter of an explicitly ideal individuality could essentially never be, *and* what the non-categorically existent social individual of historical materialism—the absolutely social individual conceived monistically—could formally never be, viz., the materialized sense of a new humanity, the organized sensation of a new world, the experience of the total presence of the God-quality. This much of a new universe is no longer awaited. In Altizer the experience of the totality of society as the silent Nothing in the 'interior depths' of individual consciousness, that is, every person's actual experience of the abyss which is the unspoken total publicity of individual identity, *is* the *existential actuality* of the sense of a new world. The perception alternative to this actuality of 'total presence' is that of a pragmatic instrumentalism unintentionally oblivious to the transcendent actuality of a new universe which unconditionally reduces perception at the furthest extreme of the intentionality of modern consciousness to doing, thereby making, in the face of an actually new world, a seeing of not-seeing, thereby making reflective community-making self-making. McDermott writes in "The Community of Experience and Religious Metaphors:"[4]

> Now if we can be pleased that contemporary culture has submitted to critical examination the last remnant of a world not

[3] W. James, *The Will to Believe* (Cambridge and London, 1979), p. 6.

[4] J. J. McDermott, *The Culture of Experience: Philosophical Essays in the American Grain* (New York, 1976), pp. 65f.

> of our making, but yet filled with demands which have kept us from our true problems, we cannot say that the end of outworn certitudes and the liberation of man from historical ideologies, religious or otherwise, are themselves adequate to our situation. For death of God or no, where there is no vision, the people perish. . . . Having been seduced over and over again by our own commitments, can we again galvanize our energies to build a truly human order in response to emerging needs rather than as a continuity of some prefabricated view of man's destiny? Stripped of the religious symbolism of the past, can we develop an entirely new sense of affectivity, a new liturgy, a new source and way of celebration? Can we learn how to gather together out of a sense of human solidarity rather than in response to ritualized obligations?

Unlike this final sense of pragmatism which as such is the desire for reconstruction, the actual experience of total presence, *qua* existential actuality of a new world, focuses *finally* on the fact that 'our own' is inevitably 'not our own'. The totality of presence does not make a seeing of not-seeing, but makes reflective making other-making. As the furthest possible extension of the essence of modern consciousness it is conscious of its own darkness of vision, perceiving clearly in the darkness the presence of a new universe.

This is the pelican-stew of contemporary consciousness. This is the unredeemed polarity at the revolutionary extremity of modern thought, the double-edged blade in American thought: either reconstruction or reception, either unarticulated vision or articulate total darkness, either self-reconstruction as the recovery of primitivity in a totally transformed landscape, or self-transcendent reconstruction as the hearing of an irrevocable speech. Such, unredeemed, is the powerful reality of the intersection of the only-body and the only-negative society; such is the analogue of the situation presented in the words of Coleridge:

> Instead of the cross, the Albatross
> About my neck was hung.[5]

[5] S. T. Coleridge, *Poetical Works* (London, 1967), p. 191.

The experience of the presence of the totality of the body is no more the pure experience of another/a new body, of the *existence* of a new humanity, of an *essentially* new universe, than is the desire to 'gather together out of a sense of human solidarity' in the face of the end of a 'world not of our making' in the hope that we can 'galvanize our energies to build a truly human order in response to emerging needs'. The pure experience of another self completely not-self, the American Death of Self, is in fact yet another self transcending the *a priori* not-self, that is, the *othering* of the transcendental unity of self-consciousness—the pure voiding of the Kantian ego—the self-transcendence of *everything + nothing*—the self-multiplication of an uncentered unity. The Death of the American Self is the transcendental void *qua* unit, the very embodiment of the fundamental situation of the self not self, namely, that the *a priori* existence of a new world (perfectly the analogue of the existence of the *a priori* body) precludes the reconstruction of a new human order: *pure self-experience precluding situation.* Indeed, the experience of the death of God finally precludes the final closure of the situation. Very Nothing finally precludes the conception of the object, finally precludes the final closure of the new-world/one-world construction. For its own part very Nothing precludes the experience of the Body of God, the actual conception of the Divine Society. The actual material for a new world, it turns out—abysmal apocalypse! —is, *pace* Aristotle, *sola prima materia*! The pragmatic instrumentalist's messianic hope in the capacity of self-'galvanized' energy to reconstruct the situation is reduced to Nothing, that is, to the pure potentiality of self from self, to the pure absolute of self-sourcing as the absolute quality of the perception/conception of Nothing. At this point, in the depths of individual/social 'inwardness', where the totality of particular individuality is the experience of the identity of Nothing/nothing, where the experience of another self completely not self is another self completely self, the experience is ourselves not experienced, the experience of not experiencing ourselves:[6] the total anesthesia of the other-experiencing self/of the self-experi-

[6] Cf. above, pp. 226ff.

encing other. This, then, before now, is the self-affirmed central reality of modern self-consciousness at the end of the world 'not of our making', the affirmed reality of modern other-consciousness at the end of the world. Here is the 'joy' of 'absolute solitude', the form of the modern affirmation of the end of the world the perfectly modern affirmation of the end of the modern world. This 'joy' *is* nothing/Nothing to prevent the creation of a new world, is, that is, the pure non-categorical act of creating ourselves, but then, in the end, the absolute avoidance of self-identity, the avoidance, at the last, of absolute responsibility. If William James' insistence on *avoiding* Kant[7] was peculiar to the moment of particularity in the internal history of American thought, to the moment of resistance which James' thinking was to the transcendental form which, in effect, Peirce had understood to be essential to the originality of pragmatism,[8] and which, as such, was destined to be taken up in the 'higher continuity' of Dewey's logic as the particularity of thinking situationally identified, as the acknowledgment at once of the unnecessary metaphysical dualism unfortunately underlying what was otherwise understood by Dewey[9] to be Kant's originality (*made practical* by Peirce) in affirming the necessity of uniting percep-

[7] W. James in "Philosophical Conceptions and Practical Results" (in *Pragmatism* [Cambridge and London, 1975], Appendix I, p. 269): "I believe that Kant bequeathes to us not one single conception which is both indispensable to philosophy and which philosophy either did not possess before him, or was not destined inevitably to acquire after him through the growth of men's reflection upon the hypotheses by which science interprets nature. The true line of philosophic progress lies, in short, it seems to me, not so much *through* Kant as *round* him to the point where now we stand. Philosophy can perfectly well outflank him and build herself up into adequate fulness by prolonging more directly the older English lines."

[8] If not to the essence of pragmatism. Cf. C. S. Peirce, *Collected Papers* (Cambridge, Mass., 1933), 5.494: ". . . the pragmatism of James, whose definition differs from mine only in that he does not restrict the 'meaning', that is, the ultimate logical interpretant, as I do, to a habit, but allows percepts, that is, complex feelings endowed with compulsiveness, to be such." Cf. also, ibid., 5.414 and 5.466.

[9] J. Dewey, *The Later Works,* vol. 12 (1986), pp. 510f.

tion with conception if there is to be scientific knowledge of the world, then in the total presence of the death of God in the form of 'absolute solitude', in that night in which all these cats are gray *essentially*, in which the essence of pragmatism is reduced to Nothing, it is clear that along with the particular self's instinctual belief in the reality of the mind of God in Peirce,[10] and along with the imperative for social self-reconstruction in Dewey, the avoidance of Kant in James is likewise reduced to Nothing. It is clear, that is, that what occurs at the deepest point is the absolute self-undoing of the transcendental *ego*,[11] Kantian self-avoidance become identically *instinctual* belief in the reality of the death of God, identically the abyss of the imperative of self-reconstruction. In this way both the originality as well as the finality of American thought *as modern* get their due, participating the Void which is the final transcendence of the death of God, the final (self-)reduction of James' Finite God[12] to Nothing.

If McDermott's 'sense of human solidarity' is the radical reduction of 'instrumentalism' as the 'philosophy of the possibilities of experience'[13] to the desire for the reconstruction of 'vision', and, as such, actually the matter of a 'gathering together', then the fact that the form of this matter in Altizer is the apocalyptic *our own not our own*, that is, the fact that the form of this desire is the immediate self-doubling of the matter, the self-undoing of the matter—this fact that desire speaking is immediately a new Nothing—is the ultimate result of *the rupture of desire from apocalypse effected in the depths of modern self-consciousness.* The pragmatic instrumentalist's desire for a new vision in the face of

[10] Peirce, *Collected Papers*, 6.494–503.

[11] The absoluteness of this Nothing is such that it is at once the Heideggerian 'incarnation of the point of view in perpetuity' (cf. D. G. Leahy, *Novitas Mundi: Perception of the History of Being* [reprint, Albany, 1994], p. 7; cf. also, pp. 18, 270–91) reduced to Nothing, that is, the Nothing-form of eternal perception of the transcendental incarnation, the eternal self-negation in the form of the outwardizing of the within of self (cf. above, pp. 215ff.).

[12] W. James, *A Pluralistic Universe* (Cambridge and London, 1977), pp. 60f.

[13] Cf. Dewey, *Later Works*, vol. 5, p. 275.

the end of past constructions is equivalently the desire for μετάνοια. But the desire for reconstruction (even if everyone is gathered together as one) is equivalently the demand for repentance without an apocalypse, which is to say—the other way round—without an apocalypse the *demand* for a new thinking is reduced to the *desire* for reconstruction, while the apocalyptic abyss/the apocalypse which is not an apocalypse, the final revelation of darkness, is the absolute liquidity of a new mind, the repentance of nothing. The desire for an after-thought, reduced to Nothing after thought, is the inversion of thought to the nothingness of God, but then the pure self/sense of a new world, the *totality* of the presence of a new world the very embodiment of the "thought that represents the transition from thinking to afterthinking,"[14] the dark *sense* of a new theology, indeed, of a new thinking,[15] the voiding, apparently to all appearances, in the totality of appearance, of the being of God. If James, for whom it was appropriate to inquire of an idea its 'cash value', could have imagined this extreme situation, he might have understood the apocalyptic absence of vision as the withdrawal of every last dollar from investment, or better yet, as the absolute refusal to reinvest in reconstruction, as the bankruptcy of new conceptions at their very source, as the reduction to nothing of the source of a new development of thought. The self-disinvestment in the other which is the final precluding of foreclosure, the absolute liquidity of 'inwardness', preserves indeed the 'sense of human solidarity', but in the form of a perpetually illiquid liquid, in the form of the Nothing-worth of perfectly unconditioned cash: the voided cash value, or cash avoiding value. Just that which is so ardently desired is reduced to Nothing, and just insofar as it is desired. The self-rendered justice of the non-apocalyptic demand for repentance is identically the apocalyptic other rendering justice to the desire for self-construction. The essence of this justice is that the desire to 'develop' 'a new source and way of celebration' is of necessity the pure non-existence

[14] Cf. above, Section II.4, p. 244, n. 52.

[15] For the demonstration of the historical identity of thinking, theology, world, and the being of God, cf. Leahy, *Novitas Mundi.*

which is the *presupposition of existence in presence* itself, the non-existence of the presupposed pre-existence, the very lack of the presupposed potentiality for a self which governs the situation, the reversed firstness of the inverted secondness[16] which desire is, the very lack of a pre-self, the Nothing without reference to Nothing including (any)thing, *the Nothing without reference to itself as the quality governing the essential situation of pragmatism.* This is the very lack of the pre-self which was first the transcendental originality of the essence of pragmatism in Peirce, the infinite self-postponement in the form of the belief in the reality of God, *qua* instinctual object, then in James the originality of the notion of the finite God who *qua* 'relative being' 'may conceivably have *almost* nothing outside of himself', and finally in Dewey the originality of the logical distinction of the person, self, or organism (terms interchangeable in Dewey as generally in pragmatism) as an object with a 'capacity for inquiry', but which, *qua* 'knowing subject', does not exist 'independently' of, nor 'antecedently' to, 'engaging in operations of controlled inquiry'.[17] In the new one-world situation the nothing-less quality ruling the situation is at once the situation-less quality ruling, absolutely excluding, nothing/Nothing. The quality ruling the one-world situation is situationless nothingless abyss. If the sense of pure self-experience is the sense of the *a priori* other, and the organism is a system of organs, and an organ, *qua* organ, an other/a tool, a system of tools/of others, and the individual a product of the system of others/of tools, that is, of the body/society, then that which precludes the final closure of the situation is the *a priori* existence of sense/the *a priori* sense organs, the essentially non-qualitative sense of existence, the transcendence of the non-sense of the *cogito*/the non-transcendence of the sense of the *cogito*/the non-I sense of Identity, the sense of the non-I thought

[16] Peirce's terms, respectively, for quality and existence, which are succinctly defined by Dewey (*Later Works*, vol. 11 [1987], p. 90): "Considered in itself, quality is that which totally and intimately pervades a phenomenon or experience, rendering it just the one experience which it is. Of course, then it is 'ineffable'. . . . As Peirce points out, a quality does not *resist* while existence involves reaction and resistance."

[17] Dewey, *Later Works,* Vol. 12, p. 518.

of transcendence, the non-qualitative sense organs of the I, the non-sense/nonsense of the I: pure representing-thought, thought representing absolutely nothing, pure reconstruction of the present/total presence of the I: the very body representing the being of God: the body representing itself/the body itself not itself: the very body of Christ the non-being of God/the very body of God the non-being of Christ/the very body of 'the eternal death of Jesus', the body of Jesus Christ reduced to Nothing.[18] This is the body excluding '*almost* nothing' at once the self-embodiment of the almost-actual God. This is the pure total experience of the essentially historical reality that the form of thought before now *represented* God, whether it did so positively in the form of the essentially self-transcendent reason of the world order (Socrates *et al.*), or in the complementary form of sacred doctrine's formally self-less supposition of the transcendental rationality of nature (Augustine *et al.*), or whether it did so negatively in the form of the transcendental appropriation of nature as reason, the effective denial of the 'real presence' of the body[19] in the form of a real rational sub-

[18] Cf. above, Sections II.4 and IV.2, passim.

[19] What is thought through to and thought through in *Novitas Mundi* is the historical fact that the Incarnation was the appearance in time past of the transcendental essence of existence itself, which appearance became, in the course of time, the very form of thought. This formally incarnational thinking was the transcendental form of natural reason elaborated in the work of Thomas Aquinas. In Thomas, the Augustinian principle of the Love of God even unto contempt of self, the vital faith of Thomas, precluded the self-ascription of the transcendental perception of nature, of the knowledge of what is transcendent, except insofar as thought began with faith, except insofar as thought affirmed the existence of the world on the basis of the divine revelation, and except insofar as theology was natural or there was a natural theology. With Descartes began the process of the absolute appropriation of the intelligible existence of the appearing essence, at once the appropriation of the form of divine self-love, together with a concomitant contempt for the immediately human (formally non-divine, merely empirical) self (a possibility open to modernity in light of the imperfect transformation of consciousness effected in medieval faith, wherein God was thought of as an infinite nature, or infinite reason, over against the finite nature or reason of the creature), a process the extension of which in Kant took shape as the elimination of

stance conditioning the body's being known to exist (Descartes *et al.*), or in the contrary form of the appropriation of nature as sensation, the effective denial of the 'real presence' in the form of the real sensible immaterial body (Berkeley *et al.*), or, finally, whether it did so negative-positively in the form of the self-postponement of the body in the form of reducing the rational to belief, the effective denial of the 'real presence' in the form of

the formal necessity of divine transcendence to the scientific enterprise, and a process, finally, the completion of which in Hegel took the form of identifying the Divine Person as Man. (For Hegel on the eucharistic implications of the movement from medieval to modern thought, cf. above, p. 468, n. 15.). Let it be noted, here, that in Berkeley there is the appropriation of the eucharistic essence of the Incarnation, indeed, of the very conception of the eucharist, the appropriation (in the direction opposite to that form of appropriation implicit in Descartes' doubting the evidence of his senses) of the transubstantiated form of the eucharistic species as the self-emptying *in the form of God* of the substance of material self-consciousness. If this is understood, then Berkeley's "absolutely pragmatistic" "critique of matter" (cf. James, *Pragmatism*, p. 47), insofar as, *pace* James, it came to Peirce *through* Kant, and not *round* him, arrived in America by way of the reversal of Kant's belief in the self as the source of the synthetic unity of perception (by which belief precisely Kant had rendered Berkeley's God obsolete) to the form of belief in God as the "analogue of a mind," the "Name" meaningful ". . . because the discoveries of science, their enabling us to *predict* what will be the course of nature, is proof conclusive that, though we cannot think any thought of God's, we can catch a fragment of His Thought, as it were" (cf. Peirce, *Collected Papers*, 6.502). It is the passage *through* Kant which reverses, as a passage through the looking-glass or through the center of the earth would, the belief in the self of which the transcendental ideal was the symbol to the belief in the God to Whom the soul's relation (instinctual belief) is its consciousness, and which, by way of restoration of the 'pragmatic critique', ironically transforms the 'understandable' and 'approachable' God of Berkeley's belief into the belief of Peirce in the Name which is an analogue of mind, but of which, *qua* "performance", it is not possible to "frame any" *meaningful* "notion" (ibid., 6.508), nor to say, strictly speaking, that it "exists" (ibid., 6.495), the Name neither understandable nor anything more in fact than the "precise" "pragmatistic meaning" of God, just that: "the soul's consciousness of its relation to God" (ibid., 6.516). In this way, finally, it is possible to understand the history of the insubstantial non-eucharistic (after the reversal of Kant, unintelligible *per se*) sensible properties and relations which are the fragmentary objects of pragmatism.

positing the necessary interaction of methodological, essentially functional, mind and matter in the production of the subject of self-consciousness (Peirce *et al.*). Christ the non-being of God, at once itself, God the non-being of Christ, the 'eternal death of Jesus', is the intelligible form of the otherwise purely non-conceptual experience of the fact that the history of past thought represents Jesus Christ as a matter of fact as the real locus of the conception of the identity of God, indeed, as the place of the real body. The Nothing-after-thought of the death of God is the embodiment of the *fact* of Jesus Christ before now (prescinding from what might be believed or not believed of Jesus Christ), viz., that 'thinking in its most proper sense', to rearrange Scharlemann's language, *was* 'theological', that positively or negatively, or both, the very 'substance' of 'our' thought was (His) Body. Thus in the end the ubiquitous conception of the body is the self doubling as the theological other/the self-doubling of identity[20] the self-doubling of the theological other. Before now the absolutely representative identity of pragmatism, actual symbolic identity, the essential double-mindedness of the self of pragmatism is reduced to Nothing. The purity of this situation is neither thought nor God, the *cogito* in its severalty and as such, that is, the essence of pragmatism in the final extremity of its desire for reunification, reduced to Nothing: neither "I" nor "*think*," but the pure experience of the presence of a 'new humanity'.

Now the form of thought is the relating of 'desire' to Nothing, that is, the new *form* of thought *is* "the quality ruling the situation is situationless nothingless abyss," and is in Peircean terms a thirdness, a mediation of the existential quality of the new world. But this thirdness is an element in a new situation which is the absolutely self-less repetition of the abyss in the form of the fourthness for the first time which *is* the absolute act of creation, the new *essence* of thought.[21] The new situation is 'desire' *ex nihilo.* Very want not unmindful but absolutely unencumbered of the memory of past constructions, unburdened of the present

[20] Cf. above, pp. 279ff. and 369ff.

[21] Cf. above, Section IV.1, et passim.

uselessness of the absolutely fixed capital of the past. Unencumbered of wanting—either positively or negatively—the past, the desire of the new situation *ex nihilo* is a perfectly new wanting identified as the very form of the creation of the abyss, the *creation* at once of a capital of 'no fixed bounds'. What now occurs for the first time in history is the pure fixing for the first time essentially of a fixed absolute liquidity. Creation *ex nihilo* the very identity of the universe—but, then, the apocalyptic meta-identity of desire and existence, the very conception of apocalyptic desire as the form of a 'reconstruction' which is a new world, which is not a 'reconstruction' but at once for the first time the construction of matter, the construction itself essentially the matter. What occurs for the first time in history is the form of an essentially technological existence which is the absolutely non-intuitive/objective identity of thought and absolute being. McDermott writes:[22]

> In recent years, dazzling reconstructions of essential bodily organs have given an aura of collective genius to medicine, accompanied by the capacity to outstrip human limitations long held to be inviolable. The existence of organ transplants, for example, connotes to the observer a bold transcendence of the boundaries of history and nature. In its intimacy and immediacy, the era of transplants is a more startling breakthrough than that of moonlanding the astronauts. The latter is an extension of man and continuous with nature, but the former is a rebirth, a bypassing of the heretofore inexorable laws of nature, as if man had transcended himself, albeit in single and isolated instances. At a minimum the horizon of the possible has been immeasurably widened.

In fact the 'horizon of the possible' has been essentially left behind. Not only is the human organism transcending the human organism but it is now essentially true for the first time that *the human species is the species-making species.* Pragmatic instrumentalism, insofar as it is rooted essentially and histori-

[22] McDermott, *Culture of Experience,* pp. 151f.

cally in the form of 'self-postponement', is inadequate to the essentially new reality. Not even the call for a new appreciation and transformative acceptance of the fact of the body's interactive/interpenetrative relations with what is more and more completely an 'artifactual' environment, not even the call for a new 'artifactual' aesthetic,[23] as powerfully right as, up to a point, it is, is quite the new necessity (although and because it is only infinitesimally different from the latter). Not the 'self-making man',[24] but the human species making for the first time an absolutely new humanity, absolutely creating humanity. The emergent fourthness *is* categorically self-less creation. The new necessity is the absolutely 'artifactual' body. The absolute context *is* an absolutely unconditioned individuality. The absolutely self-less apocalypse, the revelation/revolution beginning is the perception, indeed, the desired new vision *ex nihilo* that nothing short of an absolutely nothingless methodology will set up the structures of a 'truly human order', the understanding that nothing short of an absolutely self-less body is the foundation of a 'truly human' individuality, the understanding that precisely insofar as the individual is the (merely) living product of society the impossible is not possible, or that where the impossible is made possible in the form of an absolute inversion there is no (merely) individual consciousness/existence, that is, that while life is not an impossibility, is an actual possibility, that this possibility is not yet the actuality it is when and as the individual is the product which meta-identifies society, that is, when, the self absolutely eliminated, there is no room whatsoever for the conception that the individual product of society, *qua* other, is other than society. Then it is recognized essentially that the means is the end absolutely, that society is the moral-scientific context which *is* absolute negotiation, and that the other/the tool is the absolute end/the absolute consequence. Before now a 'capital of no fixed bounds' was posited in the form of the social imperative for self-reconstruction, but faced with the totality of the new world situation, in the face of *the* sit-

[23] Ibid., pp. 179–225.
[24] Ibid.

uation of the end of the world of everything past, it came face to face with its own inadequacy, the inadequacy of 'its own', in the bifurcation which is, on the one hand, the unfunded desire for a new vision, and, on the other hand, the absolute refusal to fund a new construction, which latter was at once the absolute recognition of the inevitability that a new thinking would be a new conception of the body of Jesus Christ, which is to say that as a matter of the reality of the historical essence of the world's existence there was no way to fund a vision the novelty of which sincerely pretended to be inessentially formal, to have little or no use for the so-called 'symbols of the past', or, more precisely, which imagined that the order existing among those symbols either was or could be an arbitrary and capricious order, as if it might in fact believe in the belief that world history was finally either but a dream or a collage, as if it were conceivable that the end of history was not an essentially historical end in which the new beginning is of necessity the absolute capitalizing of the reality of the world, the realization, for the first time, of the truth of an absolute actuality. Indeed, it turns out that in the end modernity has Nothing/nothing in reserve,[25] whether in the form in which Derrida differs from the having of "anticipation in reserve" of Heidegger, viz., in the form of "there is nothing outside the text",[26] or, at the final extremity, in the form of Altizer's equivocal[27] predication of the solitude of the act of self-judgment, in fact the very form of 'absolute solitude' where nothing in reserve is embodied in the form of unreserved anticipation, viz., "nothing whatsoever stands outside of this presence, or nothing, which can be heard, as presence itself now becomes identical with judgment."[28] The fact of the absolute clarification of the absolute now occurring for the first time in history,[29] the appearance for the first time of a new absolute, is

[25] Cf. above, Section IV.2, passim.

[26] Cf. above, Section II.3.

[27] The equivocation embodied in the realization of the death of God is of the very essence of the voided pragmatism.

[28] Cf. above, Section II.4.

[29] Cf. Leahy, *Novitas Mundi*, p. 357: "In the absolute clarification of the absolute now occurring in reality the absolute intention of that thinking essen-

essentially the perception that to have nothing in reserve, even in the form of unreserved anticipation, is not sufficient, but that what is necessary is *to have no reserve whatsoever, to have no notion of reserve,* but to have the notion of absolutely unconditioned commitment of the totality of funds to the work of construction. Anything less than absolute investment in the beginning of the new world is in fact the attempt, in the face of the loss of self, to undo, to retreat from the ultimate implication of the Cartesian enterprise of reconstructing the universe which is, as it quite unexpectedly turns out, the ultimate implication of humanity in what now for the first time in history is clearly seen to be the absolutely self-less divine creation of the world. The least disinvestment in the face of this surprising development is the attempt to draw back eternally from the thoroughgoing going-through beyond self absolutely without self which is, as never before, the apocalyptic requirement. What now actually occurs for the first time is the transcendental implementation of the law enunciated by Jesus in the 'parable of the talents' which, as part of the eschatological discourse in the Gospel of Matthew,[30] describes the *essential structure* of the King-

tially in the past is immediately comprehended (in the form of its truth [its immediate appearance], as well as in the disappearance of its substance [its self-clarification]) as formally divine, but essentially human. That is, that thinking is the essentially transcendental repetition of its own intention. Formally it is the transcendental thought of God, appropriated to all appearances without exception. But, in essence, it is the transcendental repetition of nothing but itself essentially unchanged. Essentially that thinking is the diversion to its own end of the transcendental repetition of the creation itself now occurring for the first time in history without being other than itself in essence. It is the temptation of faith itself in essence to be for another in essence rather than being simply at the disposal of another in essence. This final temptation to place one's self in the place of God is overcome in that thinking now occurring, absolutely unhindered, as it is, in essence by the Notion of Self. The absolute intention of this thinking is not merely formally divine, as was the case with the thinking belonging in essence to the past, but essentially divine, thereby transforming the form itself of the divine into the body itself in essence, essentially into the Lamb of God. "

[30] Mt. 25:14–30.

dom of Heaven. This law may be formulated (where C is the capital available for investment, V is the amount ventured or risked in investment, and R is the return on investment):

$$R = \frac{V^2}{C}.$$

This law of incipient technological transcendence states not only that nothing ventured is nothing gained, but that venturing everything is gaining everything, and that every partial venture is likewise partially rewarded. It states that the return is essentially a function of the ratio of investment to available funds, and, in effect, that where total investment is less than one hundred percent of available capital, the superstition of reliance on God or reliance on Self continues in the form of thought, in the form of the thought that there is such a thing as an uncreated matter or uncreated world, which betrays the fact that the beginning and end of available resources is 'a hard man, reaping where he has not sown and gathering where he has not scattered', who makes what he makes without utilizing a pre-existent matter, and for whom, therefore, an uninvested capital is less than the non-being of capital, indeed, the warrant for taking the 'little' from the servant who has 'little' and adding it to the abundance of the servant who has the most, while consigning the former to the 'darkness outside'.

Before now the infinitesimal difference between mind and reality, the relative objectivity of consciousness essential to pragmatism, was the basis of the truth of what in effect was the notion of the 'unfinished beginning', and made it possible in fact that James could write: "We can *create* the conclusion [the perfected world], then. . . . Only through our precursive trust in it can it come into being,"[31] where there is no dispute over the propriety of the use of the word 'create' but rather with its self-restricted *meaning* when coupled with the word 'can'. In the

[31] W. James, *Some Problems of Philosophy* (Cambridge and London, 1979), p. 116.

same way James could say: "Mind *engenders* truth upon reality. . . . Our minds are not here simply to copy a reality that is already complete. They are here to complete it, to add to its importance by their own remodeling of it, to decant its contents over, so to speak, into a more significant shape."[32] But it is just this pouring of old wine into new bottles, this wine *like* new, which is now seen to be the belonging to the past which belongs to the past.[33] Now for the first time in history it is perceived that *mind creates now willy-nilly the reality of the truth, the perfect truth of the world, the truth of the perfected world,* that for the first time the absolute alternative is now, that for the first time "*It is finished*" is thought in essence. What now occurs is the infinitesimal end of the 'additive' notion of creation. Now in fact for the first time the creature shares absolutely and essentially 'the creator's atoning vision'.[34] As never before, the quality of the absolute body is shared. This is the beginning of the absolute transparency of the Body, the body as the absolute window: the infinitesimal beginning of the absolute, the minimum for the first time. Before now the 'new reality' of Thomas Aquinas was transcendent not transcendental, while the 'new thought' of Descartes was transcendental not transcendent;[35] in Kant the transcendental ordering of transcen-

---

[32] W. James, "Interview in [The] New York Times," in *The Writings of William James,* ed. J. J. McDermott (Chicago, 1977), p. 448.

[33] James' notion of 'decanting', with its suggestion of reshaping the old wine while leaving behind its accumulated sediment, is an exact analogy to the self-postponement effected in the transition from European to American thought, and in its own way a complete proof of the identity of thinking and being. The extent to which pragmatism overcame the Cartesian dualism never overcome in Europe, was in the final analysis radically limited by its continuing to take seriously that last vestige of the mind-body dualism, viz., the very notion of 'self', by its continuing, even if by way of postponement, to confuse self with person, *ego,* organism, object etc., by its continuing to think in terms of a merely relative beginning of novelty, in one way or another in terms of James' productive intercourse of mind and reality. Pragmatism essentially recognized an irreducibly functional distinction of matter and thought, or percept and concept.

[34] Cf. James on Leibniz, in *Pluralistic Universe,* p. 58.

[35] Cf. Leahy, *Novitas Mundi,* pp. 54–92.

dence was the new method not the thing itself, while in Hegel the new thought of reality is the historical realization of the thing itself. In Europe, there was *essentially* no thought of 'beginning', no thought of beginning in essence. In America, there was indeed the problem of the beginning of thought, the beginning of the problem of thought. The problem of the beginning of thought in Peirce was conceived materially as the problem of the beginning of existence, in James conceived formally as the problem of the beginning of particular consciousness, and finally in Dewey conceived essentially as the problem which is the beginning of inquiry. In Peirce the transcendental conception of the problematic beginning was that it was a pure feeling without reference to anything else, in James that it was the 'fringe' surrounding each particular experience, in Dewey that it was a situation demanding resolution. In each of these cases was involved, *qua* essential perception of the problem of the beginning of thought, a form of the infinite postponement of self-consciousness, a form of the postponement of the 'knowing subject', the primacy of which latter had been of the essence of European thought. The essential originality of American pragmatism is able to be appreciated for the radical shift in consciousness which it was, when, for example, its notion of the God-relation is compared to that of the English associationist psychologist and philosopher, David Hartley, which the latter set out in a Scholium following Proposition 72 of Part II of *Observations on Man, His Frame, His Duty, And His Expectations* in the form of a law which formally coincides the above 'law of incipient technological transcendence', and somewhat ironically since the last is the transcendence of the very relative objectivity of consciousness essential to pragmatism by which latter the operation of Hartley's law is essentially turned aside from its intended end. The English thinker writes:

> Let us suppose the Fear of God to be a middle Proportional between the Love of the World and the Love of God in all the intermediate States of these Affections, from their first Rise in Infancy [where the second mentioned is "infinitely greater"

than the first and the first than the last], till their ultimate Absorption and Evanescence in the Love of God; and see how this Supposition will tally with Experience, and how each Affection varies in respect of the other two. Call therefore the Love of the World W, the Fear of God F, and the Love of God L. Since then W : F :: F : L,

$$W = \frac{F^2}{L}.$$

If now F be supposed to remain the same W :: L, i.e., every Diminution of the Love of the World will increase the Love of God, and *vice versa*; so that, if the Love of the World be nothing, the Love of God will be infinite, also infinitely greater than the Fear, *i.e.,* we shall be infinitely happy. If, on the contrary, the Love of the World be greater than the Love of God, the Fear will also be greater than it, and our Religion be chiefly Anxiety and Superstition. If, farther, F, supposed still to remain the same, be greater than W, it is our truest Interest to diminish W as much as we can, because then the Gain in L is far greater than the Loss in W. If L remain the same, then W = F^2; *i.e.,* every Increase of W will increase F also, *i.e.,* every Increase of the Love of the World will increase the Fear of God, which therefore, since the Love is not increased by Supposition, must incline to a superstitious Dread: As, on the contrary, if W vanishes, F must vanish also; *i.e.,* the Love of the World and Fear being both annihilated, we shall receive pure Happiness, of a finite Degree, from the Love of God. If W remain the same, then F^2 :: L; *i.e.,* every Accession made to the Fear of God will be the Cause of a greater Accession to the Love, and every Accession to the Love the Cause of only a less Accession to the Fear; *i.e.,* we shall be Gainers upon the Whole by all Motives either to the Fear or Love of God, Losers by all contrary Motives. For if F be supposed even infinite, L will be infinito-infinite, *i.e.,* will absorb it infinitely; and, if F be infinitesimal, L will be infinito-infinitesimal; *i.e.,* we shall become mere selfish Worldlings; which is the Case with those practical Atheists, who succeed in their Endeavours to put God, and a future State, out of their Thoughts, that they may give themselves up to this World. W now occupies the Place of L, and extinguishes both F

> and it; *i.e.*, Self and the World are their God. Upon the Whole, it follows from this Speculation concerning the Quantities W, F, and L, that W ought to be diminished, and F and L to be increased, as much as possible, that so W may be indefinitely less than F, and F indefinitely less than L; *i.e.*, we ourselves indefinitely happy in the Love of God, by the previous Annihilation of Self and the World.[36]

The most striking aspect of Hartley's law as compared to the perfectly objective terms of the law of incipient technological transcendence (the precise formal correspondence of the analogies is $[L = F^2/W] = [R = V^2/C]$) is the radical subjectivity which is the matter of the former, the embodiment of what is essentially the notion of self-transcendence in the form of what otherwise is the form of the law of centripetal acceleration in circular motion ($a_c = v^2/R$ [where v is tangential velocity and R is the radius of the circle]). Indeed it is to the "central point" that Hartley, at the end of Proposition 72, would have one flee away from "all human Supports and Comforts"; as he says, "we must have no *Comfortor, no God, but one*; and happy are they who make haste towards this central Point, in which alone we can *find Rest to our Souls*."[37] The *relative* objectivity of consciousness essential to

36. D. Hartley, *Observations on Man, His Frame, His Duty, And His Expectations*, vol. 2 (Delmar, N. Y., 1976), pp. 329f.
37. Ibid. Coleridge, in his "Religious Musings" (cf. *Poetical Works*, pp. 108–25), married this last thought of Hartley's with the demonstration of the Scholium:

    From Hope and firmer Faith to perfect Love
    Attracted and absorbed: and centered there
    God only to behold, and know, and feel,
    Till by exclusive consciousness of God
    All self-annihilated it shall make
    God its Identity: God all in all!
    We and our Father one! (ll. 39–44)

    That self-annihilation is no end of Self, that it is infinite Self, was not only known to Coleridge, but celebrated by him later in this poem:

    . . . Toy-bewitched,
    Made blind by lusts, disherited of soul,

pragmatism can be clearly delineated not only by noting James' fuller attitude toward Hartley's work in psychology, viz., that it was flawed by its notion of the association of 'ideas' rather than of *things*,[38] but also by comparing the 'centripetal' theology of

---

> No common centre Man, no common sire
> Knoweth! A sordid solitary thing,
> Mid countless brethren with a lonely heart
> Through courts and cities the smooth savage roams
> Feeling himself, his own low self the whole;
> When he by sacred sympathy might make
> The whole one Self! Self that no alien knows!
> Self, far diffused as Fancy's wing can travel!
> Self, spreading still! Oblivious of its own,
> Yet all of all possessing! This is Faith!
> This the Messiah's destined victory! (ll. 145–58)

Later yet in this poem written before he abandoned Hartley's materialism for Berkeley's idealism, Coleridge spies Hartley resurrected in the Millennium:

> . . . he of mortal kind
> Wisest, he first who marked the ideal tribes
> Up the fine fibres through the sentient brain. (ll.368–70)

[38] The important influence of Hartley's work on American thought is indicated by what James says of him in *The Principles of Psychology* , vol. 1 (Cambridge and London, 1981), p. 522: "Hartley. . . suggested habit as a sufficient explanation of all connections of our thoughts, and in so doing planted himself squarely upon the properly psychological aspect of the problem of connection, and sought to treat both rational and irrational connections from a single point of view. . . . I believe that he was in many essential respects on the right track, and I propose simply to revise his conclusions by the aid of distinctions which he did not make." But Hartley was not excluded from James' judgment that ". . . the whole historic doctrine of psychological association is tainted with one huge error—that of the construction of our thoughts out of the compounding of themselves together of immutable and incessantly recurring 'simple ideas.' It is the cohesion of these which the 'principles of association' are considered to account for. . . . [But *a*] *ssociation,* so far as the word stands for an *effect, is between* THINGS THOUGHT OF—*it is* THINGS, *not ideas, which are associated in the mind.* We ought to talk of the association of *objects,* not of the association of ideas. And so far as association stands for a *cause,* it is between *processes in the brain*—it is these which, by being associated in certain ways, determine what successive objects shall be thought" (ibid., 522f.). For the specific inclusion of Hartley, ibid., p. 529, n. 9.

Hartley (the Eckhartian outlines of which are fully realized in Coleridge, where, however, the Meister's identity with the One is in its modern setting the active making of the creative subject) to James' belief in the irreducibly tangential relation of the religious subject to "the wider life of things," which belief fundamentally undermines the operation of Hartley's law by infinitesimally dividing its premise. For James life is a generically polytheistic experience the whole point of which is no one point to which everything can be reduced, and which, to that extent at least, guarantees that insofar as there is a self, it is always and everywhere the self of the particular individual, which, since it not only does not exist tangentially to a circle about *the* one, *the* central Point, but rather is tangent "to curves of history the beginnings and ends and forms of which pass wholly beyond [its] ken,"[39] does not, therefore, exist apart from the experience of some part of this indefinitely wide life, but exists indeed in a circle which is no circle, just as pragmatism "has no dogmas, and no doctrines save its method".[40] Now, the method of pragmatism is *"The attitude of looking away from first things, principles, 'categories,' supposed necessities; and of looking towards last things, fruits, consequences, facts."*[41] In the form of the (merely) relative objectivity of its consciousness it remains bound tightly to its rejection of the One, turned to the future but looking over its shoulder. In this, its essential failure to categorically transcend the past-

[39] In this polytheism the heroes of the ancient world have been replaced by dogs and cats: "I firmly disbelieve, myself, that our human experience is the highest form of experience extant in the universe. I believe rather that we stand in much the same relation to the whole of the universe as our canine and feline pets do to the whole of human life. They inhabit our drawing-rooms and libraries. They take part in scenes of whose significance they have no inkling. They are merely tangent to curves of history the beginnings and ends and forms of which pass wholly beyond their ken. So we are tangents to the wider life of things. But, just as many of the dog's and cat's ideals coincide with our ideals, and the dogs and cats have daily living proof of the fact, so we may well believe, on the proofs that religious experience affords, that higher powers exist and are at work to save the world on ideal lines similar to our own" (James, *Pragmatism*, pp. 143f.).

[40] James, *Pragmatism*, p. 32.

[41] Ibid.

future distinction, in its failure to think past the future, pragmatism as the self-postponement which it essentially is shares with the uchronistic postponement of the 'higher communism' of historical materialism the distinction of embodying the last vestiges of Western idealism. But unlike the monistic pragmatism of its spiritual counterpart, American pragmatism, which otherwise shares in the understanding that the individual is a product of society, is essentially a pluralism for which the whole point of life is absolutely no one point. This pluralistic pragmatism points absolutely at no one. It is the experience of final anonymity, the refusal of responsibility in the form of the absolute experiment, the formal refusal of the responsibility of the absolute, the refusal of absolute responsibility, the responsible refusal of the form of absolute existence. It is life at the balance point of the superstition of self-reliance and God-reliance/other-reliance. The essence of this pragmatism is the abyss of dogma, the dogma of no dogma (the *a priori* impossibility of the knowledge of what is actually transcendent), the inevitable 'perhaps'. It is the decision to believe in the abyss, the abyss decided upon, nothing decided upon absolutely. When it comes then to Hartley, if the latter demonstrates the ultimate rational necessity of the self-transcendence underlying the practical experience of free will, pragmatism is essentially the self-postponement of the necessity of the self-transcendence of free will, the pure fragmentation of consciousness conceived essentially as the finite consciousness of the superhuman being,[42] at once the denial of the intermediation of an ideal self,[43] literally the fragmentation

[42] Cf. James, *Pluralistic Universe,* pp. 143f. : "We are indeed internal parts of God and not external creations, on any possible reading of the panpsychic system. Yet because God is not absolute, but is himself a part when the system is conceived pluralistically, his functions can be taken as not wholly dissimilar to those of the other smaller parts—as similar to our functions consequently. Having an environment, being in time, and working out a history just like ourselves, he escapes from the foreignness from all that is human, of the static timeless perfect absolute." This 'superhuman being' becomes in Dewey the community of the 'mysterious totality of being' (cf. below, p. 576, n. 53).

[43] At once the affirmation of the experience of self-transcendence, of the association of things in the mind. Cf. above, p. 568, n. 38.

of Hartley's rational demonstration such that, absent the actual fear of God, absent the existence of the mean proportional, absent the rational middle, there is no unifying identity of the world other than, perhaps, the God of whom we are the 'internal parts'. Hartley had anticipated a 'practical atheism' in the event of the infinitesimal Fear of God. But the fragmentation of consciousness which is the essence of pragmatism is not the supposed infinitesimal Fear of God of Hartley's rational demonstration, but rather the absolute focus of experience at the infinitesimal point itself of the curve, of the circle, of the center, at which infinitesimal point the dichotomous experience is irreducibly self-postponement, a having and a not-having of Self, a having and a not-having of God. So James on the infinitesimal point of novelty:[44]

> Novelty, as empirically found, doesn't arrive by jumps and jolts, it leaks in insensibly, for adjacents in experience are always interfused, the smallest real datum being both a coming and a going, and even numerical distinctness being realized effectively only after a concrete interval has passed. The intervals also deflect us from the original paths of direction, and all the old identities at last give out, for the fatally continuous infiltration of otherness warps things out of every original rut. Just so, in a curve, the same direction is *never* followed, and the conception of it as a myriad-sided polygon falsifies it by supposing it to do so for however short a time. Peirce speaks of an 'infinitesimal' tendency to diversification. The mathematical notion of an infinitesimal contains, in truth, the whole paradox of the same and yet the nascent other, of an identity that won't keep except so far as it keeps *failing*, that won't *transfer*, any more than the serial relations in question transfer, when you apply them to reality instead of applying them to concepts alone.

Thus not practical atheism in the event of the rejection of the formal anticipation of the 'central Point', but the formally unanticipated point of an essentially pragmatic theism, the 'central Point' anticipated *essentially*, in the primacy of the non-concep-

[44] James, *Pluralistic Universe*, pp. 153f.

tual reality of the pragmatism in which 'God, and a future State' are fully integrated with 'this World'. Just as the infinite postponement of self-consciousness makes room essentially for the experience of the *partial* novelty which is 'the fatally continuous infiltration of otherness' which 'warps things out of every original rut' in such a way that 'all the old identities at last give out', that is, *retrospectively and not all together for the first time*—this is the strategic point the defense of which against all penetration is absolutely necessary for pragmatism lest it be surprised by the absolute, lest there be an absolutely unanticipated thinking—just as the partial opening to a formally prospective but essentially retrospective novelty is the doubly limited opening to the new, so God is irreducibly the self and not the self, the same and not the same as ourselves. The infinitesimal point itself of this practical theism in which 'we are the internal parts of a finite God' is the inversion of the absolute religion of Hegel, the God-Man relation *qua* experience and at once—Kant reversed or avoided, as the case may be—the belief in God, and as such the finite doubling of the non-being of infinite being in which God 'escapes from the foreignness from all that is human' and is 'just like ourselves'.[45] In Altizer's reduction to Nothing of this pragmatic infinitesimal doubling of the 'central Point', the infinite multiplication of the doubly uncentered self, the reduction to Nothing of the essential anticipation of the 'central Point' (at once the absolute material grounding of the infinite anticipation of self-consciousness which is historical materialism [the categorically ungrounded absolute]), the inversion of the absolute religion *is* not-the-inversion of the absolute religion, that is, the 'internal parts of God' which are 'not external creations' *are* 'external creations', that is, the internal parts of the divine feel themselves outside the within, feel the outside within themselves, purely sense the other than self in the intimate depths of self-identity. This is the radical realization/actualization of the

[45] This inversion of Hegel is the God-Man identity 'mediated' not as in Hegel 'by the negation of finitude' (cf. G. W. F. Hegel, *Lectures on the Philosophy of Religion*, vol. 2, trans. E. B. Speirs and J. B. Sanderson [New York, 1962], p. 327), but by the negation of infinitude, by the finite body which is conceivably almost infinite, but always and everywhere tangent to the unseen.

incompleteness of identity, indeed, the very identity of the essence of pragmatism itself embodying its own rule that 'all the old identities at last give out'. In Altizer the experience is the postponement of the giving out of the self-transcendence of pragmatism. Indeed, the pure feeling of 'total presence' is the experience of the God infinitesimally differentiated who is 'just like ourselves' irreducibly self and other, as the Nothing the very embodiment of the abyss of self and other. If the Finite God beyond whom is '*almost* nothing' is the embodiment of the essential tentativeness of pragmatism, then, at the last, pragmatism tries the Abyss, the Finite God together with his 'internal parts' in the final darkness outside of which *for the first time* is nothing whatsoever or 'at least nothing which can be heard'. In this dark inversion of the void the essence of pragmatism undergoes the nothingness of its own identity rather than thinking nothing possible beyond the becoming of the totality of presence. American thought, *qua* furthest possible extension of modernity, within the limit of the fact that the self postponed essentially exists, does and does not give out, makes the impossible possible, that is, accomplishes as self-postponing-self what was simply impossible in European thought, viz., the undergoing of its own conception in essence, its own voiding. The Nothing/nothing which is pragmatism's own final identity is the making explicit in Dewey's terms of the fact that its notion of the 'historical relativity' of all systems of thought[46] applies *even and*

[46] Cf. J. Dewey in "The Future of Liberalism," in *Later Works,* vol. 11, pp. 291f.: "In the first place, [non-absolutist] liberalism knows that an individual is nothing fixed, given ready-made. . . . knows that social conditions may restrict, distort and almost prevent the development of individuality. It is as much interested in the positive construction of favorable institutions, legal, political and economic as it is in removing abuses and overt oppressions. In the second place, liberalism is committed to the idea of historic relativity. . . . The connection between historic relativity and experimental method is intrinsic. Time signifies change. The significance of individuality with respect to social policies alters with change of the conditions in which individuals live. The earlier liberalism in being absolute was also unhistoric. . . . The same thing is true of any theory that assumes, like the one usually attributed to Marx, that temporal changes in society are inevitable—that is to say, are governed by a law that is not itself

at the last to that system of thought which self-effacingly essentially deferred to the primacy of non-cognitive experience.

It could be imagined that Dewey's reply to the intellectual implications of the actual death of God as the self-reduction to Nothing of the essence of pragmatism might be along the lines of what he said in *Liberalism and Social Action*, viz.:

> The objection that the method of intelligence has been tried and failed is wholly aside from the point, since the crux of the present situation is that it has not been tried under such conditions as now exist. It has not been tried at any time with use of all the resources that scientific material and the experimental method now put at our disposal.[47]

But the absolute inversion of the abyss is absolutely and precisely just the essential recognition that 'the point' is 'wholly aside' from *itself*, that the notion of 'resources' 'put at our disposal', whether by 'scientific material and experimental method', or, indeed, by the God whom these latter in their self-doubling identity have replaced, is essentially—to borrow an expression of Hartley's—an infinito-infinitesimally different use of the actual 'now'. What the presence of totality mutely but essentially witnesses is the essential and final limitation of any thought not being absolutely at the disposal of another,[48] of any thinking not absolutely transcendent to the distinction *a priori/ a posteriori*, of

historical. The fact is that the historicism and the evolutionism of nineteenth century doctrine were only half-way doctrines. They assumed that historical and developmental processes were subject to some law or formula outside temporal processes." Note here the continuing confusion, fundamental to modern thought, of the notions of time and history (cf. Leahy, *Novitas Mundi*, pp. 1–21; cf. also pp. 303–96), which confusion is further connected with the fact that it does not occur to Dewey that the very notion of 'process' contains an essentially non-temporal element, viz., the time *taken*, the *passage*, the *course* of time, that the very category of 'process' is a half-way house to the creation of a new world, which latter can never be anything other than the absolute act of creation.

[47] Dewey, *Later Works*, Vol. 11, p. 37.

[48] Cf. Leahy, *Novitas Mundi*, pp. 334–96.

any thought which thoughtlessly takes for granted the notion of 'process', which thinks of direction apart from time, which thinks that time takes time,[49] which does not think the essence of temporality. The realization of the death of God is the abyssal apocalyptic recognition of the necessity of the apocalypse, of the necessity at once the impossibility of separation from self. It is the apocalyptic self-separation from the desire to reconstruct, the immanently awaiting Nothing. It is the acknowledgment of the fact that experience has demonstrated in the end the essentially self-limited usefulness of the pragmatic understanding of the apparent necessity of turning from the primacy of concept to that of immediate experience (the analogue of turning from the past toward the future), an acknowledgment such that its becoming the totality of presence is at once the real but imperfect indifference to the distinction of qualitative and propositional thought evidenced in the form of 'the eternal death of *Jesus*' as the form of an essentially *anonymous* existence. In the perfect purity of this 'imperfect indifference' the absolute quality at once the transcendental Nothing reveals to its counterpart, the pragmatic instrumentalism which hopes for a new construction 'out of a sense' of corporate intention, the continuing abyss which is its own absolutely impossible Name, its own impossible relation to existence.[50] If the furthest possible extremity of intentionality in McDermott is the intentional primitivity of the body, the reduction of human solidarity to a return to a primitive aesthetic intention albeit in and in virtue of the new post-

[49] Ibid., pp. 303–27. In this connection note the reaction of the scientific community to the theoretical calculations of a group of Indian physicists who concluded that faster-than-light messages are feasible, as reported by J. Gleik in *The New York Times*, October 27, 1987, in an article entitled "In Defiance of Einstein, Physicists Seek Faster-Than-Light Messages:" "Even physicists who cannot instantly see an error in the Indian calculation say the error must be there, since otherwise the theory of relativity will have to be re-thought." Particularly interesting in the context of a discussion of pragmatism is the fact that, according to *The Times*, these same representatives of scientific orthodoxy admit a faster-than-light 'kind of influence'. But *ex hypothesi* not a message.

[50] For Peirce on the Name cf. above, p. 556, n. 19.

Deweyan situation,[51] a situation past Dewey's synthesis of Peirce's panpsychic ideal with James' real pragmatic God which was his faith in the pragmatic divinity of the actual community,[52] and if, faced with the failure of even the logic of logic-exceeded-by-life, the desire for a recovery of an *original* primitivity in the *new* situation is the extreme application of the infinitesimal purity of anticipation, this fall-back, back-filling pragmatic position is nevertheless here and now essentially doomed by the reality of the intentional death of God. The form of the 'eternal outwardizing of the within' in fact makes sense of, *senses* in its own absolute inwardness, the inaesthetic understanding of the body now actually occurring, makes of the aesthetic intention of the body the non-being of the actual body itself, discloses to the furthest possible extremity of intentionality its very own negative. The negative of the intentional primitivity of the body, is, however, just that. It is 'absolute solitude'. This is that 'joy' which at/as the furthest extremity of modernity is, conceived logically, *imperfect indifference to distinguishing qualitative from propositional thought, but no more.*[53] This is the absolute silence short of the absolute actuality of the transcendental dichotomy. Insofar as the Nothing in the self-reduction to Nothing of the essence of pragmatism in Altizer is, *qua* furthest possible extension of modern consciousness, at once the reduction of the Heideggerian

---

[51] Cf. McDermott, *Culture of Experience,* pp. 138f. : "Given the events of the last two decades, it would be fair to question Dewey's confidence in science as the exemplary method for the development of social intelligence. On the other hand, he was prescient in his emphasis on aesthetic sensibility as central to a liberated human life. Indeed, Dewey's understanding of experience as aesthetic may turn out to be more politically significant than his explicitly political writings."

[52] Cf. Dewey, *Later Works,* vol. 9 (1986), p. 56: "The community of causes and consequences in which we, together with those not born, are enmeshed is the widest and deepest symbol of the mysterious totality of being the imagination calls the universe. It is the embodiment for sense and thought of that encompassing scope of existence the intellect cannot grasp. It is the matrix within which our ideal aspirations are born and bred. It is the source of the values that the moral imagination projects as directive criteria and as shaping purposes."

[53] Cf. Dewey, *Later Works,* vol. 5, pp. 243–62.

Dasein to Nothing, that is, insofar as the self-reduction to Nothing of the 'infinite self-postponement' which is of the essence of pragmatism is at once the reduction to Nothing of the finite self-postponement of the phenomenological essence (which latter, as such, lacking the scientific objectivity essential to pragmatism, is at once without the *a priori* generic essence/(other) [which last in Husserl[54] was, however, the work of an infinitely immediate self]), then it is as well the perfect indifference to Heidegger's notion that 'the essential nature of existence' can not be 'caught and completely explicated in a proposition'.[55] In a word, this Nothing is the perfect barrier of absolute inaction, the perfect elimination of every obstacle to the creation of a new world without in fact creating that order. Its unreserved anticipation is Heidegger brought to nought. No notion of reserve in the form of the pure Nothing: the absolutely ultimate distancing from self in the form of the beginning in reserve. Indeed, the equivocally absolute solitude which is the act of self-judgment outside of which is nothing, 'or nothing which can be heard, as presence itself now becomes identical with judgment', is the abysmal inversion of anticipatory thinking in the form of the absolutely anticipatory Nothing, at once the Abyss now anticipating the Final Judgment. This is the Abyss eternally anticipating the absolute conception for the first time of the fact that 'outside the church there is no salvation'. In the form of the absolute avoidance of responsibility, in the form of the self forgiving itself self, in the pure separation from self, in the form of unreserved anticipation the unanticipated is anticipated as such. But the latter turns out to be nevertheless the incipient transcendence which is the absolute realization that there is now for the first time absolutely no outside of existence in the Mind of God, no outside of the Body of God, and therefore no inside outside of the 'internal parts' of the Finite God, but rather the absolute exteriority of the inside of the Body, the absolute individuality of the parts of the Divine Body, the radically complete

[54] Cf. E. Husserl, *The Paris Lectures* (trans. P. Koestenbaum, The Hague, 1929).

[55] Cf. above, Section III. 5, p. 358, n. 14.

identity of the perfectly interchangeable absolutely existing parts of the Body of God, of the organism transcending the essentially binding ties of the 'common faith of mankind' since the latter,[56] in effect, would deny the fact of the *absolutely historical essence of the incipient technological transformation of the world,* would deny, in effect, the new/specific faith of humanity. The unanticipated as such turns out to be unexpectedly the beginning of the body, of society, of the new humanity conceived essentially, i.e., conceived *qua* historical actuality as *the Artifactual Body of Jesus Christ,* the infinite divine objectivity, the infinite artifactual existence in which the perfect interchangeability of the parts is a function of the fact that the unicity of the parts identical with the totality is the sameless absolute, change itself:[57] for the first time the existence in thought of the Kingdom of Heaven (the essential structure, $R = V^2/C$, *every* 'where'/'here' one absolutely existing center), the incipient existence of the absolute upbuilding of infinite totalities—or Nothing/'the darkness outside'. Not the bogeyman of James, the 'static timeless perfect absolute',[58] but the perfect dynamic of time itself the very form of the new world, not 'the same direction never followed', but *no direction but that time itself is that direction.*[59] Nothing short of a Resurrection of the Divine Intention shall provide the necessary foundation for the New Jerusalem, call it what you will. But the Resurrection of the Divine Intention is, of actual historical necessity, therefore, at once of the necessity of the actual reality of the Incarnation in time and thought, identically *for the first time* and in the form of the proof of the historical relativity of the very notion of the immediate lack of the self of experience which is the Glorified Body of the Finite God. Not the abyss of the Mass of the Resurrection, not the-Body-not-the-Body,[60] but the Glorified Christ *essentially* in the form of thought, neither reserved nor unreserved but existence itself the beginning of an

[56] Dewey, *Later Works,* vol. 9, p. 58.

[57] Leahy, *Novitas Mundi,* pp. 315–20.

[58] Cf. above, p. 570, n. 42.

[59] Leahy, *Novitas Mundi,* pp. 303–96.

[60] Cf. T. J. J. Altizer on Joyce, in *History as Apocalypse* (Albany, 1985), pp. 209–54. Also, above, Section IV.2.

essentially temporal temporality. What now actually occurs is the experience of a new transcendental *ego* which *is* the absolutely self-less *ego experior* at once the experience—where experience is thought essentially without the other-self distinction—of the infinite existence for the first time of forgiveness, the other-experience of every thing/person saying, *qua* body, *qua* essentially species-making species, *in nomine christi ego absolvo te.* An absolute pragmatism in which the severalty of the many is identical with, i.e., shares, the unity of the one. In the thinking now occurring the creature is identical with the creator without any trace of the idealism which has hitherto dominated all forms of Western thought, i.e., essentially without any form of self-reference. God is no longer thought to stand (or to have stood) between the creature and nothing, or, in the case of the essentially pluralistic pragmatism, between the creature and the *almost* nothing which is outside of God, as if his removal were the reduction of the creature to nothing or to the *almost* nothing which in the absence of God *is* his total presence—the Nothing which is almost a new humanity, almost the body—as if God's presence alone, or his co-presence, gave standing to the creature, as if he had not *actually* created the world together with everything in it, as if he had not in the very *act* of creation transcended once and for all essentially and absolutely the causative dependence of the world upon himself, as if he might change his mind, or as if he had created the world in a moment of self-forgetfulness and coming to himself, the world might *return* to nothing, or to *almost* nothing—as if in fact dependence on God were not the being created by God, the absolute independence of the existence of the body *ex nihilo.* In the mind of God the creature exists absolutely. In the mind of the creature God exists absolutely. This is for the first time the *absolute* analogy of being. Not merely the Name conceived by Peirce, but *the Name* identically *for the first time* the embodied soul's consciousness of its *essentially corporeal,* i.e., *artifactual, relation to God,* for the first time its awareness of its Body-of-Christ-essence, at once its incipient knowledge, in the form of the absolute readability of identity and the body, of every other existent. What occurs for the first time is the created absolute independence of the existing creature. The Resurrection of the body beginning in the body itself. The beginning in reserve, the buried talent, has now been taken away and given to those who have everything to gain and nothing to lose as an absolute identity to be absolutely invested, as the foundation of an infinite multiplication of totalities, the absolutely unreserved beginning. Not, as before now, the end of theology in Nothing, not 'theological thinking in its most proper sense', not thought representing the body, representing the 'transition from *noein* to *metanoein*', but theology ending in essence,[61] where essence *is* the existence of the body: thought the body itself: the transition from *metanoein* to the existence of thought: revolutionary μετανόησις: existence essentially transcendental, the absolute elimination of the notion of 'nowhere else to go' for thought or 'nothing else to do' but the transition to pure reflexivity. The beginning of the absolute emptying of the emptiness of thought: the perception that thought is absolutely-non-self-referentially the fullness of being, the conception that the being of God is the existence of thought. What now actually occurs for the first time is the transcendence of *metanoein*. The incipiently perfect existential objectivity.

[61] Leahy, *Novitas Mundi*, pp. 383–96.

2

TO CREATE THE ABSOLUTE EDGE[1]

> Like William James, I too believe that experience grows by its edges. By nature, the child comes into the world on edge, on the *qui vive,* with a penchant for making relations.
>
> J. J. McDermott, *Streams of Experience*[2]

> Beginning itself is becoming a surd in our consciousness, a cipher without a code, the only code ready to hand being one which reverses our given identity of beginning by apprehending it as the beginning of the end.
>
> T. J. J. Altizer, *History as Apocalypse*[3]

The thing embodied in the essentially American philosophy of Peirce, James, and Dewey—the thing which is really where it's at, but does not share the edge of where it's at—this thing is more or less where it's at: at a definite place indefinitely, or definitely at an indefinite place. This alternative is in fact the structure of the actual phenomenology of quantum mechanics in which Heisenberg's 'principle of indeterminacy' says the observer may choose to know precisely *either* the position *or* the velocity of a particle

[1] Originally presented June 2, 1988, at the International Conference on "Frontiers In American Philosophy," Texas A&M University, College Station, Texas. Originally published as "To Create The Absolute Edge," *Journal of the American Academy of Religion,* vol. 57, no. 4: 773–89. Reprinted here with permission.

[2] J. J. McDermott, *Streams of Experience: Reflections on the History and Philosophy of American Culture* (Amherst, 1986), p. 186.

[3] Altizer, *History as Apocalypse,* p. 8.

but not both at once. Dewey welcomed the discovery of this principle as "the acknowledgment, within scientific procedure itself,"[4] of pragmatism's understanding of the essential finitude of the intellectual organization of experience, an acknowledgment "of the fact that knowing is one kind of interaction which goes on within the world." The emergence of the principle of indeterminacy was for him the "final step in the dislodgment of the old spectator theory of knowledge,"[5] in effect, the recognition of the inseparability of synthetic *a priori* judgments from active methodology, and the acknowledgement that universal laws are but *instrumentalities* directed toward the "observation of a new phenomenon, toward an object actually experienced by way of perception," which is always an individual.[6] Dewey instantiates the philosophic understanding of the scientific enterprise as that which is ordered to the production of new individuals. The un-Aristotelian conflation of intellect with reason in European thought had been *formally* prepared in Aquinas' notion of the human intellect as 'defective',[7] and essentially carried through in Descartes' *Meditations.*[8] When James insisted on substituting *things* for 'ideas' in the psychological doctrine of association,[9] and, analogously, when he translated the 'meaning' of pragmatism from the realm of Peirce's transcendental habits to the world of percepts,[10] he, in an un-Aristotelian direction, restored *qua* species, as Peirce had *qua* universal, the Aristotelian irreducibility of intelligence to reason.[11] In his *Logic,* Dewey complet-

[4] Dewey, *Later Works,* vol. 4 (1984), pp. 163ff.

[5] Ibid.

[6] Ibid.

[7] *The Summa Theologica of St. Thomas Aquinas,* trans. Fathers of the English Dominican Province (New York, 1947), I,1,5 ad 2. Cf. Leahy, *Novitas Mundi,* pp. 57ff.

[8] R. Descartes, *Meditations on First Philosophy,* trans. J. Cottingham in *The Philosophical Writings of Descartes,* vol. 2 (Cambridge, 1984), pp. 16ff. Cf. Leahy, *Novitas Mundi,* pp. 76ff.

[9] Cf. above, pp. 568ff.

[10] Cf. above, pp. 552, n. 8.

[11] Cf. Leahy, *Novitas Mundi,* pp. 41ff.

[12] Dewey, *Later Works,* vol. 12 (1986), pp. 125ff.

ed this restoration *qua* individual,[12] producing in American thought a scientific Aristotelian realism without the latter's *transcendent* intuitionism: a new perception is essentially a construction of the acting mind within the actual world. There remains, however, in Dewey, for whom 'mind' is the active background abiding change,[13] an *immanent* intuitionism, the reversal of Aquinas' negative 'defect' of intellect (the fact that it "is more easily led by what is known through natural reason")[14] to the mind's positive ability to undergird 'consciousness' (here in the place of 'natural reason'). 'Mind' is to the incessantly changing foreground which is 'consciousness' as the Aristotelian active intellect was to reason, or, in Hegelian terms, as a 'higher continuity' of self is to the point of contact where self and world interact, but this 'mind', unlike its predecessors, is a thoroughly naturalized product of "prior interactions" of the self "with environment."[15] The implicit indefiniteness of origins in this account is fundamental to pragmatism. Pragmatic objectivity first had been Peirce's divine analogue of mind,[16] the operational understanding of which we do not possess, a matter of instinctual belief, although we can "catch a fragment" of its thought in science; then it was James' pluralistic universe of intelligent existents, constituting "the wider life of things" to which we are "tangent", a matter of the "proofs of religious experience,"[17] but finally it became Dewey's synthesis of Peirce and James: the ideal/instinctual and the particular/emotional realms embodied in the "mysterious totality of being," a matter of constructive imagination, the "matrix" of "ideal aspirations" and the "source" of "moral values," "the encompassing scope of existence the intellect cannot grasp," the mystery of existence in which we are "enmeshed."[18] As Dewey says, the fact that "the object of knowledge is a constructed, existentially produced,

[13] Dewey, *Later Works,* vol. 10 (1987), p. 270.

[14] Cf. *Summa Theologica,* I,1,5 ad 2.

[15] Dewey, *Later Works,* vol. 10, p. 269. Cf. also ibid., vol. 1 (1981), pp. 229ff.

[16] Cf. above, p. 556, n. 19.

[17] Cf. above, p. 569, n. 39.

[18] Cf. above, p. 576, n. 52.

object" is a "tremendous" "shock" to traditional notions, which fact, however, clearly and effectively "installs man, thinking man, within nature."[19] But not only is 'thinking man' comprehended in Dewey's pragmatic objectivity: the 'Almighty', the 'Creator', is installed analogously, by way of Dewey's synthesis of Peirce and James, in the existential mystery of the 'totality of being' as, in effect, *the imagination's symbolic analogue of the mind of the* finite '*creator*'. Where the Torah says *"In the beginning God created the heaven and the earth,"* Dewey, in *Art as Experience*,[20] takes the creation of heaven and earth to be an act of *self-expression* on the part of the Creator:

> Even the Almighty took seven days to create the heaven and the earth, and, if the record were complete, we should also learn that it was only at the end of that period that he was aware of just what He set out to do with the raw material of chaos that confronted Him. Only an emasculated subjective *metaphysics* has transformed the eloquent myth of Genesis into the conception of a Creator creating without any unformed matter to work upon.

But the textual epitome, בראשית ברא אלהים את השמים ואת הארץ, relates the beginning of the *totality* of the universe to divine creating. The 'seven days' of creating are comprised in this beginning of 'heaven and earth'. Indeed, ברא, 'to create', is spoken exclusively of divine creation[21] exactly to distinguish it from the human making which is "the prolonged interaction of something issuing from the self with objective conditions, a process in which both of them acquire a form and order they did not at first possess."[22] It is not that the Creator creates 'without any unformed matter to work upon', but, more precisely, that the Creator creating transcends the matter/form distinction, that *the distinction matter/form* is *created*. The notion of the 'mysterious totality of

[19] Dewey, *Later Works,* vol. 4 (1984), p. 168.
[20] Ibid., Vol 10 (1987), p. 71.
[21] *The New Jerusalem Bible,* p. 17, n. b.
[22] Cf. above, p. 583, n. 18.

being' supports the otherwise clearly unwarranted projection onto the creation of the universe as a whole, of a process of subjective-objective identification actually experienced only as interaction with a universe which by its very nature is partial. The 'mysterious totality of being' is the cosmic counterpart to pragmatism's essential way of having *and* not having the *individuality* which for Dewey is *the* necessity. The 'mysterious' is the soft underbelly of a thinking that essentially, if not formally, continues to take seriously the *a priori* other, and, therefore, will have, but not *finally* have, the existence of the individual. Dewey's objective subjectivity, essentially a form of pragmatism's infinite self-postponement of consciousness, confronts the divine with *chaos.* 'Chaos' is the 'raw material', the 'objective condition' confronting 'a self not consciously known', a self itself—since chaos is inexhaustible—inexhaustibly not-consciousness. But 'to create', ברא, is objectivity itself: to create is the absolute edge upon which cannot be projected any *a priori* thing, (any)thing from before the edge of 'the totality of being', (any)thing of mystery, (any)thing of that most subtle residue of European subjectivity in American thought, the *a priori* other, the matter matter *a priori,* the unformed matter not in fact experienced but *affirmed to be,* self-projectedly, present at the edge of the totality. But strike out pragmatism's projective 'nature', the *a priori* other, strike out the 'mystery' of pragmatism, strike out the dogmatic assumption of a postponed reality *finally* intelligible self-referentially, jettison at last that last remnant of Cartesian dualism, the "functional" self:[23] then the edge of totality is *necessarily* the edge of creation, the edge of existence *ex nihilo.* In the 13th century Thomas Aquinas[24] distinguished the meanings of *ex nihilo* in a way ignored for the most part until now: on the one hand, that the universe had a beginning (where *ex nihilo* means *after* nothing), and, on the other hand, that the universe was not made out of anything (where *ex nihilo* means *out of* nothing). Aquinas *denied* that when the world is said to be made from nothing this signifies the material cause. Dewey with 'chaos', like Heidegger

[23] Cf. McDermott, *Streams of Experience,* pp. 53f.

[24] *Summa Theologica,* I,45,1 ad 3.

with 'nothing',[25] is caught up in an argument absent both from Aquinas and the Torah, an argument projected indirectly or directly from the essentially unhistorical self-reception by consciousness of the fundamental historical facts of faith, Creation and Incarnation.[26] Indeed, Aquinas' own historically conditioned share in the essentially reactive self-consciousness prevented him from being able to understand the 'species' or essence *except* as "abstracted from *here* and *now*,"[27] so that he was not able to *think* what now begins essentially to be conceived *in the wake of the actual death of God*—when the essence is now understood to be *existence* 'here and now', when time is now the absolute totality of being—namely, that the Torah speaks with perfect intelligibility of the perfect beginning of the universe as "an integral part of history,"[28] in effect, speaks essentially of an absolutely historical universe.

But where *is* the point of contact with the world within the world? The meshing takes place at the edge. The mesh is the place where we tangle with the world. But we are 'on edge' 'enmeshed' in the world. What of the edge? The edge is not before the thing. The edge is not after the thing. The edge of a definite thing is an indefinite thing. But the edge of an indefinite thing is a definite thing. Definition: *the edge is the essentially narrow part of the thing* (as the *surface* is the essentially *thin* part of the thing).[29] The edge separates the greater part of the thing from not-the-thing. The edge of a thing is not to be confused with what is *at* the edge of the thing. The bank of a stream is not the edge of the flow. The edge of the stream is precisely that essential narrowness of the stream by which it separates itself from the emptiness-of-the-flow that is the land. The edge of the land interacting with the edge of the stream is the real indefiniteness of the respective edges of definite stream and definite

[25] M. Heidegger, "What is Metaphysics?" trans. A. F. C. Hull and A. Crick, in *Existence and Being* (Chicago, 1949), p. 345.

[26] Cf. Leahy, *Novitas Mundi.*

[27] *Summa Theologica,* I,46,2.

[28] *The New Jerusalem Bible,* p. 17, n. b.

[29] But cf. A. Stroll, *Surfaces* (Minneapolis, 1988), pp. 204ff.

land, reflecting the functionally irreducible distinction of perception and conception (the latter, in turn, a function of an irreducibly 'functional' self), respectively, the indefinite edges of two definite things at the point of contact supported by their infinitely indefinite separation (= almost nothing between), and, conversely, the definite edges of two indefinite things at the point of contact supported by their absolute separation (= nothing between). But now for the first time 'nothing' is no more. Now for the first time 'almost nothing' is no more. Now in history the beginning of the *conception* of resistance *identical* with the zero-resistance of the medium to the flow. What now actually exists is the elimination of the necessity of reducing the motion of the world to 'nothing' or to 'almost nothing' in order to defeat the consequences of an inertial framework. The construction of the frame of reference is the essence of motion *ex nihilo*, that is, *following* nothing, *not* 'not made *out* of anything', not made out of nothing (European consciousness), but also not made doubly redundantly of matter, not 'not made out of almost nothing', i.e., not 'not created but fashioned' (American consciousness), but the unprecedented construction of the frame of reference made out of actual existential matter: motion itself beginning to be constructed (New World consciousness). Now conceived for the first time: the reduction to 'nothing' or nothing 'almost' itself of the elimination of motion identically the perfect ordering of motion: neither the ideal definite, 'nothing', nor the real indefinite, 'almost nothing', at the *vanishing* of the points between edges, respectively, of two indefinite and two definite things, but the infinitely shared edge, the existence itself of order. The threshold of a new universe is traversed for the first time.

But the final frontier of American thought is the bifurcation: either 'almost nothing' or 'nothing': the polarity of subjective edge and edgeless subjectivity, the polarity, at once, of consciousness and mind. In McDermott, American thought experiences the death of God as the death of an *empty* belief in the Finite God, i.e., experiences the death of God as the disappearance of an Emptiness, a leaving behind of the divine symbol, Dewey's 'eloquent myth' relegated to the past. In Altizer, American thought transcends the disbelieving belief of McDermott (the mere belief in the reality of the death of God), experiences the death of God *as the reality*, experiences the *total* collapse of the ungraspable environment, the collapse of the 'mysterious totality of being' into emptiness *in the wake* of the divine disappearance, and, believing belief that it is, experiences *the unreality of the emptiness,* the presence of the totality of the body remaining after the disappearance of divinity. The American theology of the death of God takes the form of the self-separation of the edge from the thing for the first time, or, the actual elimination of the edge of the self of the thing, but not for the first time. In the form of the inversion of the abyss itself, the edge is not the abyss. Before now the realization of the death of God is the edge of not-the-abyss, the furthest possible extension of modernity, at once the impossible of pragmatism made real. The residue of the disappearance, at once *the disappearance of the possibility of reconstructing the world.* It turns out, in the final extremity of modernity, in the American death, that the *existential* embodiment of the 'principle of indeterminacy' is *existence or a beginning, but not both at once.* Altizer chooses beginning without existence, substituting for the latter precisely the unknown 'presence'. Beginning itself is 'apprehended' as the beginning of the end: not as the beginning of the other at the point of contact, but as the beginning of the other at the edge itself of our separation from self, which, because it is at a beginning that cannot be our own beginning, *inessentially* is our own beginning: the beginning in reserve, the beginning as the beginning apprehended. Altizer writes in *Total Presence*:[30]

> Genuine solitude is a voyage into the interior, but it is a voyage which culminates in a loss of our interior, a loss reversing every manifest or established center of our interior so as to make possible the advent of a wholly new but totally immediate world. The joy of solitude comes only out of a breakthrough releasing us from our own interior, a breakthrough and a joy which is

[30] T. J. J. Altizer, *Total Presence: The Language of Jesus and The Language of Today* (New York, 1980), pp. 106f. Cf. above, pp. 229–30.

> clearly present when we fully listen to music, and it is no less present in the presence of another, but only when that other has no point of contact with our own within.

'Absolute solitude' embodies the pragmatic extreme of modern scepticism[31] in the paradoxical form of an *Epicurean rationalism* which actually *experiences* a new universal humanity in the only way open to it in its perfect withdrawal as "a humanity which we can neither conceive nor define":[32] this is the oxymoronic depth of the immediate world: the essentially mute acknowledgment of a newly intelligible universality: the purely material elimination of the *a priori* other in the form of 'our own'.

In McDermott the other extreme of the modern disbelieving reason reduced to belief is embodied in a *sensible Stoicism*,[33] which, facing Altizer's 'eternal death of Jesus',[34] or absolute death, seizes upon "the journey itself" as the embodiment of the perpetual challenge of experience. Faced with the necessity of existentially embodying the 'principle of indeterminacy' McDermott chooses existence without a beginning, substituting for the latter 'transience'. He writes in *Streams of Experience*:[35]

> We are the species *Homo viator*, persons on a journey, human travelers in a cosmic abyss. Actually, in my judgment, transients is a better word than travelers, for the latter often connotes a definite goal, an end in view, or at least a return home. A transient however is one who is passing through. The meaning of a transient's journey is precisely that: the journey itself. . . . We should make our journey ever alert to our surroundings and to every perceivable sensorial nuance. Our journey is a kaleidoscope of alternating experiences, mishap, setback, celebrations, and eye-openers, all undergone on the *qui vive.*

For the radical experience of the death of God, the inversion of

[31] Cf. Leahy, *Novitas Mundi*, pp. 340ff.
[32] Altizer, *Total Presence*, pp. 106f. Cf. above, pp. 229–30.
[33] McDermott, *Streams of Experience*, p. 198.
[34] Cf. above, Section II.4.
[35] McDermott, *Streams of Experience*, p. 165.

the *rational* abyss wherein is glimpsed "a new world in the very advent of a new and universal humanity," the only possible question is "whether or not that humanity is our own."[36] The ultimate answer embodied in this reversal of 'our given identity of beginning' is that our own humanity is not our own. The alternative to this absolute advent of a new humanity, the alternative to the *interior* arrival of the death of God, the alternative to the arrival of an actually novel reality, the alternative to the *owning* separating itself from the novelty of the world in the form of 'total presence', is McDermott's absolute journeying: non-arrival absolutely prescinding arrival. While denying the world's novelty,[37] it prescinds the advent of an abysmal *reason*, inverts the '*cosmic*' abyss to the ideal of making ours what is *originally* not ours, inverts the *exterior* abyss to the ideal of making ours 'every perceivable sensorial nuance', inverts the nothingness of experience, the inevitability of our death, to our ideal "capacity" "to eat experience:" inverts the fact of death to "personal growth" as "the only sure sign that we are not yet dead,"[38] *believes* in Altizer's 'absolute solitude' but experiences it as *not yet*. For McDermott the perpetual challenge of life certifies we are *not yet* absolutely alone. In the return to an original primitivity in a new situation is embodied the attempt at the self-postponement of self-postponement, indeed, the reduplication of the very essence of pragmatism: at once *after Dewey* a return to James: precisely, a Deweyan retreat to James which identifies mind with consciousness, the aesthetic with the rhythmic "run" of things,[39] Dewey's "ordered movement of the matter of . . . experience to a fulfillment,"[40] with the *essential* forsaking of fulfillment: a post-Deweyan pragmatism reducing the meaningful to the *search* for meaning: indeed, purely theoretical *existence*: beyond Dewey the *final* existence of the individual in the form of the pre-Deweyan untheoretical existence of the *a priori* other, in the form of the purely theoretical

[36] Altizer, *Total Presence,* p. 89.
[37] McDermott, *Streams of Experience,* p. 168.
[38] Ibid., p. 166.
[39] Ibid., pp. 138ff.
[40] Dewey, *Later Works,* vol. 10 (1987), p. 334.

elimination of the *a priori* other. Thus, the final extremity of European-American consciousness, the total undergoing of the 'immediate world', is split down the middle: *either* the appetite for the satiable experience of relational, i.e., human-made, novelty, the 'passing through' on the edge of the same, the relation-making prehension of the same, the perpetually new seizing of the same old world, the perpetually *formal* fulfillment, *or* the insatiable satiety of the experience of a new humanity in the depths of the individual, the perpetual arrival of the totality, the seizing upon, the securing of sameness, taking possession of the new in the name of the same: the *material* fulfillment prescinding the matter/form distinction in the form of unreserved anticipation.

But for the first time, just in time, the edge of mind is a consciousness the edge of which is absolute. The edge is essentially perfect as never before. For the first time in history the fact is perceived that the essentially narrow part of mind is the edge of consciousness now *after* nothing. Mind is absolutely edged out of the edge after nothing. The edge is actually the totality of Identity after nothing. As never before the edge of the ocean is the edge of an absolute stream: the explosion of the universe itself, the advent of genetic engineering, the beginnings of the practicability of superconductivity, the incipient technology of thinking: there *is* no land the stream passes through, no same, neither in imitation of the stream to 'pass through', nor to occupy in refusing to imitate the stream, neither to seize upon nor to seize: the banks are identical with the stream for the first time: in the cosmological flood of the stream of consciousness both banks flow as the stream itself flows: there is neither the possibility of an *absolute* hanging back from a sameness, the same 'hanging back from', nor the possibility of "participating in the flow" which possibility is already too much of a "hanging back,"[41] a hanging back *from* the flow *in the relationship to* the flow, the same 'taking part'. Now for the first time in history the Christ is the god of the stream: thought in essence for the first time, the Christ of the stream eliminates the 'eternal death of Jesus': not the god of this or that stream but the god of the stream of exis-

[41] McDermott, *Streams of Experience*, pp. 166f.

tence itself beginning the absolute elimination of the death of God. As never before the divine flows absolutely. In this flow every notion of self is completely dissolved. The nakedness of the species is essentially eliminated. There remains neither the 'almost nothing' enveloped in the pure 'nothing', nor the pure 'nothing' enveloped in 'almost nothing'. The consciousness of man is the creating edge. The essentially narrow part of man, the narrow itself of man—the edge by which man grows is existing *ex nihilo.* What now actually occurs is the perfect envelopment of the beginning of which the Torah speaks essentially. The *totality* of being *after* nothing, the totality *not* after (either) being (or) nothing (the totality of being *not* after 'either nothing or . . . '), i.e., not *from/out of* nothing, is the absolutely existing edge, the edge every part of which is identical with the edge itself.

What now for the first time is conceived essentially is the Apocalyptic vision: there is no temple in the city,[42] nothing whatsoever is hidden, the body itself *is* clothing itself, clothes do not cover the body but reveal the essence of the body, manifest the essentially artifactual structure of the body, reveal the world to be such a novelty that man cannot stand even so much apart as to be a participant, so as to (merely) *take* part in the creation of the world, avoiding thereby the absolute responsibility of creating a new world. The literal truth of the fact that the body is the temple of the divine spirit now begins to be understood: since the divine spirit, *qua* first-time experience of the perfect edge of the other, takes up no room whatsoever, there is no end to the artifactual surface of the body in the so-called 'interior depths'. The essentially thin part of the artifactual body (surface) is its essentially narrow part (edge) infinitely after nothing. The reality of the body is the absolutely unconditioned exteriority of the world. Humanity can hide no longer in its clothes, nor in its nakedness: everything begins to be fabricated. For the first time the network is absolute. The essentially narrow part of existence *ex nihilo* exists everywhere. The edge of consciousness begins to be an essential objectivity, not the edge of mind, but the edge sharing

[42] Rv. 21:22.

the edge of the other for the first time, the edge of the mind of the other, transcending the 'functionally' self-referential polarity of the definite/indefinite vanishing of separation at the point of contact, eliminating for the first time this vanishing of separation by sharing the edge *after* nothing of the essentially different reality of the other, experiencing the other as identical with the novelty of every part of the edge. *For the first time* the transcendental is absolutely separate from the edgeless. Thought is the edge of the thing. Consciousness, at once absolute, begins to *share* the edge of the mind of another consciousness. *After* nothing the absolutely *from*-less totality: for the first time the perfect elimination of the space of time:[43] no possibility of the essential redundancy of placing time: *whether* inside an exterior space, "a totally present objectivity" "dissociated from all . . . interior identity,"[44] or outside an "interior space" which has been made "our place."[45] Time is *absolutely* the place. For the first time the *Ego*, minus the *a priori, transcendental* other, is absolute act. To create the absolute edge is to begin to operate *essentially* without reference to self: time *after* nothing is neither not 'our' now, nor 'our' place. The infinitely shared edge has no within to be eternally outwardized, and *a fortiori* no within to transform existence into a body in the absence of the divine spirit ideally interiorizing the world. The absolute exteriority of time-consciousness is the resurrection itself of the Body of the Finite God absolutely at the disposal of another.[46] For the first time the clearly perceived reality is that objectivity is to create objectivity itself. Time itself for the first time is המקום, The Place, in which we live and move and exist,[47] in which we have not 'our being', but the being of the other being at the disposal of another. The temporality of time is The Place which we, embodying, intimately comprehend as the pure 'at the disposal of another'. *Qui vive?* The person who begins to fabricate an *essentially* new world.

43. G. W. F. Hegel, *Philosophy of Nature*, vol. 1, ed., trans., M. J. Petry (London, 1970), pp. 236f.
44. Altizer, *Total Presence*, pp. 91ff.
45. McDermott, *Streams of Experience*, pp. 132ff.
46. Cf. Leahy, *Novitas Mundi*, pp. 341–96.
47. Ac. 17:28: ἐν αὐτῷ γὰρ ζῶμεν καὶ κινούμεθα καὶ ἐσμέν.

3

THE NEW BEGINNING: BEYOND THE POST-MODERN NOTHINGNESS

> . . . our time as well as the late Middle Ages may well be a time of profound transformation, and if that late medieval world gave birth to modernity, and a modernity which both to the non-sectarian Protestant and to the modern Catholic is a modernity which is Christian modernity, then our time may well be giving birth to a universal faith, and a universal faith that will both negate and transcend everything that we have known as Christianity.
>
> T. J. J. Altizer, "Hegel and the Christian God"[1]

As the human cell contains the rational essence of the totality of the organism, so the fundamental ratio of the historically developed modern consciousness is found in the *residuum* of Descartes' meditation, in the *cogito ergo sum.* Descartes arrived at the philosophical foundation of modernity after rejecting the philosophy of the schools and while recognizing that he had no calling for theology. The latter science did not beckon to him. The door open to him he declined to enter. Faced with this double of barriers he was cut off from the intellectual pursuits of the past. He resolved to think a new revolutionary science. From the philosophical tradition the inventor of the method took his subject, the universe; from the theological tradition he took his substance, the human self-consciousness of God. The essential foun-

[1] T. J. J. Altizer, "Hegel and the Christian God," *Journal of the American Academy of Religion,* vol. 59, no. 1 (1991):71. This article is the point of departure and continuing point of reference for what follows.

dation of the method of the inventor was the invention of himself. The invention of the inventor was the fact that he was a *mere* man. In the beginning the method was not to be applied to the faith and morality of the inventor. However, his faith was the substantial form of his invention of himself, while the morality of the inventor was the substrate of the invention of the universe as subject. In the course of a century and a half there burgeoned forth from this inauguration a great branch upon which all the birds of the air nested: in time it came to pass finally that in the beginning the invention of the absolute idea—as Descartes would say, the invention of a *mere* man—was itself the Absolute Idea. It came to pass that the nothingness of God was understood to have been in the beginning God's absolute idea of God. It came to pass that the beginning of the Absolute Idea was the Nothing which was God, yes, that the beginning of the absolute invention was the nothingness of the Trinity by the Trinity. Not that the Nothing that was God was merely the beginning and ending of God; the beginning of God was not merely the death of God, but the death of God 'who could not truly become incarnate', the beginning of God was really the Nothing that was the Divine Trinity. The beginning of God was the form of the human self-consciousness of God empty of the Trinity. The beginning and ending of God was the consciousness of the form of self-negation as the form of personal distinction in God. The ending of God was the form of the absolute death of the Three Persons: the absolute movement of self-consciousness as the form of the Trinity. The beginning and ending of God was, indeed, self-urging movement as the form of the divine otherness, the absolutely human self-consciousness of God, the death of an absolutely human God, the conception of the nothingness of God as God. The eternal incarnation of God in man which is the death of the Godhead, the incarnation conceived as the eternal death of God in God, is the incarnation which is the death of the Trinity. 'Thus God has revealed Himself through Christ, and fully and finally through Christ, a Christ in whom the infinite becomes finite, and it is by God's unity with the Son, "by this being-for-himself in the Other," that God is absolute Spirit'.[2]

2. Ibid., p. 77.

The abyss of God in God, the Godhead as Nothing, Hegel's centering of 'thinking as such' upon the Incarnation, is in effect the introduction by Hegel of the form of Augustinian self-consciousness into the Godhead itself. But, then, it is not Christian belief but the disbelief of the Christian mind that is in fact negated and transcended. The thinking which 'centers' on the 'uniquely Christian God' is the thinking of disbelief, indeed, very thinking identically the disbelief of thinking. Modernity is the essentially unhistorical historical thinking which essentially itself restricts Christianity not, it is true, to 'a particular and historically individual faith and movement' but rather restricts it to an historically individual and reactionary faith in the movement of history. It is this thinking identically the disbelief of thinking which is *as thinking* transcended in the thinking now actually occurring for the first time in history, together with the thinking of belief (the unselfconscious transcendental form of natural reason in Aquinas, not substantially Aristotelian except in its unselfconscious formality), while *as disbelief* the thinking identically the disbelief of thinking is transcended in the very thought-form of the existence of a universal faith. Before now, in Hegel, the beginning of God is not essentially historical, the absolute cannot actually die. The actual death of God is not actually possible: the non-being of the Trinity is the being of God, i.e., the non-being of the Divine Trinity is the being of the Absolute Trinity, precisely as the non-being of the finite is the being of the infinite. The death of the Three Persons is an infinite actuality infinitely itself a finite nothingness, but never a once and for all occurrence, never the uniquely finite act of the Godhead of God, never the form of the Godhead absolutely. The historical limitation of European self-consciousness precludes in fact the realization of its own demand that God actually die. The realization or complete actuality of the death of God occurs for the first time in history in American consciousness, concretely and essentially in Altizer's own theology, historically and essentially founded, as that theology is, in the infinite postponement of self-consciousness which very essence of American thought is the actual condition for the realization of the final fall of God. The perfect postponement of absolute self-consciousness in

American consciousness for the first time makes possible the actual death of the Godhead. In American theology the death of God is for the first time the form of the Godhead of God: for the first time the death of God is the actual death of the Godhead not merely the eternal death of an absolute self-consciousness. This is the complete realization of the death of God as the consciousness of the unique nothingness of death in time for the first time: pure Nothing for the first time. The death of the 'uniquely Christian God' which is not perfectly begun in European consciousness is in American consciousness the absolute beginning. This is the beginning of the selfless self. This is for the first time absolute death. American consciousness transcends and negates the imperfect realization of the death of God by going resolutely back beyond the trinitarian structure of the divine absolute self-consciousness, by infinitely back-tracking into the primal nothingness of the Godhead, by infinitely leaving behind the *a priori* distinction of for-itself from in-itself so that finally the for-itself is absolutely in-itself the absolute totality of existence. Here and now finally the transcendence of *Dasein* to Nothing is Nothing, Heidegger is brought to nought, Nothingness itself is Nothing, for the first time in history the non-being of the finite nothingness is the *groundless* infinite. This is the Nothing as the beginning of the groundless non-being of the unique God. This is the beginning of the real death of the Godhead: for the first time God back-tracking Nothing. This Nothing is the beginning at once the ending which is the ending of the inwardness of beginning itself, and this ending of the inwardness of beginning itself is the absolute and final end of every ground of past theology, the very embodiment of the now complete fluidity of the absolute ground of Christian theology. As never before this is the complete dissolution of the Godhead of God.

Before now, in medieval consciousness, *ipsum esse*, the Godhead of God, experienced death in the person of the Word made flesh. This was the experience of the abyss of the Godhead conceived in essence. In accord with the fact that 'God's nature eternally remains impassible', being itself experienced the abyss absolutely in the form of an instrumental humanity: the abyss of the Godhead was conceived in the form of *a man*. God was made nothing in the form of the Trinity. This—despite the eternalizing form of the Kierkegaardian 'leap out of . . . Christian history', which leap truly betrays the essentially unhistorical foundation of the formally historical thinking of Hegel, since, indeed, Kierkegaard is 'at bottom an Hegelian thinker'—this was the beginning of the transcendental form of the death of God. The fact is that there is no logical or historical possibility of the form of modern historical thinking apart from the fact that in medieval consciousness God was made nothing in the form of the Trinity, that is, apart from the fact that God was made nothing in the very form in effect of an infinite human reason, and made nothing in the form of an instrument of divinity. It was this transcendental form of the death of God which was absolutely the essence of the modern consciousness of God. In modern consciousness *ipsum esse* experienced death in the person of the Word made flesh in essence, i.e., in the person of God made man in essence. This was the experience of the abyss of the Godhead conceived absolutely: being itself experiencing the abyss absolutely in the form of God, i.e., in the form of the essentially transcendental man: the abyss of the Godhead conceived in the form of the God-man. God was made nothing in essence, i.e., in the form of God or in the form of man. If medieval consciousness of God made God nothing in the form of an infinite human reason, the modern consciousness of God made God absolutely nothing in the form of Absolute Reason. If, for Aquinas, Good Friday was the death-day of *divinitatis instrumentum*,[3] the death-day of the instrument of the Godhead, the death-day of the humanity of Christ, then, for Hegel, Good Friday was the death-day of *divinitatis principalis*, the death-day of the very principal of the Godhead, the death-day of the divinity of the man Christ. This was the death of God for the first time. This was the issue of history at once for the first time essentially the denial of history, the very essence of revolutionary protestant consciousness. This was the abyss. This was the beginning of the abyss. This was the beginning not the beginning, but not

[3] *Summa Theologica*, III,48,6.

yet the beginning of Nothing. Before now, in the form of American consciousness, *ipsum esse* experienced death in the person of the Word made flesh absolutely, i.e., in the person of God made man absolutely. This was the experience of the abyss of the Godhead conceived as absolute occurrence: being itself itself experiencing the abyss in the very form of the Godhead, i.e., in the form of totality. Not merely the abyss of being itself, not merely the abyss of the Trinity, not merely the self-consciousness of the eternal movement of God, but the very abyss of the Godhead absolutely in the form of an instrumental humanity. God is made nothing absolutely, i.e., in the form of the Godhead. For Altizer, Good Friday is the death-day of *divinitatis instrumentum et principalis.* This is the second death of God. This is the beginning of the eternal death of God. This is the first day of the eternal damnation of the Godhead. Good Friday is the first day of the universal kingdom of the Prince of Death. This is the beginning of the Christ, the God-man, the Godhead, as Satan. This is the abyss of the Godhead of Christ, the beginning of the death of the Godhead, the beginning of the Godhead of Satan. This is the beginning of the pure Nothing. This was and is in American consciousness *ipsum esse* for the first time purely Nothing, Being Itself for the first time the Nothingless Nothing, the beginning of the pure fullness of being nothing, the absolute and total abyss of purely beginning and ending. The complete realization in American consciousness of the death of the 'uniquely Christian God' is the ending at once the beginning of the eternity of death. This is the 'philosophical conceptualization of the Crucifixion' which does not really occur in Hegel's thought, but the full actuality of which is at once the crucifixion of philosophical conceptualization uniquely possible in America, at once the beginning which is itself the complete dissolution of the infinite God.

The philosophy which ends in Europe, which ends violently there, is, in America, crucified. Before now, in the form of American consciousness, and for the first time in history absolutely and actually, Satan is triumphant in the form of a universal consciousness. Not merely 'very close to the deep "offense" of Hegel's system', as are the forms of European consciousness, literary, artistic, and philosophical, we are here in consciousness actually in the midst of the full realization of the "offense" of the modern system for the first time. Thus in America there is the pure beginning of a universal nothingness in the very depths of consciousness. For the first time there is absolutely nothing theoretical about this actual experience. For the first time there is absolutely nothing provisional about this experience. For the first time, in the very form of American consciousness, there is nothing but this experience. This is the experience of the absolute silence of the beginning, at once the experience of the actual quiescence of nothing. This Nothing is the pure beginning of a new world: the absolute first nothing, God the Creator nothing. Beyond the abyss of beginning which is the essence of modernity, this post-modern consciousness is the abyss of the first: not the beginning of the abyss, but the first abyss: the realization of the beginning of the abyss: not merely the beginning not the beginning, but the first not the first: *the beginning not the beginning absolutely*, the beginning of the beginning of existence, the beginning of Nothing. This abysmal quality is the Nothing confused with the abyss of being itself. This beginning of Nothing is the pure form and substance of the very limit of the modern imagination in the form of an impure nothing. This pure beginning of Nothing not absolute is the form of the absolutely unconditioned porosity of consciousness itself, the absolute limit which is the absolute porosity of mind. This is the beginning of nothing in the form of the absolute existence of the birth canal: the beginning itself the end of nothing in the form of the absolute chute. This beginning is the end of Nothing in the form of the infinitely minute opening, in the form of an infinity of minute orifices, the infinite end of Nothing in the form of the absolutely unconditioned pure possibility of imagination. This is the form of Nothing in the form of the infinite expanse of consciousness itself as the Sea of Reeds: nothing beginning in the form of a universal consciousness essentially the embodiment of modernity's sea of infinite possibility. Through the infinite porosity of this limit of the transcendental imagination, in this afterlife and eternal death of God, absolutely nothing *essentially* new is able to begin to actually enter. For the first time God is really and actually dead. The novelty that is able to begin to enter the gate of this dead body of the living God is the essential novelty of death, nothingness. The Godhead itself actually dead for the first time in the form of an instrumental humanity transcendentally transcending the distinction being-in-itself/being-for-itself, identifying its own nothingness as the being-for-itself of another. If the original necessity of realizing God as the Hegelian being-in-itself was the necessity of the death of God, the formal necessity of the resurrection and ascension of God in the form of the absolutely unconditioned totality in the freedom of its own creation, then in American consciousness for the first time the absolute and entire end of this original necessity is the necessity of the death of Christ, the necessity of the actual death of the actual embodiment of the divine-human instrumentality, the necessity of the resurrection and ascension of God in the form of the pure freedom of the actual totality to create its own other, the Godhead of God in the form of total presence, in the form of the infinitely porous totality of the present, but completely and essentially the beginning of Nothing. Thus the ascension and resurrection of God is the absolute fall which is the abyss of existence for the first time: existence for the first time not existence for the first time. Indeed, this infinite channeling of the surface of the active imagination is in fact concretely and actually modernity's last chance—taken absolutely—to think nothing in essence in face of the reality of the beginning of a new universe. This infinite furrowing of the transcendental plane is the infinite postponement of the end of self-consciousness. The beginning of life itself death. The 'atonement of God with God' realized fully and actually for the first time in the form of the death of Christ—this death in American consciousness of the divine-human instrumentality in the form of the very Body of God—is, faced with the beginning of a new form of thinking and a new universe, the swerve and swivel into Nothing of consciousness itself. It is its very own form—the death of the Godhead of God in the form of the absolutely protestant conception of the *novum*—which is the impossibility of beginning the absolute imitation of the death of the 'uniquely Christian God': it is its very own form which is the impossibility of the *imitation* of the death of the divinity. It is its very own shape which is the impossibility of the beginning of a *pure* and *absolute* groundlessness of existence, the fact that it is the thought-form of creation finally the activity of the transcendently inactive Godhead of God, the 'unmediated immediacy' of the absolutely lasting creative act of a transcendently non-existent Christ. This is the pure Nothing or impure nothingness or being and nothing first and last: the first being finally nothing: the first nothing finally being. This is the impure shape of the beginning as the absolute act of nothing, but, then, the abysmal nothing of the beginning of nothing, the nothing of the beginning of nothing not nothing: the abysmal nothing of the beginning of nothing as act: the act of beginning not the beginning as act, the beginning of God not the beginning of God. Thus the 'profound ambiguity at the very center of the Hegelian system', put in the form of the question 'whether or not Hegel's absolute Spirit truly is the Christian God', 'whether or not Hegel is a Christian', 'whether or not Christianity is and only can be a pre-modern form of faith', this systemic ambiguity in the protestant revolution in thought which is the very form of the consciousness of modernity, is *realized as final* in the form of, is the *very form of finality* in, the American theology of the death of Christ. In its very own shape, then, this theology of absolute death is in fact the realization that Hegel *is* and *is not* a Christian, that Hegel's absolute Spirit *is* and *is not* 'uniquely Christian', and, further, that Christianity *is* and *is not* unique, *is* and *is not* founded on the 'death or self-negation of God'. If the form of that realization of God's own absolute otherness *is* the form of Christianity itself, then, for the first time the transforming of Christianity into, and into 'even' the realization of, that 'universality of faith which is the manifest center of [Hegel's] system' is *possible*. It is really Hegel who effectively asks 'if Christianity can transcend the end of Christendom, and even more decisively be itself precisely through that ending, an ending which would then be the ending of a deep negation of Christianity within its own original body or world'. But it is Altizer who actually asks not merely whether such is *possible*, but whether such is *possibly occurring*. For Altizer, the answer to the question posed by Hegel's system is possibly beginning, that is, the beginning of the end of the ambiguity is possible. But, then, this beginning now actually occurring is not actually the end of ambiguity. The beginning of a universal faith is now still actually thinkable as non-existent, that is, thinkable as but possible. Here we are upon the supreme point of the matter: the beginning of a universal faith in the form of the absolutely and essentially religious thought of modernity, it turns out, is not actually thinkable at the very extremity of modernity, or is thinkable as but actually possible. Whereas in Hegel the religious beginning of the form of thought as faith was not thought in essence, in Altizer the beginning of a universal faith in the form of an essentially religious thought is but the possibility of a new faith. This beginning of the absolute universality of faith thinkable as possibly non-existent is the actual failure of the transcendental imagination—in the form of the absolute lure—to exist religiously, the beginning of a universal faith conceived as actually possible, at once the transcendental reduction to Nothing of Dewey's conception of the generically religious.[4] This failure of the transcendental imagination absolutely grounded in the radical intentionality of modernity is at once the inversion and reversal of the beginning of a universal faith, for the first time the loss of the Godhead's own absolute self-consciousness, the beginning of the loss of God's own subjectivity in the very form of the self-consciousness of the Godhead of God in man.

But Christianity transcends 'the end of Christendom' in the beginning of a universal faith now actually occurring. The question, then, 'whether or not Christianity is and only can be a pre-modern form of faith' is answered: Christianity *is* a pre-modern form of faith which need not only be so *and* Christianity *is not* a pre-modern form of faith which only can be so. The death of God *is* and *is not* the foundation of Christianity itself, that is, it is not *qua* history, and it is *qua* essentially historical form. The essentially historical form of the death of God which is the foundation of Christianity itself is the necessity to create the elimination of history, that is, the essentially new foundation of Chris-

[4] Dewey, *Later Works,* vol. 9, pp. 1–58.

tianity itself is the necessity to create the elimination of the actual death of the Godhead of God. The new Christianity is essentially the conception of the necessity to create the absolute elimination of nothingness. For the first time in history the very form of Christianity is the necessity of the elimination of nothing. The essentially historical necessity of the new actuality is the elimination of the beginning of Nothing, i.e., the necessity is the beginning of the *existence* of *ipsum esse*: the beginning of the non-existence of the transcendent God but *not* in the form of the nothingness of the finite consciousness as the realization of the infinite groundlessness of the transcendental consciousness, *not* in the thought-form of the 'uniquely modern realization of the death of God', *not* in the form of 'consciousness fully and finally become metaphysically and religiously groundless'. The necessity now actually realized in the form of thought in essence is the beginning of the elimination of the nothingness of the Godhead of God which is the foundation of the essentially protestant form of the transcendence of the end of Christendom, the beginning of the elimination of the necessity of saying yes through saying absolutely nothing. This is the beginning of saying absolutely yes through saying yes absolutely to nothing. This is the beginning of the absolute transcendence of thought in essence, the immediately mediated immediacy of the realization of the uniquely modern intentionality. This realization is precisely the transcendent realization of the fact that for the first time thought is essentially the transcendental imagination. What now actually occurs is the new existence of the transcendent God in the form of the beginning of the realization of the infinite ground of the transcendental consciousness of existence: the resurrection of God after the death of God: after death the resurrection of God in the form of existence itself the very body of the resurrection. The crucifixion of the God of philosophy and religion in the form of the modern abyss, in the form of the modern-not-the-modern, in the form of the post-modern 'our time may well be giving birth to a universal faith, and a universal faith that will both negate and transcend everything that we have known as Christianity', is the beginning in the form of the death and resurrection of God, at once the beginning in the form of the death and resurrection of Christianity itself. This is the beginning as the absolute loss of philosophy and religion, indeed, of Christianity itself. But it is not what now actually exists, the beginning of existence. It is not what is now thought, the beginning of *the absolute yes-saying of a universal faith.* It is not what now actually occurs, viz., the resurrection after death of a New God, so that 'what is sown a body of flesh is raised a spiritual body': the God God after His death, the transcendent God after His death, the transformation of God as God, conceived in essence, the form of thought the very form of the resurrection, the very form of thought an essentially new thought now actually existing.

The beginning of a universal faith is the faith which *is* the novelty of God the novelty of the Godhead itself. The beginning of the actuality of a new faith leaves behind not only the essential religiosity of the thought of modernity, but also, in the forsaking of that religiosity, faith for the first time leaves behind the necessity of 'negating and transcending' either the form of the historical thinking essentially bound to the past, the philosophical form of Christianity itself, or the historical form of Christendom. Indeed, the necessity of the faith which is the very form of the beginning of an *essentially* new existence is the necessity of leaving behind the necessity of negating and transcending the form of 'negating and transcending' the past. For the first time the actuality of a new faith is able to think the novelty of God *absolutely* without appropriation, i.e., without thinking its own thought or the thought of another. Faith thinks in essence the New Christ. For the first time faith thinks in essence revelation itself.[5] This is the beginning of the nothingness of God conceived essentially without nay-saying. The Christ which for the first time was, but no longer is, Satan is today for the first time the New Christ. The Godhead which for the first time was, but no longer is, the life which was death is today for the first time the New Life of the Godhead finally and absolutely life. The life which was, but no longer is, the Godhead of God *evolution* 'beginning and ending at once', Nothing beginning, is today for the first time in history the life which is the *resurrection* of God

[5] Leahy, *Novitas Mundi*, pp. 328–43, and pp. 387ff.

the beginning even the end, the *beginning* of the divine life which knows not death: the beginning of the life of the Godhead of God which is ignorant of death: the beginning of the Very Life which is ignorance of the absolute death: the beginning of the life of God which is ignorance of the Nothing: the beginning of the life of the Godhead of God absolutely ignoring the abyss. Now for the first time in history those standing in the darkness hear the words of the bridegroom: "I do not know you."[6] The very Knowledge of the Godhead of God perfectly ignorant—not before now—of those who do not know the new form of the universe, the Word perfectly ignorant of those who do not think *essentially* in the form of faith. This is the absolute finality of the resurrection of the Godhead which now actually occurs for the first time. This is the beginning of the Resurrection which is the form of the End of the World.

The Godhead whose beginning was, but no longer is, death now begins to live a new life as existence itself absolutely unconditionally life itself: for the first time the Word of God absolutely displaces the ignorance of God. What now actually occurs as never before leaves behind even the beginning which was the final ending of the mystery, and leaves behind, as well, even the beginning which was finally the mystic recollection upon itself of the final ending of the Godhead of God. What now actually occurs as never before is the absolute exteriority of the Godhead, the absolute act ending the beyond of the Godhead, Christ Absolute.[7] If modern European consciousness in the face of the creation of the world is the absolute self-envelopment of human rationality in the form of the question formulated by Leibniz, "why is there being rather than nothing," modernity in America answered the question by 'flatly denying' the Parmenidean premise of the question, that "being is, and not-being is nothing," and by declaring its contradictory, in the words of Peirce, "that being is a matter of more or less, so as to merge insensibly into nothing."[8] In the very midst of the absolute subjectivity of

[6] Mt. 25:12.

[7] Leahy, *Novitas Mundi*, pp. 393ff.

[8] Peirce, *Collected Papers*, 7.569.

modern thought there was the beginning in American consciousness of a new conception of objectivity, the absolute inversion of perception wherein the persistent existence of anything in face of the nothingness of existence is the measure of its reality, a form of creation wherein objectivity is the achievement of the objective. This was the form of the infinite delay of the subjective consciousness, the opening up for the first time of a space for objectivity in the very midst of the absolute subjectivity of modernity. For the first time there was conceived in essence a perfectly spacious subjectivity, a subjectivity extraordinarily slow or loose. This was, in effect, the beginning of a subjectivity infinitely delaying the day of judgment. This American consciousness was infinitely the beginning: the verge of creation in the midst of itself, the consciousness of nothing perfectly slack, nothing loosed, the big easy nothing. It had been prepared for in the philosophical theology of Jonathan Edwards for whom God was 'being in general', in effect 'the universal system of existence'.[9] In Edwards the created universe was as nothing compared to being in general which 'has infinitely the greatest share of existence'.[10] For Thomas Aquinas' exclusive *ipsum esse*, the magnitude of which *being itself* was not at all to be understood dimensively, Edwards substituted the inclusive *being in general*, understood by him to be intelligible in effect in terms of *dimensive degree of existence*. But for Edwards there was 'no such thing as absolute nothing',[11] that is, in effect, there was no such thing as the absolute contradiction which necessitates the beginning of being in general. Edwards could not conceive of a mind which could conceive of 'a state of absolute nothing' which 'is a state of absolute contradiction'. But Peirce essentially understood that 'no contradiction can be involved in mere non-existence',[12] and therefore that it was conceivable that there might be a mind, albeit unlike ours, capable of thinking nothing. In the positions of the puritan and the pragmatist there is the essential agree-

[9] J. Edwards, *The Nature of True Virtue* (Ann Arbor, 1960), p. 5.

[10] Ibid., p. 14.

[11] J. Edwards, *Scientific and Philosophical Writings* (New Haven, 1980), pp. 206f.

[12] Peirce, *Collected Papers*, 6.490.

ment of American consciousness, viz., that being is not the identity of consciousness and mind, and the apparent contradiction in their positions is resolved by noting that for Edwards being is consciousness, and therefore the mind of God is in effect consciousness in general, while for Peirce, who distinguishes 'psychic life' and 'consciousness', it is possible to say 'God probably has no consciousness'.[13] Consciousness in general cannot conceive of absolute nothing, and, therefore, as being in general, cannot be conceived as beginning. But a mental life in an other-than-conscious state, Peirce's 'pure mind', might conceive a 'state of nility', and, therefore, might be conceived as beginning. The synechistic tychism of the pragmaticist Peirce is the synthesis which in effect identifies the utter generality of the divine being in American consciousness (Edwards) with the beginning of the abyss in European consciousness (Hegel). In Peirce, in effect, being in general begins as an absolutely necessary result of 'a state of utter nothingness'.[14] This was essentially and historically the consciousness for the first time of the infinite generality of everything including nothingness itself, at once the emergence of objectivity in the consciousness of being within the final ending of the beyond of the Godhead. This was for the first time the emergence in consciousness of the objective subjectivity of the absolute purity of the divine mind achieving reality. Edwards essentially understands the objective of the divine being in creating the world to be His own glory, the objective righteousness of which subjective end is logically demonstrable on the ground that divine self-love is not private self-love, i.e., that the divine self is a public self.[15] This was the objectively demonstrable righteousness of the divine self-love in the very midst of that divine subjectivity which infinitely exhausts the consciousness in which creatures participate as parts whose own being is as nothing. Analogously, Peirce essentially understands the objective of subjectivity to be the achievement of the ideal objectivity of the universal mind. In James, for whom the begin-

[13] Ibid., 6.489.
[14] Ibid., 6.490.
[15] J. Edwards, *Ethical Writings* (New Haven, 1989), pp. 422ff., 445ff.

ning was the beginning of a particular being, in effect the beginning of the radical particularity of the universal system of existence, the objective of subjectivity was the achievement of the actual objectivity of the particular mind. In Dewey, for whom the beginning was the beginning of a community of being, in effect the imaginative beginning of the totality of the universal system of existence, the objective of subjectivity was the achievement of the actual objectivity of the ideal unification of the mind of the community. For Dewey, then, the objective of subjectivity was the achievement of the divine order, that is, it was religiously qualified achieving. In Edwards there was consciousness or being in general without beginning and without absolute nothing. In Peirce there was the state of nility the beginning of mind in general, or, nothing in particular the beginning of being in general. In James there was the nothingness of the absolute the beginning of particular being, or, nothing in particular the beginning of the particular. In Dewey there was the particular nothingness the beginning of mind in general, or, nothing in particular the beginning of the ideal state of the universe, the actual beginning of the universe the ideal beginning of the universe. In Altizer, there is the transcendence of the three universes, i.e., the transcendence of the ideal universe or mind (Peirce) in the form in which it is at once identical with the actual universe or mind (James) identical with the unification of the ideal and actual universes or minds which is the universe or mind of a common consciousness (Dewey). There is the transcendence, in Altizer, of the three universes in the form of the totality of concrete mind the absolute consciousness in general of a particular community in the form of the beginning of nothing, conceived in essence, at once the ideal transcendence of the Trinity in the form of the non-sectarian protestant consciousness of beginning in general. This, then, is identically the non-sectarian protestant consciousness of the beginning of being in general, at once, therefore, the historically sectarian non-sectarian consciousness of the beginning of God. In this beginning of Nothing lurks the failed transcendence of transcendence, the transcendent form of the failed transcendence, in the form of the intrinsic failure of the transcendental imagination of a 'universal faith', in the form of the failure to imagine the new 'universal faith', i.e., in the form of the failure to *imagine* the reality. The intrinsic iconoclasm of the revolutionary protestant consciousness is for the first time absolutely and evidently intrinsically inadequate, i.e., it needs must imagine the requirement to imagine a new universal faith, and imagine itself inadequate, when faced with the requirement to imagine the reality. In the final analysis the beginning of Nothing is the form in American consciousness of the achievement of the pure objectivity of subjectivity. In this form American consciousness is the achievement of the beginning of objectivity in the form of the actually existing emptiness of objectivity/objectivity of emptiness: for the first time in the very midst of the divine subjectivity the divine self-love which exhausts the consciousness in which creatures participate as parts whose own being is as nothing is objectively demonstrable as the very form of self-righteousness: the self-embodiment of God in the form of the Satanic identity of Christ. Instead of imagining the beginning, there is this infinite backtracking into the nothingness of the Godhead: Nothing beginning, the beginning of being in general without nothing, *the beginning of nothing without being in general.* This for the first time is to actually think James' 'logically opaque' 'bottom of Being',[16] that is, to actually think the 'bottom of Being' in its very opaqueness: for the first time this is the actual absolutely opaque end of history, the absolutely opaque beginning of the end of the world.

But to imagine the reality of a new universal faith for the first time is to imagine the transcendental imagination, to imagine imagination itself, to imagine the transcendence of the transcendental. If there lurks in the beginning of nothing the failed transcendence of transcendence, the body of the dead God, then the actual achievement of the beginning of a universal faith is the absolute elimination of the former form of the transcendental imagination with which this body is identified, the absolute elimination of the opaqueness of the opaque bottom of Being. The perfect elimination of this former form of

[16] W. James, *Essays in Philosophy* (Cambridge, 1978), p. 59.

the transcendental imagination which is the Nothing, at once the form of its extreme limit, at once the transcendental limit of the transcendental, is the pure First which as such and for the first time in history is absolutely not absolutely inconceivable. This is *the* First which is the absolute end of existence in existence, the absolute end of the existence of the absolute. What now actually occurs is not the Absolute First which is God beginning the universe identically the Absolute Last which is God finally completing universe, but the First the Absolute Last, the First, neither relative not absolute nor absolute not relative, but the very First the Absolute Second, the First absolutely existing, absolutely relative. For the first time in history essentially without self-consciousness there is the consciousness which is the absolute unification of the ideal universe and the actual universe. Consciousness is for the first time the Absolute Third, no longer the Third completely relative to, merely the relating of, Absolute First and Absolute Last. What now actually occurs is the Absolute Midst of Consciousness for the first time. For the first time in history the transcendental imagination actually transcends the transcendental limit which was, but no longer is, the lack the very verge of creation in the midst of self-consciousness. The space for objectivity which is the very midst of American consciousness hitherto and essentially opened up within itself in the form of the postponement of the infinite self-consciousness, and which surfaces as such in the theology of Altizer as the form of the absolute opaqueness, is now for the first time in history absolutely displaced by the very midst of the Absolute Third—by the very midst of the Absolute Middle—which is the absolute displacement of that self-consciousness which was, but no longer is, the perimeter. This is the objectivity of the absolutely pure First identically the Absolute Third absolutely displacing self-consciousness. This absolutely pure First is relatively and absolutely a new thought. This essentially and historically thinkable First is the objective placing of the divine consciousness as the very midst of itself. This is the beginning itself in the very midst of being. This First is the Universal Joy in the depths of being surfacing. This is the Conscious Joy of the Absolute First, this is the Very First. This Very First, surfacing the very midst of the Idea, speaks: "Look! I make all things new!"[17] This First is the immediate existential reality of the new world we now actually *live.* For the first time in history pure First is absolutely conceivable as existence. For the first time the very substance of divinity is actually, at once ideally, the essential actuality of existence as a new universe. This *pure* Absolute First, *qua* transcendence of the Absolute First identically Absolute End, is the absolute beginning. The 'unmediated immediacy' which is the First *is* the beginning of the 'absolute mediation' which 'is absolute immediacy'. Before now God was actually dead. Now after death, absolutely eliminating the former-form, the God of the Resurrection lives. The Very Shape of Very First: the 'history of God' 'finally the actuality of God' 'with an absolute beginning and an absolute ending', the 'unmediated immediacy' actually identical with the 'mediated immediacy': but not the solitude of Christianity, rather the catholicological being of Christ: for the first time the immediate identical with the Idea. This is the beginning of the Absolute Idea of Another Absolute, the Absolute Third.

The necessity of this *pure* Absolute First is the Trinity, i.e., the transcendence of the synthetic unity of the Absolute First and Absolute Last of modernity. The Third Absolute is the real, i.e., actual and ideal, unification of Absolute First and Absolute Last. The Third Absolute, the Person of the Spirit as Absolute Existent, is the absolute middle the actuality of the beginning of the absolute mediation of existence. The new universe actually existing is the first beginning of the mediation of existence, at once the absolute beginning of the mediated First. The very first necessity of the Resurrection of the Godhead now actually occurring in the form of the Trinity is the perpetual existence of the instrumental humanity of Christ. For the first time the other 'through which beginning occurs' is conceived in essence as the absolute instrument. For the first time the other absolutely exists as the instrument of divinity. The necessity of the First now actually existing is the Godhead of God the instrument of divinity, that is, the Godhead of God *principalis et instrumentum*

[17] Rv. 21:5.

absolutely: after the death of the Godhead the Resurrection of the Godhead of God *principalis et instrumentum* actual flesh. This is the 'identity of God' for the first time, the Godhead of God identifying itself as the beginning of God in the form of the Resurrection of the Trinity, in the form of the Unity actually and ideally transcending the Difference within the identity of God. This is the beginning of the Trinity as the simple identity of the Godhead as nothing. For the first time the Triune Identity is the actual and ideal simplicity of the nothing. This is the first beginning of the ideal nothing, the absolutely pure First. The 'universal faith' now really and actually here is the first completely actual beginning of divinity in the very form of nothing. The other of this beginning of the absolute simplicity of God conceived in essence is the absolute exteriority of existence. This is the absolute elimination of the existence of the beginning of nothing which is the form of the former existence of the failed transcendence. This is the existence of the beginning of nothing identically nothing. The simplicity of this beginning of nothing is the elimination of absolute death, the elimination of the form of the death of a *former God*. The very simplicity of God, this resurrection of the Godhead of God, is the beginning of the complete elimination of the *former-form* of the realization of the death of God. This for the first time is the now the very form of nothing. The beginning of the absolutely divine simplicity of existence is the elimination of the former abyss of the transcendental imagination, the absolute elimination of the *former*-identity of nothing as the immediacy of existence, as the abyss of the elimination of the former ideal form of the beginning of existence, i.e., as the beginning of nothing the beginning of existence: the actual and ideal elimination of that beginning of existence which is the beginning as but the threshold of existence. Actually and ideally the now is for the first time in history the elimination of the essentially redundant former-form. The beginning of the *simplicity* of nothing is the *simplicity* of existence: this for the first time is the absolute elimination of the former disjunction of being and nothing: the absolute now the disjunction of being and nothing: the beginning of the finite, the finite beginning, the beginning of absolute finite existence. This is the beginning of the *novitas mundi* conceived in essence. This is the first universal now, the beginning which is the ending of the ending of the eternal now in the form of the *absolutely* pure nothing. The absolute simplicity of this beginning of God is the fact that there is now conceived in essence for the first time actually no otherness of existence and nothing. If there is no otherness of the beginning of existence and nothing, there is for the first time the finite existence of otherness, indeed, the finite otherness of God, and the beginning is finite, and the beginning is the end of the finite otherness which is identically nothing. The nothingness of this beginning is the absolute discontinuity of the continuum of being and nothing. This is the beginning of infinite otherness, for the first time the actual and ideal discontinuity of the continuum. If existence is no longer the contrary of nothing, and if existence is no longer the contradictory of nothing, and if, further, existence is no longer the threshold of nothing, then the identity of existence and nothing is actually and ideally unconditional difference for the first time. The difference beginning to exist between being and nothing is not the pairedness of being and nothing but the boundary is what being and nothing have, but do not share, or share, but do not have, i.e., the absolute edge.[18] If Altizer is able to think "now death is otherness itself,"[19] what is now thinkable is otherness itself after the death of God: otherness itself after absolute pure nothing: a new otherness itself after the nothingness of otherness itself: the beginning of otherness itself very life. Actually and ideally the unconditional difference of existence and nothing, and therefore of life and death, is "for the first time death is not otherness itself." The finite beginning is the perfect discontinuity of the abyss and existence, the perfectly finite continuity. The finite beginning is *ex abysso*. The finite beginning is the beginning itself, the perfect beginning. This for the first time is the absolute displacing of the intrinsicality of absolutely everything: the Very First displacing the intrinsicality of everything, the Very

[18] Cf. above, Section V.2.

[19] T. J. J. Altizer, *Genesis and Apocalypse: A Theological Voyage Toward Authentic Christianity* (Louisville, 1990), p. 34.

First absolutely displacing intrinsicality. This is the beginning of the absolute exteriority of every existing body, the beginning of the body of the resurrection. For the first time the instrument is absolutely the end. Mind begins in every now. Universe begins in every now. Christ begins in every now. The Very First is the New Christ, the Christ of the Resurrection. The universe now beginning is the mind of Christ. The beginning of mediation is the mind of the Resurrected Christ now not knowing nothing, thinking not nothing. The beginning of the mediation of existence is the mind *ex abysso* conceiving *ipsum esse.* The pure First, then, bodies forth the absolute exclusivity of being itself, the very being of the 'uniquely Christian' Godhead, the very unicity of the divine being. This birthing body of the resurrection the very unicity of the instrument of divinity is the absolute imperative of the beginning mediated: "Friend, do the will of the Father. Friend, create the world." Before now the self-consciousness of the nothingness of the creation displaced the very ground of mind in the form of the end of history. The beginning of the mediation of existence now occurring is the absolute immediacy of the Word displacing this groundlessness of the mind. For the first time the Very Godhead speaks the Word intimately to everyone living the universe in the form of the absolute exteriority of existence. The experience of this First is the essential elimination of the consciousness of the *a priori* other, the essential elimination of the not-experienced other, the absolute elimination of the form of self-experience in the form of the elimination of the nothingness of the infinite postponement of self-consciousness.

The First thought in essence is the absolute elimination of what is essentially the preconception of the universal faith in the form of its conceivable non-existence. The American theology of the death of God is effectively Peirce's 'insensible merging' of being and nothing in the form of the beginning of a universal faith. The realization of the death of God which is the selfless self-consciousness of the Godhead, the infinite backtracking of the infinite nothingness of the Godhead, is not *seeing* the beginning of the difference between being and nothing, is not seeing the beginning of nothing. But actually and ideally to *see* the beginning of the difference between being and nothing is the universal faith now actually existing in the form of the very essence of thought. To *see* the beginning of nothing: to see for the first time the midst of nothing and being and between being and nothing the difference of nothing and being, to see the beginning the midst of nothing and nothing in the midst of nothing and being, to see for the first time the nothingness of nothing as not the nothingness of the finite but as the nothingness of the infinite. For the first time this is the voyage reaching the end of the infinite backtracking of the infinite nothingness of the Godhead. This is the arrival for the first time at the triple nothingness of the Trinity, at the infinitely finite nothingness of the Godhead of God, at the finite Trinity, at the "absolute nullification of the Trinity now occurring for the first time in thought." For the first time the nothingness of the transcendent God is the actual existence of the transcendent God: now actually existing for the first time in history actually and ideally, the absolute and pure nothingness of the Creator—neither the perfectly impure nor the imperfectly pure negativity of '*Trieb or kenosis*'—the absolute and manifest very omnipotence of *ipsum esse.*[20] What now essentially occurs for the first time in thought is the perfect elimination of the *a priori* form of the beginning of nothing: for the first time in history the beginning of nothing *a posteriori* at once the absolute exclusivity of existence.

The absolute apocalypse which is the complete incarnation of God now actually occurring is the actual realization for the first time of the absolute exclusivity of existence, at once the conception of the intelligible order of the life of the Trinity as the very conception of existence identically actual and ideal. Before now Peirce wrote "there is no absolute third, for the third is of its own nature relative, and this is what we are always thinking, even when we aim at the first or second. The starting point of the universe, God the Creator, is the Absolute First; the terminus of the universe, God completely revealed, is the Absolute Second; every state of the universe at a measurable point of time is the third."[21]

[20] Cf. Leahy, *Novitas Mundi,* pp. 363f., and above, pp. 384–87, 474–78.
[21] Peirce, *Collected Papers,* 1.362.

This was the metaphysico-logical form of the death of God, the physico-logical form of the Creator, the physico-logical form of the beginning of the Godhead, the psychical-physical form of the universe. For James the physico-logical form of the Creator, the psychical-physical form of the universe, was finite; for Dewey ideal. This was the beginning of the nothingness of the Third Person of the Godhead in the form of the infinite postponement of self-consciousness immediately and ideally the beginning of the universe not the absolute beginning. In the realization of the death of God, in Altizer, there is for the first time the metaphysico-logical form of nothing, the physico-logical form of the absolutely selfless beginning, the death of God in the flesh. This is the psychical-physical form of the essence-less beginning of nothing, the not seeing of the beginning of nothing. If in Peirce and James and Dewey "we are always thinking, even when we aim at the first or second," nothing absolute, that is, if our always thinking is not our always thinking or our not always thinking "when we aim at" the Absolute First or Absolute Second, if in pragmatism the psychical-physical universe is really essentially beginning-less, i.e., merely beginning formally, then, in Altizer, the death of God is the realization that we *are* always thinking nothing, nothing pure, the *pure* nothing, when we aim at the beginning or the ending of the Godhead. In Altizer, the beginning of the psychical-physical universe is a real nothing. If, in the consciousness that is pragmatism, "every state of the universe at a measurable point of time is the third," then, in Altizer, the totality, i.e., the *absolute* state of the universe, i.e., the *full and final actualization* of Dewey's 'ideal unification of ends' 'which imagination calls the universe', is the third relating beginning and end to nothing. This is the absolute perception of the nothingness of the Third Person of the Godhead itself as the beginning itself not the beginning, purely the beginning of nothing. This nothing in the form of American consciousness is for the first time the death of the Divine Third, the actual death of the Absolute Spirit, the complete and final death of the Spirit. For the first time in the form of the death of God "we are always thinking" the nothingness of the Godhead, the nothingness of the Spirit, the nothingness of the 'uniquely Christian' Godhead of God. "The starting point of the universe" is "God completely revealed" *in death*. This beginning in the form of a uniquely American ideal is the totality of the present, the total presence of the totality "we are always thinking," the total presence of the ideal whole "we are always" imagining, but then the end of desire and action in the *realization* of this total-presence-form of the actually new world. This for the first time is the absolutely pure impasse, indeed, the existence of the absolute impasse, *passim* the impassible essence of the modern imagination. This beginning of the pure nothing is the essentially impassable limit of self-consciousness actually and ideally the residuum of the divine impassibility which clings to the 'self-emptying' surface of consciousness: the impassible impassable of self-consciousness, the passibility of nothing the passability of nothing, the absolutely pure quality of the impassable imagination the actual transcendence of the impassible mind. Here, indeed, in America, in the form of the absolute and extreme limit of the modern imagination, there is for the first time the actual existence of the 'real presence' of the 'very substance of divinity', the materialization of the 'real presence' of the *instrumental humanity* of the Godhead, the very universe the 'real presence' of the Body of Christ, so that Altizer is able to write "the advent of [the totality of history] is inseparable from an absolute movement of reversal, a reversal in which the backward movement of return fully and wholly passes into the forward movement of history, and a reversal in which the beyondness of the Alone passes into the total presence of Godhead, a reversal which the Church knows as a real presence in the eucharist, yes, but a reversal which the world ever more gradually knows and realizes as a real presence in the totality of history."[22] But the 'real presence in the totality of history' is the advent of God inseparably the reversal of God which is the beginning of nothing or real total presence. This beginning is the real presence of the church in the world in the form of the totality of history. The form of this beginning is the historical presence of the church in the city of the apocalypse. But, then, this is not the

[22] Altizer, *Genesis and Apocalypse,* p. 115; but see Leahy, *Novitas Mundi,* pp. 344ff.

real, actual and ideal, beginning of the apocalypse, this is not the beginning of the Jerusalem described by John when he writes "I could not see any temple in the city since the Lord God Almighty and the Lamb were themselves the temple."[23] Thinking the end of theology a 'seeming' the consciousness of the 'self-emptying' of the 'very substance of divinity' for the first time seeing the Godhead sees nothing. The disbelief of the Christian mind, the disbelief of thinking, faith not the essence of thinking, but faith wholly and simply the form of thought, displaces the 'real presence' with 'total presence', as if the reality of history were not in fact to create, actual beginning, but rather a 'seeming' beginning, in fact the beginning not a transformation of nothing, but the complete transformation of the divine not a beginning, but the advent inseparably absolute reversal, the beginning of nothing in the form of the advent of the totality of history. But the transformation of the divinity of the divine which is an actual beginning is not the total 'presence' of divinity, not in fact the ultimate form of the modernization of the disbelief of the Christian mind, the universalized form of the disbelief of the mind, but rather the actual elimination of 'total presence', the immediate elimination of the very notion of the *presence* of divinity: *the form of the divine actually beginning is very existence very divine.* This beginning is the *immediately* mediated immediacy of divine existence, actually and ideally the absolute elimination of the divine *presence.* Just as John writes "the city did not need the sun or the moon for light, since it was lit by the radiant glory of God, and the Lamb was a lighted torch for it,"[24] so now for the first time in history the *absolutely self-less distance* of the Godhead of God in the form of *sensible very existence*: the very existence of the Godhead of God for the first time the actual universe *qua* sensible existence. What now absolutely occurs for the first time in history is not the beginning of what is, strictly thought, the superstition of total presence, the strictly non-actual ideal beginning of nothing, the completely actual superstitious presence of the beginning, the beginning in the form of the self-embodiment of God, no, what

[23] Rv. 21:22.
[24] Rv. 21:23.

now absolutely begins is the very embodiment of the transcendent other of superstition. For the first time the other of superstition is made perfect flesh. You, the actual reader, you who are not able to say "I am Christ", you, nevertheless, *are* the Jesus Christ who is the beginning. *For the first time* "who touches this book touches a man" *absolutely*. Divine omnipotence is for the first time the absolute elimination of the impediments of superstition, distance itself, and identity. Divine omnipotence is for the first time superstition itself, itself distance itself, identity itself. For the first time divine omnipotence *is* the actual and ideal totality of existence absolutely. This is the beginning of the advent of the totality of history as the advent of completely sensible very omnipotence.

The arrival of very omnipotence completely sensible which *is* the absolutely pure beginning of a universal faith is the very simplicity of the Godhead of God. William James asked dismissively, "What specific thing can I do to adapt myself to his 'simplicity'?"[25] The answer for the first time absolutely eliminating dismissal is the imitation of the divine simplicity in the very thought of existence. What the I of the actual thinker, indeed, the I of the *cogito*, is able to do to adapt itself to the divine simplicity is for the first time to conceive the resurrection of the Trinity as the very form of the passibility and passability of omnipotence, to think this simplicity of existence as the very passability and passibility of the I, and to actually imitate in the essence of thought the death of the 'uniquely Christian' God, to imitate in the very form of thought the death of Christ. For the first time the do-able is in fact the actual achievement of I conceiving I, I thinking the passibility and passability of I in the face of very omnipotence, and, in the immediately mediated immediacy of the divine, the achievement of omnipotence thinking omnipotence in the face of the I of I think. This beginning is the perfect mutuality of human and divine conceptions of existence, indeed, the perfect grace of perfect mutuality. Now as never before the non-being of the finite is not mere-

[25] James, "Philosophical Conceptions and Practical Results," in *Pragmatism*, p. 265.

ly as it was in Hegel the ground of the infinite, indeed, now as never before the non-being of the Finite God[26] is not merely as it is in Altizer the ground of the infinite, at once the actual, final nothingness of the transcendent God. Now as never before omnipotence itself, very love, actually moves to new ground: now for the first time in history the finite is absolutely, i.e., absolutely without reference to the infinite, without reference to non-being, the absolute ground of *ipsum esse*, and in the perfect mutuality of this absolute ground omnipotence itself suffers passibility without ceasing to be omnipotence, as in this mutual change the finite itself suffers passability without ceasing to be the absolute ground. For the first time omnipotence in the simplicity of being itself eliminates the necessity of conceiving the divine movement as divine self-movement, indeed, as the *kenosis* of divinity or the *Trieb* of divine self-consciousness. The motion of omnipotence which is this beginning is absolutely not restless. The motion identical with rest which *is* very omnipotence is the *absolute* beginning. The 'absolutely transcendent impassivity' of God beginning is the elimination of the impossibility of absolute impassibility itself suffering. This is the elimination for the first time of the impassibility of the Nothing, the beginning which is the elimination of the essentially impassible nay-saying of modernity. Indeed, the 'absolutely transcendent impassivity' is the very essence of the *kenosis* which *is* creation. Indeed, the 'absolutely transcendent impassivity' of the Godhead of God is the beginning of absolute pure nothing. This nothing shares the common boundary of the beginning with being. For the first time in history there is the consciousness of no self-conscious formality whatsoever. Being and nothing share the common boundary of the beginning which is the being they *are* but do not *have*. Being and nothing have the common boundary of the beginning which is the being they *are* but do not *share*. This is the beginning of the existence of the absolute exteriority of the Word, the absolute negativity of the finite absolute: the creation of the finite absolute, the beginning of the divine absolutely finite, the Word

[26] Cf. above, Section V.2.

spoken immediately as the Absolute Idea the absolute exteriority of the thing for the first time. This is the Idea of God after death: the Absolute Idea beginning. The absolute negativity of the absolute finite—absolutely unconditioned finite negativity—is the absolute and pure sharing of the beginning with God.

The ordered life of the Trinity, *ipsum esse* now manifesting itself perfectly in the very structure of existence, is the First Person Absolute, the Second Person Absolute which is the Word of the Father, the Third Person Absolute which is the Will of the Father, which Absolute Will is actually the spiration of Father and Son, that is, the Father and Son sharing the Will of the Father is the Father and Son which is the Will of the Father. The very simplicity of the First *is* the Trinity. The Trinity is itself the very First omnipotence. The resurrection of the Trinity, the beginning now actually occurring is the simplicity of omnipotence itself. The omnipotence itself of the beginning is the Word sharing the Will of the Father. The beginning is not the Absolute Will, but the omnipotence of the Absolute Will is the beginning. Not omnipotence itself, but the act of omnipotence itself is the beginning. Not 'the Word was with God' was the beginning, not the Absolute Second was the beginning, not sharing the will of the Father was the beginning, not the actual spiration of the Godhead was the beginning, not the Absolute Third was the beginning, but 'the Word was with God *in* the beginning', the Absolute Second was *in* the beginning, sharing the will of the Father was *in* the beginning, the actual spiration of the Godhead was *in* the beginning, the Absolute Third was *in* the beginning. Absolute Second and Absolute Third were *in* the Absolute First and they were the *Very* First. The Absolute First is neither the Alone nor not the Alone: what now actually occurs is not the beginning of *ipsum esse* the abyss of the alone, the beginning of the alone not alone, the beginning not alone the beginning but the ending of God, but this is the beginning of being-in-itself-essentially-without-solitude, the beginning of existence, the beginning of very omnipotence, the beginning of the sharing of God with God, i.e., the beginning of the Word sharing the Will of the Father conceived essentially. The beginning is the perfect exteriority of the divine exclusivity: the Godhead of God *in* the beginning God within God: for the first time the perfect exteriority of the *in*most being of divinity: *sharing* the beginning 'God created the heaven and the earth'. The simplicity of omnipotence itself is not the beginning of the Godhead of God, but the sharing of that beginning which is the very structure of existence. Not omnipotence itself or very being in itself without solitude is the beginning, but the sharing of the *withness of being* or the sharing of omnipotence itself is the beginning. The absolute exteriority of the absolute exclusivity of the Trinity in the beginning is the beginning now actually occurring for the first time in the very form of thought. The essential conception of the simplicity of omnipotence is the beginning of a categorical change. It is the perception that the common boundary of everything existing is the exclusivity of the beginning. This exclusivity of the being itself of the Trinity which is the beginning is the very essence of the incarnation of the Word: the Son *having* God the Father *shares* the Spirit, and the Son *sharing* God the Father *has* the Spirit, while the Son *having* God the Father does not *have* the Spirit, and the Son *sharing* God the Father does not share the Spirit. The human and divine share a common boundary had by both, or, both have a common boundary shared by both. But both do not have and share a common boundary with one another; nor does either have and share a common boundary with the other. God the Father shared *is* the *very instrumental humanity,* the Son not *sharing* but *having* the Spirit: "Anyone who has seen me has seen the Father, so how can you say show us the Father?"[27] But then God the Father does not *have* the Son who *has* the Spirit: having the Will of the Father not sharing the Will of the Father, the Son, knowing not Sin, i.e., Very Righteousness, was made Sin, i.e., suffered death, sharing the Very Being of the Father, the Very Righteousness of God, δικαιοσύνη Θεοῦ.[28] Thus it is truly thought for the first time: the Very First not knowing death suffered the death of God: the righteousness of the Son is the Father having His Will sharing the suffering of death for the first time: conceived in

[27] Jn. 14:9.
[28] 2 Co. 5:21.

essence for the first time in history this is God the beginning of the common boundary which being and nothing have without sharing, and which they share without having. This essentially conceived is the beginning of the actual and ideal righteousness and sin, death and resurrection, of the very Godhead, *which though it absolutely dies knows not death.*

The state of utter nility is the very surface American consciousness *is.* Nevertheless, for Edwards the state of utter nility was formally inconceivable. In the mind of the puritan there is the infinite postponement of the self-consciousness of the dark transparency of consciousness: the darkness transparent is hidden in the form of the infinitely finite sharing of the being of being in general. For Peirce the state of utter nility was *for us* formally inconceivable, i.e., only relatively so. In the mind of the pragmaticist there is the infinite postponement of the self-consciousness of the dark transparency of consciousness *for us*: the darkness is transparent in the form of the beginning of mind in general. For James the state of utter nility was *for us* essentially inconceivable. In the mind of the pragmatic pluralist there is *for us* the completely practical postponement of the self-consciousness of the dark transparency of consciousness: the darkness is transparent in the form of the particular beginning. For Dewey the state of utter nility is *for us* absolutely inconceivable. In the mind of the pragmatic instrumentalist *for us* there is the inevitable postponement of the self-consciousness of the dark transparency of consciousness: the darkness is transparent in the form of the totality of beginnings. In Altizer for the first time the state of utter nility *qua* inconceivable *for us*, that is, *qua* relatively inconceivable, is completely conceivable as the other, the nothing is *a priori* conceivable as the other, the *a priori* other is conceivable as the transparent darkness. The mind of Altizer conceives the for us inconceivable nothing for the first time, conceives in fact the relatively opaque logical bottom of Being. How is this impossible possible? It is not possible, for the first time the impossible is not possible. It is, for the first time the impossible *is.* This is the beginning of the nothing. This is the extreme of the space made for objectivity in American consciousness. In the form of the realization of the death of God this is the infinite backtracking at the very center of the American mind of the possible objections of self-consciousness to the resurrection of the very Godhead of God, but actually and ideally "no resurrection lies readily at hand."[29] It is the beginning nevertheless. Willy-nilly, the impossible beginning is. For Kierkegaard the 'Eternal made historical' was the temporal now made eternal. The conception of the now was *eternity touching time.*[30] History begins in eternity touching time, in the now which is the fullness of time. For Hegel the 'dissolution' of 'the *becoming* of externality as such' 'into the differences of being as passing over into nothing, and of nothing as passing over into being' immediately disappears into the self-negating '*individuality* which is the present as *now*', which now, 'as it excludes individuality and is at the same time simply continuous in the other moments, is itself merely this disappearance of its being into nothing, and of nothing into its being'.[31] But it was Kierkegaard for whom the now which is the fullness of time is eternity 'at once the future and the past', and for whom, therefore, the self-negating individuality of the now into which the differences of the dissolution of becoming immediately disappear was *the eternal fully present.* The now which was this eternal measure of a temporal individuality was the object of a faith which was neither willing nor knowing,[32] indeed, a faith not rational, but a faith holding to its object in the face of the absurdity of its object. This was impure absolute presence, the pure absence of reason, indeed, the very embodiment of the actual absence of the *in itself* of pure reason: the present eternal and full *not* measurable. In the mind of Kierkegaard the presence of the eternal was not measurable, that is, the individuality of the temporal now which the 'Eternal made historical' measures is *in itself* nothing. But in American consciousness, where the *in itself* is nothing and the Absolute First is 'the starting point of the universe'

29 Altizer, *Genesis and Apocalypse,* p. 186.

30 S. Kierkegaard, *The Concept of Dread,* trans. W. Lowrie (Princeton, 1957), pp. 76ff.

31 Hegel, *Philosophy of Nature,* vol. 1, pp. 231ff.

32 S. Kierkegaard, *Philosophical Fragments,* trans. D. F. Swenson and H. V. Hong (Princeton, 1962), pp. 76ff.

and the Absolute Last is the 'terminus of the universe', 'every state of the universe at a measurable point of time is the third', that is, the now of time is measurable, the now of time is not the measure of nothing, but rather the measure of a possible individuality, indeed, the measure of an ideal possibility. The individuality that was *nothing* in the modernity of European consciousness is, in American consciousness, *possible.* The differences of the dissolution of the becoming of 'externality as such'—'the passing over of nothing into being and of being into nothing'—disappear into a *possible* individuality. Here the thought-form of the now which is individuality is the present possibility of the past and the future. This is the pure present of the measurable now: the present the past and the future now measurable, the present now absolutely the past and the future, the past and the future measurable as now the present. This pure present which is the ideal now of American consciousness, this pure absolute presence, is the very space made for objectivity, indeed, the very possible nothingness of the nothingness of the individuality which disappears in the perfectly finite 'externality as such'. This it is, the impossible, the nothingness of the nothingness of the individuality which disappears in 'externality as such', which is the possible for the first time *conceived* as such in the American theology of the death of God: the beginning of Nothing, for the first time the nothing passing over into being and the being passing over into nothing disappearing in the individuality of the once and for all and irreversible event which is the reversal of being and nothing: the differences in the dissolution of the becoming of 'externality as such' for the first time the final actuality. The form of the actual death of God is this pure absolute present of the measurable now: the present now itself absolutely the past and the future, the now measurable present which is the past absolutely the future, the present now the measurable totality of the past and the future, the total presence of the past and the future, the past and the future now measurable as absolutely present. But, then, actually and ideally, total presence is the very distance finally standing between the past and the future. But, then, the absolutely pure presence of the measurable now of the totality, the pure unbounded presence of the totality in the form of the measurable now, the very center of absolutely nothing, the center of consciousness the very space made for objectivity now actually the totality, this—the very past being completely at an end, the very form of the absolute future the revelation of the emptiness of everything—this total presence—this nothing—is the final connection of the past and the future, the failure finally to absolutely disconnect the past and the future in the form of beginning, the failure of beginning absolutely. This is the point of the diametrical opposition of being and nothing, the totality of the diametrically opposed past and future, the dichotomous opposition of being and nothing in the form of the beginning. If, in Kierkegaard, Christianity was conceived as the absence of *pure* reason, the pure absence of reason, the absence of reason at once the complete loss of self, this was nevertheless the impure presence of reason, the presence of reason without the complete and final loss of self. Inevitably this thinking was the thoughtfully thoughtless discontinuity of being and nothing in the beginning: in the beginning pure discontinuity of being. In Altizer what is conceived as Christianity is the impure absence of *absolute* reason, the absence of reason without the absolute loss of self, nevertheless itself therefore at once the pure absolute presence of reason, the self-less *presence* of the Absolute Idea. This is the impure absence of individuality in the form of the *presence* of the diametrical opposition of the beginning. Inevitably this thinking is the completely thoughtful failure to imagine the discontinuity of being and nothing in the beginning: in the beginning the pure continuity of nothing.

The resurrection of the Trinity for the first time absolutely eliminates the necessity of thinking and saying "no resurrection lies readily at hand." The space for objectivity at the center of consciousness is absolutely eliminated in the very form of this resurrection as the Very First the Trinity the structure of existence the measurable now and the essence of thought. Inevitably this thinking is the thoughtlessly thoughtless discontinuity of being and nothing in the beginning: the beginning of an essentially new form of thought. In the beginning the absolute consciousness of being, being identically mind and consciousness, mind and consciousness having, but not sharing, or sharing, but not having, *nothing*; in the beginning mind and consciousness having, but not sharing, or sharing, but not having, being itself: mind and consciousness having, but not sharing, or sharing, but not having, being itself and nothing: mind and consciousness not having and sharing being itself and nothing. For the first time the discontinuity of being and nothing is the very form of thought: in the beginning the absolutely pure continuity of being. The Trinity conceived in essence as sharing, but not having, and having, but not sharing, the diametric identity of being and nothing, for the first time absolutely displaces—in the very form of the spiration which is the shared will of the Father, not had, the had will of the Father, not shared—the shared diametric opposition of being and nothing. The discontinuity of being and nothing thought for the first time in the form of the Trinity is the very conception actually achieving the discontinuity of past and future, very conception very existence.

APPENDIX
THE *DE TRINITATE* OF AUGUSTINE AND THE LOGIC

The trinary system of the logic of the new thinking was first set down by the writer in 1985. As has been made clear in the text,[1] powerful conceptual motives were at work in the understanding and elaboration of this 'logic of the beginning'. The central notion was that no "nothing" was to have a place in the logic of the essentially new consciousness. The working out of the implications of the logic led immediately to the discovery of the essentially mathematical reading possible when dealing with the Hebrew and Greek languages.[2] This, in turn, led to the discovery of new fundamental properties of the natural number system.[3] After several years it was discovered that the logic was in fact the ground of the Fibonacci sequence, the foundational template of the geometric and arithmetic series, and the basis for a deeper understanding of the rationality of structural rigidity.[4] While the writer had of course noticed, as anyone might, the analogy between the trinary logic and the Trinity, and had thought it was a most appropriate analogy in the context of the thinking now occurring for the first time, he did not at first take any further serious notice of the analogy. After all, there are threes everywhere! However, in the Fall of 1992, while teaching

---

[1] Cf. above, Section III.1.

[2] Cf. above, Sections III.5 and IV.2.

[3] Cf. above, Sections III.6 and III.7.

[4] Cf. above, Sections III.2, III.3, and III.4.

a graduate course in Christian literature at New York University, the writer discovered that the analogy is not at all incidental. He discovered that in fact the complex of relations which exists among the elements in this logic—where 'different terms can be differently related but it is not possible to express inequality'[5]—corresponds exactly to the complex of relations which Augustine understood to exist among the Three Persons of the Godhead, as he worked them out over many years in his *De Trinitate.* So completely and precisely does the logic correspond to the Augustinian understanding of the Trinitarian relations that it is possible to superimpose the logical terms upon the Divine Names in such a way that what Augustine concludes in each instance concerning the Trinitarian relations perfectly coincides what is now for the first time in history the universal logic of a new world.

Here follow several passages from *De Trinitate* upon which such a superimposition of the logic has been made (each passage is headed by the logical equations corresponding to the conclusions reached by Augustine):[6]

$$1 = 10\bar{0},\ 0 = 10\bar{0},\ \ \bar{0} = 10\bar{0}$$

De Trinitate 6.8.9: Since, therefore, the Father [1] alone, or the Son [0] alone, or the Holy Spirit [$\bar{0}$] alone is just as great as the Father, the Son, and the Holy Spirit together [$1 = 10\bar{0}$, $0 = 10\bar{0}$, $\bar{0} = 10\bar{0}$], He [1] is not to be called threefold in any sense.

$$10\bar{0} = 1,\ 1 = 0 = \bar{0},\ 01 = 1$$

De Trinitate 7.6.12: And when he hears that the Father [1] is the only God [1], let him not separate the Son [0] or the Holy

5. Cf. above, p. 256.

6. The passages are taken from *Saint Augustine: The Trinity,* trans. S. McKenna (Washington, D.C., 1963). The reader may wish to compare the equations corresponding to the conclusions found in Augustine's text with those above in Section III.1, pp. 255ff.

Spirit [$\bar{0}$] from Him [1], for with Him [1] they [$0\bar{0}$] are the only God [1], with Him they are also the one God [$10\bar{0} = 1$]; because when he hears that the Son [0] is also the only God [1], it must needs be taken without any separation of the Father [1] and the Holy Spirit [$\bar{0}$]. And let him so say one essence [1] as not to think that one is greater, or better, or in any respect different from another [$1 = 0 = \bar{0}$]. Nevertheless, let him not think that the Father Himself [1] is the Son [0] and Holy Spirit [$\bar{0}$], and whatever else is said of each in relation to the other, as, for example, Word [Zero], which is not said except of the Son [0], or Gift [Unum], which is not said except of the Holy Spirit [$\bar{0}$]. It is for this reason that the plural number is also permitted, as it is written in the Gospel: 'I and the Father are one [$01 = 1$].'

$$1 = 0,\ 10 = \bar{0},\ 1 = 10\bar{0},\ 0 = 10\bar{0},\ \bar{0} = 10\bar{0}$$

De Trinitate 8: So great is the equality in this Trinity, that not only is the Father [1] not greater than the Son [0] in that which pertains to the divinity [$1 = 0$], but neither are the Father [1] and the Son [0] anything greater than the Holy Spirit [$10 = \bar{0}$], nor is each person singly, whichever of the three it may be, anything less than the Trinity itself [$1 = 10\bar{0},\ 0 = 10\bar{0}, \bar{0} = 100$].

$$10 = 1 = 0,\ 10 = \bar{0},\ 1\bar{0} = 0,\ 0\bar{0} = 1$$

De Trinitate 8.1.2: But the Father [1] and the Son [0] together do not have a more real being than the Father [1] singly or the Son [0] singly. Therefore, both together are not something greater than each one by Himself alone [$10 = 1 = 0$]. And because the Holy Spirit [$\bar{0}$] also has an equally real being, so the Father [1] and the Son [0] together are not something greater than He [$10 = \bar{0}$], because they [10] do not have a more real being than He [$\bar{0}$]. The Father [1] also and the Holy Spirit [$\bar{0}$] together do not surpass the Son [0] in greatness [$1\bar{0} = 0$], because they [$1\bar{0}$] do not surpass Him [0] in truth; they do not have a more true being. And similarly the Son [0] and the Holy

Spirit [$\bar{0}$] together are something just as great as the Father [1] alone [$0\bar{0} = 1$], because they [$0\bar{0}$] are just as truly as He [1] is.

$$1 = \bar{0}0,\ \bar{0} = 10,\ 0 = 1\bar{0},\ 1\bar{0} = 10$$

De Trinitate 9.5.8: And so each one is in each two, because the mind [1] that knows [0] and loves [$\bar{0}$] itself [1] is in its own love and knowledge [$1 = \bar{0}0$]; and the love [$\bar{0}$] of the mind [1] that knows [0] and loves [$\bar{0}$] itself [1] is in the mind and in its knowledge [$\bar{0} = 10$]; and the knowledge [0] of the mind [1] that knows [0] and loves [$\bar{0}$] itself [1] is in the mind and in its love [$0 = 1\bar{0}$]; because it loves itself as knowing [$1\bar{0} = 10$] and knows itself as loving [$10 = 1\bar{0}$].

$$1 = 0 = \bar{0},\ 1 = 0 = \bar{0} = 10\bar{0}$$

De Trinitate 10.11.18: For when we speak of memory as life, mind, and substance, we speak of it in respect to itself; but when we speak of it simply as memory, we speak of it in relation to something else. We may also say the same of the understanding and the will; for they are called understanding and will with relation to something else, yet each in respect to itself is life, mind, and essence. Therefore, these three are one in that they are one life, one mind, and one essence. And whatever else they are called in respect to themselves, they are called together, not in the plural but in the singular.

But they are three in that they are mutually referred to each other. And if they were not equal, not only each one to each one [$1 = 0 = \bar{0}$], but each one to all [$1 = 0 = \bar{0} = 10\bar{0}$], they would certainly not comprehend each other. For not only is each one comprehended by each one, but all are also comprehended by each one.

$$10 = \bar{0},\ 10 = \bar{0} = 1\bar{0} = 0 = 0\bar{0} = 1,\ 10\bar{0} = 1 = 0 = \bar{0}$$

De Trinitate 15.3.5: . . . it also became clear from the reasons which we gave for those capable of understanding that not only is the Father not greater than the Son in the substance of truth [1 = 0], but neither are both together something greater than the Holy Spirit alone [$10 = \bar{0}$], nor are any two something greater than one in the same Trinity [$10 = \bar{0} = 10 = 0 = 0\bar{0} = 1$], nor are all three together something greater than each one [$10\bar{0} = 1 = 0 = \bar{0}$].

$$10\bar{0} = 1,\ 0 = 10\bar{0},\ \bar{0} = 10\bar{0}$$

De Trinitate 15.7.12: Behold these three [$10\bar{0}$], therefore: memory [1], understanding [0], love or the will [$\bar{0}$] in that highest and unchangeable essence [1], which is God, and these three are not the Father [1], the Son [0], and the Holy Spirit [$\bar{0}$], but the Father [1] alone [$10\bar{0} = 1$].

And because the Son [0] also is wisdom [1] begotten from wisdom [1], as neither the Father [1] nor the Holy Spirit [$\bar{0}$] understands [0] for Him [0], but He Himself [0] understands [0] for Himself [0], so neither does the Father [1] remember [1] for Him [0], nor does the Holy Spirit [$\bar{0}$] love [$\bar{0}$] for Him [0], but He [0] remembers [1] for Himself [0] and loves [$\bar{0}$] for Himself [0]. For He Himself [0] is His own memory [1], His own understanding [0], and His own love [$\bar{0}$]; but that He is so [$0 = 10\bar{0}$], comes to Him [0] from that Father [1] of whom He [0] was born. The Holy Spirit [$\bar{0}$], too, because He [$\bar{0}$] is wisdom [1] proceeding from wisdom [1], does not have the Father [1] as His memory [1], and the Son [0] as His understanding [0], and Himself [$\bar{0}$] as love [$\bar{0}$] for He [$\bar{0}$] would not be wisdom [1] if the one [1] remembered [1] for Him [$\bar{0}$], and the other [0] understood [0] for Him [$\bar{0}$], and He Himself [$\bar{0}$] only loved [$\bar{0}$] for Himself [$\bar{0}$]; but He [$\bar{0}$] has these three things [$10\bar{0}$], and so has them that He Himself is these three things [$\bar{0} = 10\bar{0}$]. But that He is so [$\bar{0} = 10\bar{0}$], comes to Him [$\bar{0}$] from Him [1] from whom He [$\bar{0}$] proceeds.

$$1 = 0 = \bar{0} = 10\bar{0},\ 10\bar{0} = 1,\ 1 = 1,\ 0 = 1,\ \bar{0} = 1$$

De Trinitate 15.17.28: But we should rather so conceive this, that all together possess and each one possesses all three of these in their own nature $[1 = 0 = \bar{0} = 10\bar{0}]$, that these things do not differ in them, as memory in us is one thing, understanding another, and dilection or love another, but that we should so conceive these three as some one thing which all have, as wisdom itself $[10\bar{0} = 1]$, and which is so retained in the nature of each one, as that He who has it, is that which He has, as being an unchangeable and simple substance $[1 = 1, 0 = 1, \bar{0} = 1]$.

INDEX

In the GENERAL index page numbers within { } indicate that the word or phrase appears at least once in Greek or Hebrew at the place shown, there referenced, or earlier in the section. The case of English words need not match that of the text. For example, Being and Nothing are indexed using lower case initial letters. Foreign words and phrases are included, except those in Greek and Hebrew which are separately indexed. Works cited are to be found under the author's name. Biblical citations are grouped under New Testament and Old Testament. Material within quotations, as such, is not indexed. In the NUMBERS and SYMBOLS index numbers are indexed according to the first factor in scientific notation, and symbols alphabetically as applicable. If the form of a symbol is not invariant, a negative, italic or capitalized form is indexed according to the positive, normal, or lower case form as applicable. Fractions are indexed according to the decimal form. The GREEK index and the HEBREW index list phrases as they appear in the text and, where they occur as such, individual words.

GENERAL

NUMBERS AND SYMBOLS

GREEK

HEBREW